Microsoft Office
Inside Out
(Office 2021 and Microsoft 365)

Joe Habraken

Microsoft Office Inside Out (Office 2021 and Microsoft 365)
Published with the authorization of Microsoft Corporation by:
Pearson Education, Inc.

ISBN-13: 978-0-13-756409-5
ISBN-10: 0-13-756409-0

Library of Congress Control Number: 2021949134

2 2021

Trademarks

Microsoft and the trademarks listed at http://www.microsoft.com on the "Trademarks" webpage are trademarks of the Microsoft group of companies. All other marks are property of their respective owners.

Warning and Disclaimer

Every effort has been made to make this book as complete and as accurate as possible, but no warranty or fitness is implied. The information provided is on an "as is" basis. The author, the publisher, and Microsoft Corporation shall have neither liability nor responsibility to any person or entity with respect to any loss or damages arising from the information contained in this book or from the use of the programs accompanying it.

Special Sales

For information about buying this title in bulk quantities, or for special sales opportunities (which may include electronic versions; custom cover designs; and content particular to your business, training goals, marketing focus, or branding interests), please contact our corporate sales department at corpsales@pearsoned.com or (800) 382-3419.

For government sales inquiries, please contact governmentsales@pearsoned.com.

For questions about sales outside the U.S., please contact intlcs@pearson.com.

Editor-in-Chief: Brett Bartow
Executive Editor: Loretta Yates
Assistant Sponsoring Editor: Charvi Arora
Development Editor: Rick Kughen
Managing Editor: Sandra Schroeder
Project Editor: Charlotte Kughen
Copy Editor: Rick Kughen
Indexer: Johnna VanHoose Dinse
Proofreader: The Wordsmithery
Technical Editor: Vince Averello
Editorial Assistant: Cindy Teeters
Cover Designer: Twist Creative, Seattle
Compositor: Bronkella Publishing, LLC
Graphics: TJ Graham Art

Pearson's Commitment to Diversity, Equity, and Inclusion

Pearson is dedicated to creating bias-free content that reflects the diversity of all learners. We embrace the many dimensions of diversity, including but not limited to race, ethnicity, gender, socioeconomic status, ability, age, sexual orientation, and religious or political beliefs.

Education is a powerful force for equity and change in our world. It has the potential to deliver opportunities that improve lives and enable economic mobility. As we work with authors to create content for every product and service, we acknowledge our responsibility to demonstrate inclusivity and incorporate diverse scholarship so that everyone can achieve their potential through learning. As the world's leading learning company, we have a duty to help drive change and live up to our purpose to help more people create a better life for themselves and to create a better world.

Our ambition is to purposefully contribute to a world where:

- Everyone has an equitable and lifelong opportunity to succeed through learning.

- Our educational products and services are inclusive and represent the rich diversity of learners.

- Our educational content accurately reflects the histories and experiences of the learners we serve.

- Our educational content prompts deeper discussions with learners and motivates them to expand their own learning (and worldview).

While we work hard to present unbiased content, we want to hear from you about any concerns or needs with this Pearson product so that we can investigate and address them.

Please contact us with concerns about any potential bias at
https://www.pearson.com/report-bias.html.

To my family and friends with love and regard: Isn't life wonderful and weird in equal measure?

Contents at a Glance

Part I   Getting started with the Microsoft 365 apps

Chapter 1
Getting oriented to the Microsoft 365
applications.....................................3

Chapter 2
Navigating and customizing the 365 interface....19

Chapter 3
Managing and sharing 365 files................. 49

Chapter 4
Using and creating graphics.................... 69

Chapter 5
Using the 365 Online apps 97

Part II   Word

Chapter 6
Essential Word features 125

Chapter 7
Enhancing Word documents 161

Chapter 8
Working with tables, columns, and sections 209

Chapter 9
Managing mailings and forms...................231

Chapter 10
Creating special documents 257

Part III   Excel

Chapter 11
Essential Excel features......................... 297

Chapter 12
Worksheet formatting and management....... 345

Chapter 13
Getting the most from formulas and functions... 383

Chapter 14
Enhancing worksheets with charts 423

Chapter 15
Using Excel tables and pivot tables..............461

Chapter 16
Validating and analyzing worksheet data....... 503

Part IV   PowerPoint

Chapter 17
Essential PowerPoint features 529

Chapter 18
Advanced presentation formatting, themes,
and masters 555

Chapter 19
Better slides with pictures, objects, and
SmartArt...................................... 585

Chapter 20
Enhancing slides with animation, transitions,
and multimedia 611

Chapter 21
Delivering a presentation and creating
support materials..............................641

Part V   Outlook

Chapter 22
Outlook configuration and essential features... 669

Chapter 23
Managing email in Outlook 701

Chapter 24
Using the calendar for appointments and tasks....739

Chapter 25
Working with contacts and planning meetings .. 769

Chapter 26
Securing and maintaining Outlook............. 797

Part VI   Publisher

Chapter 27
Essential Publisher features.................... 829

Chapter 28
Advanced Publisher features 861

Part VII   Appendixes

Appendix A
Microsoft 365 application integration.......... 887

Appendix B
Microsoft 365 macros......................... 903

Index 923

Table of Contents

Acknowledgments. xxiii
About the Author. xxiv

Introduction . . . . **xxv**
Who this book is for xxv
    Assumptions about you. xxv
How this book is organized xxvi
Errata, uspdates & book support xxvii

Part I   **Getting started with the Microsoft 365 apps**

Chapter 1   **Getting oriented to the Microsoft 365 applications** **3**
Introducing Microsoft 365. 3
New features and tools in Microsoft 365 8
    Collaborating in the cloud. 8
    Collaborating with Microsoft Teams 9
    Other 365 improvements and updates 10
The 365 suite applications. 12
The different versions of the 365 app suite 12
Hardware and software requirements for 365. 14
Installing Microsoft 365 15
Getting Help in the 365 applications 16

Chapter 2   **Navigating and customizing the 365 interface** **19**
Getting familiar with the 365 interface 19
    Galleries. 20
    Contextual tabs. 21
    Overview of the 365 application window 22
Navigating the 365 applications 24
    Working with the ribbon 25
    Working in the Backstage 28
Customizing an application interface 31
    Customizing the ribbon 32
    Customizing the Quick Access Toolbar 35
    Customizing the status bar 37
Configuring application options 38
    Advanced Options settings 40
    Add-ins 41
    Using Application add-ins 42

Using the Trust Center 43
    Trusted publishers 45
    Trusted locations 46

Chapter 3   Managing and sharing 365 files 49
Understanding 365 file formats 49
    Saving files as different file types 52
    Converting files to different file types 53
Configuring save file options 55
Creating and managing files 56
    Managing files 59
    Creating a new folder 60
    Creating a new library 61
    Viewing file versions in an application 62
Searching for 365 files 63
Protecting a 365 file 65
Preparing a file for sharing 67

Chapter 4   Using and creating graphics 69
The 365 options for graphics and pictures 69
    Working with SmartArt graphics 74
    Inserting SmartArt graphics 76
    Modifying SmartArt graphics 79
Working with your digital pictures 81
    Inserting pictures 82
    Adjusting pictures 83
    Cropping an image 86
    Using the Background Removal tool 86
Using shapes and the 365 drawing tools 88
    Adding and combining multiple shapes 89
    Using the Shape Format tools 91
Using the screenshot tool 93
Using WordArt 94

Chapter 5   Using the 365 Online apps 97
What the Online apps can do 97
Where the Online apps live 99
Saving Online application files to the cloud 101
    Saving a file to OneDrive or OneDrive for Business 103
    Sharing a file saved to the cloud 104
Using the Word Online app 106
    The Word Online app's File tab 107
    The Word Online app's Home tab 109
    The Word Online app's Insert tab 110
    The Word Online app's Review tab 111
    The Word Online app's View tab 112

Using Excel Online 112
    The Excel Online app's File tab 113
    Working in the Excel Online app 114
    Inserting functions and charts in the Excel Online app 115
Using PowerPoint Online 117
    Working with slides 119
    Adding pictures and SmartArt 120

Part II   Word

Chapter 6   Essential Word features 125

Introducing Word 125
    The Word interface 125
    New features and improvements 127
Options for creating a new Word document 129
Using templates 132
    Creating a template 134
    Attaching a template 136
Navigating a Word document 137
    Moving around a document with the mouse 138
    Moving around a document with the keyboard 139
    Selecting text 140
Understanding document formatting 140
    Character formatting versus paragraph formatting 141
    Manual formatting versus styles and themes 142
Working with fonts and text formatting 142
    Formatting text 143
Working with paragraph formatting 146
    Setting paragraph alignment 147
    Changing line spacing 148
    Setting line and page breaks 150
    Setting indents 151
    Working with tabs 152
Page layout: margins and page options 155
    Changing margins 155
    Changing page orientation and paper size 156
    Inserting page breaks 157
Printing documents 157

Chapter 7   Enhancing Word documents 161

Creating better documents 161
Creating bulleted and numbered lists 162
    Bulleted lists 162
    Numbered lists 164
    Multilevel lists 165
Working with borders and shading 166
Formatting with themes 168

Creating headers and footers. 172

    Inserting headers and footers. 174

    The header and footer tools 175

    Working with page numbering 178

Inserting pictures and charts. 179

    Inserting pictures 180

    Inserting stock images and online pictures 182

    Inserting a chart 184

    Integrating text and images 186

Changing the document display 187

    Using the navigation pane. 189

    Using the Outline view 190

    Splitting the document window 192

Using the Editor 192

    Running the Editor. 193

    Using the Thesaurus 195

    Using the Search feature 195

Working with Quick Parts 196

    Creating and inserting an AutoText entry. 196

    Creating and inserting building blocks 197

Configuring AutoCorrect. 199

Understanding styles. 200

    Using the Styles gallery. 201

    Creating styles. 202

    Editing styles 203

    Managing styles 204

Chapter 8   **Working with tables, columns, and sections 209**

Options for adding a table 209

    Inserting a table 211

    Drawing a table. 213

    Converting text to a table 214

    Entering and deleting text and navigating a table. 214

    Selecting and positioning a table 215

Formatting tables. 216

    Adjusting columns and rows. 217

    Formatting cells 219

    Using table styles 220

Sorting table data. 224

Using formulas in tables. 225

Adding columns to a document 226

Understanding sections 228

    Adding and removing section breaks 228

    Formatting page attributes in a section. 230

Chapter 9   **Managing mailings and forms. 231**

Options for mail-related documents 231

Creating an envelope 232

Creating a label or labels 234

Understanding mass mailings 236
Performing a mail merge. 236
    Using the mail merge commands 238
    Understanding recipient lists 240
    Creating a recipient list. 241
    Editing and manipulating a recipient list. 243
    Using merge fields. 245
    Using merge rules 248
    Previewing merge results. 249
    Completing the merge 250
    Creating merged envelopes and labels 251
Understanding Word fields. 252
Building a form with form controls. 254

Chapter 10   Creating special documents. 257
Options for large documents 257
Creating a table of contents 258
    Creating a table of contents with built-in styles 259
    Creating a table of contents with your own styles 261
    Adding entries and updating the TOC. 263
    Building a TOC with field codes. 264
Working with captions and tables of figures 266
    Inserting a caption. 266
    Inserting a table of figures. 267
    Using cross-references 269
Generating an index 271
    Marking index entries. 271
    Inserting the index 272
Working with citations and bibliographies. 274
    Creating citations. 274
    Managing citations 276
    Inserting the bibliography. 277
    Inserting footnotes and endnotes. 278
Tracking document changes. 280
    Options for viewing changes 283
    Reviewing changes 284
    Comparing documents. 285
Building a better "big" document. 287
    Creating bookmarks 288
    Inserting comments. 289
Creating a master document 290
    Working in Outline view. 290
    Creating subdocuments from scratch 292
    Inserting existing document files into a master document outline. 293
    Manipulating the master document. 294

Part III	**Excel**	
Chapter 11	**Essential Excel features**	**297**
	Introducing Excel	297
	Navigating the Excel workspace	299
	The Excel ribbon	300
	Moving around a worksheet	302
	Creating workbooks and worksheets	303
	Using Office.com templates	304
	Inserting and rearranging worksheets	306
	Managing Excel workbooks	307
	Protecting workbooks and worksheets	310
	Locking cells	311
	Specifying edit ranges	313
	Preparing a workbook for sharing	315
	Recovering unsaved workbooks	317
	Entering data in a worksheet	317
	Entering labels	318
	Entering values	319
	Using AutoComplete	320
	Filling and entering series	321
	Copying, moving, and deleting cell contents	327
	Using the Paste Special dialog box	329
	Moving cells and ranges	331
	Clearing and deleting cells	332
	Editing cell content	333
	Viewing worksheets	334
	Printing worksheets	336
	Using the Page Layout commands	337
	Setting a print area	339
	Inserting page breaks	339
	Setting print titles	340
	Working on the print page	340
	Inserting headers and footers	342
Chapter 12	**Worksheet formatting and management**	**345**
	Formatting text entries	345
	Accessing the Format Cells dialog box	346
	Changing text orientation	348
	Formatting values	349
	Using the Format Cells dialog box	351
	Creating custom number formats	352
	Adding comments and notes to cells	354
	Inserting a Comment	354
	Viewing and deleting comments	355
	Inserting and deleting notes	356
	Using themes	357

Formatting cells using borders and color 357
    Adding cell borders 358
    Using background colors 360
Using cell styles and the Format Painter 360
    Creating a cell style 361
    Using the Format Painter 362
Using conditional formatting 363
    Using highlight cell rules 364
    Using top/bottom rules 365
    Using data bars 365
    Using color scales 366
    Using icon sets 367
    Creating and copying conditional formatting rules 367
Manipulating cells and cell content 369
    Inserting cells 369
    Merging cells and wrapping text 370
    Finding and replacing cell items 371
Working with columns and rows 373
    Changing column width and row height 373
    Inserting columns and rows 374
    Deleting columns and rows 375
    Hiding columns and rows 375
Working with worksheets 375
    Freezing rows and columns 375
    Splitting worksheets 377
    Hiding worksheets 377
Naming ranges 378
    Creating range names from selections 379
    Managing range names 380
Adding images and graphics to worksheets 381

Chapter 13   **Getting the most from formulas and functions** **383**
Performing calculations in Excel worksheets 383
Relative versus absolute referencing 385
Creating and editing formulas 389
    Understanding operator precedence 390
    Entering formulas 391
    Editing formulas 391
Working with Excel functions 392
Entering a function in a cell 393
    Using AutoSum 394
    Using the status bar statistical functions 395
    Using the Insert Function dialog box 396
    Using the Function Library 397
Using range names in formulas and functions 399
    Inserting a range name into a formula 400
    Inserting a range name into a function 401
Referencing cells or ranges on other worksheets 402

Copying and moving formulas and functions 404
Choosing the right function 405
    Financial functions 405
    Logical functions 407
    Statistical functions 409
    Lookup & Reference functions 410
    Date & Time functions 414
    Text functions 414
    Other function categories 416
Proofing your formulas and functions 417
    Common error messages 417
    Using the auditing tools 419
    Using the Watch Window 420

Chapter 14   Enhancing worksheets with charts 423
Understanding Excel charts 423
    Chart terminology 424
    Using different chart types 427
Creating charts 435
    Inserting a chart from the ribbon 436
    Selecting a recommended chart 437
    Inserting charts with the Quick Analysis gallery 438
    Tools for quickly customizing a chart 439
    Moving, copying, or deleting a chart 440
Modifying a chart 441
    Changing chart type or chart data 441
    Selecting chart layouts and styles 443
Working with chart elements 444
    Modifying titles and data labels 447
    Working with the legend and data points 447
    Manipulating axes and gridlines 449
    Adding trendlines, drop lines, and bars to a chart 450
Creating a combination chart 454
    Working with a pie of pie chart 455
    Creating a custom combination chart 455
    Using sparklines 457
    Creating sparklines 457
    Modifying sparklines 459

Chapter 15   Using Excel tables and pivot tables 461
Excel and databases 461
Defining a table range 463
Creating a table using styles 464
Using the Table Design Tools 465
Sorting table data 467
    How Excel sorts data 468
    Using the Sort dialog box 468

Filtering table data. 470
    Using the AutoFilter Search box 471
    Creating custom AutoFilters 471
    Filtering tables with slicers. 474
    Creating advanced filters 475
    Creating custom sheet views 478
Using the data form. 479
Creating outlines and subtotals 480
Working with external data. 484
    Importing data from Access 484
    Importing a web table. 486
    Importing text files. 486
Connecting to other data sources. 488
    Using Microsoft Query 490
    Viewing and refreshing connections 493
Working with pivot tables 494
    Using the Recommended PivotTables command. 496
    Creating a pivot table 497
    Working with the pivot table tools 500
    Using slicers 502

Chapter 16   Validating and analyzing worksheet data 503
Taking advantage of data validation 503
    Specifying validation criteria. 504
    Configuring input messages and error alerts. 506
    Circling invalid data. 508
Performing a what-if analysis 510
    Creating a data table. 511
    Creating scenarios 513
    Viewing scenarios and creating reports. 516
Using Goal Seek, Solver, and Forecast Sheet 518
    Working with Goal Seek. 518
    Working with Solver 519
    Creating a Forecast Sheet 523

Part IV   PowerPoint

Chapter 17   Essential PowerPoint features 529
PowerPoint. 529
Options for creating a new presentation 530
    Using templates 532
    Using a theme to create a new presentation 535
    Creating a presentation from an existing presentation 535
    Inserting slides from the Reuse Slides task pane. 536
Creating a template. 537
Inserting new slides 540
    Entering text 541
    Inserting slides from a Word outline 542
    Inserting other object content 542

Modifying a slide's layout 543
Working with slides in different views 543
    Zooming in and out. 545
    Rulers, gridlines, and guides 546
    Color/grayscale commands. 547
Opening a new presentation window 548
Rearranging and deleting slides 549
Modifying bulleted lists 549
Using numbered lists. 551
Viewing a presentation during editing 552

Chapter 18   Advanced presentation formatting, themes, and masters **555**
Working with text boxes and formatting 555
    Inserting a text box 556
    Basic text formatting 557
    Formatting a text box with the Shape Format tools. 559
    Selecting quick styles and shape attributes 559
    Shape fill, outline, and effects. 559
    Using WordArt styles and text settings .563
Arranging text in tables 566
    Inserting a table on an existing slide 566
    Formatting a table 567
    Table layout commands. 567
Working with themes 570
    Applying themes 571
    Applying theme variants 571
    Creating a custom theme. 575
Using headers and footers. 576
Understanding masters 577
Altering and creating master slides 579
Creating layout masters 581
Using slide sections 582

Chapter 19   Better slides with pictures, objects, and SmartArt **585**
Using graphics to enhance slides 585
Inserting a picture 587
Adding stock images to slides 589
Creating a photo album. 591
    Adjusting picture settings 592
    Configuring album layout settings 592
Working with shapes. 593
Inserting icons. 595
Using SmartArt graphics 596
    Inserting a SmartArt graphic. 599
    Converting text to a SmartArt graphic. 600
    Using the SmartArt tools 600
Adding charts to slides 602
    Inserting a chart onto a slide. 602
    Modifying and formatting a chart. 604

Working with slide objects 606
    Grouping objects 607
    Layering objects 607
Adding hyperlinks to slides 608
Using PowerPoint Designer 609

Chapter 20   Enhancing slides with animation, transitions, and multimedia 611
Animations versus transitions 611
Assigning animation to a slide object 614
    Accessing additional animation effects 615
    Using motion paths 616
    Applying a motion path 617
    Editing a motion path 618
    Creating a custom motion path 621
Advanced animation techniques 622
    Changing effect options 623
    Adding additional animations 624
    Using the animation painter 625
    Including sound effects with animations 625
    Setting timings for animations 627
Managing slide animations 628
Adding transitions to slides 630
    Modifying transitions 631
    Using the Morph transition 632
Adding sound to a slide 634
Editing sound options 635
    The trim audio dialog box 636
Adding video to a slide 636
    Inserting online video 636
    Inserting a video file 639
    Modifying your video clips 640

Chapter 21   Delivering a presentation and creating support materials 641
Planning your presentation 641
Checking the presentation for spelling and grammar errors 642
Running through a completed presentation 644
Using the presenter coach 645
Using the presenter view 646
Using hidden slides 648
Creating a custom slide show 649
Creating a self-running presentation 652
    Setting up a slideshow 652
    Rehearsing timings 654
    Recording a slideshow 654
Creating an interactive presentation 656
Working with the notes and handout masters 659
    Setting handout master options 659
    Setting notes master options 661

Printing presentations, notes, and handouts 661
Exporting a presentation 663
Sharing your presentation 665

Part V   Outlook

Chapter 22   Outlook configuration and essential features 669
Introducing Outlook 669
Outlook and email accounts 670
        Exchange ActiveSync. 671
        Outlook.com email 672
        Internet email 672
Configuring Outlook at first start 673
Adding email accounts to Outlook. 674
Understanding Outlook profiles 677
        Creating a new profile. 678
        Managing profiles 679
        Loading profiles 681
Understanding Outlook data files 681
        Configuring Outlook for Microsoft Exchange Server 682
        Creating personal folders files 684
        Repairing Outlook data files 685
Importing and exporting data 687
        Importing data 687
        Exporting data. 689
Navigating the Outlook workspace 689
        Accessing Outlook items using the Navigation bar 691
Working with views in Outlook 692
Categorizing Outlook items 695
Searching for Outlook items. 696
        Using Advanced Find 697
        Using search folders 697
Printing Outlook items 698

Chapter 23   Managing email in Outlook 701
Working in the Outlook window 701
Creating an email message 704
Using the Outlook Address Book 706
Setting message options 708
        Specifying email format 708
        Setting message flags, importance, and sensitivity 709
        Configuring voting buttons, receipts, and delivery options 711
        The Message Properties dialog box 713
Attaching files and items to a message 715
        Attaching a business card 716
        Attaching a calendar 717
Using themes and email stationery. 718
Adding a signature 719

Sending mail 720
Recalling a message 720
Working with received email 721
    Organizing messages in the Inbox 722
    Showing messages as conversations 723
    Filtering email 724
Managing email 724
    Using Quick Steps. 725
    Answering a message 727
    Forwarding a message 728
    Saving an attachment 728
    Translating messages 729
    Deleting messages. 729
    Printing mail. 731
    Moving email. 731
Managing email accounts 732
    Editing email account settings 734
    Adding an email account automatically 735
    Adding a mail account manually 735
Setting Outlook mail options 736

Chapter 24   **Using the calendar for appointments and tasks. 739**
Navigating the calendar. 739
    Changing the calendar view 741
    Change the time scale and time zone 742
Scheduling an appointment 743
    Scheduling a recurring appointment 745
    Scheduling an event 746
    Editing and managing appointments 747
Searching the calendar. 748
Sharing calendars. 750
    Creating a calendar share invitation 750
    Opening a shared calendar 752
    Viewing multiple calendars 752
    Emailing calendar items 754
    Emailing a calendar 754
    Publishing a calendar online. 755
Setting calendar options 757
Working with tasks 758
    Using the Tasks folder. 760
    Creating a new task from the Tasks folder 761
    Creating a recurring task 761
    Assigning and accepting tasks 762
    Viewing and managing tasks 763
    Managing tasks. 766
    Setting Tasks options 767

Chapter 25   **Working with contacts and planning meetings** **769**

Navigating the Contacts list 769
Creating a new contact. 772
Entering contact details 774
Adding fields for a contact 775
Editing contact information 776
Editing a business card 777
Tagging contacts with flags and categories 779
Mapping a contact's address 780
Searching the Contacts folder 780
Organizing contacts with groups 781
Forwarding and sharing contacts 782
Forwarding contacts 783
Sharing contacts 784
Communicating with contacts 785
Contact actions 787
Printing contact information 788
Setting contact options 788
Scheduling meetings. 789
Selecting the meeting location 790
Using the Scheduling Assistant 791
Viewing and editing meeting information 792
Responding to meeting requests 793

Chapter 26   **Securing and maintaining Outlook** **797**

Security overview. 797
Malware and antivirus software. 798
Strong password protection 799
Configuring Outlook security settings. 801
Encrypting email and using digital signatures. 804
Options for encrypting email 805
Digitally signing emails. 806
The perils of HTML email 806
Dealing with message attachments 807
Coping with junk email. 810
Working with the junk email commands 810
Setting junk email options. 812
Creating email rules. 813
Creating a quick rule for a specific sender 814
Creating complex rules. 815
The Rules Wizard 816
Managing rules. 818
Archiving Outlook items 819
Configuring AutoArchive settings. 820
Setting AutoArchive options for a folder 821
Archiving manually 822
Configuring an autoreply message. 824

Part VI   **Publisher**

Chapter 27   **Essential Publisher features** 829
Introducing Publisher 829
Planning your publication 830
Working with publication templates 831
Creating a new publication 833
Using a template 833
Using blank sizes 834
Creating a new template 835
Navigating the Publisher workspace 836
Using the rulers and guides 837
Options for viewing the publication 840
Creating a business information set 841
Creating a new business information set 841
Creating additional business information sets 842
Working with text 843
Editing text in a text box 844
Creating your own text boxes 844
Formatting text boxes 844
Linking text boxes 849
Inserting a text file 851
Inserting illustrations 852
Options for inserting pictures 852
Formatting a picture 855
Inserting clip art 856
Inserting shapes 857
Using building blocks 857
Printing publications 858

Chapter 28   **Advanced Publisher features** 861
Adding pages to a publication 861
Configuring page settings 863
Changing the current template 866
Working with master pages 868
Placing objects on the master page 869
Inserting headers and footers 870
Creating master pages 871
Using tables in publications 872
Table design commands 872
Table layout commands 873
Manipulating publication objects 874
Grouping objects 875
Layering objects 876
Swapping images 876
Merging data into a publication 877
Performing a mail merge 877
Performing a catalog merge 880

Fine-tuning your publications 882
    The Spelling feature. 882
    Hyphenation 882
    Design Checker. 883

Part VII   **Appendixes**

Appendix A **Microsoft 365 application integration** **887**
Sharing application data 887
Understanding object linking and embedding. 888
    Choosing between linking and embedding. 890
Linking objects 891
    Linking with Paste Special 891
    Linking with the Paste Options gallery. 893
    Linking using the Object command 894
Updating and breaking links. 895
    Editing linked objects 897
Embedding objects 898
    Embedding with Paste Special 899
    Embedding using the Object command 899
    Embedding new objects. 900
Editing embedded objects 901
Sharing data with Outlook using actions 901

Appendix B **Microsoft 365 macros** **903**
Macros and Office 903
    Adding the Developer tab to the ribbon. 904
    Enabling macros in the Trust Center. 905
    Creating macro-enabled Office files. 907
Understanding macros. 908
Creating a macro 910
    Recording a macro. 911
    Assigning a macro button to the Quick Access Toolbar 912
Running macros 914
Editing recorded macros 914
    Exploring the VBA Editor 915
    Stepping through a macro 916
Digitally signing macros. 917

Index **923**

Acknowledgments

It has been a real privilege for me to collaborate with the team of professionals who were assembled to make this book a reality. I want to thank Loretta Yates, the Executive Editor at Pearson Education, who got the project off the ground and assembled the project team for this book. I would also like to thank my old friend Rick Kughen at The Wordsmithery who served as the development editor and copy editor on this book. Rick waded through the first-draft text and provided many great ideas for improving its content. Our technical editor, Vince Averello, did a fantastic job making sure that everything in the book was technically sound. I would also like to thank managing editor, Sandra Schroeder; indexer, Johnna VanHoose Dinse; publishing coordinator, Charvi Arora; and our project editor, Charlotte Kughen, also at The Wordsmithery, who made sure the book made it to press on time. What a fantastic group of publishing professionals!

About the Author

Joe Habraken is an educator, digital media and computer technology professional, best-selling author, and documentary filmmaker with more than 30 years of experience in the information technology and digital media production fields. He has written more than 40 books, which include numerous titles on the Microsoft Office application suite, computer networking, and Microsoft's Windows Server network platform. His titles have been translated into numerous languages and read around the world. Joe is currently an associate professor of Communication at the University of New England in Biddeford, Maine, where he teaches a variety of digital media, film, and hands-on software-related courses.

Introduction

Although I have worked with Microsoft Windows applications since 1989, it still amazes me that the Microsoft 365 application suite (formally known as Microsoft Office) continues to evolve and offer very thoughtful enhancements to these powerful software tools. The apps "get better" with each subsequent release, and this latest iteration of the apps is no different. This latest version of the suite, which includes Word, Excel, PowerPoint, Outlook, and Publisher offers new features as well as refinements of existing processes and commands.

Microsoft 365 has been the gold standard for consumer desktop applications for most of my professional life, and it continues to provide all the tools that you need for a wide variety of tasks whether you are a writer, accountant, sales representative, engineer, teacher, or pretty much anything else.

Many of the features and certainly the user interface provided by this latest version of 365 will be familiar to some of you, who have used these applications before. You will, however, also find that each interface has changed somewhat (with the introduction of Windows 11) and that each app has new tools and enhancements that make them even more effective and powerful software tools.

The challenge of writing a book like this one that covers a group of applications, rather than a single application, means that a balance must be struck in the coverage of each of the applications. I think you will find that this book not only provides a solid foundation for each of the 365 applications (Word, Excel, PowerPoint, Outlook, and Publisher) but also provides a depth of coverage that will serve any user of the Microsoft 365 suite.

Who this book is for

This book offers a well-rounded look at the features most people will use in the Microsoft 365 apps and serves as both a primer for new users of the applications as well as an excellent reference for seasoned users of Word, Excel, PowerPoint, Outlook, and Publisher. Also, this book also goes the extra mile and provides information that will be useful to advanced 365 users and the IT professionals who support them. Whatever level of 365 user you consider yourself, you will find that this book is written in an easy-to-read, conversational style that allows you to concentrate on learning and understanding. Although each of the Office applications provides multiple ways to tackle nearly every task, this book stresses best practices in using the applications of this powerful and sometimes complex software suite.

Assumptions about you

This book has been designed to get the Microsoft 365 novice up and running and to allow the experienced 365 user a chance to flex their application "muscles" to accomplish even more with the likes of Word, Excel, PowerPoint, and Outlook. Newcomers will find it an excellent hands-on tool for learning the basics of the various Office applications. Those with more experience will find it a resource that enables them to go well beyond the basic capabilities of these powerful software applications. No matter what your experience level with the 365 apps, you will find that this book is a resource for learning how to best take advantage of the capabilities of the individual Office applications and also leverage the capabilities of Office as an integrated suite of software tools.

How this book is organized

This book is divided into six parts and also includes two appendixes. Each 365 application—Word, Excel, PowerPoint, Outlook, and Publisher—is discussed in detail in its own part or section. This book also includes an introductory section (Part I) that gets you up to speed with installing the 365 apps and discusses new features in the 365 application suite.

- Part I, "Getting started with the Microsoft 365 apps," gets you oriented to the 365 application interface and geography and looks at improvements and new features in the applications. This section also discusses managing and sharing your application files and working with graphics and images in the applications. An introduction to the updated 365 Online apps is also provided.

- Part II, "Word," takes an in-depth look at the Microsoft 365 suite's powerful word processor and desktop publishing application. This section begins with an overview of the Word application environment and how to access essential Word features and tools. Subsequent chapters build your Word knowledge base, from commonly used features and commands to advanced subject matter that helps you create more complex and specialized Word documents using styles, tables, and sections. This section also provides complete coverage of advanced features, such as Word's mail merge and forms, and it details approaches for creating larger documents that require a table of contents, footnotes, and cross-references.

- Part III, "Excel," quickly orients you to this powerful spreadsheet application so that you can immediately begin to work with worksheets, text labels, values, formulas, and cell ranges. This section then focuses on worksheet management and advanced formatting and provides an in-depth discussion on Excel formulas and functions. Charts, pivot tables, and tools for sorting and filtering data are also covered in this section. This part culminates in coverage of Excel's advanced features for validating and analyzing your worksheet data.

- Part IV, "PowerPoint," provides a detailed discussion of this powerful presentation tool. This section, which begins with an overview of the PowerPoint application environment and basic presentation tools and concepts, gives you all the information you need to build complex and compelling PowerPoint presentations. Chapters in this section include information on how to build better PowerPoint slides using themes, slide transitions, and special animations. The options and best practices for presenting PowerPoint presentations are also provided, with particular insight into how printed materials such as handouts and notes can make a presentation even more effective.

- Part V, "Outlook," covers how to use this powerful information manager both at home and at work. This section provides an overview of the Outlook interface and essential features and then shifts from the general to the specific by concentrating on Outlook's diverse capabilities. This coverage looks at Outlook's different roles as an email client, contact information manager, calendar manager, and organizer of tasks, notes, and other personal information. This section concludes with information to help you secure your information in Outlook and protect your Outlook Inbox from spam, viruses, and other security threats.

- Part VI, "Publisher," discusses the 365 suite's dedicated desktop publishing application. Publisher has evolved over the last few years into a professional layout and desktop publishing tool that enables you to quickly create a variety of visually appealing and professional documents. This section orients you to the basics of creating special documents in Publisher and then builds your knowledge base in the application so that you can create more professional and complex items, including online content.

The book completes its discussion of the Office applications with Appendix A, "Microsoft 365 app integration," and Appendix B, "Microsoft 365 macros," which provide information on integrating the Office applications and Office macros, respectively. Each appendix is designed to give you additional information related to the Office applications that you can use to leverage your capabilities when using the Office suite applications.

Errata, updates & book support

We've made every effort to ensure the accuracy of this book and its companion content. You can access updates to this book—in the form of a list of submitted errata and their related corrections—at:

MicrosoftPressStore.com/Office365insideout/errata

If you discover an error that is not already listed, please submit it to us at the same page.

For additional book support and information, please visit:

MicrosoftPressStore.com/Support.

Please note that product support for Microsoft software and hardware is not offered through the previous addresses. For help with Microsoft software or hardware, go to

http://support.microsoft.com.

Stay in touch

Let's keep the conversation going! We're on Twitter: *http://twitter.com/MicrosoftPress.*

PART I

Getting started with the Microsoft 365 apps

CHAPTER 1
**Getting oriented to the Microsoft 365
applications** 3

CHAPTER 2
**Navigating and customizing the 365
interface.** 19

CHAPTER 3
Managing and sharing 365 files 49

CHAPTER 4
Using and creating graphics 69

CHAPTER 5
Using the 365 Online apps 97

Getting oriented to the Microsoft 365 applications

Introducing Microsoft 365   3

New features and tools in Microsoft 365   8

The 365 Suite applications   12

The different versions of the 365 app suite   12

Hardware and software requirements for 365   14

Installing Microsoft 365   15

Getting help in the 365 applications   16

Microsoft 365 applications continue to be the most popular and most versatile application suite available. It is certainly the standard for professionals, students, and home users who work in the Microsoft Windows operating system environment. Whether you are using Microsoft 365 or have purchased the latest perpetual version of this powerful application suite, you have access to an impressive array of applications, including Word, Excel, PowerPoint, and Outlook. These applications enable you to tackle a large variety of business and personal tasks. Whether you are creating reports, crunching budget numbers, organizing a presentation, or managing your email and contacts, Microsoft 365 gives you all the tools and features you need to get the job done.

This chapter offers an introduction to the Microsoft 365 application suite. The discussion also incorporates licensing information options and highlights some of the new features and tools in Microsoft 365.

Introducing Microsoft 365

The current Microsoft 365 suite members are built upon the interface and features of their popular predecessors; the ribbon is still the go-to tool for accessing commands and features as you work in the applications. The Backstage provides access to settings related to managing, sharing, and printing your files as well as configuring each of the Microsoft 365 applications.

NOTE

Microsoft 365 is the new moniker for the array of productivity tools that include popular applications such as Word, Excel, and PowerPoint. The name change (from Office 365 to Microsoft 365) is a reflection that the suite now includes collaboration tools that go beyond the capabilities and possibilities provided by previous versions of the popular Office application suite.

When you get past the fact that the overall look of the applications has evolved slowly (from Office 2007 to present) and does not look radically different than earlier versions of these software applications, you will find that Microsoft has continued to make improvements and enhancements to the Microsoft 365 application suite members. Those changes might not be as numerous or as high-profile as we have seen in some of the previous launches. Still, you will find that they do provide for more efficiency when working with the various productivity applications included in the suite.

For example, in the Microsoft 365 version of Word, we see a new addition to the Editor's Home tab. The Editor command allows you to quickly check the spelling and grammar in the current document and also provides suggestions for refinements to the document related to clarity, conciseness, and vocabulary (see Figure 1-1).

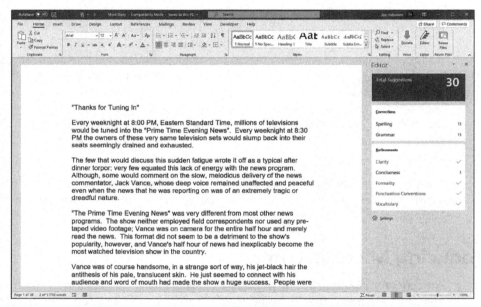

Figure 1-1   The new Editor pane provides help with spelling, grammar, and other refinements.

You will find that many of the updates to Microsoft 365 are on the subtle side. These updates don't necessarily allow you to accomplish something epic, but they do make your life easier in that the new tools anticipate your needs as you work in a particular application. This move to a "smarter" application suite really began with the inclusion of the Tell Me What You Want To Do search box at the top of each Office application window. Although this intuitive feature isn't referred to as the Tell Me What You Want to Do box in the most recent version of Microsoft 365, it still exists and has morphed into the Search box (again found at the top of each application).

Inside OUT

Upgrading Microsoft 365 versus Perpetual Office

When you subscribe to a Microsoft 365 subscription (or if your school or workplace has a subscription that you use), your Office application features and tools are upgraded over time. If you purchase a nonsubscription version of Office at a store or online, all the new Office features available at the time this software is released will be present in your version of Office. This nonsubscription version of Office will receive bug fixes and updates over time but will not necessarily be updated in terms of new features. Your first opportunity to get a complete makeover for your Office product would be when Microsoft releases a new "dated" or perpetual version of Office.

A Microsoft 365 subscription will be updated over the time of your subscription, so you will end up with some new features and possibilities as Microsoft develops them. However, there is a big caveat related to updates. If you get your Office applications through your work or school, the updating of your Office installation on your computer is controlled by the IT folks who maintain your network. This means that your Office installation will be updated only when IT determines that they will roll out a particular upgrade provided by Microsoft. If you purchase your Microsoft 365 subscription for home or a small business, your Office installation(s) will be updated (by your leave) whenever an update is available from Microsoft.

The Search box also allows you to locate commands, application help, and information on the web quickly by entering a text string that tells the application what information you need. For example, let's say I am new to working with an Excel worksheet that contains a lot of data, and I want to organize it as a table. However, because I haven't worked with the Excel data tools very much, I can get command-specific help on organizing the table data. Figure 1-2 shows the results of the text string, "organize the data." At the top of the Search box, actions related to your search string appear; in this case, the Sort & Filter and Data Validation commands appear. There is also a Get Help On area that allows you to access the Help system for the application you are using (in this case, Excel).

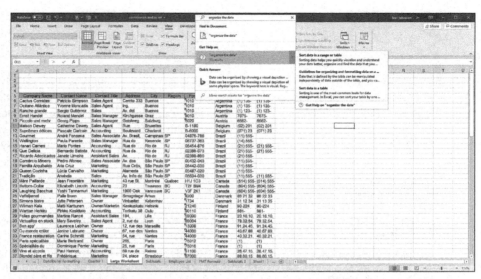

Figure 1-2   The Excel Search box helps you find actions and help related to any text search string.

To take advantage of a command provided in the search list, just select it; options related to the command (if any) will appear in a secondary box and can be accessed with a click of the mouse. For example, if you choose Sort & Filter, you will be provided with the option of doing an ascending or descending sort or creating a custom sort. The Search box's hands-on approach to providing help also links to more traditional help by selecting the results in the Get Help On area of the Search box. You can also use the Search feature when you are working with text in an application. In Word or PowerPoint, just right-click a word or text string and then select Search (in Excel, right-click the text and then select Smart Lookup). The Search feature uses Bing to search the web using keywords from the text string that you inserted into the search box. The results of the Bing search are displayed in the Search pane.

Other updates to the Microsoft 365 suite relate to collaborating with others in real time, which has been an evolutionary mantra for the 365 suite since the Office 2016 release. For example, Word now makes it easy for collaborators to view and act on comments in a Word document. These comments are referred to as "modern comments" and are also available in Excel and PowerPoint. Figure 1-3 provides a look at a comment in a shared Word document. The comment appears as a note icon within the text and also appears in the right-hand margin of the document. When a comment is selected in the text, a border appears around the comment, and you are also provided with easy access to commands such as Edit Comment, Delete Thread, and Resolve Thread. A Reply box also provides you with a quick way to message other users who are working in the same shared document.

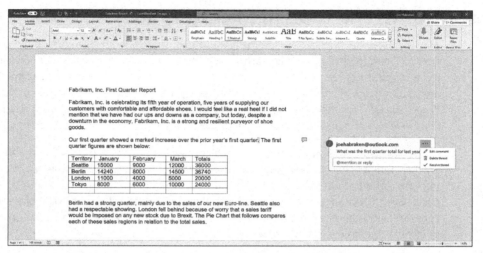

Figure 1-3   Modern comments provide the 365 apps with powerful collaboration tools.

The 365 Web apps also allow you to work with the modern comments feature, making this highly portable version of the 365 applications an extremely useful fallback when you don't have access to a computer with the full complement of Microsoft 365 apps installed.

Other Office for the Web improvements include the following:

- Enhancements to Excel for creating charts and navigating lists

- A PowerPoint Standout option that allows you to overlay your video feed on the current presentation slide

- A Word For The Web feature that allows you to add borders to tables and adjust margins and tabs in a document using the ruler

A number of other subtle yet important updates to the Office for the Web apps are covered in Chapter 5, "Using the 365 Online apps."

TIP

Both the installed version of the 365 apps and the online versions have made it easier for you to share files and add comments to documents, worksheets, and presentations that you are creating through collaboration with coworkers. Share and Comments commands reside in the upper-right (just above the ribbon) portion of the application window in Word, Excel, and PowerPoint.

In the next section, we will take a look at some of the other new features you will find in the desktop versions of the 365 applications. We can then sort out the different versions of the Microsoft 365 suite and the actual applications that these different bundles contain.

CHAPTER 1

New features and tools in Microsoft 365

The Microsoft 365 applications interface and the tools provided by the various 365 suite members changed fairly dramatically, starting with the 2010 version of Microsoft Office and continuing through the Office 2013 and the Office 2016 updates. Not only were the new interface and a host of functional changes rolled out over several iterations of the 365 suite, but the introduction of the Office for the Web apps was an even more dramatic moment. The Web apps use OneDrive as a primary storage solution for files that you create using the Web apps.

As the Microsoft 365 suite continued to evolve, new features related to online storage and strategies relating to sharing files and collaborating with others in real time have become "baked into" the apps. Both the Microsoft 365 applications and their Office for the Web-based counterparts have truly changed how we use the applications to share data and collaborate with others. Let's take a look at recent enhancements to the Microsoft 365 apps and how this powerful productivity suite has continued to evolve.

Collaborating in the cloud

The Microsoft 365 application suite encourages you to save your files to the cloud via OneDrive. Different cloud storage options may be available depending on the environment where you use the 365 applications—home, small business, or corporation. If you are a home user, you can take advantage of OneDrive to store your files. You can then access your files on any device running 365 or any device with a web browser that provides you with access to the 365 Web apps. You can use the Web apps to view or edit files that you have stored on OneDrive. You can also create documents, presentations, and workbooks using the Web apps and then store those files on OneDrive.

If you are a small business user who subscribes to Microsoft 365, you can save your files to OneDrive for Business, a SharePoint site that is part of your subscription. As with the free version of OneDrive, you can access files stored on OneDrive for Business from multiple devices. In addition, corporate users of Microsoft 365 can also store files in the cloud by taking advantage of a SharePoint site hosted by their companies or institutions.

Another aspect of sharing files in the cloud is the ability to collaborate in real time with other users. Microsoft 365 offers real-time collaboration for Word, PowerPoint, and Excel. Collaborators can edit and comment on files once you share a file and send invitations for the document, workbook, or presentation. Saving your files to the cloud becomes a requirement if you are planning on using the Web apps when you don't have access to your desktop Office applications. Saving to the cloud not only makes it easy for you to access your important files, but it also makes it easy for you to quickly share a file with coworkers and collaborators.

➤ For more information on saving files to the cloud, see Chapter 5.

Collaborating with Microsoft Teams

Another possibility for sharing information and collaborating with others is Microsoft Teams. Although Teams was initially introduced by Microsoft in late 2016, this collaboration workspace has slowly rolled out in enterprise deployments of Microsoft 365 and is now available for small business and personal use. You can sign up for a free Teams personal account at Microsoft's Teams site (*https://www.microsoft.com/en-us/microsoft-teams*). The best way to describe Microsoft Teams is that it allows you to establish a team, which consists of the people you will collaborate with on one or more projects. Channels allow you to organize your team and topics into groups such as departments or by particular topics. The chats, meetings, and content (files) available in a particular channel of a Teams site are available to all the members of the team. The great thing about Teams is that it provides easy access to files and other information, and it allows the team members to talk in real time either via chats or meetings (including video conferencing).

More importantly to our current discussion, Microsoft Teams is also integrated with the Microsoft 365 applications and allows you to work with other team members in real-time content creation. The first time you open Teams (post-intallation), you are provided a General channel designed to manage a project. The home screen (shown in Figure 1-4) provides you with easy access to the Teams command taskbar, which provides one-click commands including Chat, Teams (for building the team), Meetings, Calls, and Files. Note that in Figure 1-4, selecting the Meetings command provides you with the ability to immediately start or schedule a meeting.

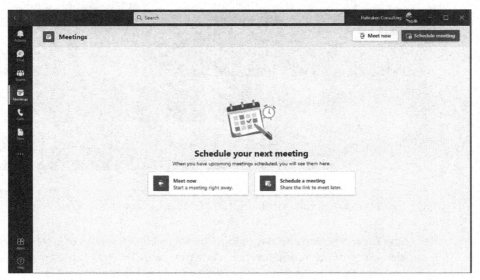

Figure 1-4   Microsoft Teams provides a new platform for collaboration.

Other 365 improvements and updates

Although Microsoft 365 is in some respects a fairly mature product, new improvements and updates—both big and small—continue to enhance the capabilities and usability of this powerful application suite. The following list highlights some of the changes that have been made to the 365 applications over the last year. More coverage is provided on many of these important changes within the chapters that cover specific applications such as Word or Excel.

- **Free Stock Images Library for Word, Excel, PowerPoint, and Outlook:** Microsoft now provides more than 8,000 royalty-free images for use with the 365 applications. In Word, Excel, and PowerPoint, these stock images can be accessed by selecting the ribbon's Insert tab, selecting the Pictures command, and then selecting Stock Images on the Insert Picture From drop-down menu. In Outlook, create a new message and then click in the body of the email. To access stock images, select Insert, Pictures, Stock Images. Figure 1-5 shows the Stock Images window, which provides access to images grouped in various categories including Tranquility, Motion, and Growth. Chapter 4, "Using and creating graphics," includes additional information on using the stock images library.

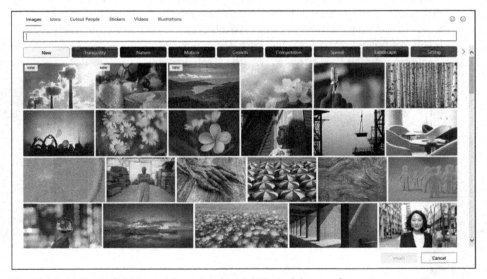

Figure 1-5   Microsoft 365 provides more than 8,000 stock images for your use.

- **New Excel function and data tools:** The Microsoft 365 version of Excel now boasts a new version of the lookup function named xlookup. This new version of the lookup function provides an exact match by default and is simpler to configure than the vlookup function. Excel also now provides linked data types that connect to source data provided by trusted sources such as the Bing search engine, Wolfram (an intelligence engine for computing answers), and Microsoft Power BI (a business analytics tool). Detailed coverage of Excel begins in Chapter 11, "Essential Excel features."

- **PowerPoint: Create Animated GIFs.** This new feature allows you to create animated GIFs using your presentation slides as source material. This PowerPoint feature even allows you to create animated GIFs with a transparent background. PowerPoint now makes it easier to create a link to another slide in the same presentation. PowerPoint is covered in detail, beginning with Chapter 17, "Essential PowerPoint features."

- **Outlook lets you dictate draft messages and commands:** The dictation toolbar provides you with the ability to draft Outlook items using your voice. You can also do a voice search (and filter the search) using everyday language. Outlook is covered in detail, beginning with Chapter 22, "Outlook configuration and essential features."

- **Create a private copy of a shared document in Word:** Typically, when you are collaborating with others on a Word document (stored via a OneDrive or Teams site), you will make annotations and edits on the document, which are then shared with all the collaborators who have been given sharing permissions for the document. In some situations, however, you might want to create a private copy of the document that you can then mark up with your own personal annotations. This feature also provides you with a link that allows access to the original shared document. Coverage of Word begins with Chapter 6, "Essential Word features."

- **Hex color values now available in Microsoft 365:** When you are working with colors for fonts, graphic objects, and the like, the Colors dialog box now includes an option for you to enter the Hex color value for a particular color. The Hex color feature is available in all the Microsoft 365 applications, including Microsoft Publisher, which is covered in Chapters 27 and 28.

- **Better Web apps:** The 365 Web apps have added features, including PowerPoint for the Web's ability to insert audio and playback settings for your slideshow. Excel for the Web now allows you to insert links to other workbooks and supports the linked data types discussed earlier in this section. The Web apps continue to evolve and can serve you well when you don't have access to the installed versions of the 365 applications.

This isn't an exhaustive list of changes to the 365 applications, but hopefully, you get the feeling that Microsoft 365 continues to evolve over time. Microsoft 365 is a powerful application suite, and you can do more in the applications and do it more effectively than ever before.

➤ **For more about the 365 Web apps, see Chapter 5.**

The 365 suite applications

The Microsoft 365 applications are bundled in different versions. The applications available in your installation depend on the bundle version that you or your company purchased. If your 365 applications installation is part of your Microsoft 365 subscription, the applications you have access to depend on your subscription level. It is also possible that your release is not part of a subscription but was purchased as a perpetual version (meaning it will not be upgraded over time in terms of new features). We sort out the different versions and subscription application mixes in the next section. In this book, we concentrate on the following applications:

- **Word:** Word has been the standard for word processing in the Windows environment for many years, and it provides many possibilities in this latest version. Whether you use Word to create letters, short reports, or lengthy documents that include footnotes, a table of contents, or cross-references, you will find in-depth coverage of Word in Part II.

- **Excel:** This powerful number cruncher continues to be the gold standard for spreadsheet software. Excel in-depth coverage can be found in Part III.

- **PowerPoint:** Your PowerPoint presentations can be even more exciting than ever, with widescreen slide formats and theme variations. PowerPoint's in-depth coverage is located in Part IV.

- **Outlook:** This versatile personal information manager and email client enables you to communicate with coworkers and friends and manage all your messages, contacts, and appointments. Part V covers this application.

- **Publisher:** With Publisher, you can create a range of publication types, from the simple to the complex. Publisher is a full-featured desktop publishing application. Part VI provides in-depth coverage.

Microsoft Teams, introduced earlier in the chapter, isn't an actual member of the Microsoft 365 application suite, but it is a useful platform for communicating with colleagues, sharing files, and collaborating with others. Your 365 installation might also include other applications, such as Microsoft Access, which is a relational database application. We do not cover Access in this book. If you are more than a casual user of this powerhouse database software, a good resource is the *Access 2019 Bible* by Michael Alexander and Richard Kusleika. The Microsoft 365 applications (and associated add-ons such as Teams) are designed as an integrated group of software tools. You can easily share information between these applications and use multiple applications to build powerful reports, presentations, and shared content.

The different versions of the 365 app suite

Microsoft 365 (or Microsoft Office as it has been known for years) licensing has changed a lot in the past few years. If you do not work for a business or institution that uses Microsoft's volume licensing, you probably choose to license Microsoft Office through a Microsoft 365 subscription.

Volume licensing and retail versions of 365 certainly exist, although, at the time of the writing of this book, the large business and enterprise options for Office were somewhat vague. It is assured, however, that the DVD Office installation is dead, and most users will install their 365 applications through their Microsoft 365 subscriptions online using Click-to-Run. Enterprise business information technology gurus will install 365 on Windows PCs using MSI (Microsoft Installer) files, and these might pull the software files from the online software repositories.

If you derive your 365 software through your workplace, you really don't have to worry about acquiring or installing the Microsoft 365 suite, so you may want to skip this section of the chapter. However, there is one thing related to institutional licensing that you might find interesting.

If you work at a large company or institution (particularly an educational institution), the licensing agreement purchased by your organization might even include perks such as allowing the installation of 365 applications on home PCs or personal devices. You might want to check with your IT department.

NOTE

If you don't want to go the Microsoft 365 subscription route and want more Office applications than are provided by the Home & Student versions, you can purchase the full-blown application suite at a tech store or online. This will be the perpetual version (the latest perpetual version was released in 2019), which does not get upgraded over time; the Microsoft 365 subscription version updates as long as you continue your subscription.

In terms of the home or small business user looking for a consistent bargain with continued updates, your future use of the 365 applications will be tied to a Microsoft 365 subscription. An exception to this statement does exist: An Office Home & Student version of the 365 applications is available as a one-time purchase. This is a perpetual version of the application suite and will receive application fixes and upgrades only for a limited time. Also, some new laptops come with different preinstalled versions of Microsoft applications. However, most of these preinstalled packages do not include Microsoft Publisher or Microsoft Access. The Home & Student version also does not include Outlook. You can review pricing for these bundles at http://www.microsoftstore.com.

Office 365 subscriptions also come in a number of different flavors and can be reviewed at the Microsoft store. If you use Office for a small business, you might want to look at some of the business options that Microsoft offers. One of the advantages of some of these subscriptions is that you can install the 365 apps on multiple computers and devices. Some of the available Office 365 subscriptions are as follows:

- **Office 365 Family:** This subscription provides Word, Excel, PowerPoint, OneNote, and Outlook. You can install the Office software on up to six PCs, Macs, or other devices, and this subscription is not user-specific. The subscription provides 1 TB of OneDrive cloud storage for each member of the family.

- **Office 365 Personal:** This subscription provides Word, Excel, PowerPoint, OneNote, and Outlook. You can install Office on one PC or Mac, and you can install the applications on one other smart device running Windows 10, IOS, or Android. The subscription also supplies 1 TB of OneDrive cloud storage.

- **Microsoft 365 Business standard:** This subscription (which is currently priced per user per month) provides Word, Excel, PowerPoint, Outlook, Publisher, and Access. This subscription also provides specific cloud services such as Microsoft Teams, OneDrive, and SharePoint.

- **Microsoft 365 Business premium:** This subscription is similar to the Business standard subscription and also includes Microsoft Azure Information Protection and Microsoft Intune, which provides for greater security and control of organizational devices including phones, tablets, and laptops.

All the available versions of Microsoft 365 (both purchase and subscription) provide the core applications (Excel, PowerPoint, and Word). You will want to determine your own needs in relation to the application mix that you purchase or receive as part of a subscription.

Hardware and software requirements for 365

All the bells and whistles of the Microsoft 365 apps come with hardware requirements. It is always better to have a computer that exceeds the minimum hardware requirements for a software application. The more memory your computer has and the faster its processor is, the more enjoyable your experience will be as you use the suite applications. This book concentrates on Microsoft 365 installations on a PC running Windows 10. Office is available on different operating system platforms across a range of devices. Research the 365 hardware and operating system requirements for your device before you purchase the software or attempt to install it. A good place to start gathering information is www.microsoft.com.

Running Office on a PC requires Windows 10. There are also hardware requirements. The minimum hardware requirements for Office on a PC and some realistic recommendations are as follows:

- **Processor:** 1.6 GHz processor (at least). I recommend at least 1.6GHz or better to really take advantage of what Office has to offer—the faster, the better. Any new computer with a dual-core processor (or better) runs the Office applications at peak performance.

- **Memory (RAM):** 2 GB for a 32-bit system, and 4 GB for a 64-bit system. I recommend a bare minimum of 4 GB on a 32-bit system and 8 GB for a 64-bit system. Memory is relatively inexpensive. The more RAM you have, the better these applications run, particularly when you want to run multiple applications at the same time.

- **Hard drive space:** A minimum of 4 GB is required for installing the Office suite. If you are running low on space on the hard drive that also contains your Windows installation, get an external drive such as a USB drive, and clean up and move files off the main drive. You can then install 365.

- **Graphics card:** You need a DirectX 12–compatible (or newer) graphics card with a resolution of 1280x768. As with everything else, the more powerful your video card is, the better the graphic-intensive Office features run.

In terms of the Windows operating system and Microsoft 365 compatibility, you can run the 32-bit version of Office on a computer that is running Windows 10. Make sure that your Windows installation is up to date on service packs before installing the 365 apps. Although it is not a hardware or software requirement for installing Office, get a Microsoft ID if you do not currently have one, particularly if you purchased an installation version of 365 rather than a subscription that includes OneDrive. A Microsoft ID enables you to use Microsoft's free OneDrive. You can connect your OneDrive to your 365 applications, which gives you another possibility for saving your files to the cloud. Having access to OneDrive also gives you access to the Office Web apps.

Installing Microsoft 365

If you work for a company or institution, chances are Microsoft 365 (at least a subset of the applications) is installed and updated for you. If you purchase a nonsubscription installation of 365, the installation instructions are provided with your purchase.

If you subscribe to Microsoft 365, you will have an account page that can be accessed via https://store.office.com. All you must do is log on and then select the My Account link in the upper right of the browser window. To install software on a PC or other device, select the Install link and follow the instructions to install your software.

You will find that the 365 installation on a Windows PC pretty much takes care of itself. You do have a role at the end of the installation process, though: You must activate the 365 apps suite the first time you launch one of the 365 applications.

To activate your installation, you will use the Microsoft ID that is associated with your Microsoft 365 subscription. If you purchased the software rather than subscribed, you do have the option of entering a product key to activate the 365 applications.

NOTE

If you use 365 on a corporate network, your network administrator more than likely dictates how you upgrade to or install the 365 application suite.

After your 365 installation is activated, you can begin to use your installed applications. If you are new to 365, you may want to take a look at Chapter 2, "Navigating and customizing the 365 interface," and Chapter 3, "Managing and sharing 365 files," before tackling the sections of the book that are devoted to specific applications, such as Word, Excel, and Outlook.

Getting Help in the 365 applications

We briefly discussed the Search box earlier in the chapter and how it provides you information and help when you are working in one of the suite applications such as Word or PowerPoint. The 365 applications provide an intelligent Help system that provides access to application-specific Help files as well as access to web-based information without exiting the application. You can search for commands and features as needed. Selecting one of the commands provided by a successful search in one of the 365 applications allows you to actually access that feature or tool (rather than just read about it on a help page).

As already mentioned, the Search box also provides you with access to more traditional help with an application. The search results go beyond traditional help, however, and supply you with the option of accessing additional information by using Bing to do a web search based on your search terms. The Search results from the Bing web search are shown in the search, which opens on the right of the application window.

Figure 1-6 shows the Word application window and the results of a search using the Search box; the search string used was "create chart." Note that the results provide the three possibilities that we discussed earlier: commands related to the search terms are provided in the Search box results (one of the possibilities shown is Add A Chart). The Search box also provides a link to get traditional help (by selecting Get Help On "Create Chart").

When you select More Search Results (at the bottom of the Search box), the Search pane opens on the right of the application window. The Search pane provides both traditional help (based on your search string) and information found by Bing.

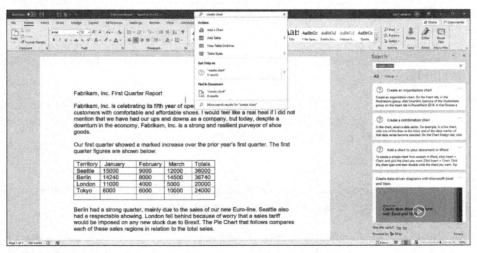

Figure 1-6   The Search box and pane provide you with help and information based on your search string.

Obviously, selecting a command provided by the search results allows you to return to your work immediately and access that feature or tool. However, for more conceptual help and background information on a particular task, you can take advantage of the traditional help links in the Get Help On area of the Search box or the More Search Results link at the bottom of the Search box. Both options will open the Search pane, which provides information from the application help system. Getting additional information via a Bing web search (based on your search terms) is a bonus and will often give you information that allows you to understand and successfully use any of the myriad features and functions provided by the Microsoft 365 application suite.

Once you have the Search pane open, you can run additional searches by typing keywords into the text box at the top of the Search pane. As already mentioned, links are then provided in your search results that enable you to explore related information. To close the Search pane, either select the Close button at the top right of the pane or press the ESC key on the keyboard.

TIP

You can access Help at any time in the Office applications on your PC by pressing the F1 Function key.

The Backstage—first mentioned at the beginning of this chapter—can also serve as an informational tool. It doesn't give you help on a particular feature or command or let you search for help by topic. It can, however, give you information on the current document (or file you are working with) as well as information about your 365 installation and connected services.

Enter the Backstage by selecting File on the ribbon. To access the Info page for the current document, select Info from the Backstage commands. This page gives you the properties for the current document. This page also lists the authors who have modified the document. The Info page provides tools that enable you to protect and inspect your file. We discuss how to use these tools in Chapter 3.

Another source of information in the Backstage is the Account page. This page gives you a list of the 365 applications installed on your computer and provides a list of all your connected services. Connected services can be your OneDrive, OneDrive for Business, and even YouTube. The Connected Services list enables you to manage these connected services, and you can remove a service by clicking the Remove link. Any service that you disconnect can be reconnected at any time.

This page also provides you with information on Office Updates and allows you to manage your 365 account. When you select Manage Account on the Account page, a browser window will open, providing you with access to your account's Admin page.

You might find that in terms of helping you complete your day-to-day tasks and satisfy other people's excessive expectations of what the 365 applications can actually do, your most valuable resource is your sense of humor. You are going to make mistakes—and sometimes the 365 applications can be frustrating—so don't be afraid to laugh once in a while.

Navigating and customizing the 365 interface

Getting familiar with the 365 interface   19

Navigating the 365 applications   24

Customizing an application interface   31

Configuring application options   38

Using the Trust Center   43

The Microsoft 365 applications are designed to make it easy for you to concentrate on your work, regardless of whether you are working on a Word document, Excel Worksheet, or a PowerPoint slide presentation. These powerful applications are also designed so that you can quickly access the commands and features that you need to get the job done. The 365 suite applications' easy-to-use interface centers around the ribbon, which is the place to go when you need to access an application command or feature. In this chapter, we take a look at the interface shared by the 365 applications (primarily Word, Excel, PowerPoint, and Publisher) and explore how to stay productive as you navigate the various command elements, such as the ribbon tabs, galleries, dialog boxes, task panes, and even the status bar.

We look at options for customizing the ribbon, and we explore the application Backstage. Our discussion also includes the Trust Center, which enables you to specify trusted locations for opening files and other security settings.

Getting familiar with the 365 interface

The 365 applications employ a ribbon-centric user interface that uses each ribbon tab to group commands into somewhat broad yet related categories. For example, in Word, the Review tab (shown in Figure 2-1) provides groups of commands related to reviewing and finalizing a document.

These groups include the Proofing group, the Speech group (which only contains the Read Aloud command), the Language group, the Comments group, the Tracking group, the Changes group, the Compare group, the Protect group, and the Resume Assistant. All these groups, except for the Resume Assistant (see note), provide commands related to reviewing and fine-tuning a Word document. Most of us will at least take advantage of the Editor command, which checks for spelling and grammar problems and also provides suggested refinements related to clarity, conciseness, and punctuation conventions, among other things.

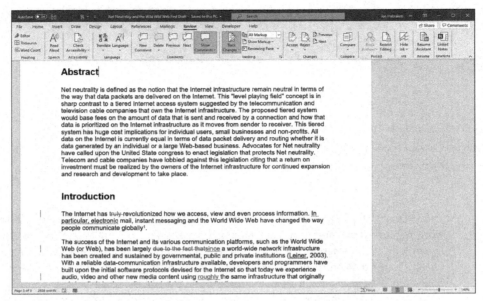

Figure 2-1   Ribbon tabs house related command groups.

NOTE

The Review tab's Resume Assistant doesn't provide a group of commands as do the Compare and Protect groups. The Resume Assistant's job is to help you create a great resume by viewing resume information and people's work experiences on LinkedIn. Select the Resume Assistant and then click Get Started in the Resume Assistant pane on the left side of the Word workspace.

The 365 application user interface does its best to provide consistency across the 365 applications. The Home tab in the Word, Excel, PowerPoint, or Publisher application window contains the Clipboard group and other groups related to font formatting, text alignment, and styles. Considering the different purposes of the 365 applications, the ribbon tabs and accompanying command groups obviously vary from application to application in the suite. However, the similarities help you quickly adapt your knowledge of one of the applications that you know well (such as Word) to an application that you have not used as much (say, PowerPoint).

Galleries

Certain commands on the ribbon tabs require that you select from a list of choices. Some of these commands provide a simple list of choices, whereas other commands provide a more visual representation of the choices in a gallery.

A gallery supplies the actual results related to a command. For example, if you want to apply a theme to a PowerPoint presentation, access the Design tab and select from the available theme choices, as shown in Figure 2-2. As you work in the 365 applications, you can select theme choices for your documents; each theme also supplies variants, which provide subtle changes to the theme colors, fonts, and effects.

Figure 2-2   Galleries provide results-driven options.

Many of the galleries are related to the visual appearance or formatting of objects (such as tables or charts) in your documents, slides, and worksheets. Consequently, a live preview of how that particular option would apply to your application's content is supplied when you place the mouse on that option. Being able to immediately preview an option and then apply a particular gallery option gives you greater flexibility and efficiency as you work with gallery-driven commands on the various ribbon tabs.

> **NOTE**
>
> **The ToolTips in the 365 applications can be really helpful. Just place the mouse on a particular command to get a short description of that command.**

Contextual tabs

As you work in a Microsoft 365 application, the ribbon tabs that are available do not remain static; they change depending on the task you are currently undertaking. These Contextual tabs become available when you are working with a particular object or feature that provides multiple options.

CHAPTER 2

For example, if you insert a table into a Word document or PowerPoint slide and then place the insertion point inside that table or select a row or column in the table, two Table Tools tabs appear: Table Design and Layout. Figure 2-3 shows the Design and Layout tabs of the Table Tools tab, with the Layout tab selected.

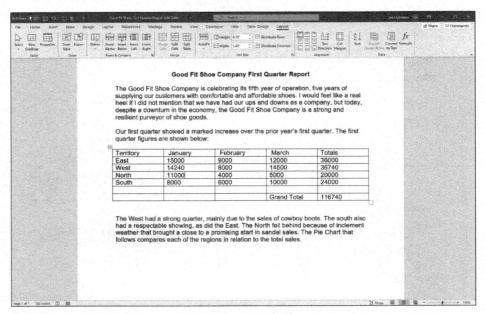

Figure 2-3   Contextual tabs provide tools for the task at hand.

You can use the commands on these contextual tabs related to tables as long as the table object is active. As soon as you click outside the table, the contextual tabs disappear, and you return to the ribbon with only the core tabs available. The core tabs include Home, Insert, and so forth; the specific tabs available depend on the application you are using and the task you are undertaking.

Overview of the 365 application window

If you are new to the 365 interface, it makes sense to take some time to gain familiarity with its various parts. Figure 2-4 shows the Excel application window. You will find that the most often used applications (Word, Excel, and PowerPoint) have very similar workspace geographies.

The following list provides a short overview of several elements common to the application interface:

- **Title bar:** The title bar supplies the application name and the name of your file (after you have saved it). The title bar also includes the Minimize, Maximize/Restore, and Close buttons on the far right.

- **Quick Access Toolbar:** The Quick Access Toolbar is nestled on the left side of the title bar. The Quick Access Toolbar provides the Save, Undo, and Redo buttons by default. You can customize it to include other commands by using the Customize Quick Access Toolbar button.

- **Ribbon:** The ribbon is the primary tool for accessing commands and features in the 365 applications. It contains a set of default tabs for each of the applications. Each tab includes command groups, which then contain individual commands. The Help button resides on the far right.

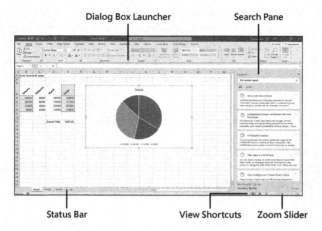

Figure 2-4   The Excel application window

- **Dialog box launcher:** Some command groups on the ribbon tabs provide a dialog box launcher to the right of the group's name. The launcher enables you to open a dialog box that contains options related to that particular group. For example, the Font group on Excel's Home tab provides a dialog box launcher that opens the Format Cells dialog box with the Font tab selected.

- **Task panes:** A task pane is a multipurpose, feature-related window. A good example of a task pane is the Insights task pane, which opens via the Smart Lookup command on the ribbon's Review tab. Different task panes are found in the individual applications. For example, in PowerPoint, there is a task pane that allows you to quickly format objects such as text boxes and other shapes.

- **Shortcut menus:** Shortcut menus have been a mainstay of the 365 applications for many years. Right-click a selected object to see options related to that object. The shortcut menus are often referred to as contextual menus because they provide commands that are within the context of the selected object.

- **Scrollbars and rulers:** Both vertical and horizontal scrollbars are available in the applications. The rulers enable you to align objects more precisely and to set tabs and indents in applications such as Word and PowerPoint.

- **Status bar:** The status bar provides application information, feature indicators, and view commands. For example, in Word, the left side of the taskbar provides information such as the page number and other application-specific information, including word count and section number. The far right of the status bar provides the View shortcuts and the Zoom slider, by default.

It goes without saying that the individual application windows vary depending on the application you are using. Word, Excel, PowerPoint, and Publisher share the most elements of the 365 applications (although Publisher does have some specialized interface tools); Outlook adheres to the "typical" ribbon-centric interface as much as possible but also provides unique tools for navigating the application. For example, Outlook provides a Folders pane that enables you to quickly access folders such as your Inbox, Sent Items, and Junk Email.

Although the 365 applications share many navigation and command elements, the "one-size-fits-all" application geography breaks down when you work with some of the more "specialized" applications, such as Outlook. And because each application is built around a specific purpose, even Word, Excel, and PowerPoint require unique command elements that enable you to tackle a particular task or work with a specific feature.

NOTE

Although it's called a dialog box launcher, some of the items that a launcher opens are really task panes instead of dialog boxes. For example, when you select the dialog box launcher for the Clipboard group, the Clipboard pane opens rather than a floating dialog box.

➤ Outlook is discussed in depth in Part V, "Outlook," beginning with Chapter 22, "Outlook configuration and essential features."

Navigating the 365 applications

Because the 365 applications take advantage of the same core user interface, some universal procedures work for navigating and using the individual applications. However, because each 365 application creates different things (say, worksheets versus documents, calendars, or contacts lists), the nuances that make up the more detailed command structures of the individual applications require that you develop some specific knowledge for each application.

As mentioned earlier in this chapter, at the center of the Microsoft 365 user interface is the ribbon. Therefore, the ribbon is a good place to start an investigation of common features and tools in the 365 applications.

Working with the ribbon

The ribbon tabs provide a results-driven grouping of application commands that places closely related commands into specific groups. Accessing ribbon commands is just a matter of selecting the appropriate ribbon tab and then accessing the command you want from a group on that tab.

For example, in Excel, you might want to insert a Sum function into a selected worksheet cell to total a column of values. You select the ribbon's Formulas tab, look in the Function Library group, and then select the AutoSum command. The ribbon's structure makes it easy to quickly drill down to a specific command or feature.

Some of the individual commands in the command groups include a drop-down arrow. Clicking this arrow on some commands gives you a simple list of options related to the command, which might also open dialog boxes associated with that particular feature. For example, clicking the Insert command on the Excel ribbon's Home tab provides the options Insert Cells, Insert Sheet Rows, Insert Sheet Columns, and Insert Sheet. The Insert Cells option opens the Insert dialog box, where you can specify how the inserted cells should affect existing cells or whether Excel should insert an entire row or column.

Other commands provide access to a gallery of choices related to the command. For example, if you have selected text in a Word document and you want to apply a new style to the selected text, you can do so from the Style gallery, which is available in the Style group on the ribbon's Home tab.

When you place the mouse pointer on one of the styles provided in the Style gallery, you can preview the style on the selected text (see Figure 2-5). This feature, called Live Preview, enables you to test various options as you work in a 365 application and apply only the option that works best. This saves you from having to apply a certain option to see how it looks and then using the Undo command to start over when you don't like the results.

The Live Preview feature is most prevalent in Word, Excel, PowerPoint, and Publisher. For example, a number of Word commands bring up Live Preview, including the Line and Paragraph Spacing command in the Paragraph group on the Home tab and the Header, Footer, and Page Number commands on the ribbon's Insert tab (in the Header And Footer group).

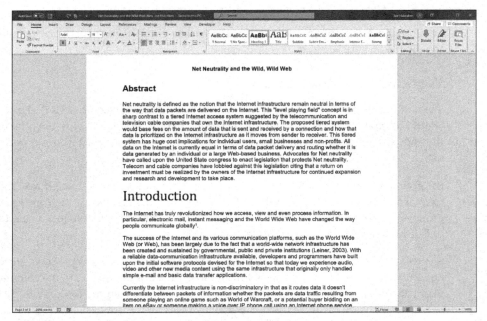

Figure 2-5   Galleries provide visual options and Live Preview.

Minimizing the ribbon

The ribbon takes up a big chunk of the application window because it provides visual cues for accessing commands and typically contains different galleries on the ribbon tabs. You can configure how you want the ribbon to behave in an application window. At the upper right of the application workspace (the application window) is a ribbon Display Options button, which is just above your name.

The Ribbon Display Options button gives you three options for dealing with the ribbon:

- **Auto-Hide Ribbon:** This option hides the ribbon. You can access the ribbon by clicking at the top of the application window.

- **Show Tabs:** This option shows the ribbon tabs only. Click a tab to view the associated commands.

- **Show Tabs And Commands:** This option is the default setting and shows the entire ribbon, including the tabs and the commands available on the currently selected tab.

All the 365 applications provide the Display Options button except for Publisher. Publisher also does not have the Search box (in the middle of the application title bar) that is provided by the other 365 applications; the Publisher's Help button is on the far right of the Publisher application window.

Accessing the ribbon with the keyboard

You can also access some ribbon commands using the keyboard. The keystrokes aren't typical keyboard shortcuts, such as Ctrl+B for bold, but they can work for you when you want to keep your hands on the keyboard.

Press (and release) the Alt key, and individual shortcut keys appear for the tabs on the ribbon. For example, the Home tab is assigned the H shortcut key, the Insert tab is assigned N, and so on. Select one of the ribbon tabs using the appropriate shortcut key. The tab is selected, and keyboard shortcuts are assigned to the commands on the tab. Figure 2-6 shows the keyboard shortcuts assigned to the Word ribbon's Home tab (activated by pressing H to access the Home tab).

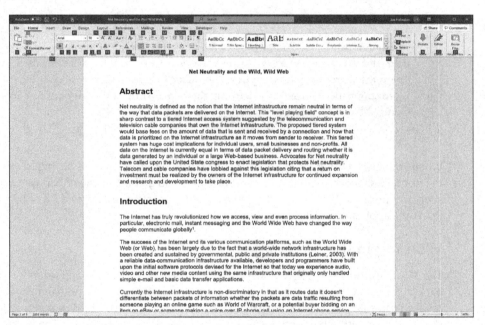

Figure 2-6   Access ribbon commands from the keyboard.

Individual alphanumeric keystrokes and multiple alphanumeric keystrokes define the commands on the ribbon tab. To access a particular command, press the key or key combination for that command. For example, you press the N key to access the Numbered List command. Some commands, however, such as the Font Color command, require that you press two keys in sequence—in this case, F and C.

Inside OUT

Take advantage of all the Quick Access Toolbar has to offer.

When you press Alt to access the ribbon using keyboard shortcuts, the Quick Access Toolbar buttons are also assigned numerical shortcuts. The Quick Access Toolbar might be one of the most misunderstood and underutilized parts of the 365 applications' ribbon-centric interface. The Quick Access Toolbar lives in the upper left of the application window. It provides quick access (thus its name) to any command or commands that you want to add to a particular application's Quick Access Toolbar. For example, in Word, the Quick Access Toolbar provides the Save, Undo, and Redo commands by default. When you select the Customize Quick Access Toolbar menu, you are provided a list of commands that you can quickly add to the toolbar with just a click of your mouse. For example, again in Word, you can add Quick Print, Draw Table, and several other commands from the Customize Quick Access Toolbar menu. If the commands provided by the list don't meet your needs, you can select More Commands on the menu, which opens the Word Options dialog box. This dialog box provides access to all the various Word commands and allows you to add them to the Customize Quick Access Toolbar menu.

When you select a keyboard shortcut, that command activates, and the keyboard shortcuts on the ribbon disappear. To exit the current command and go back to the ribbon with keyboard shortcuts, press Esc. You can toggle off the keyboard shortcuts by pressing Alt or by clicking inside the application workspace.

Working in the Backstage

The 365 Backstage has been designed to provide easy access to tasks and settings that relate back to the actual work that you are doing in the application window. Accessing information related to the file you are working with in the application window, accessing print settings, and sharing the file with other users are all possibilities found in the Backstage. The Backstage pages found in the 365 applications differ slightly. Word has the most options in the Backstage, and its Backstage is similar to the Backstage you will find in Excel, PowerPoint, and Publisher. Outlook's Backstage is different because of the type of "products" that you create in Outlook (emails, appointments, and meetings). So, Outlook's BackPage is more attuned to things like mailbox settings and email rules and alerts. Because Word provides the greatest number of choices in the Backstage, it makes sense to walk through the possibilities it provides.

To access the Backstage, click the File tab on the ribbon. When you enter the Backstage, the Home page is selected, which provides access to templates for new documents and lists recently opened documents. To view information related to the document you currently have open in

Word, select Info. This page provides information related to the file's properties and enables you to access document-protection features and inspect a document that you might want to share. Other pages in the Backstage are accessed using the navigation list on the left of the Backstage. If you want to return to the application window, click the Back button at the top of the navigation list. Figure 2-7 shows the Word Backstage with the current document's Info page selected.

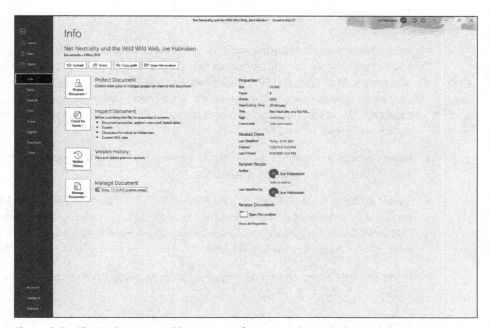

Figure 2-7   The Backstage provides access to features such as printing and sharing.

As already mentioned, Word, Excel, PowerPoint, and Publisher share several of the same Backstage pages. The shared (across the apps) Backstage commands include Home, New, Open, Info, Save, Print, Share, and Export. To give you an idea of the type of information, commands, or features you can access in the Backstage, let's look at what you would find if you accessed the Backstage in Word; a list of the Backstage pages follows:

- **Home:** Lists some standard document templates, lists recently opened documents (under Recent), and provides access to Pinned and Shared with Me documents. A Search box is also provided that allows you to quickly search for a particular document in the Recent list.

- **New:** Gives you access to templates and themes, which you can use to create a new file. The Search box enables you to search for other templates available on Office.com.

- **Open:** Provides a list of "places" you can use to store and retrieve your files. Your places include My Computer and any cloud storage that you have access to, such as OneDrive or a SharePoint site. Access to cloud storage requires that you log in to your OneDrive or other cloud storage resources using the username and password for these cloud storage possibilities. You can sign in to 365 when you complete the installation of the application. You can also add cloud storage places by using the Login service at the top right of the Backstage. These storage options can include your personal and corporate OneDrive accounts, and they might also include SharePoint sites hosted by your company or institution.

- **Info:** Provides access to permission settings (Protect Document) for the file and enables you to check the file for any issues that might cause problems if you share the file with other users. The Info page also provides access to versions of the file that are automatically saved during your application session (if you don't save a file when exiting). This page provides access to file properties, such as file size and editing time, and it lists authors who have worked on the file.

- **Save:** Saves changes to the current file. The Save command is also available on the Quick Access Toolbar in the application window.

- **Save As:** Shows all the "places" you have available for file storage. The list of places provided includes My Computer and any cloud storage you can access, such as your OneDrive, OneDrive for Business, or a SharePoint site. Recently accessed locations are also listed on this page. You can use the Browse button to open the Save As dialog box.

- **Print:** Provides access to print and page setup commands. It also provides a Print Preview pane.

- **Share:** Enables you to share the current file with other users. Options include email sharing invitations and the capability to present the document or presentation online.

- **Export:** Enables you to create a PDF or XPS version of your file that you can then share with other users. The Export page also provides the Change File Type command, which makes it easy to save the file using a different file type.

- **Transform:** This new Backstage option is designed to help you convert a Word document into an interactive web page.

- **Close:** Closes the current document (workbook or presentation).

- **Account:** Lists user information and shows the 365 background and theme that you are using by default. The Account page also shows the connected services you are accessing, such as your OneDrive or Flickr (for online photo storage). The Account page shows the Microsoft 365 product that is activated on your computer and the individual applications that the product contains.

- **Feedback:** Provides a quick way to send feedback related to the application you are working with directly to Microsoft. You can send a Smile (I like something), a Frown (I don't like something), or you can send a suggestion (I have a Suggestion). When you select one of the Feedback options, you will be taken back to the application window, and the Feedback to Microsoft pane will open on the right side of the screen. Enter your like, don't like, or suggestion in the text box provided, and then click Submit.

- **Options:** Provides access to the configuration options for the application. We discuss how to change application options later in this chapter.

Although using the Backstage requires that you leave behind the application interface where you are actually doing your work, the Backstage is designed so you can concentrate on file settings and other options related to processing a document or sharing a file. Once you've made your choices in the Backstage, you are only a click away (select the Back arrow at the top of the Backstage command list) from returning to your document, workbook, or presentation.

Customizing an application interface

You can customize any of the 365 application interfaces to suit your own needs. These customization options include customizing the ribbon, the Quick Access Toolbar, and the status bar.

Before we look at customizing the ribbon and the Quick Access Toolbar, which allows you to be selective about the commands and features available, we should briefly discuss the fact that customizing the application interface also relates to whether the application window shows certain elements or tools.

We have already discussed ways to show or hide the ribbon. You also have control over other elements of the application window, such as task panes. Task panes give you the capability to fine-tune a particular feature. For example, when you are formatting elements of a chart in Excel, you can configure each chart element separately in an associated task pane. Figure 2-8 shows the Format Legend task pane, which enables you to configure the various legend options, including position, colors, and effects. A quick way to open this task pane is to right-click the Legend in the chart and then select Format Legend.

When you open a task pane in an application window, you can choose to leave that task pane floating in the application's window, or you can close it immediately after using the commands it provides. For example, the Format Legend task pane (shown in Figure 2-8) enables you to quickly click an element in a legend to access the settings. If you are going to configure multiple elements, it makes sense to leave the task pane in the Excel application window until you have finished with it.

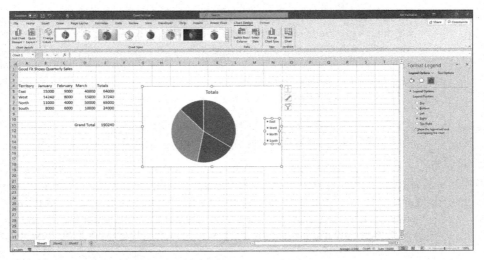

Figure 2-8 The Format Legend task pane in Excel

Inside OUT

When working in Word, PowerPoint, or Publisher, the ruler can really rule.

You might find it advantageous to have the ruler available in the application window, particularly if you are aligning objects on a page or are working in Word or PowerPoint and want to set tab stops or indents using the ruler. To place the vertical and horizontal rulers in the application workspace, click the ribbon's View tab and then select the Ruler check box. In an application such as Publisher, the ruler is particularly important for aligning objects in your publications, and you can drag guides from the rulers to help you position items on the page.

Customizing the ribbon

Because the ribbon is the command center for the 365 applications, it certainly makes sense for you to be able to customize it as you see fit. You have control over the tabs available on the ribbon, as well as the commands available on those tabs. Each application has an Options window. One of the options relates to tailoring the ribbon to your needs. You access the application options, such as Word Options, via the Backstage. Click File to open the Backstage and then select Options. The Options window for that application opens.

Each Options window provides an options list on the left side of the window. To work with the ribbon, select Customize ribbon. Figure 2-9 shows the Customize ribbon settings in the Word Options window.

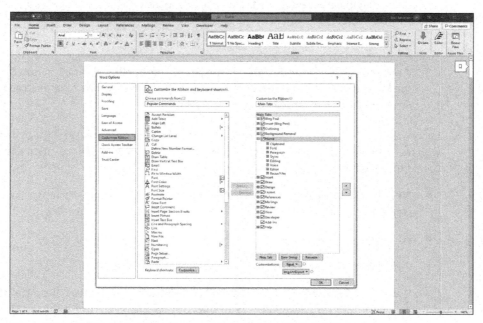

Figure 2-9   The Word Options window with Customize Ribbon selected

Let's start our ribbon customization discussion on the right side of the Customize Ribbon window. The list box on the right lists available tabs for the ribbon. By default, the Customize The Ribbon drop-down menu is set to Main Tabs (explained shortly). Some of the tabs are enabled, and the checkbox for each enabled tab is selected. Tabs not enabled (checked) will not be available on the application's ribbon.

You can use the Customize The Ribbon drop-down menu to view different lists of the tabs available in an application; to see all the tabs available, select All Tabs. As already mentioned, the main tabs are listed by default. The main tabs are the tabs that remain available on the ribbon no matter what you are working on in the application. The main tabs include the default tabs, such as Home, Insert, and so forth, and other tabs that are not available by default, such as the Developer tab. The tool tabs are a different story; these tabs are the contextual tabs that appear when you are working on a specific application object or element. For example, in Word, Table Tools is a set of contextual tabs (Design and Layout) that appear when you are working on a table. You can enable (show) or disable (hide) either main tabs or tool tabs. Just remember that you don't normally see the tool tabs until they activate when you perform a particular task in the application.

CHAPTER 2

You can expand a particular tab in the Tabs list to view the groups available on that tab. You can then expand a group on the tab to view the commands available in a group. You can enable a tab in the tabs list if you want. For example, if you want to create macros in a particular application, you need to have access to the Developer tab. To include the Developer tab on the application's ribbon, select the Developer tab check box.

TIP

If you want to rearrange the order of the tabs on the application's ribbon, you can use the Move Up and Move Down buttons to the right of the Tabs list. Click a tab and then use either button to move it.

Below the Tabs list is a set of buttons that are useful if you want to create new tabs and groups (with the intention that these groups will contain commands). A brief description of each command button follows:

- **New Tab:** Creates a new tab below the currently selected tab in the Tabs list. When you create a new tab, a new group is automatically created for the new tab.

- **New Group:** Creates a new group below the currently selected group.

- **Rename:** Enables you to rename a tab or group in the Tabs list.

- **Reset:** Enables you to reset the selected ribbon tab or reset all the customizations that you made to an application's ribbon. This is useful when you have been overzealous in creating tabs and groups.

- **Import/Export:** Enables you to import a customization file or create a new customization file based on the changes you made to the application's ribbon. After you have created a customization file for an application's ribbon, you can import it on other computers running the same version of 365. This gives you access to your custom ribbon at home or work.

Creating custom tabs with custom groups requires that you use the New Tab, New Group, and Rename commands. After you create your custom tabs and groups, you can add commands to them.

You can add commands to the groups on the existing ribbon tabs. You can also add commands to a group or groups contained in any new tabs you have created. On the left of the ribbon settings window is a list of available commands. By default, popular commands are shown.

You can use the Choose commands from the drop-down menu at the top left of the window to select the type of commands listed. You can select from command lists such as Commands Not In The Ribbon, All Commands, and Commands By Tab (such as File Tab and All Tabs). If you want to see all the commands available in an application, select the All Commands option.

Adding a command or commands to a ribbon tab's group is straightforward. Select the group in the Tabs list. Then select the command you want to add to the group in the Command list. Click the Add button to add the command to the group. You can repeat this procedure as needed to add commands that you frequently use to existing groups on the main or tools tabs. You can also populate the custom groups that you have created for any custom tabs.

Removing a command from a group only requires that you locate the command (in the group and on the tab) in the Tabs list. Select the command and then click Remove to remove the command.

When you finish modifying the ribbon, you can close the application's Options window. The changes you made to the ribbon become available as soon as you return to the application's workspace.

TIP

You can customize (or add) keyboard shortcuts for the various ribbon commands. Select Customize (below the Command list). Use the Customize Keyboard dialog box to locate a particular command, and then set the new shortcut key for that command.

Customizing the Quick Access Toolbar

You can also add commands to the Quick Access Toolbar, which resides in the upper left of the 365 application windows. Click the Customize Quick Access Toolbar button to the right of the Quick Access Toolbar to access the Customize menu. When you want to add a command button to the toolbar, select a command on the menu. A check mark appears to the left of the command, and the command button is placed on the Quick Access Toolbar. You can also remove any command button from the toolbar by deselecting it on the menu.

TIP

To place the Quick Access Toolbar below the ribbon in the application window, select Show Below The Ribbon on the Customize Quick Access Toolbar menu.

The Customize Quick Access Toolbar menu provides only a short list of commands to add to the toolbar. If you want to add a command not listed, you need to access the Customize the Quick Access Toolbar window. This window gives you a complete listing of all the commands available in the application.

On the Customize Quick Access Toolbar menu, select More Commands. Doing so opens the application's Options window with the Quick Access Toolbar options selected. Figure 2-10 shows the Excel Options window with Quick Access Toolbar selected.

On the right of the Quick Access Toolbar options is a list of the commands currently on the Quick Access Toolbar. On the left side of the Options window is a list of the popular commands. You can use Choose Commands From List (on the top left of the window) to view other command sets, such as Commands Not In The Ribbon and All Commands. You can also select a particular ribbon tab in this list to view the commands on that tab.

To add a command from the Command list, select the command and then click the Add button. The command appears in the Quick Access Toolbar list on the right side of the window. To rearrange the commands in the Quick Access Toolbar list, you can use the Move Up and Move Down buttons as needed. The list order determines the order in which the commands appear on the Quick Access Toolbar. If you decide that you don't want a command on the toolbar, select the command and then click Remove.

You can also create a secondary Quick Access Toolbar for the current file (a Word document, an Excel workbook, and so forth). Note the Customize Quick Access Toolbar drop-down menu above the Quick Access Toolbar command list (on the right side of the window).

NOTE

You can add macros that you create to the Quick Access Toolbar and the ribbon. For a primer on creating macros, see Appendix B, "365 macros."

By default, you are customizing the Quick Access Toolbar for all the documents that you create in the application, such as all the workbooks you create in Excel or all the presentations you create in PowerPoint. Any changes you make to the Quick Access Toolbar will be available whenever you use the application.

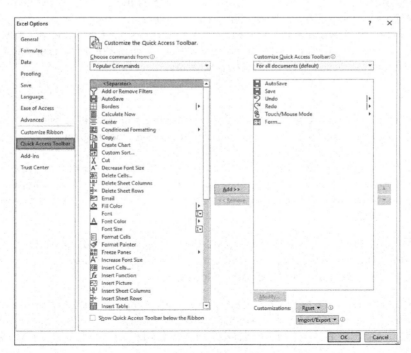

Figure 2-10   Customize the Quick Access Toolbar in the Options window

If you are creating a template or a document and want to create a Quick Access Toolbar that is available only in that document, you can use the Customize Quick Access Toolbar drop-down menu to select the current document. This empties the Command list (on the right side of the Options window); you can select commands in the Command list (on the left side of the window) and then use the Add button to populate the special Quick Access Toolbar for that document.

This new Quick Access Toolbar appears to the right of the default Quick Access Toolbar, above the ribbon, in the application window after you close the Customize The Quick Access Toolbar Options window.

A couple more points about the Quick Access Toolbar options are relevant: If you decide that you don't like the changes you have made to the Quick Access Toolbar, you can click the Reset button at the bottom right of the window. As with custom ribbons, you can use the Import/ Export button to import custom Quick Access Toolbars that you have created on other computers. You can also export your Quick Access Toolbar configuration to an exported 365 UI file that can be used on any computer with 365 installed.

TIP

The type of work you do in an application influences the commands you add to that application's Quick Access Toolbar. However, in terms of good additions to the toolbar in any application, I'm partial to the Open, Open Recent File, Paste Special, Save As, and Quick Print commands.

When you finish working in the Options window, click OK. This closes the window and returns you to the application workspace. The changes you have made to the Quick Access Toolbar are immediately available.

Customizing the status bar

The 365 applications' status bar has historically served as an informational tool at the bottom of the application window. It provides information related to the file that you are working on and lets you know whether certain features (such as overtype) are enabled.

The 365 applications' status bar is customizable, allowing you to determine what kind of information it provides. We have already discussed the fact that the View shortcuts, Zoom, and Zoom slider tools are on the right side of the status bar and let you control your view of your document in the application window.

You can customize the status bar to show additional information related to your current document (or worksheet or slide). For example, you can enable the status bar to show you if the Caps Lock has been enabled.

You can also place options on the status bar that perform an action when you click them. For example, in Word, you can add Word Count to the status bar and use it to quickly open the Word Count dialog box and view the statistics for the document. A useful status bar option in Excel is the Num Lock option (which not all the applications have) if you often use the numerical keypad on the keyboard to enter values into Excel worksheets.

To customize the status bar, right-click anywhere on it, and the Customize Status Bar menu appears. To add an item to the status bar, click the item. You can also remove items from the status bar by deselecting them (removing the check mark) on the Customize Status Bar menu, as needed.

Configuring application options

Microsoft has done a good job of making the tools for configuring the various 365 members extremely consistent across the applications. Excel, Word, PowerPoint, and Publisher use many of the same option categories, such as General, Customize Ribbon, and Add-Ins. Even Outlook provides pretty much the same approach to configuring the application using the Options window.

Obviously, some differences exist in the configuration options provided for the 365 applications because each application serves a different function. For example, Excel has a Formulas option category, which makes sense because of Excel's capability to do calculations. In Outlook, configuration options are available for the Calendar, contacts, and mail, which makes sense because of the type of work you do in Outlook.

All the applications in the suite provide an Options link in the Backstage. Select File and then Options to open an application's Options window. Figure 2-11 shows the Excel Options window with the General category selected.

The Options window breaks down the various application configuration possibilities into a series of categories. Each category provides a set of tools for configuring associated features. In Figure 2-11, the General category is selected and provides user interface options such as enabling the Mini Toolbar and Live Preview. The User Name option, available under Personalize Your Copy Of Microsoft 365, is a universal setting, and any change to the username in Excel ports over to other applications such as Word and PowerPoint.

Two other option categories contain settings that can affect multiple 365 applications: Proofing and Language. The Proofing options enable you to set the AutoCorrect settings specifically for an application. However, when you select options related to how spelling is corrected in the application or the default dictionary language, other applications also use those settings. Figure 2-12 shows the Excel Proofing options.

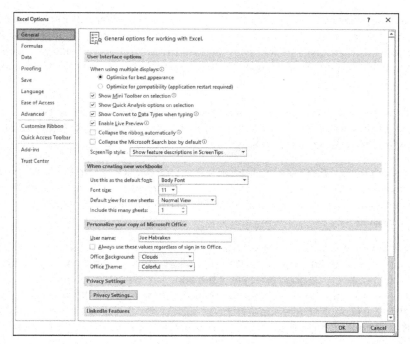

Figure 2-11   Excel General Options window

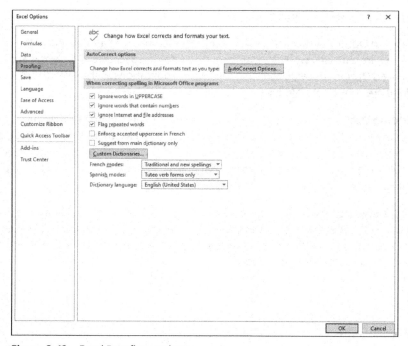

Figure 2-12   Excel Proofing options

Note that many spelling options are controlled using checkboxes, and drop-down menus provide options for different language modes and the main dictionary language. The Proofing category provides similar options when accessed in Word or PowerPoint. You need to change Proofing options in only one application, however, for them to be in force in the other applications.

The settings available in the Language options are also 365 global preferences rather than individual application preferences. Changing settings such as the Editing, Display, and Help Languages affects the other 365 applications.

In terms of options specific to an application (other than the ribbon and Quick Access Toolbar settings that we have already discussed), most of these are housed in the Advanced category. Advanced options are divided into subcategories such as Editing, Print, Display, and a catch-all General subcategory.

The Advanced options available for each application vary; however, the subcategories (such as Editing and Print) are consistent across the applications, particularly Word, Excel, PowerPoint, and Publisher. Outlook is a good example of the odd man out: It has configuration options that you don't have to deal with in the other applications. These relate to the different types of information that you create and manage in Outlook, such as emails, calendars, and contacts. Outlook's use and configuration is discussed in detail in the Outlook section of this book.

➤ Outlook's configuration is discussed in Chapter 22.

Advanced Options settings

The Advanced Options settings allow you to change settings that are specific to the application in which you are currently working. Even though these are specific to the current application, the Advanced Option subcategories that you use in applications such as Word, Excel, and PowerPoint are consistent as follows:

- **Editing Options:** These options relate to editing and selecting items in the application. For example, Word provides an Editing option related to whether selected text is replaced when you type. Excel provides an Editing option that enables or disables Auto-Complete. Look for features in this subcategory that make it easier for you to select and edit information in the applications.

- **Cut, Copy, and Paste:** True to their names, these options relate to settings such as whether the Paste Options button is enabled when you paste an item. These settings also include Word formatting options related to pasting within the same document, between documents, or between programs.

- **Display:** This set of options provides settings for the number of recent files that are displayed in the Backstage and contains other settings related to whether formatting marks, such as tab characters and spaces, are shown on the screen.

- **Print:** These options relate to the quality of certain objects when they are printed. For example, in Excel, you can set a high-quality mode for graphics. In PowerPoint, you can specify that all printing is high quality. Word and PowerPoint also provide options for background printing so that you can continue to use the application as you are printing.

Many of the Advanced options available for 365 applications are easy to work with. Most are enabled or disabled via checkboxes. You can try out a particular setting by enabling it with a click of the mouse. If it isn't particularly useful, you can return to the Advanced options and easily disable the option with another click.

Add-ins

One other category of application options to be aware of is the add-ins. Add-ins are additions to an application that increase the application's functionality. Each of the 365 applications has add-ins available. Some are added by default when you install the application. Other add-ins are installed when you install 365 but are not added to the application by default. This means that they are inactive add-ins.

For example, Excel has add-ins such as the Solver and the Euro Currency Tools. To use either of these, you must add them to your Excel configuration.

When you select the Add-Ins category in the application, you can view the active and inactive add-ins. To enable an inactive add-in, follow these steps:

1. Select Add-Ins in the Manage drop-down menu at the bottom of the Options window (when the Add-Ins category is selected). Then click Go.

2. An Add-Ins dialog box appears that is specific to the application (such as Excel or Word). The dialog box lists the available add-ins.

3. Select an add-in. If you have downloaded an add-in, you can use the Browse button to locate it.

4. After selecting an add-in (or add-ins) to activate, click OK. The Add-Ins dialog box closes.

When you return to the Options window for the application and select Add-Ins, the Active Application Add-Ins list includes any add-ins you activated. You can now use these add-ins as needed in the application.

CHAPTER 2

Using Application add-ins

Microsoft 365 provides you with another way to add functionality to your applications: add-ins. Microsoft 365 add-ins (also referred to as Office Apps in the Office Store) are basically mini-applications that have a particular function.

The add-ins are downloaded from the 365 (Office) store; you will find free add-ins and add-ins that you can purchase. Most of the add-ins for purchase provide you with the option of down-loading a trial version of the add-in so you can try it out before you buy it. Once you download an add-in, it becomes available for use in your suite applications such as Word, Excel, and PowerPoint.

Figure 2-13 shows the Bing Maps add-in. This add-in allows you to visualize location data in your Excel worksheets. To access an add-in in an application such as Excel, select the ribbon's Insert tab, and then select the My Add-Ins command to view the add-ins available in 365. Add-ins are a great way to enhance your application experience.

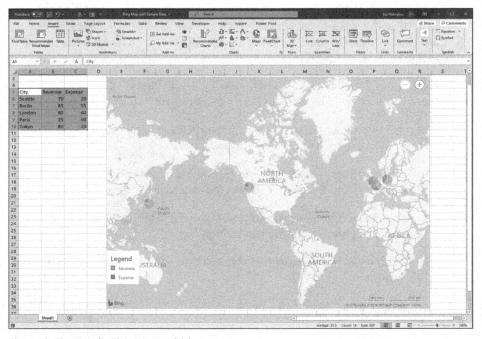

Figure 2-13   Excel's Bing Maps add-in

Inside OUT

Not all 365 add-ins are equal.

You will find that there are many add-ins available on the Microsoft Store for your 365 suite applications. Some of these add-ins (or, again, apps) are free, and some require purchase. You will also find that some are easier to install than others. For example, the Bing Map add-in is free and actually assists in its own installation. This is a case where you download the add-in, and a worksheet will open in Excel and walk you through a very simple installation. Some add-ins and apps might require a little more coaxing in terms of getting them up and running in a Microsoft 365 application.

Using the Trust Center

Keeping your computer secure from attack and protecting personal information on your computer has become a greater challenge as connectivity to the somewhat untrustworthy networking infrastructure of the Internet has become common. We use the Internet in many instances for private communication and to share files (by email and other means) without necessarily considering that we are opening up our files and computer to a public, global network. Even extremely secure corporate networks that protect users from the risks of a persistent connection with the Internet can have problems with security and privacy issues.

Microsoft has worked hard to build security and privacy protections into the 365 applications themselves, and this is where the Trust Center comes in. Each application has its own Trust Center, which provides access to security and privacy settings for the application. You access the Trust Center settings via the Options window of the specific application. To open the Trust Center for an application, follow these steps:

1. Select File on the ribbon to access the Backstage.

2. Select Options to open the Options window.

3. In the Options window, select Trust Center. Because the Trust Center is related to privacy and security settings, the Options window provides a link, "Microsoft Trust Center," which takes you to security information on the Office.com website. Microsoft recommends not changing the settings in the Trust Center if you want to keep your computer secure. Unless you have a compelling reason to change these settings, it makes sense to go with the defaults. Changing the security settings could open your computer to attack, particularly if you use macros from a source unknown to you.

CHAPTER 2

4. Select Trust Center Settings to open the application's Trust Center. Figure 2-14 shows the Word Trust Center with the Trusted Locations options selected.

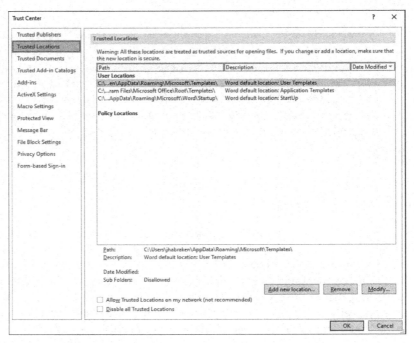

Figure 2-14 The Trust Center

The Trust Center for each of the 365 applications differs in the options available. For example, Outlook also provides Email Security settings and Automatic Download options (related to pictures in HTML emails). Outlook does not have Trusted Documents or Add-Ins options (in the Trust Center) as Word does. Word, PowerPoint, and Excel have similar options available in their Trust Centers. Outlook and Publisher provide only a subset of the options in the other applications, but they include some special options related to the function of the application (such as the Trust Center options found in Outlook, as I've already mentioned).

CAUTION

If you work on a corporate network or are a small office or home user and don't have a need that requires changes to the Trust Center, don't change the settings. A compelling reason might be that you are working with macros or are considering using add-ins from a source other than Microsoft, and you want the add-ins to be signed by a trusted publisher.

Because Microsoft sees the Trust Center as a way to make your application environment more secure, only make changes to these settings if a change provides greater security or privacy as you work. Although it is easy to select a Trust Center option category and begin to make what seem like good choices, Trust Center options are really "if it isn't broke, don't fix it" settings; don't change them unless you have a compelling reason to do so.

Two options related to the Trust Center that make it easier for you to take advantage of files containing active content, such as macros or ActiveX controls, are the Trusted Publishers and Trusted Documents settings. Both settings are available in the Word, Excel, and PowerPoint Security Centers. This makes sense because Word documents, Excel worksheets, and PowerPoint presentations are most likely to use active content, such as macros. The following information looks more closely at trusted publishers and trusted locations.

Trusted publishers

If you use macros, add-ins, or ActiveX controls to enhance the capabilities of your Microsoft 365 applications and you acquire these application additions from a legitimate developer, you can add the publisher to the Trusted Publishers list. For you to add a publisher to the list, the developer's add-in or ActiveX control must be digitally signed using a digital certificate that the developer or publisher has acquired. The certificate must be from a reputable certificate authority. Some certificate authorities are available online, such as A-Trust (www.a-trust.at) and Digicert (*http://digicert.com*). Make sure that you carefully vet any certificate authority that you are considering using.

TIP
Remove publishers from the list only when the digital signature has expired, or you no longer use content from that publisher.

You don't actually add the publisher to the Trusted Publishers list in the Trust Center. You can use the Trust Center only to view details related to a trusted publisher or to remove a publisher from the list. To remove a publisher, select the publisher in the Trusted Publishers list and then click Remove.

When you attempt to run a macro or ActiveX control that you have acquired, it is disabled by default. A message bar appears below the ribbon in the application window letting you know that the macro or ActiveX control is disabled. When you click the Options button in the message bar, the Security Options dialog box for that item opens. In the dialog box, you can see whether the developer/publisher digitally signed the item. You can view details related to the digital signature by clicking the Show Signature Details link.

If you are satisfied that the signed item is using a legitimate digital certificate and you want to add the publisher to the Trusted Publishers list, select the Trust All Documents from This Publisher option in the Security dialog box. Then click OK to add the publisher to the list in that application.

Trusted locations

The Trusted Locations list contains the default paths for add-ins (in Excel) and documents, templates, startup files, and other items in Word, Excel, and PowerPoint. If you are a user on a sophisticated network (other than a home network), some of these locations might be local paths on your computer or might have been edited by your network administrator to use network paths.

The whole purpose of trusted locations is that these folders are used to store files you trust; you do not want the Trust Center to raise a fuss when you open a file stored in a trusted location. This enables you to place files that contain macros or other content, such as add-ins, in a trusted folder and not have the Trust Center disable any of the content when you open them.

You can edit the default trusted location path if you want. Select a user location in the list and then click the Modify button in the Trusted Locations pane. The Microsoft Office Trusted Location dialog box opens. Change the path in the Path box and then click OK to close the dialog box.

In most cases, it is probably advisable not to change any of the default trusted locations, particularly if your 365 applications were configured specifically to run on your corporate network. This doesn't mean that you can't create your own trusted locations and use them as depots for files containing content that must be trusted to run correctly (such as macros, ActiveX controls, and so forth).

To create a new trusted location, click the Add New Location button. The Microsoft Office Trusted Location dialog box opens, as shown in Figure 2-15.

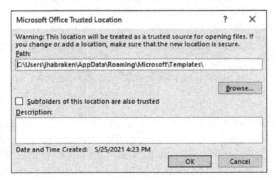

Figure 2-15   You can use the Microsoft Office Trusted Location dialog box to create a new trusted location.

Type the path for the new location in the Path text box or use the Browse button to locate the folder on your computer or your network. If you want to have all the subfolders in the new trusted folder also be trusted, select the Subfolders Of This Location Are Also Trusted check box.

NOTE

If you create your own macros or use macros created by coworkers, changes to Trust Center options related to macros might come into play. Appendix B discusses macros in more depth.

You can add an optional description for the new trusted location in the Description box. When you have finished entering the information for the new trusted source, click the OK button.

The new trusted location is added to the Trusted Locations list. If you want to remove a location that you no longer use or need, select the location in the list. You can then click the Remove button to remove the trusted location.

CHAPTER 2

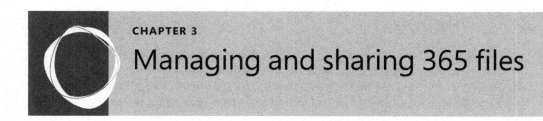

Managing and sharing 365 files

Understanding 365 file formats   49

Configuring save file options   55

Creating and managing files   56

Searching for 365 files   63

Protecting a 365 file   65

Preparing a file for sharing   67

The Microsoft 365 applications provide you with all the tools you need to create documents, presentations, workbooks, and publications. After you create your various files using the 365 applications, it is up to you to manage your files and share them with colleagues and coworkers.

In this chapter, we take a look at the 365 file formats used in each of the Microsoft 365 applications. We also look at your options for managing and sharing files.

Understanding 365 file formats

The default file formats for each of the 365 applications (excluding Outlook) take advantage of the open XML (eXtensible Markup Language) file standards. The file formats benefit file compression, improved damage recovery, better detection of files containing macros, and better compatibility with other vendor software.

Although some backward-compatibility issues may be involved when you attempt to share a file using one of these file formats with a user who still works with an earlier version of a particular 365 application (think pre-2010 versions), most problems have been ironed out. Users still working with earlier versions of the applications can take advantage of various conversion utilities and software updates that enable them to convert or directly open a file using one of the new file formats.

You can also save your files in file formats that offer backward compatibility for coworkers still using older versions of the Microsoft (formerly Office) suite applications. And the applications (such as Word and Excel) provide you with compatibility-checking tools that help negate any issues with files shared with users of legacy Microsoft applications.

As already mentioned, Word, Excel, and PowerPoint use the open XML file formats by default when you save a file in these applications. And you have some other file format options in these applications if needed.

Publisher, on the other hand, saves publications by default in the .pub file type. The .pub file type is "directly" compatible with versions from Publisher 2003 through Publisher 2013. Although Publisher does not enable you to save a publication in the open XML file format (like Word and Excel), you can save Publisher files in the XPS file type, which is an XML file format for "electronic paper." Publisher also has file types available that you can use to make your publications backward compatible with collaborators who are using previous versions of Microsoft Publisher.

➤ For more about Publisher file types, see "Creating a new publication," in Chapter 27.

The following lists provide an overview of some of the file types used in Word, Excel, and Power-Point, respectively.

Word:

File Extension	Description
docx	XML file type; default file type for Word 2010, 2013, 2016, and 2019 documents
docm	XML file type; macro-enabled document
dotx	XML file type; Word template
dotm	XML file type; macro-enabled Word template
doc	Binary file type; document compatibility with Word 97–2003
dot	Binary file type; template compatibility with Word 97–2003

Excel:

File Extension	Description
xlsx	XML file type; default file type for Excel 2007, 2010, 2013, 2016, and 2019 workbooks
xlsm	XML file type; macro-enabled workbook
xltx	XML file type; Excel template
xltm	XML file type; macro-enabled Excel template
xls	Binary file type; document compatibility with Excel 97–2003
xlt	Binary file type; template compatibility with Excel 97–2003

PowerPoint:

File Extension	Description
pptx	XML file type; default file type for PowerPoint 2007, 2010, 2013, 2016, and 2019 presentations
pptm	XML file type; macro-enabled presentation
potx	XML file type; PowerPoint template

potm	XML file type; macro-enabled PowerPoint template
ppsx	XML file type; PowerPoint show
ppsm	XML file type; macro-enabled PowerPoint show
ppt	Binary file type; presentation compatibility with PowerPoint 97–2003
pot	Binary file type; template compatibility with PowerPoint 97–2003

The 365 applications also provide other file formats that make it simple for you to share your documents or workbooks in a format designed for easy viewing. A good example is the PDF file format (created by Adobe Systems), which allows users who have a PDF reader, such as the free Adobe Reader software installed on their computers, to view your files. Windows 10 also provides a PDF viewer (Windows Reader) to view a PDF document. The viewer enables you to search the PDF document using the Find tool.

The XML Paper Specification (XPS) file format also makes it easy for others to view your work. Windows 10 supplies an XPS viewer that enables any Windows 10 user to open and view files in the XPS file type. Figure 3-1 shows the Windows 10 XPS viewer containing a Word document converted to an XPS document.

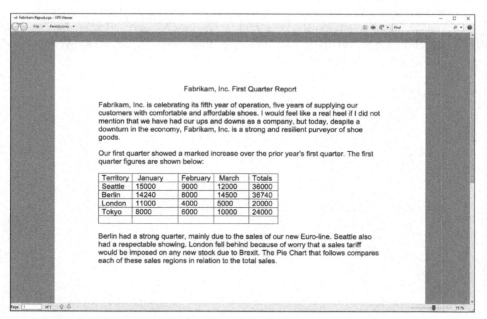

Figure 3-1   A Word XPS document in the XPS viewer

Both the PDF and the XPS file formats are primarily designed to enable you to share a view of a particular file without requiring that the applications themselves be installed on the computer of the user who will view the file. Although both the PDF and XPS file types require a particular viewer type to view the file, viewers such as Acrobat Reader and some XPS viewers (including

Microsoft's XPS viewer) are available for free download on the web. Most operating systems, including Windows 10, have their own native PDF and XPS viewers.

NOTE

This chapter doesn't address Outlook because of how it stores and works with different items such as emails and contacts, which is very different in how applications such as Word and Excel where you create discrete files. Part V, "Outlook," covers everything you need about this powerful email, contact, and calendar application.

Saving files as different file types

When you create a new Word document, Excel workbook, or PowerPoint presentation, you eventually need to save your work to a file. As already mentioned, each of these applications uses the open XML file format by default. So, if you save a new Word document and do not change the Save As Type setting, you get a file with the extension .docx (the open XML format for Word).

When you save a file for the first time, the Save As dialog box opens. At a minimum, you must provide a file name for the new file, and you have the option of specifying the location where the file will be saved. You also have control over the file type used when the file is saved. You can select the file type in the Save As Type drop-down menu. Figure 3-2 shows the Word Save As dialog box with the Save As Type drop-down menu selected.

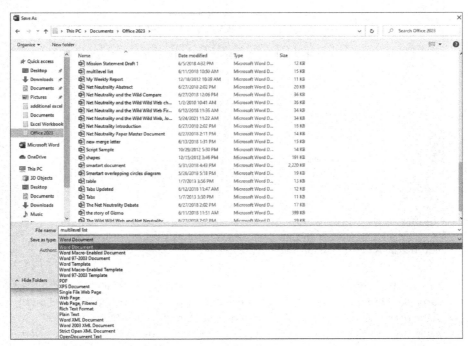

Figure 3-2   Selecting the file type for a Word document

After selecting the file type, click Save. When you have saved the file for the first time, use the Save button on the application's Quick Access Toolbar to save the changes that you make as you add to and edit the document.

You can also convert an existing file to another file type by using the Save As dialog box. After you save a file, the only route to the Save As dialog box is via the application's Backstage. Follow these steps to open the Save As dialog box for a previously saved file:

> ### TIP
>
> **You can also save 365 files such as Word documents, Excel worksheets, and PowerPoint presentations in various web page formats, making it easy to include the content on a website.**

1. Select File to access the Backstage.

2. Select Save As. The Backstage Save As page opens.

3. Select a place (location) to save the file on the left side of the Save As page. You can choose from This PC and cloud places such as your OneDrive or a network drive. You can also choose from existing Windows folders, such as Documents, Desktop, and Downloads.

4. Select Browse to choose your location and open the Save As dialog box.

5. In the Save As dialog box, use the Save As Type drop-down menu to specify the file type for the file.

6. You also have the option of changing the name and location for the newly created file.

7. Click Save. The Save As dialog box closes.

The file is saved using the new file format you selected. The file has a new name and save location if you changed these settings in the Save As dialog box.

Converting files to different file types

Save As gives you the capability to change a file's current file type to another file type. Another avenue for converting a particular file to a different file type is the Export page in the Backstage. You can access this page by selecting File and then selecting Export.

The Export page provides two possibilities: Create PDF/XPS Document and Change File Type. By default, the Create PDF/XPS Document is selected on the Export page, so to quickly create a PDF or XPS "copy" of the current file, click the Create PDF/XPS button. When the Publish As PDF Or XPS dialog box opens, it looks much like the Save As dialog box. By default, the file is saved as a PDF, but you can switch to XPS using the Save As Type drop-down menu. Specify a location file name, and then select Publish to save the PDF (or XPS) file.

The Export page also provides the Change File Type pane, which is accessed by selecting Change File Type on the left side of the Export page. The Change File Type pane makes changing the file type less confusing than just picking a file type from the Save As Type drop-down menu in the Save As dialog box. File types are visually represented in the Change File Type pane, and short descriptions of each file type are provided. Figure 3-3 shows the Excel Change File Type pane in the Backstage.

To create a copy of the current file in a new file type, select one of the alternative file types provided in the Change File Type pane. For example, you might want to save an Excel workbook that is currently in the Excel .xlsx file format (the default) to the Excel 97–2003 workbook file type (.xls) so that you can share the file with a colleague who uses an earlier version of Excel.

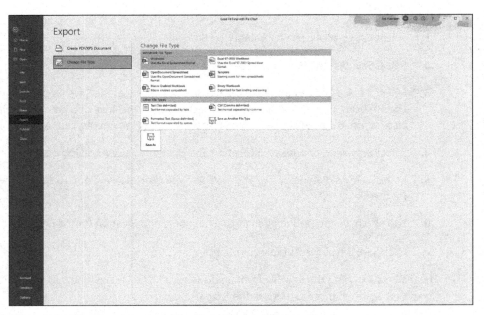

Figure 3-3   The Export page and the Excel Change File Type pane

Select the new file type in the Change File Type pane, and the Save As dialog box opens. The file type that you chose in the Change File Type pane is selected in the Save As Type drop-down menu. You can change the file name or the file location as needed and then click Save to save a copy of the original file in the file type.

Although going directly to the Save As dialog box via the Backstage Save As command might seem to be a faster option than getting to the Save As dialog box via the Change File Type pane, the latter option does a better job of laying out the possibilities. Until you have a good feel for which file type is which on the Save As Type drop-down menu in the Save As dialog box, use the Change File Type pane as an aid to select the appropriate file type for the file. Obviously, "appropriate" depends on what you are going to do with the file in its alternative file type.

Configuring save file options

When you save a file for the first time in one of the 365 applications, you obviously will have the option to specify the location where the file will be saved. By default, the applications are configured to save your files in your Documents folder. However, when you save a new file, you are ushered to the Backstage, and if you don't provide an alternative location, the files end up in the default folder—your Documents folder.

You can actually control the save options for an application and specify both the default file format for saving files and the default location for files and templates. You can even set an option so that the Backstage won't open every time you save a new file; this option enables you to "jump" right to the Save As dialog box. Other options that you control include the default file location and the default file format used to save files in a particular 365 application. The settings for these various options are in the Save pane of an application's Options window.

To open the Options window for an application, select File to open the Backstage. Then select Options. The Options window for the application opens. Click Save to view the save settings for the application. Figure 3-4 shows the Save pane for PowerPoint. The Save options for Word and Excel are similar.

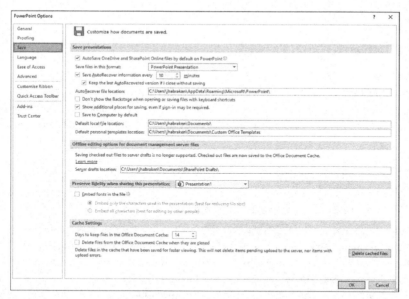

Figure 3-4   The PowerPoint Save options

To change the default file format, use the Save Files In This Format drop-down menu. Change the file format only if you have a good reason, such as the fact that you always work with people who use a legacy version of an application, and you want to match the file type that they use.

CHAPTER 3

You can also edit the default file location. The default file location is used only if you also select Don't Show The Backstage When Opening Or Saving Files With Keyboard Shortcuts. Selecting this option takes you right to the Save As dialog box when you save a new file for the first time (instead of going to the Save As Page in the Backstage).

If you do want to specify the location where your files are stored by default, you can edit the entry in the Default Local File Location box. You are required to type the path, so you may want to use the Windows File Explorer to browse for the path so that you enter it correctly in the Default Local File Location box.

Other options provided by the Save pane relate to the AutoRecover feature and offline editing options when you work in an environment that uses network servers running SharePoint Server. Leave most of these options at the defaults—particularly those related to offline editing in a server environment.

CAUTION

If you work in a networked environment other than a home or small office environment, you might drive your network administrator completely insane if you change the default Save settings for your 365 applications. Check with your administrator before you attempt to change these settings.

Creating and managing files

The Microsoft 365 applications provide you with different ways to create new files. When you open one of the applications, such as Word, Excel, or PowerPoint, you are taken to the Start screen. The Start screen enables you to create a new blank file (such as a new blank document in Word), open files from the Recent list, or take advantage of a huge library of themes and templates.

Inside OUT

Choose or create the right template for your file

Everything that you create in the 365 applications is based on a template. Each application has a default template. For example, in Word, the default template is the Normal template and is used when you create a new blank document. By design, templates are ready-made blueprints for documents, workbooks, or other application files. For example, you might want to create a monthly budget for your household. If you want some help in creating the overall layout that goes into making this budget in Excel, you can take advantage of the Simple Monthly Budget template that is provided by Office.com and easily opened via the Excel Backstage. Remember, you are not limited to the templates that are provided by the various applications such as Word and Excel. You can also create your own templates so you have greater control over a particular Word document or Excel workbook.

When you want to create a more specialized document, workbook, or presentation, the easiest route is to take advantage of one of the templates provided by the application in which you are working. Templates often provide layout attributes, text formatting, and even placeholder text. The sophistication of the file created using a particular template depends on the actual template. For example, you might use a Word Memo template that creates a simple memo containing some placeholder text (that you replace) in the To, From, and Re: areas of the memo. Or you might take advantage of the Simple Monthly Budget template mentioned a moment ago. It provides individual tables in a worksheet for items such as projected costs and projected monthly income, and it supplies ready-made charts for your monthly expenses and expenses by category. Figure 3-5 shows a new Excel worksheet started using the Simple Personal Budget template.

You can also start a new file using a theme. A theme is a collection of colors, fonts, and text effects. Most of the possibilities provided on the Start screen and the Backstage New page are actually themes (unless you do an online search for templates on the Start screen or New page). Themes provide you with an overall document look, as a template does, but using a theme negates having to work within the confines of a template's placeholder text and other document settings. However, using themes or templates is a quick way to begin the process of creating an eye-catching document, presentation, or worksheet.

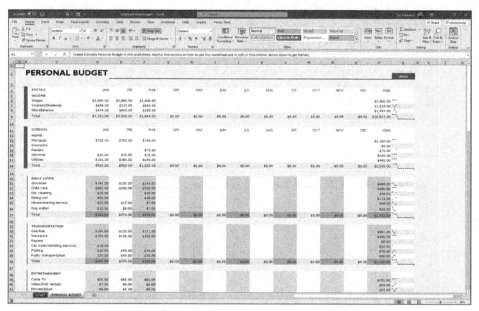

Figure 3-5 Excel's Simple Personal Budget template

You can take advantage of themes and templates in Excel, Word, PowerPoint, and Publisher. To start a new file based on a template or theme, follow these steps:

1. Select File to open the Backstage.

2. Select New in the Backstage. The New page opens (which is similar to the Start screen). Figure 3-6 shows the Excel New page.

3. Select a template or theme in the New window to preview the template or theme. The Preview window also describes the theme or template.

4. If you want to search for an online template or theme, select one of the suggested searches at the top of the New page or enter keywords in the Search box and run the search.

5. The search results show all the templates available online that match your search criteria. On the right side of the Search results, you find a Category list. The categories listed are keyword subsets of all the templates that were found using your search terms. Each category has a number to the right showing how many of the listed templates fall into the category. You can view a subset of the search results by selecting a category.

6. If you selected a template stored locally on your computer, click Create. If the template is an Office.com template, click Download. In either case, a new file opens in the application window based on the template.

You determine whether to create your files from new blank documents, workbooks, or presentations or to take advantage of the various themes and templates available. Working with themes and templates can help you determine how a special document, such as a newsletter, or a special worksheet, such as an invoice, should be laid out. So instead of reinventing the wheel, it makes sense to take advantage of the benefits a template can provide. You can also use themes to great advantage when you are creating a "family" of documents that are related. For example, you might use the same theme for a Word document, an Excel worksheet, and a PowerPoint presentation that are related to a specific project you are developing.

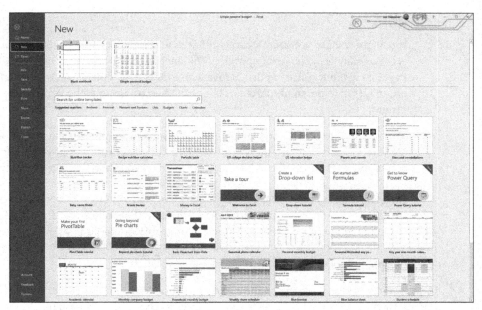

Figure 3-6 Create a new file based on a template or theme.

Managing files

Managing files effectively is a bit of an art form. You need to create some sort of structured environment that keeps your saved files organized but also makes it easy for you to find the files you work with often. Your particular situation might also require that you store your files in particular network shares (folders) so that others can easily access them. The Microsoft applications have adopted a cloud storage strategy that also makes it possible for you to easily store files on your OneDrive (both the free version and the version available with a Microsoft 365 subscription—OneDrive for Business), or a corporate SharePoint site.

Whether you store your files on your computer's hard drive, on a shared drive on a network server, or in the cloud on your OneDrive, you still must adopt a strategy for organizing your files. And whether you are talking about a hard drive or OneDrive, these storage containers can still be seen as the electronic equivalent of a filing cabinet. Each drawer in the filing cabinet is equivalent to a folder on the drive. The hanging file folders inside filing cabinet drawers are equivalent to the subfolders inside the main folders.

The naming conventions you use for the folders and subfolders you create are really up to you but should reflect some sort of system. For example, you could have a folder named Projects that contains subfolders named for each of the specific projects you are working on. Take some time to figure out your folder taxonomy. If you end up with a folder named Miscellaneous, I recommend that you rethink your naming system.

CHAPTER 3

NOTE

You might want to use your Documents folder as the parent container for the subfolders you create for your various projects. This enables you to create the necessary folder structure without cluttering the C: drive with a lot of new folders. This method of organizing files in folders and subfolders has been around as long as the Windows operating system.

An alternative to organizing files in folders and subfolders is to take advantage of the file library that is provided by Windows 10. The library approach helps you organize and access your files, no matter where you store them on your computer (or your network).

In Windows 10, a library is a container that gathers files from different locations on your computer and your network and displays them as a collection that you can access. By default, Windows 10 provides the Documents, Music, Pictures, and Videos libraries. You can toggle the libraries on (if you don't see them) in the File Explorer by right-clicking the Navigation pane and selecting Show Libraries.

So you can go "old school" and create folders and subfolders on your computer's hard drive, or you can take advantage of libraries to give you easy access to the files you use. Whether you are creating new folders on your computer or on a network share assigned to you, you can use the File Explorer as your primary tool. The same goes if you want to create new libraries: Use the File Explorer.

The next two sections look more closely at creating folders and libraries on your computer's hard drive. Working in the cloud and organizing cloud storage is similar in most respects to organizing a "physical" drive. You can create folders on both your OneDrive or other network drives that you access. OneDrive for Business also gives you the capability to create and manage libraries. Both OneDrive for Business and Windows 10 allow you to create libraries that serve as virtual containers for the files that you create and share.

Creating a new folder

In Windows 10, switch to the desktop and then click the File Explorer icon on the taskbar. File Explorer (shown in Figure 3-7) provides links on the left side of the window, such as various links to the desktop or your current libraries (Documents, Music, and so on). In its main pane, you can see a listing of the hard drives, DVD drives, CD drives, and so forth on your computer and any network shares (in the Network Location area) configured for your use (including SharePoint sites).

TIP

You can also create new folders in a 365 application's Save As dialog box. Navigate to where you want to create the new folder, and then select New Folder on the toolbar in the Save As dialog box. Provide a name for the folder. You can now use the folder as a location to save the current file (and subsequent files) as needed.

To view the folders on a particular drive, such as the C: drive (which is typically the default drive on most PCs), double-click the drive. You can create new folders on any drive or in existing folders, such as the Documents folder. Navigate to the drive or folder you want to serve as the parent container, and then click the New Folder button on File Explorer's ribbon. Type a new name for the folder, and you are good to go. You can drag existing files and folders into the new folder (using File Explorer) and specify the new folder when you save a file in the Save As dialog box.

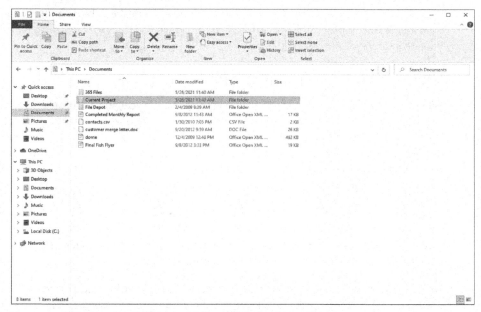

Figure 3-7   Create new libraries or folders using File Explorer.

Creating a new library

As already mentioned, a Windows library enables you to view and access files from different locations on your computer and your network. A library isn't really a container because a library doesn't store the actual files. A library is a kind of virtual container that can point to different folder locations and enable you to access related files (such as all the files related to a particular project).

To create a new library in File Explorer, follow these steps:

1. Right-click the Navigation pane and select Show Libraries. This places the Libraries icon in the Navigation pane.

2. Right-click the Libraries icon and point at New on the shortcut menu.

3. Select Library and a New Library appears in the Details pane.

4. Click on the default library name (New Library) and then type a name for the library.

Once you have created a library, you can add folders to the library as needed. Use File Explorer to navigate to any folder on your computer or your network. Right-click the folder and then point at Include In Library. A list of available libraries appears. Select the desired library.

When you are working in one of the 365 applications and want to open a particular file from one of your libraries using the Open dialog box, select the desired library in the Location list and then locate the file you want to open. You can also save your files to folders in a library when you are in the Save As dialog box.

Viewing file versions in an application

When you are working in an application such as Word or Excel, the application uses the AutoRecover feature to create different versions of the file on which you are working. By default, the 365 applications save AutoRecover information for your current file every 10 minutes. If you accidentally close a document or workbook in Word or Excel without saving, the last AutoRecovered version of your file is saved so that you can access it. This is also a default setting in the application's Save options.

When you save a file and close it, all the AutoRecovered versions of the file are deleted. But you can peruse the different versions of your file saved by the AutoRecover feature as you work on the document. This includes any unsaved versions of the document that exist because you did not save changes that you made to the file before you closed it.

To view any unsaved versions of the current file, such as a Word document, select File to open the Backstage and then click Info. Figure 3-8 shows the Info window for a Word document. The area of interest in this window is the Manage Document area. Note that in Figure 3-8, a version of the file exists (from earlier in the day) because the Word document was autosaved (which happens by default every 10 minutes).

You can also browse for unsaved versions of a file by clicking the Manage Document button and then selecting Recover Unsaved Documents. This enables you to browse for any unsaved versions stored on your computer. Any unsaved versions of the current document that have been automatically saved are listed in the Versions area of the window.

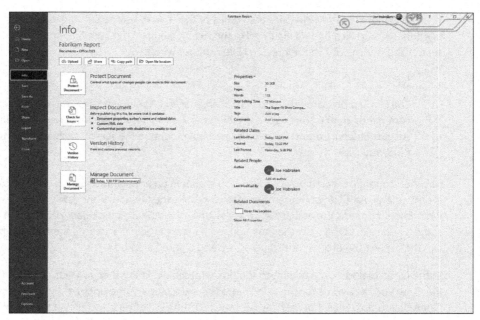

Figure 3-8   The Word Info page

You can open a version of the file from the list by selecting it. When you open the automatically saved version of the file (which is labeled "Unsaved"), a message bar appears at the top of the document window below the ribbon. It states that the current document is a "Recovered Unsaved File" and the file is temporarily stored on the computer. You are provided two options: Compare and Restore. You can select Compare to compare this version of the file with the current version of the file. Any differences between the two files are detailed using the Track Changes feature and are displayed in the document and the Reviewing pane. You can go through each of the changes marked in the document and accept or reject them as needed.

You also have the option of selecting Restore. This option saves the AutoRecovered version of the file over the current copy of the file. A message box opens, letting you know that the current version will be overwritten by the restored version. Click OK to overwrite the current version.

Searching for 365 files

If you haven't done a good job of keeping your files organized and can't seem to locate the file you need, you have a couple of ways to search for files. One option is to use the Search box provided by File Explorer. Open File Explorer, and then select the location for the search using the icons on the left of the File Explorer window. You can then type the file name or a portion of the file name in the search box; the search begins automatically.

The File Explorer window supplies the results of the search. You can modify the search as needed. You can also open a file listed in the search results. The Close Search button closes the search and returns you to the previous File Explorer window.

NOTE

The File Explorer provides you with a tab of Search Tools when you run a search. Location commands enable you to specify where the search should take place (current folder versus subfolders). Commands are also available to refine the search, such as Date Modified, Kind, and Size.

Another option for searching your files is to search in an application's Open dialog box. This is particularly useful if you remember at least part of the file name but don't really remember what folder contains the actual file. To access the Open dialog box, select File to open the Backstage. Then select Open. On the Open page, select a particular location, such as Computer. You can then select the Browse button to access the Open dialog box.

In the Open dialog box, navigate to the drive, folder, or library that you want to search for the file. Type your keywords for the search into the Search box in the upper-right corner of the Open dialog box. Files that match your search criteria have the search keywords highlighted in both the document title and document content, as shown in Figure 3-9.

Figure 3-9   The Word Open dialog box, as it appears after you have searched by keyword

If you want to search a different folder using the same search, select that folder in the Organize list and then click the Search box to select your recently used keywords. When you want to open a file that has been identified by the search, double-click the file name to open it in the current application.

Protecting a 365 file

The 365 applications enable you to protect a file (such as a document or workbook) that is shared with other users (particularly users on a network). The Protect Document settings help protect the content of the file and can also potentially restrict what can be changed in the document and by whom. To view these options, click the Protect Document button in the Info window, as shown in Figure 3-10.

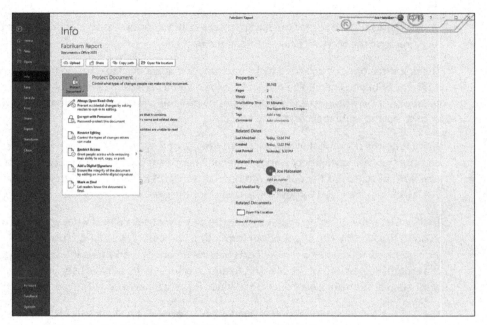

Figure 3-11   Select a document protection strategy on the Info page.

The following options are available:

- **Always Open Read-Only:** When you choose this option, documents you share are opened in read-only mode. This feature is primarily designed to keep users from inadvertently making changes to a file upon first inspection.

- **Encrypt With Password:** The file is encrypted and protected with a password. When you select this option, you are required to enter a password for the file. Only users with the password can open the file.

- **Restrict Editing:** This command opens the Restrict Formatting and Editing task pane in the document, presentation, or worksheet window. You can restrict formatting to a selection of styles and specify editing restrictions for the document, including making the document read-only.

- **Restrict Access:** This option enables you to take advantage of a Digital Rights Management server. This type of service allows you to assign users different permission levels for the file.

- **Add A Digital Signature:** You can digitally sign a file to prove its authenticity. Signing a file digitally requires that you obtain a digital certificate. A certificate authority can provide digital certificates.

- **Mark As Final:** This command marks the file as final and makes the file read-only. All editing commands for the file are disabled; however, any user opening the document can remove the Mark As Final setting in the Backstage.

The first three options provided by Protect Document are available to 365 users (home, small business, or big business). The Always Open Read-Only option is useful when you want your collaborators to opt-in to editing privileges by providing for a read-only look at the document prior to having editing access to the file.

Encrypting the document with a password (the second option) definitely limits access to the file because the password is necessary to open it. This means that you also must keep track of the password because it is the only way to open the encrypted file. This is a strong security measure, but it can backfire if you forget the password for the file.

The Restrict Editing setting enables you to be somewhat selective in what you allow other users to do to the file. You can specify both formatting and editing restrictions using the Restrict Editing task pane. You can also choose parts of a document or worksheet and specify the users who can edit those portions of the file. This feature requires that you have user groups on your network, such as domain user groups on a Windows Server network.

The Restrict Access setting requires that you have access to a Digital Rights Management server (DRM server). So if you work in a corporate environment that provides a DRM server, you can take advantage of this way of securing your files. Restricting access using a DRM server enables you to specify a particular user (by username or email address) and then assign a level of access to that user.

Digitally signing a file is a way to authenticate that a file is from a trusted source. So adding a digital signature to a file is more about letting users with whom you share the file know that the file is authentic and does not contain any malicious code that might damage their computers or computer files. Adding a digital signature to a file protects your collaborators—the people who review the shared file—more than it protects you from a particular security problem.

To digitally sign a file, you need a digital certificate. You can obtain digital certificates from an online certificate authority such as Global Sign (*globalsign.com*) and Digicert (*digicert.com*); depending on the size of your business, you might find digital certificates cost prohibitive. CAcert (*www.cacert.org*) is a community-based certificate authority that offers certificates to members for free.

You can also create a digital certificate using the Digital Certificate for VBA Projects utility provided with 365. Appendix B, "365 macros," provides a walkthrough of using this utility in the section "Digitally signing macros."

You should digitally sign a file only when you are providing a final draft to your collaborators. Signing the file marks the file as final, which makes it read-only. That means when you have a final file, and the certificate is on your computer, you are ready to go.

Click Protect Document and then Add A Digital Signature. The Sign dialog box opens. Enter the commitment type and the purpose for signing the file. Your default signing certificate is listed in the dialog box in the Signing As pane. You can click the Change button to locate a different certificate if you have multiple certificates on your computer.

When you are ready to sign the document, click Sign. The Signature Confirmation box opens, letting you know that your signature has been saved with the document. However, if the document is changed, the signature becomes invalid.

Preparing a file for sharing

The Microsoft 365 applications also give you tools for checking a document before you share it. These features are primarily designed for both security and accessibility issues. For example, you can check the document for any personal information that might be contained in it; this is a security check because you don't necessarily want to share personal information in the shared document. Or you might have text in the document that will be difficult for people with disabilities to read; this is an accessibility issue.

The Check For Issues button on the Info window in the Backstage provides three tools that check your file for possible issues related to sharing:

- **Inspect Document:** This tool inspects the document for specific content such as comments, annotations, document properties, and hidden text. The main purpose of the inspector is to help ferret out personal information that you might have inadvertently stored in the document.

- **Check Accessibility:** This tool opens the Accessibility Checker task pane in the document and provides a list of warnings related to accessibility issues in your document. For example, several blank lines between paragraphs might signal to a person using a screen reader that the document has ended. As you select each warning in the task pane, you are presented with information on why you should fix the issue and suggestions on how to fix it.

- **Check Compatibility:** This tool checks the file for items that are not supported by earlier versions of the application you are using. For example, you might have used the Citation and Bibliography features in Word, but the Compatibility Checker tells you the earlier versions of Word (Word 97–2003) need to convert these items to static text.

As already mentioned, you can run these tools from the Backstage in the Info window. The purpose of these tools is to negate the chance of sharing personal information (Inspect Document), to make sure that the file is accessible to users with disabilities (Check Accessibility), and to ensure that users of earlier versions of Microsoft products can access the file and view its content (Check Compatibility).

Using and creating graphics

The 365 options for graphics and pictures   69

Working with your digital pictures   81

Using shapes and the 365 drawing tools   88

Using the screenshot tool   93

Using WordArt   94

Each Microsoft 365 application is designed for a particular purpose. Excel is a number cruncher, Word is a powerful word processor, and PowerPoint is an extraordinary presentation application. Although you use the different applications for different purposes, graphics (images, shapes, and clip art) are used for pretty much the same purpose in all the applications. Graphics enable you to enhance information and add interest to the worksheets, documents, and presentations you create. In 365, the commands and tools used to insert and modify images, shapes, SmartArt graphics, and icons are pretty consistent across the different applications in the Office suite. So if you know how to use graphics in Word, you can apply that knowledge to another application, such as PowerPoint.

This chapter provides an overview of the options for adding graphics to your Office application files. We look at how to insert shapes, SmartArt graphics, and images. We also look at how you can manipulate images and take advantage of two new sources of images: the new Stock Footage library and the 3D Models library. These new options make it easy for you to quickly design compelling presentations and reports using the 365 applications.

The 365 options for graphics and pictures

The Office applications offer you ample ways of enhancing the files you create with graphics. Options for graphics range from basic shapes to the insertion of customizable SmartArt graphics to options from Microsoft's new stock image library. There are also your own digital images, which also can be added to your files. How you use graphics in your application documents (or files, if you prefer) is as important as the type of graphics you use. Graphics are meant to enhance a Word document, Excel worksheet, or PowerPoint slide.

Enhancing your work with graphics can have a different meaning, depending on the type of product you are creating in an Office application. For example, a neighborhood newsletter created in Word might benefit from the use of images as design elements or headlines formatted as graphics using WordArt. In another scenario, a PowerPoint slide detailing a particular business process could be greatly enhanced using a SmartArt graphic diagram that provides a visualization of the process described on the slide. An Excel worksheet that details a particular process could also be enhanced visually using a stock image or two. Weighing the benefits of adding a graphic or an image to a 365 document definitely makes sense; however, you should avoid graphics that make a document, worksheet, or slide too busy or that do not enhance the information provided. Make sure that your use of graphic elements increases the impact of information being presented.

Charts, for example (which are discussed in the context of their use in specific applications such as Excel and PowerPoint), are extremely useful graphics that provide a visualization of numeric data. Charts can be particularly useful when they accompany worksheet data in Excel or help explain numerical data provided on a PowerPoint slide or in a Word document. Consider the chart as your measuring stick in terms of weighing whether to use a particular graphic type in an application. We know how charts enhance the understanding of numerical values in tables, so try to apply the same measuring stick when you plan to use digital images, clip art, and diagrams. Make sure they add to the document and don't just serve as a cute distraction. I realize that pictures of puppies and kitties are popular on the web (they melt nearly anyone's heart), but using puppy pictures to mask poor sales data on a PowerPoint slide is just plain wrong.

➤ **For information on creating charts in Excel, see Chapter 14, "Enhancing worksheets with charts."**

➤ **For information on using charts and other graphics in PowerPoint, see Chapter 19 "Better slides with clip art, pictures, and SmartArt."**

As already mentioned, the applications provide different types of graphical elements that you can use in your files. The following list briefly describes the possibilities:

- **Picture:** You can insert your own digital pictures into your documents and presentations. The 365 applications support different file formats, including Windows Bitmap (.bmp), Graphics Interchange Format (.gif), Joint Photographic Experts Group (.jpg), Portable Network Graphics (.png), and Tagged Image File Format (.tif) formats.

- **Stock Images:** Microsoft 365 now has a huge library of stock images that you can use in your documents, presentations, and worksheets. The stock images come in five different types: Images, Icons, Cutout People, Stickers, and Illustrations. Each of these image types are further broken down into subcategories based on the image content or theme. For example, the Images group is further divided into categories such as Communication, People, Flowers, Creativity, and Sunlight. The Icons are divided into categories such as Location, Interface, and Animals (just to name a few). These categories change periodically.

- **Online Pictures:** You can also search for online pictures using the Bing search engine. Online pictures can also be accessed by categories such as Airplane, Animals, Fireworks, Flowers, and Fish. Images are typically protected by copyright law, but you can configure the Online Pictures tools to limit the pictures found in the search to images that use a Creative Commons license, which typically allows the image to be used in most circumstances. However, using online images that do not readily provide a clear provenance might not be the best idea nor make it readily apparent if there is a fair use exception to the use of a particular image.

- **Shapes:** The capability to insert different drawn shapes into an application has been around nearly as long as the Microsoft applications. A Shapes gallery provides different shape categories that make it easy to add lines, rectangles, stars, and even callouts to your Office documents. You can also edit and group shapes for all sorts of possibilities. PowerPoint provides new Merge Shapes commands that enable you to combine several shapes into a single shape.

- **Icons:** Icons are two-color (black and white) drawings that can be used to enhance a document or presentation. The Icons are broken down into groups such as Communication, Education, Food And Drink, and Holidays.

- **3D Models:** This library of images is another recent addition to the 365 applications. These 3D images can be panned or tilted in any direction and can be rotated clockwise or counterclockwise. A number of the 3D models in the Microsoft online library are animated. For example, there is a cross-section of a human heart that beats. The 3D model files are organized into categories such as Animated Animals, Anatomy, Clothing, Space, and Vintage Cartoons (to name a few).

- **SmartArt:** This graphic type provides SmartArt diagrams, which include lists, processes, hierarchies, and relationships. Even the most complex SmartArt graphics are designed so that you can easily add text labels and other information to the various parts of the SmartArt.

- **Screenshot:** This tool gives you the ability to take a snapshot of the Windows desktop and any windows open on the desktop. This can be particularly useful if you want to visually document the steps required in a particular feature in one of the 365 applications (or any application open on the Windows desktop). You can also use it to capture any screen on your computer, including messaging platforms such as Skype .

- **WordArt:** WordArt styles provide a quick way to add special effects to text in objects such as text boxes. A WordArt quick style includes many different text options (formatting possibilities), including Shadow, Reflection, Glow, Soft Edges, and 3D Format. WordArt is designed for when you want the text to stand out and add visual interest to your document.

Although Word, PowerPoint, and Excel provide easy access to the above-mentioned graphics, each application has the necessary commands sequestered in a slightly different way on the Insert tab of the ribbon. For example, Word has a single group called Illustrations. Excel's

Insert tab also provides an Illustrations group, which is very similar to the Word grouping of the graphic-related commands. PowerPoint divides the these commands into two groups on the ribbon's insert tab: Images and Illustrations. Figure 4-1 shows the PowerPoint application window with the Insert tab of the ribbon selected.

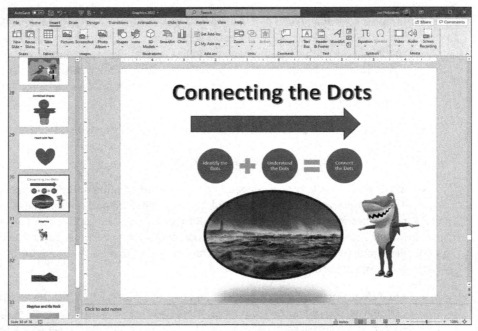

Figure 4-1   The ribbon's Insert tab enables you to insert objects such as pictures, icons, and SmartArt.

TIP

The Insert Picture dialog box also provides a Search Pictures box. Rather than hunting for your images using the folder and library icons in the navigation pane of the dialog box, you can do a keyword search to locate your images.

Although the Pictures command is housed in the Insert tab's Images group in PowerPoint and the Illustrations group in Word and Excel, its purpose is the same in all three applications. It allows you to access pictures on your computer (including your OneDrive), pictures in the Stock Images library, and pictures available online. To access pictures on your computer, select the Pictures command and then select This Device. An Insert Picture dialog box will open with the Pictures library on your computer selected. If your images are scattered throughout your computer's hard drive, you can use the folder and library icons available on the left of the Insert Picture dialog box as needed to locate your pictures.

Pictures and images stored on your OneDrive can also be accessed using the Pictures command because your OneDrive is considered one of the other "places" you might potentially store images. So think of—at least for the purposes of accessing pictures using the Pictures command—OneDrive as local storage.

To take advantage of the new Stock Images library provided by Microsoft, select Pictures and then select Stock Images. The Stock Images window opens, as shown in Figure 4-2.

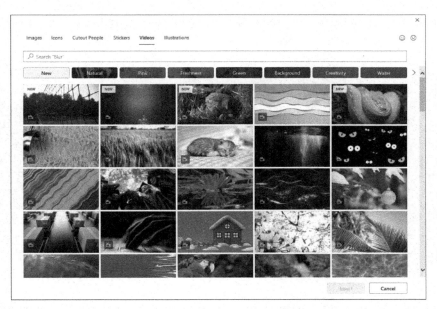

Figure 4-2   The Stock Images command opens a library of images, icons, and other visual content.

The Stock Images window provides access to Images, Icons, Cutout People (no background on these candid people shots), Stickers, Videos, and Illustrations. So, in this particular case, we have opened the Stock Images window via the Pictures command (followed by the Stock Images command). If you select Icons from the Insert tab on the ribbon, you will also end up in the Stock Images window. This image library actually provides you with more than just photographic images; the images library also includes Icons, Cutout People, Stickers, and Illustrations. You can switch between these image types by selecting the appropriate heading at the top of the window.

You also have the option of using the Search box to find particular types of images, or you can select any of the provided thematic groupings, including Expertise, Vacations, Adventure, and Blue. By default, new images are provided when you open the Images window. Once you find an image you want to use, select it and then select Insert. If you want, you can actually select more than one image and then have all your selected images placed in the current document, worksheet, or presentation slide.

For accessing pictures available on the web (using a Bing Search), use the Online Pictures command to open the Online Pictures window. Images are divided into different groupings, including Animals, Coffee, Fish, and Swimming. If you would rather not browse for images, you can run a search using the Search Bing box at the top of the window. To run a search, type a keyword or phrase in the Search Bing box and then select Search. By default, Bing shows you images that are licensed under Creative Commons or available in the public domain. It is your responsibility to secure permissions to use online images that are copyright protected. You will find that you can also access your OneDrive via the Online Pictures dialog box. This is because (at least in the Online Pictures dialog box) your OneDrive is considered an online resource even though it is also available in the Insert Pictures dialog box.

Inside OUT

Microsoft 365 does not provide traditional clipart.

If you have been a user of Microsoft 365 as long as I have (I must confess I used Microsoft Word for DOS back in the day), you have probably put together presentations and documents and thrown in a few clipart images along the way. Microsoft 365 does not supply clipart, although it does provide stock images, icons, and 3D models. Even if you are convinced a cute piece of clipart will make a PowerPoint slide attain perfection, I would suggest you avoid "clipping" clipart from the web. Every image has a source, and the originator of an image (in most cases) holds the copyright for that image. Do not violate copyright law trying to attain cuteness.

Once you have located the web image file that you want to insert via the Insert Pictures window, select the image and then click the Insert button. Once the image is in your document, your worksheet, or presentation slide, you can then manipulate the photo using the Picture Tools Format tab, which provides adjustment, style, and arrangement settings. We will take a closer look at manipulating pictures in the various Office applications later in this chapter. Let's take a look at working with SmartArt graphics, and then we can continue our discussion of other graphic possibilities, including pictures, screenshots, and WordArt.

Working with SmartArt graphics

SmartArt provides a large gallery of complex graphical elements that you can use to create eye-catching lists and diagrams. You can create lists that use shapes to better define the relationship between text entries in a list, and you can create lists that make it easy to combine text and pictures. Figure 4-3 shows a vertical picture list SmartArt graphic that includes thumbnail photos and text.

SmartArt lists enable you to go beyond the possibilities normally associated with numbered and bulleted lists. SmartArt lists can be particularly useful in PowerPoint, where you can replace bulleted lists on slides with SmartArt lists. SmartArt lists are better at showing how the different items in a list are related than the typical bulleted list found on a PowerPoint slide.

➤ **For information on converting text to SmartArt in PowerPoint, see Chapter 19.**

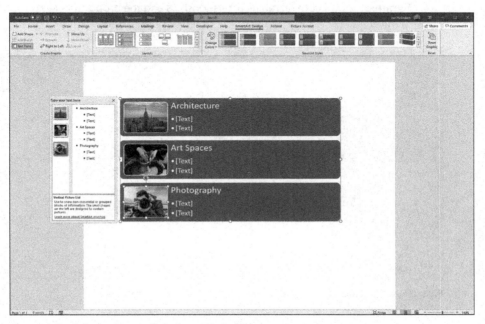

Figure 4-3   A SmartArt vertical picture list in Word

The SmartArt gallery also provides many different diagram types, including process diagrams, relationship diagrams, and hierarchy diagrams, just to name a few. For example, you can use a hierarchy organization chart in an Excel worksheet to provide information related to how different departments shown in a worksheet relate to each other in terms of corporate structure. Figure 4-4 shows a half-circle organization chart in an Excel worksheet.

Each SmartArt diagram category gives you a specific way to represent information visually in your Office documents. The following list briefly describes each SmartArt graphic category:

- **List:** Places text in nonsequential vertical or horizontal lists.

- **Process:** Shows a logical progression or flow to break down the steps in a process or cycle.

- **Cycle:** Shows the steps in a continuous process.

CHAPTER 4

- **Hierarchy:** Shows the hierarchical relationship between items in the diagram. A hierarchy diagram can also show a decision tree.

- **Relationship:** Shows how elements in the diagram are related or connected.

- **Matrix:** Shows how the parts relate to the whole.

- **Pyramid:** Shows both hierarchical relationships and the proportional importance of items in the hierarchy.

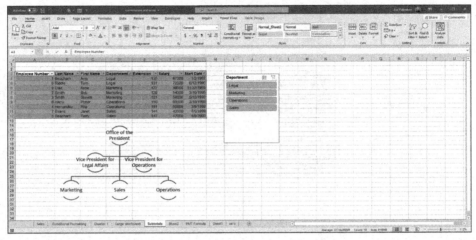

Figure 4-4   Organization charts can be inserted into Excel worksheets.

- **Picture:** Lists all the SmartArt lists and diagrams that enable you to incorporate images into the SmartArt structure.

- **Office.com:** Provides additional SmartArt graphics offered online via the Office.com website.

SmartArt graphics are easy to create. They are also easy to edit and modify. Let's take a look at inserting SmartArt graphics into the Office applications and then look at the tools available for modifying and enhancing SmartArt lists and diagrams.

Inserting SmartArt graphics

SmartArt graphics are inserted using the SmartArt command, which is housed in the Illustration group on the ribbon's Insert tab. To insert SmartArt into an Office document, follow these steps:

1.   On the Insert tab, select SmartArt. The Choose SmartArt Graphic dialog box opens, as shown in Figure 4-5.

2.   Select a SmartArt category to view the individual diagrams provided by a particular category.

3. Select the list or diagram you want to insert.

4. Click OK. The list or diagram is inserted into your current Office document.

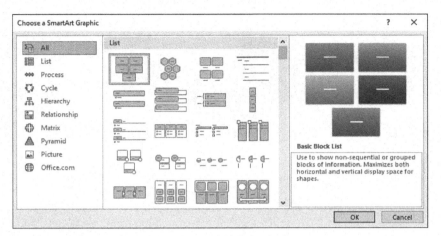

Figure 4-5   The Choose A SmartArt Graphic dialog box

You can now enter the text that you want to place in the diagram. Figure 4-6 shows a Venn diagram SmartArt graphic that has been inserted into a Word document.

You can enter the text for the diagram directly onto the diagram parts by replacing any of the [TEXT] placeholders. You can also make text entries and edit them for the diagram in the Text pane that accompanies each SmartArt graphic (to the left of the SmartArt). You can collapse the Text pane by clicking the pane's Close button. If you want the Text pane to reappear, click the Expand button on the left edge of the SmartArt frame.

Some SmartArt lists and diagrams enable you to include pictures as part of them. After you insert a SmartArt graphic that includes placeholders for pictures, picture placeholders are provided in the different diagram parts and the Text pane for the SmartArt graphic. To replace a picture placeholder, click the placeholder in either the diagram or the Text pane. The Insert Picture dialog box opens. Navigate to the folder that houses the picture graphic, and then select the file. Click Insert to place the picture in the SmartArt graphic.

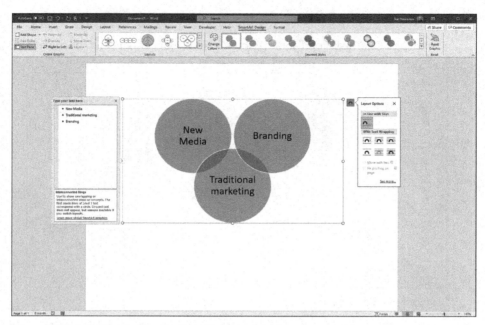

Figure 4-6 Enter the text for the SmartArt list or diagram.

CAUTION

If you are going to use SmartArt graphics in a 365 application, save your file using the current Office file formats. For example, Word uses the file format .docx, and Excel uses .xlsx (by default). Saving a file containing SmartArt graphics in one of the earlier Office formats (such as .doc or .xls) can lead to a loss of functionality and capability when attempting to edit the SmartArt graphic once it is in the legacy file type.

The picture is sized according to the space allotted for it in the list or diagram. For example, if you insert a picture into a circle that is part of a particular diagram type, the picture is sized to fit in the shape (meaning the circle). This means that you do not have to size or crop images before you insert them into a SmartArt list or diagram. Even the largest digital photo will be sized to fit appropriately into the SmartArt graphic shape.

When you have finished entering the text and pictures (if applicable) for the SmartArt graphic, click outside the graphic's frame. You can now continue to work on the document, worksheet, or presentation that you are creating. The SmartArt graphic is like any other object in that you can move or size it as required.

Modifying SmartArt graphics

When you select a SmartArt graphic in a 365 file such as a document or presentation slide (it is selected when you first insert it), the SmartArt Tools become available on the ribbon. The SmartArt Tools consist of a Design tab and a Format tab. For example, look back at Figure 4-6, which shows a SmartArt graphic in process with the SmartArt Design tab selected.

The Design tab is devoted to modifying the SmartArt elements. For example, the Create Graphic group on the Design tab enables you to add shapes and bullets and promote or demote items in the SmartArt list. The Design tab also enables you to change the SmartArt layout and assign different styles to the elements in the SmartArt. For example, from the Layouts gallery, you can choose from among different layouts for the particular type of SmartArt list or diagram that you inserted into your Office document. The Change Colors command in the SmartArt Styles group enables you to specify a color combination for the SmartArt graphic based on the current theme and many other color categories. After you have specified a color combination for SmartArt, you can use the SmartArt Styles gallery to fine-tune the color scheme selected for the graphic and apply 3D styles to the SmartArt.

Two other command groups serve as the end caps for the Design tab. On the far left is the Create Graphic group, and at the far right is the Reset group. In the Create Graphic group is the Add Shape command, which enables you to add shapes (the same shape used as the primary building block for the SmartArt graphic) to the graphic.

So if you have inserted a SmartArt list that provides three list boxes, you can increase the number of boxes using the Add Shape command. The Create Graphic group has other commands that enable you to promote or demote and move up or move down shapes in the SmartArt graphic. The availability of these commands depends on the type of SmartArt graphic you have inserted into your Office document.

If you make design changes to your graphic using the Change Colors command or the SmartArt Styles gallery, and you just don't like the way things turned out, you can reset the graphic and start over (or just leave well enough alone). Click the Reset Graphic command in the Reset group. The Reset Graphic command does not reset changes that you make using the Layouts gallery or the commands in the Create Graphic group.

The other SmartArt Tools tab is the Format tab, shown in Figure 4-7. The Format tab commands are geared to modify shapes and assign shape styles to the SmartArt graphic. WordArt styles are also provided so that you can manipulate the text elements in the SmartArt graphic.

Many of the command possibilities the Format tab provides can apply to the entire SmartArt graphic or the individual shapes (elements) that make up the graphic. This enables you to fine-tune the look of a SmartArt graphic and modify an existing graphic as you require.

For example, you might want to change the shape of a specific element (which is referred to as a shape, so this can be confusing) in the SmartArt graphic. You can select a specific shape and modify it, or you can select a number of shapes (select the first shape or element and then hold down the Ctrl key when selecting the other shapes) and modify them collectively. The Shapes group on the Format tab enables you to change the shape of a selected element or elements using the Change Shape gallery. You can also change the size of a shape or shapes using the Larger and Smaller commands.

TIP

If you are working with a 3D SmartArt graphic, you might find it easier to edit the shape settings in 2D. Select the Edit in 2D command in the Shapes group.

Also, the Format tab enables you to modify the style for a selected shape or shapes and modify shape fill, outline, and effects. The Shape Styles group provides access to the Shapes Styles gallery, which provides different border fill and text styles. Shape Fill, Shape Outline, and Shape Effects enable you to modify these style elements individually.

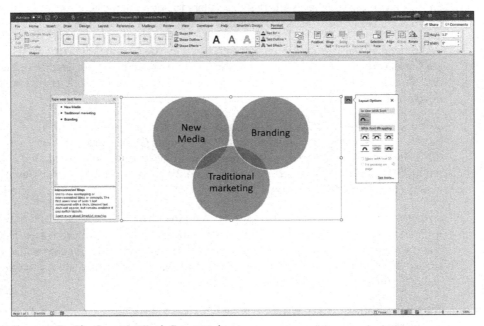

Figure 4-7   The SmartArt Tools Format tab

The WordArt Styles gallery offers WordArt text styles that you can apply to the text in a shape. These styles include color, outline, shadow, and text effects. If you want to fine-tune the WordArt style assigned to a particular shape or a number of selected shapes, you can use the Text Fill, Text Outline, and Text Effects commands as needed. For even greater control over the shape and text options for a SmartArt graphic, select the SmartArt graphic and then navigate to the SmartArt Tools Format tab. Select the dialog box launcher in the WordArt Styles group to open the Format Shape task pane.

TIP

You can toggle the SmartArt graphic's Text pane on or off using the Text Pane command in the Create Graphic group on the SmartArt Tools Design tab. The Arrange group commands relate to how a shape is layered with other shapes and how the text in a document such as a Word document deals with the SmartArt graphic. To layer shapes in a graphic, use the Bring Forward and Send Backward commands. You can change the alignment and rotation of an entire SmartArt graphic or shape by using the Align Objects and Rotate Objects commands, respectively.

TIP

If you are attempting to select a shape in a SmartArt graphic that is behind another shape, the easiest way to select it (instead of using Bring Forward) is to select the shape's text in the Text pane.

Working with your digital pictures

You can work with a number of different digital picture file formats when working in the applications. It is true that a picture is worth a thousand words, and you can use pictures to enhance your Word documents, PowerPoint slides, Excel worksheets, and even Outlook emails. Some of the commonly used digital picture file formats are as follows:

- Windows Bitmap (.bmp)

- Graphics Interchange Format (.gif)

- Joint Photographic Experts Group (.jpg)

- Portable Network Graphics (.png)

- Tagged Image File Format (.tif)

- Windows Metafile (.wmf)

Digital image files are compressed, and the compression scheme a particular file format uses can affect the overall quality of the image. Lossless compression schemes compress the file without discarding any of the file data; the lossy compression scheme actually discards some of the file's data to compress the image file. Image files also differ in the number of colors they can provide, so you will find that each file format definitely has its own plusses and minuses.

For example, GIF files, which are typically only used on the web are relatively low resolution when compared to some of the other image file formats. The PNG format provides millions of colors and uses a lossless compression scheme, so you get a fantastic-looking image, but the file size can be quite large. A JPEG image uses a lossy compression scheme; it might not look as good as a PNG file, but it definitely provides you with a smaller file size, particularly if you are trying to email photos.

Most digital cameras shoot either JPEG or PNG files by default. Most digital cameras also enable you to adjust the number of megapixels used in a shot, which relates to the resolution of the picture and the file size created.

Inside OUT

Not all photo file types are created equal.

Most cell phone cameras shoot photos in the JPEG format, which looks good and commonly has a file size (even at maximum resolution) that is still reasonable to work with. If you want to work with photo files for print publications that you've created in Publisher, you might want to use a higher resolution image file that you would use with a lossless compression strategy. There are many possibilities, including BMP (which has been around since the very dawn of Microsoft Windows) and TIFF (Tagged Image File Format). If you use an actual camera to shoot your photos, the file type possibilities will be greater than those offered by your cell phone.

When using digital images in the 365 applications, you don't really need to worry about file size, megapixels, or file type. The applications can deal with most of the common file types and typically size the image to fit into the shape or frame that will contain the image.

Inserting pictures

The Pictures command is on the Insert tab. To insert a picture, follow these steps:

1. Select the Pictures command, then select This Device. The Insert Picture dialog box opens, as shown in Figure 4-8.

2. Locate and select the picture file you want to insert.

3. Click the Insert button. The Insert Picture dialog box closes, and the picture is inserted into the document.

Figure 4-8   The Insert Picture dialog box

After the image has been inserted into the document, you can size the document using the handles provided on the picture frame. You can also modify the image size using the Shape Height and Shape Width spin boxes, which are provided in the Size group of the Pictures Tool Format tab. The Picture Tools become available on the ribbon when the picture is selected.

Adjusting pictures

The Picture Tools Format tab provides commands that modify different aspects of the picture. For example, the Picture Styles gallery enables you to change the border type and the shape, and it allows you to apply some 3D effects to the picture. You can access the picture border and the effects applied to the picture, such as settings for the shadow, glow, and 3D rotation, using the Picture Border and Picture Effects commands, respectively.

Many of the commands provided on the Picture Tools Format tab are the same as those found on the SmartArt Tools Format tab. For example, the Position, Wrap Text, and other Arrange group commands are the same for a picture, SmartArt graphic, or shape; however, the Picture Tools Format tab does provide the Adjust group, which contains extremely useful commands specific to digital pictures. The Adjust group commands are as follows:

- **Remove Background:** This command enables you to remove the background from the picture. We look at using this tool later in the chapter.

- **Corrections:** With this command, you can select from a gallery of choices that enable you to sharpen and soften the image or adjust the brightness and contrast. Thumbnails of your image are provided in this gallery, with different correction settings applied to them. All you need to do is select one of the possibilities. To view the brightness and contrast settings for one of the gallery thumbnails, place the mouse on that thumbnail to view a ScreenTip that provides the percent brightness and contrast.

- **Color:** This command provides a gallery of color saturations and tones, as well as recolor settings for your image. Figure 4-9 shows the Color gallery. Color saturations are denoted by percent saturation, such as 100%, 200%, and so on. The color tones are denoted by degrees Kelvin (lower numbers are "cooler" and tend toward the blues; higher numbers are "warmer" and tend toward yellow). To apply a setting from the gallery, select the thumbnail of your image that provides the color changes you want to make to your picture.

TIP

To add a caption to a picture (or clip art) in the Office applications (excluding Excel), right-click the selected picture and then select Insert Caption. You can then set up the caption in the Caption dialog box.

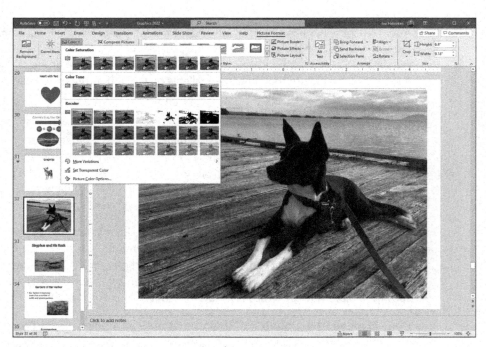

Figure 4-9   The Color Adjustment gallery for a picture

- **Artistic Effects:** This command provides a gallery of photo effects, such as Pencil Sketch, Cement, and Plastic Wrap. You can preview any of the effects on your picture by placing the mouse on a particular effect in the gallery. Some of the possibilities are mind-blowing and really groovy (of course, I grew up in the 1960s).

- **Compress Pictures:** This command enables you to compress the image so that its size—in terms of file size, not the size of the image in the document—is smaller. Therefore, your entire document file size will be smaller. When you select Compress Pictures, the Compress Pictures dialog box opens. It enables you to delete any cropped areas of the picture and to select a target output size, such as 96 ppi (pixels per inch) for emails and 150 ppi for web pages.

- **Change Picture:** Use this command to open the Insert Pictures dialog box and select a picture to replace the current image.

- **Reset Picture:** This command throws out all the formatting changes you have made to the picture. You return to square one.

Although the galleries provided by a number of the Adjust group commands might be sufficient for your needs in changing an image's attributes, you can fine-tune these settings using the Format Picture task pane. You can display the Format Picture task pane by selecting the options link provided at the bottom of the Corrections, Color, and Artistic Effects galleries. For example, if you select Picture Corrections Options at the bottom of the Corrections gallery (select Correction then Picture Corrections Options), the Format Picture task pane opens with Picture Corrections selected, as shown in Figure 4-10.

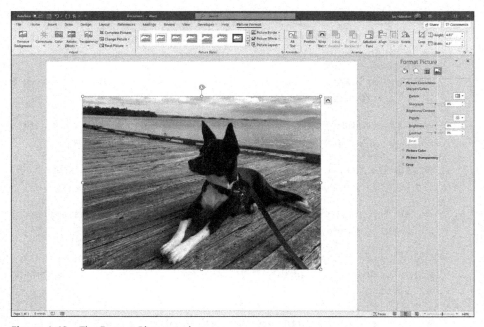

Figure 4-10   The Format Picture task pane

You can use the different settings in the Format Picture task pane to specify the fill, the line color, the line style, and the 3D format and rotation for the image. You can also fine-tune changes that you have made to the picture, such as brightness and contrast corrections, color changes, and artistic effects. For example, you can adjust the Picture Corrections settings (shown in Figure 4-10) using slider bars that soften or sharpen an image or change the brightness and contrast of the image.

TIP

The Format Picture task pane appears in Excel and Word as a fixed pane on the right side of the application window. In PowerPoint, the Format Picture task pane is a floating pane and can be moved on the screen as you wish.

Cropping an image

Another useful command for adjusting an image is the Crop command. Although this command isn't included in the Adjust group, the Crop command is useful when you want to trim unneeded parts of the image. It is located at the other end of the Format tab in the Size group.

The Crop command offers more than one possibility for cropping an image. When you select the Crop command, the following options are provided:

- **Crop:** Select Crop to place the crop frame around the image. You can then adjust the cropping handles as needed. Select the Crop command again to apply your cropping settings.

- **Crop To Shape:** You can apply a shape to the image from the Shape gallery and have the image cropped to that specific shape.

- **Aspect Ratio:** You can have the image cropped using a specific aspect ratio, such as 1:1 (square), 2:3 (portrait), or 3:2 (landscape).

- **Fill:** The image is resized to fill the entire picture area (such as a picture box), and the portions of the image that fall outside the picture area are cropped.

- **Fit:** The image is resized to fit in the picture area, maintaining the original aspect ratio of the image. This is the opposite of cropping.

If you find that you have gone overboard on the cropping, you can remove the cropping by using the Undo command on the Quick Access Toolbar. The Reset Picture command does not undo cropping.

Using the Background Removal tool

The Background Removal tool can be extremely useful in removing unwanted background information from a picture so that the resulting image completely highlights the subject of the picture. The great part about this tool is that it can differentiate the background from the foreground elements in your photo and automatically selects the background areas to be removed from the photo. How well this works depends on the photo. Some photos contain color combinations or low contrast between the elements in the photo that make it difficult to separate the background from the foreground elements easily. However, after the Background Removal tool takes the first cut at selecting the background of the photo, you can step in and fine-tune the selection so that you end up with some good results.

To use the Remove Background tool, select a photo in the Office application. Then click the Remove Background command. The Background Removal tab appears on the ribbon, as shown in Figure 4-11.

The commands provided on the Background Removal tab are self-explanatory. Two command groups are provided: Refine and Close. The Refine group provides commands that enable you to refine the initial selection of the background. The Close group provides you with two possibilities that enable you to either discard the changes or keep them.

Upon the first inspection, after you select the Remove Background command, the background areas marked in the photo for removal are designated by a magenta overlay. A marquee with sizing handles is also floated on your image to specify the area of the image that contains the foreground elements to keep. If the marquee has excluded foreground items that you want to keep, you can change the size of the marquee or move the marquee's position as required.

CHAPTER 4

Figure 4-11   The Background Removal tab and a selected picture

Adjusting the marquee isn't going to get you much, so for greater refinement, you need to take advantage of the Refine group commands. Let's start with marking areas that you want to keep: Select the Mark Areas To Keep command. The mouse pointer becomes a pencil. Use the pencil to outline each area that you want to keep that has been marked for removal. Click the pencil to place a mark point on an area, and then continue to drag the mouse. Marking points makes it easier to connect the dots and mark the entire area you want to keep. While using the mouse, you might find that you've only enclosed a portion of an area to keep when the Background Removal tool suddenly catches on and finishes the selection for you by removing the magenta overlay from that area.

You can also mark areas to remove. Select the Mark Areas To Remove command and use the Pencil to mark areas that should be removed. When the area has been marked for removal, the magenta overlay is applied to that area of the image.

When you are ready to complete the process by keeping all the fine-tuning that you did with the Mark Areas To Keep and the Mark Areas To Remove commands, select the Keep Changes command. The background is removed from the image. Now you can take advantage of the picture styles that provide background fill colors or shadow effects.

If you have ever attempted to manipulate digital photos, you are probably aware that many of the possibilities we have discussed here would normally require a sophisticated piece of digital image editing software. It is pretty amazing that you can quickly correct such image parameters as brightness and contrast and apply artistic effects to an image from within the various Office applications such as Word and PowerPoint.

Using shapes and the 365 drawing tools

The Microsoft 365 applications enable you to add a variety of shapes to your Office documents. The Shapes gallery, which you access via the Shapes command on the Insert tab, provides shape categories. You can add lines, rectangles, block arrows, callouts, and other shape types.

One of the available shapes is a text box, which, as its name implies, adds a box containing text to a document. However, other shapes can also contain text; this means that you can use any shape as a design element and get double duty out of it as a text container. This can be useful when you want to add text to a document along with some visual interest, say, in a Word document or a PowerPoint slide. You format the text in a shape using WordArt styles and text fill, outline, and effects tools. This enables you to create shapes with eye-catching text entries that serve an informational purpose in your document.

You can insert multiple shapes into a document, worksheet, or PowerPoint slide. When you insert a shape onto a document page or slide, the shape resides in a layer that is superimposed on the text that already exists on the document page or slide. You can move a shape to any location and size the image. In Word, you can determine how the image coexists with the surrounding text by clicking the Layout Options button, which appears next to the selected shape.

This opens the Layout Options pane, which enables you to quickly determine whether the shape should be in line with the text or whether the text should wrap around the shape in a pattern. Options include Square, Tight, Through, Top and Bottom, Behind Text, and In Front Of Text.

To insert a shape onto a slide or document, navigate to the ribbon's Insert tab and then select Shapes. The Shapes gallery appears, as shown in Figure 4-12.

Select a shape in the gallery. The pointer becomes a drawing tool, and you can use it to "draw" the shape on the document page, sheet, or slide. After inserting the shape, you can size it using the sizing handles provided when the shape is selected. You can also drag the shape in the document to position it. When the shape is selected, the Drawing Tools Format tab becomes available on the ribbon. It supplies commands for formatting the shape and the text that appears in the shape.

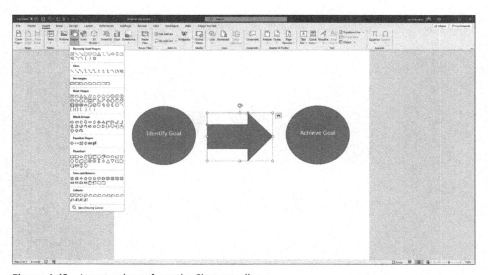

Figure 4-12   Insert a shape from the Shapes gallery.

Adding and combining multiple shapes

Although the SmartArt graphics provide many composite drawings and diagrams that contain different shapes (and can be manipulated individually), you can use the shapes in the Shapes gallery to create pretty much anything you require. In the Office applications, you can insert multiple shapes and then group them. After the shapes are grouped, you can treat them as a single object on the page.

To create a design element from multiple shapes in Word, Excel, or PowerPoint, insert the required shapes and position them as needed. Then use the Arrange commands to further position and layer the shapes.

You can use the Selection pane to change the layer position of the shapes by changing the shape's position in the Selection list. You can also select shapes in the Selection pane (instead of trying to click items on the page) when you want to specify the shapes to be grouped. Figure 4-13 shows multiple shapes selected on a Word document page. To open the Selection pane, select Selection Pane in the Arrange Group on the Shape Format tab (make sure one of your shapes is selected to access this tab).

When you are ready to group the selected shapes (and other objects), select the Group command in the Arrange group and then select Group from the drop-down menu. Now, when you move or size one shape in the group, all the shapes in the group are moved or sized.

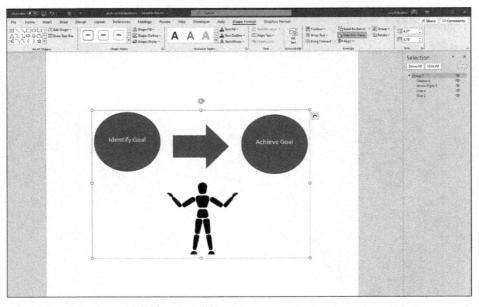

Figure 4-13   Group multiple shapes and images.

PowerPoint takes the capability to combine multiple shapes even further by offering a Merge Shapes command. Select the shapes on the slide that you want to combine. Select the Shape Format tab. The Merge Shapes drop-down menu is available in the Insert Shape group. When you select Merge Shapes, you have five possibilities:

- **Union:** Combines all the shapes into a single shape. You basically end up with a shape that incorporates the outline and internal volume of the original shapes. A one-color shape is created.

- **Combine:** Combines the shapes into a single shape, where any overlapping parts of the original shapes are omitted. A single, color shape results, as shown in Figure 4-14.

- **Fragment:** Combines the shapes into a one-color shape that outlines the exterior shape and any parts where the shapes originally overlapped.

- **Intersect:** Creates a combined shape that shows only the parts that originally overlapped.

- **Subtract:** Subtracts the overlapping shapes. For example, if you place an arrow on top of a circle and select Subtract, the circle would have an empty space within it in the shape of an arrow.

TIP

You can add text to any shape. Select the shape and then click the Text Box tool in the Insert Shapes group. The Insertion point is placed in the shape. From there, just type the text.

Using the Merge Shapes commands gives you another way to create custom shapes for your PowerPoint slides. No matter how you create your shapes (using Insert Shape, Group Shapes, or Merge Shapes), you can use the various tools in the Shape Styles group to modify their fill color, outline, and effects. Figure 4-14 shows a group of selected shapes on a PowerPoint slide and the Merge Shapes gallery on the Drawing Tools Format tab.

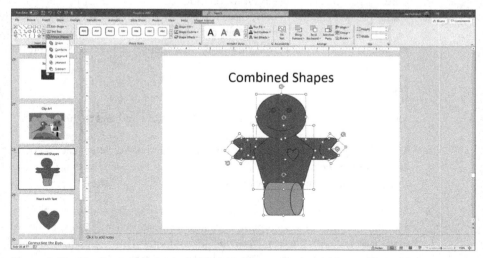

Figure 4-14   Use PowerPoint's Merge Shapes commands to combine multiple shapes in different ways.

Using the Shape Format tools

As you work with shapes in the 365 applications, selecting a shape or shapes will add the Shape Format tab to the ribbon (a similar tab for pictures and 3D models appears when either of these object types is selected). The Shape Format provides all the tools you need for formatting a shape. The Shape Format ribbon command groups are as follows:

- **Insert Shapes:** This group provides the Shapes gallery and the Edit Shape, Draw A Text Box, and Merge Shapes commands. The Edit Shape command enables you to replace a selected shape or view the edit points on a shape. The edit points enable you to manipulate different parts of a single shape. For instance, on a Smiley Face, the edit points give you control over the placement of the eyes and mouth on the face.

- **Shape Styles:** This group enables you to apply shape styles to your shapes that include fill, outline, and text color formatting. You can fine-tune the style for a shape using the Shape Fill, Shape Outline, and Shape Effects commands. The Shape Effects command enables you to apply different effects to the shape, such as Shadow, Reflection, and Glow. You can also use the 3D Rotation option to add 3D effects to the shape.

- **WordArt Styles:** This group becomes available when you have added text to the shape. You can apply WordArt styles to the text and manipulate the fill, outline, and effects for the text. The Text Effects command provides Shadow, Reflection, and Bevel effects, as well as 3D rotation effects.

- **Text:** This group (available in Word) provides commands for formatting the text in the shape. You can change the text direction and alignment within the shape. When you create multiple text boxes (which, again, can be any shape), you can link the shapes containing text using the Create Link command, which causes the text to flow through the linked text containing shapes.

TIP

You can also right-click a shape and select Add Text to add text to the shape.

- **Accessibility:** This group provides the Alt Text command, which allows you to create a description of the objects and the information on the screen so that the subject, setting, and actions are clear to someone who is blind or has low vision.

- **Arrange:** This group enables you to position the shape (or multiple shapes on a canvas) with the text layer in a document. In Word, the Position command specifies whether the shape is in line with the text. The Wrap Text command then specifies how the text actually wraps around the shape. This group also provides the Bring Forward, Send Backward, and Group commands. PowerPoint includes this group but does not provide the Position Wrap Text commands.

- **Size:** This group contains the Shape Height and Shape Width spin boxes, which are used to size the selected shape.

If you have layered a number of shapes, you might find it difficult to select a specific shape, particularly a shape that is at the back or behind another shape. You can view a list of shapes and the canvas with which they are associated using the Selection pane.

Using the screenshot tool

The screenshot feature enables you to capture a screenshot of an open application or a specific area of an application window by using the Screen Clipping tool. This enables you to place screenshots of any application, utility, or web browser window into your Office application documents. For example, you can place a screenshot of an Excel worksheet in a Word document as part of a report, or you can include a screenshot of a website page on a PowerPoint slide. The possible uses of the screenshot feature are really up to you; this feature can be useful if you are writing a set of procedures on how to use a particular application for a certain purpose.

You can capture screenshots in Word, Excel, PowerPoint, and Outlook (when creating new email messages, appointments, tasks, and contacts). The Screenshot command is housed in the Illustrations group on the ribbon's Insert tab, except for in PowerPoint, where it resides in the Images group on the Insert tab. As already mentioned, you can create a screenshot of an entire application window or specify an area to be captured. To capture an entire window, follow these steps:

1. Open the application window that you want to capture in the screenshot.

2. Switch to the application that will serve as the destination for the screenshot. For example, you might insert the screenshot into a Word document or onto a PowerPoint slide.

3. Select the Screenshot command. An Available Windows gallery appears.

4. Select the window you want to capture. The entire application window is pasted as a screenshot into the current Office application.

You can size or move the inserted screenshot; it is no different from any other graphic object. In fact, when the screenshot is selected, the Picture Tools Format tab becomes available on the ribbon. You can use the commands available to manipulate and format the screenshot as you would a digital image, which we discussed earlier in this chapter. For example, you can crop the screenshot or adjust brightness and contrast settings using the Correction command. You can also add styles to the screenshot using the Picture Styles gallery.

Also, you can capture screenshots of specific areas of a window. The Screen Clipping tool provided by the Screenshot command makes it easy to use the mouse to specify the area to be captured.

Before you use the Screen Clipping tool, you need to get the open windows cued up so that you have access to the correct application window when you select the Screen Clipping tool. This is particularly important if you have more than two windows open on the Windows desktop; select the application window that contains the area you want to capture using the appropriate icon on the Windows taskbar. This places that window at the top of the windows that are currently open. Switch back to the Office application that will serve as the destination for the screenshot using that application's icon on the taskbar.

Now you can capture the screenshot: Select Screenshot and then Screen Clipping. You are switched to the application window, where you make the screenshot. The mouse pointer becomes a screen-clipping tool. Click and drag the mouse as needed to specify the area of the window that you want to capture. When you release the mouse, you return to the screenshot destination application, and the screen area you selected is pasted into the current Office document as a screenshot.

You can save your screenshots as image files for further use. Right-click a selected screenshot and then select Save As Picture. The Save As Picture dialog box appears. Provide a name for the screenshot and then navigate to the folder that serves as the destination for the file. By default, the screenshot is saved as a PNG file. You can also save the file in another digital image format, such as GIF or JPEG, and as a bitmap file.

Using WordArt

WordArt enables you to create interesting text effects within your 365 application documents. You can use WordArt boxes on PowerPoint slides or as graphic elements in a Word document or an Excel worksheet. You can create a WordArt object from existing text, or you can create a blank WordArt object and then type the required text directly in the WordArt frame.

The WordArt command is on the ribbon's Insert tab. It is available in Word, PowerPoint, Excel, and Publisher. It is also available in Outlook when you are creating new Outlook items such as emails, contacts, and appointments.

Inserting a WordArt object into a document is really just a matter of selecting the WordArt command and then selecting one of the WordArt styles from the WordArt gallery.

If you formatted selected text as WordArt, your existing text appears in the WordArt frame and is formatted with the selected WordArt style. A new WordArt box contains the placeholder text "Your text here," which you can replace with your own text.

You can move the WordArt in the document as needed and size the WordArt box. When the WordArt box is selected, the Shape Format tab appears on the ribbon. Select Shape Format to access the various commands it provides. You can change the style of the WordArt box (or frame) by using the shape styles and shape-related commands (such as Shape Fill and Shape Outline) in the Shape Styles group.

The commands that affect the way the WordArt text looks are found in the WordArt Styles group. You can change the WordArt style that you have assigned to the selected WordArt by using the WordArt Styles gallery. The gallery provides styles that incorporate interesting effects, such as bevel and reflection.

The Text Fill and Text Outline commands enable you to control the fill for the WordArt text characters and the outline of the characters, respectively. The really cool part of using WordArt, however, lies in the different text effects that you can apply to the WordArt via the Text Effects command. Figure 4-15 shows the Text Effects gallery, including the Transform gallery.

Figure 4-15   The Text Effects gallery

The Text Effects gallery enables you to apply effects to the WordArt text, including Show, Reflection, Glow, and 3D Rotation. In terms of working with the WordArt object, the other Format tab command groups enable you to manipulate the text direction and alignment as well as determine how the object is positioned in relation to existing text in the Office document. For even more control over the WordArt text effects, right-click the WordArt and select Format Shape to display the Format Shape task pane, which provides Shape Attributes such as Fill and Line Color. The Format Shape task pane also enables you to manipulate text effects such as 3D Format and Rotation.

Using the 365 Online apps

What the Online apps can do   97

Where the Online apps live   99

Saving Office application files to the cloud   101

Using the Word Online app   106

Using Excel Online   112

Using PowerPoint Online   117

We have all found ourselves in situations when we are away from the office (and our computer) and need to take a quick look at a Word document or a PowerPoint presentation that has been created but didn't really get completely fine-tuned. Recent versions of the 365 application suite have shifted away from the notion of storing files on your computer. Rather, Microsoft has wholeheartedly adopted a cloud strategy for file storage where you are encouraged to save your files to your OneDrive or a location on a SharePoint server site (for 365 subscribers who use OneDrive for Business). Both cloud options then make it easy for you to access your files from any location and device; all you need is a smart device that runs an operating system that provides access to Microsoft 365 apps. For example, Microsoft apps are available for both iOS and Android devices. Devices shipped with Windows installed have the Office apps built in.

Even if you are using a device that doesn't provide for native 365 apps, any device that provides a web browser application allows you to access the 365 Online apps. The Online apps allow you to view and modify the files that you store in the cloud. You can also use the Online apps to create new files and save them to your OneDrive. As already mentioned, all you need is a device that provides a web browser. A version of the Online apps is also available to users who have access to a SharePoint site, such as Microsoft 365 Business (there are different levels of the Business subscription) and Enterprise subscribers. Online apps are available for Word, Excel, and PowerPoint.

In this chapter, we will take a look at the 365 Online apps and what they can do for you. The discussion includes how to save files to the cloud and share your files with collaborators and coworkers.

What the Online apps can do

The Online apps provide you with the ability to view, edit, and save files to an online workspace that can be accessed from any computer or smart device with an Internet connection and a supported web browser. But the Online apps are only part of Microsoft's cloud computing initiative. Microsoft continues to provide users with a free OneDrive account. To take advantage of OneDrive, you just need to obtain a Microsoft account using Outlook.com. The OneDrive website (*https://OneDrive.live.com*) provides free storage space for your files and access to the Office Online apps.

If you subscribe to Microsoft 365 (Home, Personal, Small Business, or Enterprise), you are provided access to OneDrive as well. This "paid" version of Microsoft's online storage strategy will provide you with more storage space than the free OneDrive. For example, the Home version of 365 provides you with 1 TB of OneDrive storage space for up to six people. The Personal version provides a single OneDrive license, but it also provides 1 TB of storage.

The Online apps are designed to provide you basic capabilities for working with files that you have created using the installed versions of Microsoft applications, such as Word, Excel, and PowerPoint. The Online apps also provide you with the capability to create new files. So, in many circumstances, you will find that the Online apps are as functional but not as full-featured as the installed versions of the 365 applications.

You can do a lot with the Online apps, Figure 5-1 shows a PowerPoint presentation that was opened using PowerPoint Online.The online app allows you add new slides to the presentation, modify existing slides, and format text on the slides. You can even add a picture or SmartArt to a new slide and then view the presentation as a slide show—all within the Online app.

NOTE

The PowerPoint Online workspace looks similar to the installed version of PowerPoint. However, the ribbon provided by default—the "simple ribbon"—spreads the commands across the ribbon and does not divide the commands provided into groups (as they are on the desktop versions of PowerPoint and the other 365 applications). The simple ribbon is actually easier to work with (particularly on a small laptop screen) than the traditional ribbon. However, if you prefer having the commands divided into groups (in a similar way to the desktop apps), select the Switch Ribbons command on the far right end of the currently selected ribbon tab.

Although the Online apps have greater capabilities with each new version, they typically are used as a fallback plan when you just don't have access to a device that hosts the installed Office application suite. The fact that they are available from any computer (and many other devices) with a web browser and an Internet connection means that the Online apps provide you with a lot of portability and possibilities for accessing your files in the cloud and sharing them with coworkers or colleagues.

NOTE

Whether you use the Online apps via your free OneDrive, your Office 365 subscription or your company's hosted SharePoint site, you are still using the same SharePoint Server technology. The Office Online apps are pretty much the same in terms of functionality no matter which of these three options you use to access them. As time has passed, the online apps have become more full-featured and serve as an excellent option for computing on the go.

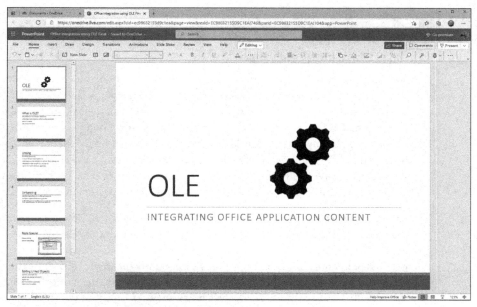

Figure 5-1   Files stored on OneDrive can be opened in the Online apps.

Where the Online apps live

As already mentioned, the Online apps operate in your web browser whether you are using the Online apps via the Microsoft OneDrive website, OneDrive for Business, or a SharePoint Server installation at your company or institution. The Office Online apps work in most web browsers, including Microsoft Internet Explorer, Google Chrome, Mozilla Firefox, and Apple Safari. To avoid any browser issues, make sure that you are using the most recent version of your chosen web browser.

Accessing OneDrive, OneDrive for Business, or a company-run SharePoint server requires log-in credentials: a valid username and password. When you sign in to OneDrive (*https://OneDrive.live.com*), the OneDrive main page provides a list of the folders and files you have stored on the site. On the left of the OneDrive main page, a Navigation pane makes it easy for you to view your recently saved documents (Recent) and view files that you have shared (Shared). Figure 5-2 shows the OneDrive main page.

> **NOTE**
>
> OneDrive (both the free and subscription versions) now provide an additional security feature called Personal Vault, which basically is a special place (or virtual drive) that has greater security than the My Files area of your OneDrive. Personal Vault provides two-step verification and will auto-lock after 20 minutes of inactivity. Once you set it up, the Personal Vault can be accessed on all the devices you use when you work with your OneDrive.

Inside Out

Faulty Wi-Fi and the Online apps

You basically have two options for accessing the 365 files that you store on your OneDrive or other cloud storage. You can take advantage of the Online apps that we discuss in this chapter. Depending on your smartphone, you might also be able to take advantage of apps that are designed to operate in the most popular phone operating systems such as Apple iOS, Android, and Microsoft. The choice of whether you prefer to work in the cloud with the Online apps or you like the idea of having 365 apps, such as Word and PowerPoint, installed directly on your smartphone is really up to you. Both of these options allow you to access the files that you keep on your OneDrive.

Regarding which of these options is best, for me, it really comes down to how much work you need to do on a particular cloud-stored file and the speed of the Wi-Fi connection that you will use (which can be particularly tricky when traveling). Regarding richness of features, the Online apps provide a slightly greater breadth of features when compared to the OS-specific apps you can install on your phone, particularly those available for iOS and Android. However, if you are working with a dodgy Wi-Fi connection, you are going to find that the Online apps run pretty slow. And even though the installed Office apps are rather cramped on a phone in terms of working space (and depending on your age, might also require reading glasses), these apps are running directly on the phone. This means that you will typically experience less lag time than the Office Online apps when you don't have a solid Internet connection. This is not to say that the apps you use directly on the phone are more robust or full-featured than the Online apps. You will find that when you have access to good Wi-Fi, the Online apps will perform quite well and provide a very useful set of the features and commands that are provided by the full-blown 365 application suite.

To view a file in an Online app viewer, select the file. You are certainly not limited to viewing files when you work in your OneDrive. You can edit an existing file, or you can create new Word, Excel, and PowerPoint files by launching the appropriate Online app via the New command. When you choose to edit an Office file stored on your OneDrive, you can edit the document in Word (if you have Word installed on the device) or you can edit in the Word Online app (see Figure 5-2).

There is no doubt that the Online apps are very intriguing and fun to work with. However, they are best thought of as one aspect of the cloud storage and sharing framework that Microsoft has created. Using the Online apps in concert with the installed Office applications should allow you to take full advantage of these productivity tools.

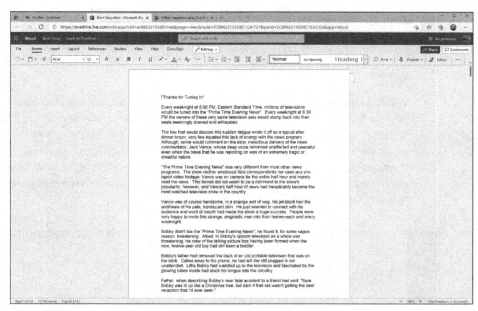

Figure 5-23   A Word document open in the Word Online app

Saving Online application files to the cloud

The installed versions of the Office applications actually encourage you to save files to the cloud. In fact, saving your 365 files to a cloud server such as OneDrive or OneDrive for Business is configured at the end of the 365 desktop application installation process. If you work at a company or institution, your desktop installation may be handled by your network administrators. Therefore, at least one cloud location is available by default in all your 365 applications. Saving your Excel, Word, and PowerPoint files directly to one of these cloud options allows you to access your files from multiple devices easily, and it allows you to share files with colleagues or coworkers easily.

Even though you choose a cloud server possibility from the get-go with your Office applications (for example, the free OneDrive or the 365 OneDrive for Business), you can add additional "places" to your Office configuration. This means that you can configure Office so that you can save to both your free OneDrive and OneDrive for Business (from your 365 subscription), or you can access your free OneDrive and your corporate SharePoint site. If you work for a company that provides multiple SharePoint sites, and you have access to these sites, you can add them to your applications as places (cloud locations to save and retrieve files).

Figure 5-3 shows the Save As page in the PowerPoint Backstage. One cloud location, OneDrive–Personal, has already been configured. You can add additional cloud locations, including free and business OneDrive sites, by selecting Add A Place. The Add A Place options are OneDrive and OneDrive For Business. You will be required to log in to one of these cloud options and add it as a place.

> ### NOTE
>
> **Windows 10 can be configured so that you sign in using login credentials such as your Microsoft ID. This configures Windows 10 to include your OneDrive as a default location (which you can access on the Windows Start page using the OneDrive tile). Your 365 installation can "pick up" on your Windows 10 configuration (and vice versa). This means if you are using your Windows Live or Office 365 credentials to log in to Windows, you might find your OneDrive or OneDrive for Business has already been configured as a "place" in the 365 applications.**

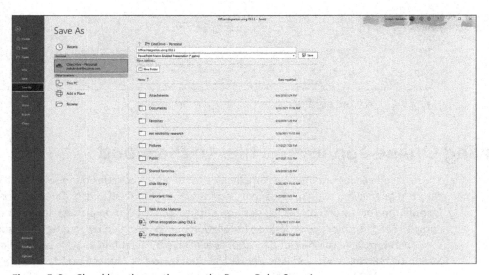

Figure 5-3   Cloud location options on the PowerPoint Save As page

When you select one of the Add A Place options, the Add A Service dialog box opens. Enter the email address that serves as the log-in name for the service and then select Next. On the next screen, supply the password for the account and then select Sign In. The new service will be added to the list of cloud options on the Save As page.

When you add a place, such as a OneDrive site, to one of the 365 applications, you are adding it to all the 365 applications. You will find that the process for accessing these sites is very consistent and similar across the applications, particularly Word, Excel, and PowerPoint.

TIP

You can also add a service to your Office configuration on the Backstage's Account page. Just select the Add A Service button at the bottom of the Connected Services area. When you add a service to your Office installation, you are not limited to services associated with the user account that was used when you (or someone else) initially installed Microsoft Office on your computer. This allows you to access resources such as different OneDrives that you might have tied to other Microsoft ID accounts. For example, your Office installation might be tied to your business email, which will have its own OneDrive. If you wish to access another OneDrive—perhaps one that you created using a personal email—you can add the OneDrive as another connected service.

Let's take a look at saving files from the Office Backstage to a cloud location such as OneDrive. We can then take a close look at how best to use the Office Online apps when you do not have access to the installed version of the Office suite.

Saving a file to OneDrive or OneDrive for Business

Saving a file to your OneDrive or OneDrive for Business (or any other SharePoint site) is very straightforward. Obviously, from our discussion so far, you might think the fastest way to save a file in a 365 application is to go to the Backstage and access the Save As page. You are correct, but read on for a slightly different path to a solution.

For example, let's say that you want to save a new Excel workbook to your OneDrive. With the workbook open in the Excel application window, click Save on the Excel Quick Access Toolbar. Excel opens the Save This File dialog box as shown in Figure 5-4. The Save This File dialog box provides a File Name box and a Choose A Location drop-down menu, which provides a shortlist of recently used locations, including your cloud drives and hard drive(s).

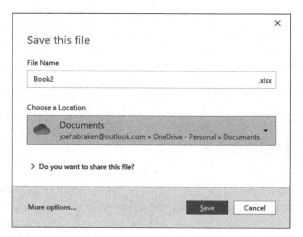

Figure 5-4   The Save a new file using the Save this file dialog box

All you have to do is provide a name for the file and choose a location where you want the file to be saved. If you want to share the file, you can take advantage of the Do You Want To Share This File? link. Click the link in the Save This File dialog box and the Enter A Name Or Email Address dialog box will open. Enter the appropriate information to share the file. You can add multiple names or email addresses to the list as necessary. Once you have entered a name, location, and optional sharing information in the Save This File dialog box, select the Save button to save the file.

NOTE

Think of the free OneDrive as "SharePoint Lite." OneDrive uses SharePoint technology (as does OneDrive for Business) to provide you with the Online apps and file-sharing capabilities. However, the file-sharing environment provided by the free OneDrive is probably not as secure as a storage and sharing environment as is a OneDrive for Business account or a corporate SharePoint site. You can always make your accounts more secure (whether they are free or by subscription) by using more secure passwords that take advantage of alphanumeric capital characters and a clever combination of numbers and letters of the alphabet. Don't make it easy for others to guess your password. A new option for securing OneDrive (including the free version) is the Personal Vault. If you haven't used your OneDrive for a while, you might want to log in and take a look at this new option for securing your files on OneDrive.

If the Save This File dialog box doesn't provide you with the location you want to use, or if you would like additional options for saving the current file, you can abandon the Save This File dialog box by selecting the More Options link in the lower-left corner. The Save As page will open in the application's Backstage. You can then select a location using any of the tools provided, including the This PC icon, the Add A Place option, and the Browse command. Once you name the file and choose a location, select the Save button, and you are good to go.

So, now you have a new file in the cloud—and even if you haven't used cloud storage much in the past—you will find that opening a file you saved to your OneDrive or other cloud place is no different from opening a file stored locally. In the 365 application's Backstage Open page, recently saved files are listed. If you saved a file to the cloud and it's listed in the Recent list, select the file to open it. If a cloud-based file isn't listed in the Recent list, you can select the appropriate cloud location (in the Open window) and then locate and open the file using the Open dialog box.

Sharing a file saved to the cloud

Microsoft 365 makes it very easy for you to share a file that you have saved to one of the cloud-based places such as your OneDrive or OneDrive for Business. In the case of OneDrive for Business or corporate SharePoint sites, you can save your files to folders that are already shared with other users. The sharing process is basically the same for the different cloud options. Let's take a look at how you share an Excel workbook that has been stored on OneDrive. Sharing a cloud-stored file via Word or PowerPoint uses the same process. Before you can share a cloud-stored file, the file actually needs to be saved to your OneDrive (or other cloud location). In Excel, Word, or PowerPoint, use the Backstage's Save As page to save the file to the cloud. Then you can return to the application window (such as an Excel worksheet) and share the file with other users.

With the workbook you want to share open in Excel (again, the process is the same for Word or PowerPoint), select the Share icon on the far right of the Excel application window (just above the Excel ribbon on the far right of the ribbon). This will open the Send Link dialog box (see Figure 5-5).

NOTE

As already mentioned, if the file you want to share has not been saved to one of your cloud locations (such as your OneDrive), save the file to the cloud before you attempt to share it in Excel, Word, or PowerPoint.

In the Send Link dialog box, click the share link settings just below the file name. The Link Settings dialog box will open. To allow others to edit the shared file, select the Allow Editing option. You can also set an expiration date for the link and password-protect the link if you want. Once you have selected the appropriate options, select Apply, and you will be returned to the Send Link dialog box.

Figure 5-5   The Send link dialog box

At this point, you can enter names, groups, or individual email addresses to populate the list of people with whom you will share the file. There is also an optional message box. If you want to copy the link, a Copy Link button is in the lower third of the dialog box. There is also an Outlook button, so you can port the link right into a new Outlook email and work through the sending of the link from your email client. The Send A Copy link at the bottom of the dialog box allows you to quickly send a copy (including a PDF option) of the file to your recipient list rather than providing an active link to the cloud version of the file.

When you have configured the sharing properties and provided a list of link recipients, click the Send button. A "link sent" confirmation will appear in the application window; you can clear it by clicking the Close button in the upper-right corner of the message box.

If you have been using the share option a lot in the 365 apps, you might be a little surprised that the Share page in the Backstage doesn't really do a whole lot in the current iteration of Microsoft 365. When you select Share (in the Backstage), you are returned to the application's window and the Send Link dialog box opens.

TIP

When you are working with the Online apps, remember that the Share button is available as it is in the installed versions of these applications. (The Share button is located on the far right of the application window just above the ribbon.) Select Share and then invite people via email or get a link to share with collaborators.

Using the Word Online app

The Word Online app provides you with the ability to edit existing documents (stored in the cloud) and create new documents. It supplies commands for working with text, including character-formatting and paragraph-formatting attributes. It also provides you with the ability to insert tables and pictures into a document. If you are new to the Online apps, you will find that the apps actually save your work automatically, which can be a little disconcerting if you haven't experienced it before. When you work in the desktop apps such as Word and Excel and are editing a file stored on OneDrive, the file changes are also updated automatically.

The document views in the Word Online app include the regular editing view (the default view where you create or edit your file), the Reading view, and the Immersive Reader view. The Reading view provides a print layout–type view of your document, where editing is disabled. The Immersive Reader is a new tool/view provided by the Word Online app and other Microsoft applications, such as the 365 versions of Word and Outlook. The Immersive reader can read aloud text and can also be used to dictate text. The Immersive reader also has translation capabilities. For more details on the Immersive Reader, check out *https://education.microsoft.com*.

You can start a new Word file from your OneDrive page (select New and then Word Document) or from the Word Online app's Backstage (select File then New to access document templates). New files created in the Word Online app are saved in the .docx file format, which means there may be compatibility issues if you share your document with users who are using older versions of Word.

➤ **For information on saving Office application files in different file formats, see the "Saving files as different file types" section in Chapter 3, "Managing and sharing 365 files."**

The Word Online app provides you with four ribbon tabs: File, Home, Insert, and View. The ribbon also provides a convenient Open in Word command that allows you to open the current document in the installed version of Word if it is present on the device you are using. Perusing the commands available on the ribbon tabs supplies you with good insight into the overall capabilities that you're afforded by the Word Online app. Let's look at each of the ribbon tabs and the command groups that they provide.

The Word Online app's File tab

The File tab (which uses geography like the File tab in the installed Office applications) provides you with access to the Word Online app's Backstage. The Home page of the Word Online Backstage provides a list of recent documents and access to a new blank document template. The New page provides additional access to new document templates, though the list of possibilities falls way short of what you would find in the desktop version of Word.

The Backstage's Open tab makes it easy for you to quickly open recent files you have worked on. If you want to open your document in the Word desktop app, select the Info tab. This tab also provides a one-click Protect Document option that changes the document to view-only. The Info tab also provides a Version History command that provides the version history of the current document.

The Save As page in Word Online provides a number of possibilities related to saving a document in different formats, as shown in Figure 5-6.

CHAPTER 5

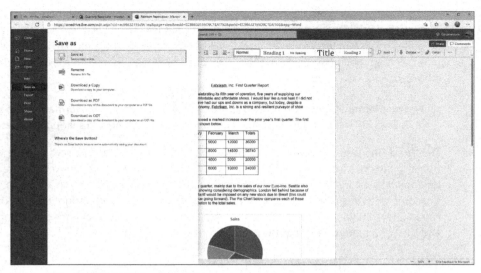

Figure 5-6   The Word Online Save As page

The Word Online app's Backstage also provides access to Info, Export , Print, Share, and About pages. These options provide the following:

- **Info**: This page allows you to open the current file in the desktop version of Word. It also provides options for protecting the document when it is shared.

- **Export**: This page is a new addition to the Word Online app. It allows you to export the current document into a PowerPoint presentation.

- **Print**: The print options have been updated for this feature, which didn't really have an option to send the current document to a printer. The Print page now contains a Print button, which opens a Print window that contains similar options to the Print page feature in the desktop version of Word. The print features also allow you to save the document as a PDF or XPS file.

- **Share**: This Word Backstage page allows you to share the document via a Share With People command. It also provides an Embed command, which allows you to embed the document in a blog or website.

- **About**: This is an informational page provided by Microsoft that provides terms of use, third-party notices, and information related to privacy and cookies.

When you have completed working in the Word Online Backstage, select the Close button, which will return you to the Word Online workspace. Because you spend most of your time working in an application's workspace, it makes sense to spend some time getting familiar with the different ribbon options available in the Word Online app. The sections that follow provide a look at each of the Word Online ribbon tabs.

The Word Online app's Home tab

The Home tab in the Word Online app provides a subset of the commands that you would find on the Word Home tab. The Word Online app's Home tab provides you with the ability to change font attributes, set paragraph alignment settings, and assign styles to your document text. Figure 5-7 shows the Home tab from the ribbon on the Word Online app. Although the document shown in the figure uses Arial 12-point, the default font is Calibri, and the default font size is 11-point.

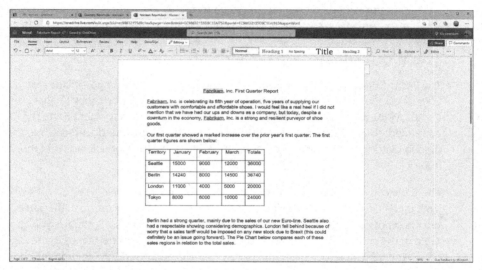

Figure 5-7   Word Online app screen

Notice that much of the ribbon's Home tab is related to copying, formatting, and aligning text in your document. The Home tab also includes the new Dictate and Editor commands. The Dictate command allows you to add text to the document by dictating the text. The Editor command provides access to the Spelling And Grammar feature, which also includes suggestions for refinements to your document.

> **NOTE**
>
> **You might have already noticed that the Word Online ribbon isn't divided into distinct groups, as is the desktop version of Word. The Online ribbon is designed for ease of use, and the commands are spread across the ribbon.**

Font commands included on the Home tab provide you with the ability to change the font and font size, as well as assign font attributes to your text, such as bold, italic, and underline. An ellipsis to the right of the Clear Formatting command opens additional text commands, including the Subscript and Superscript commands.

Commands are also included for text alignment and indents (center, right align, and so on), and commands are provided to create bulleted and numbered lists. To assign a style to document text, select one of the styles provided in the Style Gallery. Use the drop-down menu for access to more styles and the Create New Style From Formatting command.

If you are looking for the paragraph-related commands, such as Line Spacing and Special Indent, select the ellipsis just to the right of the Designer command. This opens a list of commands related to paragraph options.

➤ For information on text and paragraph formatting in Word, see the "Understanding document formatting section" in Chapter 6, "Essential Word features."

The Word Online app's Insert tab

The Word Online app ribbon's Insert tab provides you with some possibilities for enhancing your document with a table, your own photos, or Microsoft's new Stock Images. The Insert tab also provides you with the ability to force page breaks in the document using the Page Break command. You can also quickly insert a link (hyperlink) into your document. You can also upload pictures from your computer to the document and insert clip art from the Office.com library.

The Table command provides a table grid that enables you to select the number of columns and rows in the new table. After the new table is inserted into the document, the Table Tools, Layout tab becomes available on the ribbon. The Layout tab in Table Tools enables you to select the table or the current column, row, or cell. You can then use the commands in the Delete group to delete the table or selected column or row. You can also insert new columns above or below or new rows to the left or right of the currently selected column, row, or cell. Text in the table can be aligned using the commands provided in the Alignment group.

➤ For information on working with tables in Word, see Chapter 8, "Working with tables, columns, and sections."

The Insert tab also enables you to add pictures to your document. Select the Picture command and then select This Device, OneDrive, Stock Images, or Bing Pictures. The Stock Images library only provides a subset of its collection to free OneDrive accounts. So, you might be limited to the number of images you can use. As well, I caution you on using pictures sourced from the web (even if you are using the Bing Pictures option). It's often very difficult to tell if you are using an image taken from the web legally.

When you insert a picture, the Picture tab becomes available on the ribbon. This tab enables you to specify alternative text for the image (in cases where the document is viewed on the web, and the picture cannot be loaded), and enables you to enlarge, shrink, or scale the image. You will find that large picture files take a while to load when you insert them into the Online app.

If you want to take advantage of a much more complete set of picture commands, you might want to insert pictures into your documents using Word rather than the Word Online app.

➤ **For information on working with pictures in the Office applications, see Chapter 4, "Using and creating graphics."**

The Word Online app's Review tab

The Review tab provides access to the Editor feature and a number of other tools, including Track Changes, Word Count, and Comments. In terms of new features, the Translate feature is pretty much a home run. You can use the feature to translate a selection or an entire document into a number of languages. According to Microsoft, there are over 70 languages available. You have the option of translating different parts of a document into different languages.

The Review tab also provides Comments and Track Changes tools. Once you have tracked changes in the document, you can then accept or reject the changes as you want. As already mentioned, the Word Online app provides the Editor feature, which checks the spelling, grammar, and writing style of your document. Figure 5-8 shows the results from the Editor feature. The Editor results are found in the Editor pane on the right side of the document window. The Editor provides a score, a list of spelling and grammar corrections, and a list of refinements related to such things as clarity, conciseness, punctuation, conventions, and vocabulary.

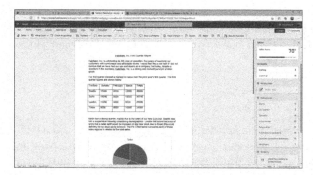

Figure 5-8   The Word Online app ribbon's Review tab

To view the flagged spelling and grammar issue, select Spelling (or Grammar) in the Corrections area of the Editor pane. When you do so, the Editor walks you through the suspected Spelling or Grammar errors and provides you with options for correcting these flagged items. You can also check whether any refinements are suggested for the document related to clarity, formality, or vocabulary (among other possibilities). To view these flagged items, click one of the Refinements categories in the Editor pane.

The Word Online app's View tab

The Word Online app's View tab provides some interesting possibilities when you are in a situation where you need to give a document a look over when using the Word Online app. The Online View tab is not as robust as the View tab provided by the installed version of Word; it provides only three possibilities: Editing View, Reading View, and Immersive Reader View.

The Editing View is the view you are using as you edit the document in the Word Online app. When you select the Reading View, you are taken to a view that strips away the ribbon and other app tools and allows you to concentrate on reading your text document. A More menu (the ellipsis in the upper-right corner) is available in the Reading View that allows you to open the Find pane and search the document. The More menu also provides access to the Immersive Reader and provides you with the ability to download or embed the file.

When you have finished viewing your document, you can then select the Edit Document menu to reopen the document in the Word Online app (Edit In Browser). You also have the option of opening the document in Word by selecting Open In Word.

The most recent version of the Word Online app also offers the Immersive Reader View. When you select this view on the View tab, you are taken to a viewing screen where the document will be read to you. This feature is surprisingly useful, and the "reader" does a very good job of reading the text. This not only allows you to review a document but also get an idea of how the text sounds when read out loud. This can be particularly useful when you are working on a document that is the script for a presentation or other talk. When you have finished working in the Immersive Reader View, select the Back button on the left side of the viewing window to return to the Editing View of your document.

Using Excel Online

The current iteration of the Excel Online app actually provides you with a great deal of the functionality you would find in the installed version of Excel. As with the Word Online app, the command groups have been removed from the ribbon and associated commands are not organized on the various ribbon tabs supplied by the Excel Online app. The app allows you to quickly add sheets to the current workbook. The New Sheet command (a + symbol) is on the status bar just to the right of the last sheet in the workbook. You can also quickly insert Excel functions using the AutoSum command (and its drop-down menu that provides access to many other functions) on the ribbon's Home tab.

The Excel Online app also provides you with the ability to create new Excel workbooks and to edit the existing workbooks that have been saved to your OneDrive folder or SharePoint site. Anytime you save an Excel workbook to the cloud using the installed desktop version of Excel, you can also access these files and edit them as needed using the Excel Online app. As with the

Word and PowerPoint Online apps, there is no Save button or option; your work is saved automatically as you use these apps.

The Excel Online app provides capabilities for formatting text labels and values on the Home tab of the ribbon, including styles. Also, access to conditional formatting settings, the ability to format worksheet data as a table, and commands for sorting and filtering your worksheet data are provided. The Excel Online app is probably strongest when working with Excel tables and provides you with the ability to specify a cell range as a table. You can then use the Sort and Filter drop-down menus provided for each field (column) heading to sort and/or filter the table. The Excel Online app also enables you to update connections in a workbook if you are editing a workbook created in Excel that includes external data sources such as a SQL Server database or another data source accessed through Microsoft Query. Use the Refresh All command on the ribbon's Data tab to refresh all external data sources.

> ➤ **For information about Excel tables, PivotTables, and data sources, see Chapter 15, "Using Excel tables and pivot tables."**

The Excel Online app's File tab

The Excel Online app provides a ribbon with 10 tabs: File, Home, Insert , Draw, Page Layout, Formulas, Data, Review, View, and Help. The File tab, which is equivalent to the Backstage found in the installed version of Excel, provides you with the ability to create new Excel files, open other Excel files stored in the cloud, protect the current workbook, or rename the workbook. The Excel Backstage supplies a Home, New, Open, Info, Save As, Print, Share, Options, and About page. A short description of each of these pages follows:

- **Home**: This page provides templates for new Excel workbooks. It also includes a Welcome To Excel tour and provides access to recently opened workbooks.

- **New**: This page provides access to several templates for creating new workbooks.

- **Open**: This page provides a list of recently opened Excel files.

- **Info**: This page allows you to open the current workbook in the Desktop app. The page also includes

    - **Save As**: This page allows you to save a copy of the current workbook to your OneDrive. It also provides the ability to rename the current workbook and download a copy of the current workbook to your computer.

    - **Print**: This page can provide you with a print-friendly view of the current worksheet that you can then print (similar to the PDF option provided by the Word Online app).

    - **Share**: This page allows you to send a share invitation to your collaborators, or you can embed a copy of the sheet on a web page or blog.

CHAPTER 5

- **Options**: This page provides a Regional Format Settings command that allows you to edit your Excel regional format settings.

- **About**: This page is purely informational. (There is no information related to the Excel worksheet you are working on.) This page provides Microsoft's terms of use for the Excel Online app and also provides a primer on how the Online apps protect your privacy.

Although the Backstage pages provided by the Excel Online app might seem lacking when compared to the installed version of Excel, you will find that all the options that you need to create files on the go are available. The Excel Online app also make it very easy to share files with collaborators, and you can open the file in the installed version of Excel from any computer.

Working in the Excel Online app

The Excel Online app provides a pretty strong subset of the Excel commands, so you can build sheets that take advantage of Excel's function library and its ability to manipulate table data as well as visually portray your data in a variety of chart types. Figure 5-9 shows an Excel Online app worksheet containing quarterly sales data that is visualized using a pie chart.

All the basic Excel features are available in the Excel Online app, and you can adjust row heights and column widths in a worksheet by dragging the row or column border. The Best-Fit column width function (double-clicking a column border) is also available in the Online app, so you can easily size columns to accommodate the longest entry in a particular column. As already mentioned, you can insert new sheets into your workbook, and you can delete a sheet in the workbook by right-clicking the sheet tab and selecting Delete. You can also rename worksheets as needed.

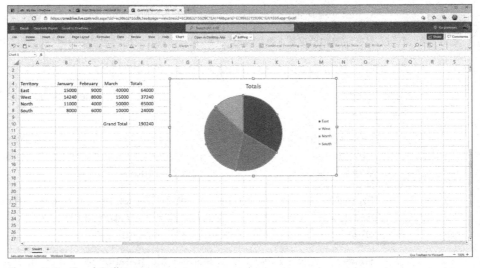

Figure 5-9 Excel Online app screen

You can view graphics that you have added to a worksheet created in Excel, such as pictures, clip art, and SmartArt, but you do not have the formatting control over them that you do in the installed version of Excel. You can move a graphic such as a picture on a page in the Online app and resize the picture as needed. You can also remove a picture (or other sheet object) by selecting the object and then pressing Delete on the keyboard.

Inserting functions and charts in the Excel Online app

Inserting functions into a worksheet when you are working in the Excel Online app can be accomplished using the AutoSum drop-down menu provided on the ribbon's Home tab or the Function command provided on the Insert tab. Selecting More Functions on the AutoSum command (on the Home tab) or selecting the Function command (on the Insert tab) opens the Insert Function dialog box, as shown in Figure 5-10.

Figure 5-10   The Insert Function dialog box

Select a function category in the Insert Function dialog box and then pick the function you want to insert into the currently selected cell. Click OK, and the function is inserted into the sheet; however, you still need to specify the range of cells to be used by the function. For example, in Figure 5-11 the MAX function is used to compute the maximum salary in a range of salary data. Simply select the range of cells that you want the function to act upon.

To finish off the function (after selecting the cell range), you must type a closing parenthesis and then press Enter. The results of the function appear in the sheet. Working with more complex functions in the Excel Online app might be more trouble than they are worth. The installed version of Excel does much more hand-holding when it comes to setting up complex functions.

You can also add your own formulas to a sheet when you are working in the Excel Online app. To add a formula, type the equal sign (=) and then specify the cell addresses and the operators required for the formula. You can use the mouse to specify the cell addresses that appear in the formula as you would in Excel. When the formula is complete, press the Enter key.

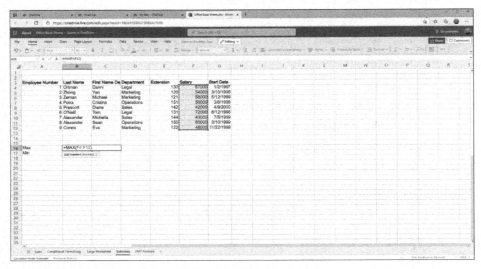

Figure 5-11   Insert a function and then select the range to use.

In terms of copying a formula or function (or extending a series), you can use the fill handle as you would in the installed version of Excel. You can also take advantage of the Clipboard group on the Home tab to cut or copy a formula or function (or any cell content). The Paste command in the Excel Online app provides a menu that enables you to paste formulas, paste values, or paste formatting. Select Paste Formulas to paste the formula.

You can also insert charts into your sheets when you are using the Excel Online app. Select the cells that will serve as the chart data. On the Insert tab, select the drop-down menu on the Chart command to view the chart types (Column, Line, Pie, Bar, and the like). Each chart type provides chart subtypes. Select one of the subtypes, and the chart is inserted into the sheet.

When the chart is selected, the Chart tab appears on the ribbon. This tab provides a stripped-down version of the chart tools found in the installed version of Excel, but they still provide you with many possibilities. You can manipulate the chart type, and you can modify chart elements, such as the chart title, axes, and legend. You can also add labels and grid lines to the chart as needed.

➤ For more information on creating charts in Excel, see Chapter 14, "Enhancing worksheets with charts."

➤ For more information on Excel formulas and functions, see Chapter 13, "Getting the most from formulas and functions."

NOTE

The Excel Online app does not include a Save button because changes that you make to an Excel Workbook in the Online app are saved automatically. If you want to save a particular version of a workbook (say, under a new file name), select the File tab and then Save As.

Using PowerPoint Online

The PowerPoint Online app provides you with a solid collection of commands for creating a new presentation or editing an existing presentation that you have saved to your OneDrive or SharePoint site library. It is probably the most full-featured of the Online apps. When you create a new presentation (via the OneDrive New drop-down menu), a new presentation opens in PowerPoint Online, as shown in Figure 5-12.

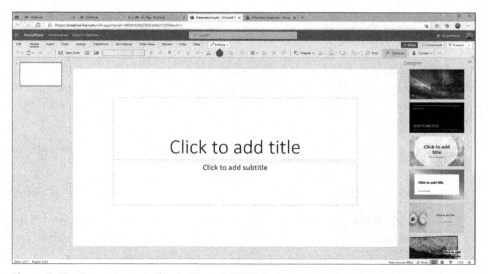

Figure 5-12   A new presentation in PowerPoint Online

When you create the new presentation and its title slide, the Designer pane will open. The Designer provides you with several different options for the slide design for your new presentation. The designs are optional, as are the themes provided by the designs. If you want to assign a theme to the new presentation), select the ribbon's Design tab and then choose one of the themes from the Themes gallery. You can also use the Variants gallery to fine-tune your selected theme.

The PowerPoint Online app's ribbon uses the simple ribbon design embraced by the other Online apps. You can switch to the "group" version of the ribbon if you want by using the toggle button on the far right of the application window.

The ribbon tabs and their contents are as follows:

- **File**: This tab provides the Backstage and access to commands for creating a new file, opening a cloud file, downloading a copy of the current file to your desktop, and sharing the current presentation with collaborators.

- **Home**: This ribbon tab provides commands for creating new slides, formatting text (both font and paragraph formatting), and inserting shapes.

- **Insert**: This tab enables you to insert objects, such as pictures, shapes, Icons, and SmartArt. There are also a Text Box command and a Comment command on the Insert tab, which allow you to insert a new text box or comment, respectively.

- **Draw**: This tab allows you to select different pen types and tools for drawing on a touch screen.

- **Design**: This tab is reserved for the Themes and Variants galleries, which allow you to change the presentation theme or modify the current theme by selecting a variant, respectively. Slide Size and Background drop-down menus are also available, as is a Designer command to open the Design pane.

- **Transitions**: This tab is dedicated to slide transitions and includes an Options And Duration feature.

- **Animations**: This tab allows you to add animation effects to your slide elements.

- **Slide Show**: This tab provides commands for starting your slideshow from the beginning or current slide and has a Rehearse With Coach feature that provides feedback on the presentation.

- **Review**: This tab provides the Check Side feature, which proofs the slides. This tab also allows you to add comments and check the presentation's accessibility.

- **View**: This tab provides you with access to the slide Notes pane (for adding notes to a slide) and also provides access to the Slide Sorter. Zoom and Fit To Window commands are also available. PowerPoint also provides access to the Immersive Reader feature discussed earlier in this chapter.

- **Help**: This tab provides Help and What's New features and also makes it easy for you to contact Microsoft support or provide feedback on the app.

The status bar of the PowerPoint Online app also provides quick access to app features, including Notes, the Editing View, the Slide Sorter, and the Slide Show command. The Online app doesn't provide a zoom slider (like the desktop application) but does have a zoom level icon. When you select it, the Zoom To dialog box opens, providing different zoom levels, including a Fit option.

➤ **For more information on working in different PowerPoint views, see the "Working with slides in different views" section of Chapter 17, "Essential PowerPoint features."**

Working with slides

You can add, delete, and duplicate presentation slides. The slide-related commands are on the ribbon's Home tab. The New Slide command allows you to quickly add a slide to the presentation using the New Slide dialog box. The New Slide command is also available on the ribbon's Insert tab.

When you create a new presentation in PowerPoint Online, you are provided with a title slide by default (just like the installed PowerPoint application). You can click the title slide and enter the title slide text as needed.

As already mentioned, you insert a new slide using the New Slide command. The New Slide dialog box opens, as shown in Figure 5-13.

Select a layout for the new slide. If you are going to add an object, such as a picture or SmartArt, select a slide layout that provides a content placeholder. Click Add Slide to insert the new slide.

After you have inserted the new slide, you can enter the text for that slide. You can format the text using the Font and Paragraph group commands provided on the Home tab. You can add other slides as needed. Changes that you make to the presentation are saved automatically.

You can delete elements on a slide; select a text box or content box, and then press Delete. You can also rearrange the slides in a presentation in the Online app by dragging the slide thumbnails to a new position in the slide list. To delete a slide, select the slide's thumbnail and then select Delete Slide on the Home tab.

CHAPTER 5

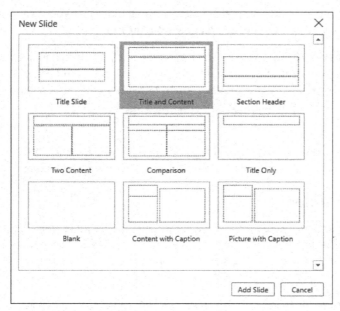

Figure 5-13   Insert a new slide.

Adding pictures and SmartArt

To add pictures or SmartArt to a slide using the PowerPoint Online app, all you need to do is navigate to the Insert tab of the ribbon and then insert the object type. For example, to insert a SmartArt graphic, select the SmartArt command on the Insert tab. The SmartArt gallery opens.

The gallery contains thumbnails of many different types of SmartArt lists and diagrams. Select a SmartArt list or diagram in the gallery to insert it into a content placeholder on the slide.

When a SmartArt graphic is selected on a slide, the SmartArt tab becomes available on the ribbon, as shown in Figure 5-14. You can change the layout, colors, and style of the currently selected SmartArt graphic.

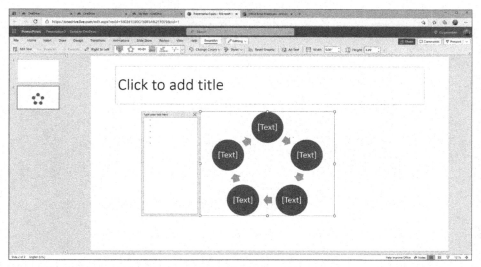

Figure 5-14   A SmartArt graphic and the SmartArt ribbon tab

To make text entries in a SmartArt graphic, click one of the text placeholders on the graphic. The text boxes on the SmartArt graphic are temporarily converted to a list; enter your text and then click outside the list; the SmartArt graphic reappears on the slide.

Pictures (such as the Stock Photos) can also be added to your slides via the Insert tab. When an inserted picture is selected, the Picture tab becomes available on the ribbon. Assign a style to the selected picture, or you can use the Change Picture command to specify that a different picture file be used in the slide.

➤ **For information on working with pictures and SmartArt in the Office applications, see the "Adjusting pictures" section of Chapter 4.**

PART II

Word

CHAPTER 6
Essential Word features. 125

CHAPTER 7
Enhancing Word documents 161

CHAPTER 8
**Working with tables, columns,
and sections** 209

CHAPTER 9
Managing mailings and forms 231

CHAPTER 10
Creating special documents. 257

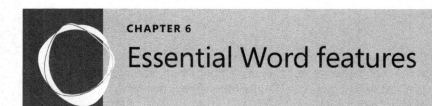

Essential Word features

Introducing Word   125

Options for creating a new Word document   129

Using templates   132

Navigating a Word document   137

Moving around a document with the keyboard   139

Understanding document formatting   140

Working with fonts and text formatting   146

Working with paragraph formatting   146

Page layout: margins and page options   155

Printing documents   157

CHAPTER 6

Word processing might not seem like the most exciting task. However, Word can make the document-creation process much more productive and creative. In this chapter, we take a look at the Word application window and the basic features and tools this powerful word processor provides.

We cover the options for creating new Word documents and look at ways to navigate the Word application window and your documents. We look at document formatting, including working with fonts and formatting paragraphs. We also work with tabs, margins, and page orientation settings.

Introducing Word

Microsoft Word has been the standard for word processing for well over two decades. And it is certainly safe to say that it is the most often used member of the Microsoft Office application suite—no matter our job or endeavor, we all need to create documents. Some of us use Word to create lists, memos, and letters; others create more complex documents, such as reports, news-letters, and forms. Regardless of the type of documents you create, Word provides all the tools and word-processing features of a full-fledged desktop publishing application. The new Word also provides some interesting new features that better integrate this powerful application with web content and cloud computing.

The Word interface

The Word application interface is centered on the ribbon as the command center (as are the other Office applications such as Excel and PowerPoint), and you will find that the ribbon pro-vides you with quick access to logical groupings of commands and features via ribbon tabs. Each ribbon tab is divided into groups of related commands and features, with related com-mands broken into visually separate groups.

Figure 6-1 shows the ribbon with the Home tab selected. The Home tab is home to command groups that include the Clipboard, Font, and Paragraph groups. Each group contains related commands. For example, the Font group contains font-formatting commands such as Bold, Italic, Font Size, and Font Color.

Figure 6-1   The Word application window and ribbon

The ribbon also provides a contextual approach to accessing the tools you need as you work on a particular task or with a particular Word feature. For example, you can quickly create a table from the Insert tab of the ribbon by selecting the Insert tab, selecting Table, and then choosing one of the methods of table creation. When you place the insertion point in the table, two contextual tabs, Table Design and Layout, appear on the ribbon. Selecting either the Table Design tab or the Layout tab provides tools specific to formatting the table. Figure 6-2 shows the layout that becomes available when the insertion point is in the table or a table is selected in a document.

The Layout tab enables you to work with rows and columns, merge cells, and change the text alignment in cells. The Design tab enables you to assign styles to the table and set style options.

➤ **For information about customizing the ribbon, see "Customizing an application interface," in Chapter 2, "Navigating and customizing the 365 interface."**

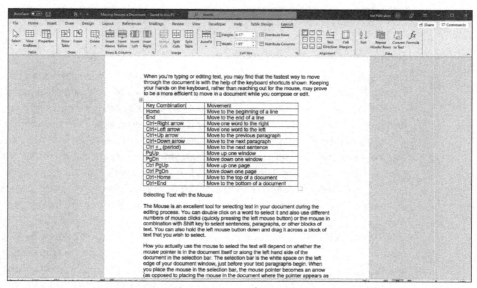

Figure 6-2   The contextual Table Design and Layout Tool becomes available on the ribbon when you work in a table.

New features and improvements

Word builds on the tools and features of previous versions of this powerhouse word processor and also provides some new enhancements. Some of the updates you will find in the most recent version of Word include the following:

- **Dictation:** Although the Dictation feature was added to Word and PowerPoint a couple of years ago, the Dictation feature has been improved and is worth trying out as a way to rough out a document without doing a lot of typing. You can dictate text in your documents and insert punctuation by stating the punctuation mark, such as "period" or "question mark." You can also edit your text using the dictation feature and a few simple phrases, such as "delete," "insert space," or "backspace."

Inside OUT

Getting your Office application updates

If you have a subscription to Office 365, new features are periodically added to your installed Microsoft Office suite subscription. These updates will range from adding a new feature (such as the addition of a new Excel function) to periodic bug fixes. If you find it difficult to wait for new features, you can sign up for the Office Insider program. This program helps you get targeted updates earlier than most other Office users. If you have an Office 365 subscription through your work or school, you might not be eligible for the Office Insider program, and your employer or school might control the actual update frequency and schedule. If you have your own home, personal, or small business subscription for Office 365, you can determine if the Office Insider program is something that you would be interested in joining. Finally, if you purchase Office as a stand-alone suite product that is not part of an Office 365 subscription, you will receive periodic bug fixes and performance updates, but you will not necessarily receive any updates relating to new features. To get all the new features (new in terms of your Office installation), you would need to buy the latest version of the Office suite. We discuss the different versions and flavors of Office in Chapter 1.

TIP

You can pin the Word Start menu icon to the Windows 10 taskbar. With the Word application window open on the desktop, right-click the Word icon on the taskbar and then select Pin to Taskbar. You still need to access the desktop to start Word from the taskbar, but this gives you another possibility for starting applications that you frequently use, such as Word.

- **Modern Comments and Collaboration:** Word now makes it easy for collaborators to view and act on comments in a Word document. These comments are referred to as modern comments and are also available in Excel and PowerPoint. The contextual view (meaning as you work in a document) of comments hides any resolved comments related to the document. This allows you to concentrate on unresolved issues related to the document. The Comments command on the far right of the Word window can be used to quickly open the Comments pane and access both resolved and unresolved comments. The Modern comments also allow you to use the @ symbol to refer to collaborators within comments quickly. This will then trigger an email that's sent to this collaborator mention. The comment that mentions a collaborator would be in the @email format, where email is the collaborator's email address. (Microsoft refers to this comment type as an @ mention.).

- **Free Stock Images:** If you like to add images to your documents (hey, every picture tells a story), Microsoft 365 now supplies the 365 applications with access to a huge library of stock images. There are more than 8,000 royalty-free images available. The images are grouped in categories such as Tranquility, Motion, and Growth. Because Microsoft is providing you with the images, you don't have to worry about rights issues related to them. You also don't have to spend time searching the web for what typically turns out to be poorly framed photos and bad clipart.

This is certainly not an exhaustive list of all the new features and improvements in Word. For example, if you collaborate on a shared document, you can create a private copy of the shared document so you can noodle around with the document a little before you mark up the actual shared version of the document. Another new improvement related to sharing files with the Microsoft 365 applications, including Word, is the Microsoft Defender Application Guard. Let's say you download a Word document from an online source that is a bit dubious. Defender Application Guard will open and isolate the file before it can do any harm to your computer system. This software can be run manually (by the user) or configured by your IT department to run in an automated mode. If you are new to the Microsoft 365 subscription environment and the 365 suite's update strategy, you will find that new features pop up periodically.

Options for creating a new Word document

When you start Word, the Start screen opens; the screen includes three windows: Home, New, and Open. The Home window opens by default. Home provides access to Word document templates, which you can use to create a variety of different document types. A single row of templates is provided at the top of the window. Select the More Templates link on the right side of the window. So, the Home window provides templates for new documents. However, this window is also geared to help you open documents that you've recently worked with. A search box is also provided, which allows you to search your computer and cloud for documents.

TIP

When you are in the Home window, you can quickly open a copy of any document provided in the Recent list. Right-click the document name and select Open A copy from the shortcut menu. You can also pin or remove documents in the Recent list by taking advantage of the options on the shortcut menu, which appears when you hover the mouse over a file name.

The Recent list provides a list of documents that you have recently accessed. A Pinned heading allows you to view documents you have pinned to the Home page by hovering next to a file name and selecting the Pin icon. The Shared With Me list shows documents that have been shared with you. It also lists recently opened documents under the Recent heading. You can also select from a list of documents that are in the Pinned list.

CHAPTER 6

If this is the first time you have started Word (or if you have removed all the recent files from the Recent list), a message stating that you haven't opened any documents recently will reside where the list of recently opened files would normally be.

Although the Home window provides you with access to the Word templates (including the Blank document template), if you select New, you are provided with a window dedicated to Word templates. The New window also provides a Search box that can be used to find online Word templates. See Figure 6-3, which shows the New window.

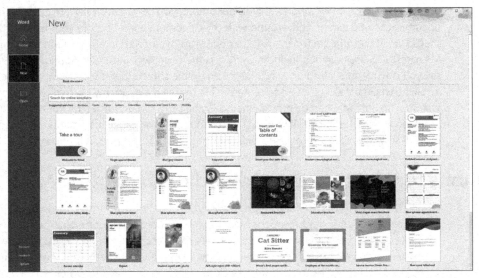

Figure 6-3 The New window makes it easy for you to create a new document using a Word template.

You can quickly start a new, blank document by clicking the Blank Document template (at the top of the window). Your new document now contains all the default page layout settings, such as margins and page orientation, and it uses Word's default font and font attributes. Starting a document from scratch affords you complete control over how the document looks, from the font to the paragraphs to the page. However, you might want to create some sort of specialized document (such as a newsletter), or you might want help with the overall design and look of a particular type of document.

Creating a particular type of new document means you need to use the appropriate template. The New window lists many template options in the lower half of the screen; in the upper-middle part of the page is a search box for locating templates stored in a large online template library. We discuss templates in more detail in the next section.

Once you have created some documents, you probably will want to edit or share some of your work. As already mentioned, the Startup screen also contains an Open window, which is designed to make it easier for you to open an existing file, including the ability to browse (or search) your computer or cloud storage for the document. Figure 6-4 shows the Open window, which provides a list of recently opened documents, a list of recent documents, and access to the various places you might have stored documents, such as your computer's hard drive or your OneDrive.

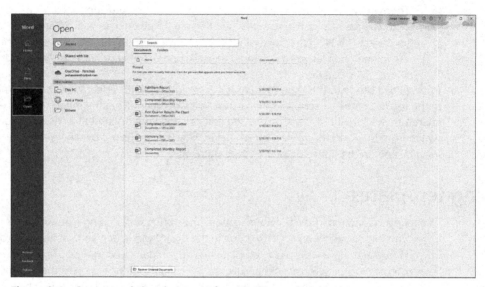

Figure 6-4   Open an existing document from the Open window.

For example, to open a file on your computer, follow these steps:

1. To access a file on your PC and/or its various folders, select Browse.

2. The Open dialog box opens. Use the folder and drive icons in the Organize menu to open a particular location on your computer. (You can also select OneDrive if you want to open a file stored online.)

3. Navigate as needed to locate the file you want to open. You can also use the Search Documents box at the top right of the Open dialog box to search for a particular file.

4. Select the document you want to open and then select Open; if you want to open a copy of the document, select the drop-down arrow next to Open and then select Open As Copy. The document opens in the Word application window.

You can now edit your document as needed. If you are collaborating with other users and would like to read through the document without distractions from the ribbon and the other functional elements of the Word application, you can take advantage of the Read Mode. Select the View tab on the ribbon and then select Read Mode in the Views group. Read Mode is designed to make it easy for you to read your document no matter what type of device you are using to run Word—a computer, a smartphone, or a tablet. Read Mode formats the document into columns and removes the ribbon to provide maximum screen space for the document.

TIP

The Start screen's Open window (select Open when the Word application window opens) also provides a quick way to access files that are stored on both your PC and the cloud. If you select This PC in the Open window, your Documents folder will be opened, displaying the folders and files you have stored there. To open a folder or file in the list, click it once.

Exiting Read Mode to the Page Layout view is straightforward. Select View (on the "mini ribbon" at the top left of the screen), and then select Edit Document from the menu that appears. You are returned to the Print Layout view, and you can edit your document as needed. You can also switch from the Read Mode view (or whatever view you are using) by taking advantage of the View button on the right side of the Word status bar.

Using templates

As already mentioned in the previous section, one option for creating a new document is to use a template provided on the New page in the Backstage. When you create a new document in Word, you actually always use a template—even for blank documents. Blank documents are based on the Normal template, which uses all the default settings, such as the default font, margins, tabs, paragraph settings, and the other document layout attributes. If you haven't changed any of the default Word settings (something we talk about later in this chapter), the Normal template presents you with all the default settings that Word provides at installation.

For example, the default margins for the Normal template are one inch for left, right, top, and bottom (of the page). The default page orientation is portrait (meaning the page is taller than it is wide, based on the default page size in the United States of 8.5 by 11 inches). The default font is Calibri, with a default font size of 11 points (there are 72 points to an inch). The default line spacing (which is a paragraph setting) is set to Multiple, which is actually 1.08 spaces between each line. This is different than in earlier versions of Word, which use one inch as the default line spacing. Obviously, suppose you want to create a special document such as a resume, flyer, or restaurant menu. In that case, you will want to edit these and other default settings to achieve the appropriate overall design and look for your special document.

By design, templates contain formatting and layout attributes particular to a certain document type. So, if you need to create a brochure, you simply select one of the brochure templates provided. The template takes care of the font, paragraph, and page-formatting attributes; all you have to do is provide the content for the document, such as text and pictures. Then you can quickly print your required number of brochures. Figure 6-5 shows one of the Word brochure templates.

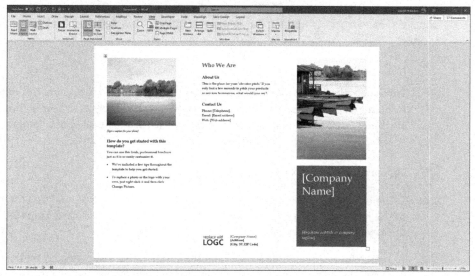

Figure 6-5   Templates, such as this brochure template, enable you to quickly create specialized documents.

Templates also often contain sample text or text placeholders. You replace the sample text with your text or click one of the text placeholders and insert your text as needed. Some templates also contain borders, shading, and even graphics (some of the graphics might take the form of watermarks on the page). The whole point behind templates is to enable you to quickly and efficiently create a specialized document that typically requires special formatting and layout attributes.

At this point, you might not have a complete feel for all the different font, paragraph, and page layout formatting attributes that a Word template can control (although you will after you have spent time in the Word section of this book). Even without a thorough understanding of all the options, you can still take advantage of the templates to create special documents. Using a template does not lock you into the formatting attributes provided by the template, though you can fine-tune your new template-based document as readily as you can tweak a simple document that you created from scratch (which, as you now know, is based on the Normal template).

If you decide to use a template, you have three options:

- You already have some templates installed on your computer from installing Microsoft Word.

- Office.com provides many templates that you can preview and then quickly download into your template library.

- You can create your own template (as you would any Word document) and base new documents on that template.

When you start Word, both the Home and New pages give you access to the Word templates. If you are already working in Word, the steps for creating a new document using a template are as follows:

> **NOTE**
>
> **Templates take advantage of styles. Styles are a collection of font, paragraph, and other formatting attributes saved under a style name. You can apply a number of formatting attributes to text by assigning a style to the text (such as a heading or a paragraph). Chapter 7, "Enhancing Word documents," discusses styles in depth.**

1. Open the Backstage (select File on the ribbon).

2. Select New in the Backstage. At this point, you can select one of the listed templates and then click Create to open the new document based on the template. Steps 3–5 walk you through a template search.

3. To search for an online template, either select one of the suggested searches (Letters, Resume, and so on) or type keywords into the Search Online Templates box and then click the search icon (or press Enter). A list of templates appears.

4. Select a template, and a window will open, providing a thumbnail of the template and additional information about the template.

5. If you want to browse through the templates that were listed based on your search parameters, use the Back and Forward arrows that appear in the template sample window.

6. To open a new document based on the template, select Create.

When your new document is open in the Word window, you can edit it as needed. Remember, your changes to the document are reflected in the document only; you are not editing the template itself. When you save the document, the Save As dialog box opens, and you can specify a name and location for the document.

Creating a template

Although an incredible number of templates are available on Office.com, you might still want templates specific to the type of Word documents you need to create. Basing your documents on templates that you have created provides you with Word documents that can be designed to meet your specific needs and have a look and function determined by you. For example, you can create a template for your business letters that includes a logo in the document header and uses a specific font for your text. Margins, page layout settings, and even page orientation can be saved as part of the template.

Templates that you create are saved (by default) to a folder named "Custom Office Templates." This folder can be found in your Documents folder, which is created when Windows is installed on your PC.

TIP

If you find that Word (or one of the other Office applications) is not saving your templates to the default Custom Office Templates folder, you can change the location specified for templates using the Word Options window. In the Backstage, select Options. In the Word Options window, select Save. The Save page is where you specify the folder for your templates. All you have to do is type a path in the Default Personal Templates Location box. An example of the syntax is `C:\Users\Joe\Documents\Custom Office Templates`, specifying the drive letter, folder, and subfolder.

When you are ready to create your own template, open a new, blank document (or an existing document). Then configure the various document settings, such as font attributes, paragraph attributes, and page layout settings, as needed. Save the document to your computer or OneDrive because creating a template can take time, and you don't want to lose all the various document attributes that you have added to the document.

When the document is ready to be saved as a template, follow these steps:

1. Select File and then select Save As in the Backstage. The Save As page appears.

2. The name of the current document appears at the top of the Save As page. If you want to change the name, select the current name, and type a new name.

3. The document's file type is shown below the File Name in a drop down-menu. Select the Save As Type drop-down arrow to view the different file types offered by Word when saving a document.

4. Select Word Template (*.dotx).

5. The file will now be saved as a template, and the default path for new templates should appear just above the file name.

6. Click the Save button to save your new template.

TIP

You can also use the Save As dialog box to save your template to the appropriate folder. When in the Backstage on the Save As page, select Browse, and the Save As dialog box will open. Specify a file name and choose Word Template from the Save As Type drop-down menu. Then navigate to the folder where you save your templates. Select Save, and you are good to go.

Now when you want to base a new document on the saved template, you can access it (and your other personal templates) by selecting Personal in the Backstage New window (File, New). All you have to do is select the template you want to use, and a new document based on the template opens in the Word window.

Templates can provide both uniformity and efficiency when you're creating new documents. If you repeatedly create documents that are similar (such as a weekly report), it makes sense to use templates to create those documents.

Attaching a template

Creating your own templates might be considered a fairly advanced move, and you might want to make sure you understand how Word documents really work (in terms of document attributes) before embarking on the template creation journey. Another advanced move is actually changing the current template for a particular document. Because each document is created using a template (like the Normal template), you can change the template if necessary. Because templates typically include building blocks, styles, and macros, you might find it advantageous to change the template currently assigned to a document so that you can take advantage of a different set of document attributes and features. Attaching a template replaces the template currently assigned to the document.

To attach a template to a document, you need access to the Developer tab on the ribbon. However, the Developer tab is not shown by default. The Developer tab provides access to the Templates And Add-ins dialog box, which is where you actually attach the template.

Select File on the ribbon and then select Options. In the Word Options window, select Customize Ribbon. On the right of the dialog box is a list of the ribbon's main tabs. Select the Developer check box and then click OK. The Developer tab now appears on the ribbon. Select Developer on the ribbon and then, on the Developer tab, click Document Template in the Templates group. The Templates And Add-Ins dialog box opens, as shown in Figure 6-6.

In the Templates And Add-in dialog box, click the Attach button. The Attach Template dialog box opens. The templates listed are either the templates you downloaded or templates that were installed with Word (Users/*your username*/AppData/Roaming/Microsoft/Templates). You can also navigate to another folder to select a template, such as the folder you are using to store the templates you created. After you locate the template you want to attach, select it and then click Open.

The template that you selected appears in the Document Template box on the Templates And Add-Ins dialog box. Click OK to close the Templates And Add-Ins dialog box. The document now has access to styles and other items (such as building blocks) saved with the template.

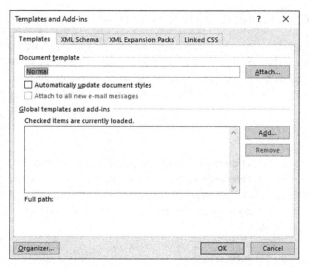

Figure 6-6   You can attach a different template to your document.

Navigating a Word document

As you create a new document or work with an existing document, you need to move around the document (say, from paragraph to paragraph or page to page). With the understanding that you use different techniques, such as taps, slides, and other manipulations of the touchscreen on a tablet (or other touchscreen device), let's take a look at the basics of moving around a Word document on a PC using the mouse and keyboard. The keyboard provides some nice shortcut key combinations. For example, to quickly go to the bottom of a document, press Ctrl+End. You can return to the top of the document just as easily by pressing Ctrl+Home. Let's look at what the mouse can do in terms of moving around a document and then see what the keyboard can do.

CAUTION

When navigating a document with the keyboard versus the mouse, remember that when you use the keyboard shortcut keys or the arrow keys, you move the insertion point to a new position. You can then immediately start typing or editing. When you use the mouse to move around a document (including when you use the mouse and the vertical scrollbar), you change your viewpoint of the document. After you locate the place you intend to go to using the mouse, you need to click the I-beam in the text to place the insertion point.

Moving around a document with the mouse

The mouse provides the easiest way to move the insertion point to a new position on the current page: Place the I-beam in the text and then click to fix the insertion point at that position. Obviously, you can also scroll through the document pages using the scroll wheel/button on the mouse. The vertical scrollbar provides different ways to move through the document, as listed in Table 6-1.

TIP

If you don't see the vertical and horizontal scrollbars, you might have to activate them via the Word Options window. Select File to enter the Backstage and then choose Options. In the Word Options window, select Advanced. Scroll down through the options until you find the Display settings. Select Show Horizontal Scrollbar and Show Vertical Scrollbar, and then click OK.

Table 6-1   Using the mouse and vertical scrollbar

Mouse movement	Your view of the document will …
Click the up scroll arrow.	Move up a line.
Click the down scroll arrow.	Move down a line.
Click Next Page.	Move to the next page.
Click Previous Page.	Move to the previous page.
Click below the scroll box.	Move to the next screen.
Click above the scroll box.	Move to the previous screen.
Drag the scroll box.	Move to a specific page.

The vertical scrollbar also provides some options when you right-click it. The shortcut menu that appears enables you to quickly go to the top or bottom of the document or to scroll to the position where you executed your right-click. (Choose Scroll Here.)

The horizontal scrollbar offers the capability to scroll to the left and right of a document page. The horizontal scrollbar does not appear if the document window is wide enough to display the entire page from left to right. The horizontal scrollbar is useful when you zoom in on a document and need to pan left and right to view all the text and other items (such as graphics) in the document.

NOTE

More complex documents that contain multiple sections can (and often do) have different page layout settings in each of the sections. For more about sections, see Chapter 8, "Working with tables, columns, and sections."

Moving around a document with the keyboard

Word also embraces a number of keyboard shortcuts that enable you to move around your document. For example, everyone is familiar with using the arrow keys on the keyboard to move around in your document. The up arrow takes you up a line, and the down arrow takes you down a line. By themselves, the arrow keys are not that efficient in moving around your document. Table 6-2 shows some more elegant keyboard shortcuts for moving around a document.

Table 6-2   Using the keyboard to move through a document

Key combination	The insertion point will …
Home	Move to the beginning of a line.
End	Move to the end of a line.
Ctrl+right arrow	Move one word to the right.
Ctrl+left arrow	Move one word to the left.
Ctrl+up arrow	Move to the previous paragraph.
Ctrl+down arrow	Move to the next paragraph.
PgUp	Move up one window.
PgDn	Move down one window.
Ctrl+PgUp	Move up one page.
Ctrl+PgDn	Move down one page.
Ctrl+Home	Move to the top of a document.
Ctrl+End	Move to the bottom of a document.

To a certain extent, your use of the mouse or keyboard for moving around your document relies on personal preference. However, it makes sense to consider keeping your hands on the keyboard as you initially type your document instead of constantly reaching for the mouse. Using the keyboard shortcuts can save you some time.

TIP

Another useful keyboard shortcut for navigating a document is Ctrl+G. This keystroke combination opens the Find And Replace dialog box with the Go To tab selected. Select an item in the Go To What list and then enter a number in the box to the right. For example, with Page selected, you can enter a page number and then select the Go To button to move to that page. Go To can also quickly move to bookmarks you have placed in a document, as well as to specific document items such as footnotes, tables, and headings.

CHAPTER 6

Selecting text

When you use the mouse to select text, you actually have a number of options depending on whether the mouse pointer is in the document text itself or along the document's left margin, which is referred to as the selection bar. The selection bar is the whitespace on the left edge of your document window, just in front of your text paragraphs. When you place the mouse in the selection bar, the mouse pointer becomes an arrow (in contrast to placing the mouse in the document, where the pointer appears as an I-beam). Table 6-3 provides the possibilities for selecting text using the mouse.

Table 6-3   Selecting text with the mouse

Text selection	Mouse action
Select the word.	Double-click a word.
Select the text block.	Click and drag. Alternatively, you can click at the beginning of the text and then hold the Shift key and click at the end of the text block.
Select the line.	Click in the selection bar next to the line.
Select multiple lines.	Click in the selection bar and drag down through multiple lines.
Select the sentence.	Hold Ctrl and click a sentence.
Select the paragraph.	Double-click in the selection bar next to the paragraph. Alternatively, you can triple-click in the paragraph.
Select the entire document.	Hold down Ctrl and click in the selection bar.

You can also select text using the keyboard. Hold the Shift key and use the arrow keys to select text as needed. If you work "old school," you can also use the Word Extend feature to select text using the keyboard. Position the insertion point before the word or sentence you want to select. Press the F8 function key to turn on Extend. Press the spacebar to select a word; each time you press the spacebar, you select the next word. To select an entire sentence, turn on the Extend feature and then press the period (.) key. You can select entire paragraphs this way by pressing the Enter key. To turn off the Extend feature, press the Esc key.

> TIP
>
> **A fast way to select all the text in the document is to use the keyboard shortcut Ctrl+A.**

Understanding document formatting

The overall look of your document depends on different types of attributes and layout settings, which many Word users lump together under the general term "formatting." However, text or character formatting relates to how the characters look (settings such as bold, 14-point, and red), whereas paragraph formatting is concerned with line spacing, indents, borders, alignment, and so on. Other document layout settings, such as margins, columns, and page orientation, fall under the Page Layout settings. So, when you create documents in Word, you must understand that although they are distinctly different in how they are applied to the document and how they change the document, the character formatting, paragraph formatting, and document layout settings all work together to give the document its overall look.

In terms of simple documents (such as a two-page letter), most people would agree that, when changing a page layout setting such as the margins, they would expect the margins on all the pages to change to the new settings. Page layout settings are pretty much all-encompassing when you change them in a document. Character formatting and paragraph formatting, on the other hand, are specific in their application. Read on to learn more about those settings.

Character formatting versus paragraph formatting

Even if you are new to Word, you have probably selected text and then clicked the Bold command on the ribbon's Home tab. The selected text becomes bold; it's a simple text-formatting operation. Character formatting relies on you to select the text you want to format and then select a character attribute, such as bold or red, to format the selected text.

Paragraph formatting, such as with line spacing, indents, borders, and other paragraph-formatting attributes, is a little different. For paragraph formatting to completely make sense, you need to understand what Word considers a paragraph.

When you click the Show/Hide command on the ribbon's Home tab, Word shows you the paragraph marks and the spaces between words. In the discussion here, the paragraph marks are extremely important. Every time you press the Enter key, which creates a blank line, you create a paragraph to Word.

TIP

You can use the Show/Hide command to show paragraph marks, spaces between words, object anchors, and hidden text. Clicking Show/Hide will turn on these formatting marks, and a second click will turn them off. If you want to have certain formatting marks always shown on-screen, open the Word Options window (click the File tab and then Options) and then select Display from the left side of the window. Select the checkbox for any of the formatting marks that you want to have always displayed on the screen.

When you click in a block of text preceded and followed by the paragraph mark symbol, you are in a paragraph—or what Word considers a separate paragraph. With the insertion point in that paragraph, you simply click the Center command on the ribbon's Home tab to center that text (all the text in the paragraph). You are not required to actually select the text (as you do when you want to change a character formatting attribute such as bold or italic). When you want to apply paragraph formatting to multiple paragraphs, you must select the paragraphs.

Manual formatting versus styles and themes

You can quickly and easily apply character formatting attributes to text in the document. Making a heading bold and then 14-point, for example, is easy. The same goes for paragraph formatting; after you click in a paragraph, you can change the line spacing using the Line Spacing command on the Home tab.

The problem with this manual formatting approach to changing the way text and paragraphs look is that building a consistent look throughout a document that consists of several pages can be a real chore.

If you desire a uniform look for a document, taking advantage of styles and themes makes sense. A style can be a collection of character and paragraph formatting attributes saved under a style name. You can repeatedly apply this style to text in the document, thus providing consistent formatting. On the other hand, a theme is an integrated set of formatting attributes that provides font, color, and effects settings.

In terms of a consistent look for a document, styles and themes give you a more controlled approach than manual formatting does. Taking advantage of styles and themes makes sense, particularly when you are working on special document types that require a greater amount of overall formatting.

➤ Read more about styles in the "Understanding styles" section, p. 200.

➤ To learn more about themes, see "Formatting with themes," p. 168.

Working with fonts and text formatting

The basic look of the text in a Word document is controlled by the font you are using. Each font set has a particular typeface, meaning the physical characteristic of the characters. Each font also has a particular look that makes it unique. An example of a font set is Calibri, which is the default Word font. A variety of other fonts exist, with names such as Arial, Courier, Times New Roman, Cooper Black, and Bookman Old Style. The fonts you have access to when working in Word depend on the fonts installed on your computer. Most of the fonts you work with are software fonts, or "soft fonts," and are Microsoft OpenType fonts (formerly called TrueType fonts) provided by your Windows operating system.

Most of the fonts you use are proportional fonts, meaning that the characters can have varying widths (as opposed to nonproportional fonts, which use a single standard width for all characters, such as in monofont type). For example, in proportional fonts, the letter *W* is wider than the letter *I*. Proportional fonts have a typeset look and not only are easier to read, but they also work well in columns and tables. Figure 6-7 shows some of the proportional fonts available in Word.

CHAPTER 6

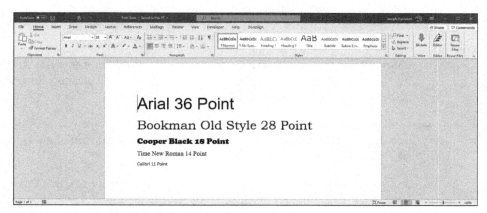

Figure 6-7   Proportional fonts in different point sizes

Proportional fonts are measured in points, which refer to the character height. Each point is ¹⁄₇₂ of an inch. For example, a 12-point font is ⅙ of an inch tall; a 36-point font is ½ inch tall.

You can change the font settings (also known as the font characteristics or attributes) before you begin typing in a document, or you can change the various text attributes after the fact and format existing text. If you want to change the font name or font size in a new document before you begin typing, use the Font and Font Size drop-down menus on the Home tab. Or if you are going to type a heading that you want in bold, press Ctrl+B to turn on the bold and then press Ctrl+B a second time to toggle off the bold. Let's look at using the various text-formatting commands that Word provides.

Formatting text

The easiest way to change a number of the commonly used font attributes (whether you are typing new text or working with selected text) is to take advantage of the formatting commands in the Font group of the ribbon's Home tab. This group includes the Font, Font Size, Bold, Italic, Strikethrough, Subscript, Superscript, Text Highlight Color, and Font Color commands, which are straightforward in their use. With drop-down menus such as Font, Font Size, Underline, and Font Color, you can preview the formatting before you apply it to your selected text (this is called Live Preview). Just point at one of the choices, such as a particular size on the Font Size list, to preview the size change directly on your selected text.

Some of the Font group commands aren't necessarily used that often and warrant additional coverage. The following list provides a brief description of these commands:

- **Text Effects And Typography:** This command provides text effects such as Glow, Shadow, Reflection, and Outline. It also grants access to styles, ligatures, and stylistic sets.

- **Increase Font Size:** This command increases the font by one increment (to the next preset). If the font is currently 18-point and the next increment on the Font Size list is 20-point, the command increases the font size from 18-point to 20-point.

- **Decrease Font Size:** This command decreases the font one increment (down one preset). It is the opposite of the Increase Font Size command.

- **Change Case:** This command provides a drop-down menu that enables you to change the selected text to sentence case, lowercase, or uppercase. It also enables you to capitalize each word in the selection or toggle the case of the text.

- **Clear All Formatting:** This command clears all the formatting on the selected text. This includes font-formatting attributes and paragraph-formatting attributes. This command also removes a style from the selected text.

Obviously, these commands are easy to use when you are formatting text that already exists and has been selected. Using these commands as you type might slow you down quite a bit. Table 6-4 provides some of the most often used font-formatting shortcut key combinations.

Table 6-4   Font formatting keyboard shortcuts

Attribute	Shortcut Keys
Bold	Ctrl+B
Italic	Ctrl+I
Underline	Ctrl+U
Double underline	Ctrl+Shift+D
Small caps	Ctrl+Shift+K
Subscript	Ctrl+equal sign (=)
Superscript	Ctrl+Shift+plus sign (+)
Increase size	Ctrl+Shift+>
Decrease size	Ctrl+Shift+<
Cycle through case	Shift+F3
Clear formatting	Ctrl+spacebar

Although these keyboard shortcuts are not all-inclusive in terms of font-formatting options, they enable you to quickly toggle a font format attribute on and off. For example, you can press Ctrl+I, type your italicized text, and then press Ctrl+I again to toggle italic off.

TIP

You can copy and then paste font- and paragraph-formatting attributes from one paragraph in a document to another (or to more than one paragraph). Select the text that has the formatting attributes you want to copy. Then click the Format Painter on the Clipboard group of the ribbon's Home tab. You can click a paragraph to paste the formatting or use the Format Painter mouse pointer to select text, which then has the formatting copied to it. To apply the copied formatting multiple times, double-click the Format Painter initially and use it as needed. When finished, click the Format Painter again to turn off the tool.

The Mini Toolbar

When you select text in a document, a floating toolbar appears near the selected text. This is the Mini Toolbar. It provides quick access to a number of the font-formatting commands (and some paragraph-formatting commands such as Bullets and Number). Figure 6-8 shows the Mini Toolbar.

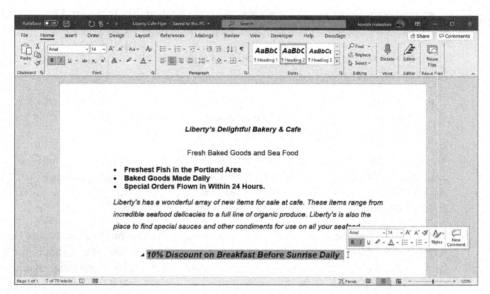

Figure 6-8   Use the Mini Toolbar to quickly format selected text.

To use the Mini Toolbar, move the mouse onto it immediately after it appears near your selected text. Select commands from the Mini Toolbar as you would any of the commands that you work with on the ribbon's Home tab.

The Font dialog box

Although the Font group on the ribbon's Home tab and the Mini Toolbar provide you with most of the font-formatting attributes you need, the Font dialog box is another place that provides access to all the font attributes and some other advanced character settings. To open the Font Dialog box, click the dialog box launcher (on the right side of the Font group on the Home tab).

The Font dialog box has two tabs: Font and Advanced. The Font tab provides access to the font, font style (bold, italic, and so forth), and font effects. You can also access text effects from the Font tab. When you select a font attribute, it is applied to selected text in the document.

The Advanced tab of the Font dialog box enables you to control features related to text spacing and OpenType features. First, the Character Spacing settings:

- **Scale:** This setting enables you to stretch or condense the text (horizontally). For example, a scale setting of 200% stretches the font characters, making them larger. A scale setting of less than 100% compresses the characters.

- **Spacing:** This setting controls the distance between the characters. Expanded increases the space between the characters; Condensed compresses the spacing.

- **Position:** This setting enables you to raise or lower the selected characters from the text's baseline position.

- **Kerning:** This setting enables you to compress the distance between characters (meaning the space between the characters). You specify a baseline font size, and all fonts of that size (and above) are then kerned.

The OpenType features on the Advanced tab relate to the capabilities of OpenType fonts, which Microsoft and Adobe jointly developed. Without going into a lengthy discussion of font outline data and font layout tables, suffice it to say that OpenType fonts provide you with more robust font families and special font features such as ligatures and stylistic sets.

A ligature is a combination of two adjacent characters by a common element. For example, the letters *f* and *i* can be combined as a ligature using the cross piece in the *f* (that is, fi). Stylistic sets are alternative sets of glyphs (the visual representations of the individual characters) for the font. Selecting a different stylistic set allows you to take advantage of a different set of glyphs; for example, a stylistic set might contain all caps and other style differences. If you are interested in typography, you might find ligatures and stylistic sets useful.

Working with paragraph formatting

Paragraph formatting encompasses many formatting attributes, including alignment. (Think of centering and aligning text left.) Paragraph formatting also includes line spacing (single-spaced versus double-spaced), tabs, and indents. However, other settings related to how paragraphs are broken between lines and pages (such as widow/orphan control) play a part in this discussion of paragraph formatting.

As discussed earlier in this chapter, Word sees a paragraph as any text block (or blank line or lines) that is preceded and followed by a paragraph mark (that is, you pressed Enter before the paragraph and after the paragraph). Each paragraph can be assigned different paragraph attribute settings, such as Center or Indent. Each paragraph can also have different tab settings.

You can access all the paragraph settings in the Paragraph dialog box, which you open via the dialog box launcher on the right side of the Paragraph group (on the Home tab of the ribbon).

Settings such as alignment and indentation are available on the Indents And Spacing tab, as shown in Figure 6-9. Widow/Orphan control and other break and formatting options are available on the Line And Page Breaks tab.

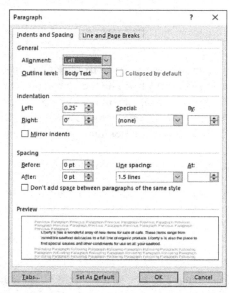

Figure 6-9   You can access all paragraph-formatting options in the Paragraph dialog box.

> TIP
>
> **You can change font settings in the Font dialog box and make them the default settings for Word (meaning that you change the Normal template). After you select the various font attributes you want to use by default, click the Set As Default button.**

To apply paragraph formatting to a single paragraph, you simply make sure that the insertion point is in the paragraph. If you want to format multiple paragraphs, you must select those paragraphs. Let's look at the various formatting attributes related to paragraphs, how you can view the formatting present in a document, and how you can copy formatting attributes from paragraph to paragraph.

Setting paragraph alignment

A basic formatting attribute of every paragraph—whether it is a 20-line paragraph or a single-line heading—relates to how that paragraph is aligned on the page in relation to the left and right margins. By default, all text uses the Align Text Left setting, which is characterized by text that is straight or unvarying on the left margin but has a ragged right-edged margin.

Paragraph alignment that varies from the norm of left alignment can set elements of a document apart from other document elements, such as a centered heading. You can also use alignment to provide a document page with a look of uniformity, such as a letter or resume that uses justification on all paragraphs. The following list briefly explains each paragraph alignment possibility.

TIP

You can also set the alignment for a new line of text using Word's Click And Type feature. Place the insertion point at the beginning of a blank line, and then move the I-beam from left to right on the page; the I-beam becomes an indent pointer, a center point, and a justify-right pointer. Double-click the mouse to place the insertion point horizontally on the line, based on the current mouse alignment pointer.

- **Align Text Left:** This is the default placement for normal text, aligned on the left.

- **Align Text Right:** Text is aligned at the right margin, and text lines show a ragged left edge.

- **Center:** Text is centered between the left and right margins of the page (with both margins having irregular edges).

- **Justify:** Text is spaced across each line so that both the left and right margins are straight and uniform (often used in printed publications such as daily newspapers).

The fastest way to change the alignment of a single paragraph (or many selected paragraphs) is to use the alignment commands provided by the Paragraph group of the ribbon's Home tab. For example, to center a heading, click the heading and then click Center in the Paragraph group. You can also control alignment using the Alignment drop-down menu on the Indents and Spacing tab of the Paragraph dialog box.

TIP

You can set the spacing before and after a paragraph using the spin boxes on the Spacing portion of the Paragraph group found on the ribbon's Layout tab.

Changing line spacing

Line spacing is the vertical space between lines of text in the paragraph. The default line spacing is Multiple 1.08 (the actual spacing depends on the height of the font you are using). You can control line spacing options using the Line And Paragraph Spacing command, which is in the Paragraph group on the ribbon's Home tab. Click Line And Paragraph Spacing and then select one of the line spacing options, such as 1.0, 2.0, or 3.0.

If you want to set a custom line spacing, you can do so in the Paragraph dialog box in the Spacing section of the Indents And Spacing tab. The Before and After spin boxes allow you to set spacing before and after a particular paragraph or paragraphs. This is particularly useful for headings or other special text items. Be advised that adding space before and after paragraphs can be tricky. For example, if you have a paragraph configured with an After setting, that additional space is added to the paragraph that follows—if that following paragraph has a Before setting—that additional space is added before that paragraph (the paragraph that follows). So, inadvertently using both After and Before settings on adjoining paragraphs can open way too much white space between them.

You can also control the line spacing for paragraphs using the Line Spacing drop-down menu. It provides the following options:

- **Single:** Spacing accommodates the largest font size found on the lines and adds a small amount of whitespace (depending on the font used) between lines.

- **1.5:** The line spacing is one-and-a-half times greater than single spacing.

- **Double:** Spacing is twice the size of single-line spacing.

- **At Least:** This is the default setting. Line spacing adjusts to accommodate the largest font on the line and special items such as graphics.

- **Exactly:** All lines are equally spaced, and special font sizes and items such as graphics are not accommodated. If these items are larger than the setting used here, they appear cut off in the document. You can still accommodate these items by using the Multiple box (described next) to shift all the text lines to a higher spacing percentage that accommodates special items.

- **Multiple:** You specify the line spacing by a particular percentage. This feature is used in conjunction with the Exactly option to set a line-spacing percentage that accommodates special font sizes or graphics in the document. For example, if you want to decrease the line spacing by 20 percent, you enter the number 0.8. To increase the line spacing by 50 percent, you enter 1.5.

TIP

If you are using two different fonts in a document, you might find that setting line spacing to Exactly (and a specific point size) in the Paragraph dialog box gives you a more uniform look in the document; this is because different font families can look bigger or smaller than others when you use the default Single or Double settings for line spacing.

Some of the setting options that you select from the Line Spacing list are influenced by the point size you enter in the At box (this applies only when you have selected At Least, Exactly, or Multiple). Use the click arrows to increase or decrease the point size of the line spacing. The

CHAPTER 6

Preview pane gives you an overview of how the line spacing that you set will actually look for the paragraph or paragraphs affected by the line settings.

Setting line and page breaks

The Paragraph dialog box also gives you control over how line and page breaks affect a paragraph or paragraphs. Figure 6-10 shows the Line And Page Breaks tab of the Paragraph dialog box.

By default, Widow/Orphan control is set (note the selected check box for Widow/Orphan control in Figure 6-10). A widow is the last line of a paragraph that appears by itself at the top of a page. An orphan is the first line of a paragraph left by itself at the bottom of the page. Widow/Orphan control keeps the last line or first line of a paragraph from printing on the next or previous page, respectively. The Keep Line Together option keeps the entire paragraph together on a page, and the Page Break Before option forces Word to start the paragraph on a new page if the entire paragraph cannot be kept on the previous page.

The Line And Page Breaks options also provide formatting exception settings that you can apply to your paragraphs. Word can assign line numbers to all the lines in a document. The line numbers setting is in the Page Setup group of the ribbon's Layout tab. If you are using line numbering, you can use the Suppress Line Numbers formatting exception if you want to suppress line numbers for specific paragraphs in a document.

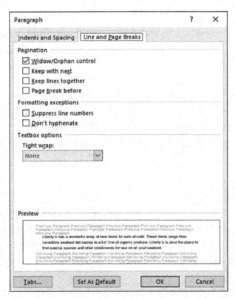

Figure 6-10 The Paragraph dialog box's Line And Page Breaks tab

Word does not automatically hyphenate words in paragraphs; it wraps them to the next line. If you have enabled hyphenation (the Hyphenation command is on the Page Setup group on the ribbon's Layout tab), you can use the Don't Hyphenate check box on the Line And Page Breaks tab in the Paragraph dialog box—click the launcher on the Paragraph group—to turn off the hyphenation on a paragraph or paragraphs.

Setting indents

You can use indents to offset paragraphs (including individual lines such as headings) from both the left and right margins. By default, indents are set every half-inch. The Increase Indent command is in the Paragraph group of the ribbon's Home tab. Each time you click Increase Indent, you indent the paragraph another half-inch. To decrease the indent, use the Decrease Indent command.

> **TIP**
>
> **To view the Ruler (both the horizontal and vertical Rulers), click the Ruler check box in the Show group of the ribbon's View tab.**

You can also use the Ruler to set the indent for a paragraph. The Ruler has both a left-indent and a right-indent marker. It also has a first-line indent marker and a hanging indent marker. These two markers are stacked on the top of the left-indent marker, but you can move them independently. Figure 6-11 shows the different Ruler indent markers.

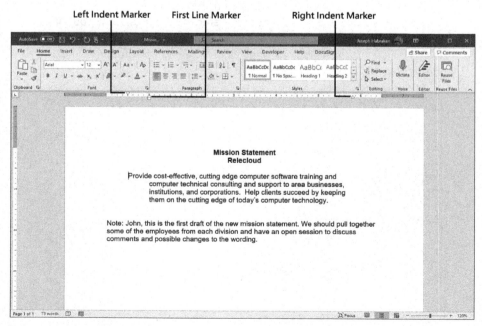

Figure 6-11   The Ruler's indent markers

You can drag the left-indent marker or the right-indent marker as needed to indent the left or right of a paragraph, respectively. You can also create hanging indents by using the indent markers. Hanging indents are created by separating the first-line indent marker from the left indent marker on the Ruler.

TIP

You can also set the left and right indents for a paragraph using the Indent settings on the Paragraph group of the ribbon's Page Layout tab.

To create a hanging indent (shown in Figure 6-11), drag the left-indent marker (using the square bottom of the marker) to the position where you want to indent the second and subsequent lines of the paragraph. Then drag the first-line indent marker (drag it by the top of the marker) back to the position where you want the first line to begin. Hanging indents are useful when you want to subordinate the remainder of a paragraph under the first line of the paragraph, such as with job descriptions in resumes.

Working with tabs

You can use tabs to align text in your documents. Most Word users typically think of the tab as a way to offset the first sentence of a paragraph (one tab stop from the left margin) from the rest of a paragraph. Word actually provides different types of tabs that you can use as a way to align items in much the same way (at least visually) that you align items in a table.

By default, Word provides a tab stop every half-inch. Every time you press the Tab key on the keyboard, you offset the text line from the left margin one tab stop. You can set your own tab stops using the Tabs dialog box or the Ruler. You open the Tabs dialog box from the Paragraph dialog box (select the dialog box launcher in the Paragraph group). Figure 6-12 shows the Tabs dialog box.

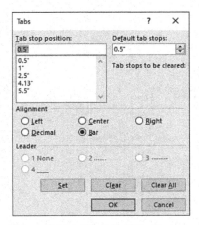

Figure 6-12   The Tabs dialog box

You can change the default tab stops from 0.5 inches to any increment using the Default Tab Stops spin box. To create a new tab, enter a tab stop position (in inches) and then select the alignment for the new tab (Left, Center, Right, and so on). You can also select one of the Leader options for your tab, such as Dot Leader (2). When you have finished setting the tab's options, click Set to create the tab. You can then create the process as needed.

Word provides different tab types; the following list briefly describes each:

- **Left tab:** Aligns the beginning of the text line at the tab stop

- **Center tab:** Centers the text line at the tab stop

- **Right tab:** Right-aligns the text line at the tab stop

- **Decimal tab:** Lines up numerical entries at their decimal point

- **Bar tab:** Inserts a vertical bar at the tab stop (it doesn't actually align text)

Because it provides a more visual medium for setting tabs, the Ruler is your best bet for quickly setting tabs and using the different types of tabs Word offers. To set a tab on the Ruler, click the Tab button on the far left of the Ruler to select the tab type (Left, Center, Right, and so on). Each time you click the Tab button, you cycle to the next tab type. If you go past the type of tab you want to set, keep clicking until the tab type appears on the Tab button.

When you have the appropriate tab type selected on the Tab button, place the mouse pointer on the Ruler where you want the tab and then click to place it. If you need to adjust the position of a tab, drag it to a new position on the Ruler. Figure 6-13 shows the different tab stop types and how they actually align text at the tab stop.

When you want to remove a tab from the Ruler, drag it off the Ruler. You can also clear a tab or all your tab settings in the Tabs dialog box.

The Reveal Formatting task pane is a useful feature when you're working with manually assigned font- and paragraph-formatting attributes. This feature enables you to quickly review the font and paragraph formatting that you have assigned to your text.

To open the Reveal Formatting task pane, press Shift+F1. To view the font and paragraph formatting in a particular paragraph, click that paragraph (or select text as needed).

CHAPTER 6

Tab Button   Bar   Left   Center   Right   Decimal

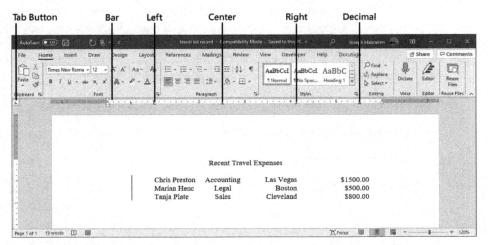

Figure 6-13   Tab stops on the Ruler

For more detail on the source of the formatting that has been assigned to text, click the Distinguish Style Source check box in the Options area of the Reveal Formatting task pane (see Figure 6-14).

The Reveal Formatting task pane also has a Show All Formatting Marks check box. You can select it to view paragraph marks, spaces, and tabs in the document.

Figure 6-14   The Reveal Formatting task pane

Page layout: margins and page options

The standard page layout options primarily relate to the document margins, page orientation, and paper size. Other page setup options, such as the paper source settings, are more closely associated with printing documents; we look at printing in the last section of this chapter. Layout settings are related to sections and headers and footers. We discuss headers and footers in Chapter 7 and then look at sections in Chapter 8.

> ### TIP
>
> **You can have Word mark formatting inconsistencies the same way it marks spelling errors and grammar problems. On the File tab, open Options and then click Advanced. Under Editing Options, select the Keep Track Of Formatting check box and the Mark Formatting Inconsistencies box. Now Word marks formatting inconsistencies with a wavy blue line.**

Margins control the amount of whitespace of the page. Four margins exist: top, bottom, left, and right. By default, each of these margins is set to 1 inch. You can change any of the margin settings for your document as needed; you can also change the margins for just a portion of a document. Select the text in the document and then change the margins. The changes affect only the selected text.

Changing margins

To change the margins for the document or selected text, use the Margins command in the Page Setup group of the ribbon's Layout tab. You can select from one of the margin presets provided, or you can select Custom Margins. This opens the Page Setup dialog box, shown in Figure 6-15.

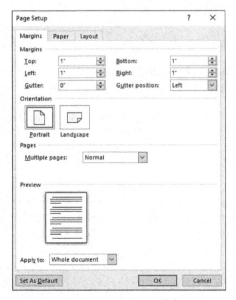

Figure 6-15   The Page Setup dialog box

NOTE

A document divided into sections can potentially have different margin settings for each section. Sections are discussed in Chapter 8.

The Page Setup dialog box enables you to set each of the margins. Use the appropriate spin box or type a new margin setting.

When you are creating a special document, such as a document with mirror margins or a book-fold document, you can change the Multiple Pages setting in the Pages area of the Page Setup dialog box so that your margins accommodate that type of document. For example, if you select Mirror Margins (the margins on the facing pages will be mirrored) in the Multiple pages drop-down menu, you have Top, Bottom, Inside, and Outside margins. You also set a gutter, which provides extra space between the inside margin and the edge of the page. This helps accommodate binding or punch holes if you plan to bind your document in a three-ring notebook.

CAUTION

Be advised that your default printer defines the minimum (and maximum) margins for a page. If you set margins less than the minimum, a dialog box appears when you close the Page Setup dialog box, letting you know that your margins are outside the printable area of the page. Click Fix to return to the dialog box and fix the margins.

When you want to change only the document margins going forward in the document from where you parked the insertion point, you can select From This Point Forward in the Apply To drop-down menu (this creates a new section in the document). When you have completed your changes to the margin settings, click OK to return to the document.

Changing page orientation and paper size

The default page orientation in Word is portrait. The default page size (in the U.S.) is Letter (8.5 by 11 inches). You can change both the page orientation and the page size as needed.

To change the page orientation, click Orientation in the Page Setup group of the Page Layout tab. Then select Portrait or Landscape, as needed. You can also change the page orientation on the Margins tab of the Page Setup dialog box.

TIP

You can view your document margins in the Print Layout and Full Screen Reading views. You can also see the margins in Print Preview. To add Print Preview to the Quick Access Toolbar, select the drop-down menu on the right of the Quick Access Toolbar and select Print Preview.

The Size command in the Page Setup group of the Page Layout tab provides a list of paper sizes, such as Letter, Legal, and Executive. You can select from the list or click More Paper Sizes to open the Paper tab of the Page Setup dialog box and select from a list of preset paper sizes. More importantly, this option enables you to set the paper size to Custom Size and then set your width and height for the paper.

TIP

The quickest way to insert a new page break is from the keyboard: Press Ctrl+Enter.

Inserting page breaks

As you type your document, Word automatically starts a new page when you fill the current page with text or other document items (such as tables, clip art, and so on). You can insert a page break in your document as needed. You insert page breaks using the Page Break command on the Insert tab of the ribbon (in the Pages group). You can also insert page breaks from the Break list in the Page Setup group on the Page Layout tab.

When you want to be able to visually differentiate between the page breaks Word placed in the document and the page breaks you inserted, select the Show/Hide command (on the Home tab) and then go to Draft view using the view icons along the bottom-right part of the status bar.

TIP

Type a range of page numbers (for example, 1–4,6) below the Print All Pages box. This changes the setting to Print Custom Range and prints only the pages you specify.

Page breaks that you insert show a dotted line and the words *Page Break*. You can select your inserted page break and then delete it, if needed.

Printing documents

Printing in Word is accomplished using the various tools provided in the Backstage Print window. This window enables you to select a printer, set printer properties, and control print settings such as page orientation, page size, and margins. The Print window also provides a print preview of a selected page in the document, and you can use the Zoom slider to zoom out and view multiple pages. Figure 6-16 shows the Print window.

CHAPTER 6

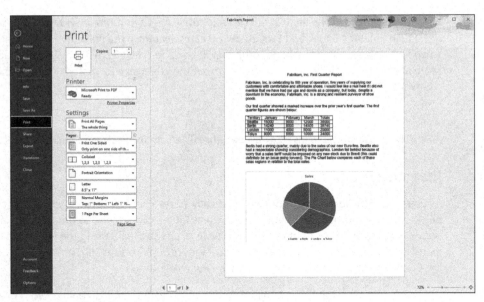

Figure 6-16   The Print window

To send the document to the printer, you click the Print button. If you need to change the number of copies, you can use the Copies spin box. Before printing, you might want to examine some of the possibilities that the new Print Backstage view provides. A number of print-related settings are listed under the Settings area. These options are as follows:

- **Selecting What To Print:** By default, Print All Pages is selected, and the entire document prints. You can select another option from the list, such as Print Selection, Print Current Page, or Custom Print (which requires that you provide a range of page numbers). You can also choose to have certain lists related to the document's properties printed, such as styles, autotext entries, and a list of customized shortcut keys.

- **Printing One or Two-Sided:** This option enables you to set up the print job to print one-sided or print on both sides (if your printer can handle duplex printing). You can also choose Manually Print On Both Sides, which enables you to flip the paper over and reload it in the printer.

- **Collated Or Uncollated:** You can choose to have your printout collated or uncollated using this setting.

- **Orientation:** You can choose the printout orientation: portrait or landscape.

- **Paper Size:** You can change the paper size before printing. Remember that this repaginates the document.

- **Margins:** You can change the margins before printing.

- **Pages Per Sheet:** You can select how many pages are printed per page. You can also have the document pages scale to the paper size.

When previewing the document, you can use the Zoom slider on the lower-right portion of the screen. The Zoom To Page button zooms you back to a single-page view if you have been previewing multiple pages.

CHAPTER 6

Creating better documents   161

Creating bulleted and numbered lists   162

Working with borders and shading   166

Formatting with themes   168

Creating headers and footers   172

Inserting pictures and charts   179

Changing the document display   187

Using the Editor   192

Working with Quick Parts   196

Configuring AutoCorrect   199

Understanding styles   200

This chapter looks at different possibilities for making your documents more communicative and professional. It begins with a look at basic bulleted and numbered lists and then examines formatting options such as themes and styles.

This chapter also explores the use of headers and footers in documents and discusses different page-numbering options in Word. We also delve into enhancing your Word documents with pictures and charts. Included is a look at different ways to view a document and how to use building blocks and document review tools, including the Editor and the Thesaurus.

Creating better documents

When you have a good feel for the baseline features used to create, save, and print documents, it's time to explore features that enable you to enhance your documents. A broader command of Word's features will not only make you more productive, but it also will enable you to create more interesting-looking documents that take advantage of bulleted and numbered lists, borders, shading, and themes. Features and tools such as quick parts and styles also enable you to create documents more efficiently and produce more uniform documents.

Additionally, tools are available that enable you to root out errors in a document. The Editor feature now combines the spelling and grammar features; it also provides additional scrutiny of your document based on refinements. These refinements are Clarity, Conciseness, Formality, Punctuation Conventions, and Vocabulary. Word also includes the Research pane and the Thesaurus, both of which enable you to improve the content of your documents.

Creating bulleted and numbered lists

Numbered and bulleted lists emphasize information on the page and provide a visual mechanism for arranging similar items. Bulleted lists work best when you want to separate and highlight items from the other text on a page; however, a bulleted list doesn't necessarily have a particular order or hierarchy. Numbered lists work well when you are detailing a procedure in which the order of the steps is important in accomplishing a particular task.

You can quickly assign both bullets and numbers to existing lists, or you can toggle on bullets or numbering and create your list as you type your text. You have complete control over the bullet type (using special characters or other graphics) used in a bulleted list and the alignment of the text lines in the list. You can also format numbered lists by specifying the numbering format, including where the numbering starts and the numbered items' text alignment.

The commands for bullets, numbering, and multilevel lists are located in the Paragraph group of the ribbon's Home tab. Each command also gives you a drop-down menu that enables you to fine-tune the formatting related to the particular list type (bullets versus numbers) that you select.

Bulleted lists

Whether you are formatting an existing list that you have selected or are planning to type the bulleted list on the fly, all you have to do is select Bullets in the Paragraph group on the ribbon's Home tab.

If you want to select the bullet character used in the list, click the arrow next to the Bullet command to choose one of the bullet characters provided by either the Recently Used Bullets list or the Bullet Library. When you are changing the bullet for a selected, existing bulleted list, place the mouse on any of the bullets to preview that bullet on the list. Figure 7-1 shows the Bullet Library; the selected bullet is previewed in the document.

> ### TIP
> **You can also turn on bulleting using the Mini Toolbar, which appears when you select text (such as several lines of text in a list). Click the Bullets command on the Mini Toolbar. This formats the existing list as a bulleted list and turns on the bullets so that each subsequent item you add to the list is also bulleted.**

When you want to use a bullet type not provided in the library, select the Bullets command arrow and then click Define New Bullet. The Define New Bullet dialog box opens and enables you to select a new bullet character from the available symbols. You can also ramp up the look of your bullets by using bullet pictures (including many available on Office.com) or importing your own pictures to use as bullets. Figure 7-2 shows the Define New Bullet dialog box.

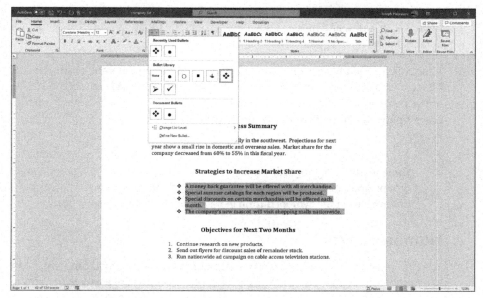

Figure 7-1   Change the bullet for the selected list.

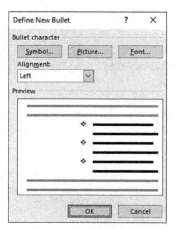

Figure 7-2   Define your own bullets for your lists.

To select a new bullet character from the various symbols installed on your computer as part of your available fonts, select the Symbol button in the Define New Bullet dialog box. The Symbol dialog box provides a Font drop-down menu that enables you to select the font or character set from which to select the new bullet character. After you select the new bullet, select OK to return to the Define New Bullet dialog box.

The Define New Bullet dialog box also enables you to select the alignment for the bullet (Left, Centered, or Right) and makes it possible to select the font family used to render the bullet (by default, the bullet uses your default font).

Although we don't typically think of bulleted lists as having different levels, you can change the list level for a bulleted item (or items) in a list. To change the list level, click the Bullets command arrow, point at the Change List Level command, and then select a list level from the list level presets provided (nine list levels are provided).

TIP

Some of the more interesting bullet characters are in the Wingdings and Webdings font groups. You can access these and other installed font groups from the Symbol dialog box; just select the Symbol button in the Define New Bullet dialog box.

Numbered lists

You can create numbered lists in your document as you type, or you can format an existing list as a numbered list after the fact. You can also take advantage of a variety of number formats.

To start numbering or to format a selected list, click the Numbering command (in the Paragraph group on the ribbon's Home tab). Doing so brings up a list using the default numbering format (1,2,3) and starting at the number 1.

TIP

You can quickly change a numbered list to a multilevel list by changing the list level for items you consider a sublevel in the numbered list.

You can use the Numbering command arrow to access different number formats in the Numbering library (such as the Roman numeral format). This gallery of number format choices also enables you to change the list level for one or more items.

If the number formats in the Numbering Library don't meet your needs, you can define your own number format. Use Define New Number Format (in the Numbering command arrow gallery) to open the Define New Number Format dialog box (see Figure 7-3).

In the Define New Number Format dialog box, you can set the number style, the number format, and the alignment of the number (Left, Centered, or Right). You can also select the font used for the numbers.

If you want to change the starting number of the list, you can open the Set Numbering Value dialog box (click Set Numbering Value on the Numbering menu). This dialog box also gives you the option to start a new list (the default) or continue the numbering from a previous list. You can continue from a previous list but set an advance value, which enables you to skip numbers.

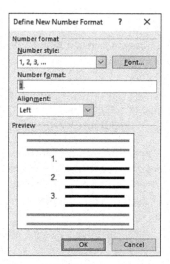

Figure 7-3   Define your own number formats.

Multilevel lists

Using the Multilevel List command in the Paragraph group on the ribbon's Home tab, you can quickly create lists and outlines that require different levels. As with other lists, you can format selected existing text or start a new list. First, select the Multilevel List command and select one of the multilevel list formats from the List Library. You also can define new multilevel lists via the Define New Multilevel List command at the bottom of the library.

You can build your list or edit an existing list when you have the multilevel list format set. With a new list, use the Tab key to demote an item to the next lower level. For example, if you have already typed a primary-level heading, press Tab and then type the secondary level items that go under that heading.

> ### NOTE
> **Multilevel lists are fine for simple outlines. However, use the Outline view when you need to use outlining as a more advanced organizational tool in complex documents. It provides tools for designating headings, promoting and demoting paragraphs, and expanding and collapsing levels. We discuss the Outline view later in this chapter.**

When you need to move the insertion point up a level in the multilevel list, press Shift+Tab. For example, you might have a secondary-level item that you want to promote to a primary level. You also can change the level of a list item using the Change List Level command. Select the line in the multilevel list you want to promote or demote. Select the Multilevel List command, and then select the Change List Level command (below the List Library). Choose a new level from the levels provided.

TIP

When you edit a multilevel list, you can use the Decrease Indent command or Promote Indent command in the Paragraph group to demote and promote items, respectively.

To select the format for the multilevel list, click the Multilevel List command arrow and select a format from the List Library. Select the Define New Multilevel List command if you need a custom list format, which opens the Define New Multilevel List dialog box, shown in Figure 7-4.

You can modify each level, including the number formatting, number style, and position for the level. If you click the More button, you can also select other options, such as specifying the start number for the level, selecting the level to be shown in the gallery, and denoting whether the number should be followed with a specific character, such as a tab, a space, or nothing (yes, nothing is a choice).

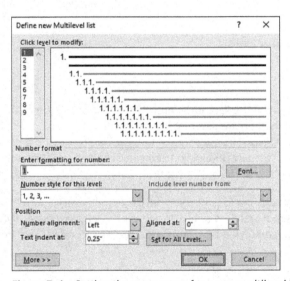

Figure 7-4 Setting the parameters for a new multilevel list

Working with borders and shading

Font-formatting attributes, such as bold, italic, underline, and increased font size, can emphasize specific text in a document. When you want to draw attention to a certain paragraph or heading and you want something a little flashier than a font attribute change or simple paragraph-formatting attributes such as centering or indents, you can take advantage of borders and shading. Borders and shading provide a simple way to add color and graphical elements to a special document such as a report, flyer, or newsletter.

You can place a border around any text paragraph or a number of selected paragraphs. To place a border around a single paragraph, make sure that the insertion point is in that paragraph. If you want to put a border around several paragraphs, select them.

To select one of the border options for the paragraph (or paragraphs), select the Borders command in the Paragraph group of the ribbon's Home tab. The border gallery provides many border options, including Bottom Border, Left Border, and Outside Borders (designed for use on tables). Select an option to have the borders applied to your text.

After you have selected your border, you can place shading behind the text (you can "shade" text that doesn't have a border as well). You apply the shading using the Shading command in the Paragraph group. When you click the Shading command arrow, a palette of theme colors appears (you can also choose from a list of standard colors). To select additional colors, click the More Colors option. This opens the Colors dialog box, where you can select standard colors or mix custom colors (on the Standard and Custom tabs, respectively). We will discuss themes and how they affect formatting options in the next section of this chapter.

TIP

The Borders And Shading drop-down menu also enables you to insert a horizontal line or draw a table at the insertion point.

If you want greater control over the borders (and shading), you assign to document paragraphs—including settings such as the border's line style, line width, and line color—you can open the Borders And Shading dialog box, shown in Figure 7-5. Select Borders And Shading on the Borders drop-down gallery. (To open the gallery, click the arrow next to Borders in the Paragraph group.)

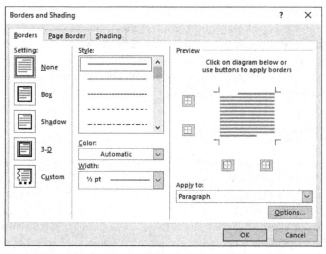

Figure 7-5   The Borders And Shading dialog box

NOTE

On the Custom tab of the Colors dialog box, you can specify a color by its RGB code. This is particularly useful if you want to make sure that you are consistently using the same color for different document elements (such as paragraph shading and font color). For example, to make sure that I am using steel-blue as my shading color, I enter the RGB (Red–Green–Blue) code of 70–130–180. Many websites provide the RGB color codes— just do a Bing or Google search.

The Borders tab of the dialog box gives you control over the style and color of the line and provides settings that enable you to include a shadow or 3D effect on the border. The Page Border dialog box (which is discussed in a moment) enables you to place a border around the entire page (or pages). The Shading tab lets you select a fill color and an optional pattern style for the paragraph shading.

Using the Page Border tab of the Borders And Shading dialog box, you can also place a border on the pages of your document. It provides you with options similar to those provided for paragraph borders, such as shadow and 3D effects and the ability to control the line style, color, and width. Page borders can also include repeating art elements (such as palm trees or gingerbread men). You select these border elements by using the Art drop-down menu. Word provides some color and grayscale elements that you can use for your page borders.

TIP

You can directly open the Page Border tab of the Borders And Shading dialog box using the Page Borders command. This command resides in the Page Background group of the ribbon's Design tab.

Word also allows you to assign a page background color to a page (or pages). Select the Page Color command arrow on the Page Background group of the ribbon's Design tab. This opens the color palette, where you can choose from theme colors or standard colors, or you can open the Color dialog box to choose from the colors or mix your own. You can configure fill effects such as gradients, textures, patterns, and pictures for your page background by selecting Fill Effects from the Page Color palette, which opens the Fill Effects dialog box.

Formatting with themes

When using a document (or family of documents, workbooks, or presentations), a uniform look can be very useful, particularly when you are putting together materials for a product-line promotion or campaign. However, working with many document elements, such as different document colors (including font, border, and shading colors), fonts, and text effects, can be somewhat difficult. The same is true when it comes to getting a group of documents that all look similar. This can be particularly tricky when you want the color and font schemes in a Word document to match an accompanying Excel worksheet or PowerPoint presentation. Keeping a document's appearance consistent—particularly when you have used some special formatting attributes—is best done using themes. A theme is a collection of colors, fonts, paragraph settings, and text effects. The Themes gallery provides many different themes, and you can modify existing themes to create your own themes.

Themes are consistent across the Microsoft Office applications Word, Excel, and PowerPoint, which means that you can create a family of Word documents, Excel worksheets, and PowerPoint presentations that are consistent in their overall look.

Each Word template (such as the Normal template) has a specific default theme. You can change that default theme to any of the built-in themes, and you can also browse for themes you have created. (Typically, they are saved to the Documents Themes folder: Microsoft\Templates\Document Themes folder on your computer.)

NOTE

Word has a Design tab with a Document Formatting group that provides theme-related commands such as Colors, Fonts, and Effects.

➤ **See Chapter 6, "Essential Word features," for more about templates.**

To take advantage of themes, you must save your document in the Word Document format provided in the Save As dialog box, which is available when you first save the file or use the Save As Command in the Backstage to change a file's name, save a copy, or save the document to a new location. Any document that has been created in a version of Word that predates Word 2007 (for backward compatibility with people who use earlier versions of Word) will require you to save the document in Word in the "new" Word file format. Otherwise, you won't be able to use themes to format the document.

Using themes provides you with the ability to create professional-looking documents that are well designed and visually interesting. Themes include multiple style sets that change the formatting of built-in styles that you have applied to your document. Although we don't discuss styles until the end of this chapter, suffice it to say that each theme available in Word gives you more choice in how your text looks. These theme possibilities are housed on the Design tab on the ribbon; the theme commands are in the Document Formatting group. The only other command group in the Design tab is the Page Background group, so most of the tab is reserved for the Document Formatting gallery and the theme commands such as Themes, Colors, and Fonts.

As already mentioned, themes include color, font, paragraph, and text effect formatting attributes. You don't really see the complete effect of a theme on your document if you don't use the built-in styles provided in the Styles gallery, which is accessed via the Home tab. A style is a collection of saved formatting attributes. Themes are collections of formatting attributes that affect styles. Each theme has a collection of style sets that change how your applied styles look. The current style set dictates the font and paragraph formatting of the text in the document.

It's really an upside-down pyramid with themes at the top, followed by the style sets (found in the Style Set gallery on the Design tab), followed by individual styles (from the Styles gallery on the Home tab). To change the current theme for your document, select Themes on the Design tab. The Theme gallery opens (see Figure 7-6).

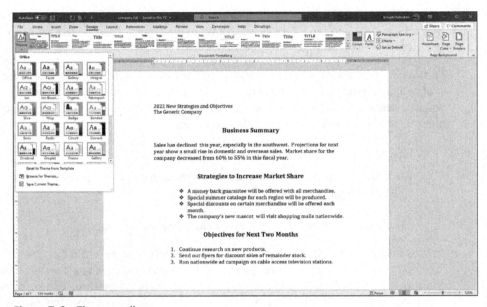

Figure 7-6   Themes gallery

Place the mouse pointer on a theme to preview how that theme affects the text in your document. When you select a theme, it is then applied to your document.

To refine the effect of the theme on the document, you can change the current style set. Click More at the bottom right of the Style Set gallery (just to the left of the Colors command on the ribbon) to view all the available style sets related to the currently selected theme. Place the mouse on a style set to see how it changes the text formatting in your document. Select a style set to apply it to your document.

As already mentioned, the Document Formatting group (on the Design tab) includes additional commands that enable you to make even finer refinements to how the currently selected theme and style set affect your document: Colors, Fonts, Paragraph Spacing, Effects, and Set As Default. The drop-down menus, such as Colors and Fonts, enable you to fine-tune the settings for the current theme and the currently applied style set (from the Style Set gallery). For example, if you select Colors, you see a gallery of color combinations. Place the mouse on one color set to see it previewed in the document. Select the color scheme when you find the one that works best for the current document.

You have control over paragraph spacing via the Paragraph Spacing command. The Paragraph Spacing gallery shows you the current style set selected in the Style Set gallery and provides access to built-in spacing such as Compact, Open, and Double. You can also preview each spacing scheme by placing the mouse on it.

If you want to change the font setting for the currently selected style set and theme, select Fonts and then make a selection in the Fonts gallery, as shown in Figure 7-7.

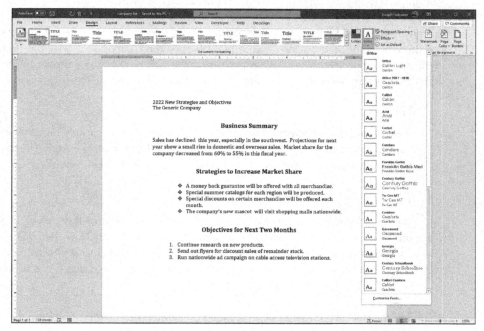

Figure 7-7   Fonts gallery

You have the option of creating your own style sets and your own themes. To create a new style set, you first modify the built-in styles that you applied to the parts of your document (such as headings, titles, and so on). See the "Understanding styles" section of this chapter for all the information on creating and modifying styles (even the built-in styles provided in the Styles gallery on the Home tab).

➤ For more about working with styles, such as those found in the Styles gallery, see "Understanding styles," p. 200.

After you modify and save the styles, go to the Design tab of the ribbon. Your changes appear as a style set in the Style Set gallery. To save this new style set as a permanent style set in the current theme, click the More button in the Style Set gallery. Select the Save As New Style Set command at the bottom of the gallery. The Save As A New Style Set dialog box opens. Be sure to save the style set in the Users*UserName*\\AppData\\Roaming\\Microsoft\\Quickstyles folder (the default folder for style sets). Type a name for the style set and click Save. The new style set appears in the Gallery. This style set is now available in the Style Set Gallery when working on a new or existing document.

You can also create custom themes; you simply modify the existing document theme (any theme you selected in the Theme gallery). To modify the current scheme, use the Colors, Fonts, Paragraph Spacing, and Effects drop-down menus to modify the current theme-formatting attributes. After you modify the theme, select the Themes command and then select Save Current Theme. The Save Current Theme dialog box opens. Supply a name for the new theme and then select the Save button. Now, when you open the Themes gallery via the Themes command, your newly created theme (and any other theme you create) appears in the gallery under the Custom heading. All the built-in themes appear under the Office heading.

TIP

If your new style set doesn't differ dramatically from the built-in style sets, and you are having trouble locating it in the Style Sets gallery, select the More button. The style sets that you created are listed under the Custom heading in the Style Sets gallery.

TIP

You can also create custom color sets and font sets. The Colors gallery (select Colors) provides a Customize Colors command, which opens the Create New Theme Colors. The Fonts gallery (select Fonts) provides the Customize Fonts command, which opens the Create New Theme Fonts dialog box. Edit the settings in these dialog boxes to create custom color and font settings for a theme.

Changing the style set or theme when working on a document changes the formatting attributes of the built-in Word styles (that you might have modified), as well as the styles you created. If you don't want to keep a custom style set or a custom theme, you can delete it. In the Style Set gallery, right-click the style set that you created and then select Delete from the shortcut menu. Select Yes to delete the style set.

Deleting a theme you created is just as straightforward; right-click the custom theme in the Themes gallery and then select Delete. Select Yes to confirm the deletion. The theme file you created is deleted, and the theme is removed from the Custom theme list in the gallery.

Creating headers and footers

In business documents such as reports, manuals, and even some correspondences, text and even images (such as a company logo) are repeated at each document page's top and/or bottom. And I'm probably safe in assuming that pretty much everyone has at some point had to create a multipage document that required page numbering on each page.

Headers and footers give you a way to include repeating information on each document page, such as a document title, the current date, or the page number. Headers and footers can also contain pictures and design elements. You can format text in a header or footer using the same formatting tools that you use for the text in the document itself.

Inside OUT

Conforming to a particular style manual

There are a number (meaning a lot) of different style guides out there (*The Chicago Manual of Style*, for instance). International style guides such as the ISO 2145 standards relate to the numbering of sections and subdivisions in a document. There are also standards for particular document types. For example, the *MLA Handbook for Writers of Research Papers* is often required for academic journal manuscripts. Many journalists follow the *Associated Press Stylebook*. These different manuals not only provide the overall organizational template for a particular document type, but they can also provide guidelines for specific parts of a document, such as footnotes and even how headers and footers are placed and formatted in a document. If you are writing a "formal" document that requires you to follow a particular style guide, consult the specific style guide before beginning your document. It is often easier to work with a document formatted appropriately from the beginning, rather than trying to make wholesale changes to the document after the fact just to comply with the style guide.

The header resides at the top of a page, and the footer resides at the bottom of a page. The header and footer areas are within the top and bottom margins of the document. Headers and footers cannot grow beyond the limits of the margins (they can't be on unprintable portions of the page). This means larger headers and footers—meaning a header or footer with many text lines or a large image such as a logo—steal line space from the regular text portion of the page.

How you use headers and footers can depend greatly on the overall structure of your document. For example, say that you have a report document with a title page. All the pages that follow the title page consist of the report details. It is common practice to avoid including headers and footers, page numbers, report titles, or draft numbers on the title page of a report (or any document).

You need different header/footer settings on the first page because you don't want to include the headers and footers that appear on the rest of the document pages. Word enables you to have different headers/footers on the first page of the document, including no headers or footers at all.

Another document structure issue that affects headers and footers arises when you want to bind a document with facing pages (where you have printed on both sides of the pages). Bound documents often use different headers and footers on the odd and even pages of the document. (Take a look at this book as an example.) Word has you covered when creating different odd and even page headers and footers.

Consider one more point related to headers and footers: When you're working with more complex documents, it is not uncommon to have different document parts that vary greatly in terms of layout, content, and purpose. For example, you could be working on a document that has a table of contents, the main body of the document, and then a bibliography or index.

Documents can be divided into sections. Sections (discussed in the next chapter) enable you to set different page layout settings, including headers and footers, for each of the sections. Because each section of the document can have its own set of headers and footers, you can give the table of contents its own headers/footers, the body of the document its own headers/footers, and so on.

➤ **For more about sections, see "Understanding sections," in Chapter 8, "Working with tables, columns, and sections."**

Inserting headers and footers

To insert a header, footer, or page number in your document, you use the Header and Footer commands on the ribbon's Insert tab (the Header & Footer group). After a header or footer has been placed in the document or section of a document, the Header & Footer Tools are activated on the ribbon. The Design tab provides all sorts of possibilities for modifying, navigating, and fine-tuning the header or footer. We talk about these tools shortly. First, take a look at how you insert a header or footer in a document.

To place a header in the header area, select the Insert tab of the ribbon and then select the Header command. The Header gallery (shown in Figure 7-8) provides several different header styles, including a blank header. Header styles make it easy for you to insert text into the header area. For example, the Sideline Header style provides placeholder text for the document. Other header styles, such as the Slice 1 style, makes it easy for you to create a header that includes a right-aligned page number. The Header gallery also provides the Edit Header and Remove Header commands.

After you select one of the header options in the gallery, the Header area appears at the top of the current page. Replace the placeholder text with your own text. If you select the blank header, type and format your text as needed in the Header area.

Placing a footer in the Footer area involves pretty much the same process as placing a header in the Header area. Select a footer style from the Footer gallery (open it by selecting the Footer command) and, when the insertion point appears in the Footer area, type and format your footer text as needed.

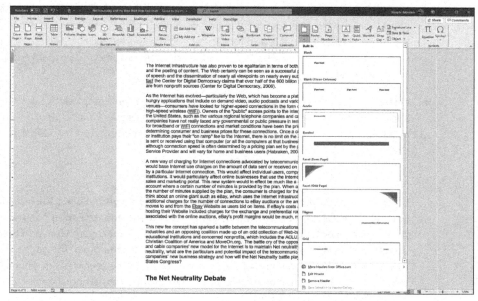

Figure 7-8   The Header gallery

The header and footer tools

When the insertion point is in the Header or the Footer area, the ribbon takes on the form of the contextual Header & Footer Tools Design tab. This special Header and Footer toolkit contains the following command groups:

- **Header & Footer:** This group provides the Header, Footer, and Page Number commands. These are the same commands found in the Header & Footer group on the ribbon's Insert tab. Earlier in this chapter, we discussed the Header and Footer commands (which place a header or footer). We look at the Page Number command later in this section.

- **Insert:** This group lets you insert items into the header and footer, including date and time information, Quick Parts, pictures (including online pictures), and clip art. The Document Info command enables you to quickly add document-creation information to the header or footer, such as the document's author (most likely, your name), the file name, and/or the file path. Inserting informational fields into a document's header or footer can help you keep track of the origin of a document and even sort out various drafts of the same document.

- **Navigation:** This group of commands enables you to jump between the header and footer in your document and navigate to a particular header or footer if you have a complex document with multiple headers or footers. An important command in this group is Link To Previous; it controls whether the current header or footer is linked to the previous header or footer in the document (when you have multiple sections in the document and, therefore, multiple headers and footers). If you have independent sections of a document, such as a document with a table of contents or bibliography, you probably do not want to link headers and footers.

- **Options:** This group provides the Different First Page, Different Odd & Even Pages, and Show Document Text check boxes. To have different headers and footers on the first page of the document (different from the rest of the document), select the Different First Page check box.

TIP

If you want to go "old school" with headers and footers, you can place the insertion point in the header or footer without using either the Header or Footer command (in the Header & Footer group). Make sure that you are in Print Layout view, and then double-click in the Header or Footer area (top or bottom margin of the page). You can then type the text for the header and footer and format the text as needed. Be advised that even the default header and footer settings include formatting: a center tab at 3.25 inches and a right tab at 6.5 inches.

- **Position:** This group enables you to set the distance for the header in relation to the top of the page and the footer from the bottom of the page (remember that this setting cannot place the header or footer into the unprintable portion of the margin, as dictated by your printer settings). This group also provides the Insert Alignment tab, which enables you to insert an alignment tab at the left, center, or right of the header or footer. Also, you can select a leader, such as a dot leader for the tab setting.

- **Close:** This group contains the Close Header and Footer command. It closes the Header or Footer area and returns the insertion point to your document text.

When you are working with headers and footers, note that the use of these commands depends on the following:

- The complexity of your document (such as the Different First Page and Different Odd & Even Pages commands)

- The number of headers and footers in the document (such as a document with sections where you need to move from header to header or footer to footer using the Previous and Next commands)

Regarding what you can place in your header and footer, the Insert group makes it easy for you to include information (such as the current date) or a picture (such as a logo). This group also makes it easy to quickly create informational headers and footers.

For example, suppose you need to insert your name (author), your company name, or other document property information (such as the file name or path of the document). In that case, you can take advantage of the fields provided by the Document Info command. The Document Property command on the Document Info menu offers many possibilities, including company, name, keywords, and category. Other potential sources of information that you can insert into a header or footer are items you have stored as an AutoText entry; you can select the Quick Parts command and then select from your various AutoText entries.

The Quick Parts command also opens the Building Blocks Organizer, which provides access to all default building blocks (including added AutoText entries and added Quick Parts). The Building Blocks Organizer contains some building blocks specifically designed for headers, footers, and page numbering.

Both the Quick Parts command and the Document Info command provide access to the Field dialog box, which enables you to insert additional fields into your header or footer. In Chapter 9, "Managing mailings and forms," we look more closely at fields as they relate to Word forms. For now, I want to stress that you can use some fields to great effect in headers and footers. Figure 7-9 shows the Field dialog box.

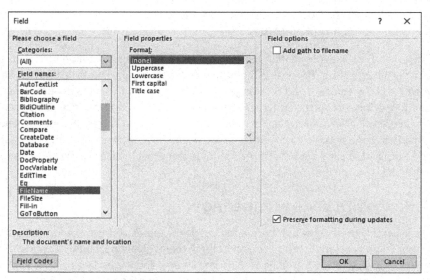

Figure 7-9   The Field dialog box

TIP

Inserting document property information into a header or footer isn't all that useful if you haven't entered any information into the document's properties. You can access the document properties via Backstage View. Select File, and then select Info. On the Backstage Info page, select the Properties heading (on the right side of the page), and then select Advanced Properties. This opens the Properties dialog box for the current document. You can add information associated with the document as needed in the provided fields. Click the OK button in the dialog box when you finish your additions.

As already mentioned, the Document Info menu provides access to useful fields such as Author, File Name, and File Path. You might want to insert other fields into a document, such as insert the PrintDate and SaveDate fields into a header or footer, to show you the last time (date) a file was printed or saved, respectively. The only place where you see a complete list of the fields available in Word is the Field dialog box.

The Field dialog box enables you to list fields by categories via the Categories drop-down menu. Three categories that are very useful in terms of document information are the Date And Time, Document Information, and User Information categories.

When you select a field in the Field dialog box, you also must select from options provided in the Field properties list. For example, if you select PrintDate as the field you want to insert into the header or footer, you also have to select a date format for the date. Or say that you select the Title field from the Document Information category. This field inserts information that you provided in the document properties.

You are inserting field information that is simple text, and the Field dialog box wants you to specify whether it should appear in the header or footer in a particular text format, such as uppercase or lowercase. Using fields in your header or footer to "tag" a document with important information such as the author, file name, and path is a good practice. Other people editing a document will always know the document's author if you have used the Author field. If you use the File Name and File Path fields, you can even find a document on your computer (or network) from a hard copy because the header or footer gives the file's name and location on your computer.

Working with page numbering

You can quickly place page numbers in the header or footer of the document using the Page Number command (on the ribbon's Insert tab). A menu gives you various options for the location of the page, such as Top Of Page, Bottom Of Page, and Page Margins. (Yes, you can place the page number in the margin or at the current position of the insertion point.)

When you select one of the placement options for the page number, such as Top Of Page or Bottom Of Page, a gallery of different page-numbering formats appears. You can also access more page number formats from Office.com by selecting More Page Numbers From Office.com.

You can modify the number format for your header and footer page numbers. Select the Page Number command (either on the Insert tab or on the Headers & Footers Tools tab if you are already in the header or the footer), and then select Format Page Numbers. The Page Number Format dialog box, shown in Figure 7-10, opens.

TIP

When you have text or field information in a header or footer, the Page Number command (from the ribbon's Insert tab or the Design tab of the Header & Footer Tools) deletes this text. For example, if you have your name and the file path in the footer, then when you select Page Numbering and Bottom Of Page, all the footer information is deleted when the page code is inserted. The remedy for this is to place the insertion point where you want the page number to appear (in relation to the other text or fields in the header or footer) and then use the Current Position command to place the page number. You can also use the Page field from the Field dialog box. Insert the field where you want the page number to appear, and format the field as needed.

Figure 7-10   The Page Number Format dialog box

Use the settings in the dialog box to change the number format using the Number Format drop-down menu. If you have chapters in your document, you can also have chapter numbers included along with the page number. (You specify the style used for your chapter titles to let Word know where the chapters start.) You can also choose to continue the page numbering from the previous section or use the Start At box to specify a number for the start of the page numbering.

Inserting pictures and charts

You can enhance your Word documents using pictures, icons, and SmartArt. Word also gives you options for inserting your own digital photos and makes it easy to insert pictures from online sources, including a large, royalty-free stock image library. Also, you can insert other graphics, such as shapes, SmartArt, charts, and icons, into your documents. As with the other

365 applications, Word offers some awesome tools for working with photos and other graphics. For example, the Live Layout shows you the position of your graphic in real time as you move or resize it. Alignment guides help you position an item, such as a photo, on the page. Options for formatting how text near the image is aligned are accessed with a single click on the Wrap Text button, which provides picture layout options; the Wrap Text button is available when a picture or other graphic is selected.

> ➤ **For a detailed overview of working with pictures and other graphics in Microsoft Office, see Chapter 4, "Using and creating graphics."**

Inserting a particular graphic or image is really just a matter of parking the insertion point in the document where you want to insert the item and then specifying the type of graphic—picture, clip art, SmartArt, and so on—that you want to insert. As already mentioned, you can use a variety of image sources, including digital photographs, scanned images, and content from online sources.

Word also gives you a robust set of image-adjustment and formatting tools. You can quickly adjust the brightness or contrast settings for a photo and change the color saturation or tone. The Picture Tools also provide picture styles and arrangement and sizing tools.

Inserting pictures

The Pictures command is in the Illustrations group, which resides on the ribbon's Insert tab. Selecting the Pictures command provides three options for inserting a picture:

- **This Device:** You can insert a digital picture that you have created using the This Device option.

- **Stock Images library:** You also can insert a picture from the new Stock Images library provided by Microsoft.

- **Online Pictures:** This option allows you to browse and search for pictures on the web.

In terms of using your own pictures (or images supplied to you), you can take advantage of many picture file formats in your Word documents. These are some of the image file formats Word supports:

- Portable Network Graphics (.png)

- CompuServe Graphics Interchange Format (GIF) (.gif)

- Encapsulated PostScript (.eps)

- Various paint programs (.pcx)

- Tagged Image File format (.tif)

- Windows bitmap (.bmp and .dib)

- JPEG file interchange format (.jpg)

- Microsoft meta files (.emf and .wmf)

To insert a picture from your computer (or OneDrive) into the current document, place the insertion point where you want to insert the picture and then select Pictures on the Insert tab. In the Pictures drop-down gallery, select This Device. The Insert Picture dialog box opens. It opens by default to the Picture folder (library) on your computer. Navigate to the folder that holds your picture file and then select the file. Click Insert to insert the image into the Word document (or double-click the image to select and insert it).

When a picture is selected on a page (such as the picture you just inserted), the Picture Tools appear on the ribbon. Figure 7-11 shows an inserted picture file (a .jpg file) and the Picture Tools provided on the ribbon.

The Picture Tools enable you to adjust the picture (such as its brightness and contrast), select a picture style, arrange multiple pictures on the page, and crop and size the selected picture. The Picture Tools groups are as follows:

- **Adjust:** This group provides tools for altering and fine-tuning the picture settings. You can correct the contrast, make color corrections, add artistic effects, and even remove portions of the photo's background. You can preview the adjustment before applying it to the picture and compress a picture in a document. (It is saved in the document as a .jpg file.) The overall Word file size is more accommodating if you share the file online or via email.

- **Picture Styles:** This group offers frame formats such as Metal Frame, Center Shadow Rectangle, and Relaxed Perspective White. Place the mouse on a style to preview the style on the picture. This group also enables you to select the color of the picture border and add effects to the picture.

Figure 7-11   The Picture Tools enable you to adjust pictures.

- **Accessibility**: The Alt Text option allows you to create alternative text descriptions for images in a document that are used by screen readers.

- **Arrange:** You can layer multiple images with this group (using commands such as Bring Forward and Send Backward). You also can group graphics, align images (left, center, right, top, middle, bottom), and rotate and flip pictures. The Position and Wrap Text commands reside in this group as well.

- **Size:** This group provides Height and Width spin boxes for sizing a picture. You can also use the Crop command to crop the image as needed.

➤ **For more about manipulating pictures and other graphics in the Office applications, see Chapter 4.**

When you have finished working with the Picture Tools, click outside the picture or graphic. This returns the ribbon to its "normal" set of tabs and command group.

TIP

You can remove all the picture-formatting changes you have made using the various tools provided by the Picture Tools (except for Change Picture and Compress Picture). Click the Reset Picture command (in the Adjust group).

Also, notice that when a picture is selected on a page, the Layout Options icon appears in the upper-right corner of the image. This option provides quick access to the layout options (in relation to the surrounding text) for the picture or other graphic. By default, the picture's layout is in line with the text; you can access other possibilities by selecting one of the options provided.

Inserting stock images and online pictures

Word also allows you to quickly access a seemingly endless supply of stock images (supplied by Microsoft) and online pictures from the web that you can use to enhance your documents. Chapter 4 provides more details on sourcing your images and the difference between the Stock Images library and pictures sourced from the web.

You always need to keep in mind copyright and the rights of the owners of images you source from the web. I am a big fan of the (relatively) new Stock Images library that is provided for use with the Microsoft 365 applications because it appears you can use these images worry-free (at least in terms of fair use).

To insert an image from the Stock Images library, place the insertion point in your document at the place where you want to add the image. On the ribbon's Insert tab, select Picture, Stock Images. The Stock Images browser opens, as shown in Figure 7-12. The library images are divided into different types, including Images, Icons, Cutout People, Stickers, and Illustrations. Each of these different types of pictures is further divided into subcategories.

Figure 7-12   The Stock Images browser

Browse the Stock Image library until you find the image (or images) you want to insert. Select an image or images; the number of images that will be inserted appear on the Insert button in the lower-right part of the browser. When you are ready to insert the image or images, select the Insert command. The image (or images) will be downloaded and inserted into your document. Multiple images will be inserted into the document in the order you selected them in the Browser. You can use the Picture Format tab on the ribbon to adjust picture settings and arrange multiple pictures using the Arrange Group commands.

Online Pictures is another image source option provided by Word (and the other Microsoft 365 apps). The Online Pictures browser uses Microsoft's Bing search tool to locate the type of image you want to insert into your document. Select Pictures on the Insert tab of the ribbon and then select Online Pictures. The Online Pictures browser will open. Click in the search box at the top of the browser window, enter keywords for the search, and then press the Enter.

Thumbnail images of pictures that Bing located online will appear in the Search browser. By default, Bing only shows you images licensed under Creative Commons, which is a licensing system that allows media creators to protect their intellectual property while also sharing their work with others who are not using the images or other media for profit.

> **NOTE**
>
> **If you would like to know more about how Creative Common licensing works, check out the Creative Commons website at http://creativecommons.org/.**

The Image Search browser also allows you to show all web results from your search. Be advised that you may be using material that is protected under copyright or trademark if you use images and media that are not licensed under Creative Commons. You can scroll through the thumbnails using the up and down arrows on the right of the Image Search browser. When you have located the image you want to use, select the image and then click Insert. You can then modify the image as needed using the various Picture Format tools.

NOTE

You can also insert charts and worksheets created in Microsoft Excel into your Word documents. See Appendix A, "Office application integration," for more about sharing information between Office applications such as Word and Excel.

The Online Pictures browser also makes it easy for you to access images or other media that you have saved to your OneDrive. You can access OneDrive directly from the Online Pictures browser. Select the OneDrive icon in the lower-left side of the browser. The drive will open and provide access to any folders stored on your OneDrive. When you select a folder containing images, thumbnails are provided. To insert an image, select the appropriate thumbnail and then select Insert.

Inserting a chart

You can insert many other types of graphics into your Word documents, including shapes, icons, 3D Models, and SmartArt (all discussed in Chapter 4). You can also insert charts, which allow you to visually present statistics or other numerical information in the form of a picture. Chart types include column, line, pie, bar, doughnut, and radar charts. Select Chart (in the Illustrations group on the Insert tab) to insert a chart at the insertion point. The Insert Chart dialog box opens (see Figure 7-13).

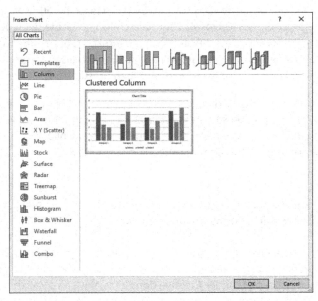

Figure 7-13   The Insert Chart dialog box

Select a chart type in the All Charts list. You can then select one of the specific chart types, such as Line or Pie. Click OK to insert that chart into the Word document. An Excel worksheet also opens that provides the datasheet for your chart (see Figure 7-14). You can change the category and series names (the column and row headings in the Excel sheet) and the data on the worksheet until they contain the information required for your chart.

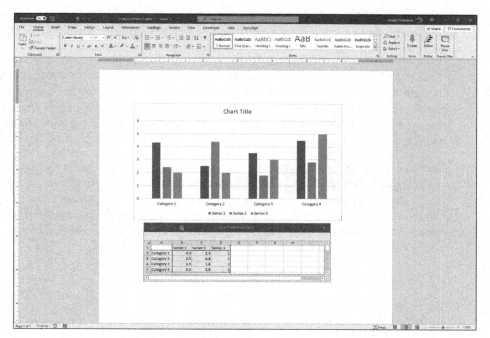

Figure 7-14   Edit the table data to create your chart.

When you finish making your changes to the Excel data table, you can close the Excel window (you don't need to save the table data). Whenever the chart is selected in your document, the ribbon provides chart tools in the form of a Chart Design tab and Format tab. The Chart Design tab provides access to the data sheet you created for the chart. Use the Edit Data command (in the Data group on the Chart Design tab) to open the data sheet. The Chart Design tab also enables you to change the chart type, add chart elements, and select one of the built-in chart styles.

> ➤ **For best practices related to using and selecting charts and entering chart data, see Chapter 14, "Enhancing worksheets with charts."**

The Format tab of the Chart Tools enables you to change shape styles and select WordArt styles for the text labels in the chart. You can use the Height and Width spin boxes to set the size for the chart.

Creating simple charts within Word is a fairly straightforward process. When you are working with more complex sets of data, you might want to use Excel to create the chart. You can then copy and paste the chart into Word (see Appendix A for more about integrating Word and Excel).

Integrating text and images

One of the most important aspects of using pictures, clip art, or charts in Word is integrating the image with the text in the document. This primarily relates to sizing the picture or clip art file and determining how you want the text to wrap in relation to the image.

You can click any image and use the sizing handles that appear on the image to change its size. To maintain the height/width ratio of the image (so that you don't stretch or distort the image), use the sizing handles on the corners of the image and drag diagonally. If you would rather change the size of the image more precisely, you can use the Height and Width spin boxes on the Size group (you can find this group on the Picture Tools and the Chart Tools).

For more precise control of the height and width of an image, you can use the spin boxes in the Size group. This group also provides cropping capabilities. For even more control over an image and to lock the aspect ratio (the height/width) of an image, you can take advantage of the Layout dialog box, particularly its Size tab. To open the Layout dialog box from the Picture Tools (with the Format tab selected), click the dialog box launcher on the Size group. Figure 7-15 shows the Layout dialog box.

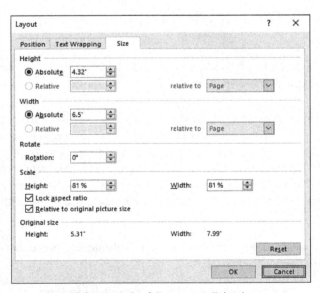

Figure 7-15   The Size tab of the Layout dialog box

You can use the settings on the Size tab to adjust the height and width and to rotate the image. When you select Lock Aspect Ratio (which is typically set by default), any change to the height or width results in a change to the other measurement; for example, if you change the height, the width changes based on the aspect ratio.

Another aspect of integrating the image with the text relates to the text wrapping you set. By default, the wrapping style is set to In Line With Text. This means that the image is placed between the margins, and text appears over and below the image. You can use the Wrap Text command in the Arrange group of the Picture Tools tab and the Chart Tools tab to change how the text wraps in relation to the image. You can use the Square setting to have the text frame run along the top, bottom, left, and right of the image.

You can also use the Behind Text or In Front Of Text settings to select the text to appear in front of or behind the image, respectively. These settings are available on the Text Wrapping tab of the Layout dialog box or by selecting the Layout Options button, which appears next to the top-right corner of any selected image.

Changing the document display

Word gives you several viewing possibilities as you work on your documents in the application window. All the viewing options are available on the ribbon's View tab. The Document Views group provides commands for the different document views, such as Read Mode, Print Layout, and Draft. The Zoom group enables you to access the Zoom dialog box and quickly zoom to 100%.

The Window group enables you to arrange the open document windows to view two documents side by side. Figure 7-16 shows the ribbon's View tab and a document in the Print Layout view with Multiple Pages selected in the Zoom group.

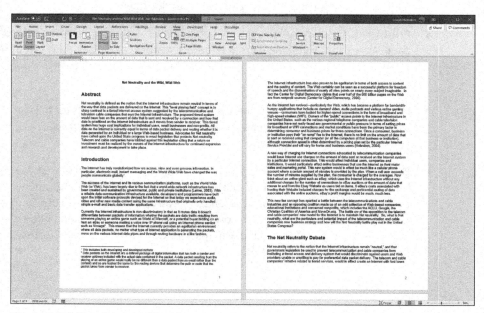

Figure 7-16   The ribbon's View tab

Using the different document views to your advantage can help you visualize and create great-looking Word documents. The following list provides an overview of the different document views in the Document Views group of the View tab.

TIP

You can quickly change the document view using the View icons on the Word status bar (on the far right). Icons for Read Mode, Print Layout, and Web Layout are provided. You can also use the Zoom slider on the status bar to zoom in and out on the document.

TIP

The View menu available in the Read Mode enables you to access the Navigation pane and show comments in the document.

- **Read Mode:** The Read Mode is designed to make reading a document easy, whether you are running Word on your personal computer or on a smaller-footprint device such as a tablet or smartphone. Read Mode provides a "magazine" format for the document, dividing the text into easy-to-read columns of information. Navigational arrows move through each screen of the document (both forward and backward). The ribbon is not available in Read Mode, but a menu containing three commands—File, Tools, and View—is available in the upper left of the Read Mode window. The File command takes you to the Backstage. The Tools command provides access to tools such as the Find command and the Search With Bing command. The View command provides a list of commands such as Edit Document, Navigation pane, and Show Comments. It also offers the Column Width, Page Color, and Layout commands, which enable you to fine-tune the Read Mode environment and make it easier to view and read your document.

- **Print Layout:** Here, you can view your document exactly as it appears on the printed page. Also, you can view headers and footers, margins, and other page layout settings. You can fine-tune graphic placement as well because pictures and clip art appear as they print in this view.

- **Web Layout:** This view is designed for creating HTML documents for the web. It does not show margins or other layout attributes; instead, it provides a workspace much like what appears in a browser window when you view a web page.

- **Outline:** This view (select Outline in the Views group) is designed so that you can see the document in an outline format. Headings appear as Level 1 of the outline; text that follows each heading displays as secondary-level body text. You can use Outline view to rearrange text in a document by moving a heading and its associated body text. Outline view is also designed for working with master documents, which are discussed in Chapter 10, "Creating special documents."

- **Draft:** This view (select Draft in the Views group) displays character and paragraph formatting that you place in the document; however, it does not display the document headers and footers or show graphics in the document as they print. It is an excellent view to find page breaks that you have placed in the document and find (and perhaps delete) section breaks that you have assigned to a document.

Each view provides a different way of looking at your document. Most people create the initial draft of a document in Print Layout or Draft view. To organize the document text, you might switch to the Outline view, particularly if you are working with a larger document containing headings and different document sections. Read Mode enables you to easily read the document and concentrate on the content rather than the layout.

Using the navigation pane

Although it is not designated as a full-fledged view (as are Print Layout and Draft), the Navigation pane enables you to navigate through a document using search results, document headings, or page thumbnails. You open the Navigation pane by selecting the Navigation Pane check box in the Show group (on the ribbon's View tab). To navigate using the Search document box in the Navigation pane, type a keyword or phrase in the box and then press Enter or click the Search icon. Select Results to view the occurrences of the keyword or phrase in the document. You can quickly jump to each result of the search by selecting the occurrences listed.

To take advantage of the Headings feature in the Navigation pane, you need to use the built-in Heading styles that Word provides to format the headings in the document (such as Heading 1, Heading 2, and so on). When the Headings feature is selected in the Navigation pane, you can quickly jump to a particular heading in the document by selecting that heading.

Figure 7-17 shows the Navigation pane with the Headings feature selected. If you didn't use the Word built-in styles (in the Styles gallery on the Home tab), you can still use the Search box or navigate through the document page by page by selecting Pages in the Navigation pane. To open the Navigation pane, select the Navigation Pane check box in the Show group (of the ribbon's View tab).

When the Navigation pane is active in the Word application window, the Collapse/Expand toggle button appears when you place the mouse just to the left of one of your document headings (headings formatted using the built-in heading styles). Click the toggle to collapse all the text that is subordinate to the heading. In effect, this hides the text that follows that heading in the document (each heading in the document controls the subordinate text that follows it).

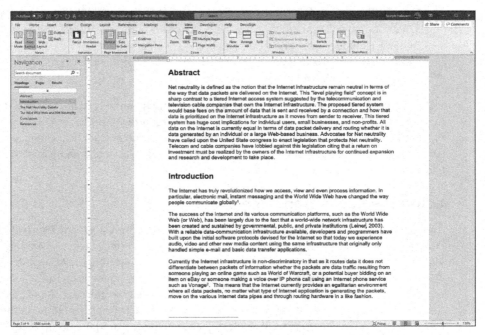

Figure 7-17   The Navigation pane

TIP

Another useful view-related tool is the View Side By Side command in the Window group. It enables you to view two different documents side by side. By default, the two documents have their scrolling synchronized. You can click the Synchronous Scrolling command to scroll independently through each document. You can then drag and drop text between the documents and compare the documents as needed.

Now, if you move the heading in the document (that is, when you drag it to a new location), the subordinate text goes with it. Expand the heading (with the toggle button) to view the text. This feature is similar to what happens when you expand or collapse text when you are working in Outline view (discussed in the next section). When you have finished working with the Navigation pane, click the Close button to remove it from the application window.

Using the Outline view

Outline view is probably one of the most misunderstood of the view-related features. Outline view is much more than just a tool for creating simple outlines; it is a different way of organizing a complex document. Outline view enables you to quickly move a heading and its associated text to a new location and also allows you to promote or demote an item to a different level in the outline hierarchy. This makes it easy to manage the headings and subheadings in the document.

You can start a new document in Outline view, which helps you build the basic organization of the document. For example, you can brainstorm the main headings and subheadings that appear in the document. You can then build the document as you would an outline by typing the text that goes under each heading (or subheading). You can use Outline view to rearrange the information in the document as needed.

To start a new document in Outline view (or work with an existing document), select the View tab and then select Outline in the Views group. An Outlining tab appears on the ribbon and gives you the Outline Tools group. When you type the first item in your document, it is assigned Level 1 in the outline hierarchy. You can use the Level drop-down menu or the Promote or Demote buttons to change the level of an item in the outline. Be advised that a Level 1 item is assigned the Heading 1 style. Level 2 is assigned the Heading 2 style. Nine heading levels are available in Outline view, and a Body Text level is assigned to text that is not a heading (the document's actual content). Figure 7-18 shows a document created in Outline view. The document currently contains three levels: Level 1 headings, Level 2 headings, and body text.

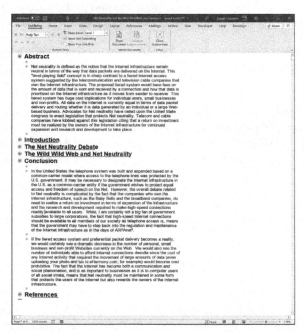

Figure 7-18   In Outline view, you can create and arrange a document's content.

When you are working with the document in Outline view, you can quickly select a heading and its associated subheadings and body text by selecting the Outline level button to the left of the heading. You then drag the heading and all the associated text to a new location in the document. If you want to concentrate on just the Level 1 headings, you can click the Show Level drop-down menu and select Level 1. This makes rearranging the document by heading easy because you are not distracted by subheadings or body text. The Move Up, Move Down, Expand, and Collapse buttons (just below the Level drop-down menu) move selected outline items up or down in the outline and expand or collapse headings and associated text, respectively.

By design, Outline view helps you concentrate on the document's organizational structure. It enables you to concentrate on specific document levels and makes it easy to move entire parts of the document based on headings. When you have finished working in the Outline view, select the Close Outline View command, which takes you to the Print Layout view, where you can finalize your document by enhancing it with pictures, charts, or other graphics.

Splitting the document window

Another useful view-related tool is the capability to split the current document into two panes. This enables you to scroll to a different part of the same document in the different panes. You can then use two panes to drag and drop information from one part of the document into another. Remember that changes you make in either of the split panes affect the document.

To split the document screen into two panes, select the Split command (in the Zoom group of the View tab). Use the mouse to position the split in the document, and then click the mouse to place the split.

Each of the separate panes can be treated as a separate document. You can use Zoom to change the zoom level of each pane independently, and you can use all the other Word tools as needed in each of the panes. When you have finished working in the split document window, select Remove Split in the Window group to remove the splitter bar from the document.

Using the Editor

Even a document that is designed and well-laid out will appear amateurish if it is not error-free. It's difficult for someone to take your information seriously if you have spelling errors, grammar issues, or other errant typos and mistakes. Word provides the Editor, which is designed to ferret out errors in your text. These flagged errors are not limited to misspelled words, and the Editor feature is much more than just a simple spell checker. The Editor does check for spelling and grammar areas, but it also helps improve the document by suggesting refinements. These refinements relate to such "readability" issues as clarity, conciseness, punctuation, and vocabulary.

To open the Editor from the ribbon's Home tab, select Editor (in the Editor group). You don't have to wait until you have finished creating your document to open the Editor. The Editor proofs your document as you type and automatically flags spelling and grammar errors as you work with your document. Spelling errors are flagged with a red wavy underscore, and grammar errors are flagged with a double blue underscore. If you like, you can right-click spelling and grammar errors to access a shortcut menu that provides suggested spellings and grammar fixes. You can use this method to correct errors on the fly, or you might find it more efficient to correct them collectively by running the Editor after you have entered all your text.

You can change the Editor's default settings associated with the automatic spelling- and grammar-checking features (meaning, turn them off). Click File to go to Backstage view, and then select Options. In the Word Options window, select Proofing. Deselect the check boxes on these two options: Check Spelling As You Type and Mark Grammar Errors As You Type, which disables both. To return to the document window, click OK.

TIP

As you become more familiar with the type of errors the Editor flags using the spelling, grammar, and refinements default settings, you can fine-tune these settings to suit your writing better. The Word Proofing Options (in the Backstage, select Options, Proofing) allow you to turn off spelling and grammar as you type and also allow you to select (or deselect) refinement options. The refinements include all sorts of options related to grammar, informal language, and slang. Inclusiveness options can also be selected, which flags age, gender, and race bias in your writing. The Refinement settings (both default and optional) can be opened by selecting Settings in the Word Options Proofing window. You can quickly access all these settings from the Editor pane by selecting the Settings icon.

Running the Editor

Waiting to run the Editor on a document until you have finished composing it enables you to concentrate on getting your thoughts down without interruption. You can then have the Editor check the entire document. You can open the Editor from the Editor command on the Home tab. The ribbon's Review tab also provides access to the Editor command and the other proofing tools—the Thesaurus and the Word Count commands.

When you start the editor," your errors are listed in the Editor task pane, which appears on the right side of the Word document window. This task pane provides the number of total suggestions the Editor has flagged and breaks down the corrections into Spelling and Grammar errors. The Refinements are broken down into five categories: Clarity, Conciseness, Formality, Punctuation, Conventions, and Vocabulary.

To run the Editor, select the Editor command on the Home tab or the Review tab. The Editor task pane opens (see Figure 7-19). Words that are flagged as misspelled can be reviewed by selecting the Spelling box under the Editor's Correction heading.

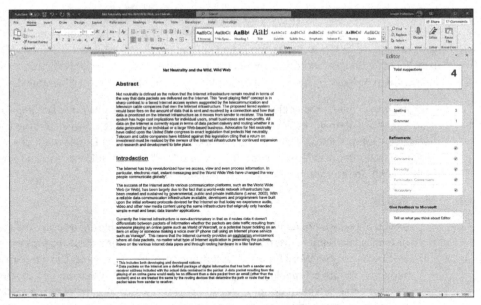

Figure 7-19   The Editor checks spelling, grammar, and other refinements in your document.

Once you select Spelling, the Editor plane becomes the Spelling pane. It shows the first spelling error found in the document and includes a list of suggested spellings (for the misspelled word) and synonyms for the currently flagged word. Select a suggestion to correct the misspelling. This will correct your document and move you to the next flagged word.

Navigation buttons on the right top of the Editor pane provide you with the ability to move forward and backward in the document as you peruse the various flagged misspellings in the document. If a flagged word is actually correct (such as someone's name that has been flagged). You can choose from Ignore Once, Ignore All, or Add To Dictionary to bypass the word and leave it as it is currently spelled. When you have completed the Editor's check of the document's spelling, a message box will open stating that you have finished reviewing the Editor's suggestions. Select OK to close the message box.

Grammar errors can also be accessed by selecting Grammar in the Editor pane. The Grammar checker will walk you through the document and show you suspected grammar errors. Suggestions will be provided for flagged content, and you can choose the suggestion and move on to the next grammar error. You also have the option of ignoring flagged, suspected errors by clicking Ignore. Select the Stop Checking For This option if you don't want the flagged issue to be included in future grammar checks.

You can also review the refinements suggested for the document. Select a refinement category that contains flagged items, such as Conciseness or Formality. As with the spelling and grammar check, the Editor will walk you through the list of potential issues. For example, let's say you have written a rather formal document and use the contraction "doesn't." By default, the Formality tracker will flag this as informal and suggest that you change "doesn't" to "does not." You can select the suggested fix in the Editor window, or you can choose to ignore the flagged item by selecting Ignore Once. You can use the navigation arrows at the top of the Editor task pane to navigate the document as needed. When you have finished using the Editor to comb through all the spelling, grammar, and refinements errors, you can close the editor by clicking the Close button at the top-right part of the pane.

Using the Thesaurus

The Thesaurus gives you a tool to find synonyms for the words in your document. Synonyms are words that mean the same thing. Because the Thesaurus can generate a list of synonyms for nearly any word in your document, you can avoid the repetitive use of a particular descriptive adjective (such as *excellent*) and add some depth to the vocabulary in your document.

Click a word in your document and then click the Thesaurus command in the Proofing group. The Thesaurus task pane opens on the right side of the Word window. To replace the word with a synonym, place the mouse on the synonym in the synonym list and then click the drop-down menu arrow that appears to the right of the synonym. In the menu that appears, click Insert.

If you prefer to forgo using the Thesaurus task pane for synonyms, you can view a shortlist of synonyms for a selected word by right-clicking the word. Point at the Synonyms command on the shortcut menu, and a list of synonyms for the word appears. Click one of the words provided to replace the word in the document.

> TIP
>
> **If you want to see a list of synonyms for one of the words that appears in the Thesaurus task pane, click that word.**

Using the Search feature

If you want information about a particular word or phrase in your document, you can take advantage of the intelligent Search feature. The Search feature provides the Search box at the top of the Word application window, and you can look up information on the web without exiting Word. You can also use the Find feature by right-clicking a word in your document. When you right-click a word (or selected phrase) in your document and then select the Search command, the Search pane will open on the right side of the Word (or Excel or PowerPoint) application window. Typically, the Search pane provides you with a definition of the word and provides additional information sourced from the web pertaining to the selected word.

CHAPTER 7

NOTE

The Review tab of the ribbon also offers a Language group that provides a Translate command. You can use it to translate selected text (or the whole document) into another language. A single document can also contain translations in multiple languages. The Translate feature now provides access to more than 70 languages.

Working with Quick Parts

As we create documents, we are always looking for shortcuts and timesavers that help us work more efficiently. The Quick Parts feature gives you access to premade document-building blocks—your own AutoText entries, document properties, and Word fields. Inserting often-used document parts, information, or words and phrases saves you time and keeps information consistent in your document or documents.

So, what is a building block compared to an AutoText entry? Building blocks are any words, text lines, paragraphs, or even entire pages that you save that are meant to help you quickly enter often-used items into your documents. Word provides many building blocks, such as different headers and footers, page-numbering formats, and even text boxes and watermarks. You can add building blocks as needed and then access your building blocks in the Building Blocks Organizer. Building blocks are organized in galleries. These galleries include possibilities such as cover pages, headers, and tables, among others.

AutoText entries are a type of building block; however, you can insert AutoText entries into a document more quickly than a building block, and the entries are saved in a specific AutoText gallery. Think of the difference between AutoText entries and building blocks as being practical rather than technical.

I recommend that you reserve AutoText for words and phrases such as company names, letter closings, and the like—short text entries that you use often. Save the building blocks for more complex items that you occasionally insert—items such as long paragraphs, a particular page type (such as a cover page), or a special table.

Creating and inserting an AutoText entry

To create an AutoText entry, select the text in the document you want to save as the AutoText entry. Select the ribbon's Insert tab and then select the Quick Parts command in the Text group. On the Quick Parts menu, point at AutoText and then select Save Selection To AutoText Gallery. The Create New Building Block dialog box opens (see Figure 7-20).

In the dialog box, provide a name for the new AutoText entry (a name based on the text content is provided by default). You can also choose options related to the entry, such as whether to insert the content only or to insert the content in a separate paragraph or on a separate page. Click OK to create the entry.

To insert an AutoText entry in your document, place the insertion point where you want to place the entry. Select the Quick Parts command on the ribbon's Insert tab and then hover the mouse on AutoText. Select the entry you want to place in the document from the choices provided in the AutoText gallery.

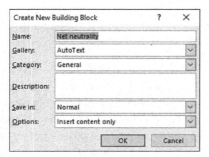

Figure 7-20   The Create New Building Block dialog box

Creating and inserting building blocks

Creating a building block is similar to creating an AutoText entry. Select the text, table, header, footer, or other object that you want to serve as the building block. Select the ribbon's Insert tab and then select Quick Parts. On the Quick Parts menu, select Save Selection To Quick Part Gallery. The Create New Building Block dialog box opens (refer to Figure 7-20).

> **TIP**
>
> **You can provide an optional description for the new entry in the Create New Building Block dialog box. This can be useful if you end up with several AutoText or building block entries that have similar names.**

Provide a name for the new building block. You can also select the gallery and category for the building block. More importantly, you can control the options related to how the building block will be inserted into the document via the Options drop-down menu.

Use the Insert Content Only option if the building block contains only text you want to insert into other paragraphs (much like an AutoText entry). The building block is then formatted the same as the surrounding text.

Use the Insert Content In Its Own Paragraph option if you are creating a building block with specific formatting or a special building block such as a table. This maintains the formatting of the block. Select the Insert Content In Its Own Page option if you are creating a building block that consists of a page such as a cover page (or a number of pages, such as front matter for a book). This places the building block into the document as a new page or pages. When you have finished selecting the various options, click OK to create the building block.

When you want to insert a building block you created into a document, you insert it from the Quick Parts menu (if you used the General category when you built the building block). Select Quick Parts and then select the building block from the menu.

You can open the Building Blocks Organizer from the Quick Parts menu when you want to use building blocks provided by Word or when you want to peruse the available building blocks (including AutoText and building blocks you have created). Figure 7-21 shows the Building Blocks Organizer.

You can insert building blocks from the organizer (select the building block and then click Insert). You can also manage your building blocks by editing their properties and even deleting unwanted building blocks. To change the text or other objects in a building block, you can insert the building block into a document and modify it as needed. You can then save it to the Building Block gallery using the same name and properties. You are asked whether you want to redefine the building block; click Yes, and the building block is modified.

Obviously, building blocks can save you a lot of time and add consistency (in terms of content) to your Word documents. If you create several building blocks, remember to use the appropriate gallery and category for each building block, to help you keep the library of text blocks organized.

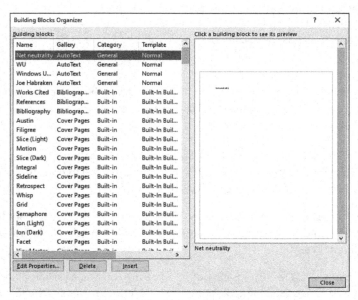

Figure 7-21   The Building Blocks Organizer dialog box

Configuring AutoCorrect

AutoCorrect has remained fairly consistent in terms of its configuration and function, and in Word, it still automatically corrects commonly misspelled words, including words that you add to it. It also corrects issues such as initial caps, automatically capitalizes the first letter of the first word in a sentence, and automatically capitalizes the names of days of the week.

You can access the AutoCorrect dialog box (see Figure 7-22) from the Word Backstage. Select File and then Options. In the Word Options window, select Proofing and then click the Auto-Correct Options button.

You can add entries to the Replace Text As You Type list. In the Replace box, enter a word as you misspell it. In the With box, enter the correct spelling of the word. To add the entry to the Auto-Correct list, click Add.

You can also access settings related to AutoFormat, such as replacing straight quotes with smart quotes, on the AutoFormat tab of the AutoCorrect dialog box. Other options, such as automatic bulleted lists and formatting list items identically, are accessed on the AutoFormat As You Type tab.

Figure 7-22   The AutoCorrect dialog box

Understanding styles

When you create Word documents that contain many different formatting attributes for the various headings, special paragraphs, and other text items you create, it makes sense to take advantage of styles. A style is a grouping of formatting attributes identified by a style name. Styles can contain text-formatting attributes, such as bold and 14-point, and can also contain paragraph-formatting attributes such as indents and other alignment settings (such as Center or Justify).

The great thing about using styles to format your text is that when you modify the style itself, the modifications will be applied to all the text that has already been assigned that style. For example, if you have used a style for all the headings in your document and decide that you want the headings to be formatted in bold (along with the other formatting contained in the heading style), you simply modify the style to include the bold attribute.

Word provides Quick Styles, which are predesigned styles. Quick Styles, or just built-in styles, if you prefer, come in families or sets of styles to provide consistency in look and formatting when you use them to format the various items in a document, such as headings, titles, and quotes. These style families are called style sets. You can change the style set currently used in the document on the Design tab. The Design tab also provides access to the Themes command, which enables you to change the document's current theme. For more about themes and style sets, see "Formatting with themes," earlier in this chapter.

Although you might think of styles as formatting that is reserved for the formatting of headings, titles, and other special text that you want to stand out in your document, styles are used to format lists and tables. For example, a multilevel list contains different levels, such as an outline; each sublevel is indented below its parent level, and a numbering system denotes parent levels and sublevels. For example, the primary level might be designated with the number 1, whereas the first sublevel is 1.1, the second is 1.2, and so on. You can create a numbered list and modify the formatting and level designations. This new list format can then be saved as a new list style.

Styles help with table formatting, too. The Table Tools Layout tab has a gallery of table styles, or you can create your own.

Clearly, styles can help you consistently format the text and other objects in your documents, and you have the freedom to create, modify, and delete your own styles if you want. Word provides various tools that you use when working with styles. For example, you can view a document's styles in the Styles dialog box, which is opened using the dialog box launcher in the Styles group on the Home tab of the ribbon. The Styles dialog box then provides access to other tools, such as the Style Inspector and the Manage Styles dialog box, which allow you to inspect styles and manage styles, respectively.

TIP

To create a list style based on a modified multilevel list, place the insertion point in the list and then click the Multilevel List icon in the Paragraph group on the ribbon's Home tab. Select Define New List Style in the gallery. The Define New List Style dialog box enables you to specify the settings for the new style and apply the style to the current document and/or all the documents based on the current template.

Using the Styles gallery

You can apply Quick Styles to selected text or a paragraph (remember that Word considers even a single-line heading to be a paragraph). The Quick Styles reside in a style gallery in the Styles group of the ribbon's Home tab.

After you specify the text that you want to format with the Quick Style, place the mouse pointer on any of the available styles to preview the style's formatting (on your text). To view additional Quick Styles in the current set, use the arrows to the right of the Quick Style gallery. You can also click the More button (just below the arrows) to expand the gallery so that you can see more of the Quick Styles in one view.

If you want to use a different set of styles in the current document, navigate to the ribbon's Design tab. Select the More button on the Style Set gallery (in the Document Formatting group) to see all the style sets available, including the style set used in the current document and the various built-in styles sets (see Figure 7-23).

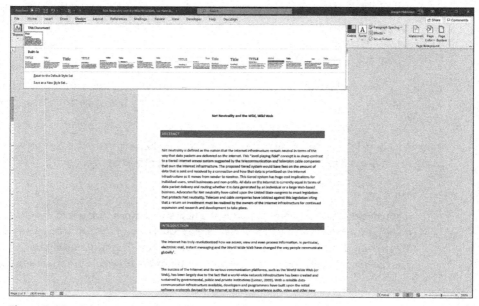

Figure 7-23   Select a new style set.

CAUTION

The Quick Styles that you have assigned to your document's text are affected (in terms of their formatting attributes, such as the fonts and font colors used) when you change the theme or style set for your document. If you plan to use themes, style sets, and Quick Styles, assign the theme to the document and/or style set before you begin to create it; then select the appropriate Quick Styles for each text item as needed (such as a heading, title, or body text).

If you place the mouse pointer on any of the style sets listed, you get a preview of how the built-in styles that you have already used in your document will look when you apply the new style set. You can also reset your document to the style set used by the current template (which, in many cases, is the Normal template); this also resets all the Quick Styles to their defaults if you have modified any of them.

TIP

If you have modified the built-in styles in your document and want to save these changes in a new style set, select Save As A New Style Set in the Style Set Gallery. Provide a name for the new style set in the Save As A New Style Set dialog box. The new style set appears in the Custom list when you expand the Style Set Gallery with the More button.

Creating styles

You can create your own styles quickly and easily by example. Apply font- and paragraph-formatting attributes to selected text. The text can be a single-line heading or an entire paragraph of text. Any of the font-formatting attributes, such as bold, italic, font color, font size, and even font type, are fair game for your style, as are paragraph-formatting attributes related to alignment, line spacing, indents, borders, and shading.

When you have the text formatted, click the More button in the Styles group (on the Home tab) and select New Style. The Create New Style From Formatting dialog box opens, as shown in Figure 7-24.

Provide a name for the new style in the Name box and then click OK. The new style appears in the Quick Style gallery. You can apply it to your document text as needed.

TIP

If you decide that you want to modify the new style before saving it to the Quick Style gallery, click Modify in the Create New Style From Formatting dialog box, and a larger Create New Style From Formatting dialog box appears. The larger dialog box enables you to change the various formatting attributes of the style before you save the style.

Figure 7-24   Create a new style from formatting.

Editing styles

You can edit any style in the document, including the built-in style provided by the current template and any styles that you have created. A quick way to view all the styles available in the current document and access a particular style for editing is to open the Styles window (click the Styles window launcher on the edge of the Styles group).

The Style window lists all the styles in the document (see Figure 7-25). If you want to see a preview of the style's formatting attributes, click the Show Preview check box at the bottom of the Styles window.

You can modify a style from the Style window in two ways. You can modify it by example or edit the style's formatting attributes manually.

To modify the style by example, reformat text that has been assigned the style with the attributes you want in the modified version of the style. Click the drop-down menu arrow next to the style you want to modify (in the Style window) and select Update (*style name*) To Match Selection. The style is updated, as is all the text that has been assigned that style.

> ### TIP
>
> To quickly view the formatting attributes of a style in your document, select text that has the style applied and then click the Style Inspector button in the Styles window. The Style Inspector provides the paragraph- and text-level formatting for the style. The Style Inspector can also be used to clear formatting attributes used in the style.

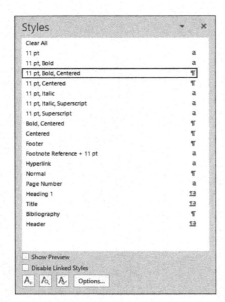

Figure 7-25   View all the styles available in the document.

You can also modify a style using the Modify Style dialog box: Click the drop-down arrow next to the style and select Modify. The Modify Style dialog box provides Formatting toolbars that you can use to change font-formatting attributes and paragraph attributes.

You can also access specific dialog boxes from the Modify Style dialog box to achieve even greater control over the formatting attributes contained in the style. Select the Format button at the bottom left of the dialog box and select Font, Paragraph, Tabs, Borders, or any of the other dialog boxes listed; that particular dialog box opens (such as the Font dialog box or the Paragraph dialog box).

TIP

If you want to delete a style, click the drop-down arrow next to the style in the Style window and select Delete (*style name*) on the menu. Click Yes to confirm the deletion.

After you have made changes to formatting attributes in one of the dialog boxes, closing the dialog box (clicking OK) returns you to the Modify Style dialog box. When you close the Modify Style dialog box, you return to your document and the Styles window.

Managing styles

The Styles window not only gives a comprehensive list of the styles in a document, but it also enables you to modify and even delete styles from the document quickly. The Styles window also provides access to the Manage Styles dialog box, which gives you even greater capability to manage the styles in your document. It even enables you to import and export styles into and from your current document.

TIP

You can also create a new style from the Styles window by clicking the New Style button at the bottom of the window.

In the Styles window, select the Manage Styles button (first button on the right). This opens the Manage Styles dialog box. The Manage Styles dialog box allows you to modify any of the styles in your document or in the template (if you are working on a template). You can delete styles or create new styles (directly from the dialog box). The Manage Styles dialog box also lets you determine which styles appear in the Quick Style gallery and Styles window. You can also specify the order in which the styles appear. Also, it provides options related to setting some of the font- and paragraph-formatting attributes for the document.

The Manage Styles dialog box provides four tabs:

- **Edit:** This tab enables you to modify and delete styles and to change how the list of styles is sorted on the tab. For example, you can change the sort order to Alphabetical using the Sort Order drop-down menu. The default sort order, As Recommended, is based on a numerical system (a style assigned a 1 appears at the top of the list), which you can set on the Recommend tab.

- **Recommend:** The Recommend list is determined on this tab by assigning a particular order number to a style (1 is the highest). The order determined by the Recommend list is basically the priority used to list the styles in the Quick Style gallery and the Styles windows. Use the Move Up, Move Down, and Assign Value buttons to assign the priority number to a style in the list. You can also choose to have certain styles hidden until you use them (via the Hide Until Used button), and you can hide styles. Any styles assigned the Hide Until Used or Hide statuses can be shown by selecting the style or styles and clicking Show.

- **Restrict:** You can limit access to formatting in the document. This is particularly useful if you are designing a template in which you want people who use the template to have restricted access to the formatting tools on the ribbon and want only certain styles to be used for formatting (in lieu of direct formatting). Select a style or styles in the Styles list to permit or restrict the style. If you want to limit formatting to the permitted styles, be sure to select the Limit Formatting To Permitted Styles check box. This feature grays out formatting commands on the ribbon's Home tab, making them unavailable.

- **Set Defaults:** This tab enables you to specify some of the default formatting attributes for the current document or documents based on the template you are creating and configuring. These attributes include Font, Font Size, Paragraph Position, and Paragraph Spacing.

CHAPTER 7

Another tool that you can access via the Manage Styles dialog box is the Organizer. It enables you to copy styles from other documents and templates into your current document (and export them to other documents and templates). After all, sometimes you want to have access to styles that you have created in other documents or that are contained in other Word templates (existing templates and templates that you have created).

➤ **See Chapter 6 for more on Word templates.**

To open the Organizer, click the Import/Export button at the bottom of the Manage Styles dialog box (the button is available on all tabs of the Manage Styles dialog box). The Organizer (shown in Figure 7-26) provides two separate panes that list the styles in the current document (on the left of the dialog box) and the styles in the current document template, which is the Normal template in Figure 7-26.

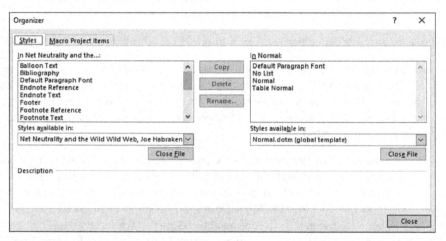

Figure 7-26   The Organizer dialog box

The trick here is to leave the current document and its styles in the Organizer (in the left pane) and use the right side of the Organizer window to open the document that you want to use when you import (or export) styles. To close the current template file on the right side of the dialog box, click the Close File button.

Now you need to open the document or template that will serve as the source for the styles you want to import or serve as the destination for the files you want to export from the current document. Click Open File on the right side of the Organizer dialog box. The Open dialog box appears. Use it to locate and open the document or template from which you want to copy the styles (or export styles to). Double-click the file in the Open dialog box to open the file.

TIP

If you want to import a style into a document (from a document or template), but that style has the same name as a style that already exists in the document that will receive the imported style, you need to use the Rename command to rename the style before you can import it.

Now all you have to do is import or export the styles. Select a style or styles (use the Shift key to select multiple styles) in the document opened on the right side of the Organizer, and then click Copy to import the styles into your current document. If you want to export styles from the current document, select them on the left and then copy them to the file on the right. The dialog box also enables you to select styles in either style list and then delete them.

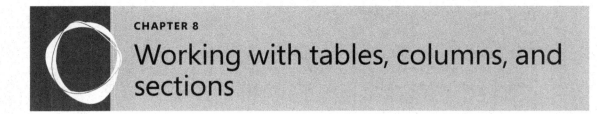

Working with tables, columns, and sections

Options for adding a table   209

Formatting tables   216

Sorting table data   224

Using formulas in tables   225

Adding columns to a document   226

Understanding sections   228

The type of documents that we create in Microsoft Word dictates how information is arranged on the pages of a particular document. For example, you might need to show sales data in a report that is best displayed in a table format, or you might need to create a newsletter that requires your text and images to appear in columns. Because we often create documents that require text and even images to be arranged on the page in ways other than the typical paragraphs you find in a simple business letter, we often find ourselves working with tables and columns in a document.

Word makes adding tables to your documents relatively simple. It also enables you to create columns on a document page or pages. You might run into a situation when you need to display a large table (in terms of columns) on a page in Landscape view, but you need to have the other pages in the document remain in Portrait orientation. Or you might want a document to have regular single-column text in paragraphs but then switch at a certain point in the document to a two-column layout.

Sections can handle these types of layout issues. Each section can have its own page layout settings, such as the number of columns, margins, and even headers and footers. This chapter begins with a discussion of Word tables, and then moves to columns and, finally, sections.

Options for adding a table

When you think about the spatial arrangement of text on a Word document page, the positioning of the information is dictated primarily by the document margins and then any paragraph alignment or line-spacing settings that you choose (such as centered or double-spaced text). Tables, however, are containers that provide a way for you to arrange information on a page in a grid-like format. Tables consist of columns and rows, and each intersection of a column and row is referred to as a cell. You enter your data (text or other objects) into the table cells.

Although you can arrange text on a page in a tabular (or table-like) format using tabs, tables are much more flexible, particularly when the amount of text to be entered into each column is not uniform. The cell's height grows as needed to accommodate your entered text, and you can easily widen the columns as needed. Tables can also contain pictures and other graphics to provide you with layout possibilities that would be nearly impossible to achieve using tab stops.

Word provides multiple options for creating a table in your document. Figure 8-1 shows the possibilities when you select the Table command on the ribbon's Insert tab. The table-creation possibilities follow:

- **Table Grid:** You can insert a table by dragging the mouse on the table grid to select the number of columns and rows that make up the table. You access the table grid by selecting the Table command in the Table group. When you insert a table using the table grid, you are initially limited to a maximum table size of 10 columns by 8 rows. However, you can easily insert additional columns and rows afterward.

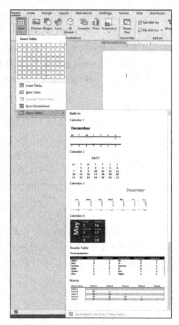

Figure 8-1   Create a new table using one of the options provided by the Table command.

- **Insert Table:** This old-school table option uses the Insert Table dialog box and enables you to specify the number of columns and rows. To open the Insert Table dialog box, select Table on the Insert tab and then select Insert Table.

- **Draw Table:** You can draw your table in the document using a "pencil" mouse pointer. You can add columns and rows using the drawing tool as needed (you can distribute the rows and columns evenly afterward via commands on the Table Tools Layout tab). To draw a table, select Table and then select Draw Table.

- **Convert Text To Table:** You can convert existing text to a table. This is useful when you have used tabs to place text in a tabular arrangement. The command is available when the text is selected.

- **Excel Spreadsheet:** This option places a new Excel sheet into your document at the insertion point. Whenever the spreadsheet is selected, Excel tabs and commands are available on the Word ribbon.

- **Quick Tables:** You can select a premade table from the Quick Tables gallery. You access the gallery via the Table command on the ribbon's Insert tab (select Table and then hover over Quick Tables). Quick Tables provide different table layouts and formatting (refer to Figure 8-1). They also provide sample text, which you can replace with your own text.

➤ For more about integrating Word and Excel, see Appendix A, "Microsoft 365 application integration."

TIP

You might think it best to use Excel for information that needs to be organized in a table and then copy and paste the Excel sheet data into Word. This makes sense when the data is already in Excel. However, the Word table feature is extremely robust and flexible and provides you with many options regarding the table format and layout. Word also enables you to insert formulas into the table so that you can do calculations (as in Excel). If the data isn't already in Excel and doesn't need to be in Excel, just enter it into a Word table.

All these options place a table (or an Excel spreadsheet) into the document at the insertion point. However, keep in mind that the differences among these different table-creation methods provide you with a great deal of flexibility in creating a table.

For example, if you want to quickly create a table such as a tabular list and are happy with the layout and formatting provided by the Tabular List Quick Table, you likely will want to use it and then replace the sample text with your own text.

If you are creating a table where you want to control the number of columns and rows more precisely, you can use the Insert Table option. This option also enables you to work through the process of setting the design and layout options for the table and formatting the cell contents (text). Let's walk through each of the options for creating a table from scratch and then look at fine-tuning tables, including using the Design and Layout Table Tools.

Inserting a table

When you insert a table, you can specify the initial number of rows and columns in the table. You also can specify the position on the page where you want to place the table; you simply park the insertion point where you want to place the table. The insertion point marks the top-left starting point of the table.

Obviously, if you use the Insert Table grid on the Table command's menu, you merely drag the mouse to specify the number of columns and rows. The Insert Table dialog box provides you with more options, so let's assume that you want to go that route to insert the new table. Follow these steps:

1. Place the insertion point in the document where you want to insert the table.

2. Select the Table command on the ribbon's Insert tab and then select Insert Table. The Insert Table dialog box appears, as shown in Figure 8-2.

Figure 8-2   Insert a table using the Insert Table dialog box.

3. Use the Number Of Columns and Number Of Rows spin boxes to specify the number of columns and rows for the table (or type a number in either box).

4. The AutoFit options enable you to specify how the columns in the table behave in relation to the amount of text placed in each column. The options are as follows:

   - **Fixed Column Width:** This setting, which is Auto by default, enables you to set a fixed width (an actual number in inches) for all the columns in the table. When you use this option, you must manually resize columns in the table (using the sizing tool) to change any of the column widths.

   - **AutoFit To Contents:** Column widths adjust to the amount of text in the column. A column grows in width (at the expense of the other columns in the table) as you enter text.

   - **AutoFit To Window:** This option keeps the table aligned between the left and right margins. It is primarily designed for web pages so that the table adjusts its size based on the web browser window size.

5. (Optional) If you want the settings you selected to become the default for new tables, select the Remember Dimensions For New Tables check box.

6. When you have finished setting the options for the new table, click OK.

TIP

To access the AutoFit settings for the table (after you have created the table), use the AutoFit command in the Cell Size group on the Table Tools Layout tab.

Drawing a table

An alternative to inserting a table into your document is to draw the table. When you draw the table, you can make the table any height and width instead of having Word determine the height and width based on the number of columns and rows. You create the outside table borders without any rows or columns; you then must manually insert the rows and columns using the Table Drawing tool.

Although you can build a highly customized table using this method, it is not as fast as inserting a table with a prescribed number of rows and columns (as when you insert a table). Follow these steps:

1. Select Table on the Insert tab and then select Draw Table. The mouse pointer becomes a "pencil" drawing tool.

2. Click and drag to create the table's outside borders (its "box" shape). Release the mouse when you have the outside perimeter of the table completed.

3. To add rows and columns to the table, use the pencil to draw (click and drag) the row and column lines.

4. When you have finished drawing the column and row borders (they do not have to be spaced evenly at this point), select Draw Table on the Design tab of the Table Tools. This turns off the pencil drawing tool.

5. To evenly distribute the drawn rows and/or columns in the table, select the Layout tab (of the Table Tools ribbon) and then select Distribute Rows and/or Distribute Columns, as needed.

The Draw Table feature is toggled off if you click outside the table (in the document's text) when using the table drawing tool. All you have to do is click inside the table and then click the Draw Table command on the Table Tools Design tab to reactivate the pencil drawing tool. You can then add tables or rows as needed. You can also use the Eraser tool to erase rows or columns that you have placed in the table. Select Eraser on the Design tab and then click and drag the Eraser to select a row or column border. When you release the mouse, the column or row border is erased. You can also use the Eraser to fine-tune borders and erase parts of a column or row to join cells.

Converting text to a table

You can convert existing text to a table, which is particularly convenient when you have used tabs to align text in a tabular format but find that you are better served by converting the text into a table. This is also useful if you have a text file that is delimited with spaces or commas, and you want to get the data into a table.

To convert delimited text (some sort of delimiter must exist between each text entry, such as a tab), select the text. On the ribbon's Insert tab, select Table and then select Convert Text To Table. The Convert Text To Table dialog box opens (see Figure 8-3).

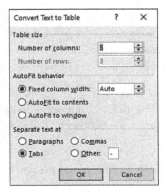

Figure 8-3   The Convert Text To Table dialog box

Select the delimiter that separates the text in the list in the Separate Text At area of the dialog box. You can select from Paragraphs, Commas, Tabs, or designate a delimiter using the Other option. Based on the delimiter, Word specifies a table size showing the number of columns and rows. You can also set the AutoFit behavior in the Convert Text To Table dialog box if warranted.

When you click OK, the text converts to a table. If the table hasn't perfectly arranged the data, you can insert columns and rows (if needed) and then drag and drop cell entries until you have the data appropriately placed in the table.

TIP

You can change the line style, line weight, and pen color when you are using the Draw Table feature. Change any of the color or line settings in the Borders group on the Design tab of the Table Tools.

Entering and deleting text and navigating a table

When you have the table in your document, you need to add data. Entering text into the table is straightforward. Click in the first cell of the table and enter the appropriate text. To move to the next cell, press the Tab key. You can continue to move through the cells in the tables by pressing the Tab key and entering your text. If you want to back up a cell, press Shift+Tab, which moves you to the cell to the left of the current cell. If you move to a cell that contains text, that text is selected. If you type new text, it overwrites the original contents of the cell.

Of course, you can use the mouse to click in any cell of the table at any time. However, if you are entering information into the table, using some of the other keyboard combinations to navigate a table is quicker:

- **Alt+Home:** Takes you to the first cell in the current row

- **Alt+Page Up:** Takes you to the top cell in the current column

- **Alt+End:** Takes you to the last cell in the current row

- **Alt+Page Down:** Takes you to the last cell in the current column

Deleting text from the table is really no different from deleting any other text in a document. Select text in the table and press Delete to remove it. If you want to delete all the text in an entire row, place the mouse pointer at the left edge of the particular row. Click to select the entire row. When you press Delete, all the text in the selected row is deleted. You can also use a column pointer (a solid black arrow; place the mouse at the top of any column) to select an entire column and delete text in that column using the Delete key.

Selecting and positioning a table

To select a table, place the mouse just above the top-left corner of the table. The Table handle appears. Click the handle, and the entire table is selected. You can also reposition a table using the Table handle. Use the handle (a four-headed arrow) to drag the table to a new position in the document.

Because the text surrounding the table (the text in your paragraphs) basically sees the table as a graphical element (kind of like a picture), you can configure how the surrounding text wraps around the table (as you can a picture or chart). Drag the table to position it within a paragraph of text. Right-click the table and select Table Properties from the shortcut menu. The Table tab of the Table Properties dialog box is selected, as shown in Figure 8-4.

NOTE

The contents of the cells in your table are not limited to text. You can place clip art, pictures, and other graphics in a cell. You can also nest a table in a table. For example, you can include a table of data (in a cell) beside a chart of that data (which is also in a cell). Tables provide a great way to arrange objects on a document page.

TIP

You can select a cell, a column, a row, or the entire table using the Select command on the Table Tools Layout tab.

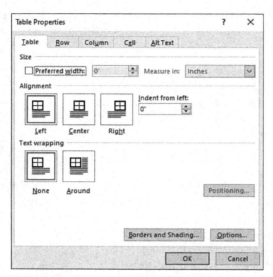

Figure 8-4 The Table Properties dialog box

Use the Alignment and Text Wrapping settings in the Table Properties dialog box to determine the alignment and text wrapping for the table. Select None in the Text Wrapping area if you do not want the text to wrap around the table. To position the table in relation to the text in the paragraph, select Left, Center, or Right. Once you have completed your selections, click OK to close the dialog box. You can also access the alignment settings in the Alignment group on the Table Design tab when the insertion point is placed inside the table.

Formatting tables

In terms of formatting tables, you work with two broad categories of tools on the ribbon: Table Design and Layout. These Table tabs appear on the ribbon when the table is selected or when the insertion point is in the table. The Table Design tools provide commands related to the use of table styles (many table styles are built into Word) and shading and borders settings. The Draw Borders group is also part of the Design tab of the Table Design tools, which is shown in Figure 8-5.

The table layout commands appear on the Layout tab. These tools include commands that enable you to insert columns and rows, merge and split cells, and change the text alignment in a cell or cells. Figure 8-6 shows the Layout tab.

Figure 8-5   The Table Design tab

Figure 8-6   The Table Layout tab

A good way to differentiate between the Design and Layout commands on the Table ribbon is to think of the Design commands as tools that allow you to control the overall look of the table by providing access to the table styles, table style options, and commands related to the format of the table's borders. The layout commands are table tools that enable you to manipulate the rows, columns, and cells of the table and the text alignment in the cells.

Adjusting columns and rows

The columns and rows provide the table's basic structure, or "bones." You have complete control over the number of rows and columns in your table. You also control column widths and row heights. Word provides you with insert controls for quickly inserting columns or rows into a table.

To insert a new column, place the mouse on the border between two columns at the top of the table. An insert control appears as a vertical element highlighting the column border. Click the plus symbol on top of the column insert control, and a new column is inserted (between the columns). You can also use the row insert control to add a new row between two existing rows. Place the mouse on the left side of the table between two rows until the insert control appears. Click the plus symbol to insert the row.

The Table Tools Layout tab gives you commands for inserting columns and rows into a table. The possibilities are as follows:

- To insert a column, place the insertion point in the column next to where you want to insert the new column. On the Table Layout tab of the ribbon, use the Insert Left or Insert Right command to insert a new column to the left or right of the current column, respectively.

- To insert a row, place the insertion point in a row, and then use the Insert Above or Insert Below commands to insert a new row above or below the current row.

- If you need to add more than one column or row, select the number of columns or rows you want to add to the table and then use the commands in the Rows & Columns group to insert columns or rows as needed (to the right or left of the selected columns or above or below the selected rows).

For adjusting column widths and row heights, you can use the sizing tool to visually change the width of a column or the height of a row. To change the column width, place the mouse between two columns until the resizing pointer appears. Drag the mouse to increase or decrease the column width.

TIP

If you are working on a table that does not have borders, click the View Gridlines command on the Table Tools Layout tab. Seeing the nonprinting gridlines makes working with the table easier.

To set a more precise width for a column (or selected columns), you can use the Width spin box in the Cell Size group of the Layout tab. Use the arrows to increase or decrease the width. Also, you can type a measurement (in inches) in the box to specify the width.

You can increase the row height by using the resizing pointer on the bottom of a row to drag the border down. To change the height for selected rows, use the Height command spin box in the Cell Size group.

You can also set column widths and row heights in the Table Properties dialog box. Click in the column or row that you want to adjust and select the Properties command (in the Table group of the Layout tab). If you are adjusting the width of a column (or columns), select the Column tab of the Table Properties dialog box (see Figure 8-7).

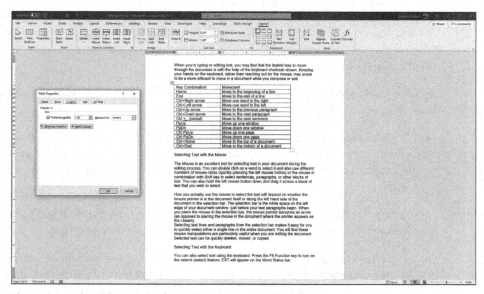

Figure 8-7   The Column tab of the Table Properties dialog box

Use the Preferred Width spin box to set the width for the column. (The default measurement is inches.) You can use Previous Column or Next Column options to set the preferred width for columns adjacent to the current column.

For row height, use the Row tab. The Specify Height spin box enables you to set the row height, and the Row Height spin box lets you specify that the height of the row is at least or exactly the height you have entered. An option is also available that enables you to specify whether the row should be allowed to break across pages.

Columns and rows can be selected and dragged to new positions in a table. You might also find it necessary to delete columns or rows in the table. Deleting columns or rows is straightforward:

1. Select a column (or columns) or a row (or rows).

2. Select the Delete command on the Layout tab.

3. Use the Delete Columns or Delete Rows commands as needed.

4. If you want to delete the entire table, select Delete Table.

TIP

The Repeat As Header Row At The Top Of Each Page check box on the Row tab enables you to specify that the current row is the header (top row of the table) and should be repeated when the table is broken over multiple pages.

Formatting cells

Word provides formatting attributes to relate directly to the cells in a table. These formatting features include the capability to merge and split cells. You also have control over how text is aligned in the cell and the cell margins.

Merging cells gives you control over the internal space of the table. To merge cells, select the cells and then click the Merge Cells command in the Merge group of the Table Tools Layout tab. You can also split a cell; use the Split Cells command to split the current cell into two cells.

Another split-related command is available in the Merge group. If you want to split a table into two tables at a particular row, place the insertion point in that row and then click Split Table.

Several other cell-specific commands are in the Alignment group on the Layout tab. These commands control the following cell settings:

- **Alignment Commands:** On the left of the Alignment group are nine commands that control where the text is aligned in a cell (or selected cells): Align Top Left, Align Top Center, Align Top Right, Align Center Left, Align Center, Align Center Right, Align Bottom Left, Align Bottom Center, and Align Bottom Right.

- **Text Direction:** This command enables you to cycle through two text-direction possibilities: On the first click of the command, the text is rotated 90 degrees and placed in the upper-right part of the cell. The next click rotates the text 180 degrees (from the previous setting) and places it in the bottom left of the cell. The third time you click the Text Direction button, the text returns to its normal text orientation and default alignment.

- **Cell Margins:** This command enables you to set the default cell margins for the table. This is particularly useful if you want to give crowded cells more breathing room and add some white space to the table's interior. When you select the Cell Margins command, the Table Options dialog box opens (see Figure 8-8). You can specify the top, bottom, left, and right cell margins and set the default cell spacing.

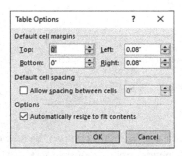

Figure 8-8   Table Options dialog box

One point to remember when working with the individual cell settings, such as the Alignment commands and the Cell Margins command, is that you need to make these types of adjustments *after* you apply a style to the table. Table styles override any specific cell-formatting attributes that you configure, except for the Text Rotation setting, which is not affected by assigning a style to a table.

TIP

You can adjust the width of an individual cell. Select the cell and then drag the cell border as needed to change the width. Note that this takes the cell out of alignment (in terms of its borders) with the rest of the cells in that column.

Using table styles

Table styles give you a unified design for your tables that includes a number of table-formatting attributes, such as fonts, borders, and shading. By default, all new tables created use the Table Grid style, which provides black borders for the table cells. This basic table style uses the default font from the current template (in most cases, Calibri and the Normal template, respectively) and applies no shading to the cells. Formatting a table with a table style doesn't mean that you relinquish all control of the table's look. Obviously, you can edit the style. Check boxes provided in the Table Style Options group on the Table Design tab also determine how the table styles will affect certain parts of the table. These options are as follows:

- **Header Row:** The header row is the first row of the table and typically contains the column headings for the table. Because the header row differs from the rows that contain regular data, the table style formats it differently. This option is selected by default.

- **First Column:** The first column often contains the row headings for the table. If you select the First Column option, the table style formats the first column differently than the other columns in the table. This option is selected by default.

- **Total Row:** Totals are typically included in the last row of the table. This option requires the table style to format the last row differently.

- **Last Column:** This option indicates that you want the table style to format the last column differently than the other columns in the table.

- **Banded Rows:** When you select this option, the style formats the odd and even rows in the table differently. This option is selected by default.

- **Banded Columns:** This option allows the table style to format the odd and even columns in the table differently.

TIP

You can access the Borders And Shading dialog box for more control over the border and shading options for your table; simply select Borders And Shading on the Borders drop-down menu.

When you decide on the options for the table styles by selecting or deselecting options in the Table Style Options group, you can preview how the various styles provided in the Table Styles gallery look when applied to the table (just point at a style to preview it). Figure 8-9 shows the Table Styles gallery (click the More button to view the gallery) and the Table Style Options group (on the left).

After you apply a particular style to the table, you can change any of the table style options as needed (deselect the check boxes or select different check boxes) and modify other table-formatting attributes supplied by the style, such as the shading or border formats. For example, you can select the Shading command to select a shading color from the color palette. You can select colors from the current document theme or from a list of standard colors. You can also select your own colors by clicking More Colors.

CHAPTER 8

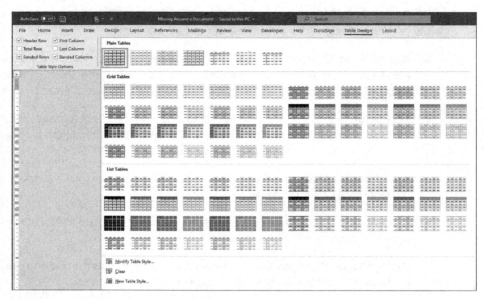

Figure 8-9 The Table Styles gallery

Also, you can actually format borders individually using the Border Painter tool, which is located in the Borders group on the Table Design tab. Select a border style in the Border Styles list, and the mouse pointer becomes a pen; this is the Border Painter. Use the Border Painter to "paint" the new border style on the borders in the table (click and drag along a border to paint the border with the new format). When you have finished working with the Border Painter, select the Border Painter button in the Borders group to deactivate this feature.

If you modify the table formatting provided by the currently selected table style, you have the option to save the modified style as a new style. You can then use this new style to format any future tables that you create. You can specify whether the new style is available only in the current document or in all new documents based on the current template. Follow these steps to save the modified table style as a new style:

1. On the Table Design tab, select the More button on the Table Styles gallery. The Tables Style gallery expands.

2. Select the New Table Style command at the bottom of the gallery. The Create New Style From Formatting dialog box appears (see Figure 8-10).

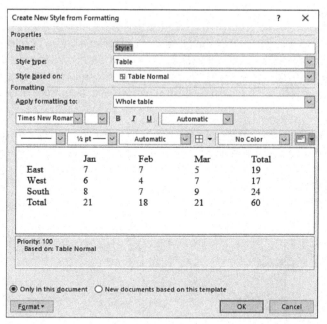

Figure 8-10   The Create New Style from Formatting dialog box

3. Provide a name for your new style. Use the Apply Formatting To list to specify whether the style is applied to the whole table, the header row, the total row, and so on.

4. Select either the Only In This Document option or the New Documents Based On This Template option.

5. Select OK to save the new style.

The new style is listed in the Table Style gallery under the Custom heading. You can modify any existing table style as needed. If you format a table from scratch (including borders, shading, and font), you can save the table's formatting as a new style.

You can also delete a table style that you have created but no longer need by simply right-clicking the style in the gallery and then selecting Delete Table Style from the shortcut menu.

TIP

You have complete control over all the format settings in a style when you are in the Create New Style From Formatting dialog box. Select the Format button at the bottom of the dialog box to access Table Properties, Borders And Shading, Banding, and other formatting attributes that you want to modify.

Sorting table data

Word enables you to sort data within the table. You can select a group of cells and then sort the data in those cells, or you can sort all the data in the table based on the contents of a particular column in the table. To sort an entire table, your table layout must be consistent; if you have split or merged cells within the table, you must select specific groups of cells for the sort to work correctly.

To sort data in the table, select the cells to be included in the sort, or click anywhere in the table when you are sorting a uniform table with no split or merged cells and no special rows (such as a total row). On the Table Layout tab, select the Sort command (in the Data group). The Sort dialog box opens (see Figure 8-11).

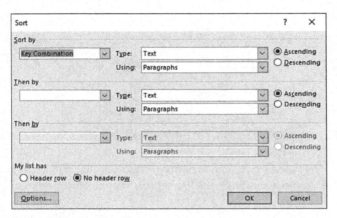

Figure 8-11   The Sort dialog box

The Sort dialog box enables you to set the sort based on a specific parameter, such as a particular column or row heading. You also can specify the type of data (Text, Number, or Data). Take advantage of the Header Row option if you are sorting an entire table with uniform cells and the table has a header row (meaning column headings in the top row). If you are working with a table or a selected area of a table with column and row headings, the Sort dialog box anticipates the Sort By parameter from the sort and can usually specify the type of data you are sorting (text versus numbers).

The Sort dialog box enables you to sort by three different sort criteria. (For example, you can sort by last name and then first name in a table of clients or employees.) After you set the various sort parameters, click OK to perform the sort and return to the table. If the results of your sort don't appear to be correct (in terms of how things are sorted), select the Undo button on the Quick Access toolbar, which will return your data to its original position in the table. Fine-tune your search as needed, and then try it again.

Using formulas in tables

Word enables you to do different types of calculations in your tables. It certainly does not provide the many functions you find in Excel, but it provides function calculations that include average, sum, maximum, and minimum.

Word (like Excel) can take an educated guess on the type of calculation you want to make in a table. For example, if you insert a formula at the bottom of a column of numbers, Word assumes that you want to act on the data above the current cell and suggests the formula =SUM(ABOVE). This Sum formula pops up first when you are attempting a calculation in a table because it is the default formula for Word tables (and if you think about it, adding a column of numbers is a very typical action in a table).

NOTE

When you need to do a lot of calculations, you might want to create the table in Excel. If you already have the table in Word, copy and paste the table into Excel. Excel provides greater flexibility and options when working with calculations (be advised that when formulas pasted are from Word to Excel, the result of the formula is pasted).

In some cases, Word might not be able to help you by recognizing the group of cells you want to include in the calculation, so you have to know how to specify a group (called a range) of cells to be acted on by a particular formula. Here is the geography of a table: The first column is A, the second is B, and so on.

The first row in the table is 1, the second row is 2, and so on. The first cell in a table—which is in column A and row 1—is cell A1. Each cell's address is dictated by its location in the table: the column letter followed by the row number.

To specify a group of cells to be acted on by a formula, you must specify the first and last cells in the group. For example, if you were adding cells B2, B3, B4, and B5, you designate the cell group with B2:B5. This tells Word where the cells to act on begin and end.

To insert a formula into a table cell, click in the cell where you place the formula. To open the Formula dialog box, select the Formula command in the Data group. Figure 8-12 shows the Formula dialog box.

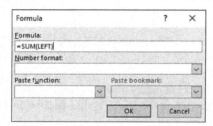

Figure 8-12   The Formula dialog box

In the Formula dialog box, you need to specify the formula. As already mentioned, if you are inserting a formula at the bottom of a column of numbers or at the end of a row of numbers, Word provides a formula in the Formula box.

You can specify a formula for the Formula box by selecting a function from the Paste function list. After you paste in the function, you must specify the cells upon which the formula will act. To do so, type the cell range (which is the starting cell address and ending cell address) between the parentheses provided in the formula.

You can also use the Number Format drop-down box to specify how the calculation result in the cell should be formatted (such as currency or a percentage). When you finish setting the formula options, click OK to insert the formula.

TIP

You can specify the cell range for a formula in a Word table using a bookmark. Select a group of cells in the table, select Bookmark on the ribbon's Insert tab, and provide a name for the bookmark. You can use the bookmark when you create your formula in the Formula dialog box.

Adding columns to a document

The columns provided by Word are called newspaper or "snaking" columns. This means that if you have two columns on a page and you fill the first column with text, the additional text snakes over into the second column and continues to be inserted there. Word columns are perfect for newsletters and brochures.

You can format a blank document for columns, or you can select existing text and then apply column settings to it. You can also have Word begin the column settings at a particular place in a document by placing the column settings at the insertion point. This will place all the text from that point forward into the number of columns that you have selected. This allows you to easily "mix" text in columns with text that is not in columns. This all works seamlessly because when you apply column settings to any selected text or at a particular insertion point in the document, Word automatically places the text (now in the number of columns you selected) into its own document section. We discuss sections later in this chapter. For now, just remember that the purpose of a section is to separate text with specific page layout settings (in this case, a section containing text in columns) from the rest of the document.

To insert columns into a document at the insertion point, select the Columns command (it provides a drop-down menu) on the ribbon's Layout tab. You can select One, Two, or Three from the Columns list that appears. Selecting Two (or more) places columns of equal width on the page. You can also select Left or Right. The Left option places a narrow column on the left and a wider column on the right (a 1.83-inches-wide column on the left and a wider right column of 4.17 inches). The Right selection does just the opposite. All the preset selections separate the columns created by a half inch, with a spacing of a half inch.

CAUTION

Word columns are not appropriate for arranging text in a tabular format (meaning side-by-side text). Use a table (my first choice and the best way to go) or tabs (only for very rudimentary alignment of text in columns) if you need to arrange text on the page in side-by-side columns.

If you want more control over the column settings, select More Columns, which opens the Columns dialog box (see Figure 8-13).

You can select the presets from the Columns dialog box or specify your own number of columns using the Number Of Columns spin box. After you specify the number of columns, you can specify the width and spacing (between the columns) using the Width and Spacing boxes.

You can also specify whether you want the column settings to apply to the whole document or from this point forward in the document (from the insertion point). If you select This Point Forward in the Apply To drop-down menu, a new section is created in the document. When you finish entering your settings for the columns, click OK.

You can edit the columns settings that you have applied to your document (or a section of the document). First, make sure that you place the insertion point within a document section formatted for columns. Then click the Columns command in the Page Setup group and select More Columns. This opens the Columns dialog box, and you can edit the current settings as needed.

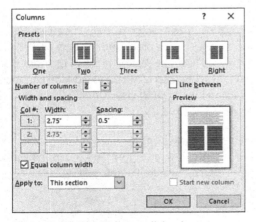

Figure 8-13   The Columns dialog box

CHAPTER 8

TIP

If you want to place a line between the columns in your document, select the Line Between check box in the Columns dialog box.

Because you are working with continuous, newspaper-type column settings, sometimes it is advantageous to force a column break in a column. This enables you to balance the text between columns or end the text in a column at a particular point and force the rest of the text into the next column. To place a column break at the insertion point, select the Breaks command on the ribbon's Page Layout tab. Select Column on the Breaks list.

Understanding sections

Most of the documents that we create (the smaller, less complex documents) typically consist of one section. The page layout attributes such as margins, page orientation, number of columns, and even headers and footers are the same for the entire document and accommodate all the text in the document. More complex documents can be more challenging in terms of page layout settings; think of a report that has a cover page, a table of contents, the body text of the report, and then a bibliography or maybe an index.

Each of these different parts or sections in this complex document might require different page layout attributes than the other document sections. In Word, a section is designed to meet the different page layouts in a single, complex document. A section break defines each section in a document, and each section can have its own page layout settings as well as its own headers and footers.

Adding and removing section breaks

When you insert new section breaks into a document, switch to Draft view (Draft on the View tab's Views group). This enables you to view the section break and the type of section break that you insert. When you have confirmed that you have the section break in the right place, you can always switch to another view, such as Print Layout, and continue to work on your document. However, when you need to deal with section breaks, Draft view is the best view to use, particularly when you want to locate and delete section breaks.

Place the insertion point in the document where you want the new section to start. On the ribbon's Layout tab, select Breaks (in the Page Setup group). Figure 8-14 shows the various Breaks options, including the section break types (in the lower half of the gallery).

TIP

You can copy the formatting from one section to another in a document by copying the section break. In Draft view, select and copy the section break. Then paste it into another part of the document. This creates a copy of the section, including all the page layout settings from the copied section.

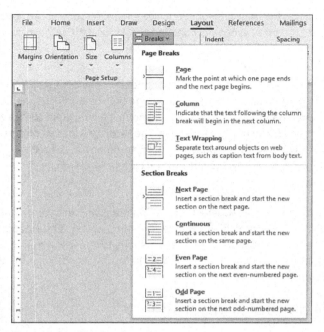

Figure 8-14   The Breaks gallery

Four types of section breaks are listed:

- **Next Page:** A page break is placed in the document, and the new section begins on this new page.

- **Continuous:** The new section starts at the insertion point and continues for the rest of the document (or until it comes to the next section break).

- **Even Page:** The new section starts on the next even-numbered page.

- **Odd Page:** The new section starts on the next odd-numbered page.

Obviously, the type of section break you select depends on the type of document you are creating. If your document has a table of contents followed by the body, using a Next Page section (starting the body of the document on a new page) makes sense. Even page and odd page sections are often used when you create a document with facing pages. Different headers and footers are then created for the even pages and the odd pages.

After you select one of the section break types in the Breaks gallery, the section break is inserted into the document. As already mentioned, you can view the section break in Draft view. This view doesn't give you any insight into the different page layout settings configured before and after the section break, but it is the only way for you to see where the section break has been inserted into the document (in Print Layout view, section breaks look the same as page breaks).

TIP

If you don't really need a new section in a document but are considering using it to add a new black page to your document, use the Blank Page or Page Break commands in the Pages group of the ribbon's Insert tab. These commands are a more appropriate way to add a blank page or page break in your document. The Pages group even offers a Cover Page command that will insert a cover page into your document. A Cover Page gallery offers you many different cover page styles, and you can also access many more possibilities from Office.com.

To delete a section break in the Draft view, select the section break and then press Delete. This removes the section from the document. It also removes all the page layout formatting that was applied to the section. In effect, removing the section resets the text that was in that section. The text does not adhere to the layout attributes configured for the section directly above the text that was contained in the deleted section.

Formatting page attributes in a section

After you establish a new section in the document, you can specify the various page layout settings for that section. When you want to format a particular section, make sure you have the insertion point in that section.

Some of the common page layout settings and other document attributes that differ from section to section in the document require the use of the Page Setup commands on the Page Layout tab. These commands enable you to change margins, page orientation, and the number of columns for each section. Other settings that you might want to configure differently for document sections relate to headers, footers, and page numbering. These commands are located in the Header & Footer group on the Insert tab.

Remember that to view the actual location of a section break, you use the Draft view. To view the effect of the page layout settings for a section, you use Print Layout view or the Print Preview pane in the Print window (in the Backstage).

Managing mailings and forms

Options for mail-related documents   231

Creating an envelope   232

Creating a label or labels   234

Understanding mass mailings   236

Performing a mail merge   236

Understanding Word fields   252

Building a form with form controls   254

Creating form letters, mailing labels, envelopes, and mass email can seem to be a rather daunting set of tasks. However, Word takes a very straightforward approach to creating all the printed and/or electronic (in case of a form email) materials necessary for a mass mailing to a group of customers, colleagues, or friends. Word also makes it easy to gather information electronically by creating forms that can be circulated on your network or via email. You can create questionnaires or other materials that make it effortless for the recipient of the form to provide you with the information you need.

In this chapter, we look at how to create mail-related documents such as envelopes and labels. We also perform a mail merge in which you merge names and addresses with a form letter or email message. Finally, we wrap up the chapter with a look at how to create forms using form controls, which provides an excellent way to build forms that the recipients can easily complete.

Options for mail-related documents

Most tasks undertaken in Word relate to communicating with others—creating documents such as letters, email, and forms. Word gives you all the tools required for letters, envelopes, and mailing labels: You can quickly create any snail mail–related document you require.

Word also enables you to quickly merge a data source, such as a list of names and addresses, into a document such as a form letter. Merges can also be accomplished using data from Microsoft Outlook that is then merged into an email. Word definitely provides a very robust set of tools for your mass mailings.

For mail-related documents, Microsoft Word provides several letter templates. You can use these templates to create a letter to send to an individual or a form letter that can play a part in a merge that produces a number of letters based on a list of names and addresses.

Along the same lines, Word enables you to create a single envelope for a letter quickly or to merge addresses into an envelope form that creates envelopes for your entire mailing list. The same goes for labels; you can create labels that repeat a single address (such as your return address), or you can create labels for each person on your mailing list.

Also, Word can build forms. Using form controls on your forms makes it easy for respondents (such as network users or email recipients) to fill out the form with their responses quickly. In addition, these controls can specify lists of responses so that your data collection using the form is more consistent across your respondent pool.

Creating an envelope

When you create a letter in Word, it typically contains the name and address of the individual you want to receive your letter. Having the name and address available in the letter makes it easy for you to then create an envelope for that letter.

Creating the letter and then using the address information in the letter when you create the envelope actually makes your life easier. Another trick that you can take advantage of is to add the envelope to the letter document in a separate section (say at the end of the letter). This will make it easier for you to print both the letter and the envelope at your convenience and save it for later reference as part of the same document file. When you initially create the letter, you can also use your own letter format or take advantage of one of Word's letter templates.

TIP

You can quickly insert the current date into the letter using the Date And Time command in the Text group of the ribbon's Insert tab.

Select the Envelopes command (in the Create group) on the ribbon's Mailings tab when you are ready to create the envelope. The Envelopes And Labels dialog box opens, as shown in Figure 9-1. Note that the Envelopes tab of the dialog box is selected.

If a delivery address was present in your letter, it should appear in the Delivery Address box (in the Envelopes And Labels dialog box). If needed, you can type in the address, or you can use the Address Book icon to add the address from Outlook. You can also type your address in the Return Address box, or you can use the Address Book icon to add your address to the box using your Outlook profile.

The Envelopes And Labels dialog box enables you to add electronic postage to the envelope. To specify the options for your envelope, such as the size and the fonts used, select the Options button in the Envelopes And Labels dialog box. This opens the Envelope Options dialog box (see Figure 9-2).

Figure 9-1   The Envelopes And Labels dialog box

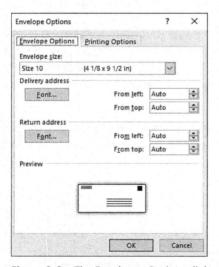

Figure 9-2   The Envelopes Options dialog box

You can specify the envelope size and the fonts to use for both the delivery address and the return address. You can also specify the distance from the left and top of the envelope for the addresses. Click OK to return to the Envelopes And Labels dialog box.

CHAPTER 9

You can now print the envelope. Click the Print button in the Envelopes And Labels dialog box. If you want to add the envelope to the current document (your letter), click the Add To Document button. When you select this option, you are creating a new section in the document (remember that different sections can have different page layout settings). Having the envelope as part of the current document means that you can print the envelope and the letter during the same print job.

Creating a label or labels

In Word, you can print a sheet of labels that contain individual names and addresses for a mailing—meaning each label will be different. (Your sheet of labels doesn't have to contain addresses; it can be any information you want to place on the labels.) You can also choose to create or print a sheet of labels that all use the same piece of information, such as your mailing address. This allows you to print a sheet of labels with your return address so that you always have ready-made labels on hand for the return address on your letters or other mailings.

TIP

If you have a letter open in Word that contains your return address, you can click the Use Return Address check box to have your address placed in the label's Address box.

To create the labels (or a single label), click the Labels command on the Ribbon's Mailings tab (print a single label by selecting Single Label). The Envelopes And Labels dialog box opens with the Label tab selected. You can enter the address for the label (or sheet of labels) in the Address box or use the Address Book icon (to left of the Use Return Address check box) to add an address from Outlook.

The default setting for printing labels is to print a full page of the same label. You can print the labels via the Print button or save them as a new document (use the New Document button) and then print them as needed.

Inside OUT

The possible perils of printing labels

Considering how straightforward the process seems to be for creating mailing labels in Word, you might think that the whole process will be a real piece of cake. (Sorry, if you don't like cake.) Unfortunately, printing labels via Word is always a bit of an adventure, and how successful your results are will depend on the printer and labels that you use. First, you need a printer that makes it easy for you to load sheets of labels so that they have a safe journey as they pass through the printer. Another hazard is your placement of labels in the paper tray or feeder just seconds before someone prints out a lengthy document and consumes all your precious sheets of labels. So, first, do some tests with your labels and your printer to make sure you get satisfactory results. Also, alert your coworkers that you are printing labels so that you can get your print job done. Finally, sheets of labels can actually be the greatest liability in terms of getting a satisfactory batch of mailing labels printed. I recommend that you purchase labels made by a company on the vendor list provided by Word and use labels that appear in the Product Number list. Peruse the labels listed in the Label Options dialog box to view the possibilities. It will make your life a lot easier because these vendor-specific labels usually work (even if they do cost more than a generic knock-off label that claims to be equivalent).

After you have specified the address for the full page of labels or a single label, you will want to specify the type of label you will use in your printer. Select the Options button (or click the default label shown in the Label box); the Label Options dialog box opens (see Figure 9-3).

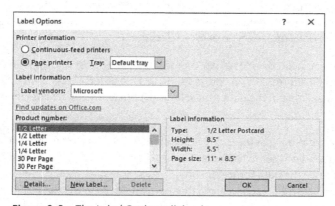

Figure 9-3   The Label Options dialog box

The Label Options dialog box enables you to specify the label vendor and the product number of the labels you are using. Select the vendor in the Label Vendors list, and then scroll through the Product Number list and identify your label.

You can access the details for a particular label by selecting the Details button. You can adjust your label's margins, pitch, height, and width. This should not be necessary if you are using a standard label.

When you select your label vendor and type of label, you can choose to print the labels immediately via the Print button. You also can create a new document (use the New Document button) for the labels, which allows you to save the labels for future printing.

TIP

If you choose the Single label option on the Labels tab of the Envelopes And Labels dialog box, you can specify the row and column of the label that you use on the label sheet when you print. This is handy if you will be using one label at a time and want to use all the labels on the sheet.

Understanding mass mailings

We normally equate mass or group mailings with form letters that are then sent by snail mail. However, Word's mail merge feature enables you to create all sorts of documents, including group emails as well as the typical, hard copy form letter. Other possibilities also include envelopes, labels, and directories. You merge information into an email and send it to coworkers or collaborators using your Outlook Contact list.

To perform a mail merge, you need two things: a mass-produced merge document (one that is created for each recipient, such as a form letter) and the data that goes into the document. The document that is merged with the data can take any form; it is most often a letter or an envelope, but you can merge data into any type of Word document.

As already mentioned, you need data for a mail merge. This can be a list of names and addresses or a list of email addresses. The data is stored in a file called a data source. So, the big question is, "How does the data in the data source know where to end up in a document such as a form letter?"

The information in the data source is inserted into the form letter, envelope, or mailing label using placeholder codes called merge fields. Each merge field in the merge document relates to a piece of information in the data source document, such as first name, last name, or street address, and the merge field gets its name from that particular field in the data source.

Performing a mail merge

The commands you use to perform a mail merge are in the Start Mail Merge group (on the ribbon's Mailings tab). As already mentioned, the merge process requires that you have a document such as a form letter and that you also have a data source. The process of performing the mail merge consists of four distinct parts: creating or opening the merge document; creating or specifying the data source; inserting the merge fields into the main document; and running the merge, which creates the form letters, envelopes, and so on.

Each of these four actions can potentially require you to perform a subset of additional tasks depending on whether you have created your form letter (or other document) and already have a list of recipients for the merge document. Obviously, you need to supply your initial form letter (or other document), but the process is flexible because you can create your letter during the merge process, or you can open an existing letter that you already have created.

The same goes with your list of recipients (the data source), you might create the recipients list on the fly during the merge process, or you might already have the list available (and it might even be in another application, such as Microsoft Outlook). Even if you have the list of recipients available, you can edit the particulars of the list during the merge process, and you can also specify that the merge uses a subset of the available recipients. Obviously, what happens during each major phase of the merge is dictated by your particular needs related to the merge document, the recipient list, and the merge fields you will use.

To perform the mail merge, you can use the Mail Merge Wizard, which walks you through the entire process. To invoke the Mail Merge Wizard, select the Start Mail Merge command and select Step By Step Mail Merge Wizard. The Mail Merge task pane opens, as shown in Figure 9-4.

Figure 9-4   The Mail Merge task pane

The wizard breaks the mail merge process into six distinct steps:

1. **Select Document Type:** This step provides option buttons that enable you to specify the type of merge document you want to create: Letters, Email Messages, Envelopes, Labels, or Directory. A directory does not create a separate document for each of the recipients; an example is a list of names and addresses created from your data source. The Start Mail Merge command also provides you with the option of creating a Normal Word

Document that can then be used as the destination for merged information from a data source.

2. **Select Starting Document:** Here, you specify how you set up the merge document. You can select from the following options: Use the Current Document, Start From Template, and Start From Existing Document.

3. **Select Recipients:** This step not only provides the list of recipients for the merge, but it also determines the merge field codes (based on the data source's fields) that are available to insert into the merge document. You can use an existing list, select from Outlook contacts, or type a new list.

4. **Write Your Letter:** In this step, you type your merge document, such as a letter or email, or you set up your envelope or labels (if you haven't already done it). This is also the step where you insert merge fields into the document. Merge fields included in the task pane are the Address Block, Greeting Line, and Electronic Postage.

CAUTION

Although the Mail Merge Wizard makes sure that you complete all the steps necessary to perform the merge, you might find more flexibility in completing the merge process if you forgo the wizard and use the various commands on the Mailings tab. Therefore, we'll take a closer look at each major part of the mail merge process and add some depth to your knowledge of the various commands on the ribbon's Mailings tab.

5. **Preview Your Letters:** This step previews your letters (or other documents resulting from the merge, such as envelopes or labels). Use the Next and Previous buttons as required to preview the results of the merge.

6. **Complete The Merge:** Finally, you either send the merge results to a printer or edit each of the individual documents that resulted from the merge (such as your letter, envelopes, and so on).

Using the mail merge commands

If you find the Mail Merge Wizard a hindrance rather than a help, you can forgo using the wizard and run through the merge process "manually" by using a series of commands available in the Start Mail Merge group. As each of these commands is initiated (in order), you basically go through the same overall process as the Mail Merge Wizard would to create merged form letters, envelopes, or labels. Simply select the commands from left to right on the Mailings tab, starting with the Start Mail Merge group commands and moving to the Write & Insert Fields group commands. Then move to the Preview Results group commands to the Finish group.

To begin the process, select the Start Mail Merge command in the Start Mail Merge group (see Figure 9-5). As you do when you use the wizard, you select the type of document you want to create using the merge: Letters, Email Messages, Envelopes, Labels, or Directory. The Start Mail Merge command provides an additional option: Normal Word Document, which opens a new blank Word document based on Word's Normal template. You can use this document to create your form letter or directory if you do not already have these documents drafted. Creating your form letter or email before you even think about the merge process probably makes sense. In the final analysis, the content of the letter or email is of primary importance because you are trying to send your message or information out to a number of people. Make sure that you spend the appropriate amount of thought and time on the correspondence itself.

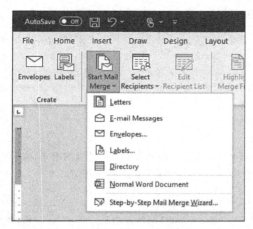

Figure 9-5   Select the type of merge you want to perform.

Once you have a letter (or email) written, you are ready to move on to the next step, which requires that you open or create a recipient list for the merge. The two most problematic parts of performing the merge relate to creating and manipulating the recipient list and then inserting (appropriately) the merge fields into your document (that are used by Word to retrieve the data from your recipient list). Let's look at some issues related to recipient lists, and then we can work with merge fields.

TIP

A form letter always contains the current date (typically at the top of the letter). To insert the date into your form letter so that it automatically updates, open the Date and Time dialog box using the Date & Time command on the Insert tab. Select a date format in the dialog box and then select the Update Automatically check box.

Understanding recipient lists

The data source or recipient list (if you prefer) consists of the information that you merge into your form letter, email, envelope, or another document type (for example, you can merge into a memo or a phone list; Word refers to a list as a directory). As already mentioned, data sources used in mail merges are typically names and addresses, but they can also include other information, such as email addresses and telephone numbers. Data sources can include any information that is important and necessary for the merge.

I want to introduce a couple of terms that can help you work with data sources: records and fields. A record is the information related to a particular person (or place or thing). So, each person in your recipient list has their own record.

More importantly (for understanding the merge process), each piece of information in a record, such as the first name or street address, is called a *field*. The fields in the data source relate directly to the merge field codes that you will insert into your form letter or envelope. This means each field code directly relates to a piece of information (a field) in each record in your recipient list.

NOTE

If you are using the Mail Merge Wizard, the recipient list is created or specified in step 3 of the wizard's merge process provided in the Mail Merge task pane.

When specifying a recipient list for a particular merge, you have options. You can access these options via the Select Recipients command in the Start Mail Merge group (see Figure 9-6).

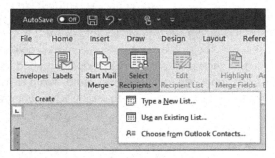

Figure 9-6   Select or create a recipients list.

The options related to the recipient list are as follows:

- **Type A New List:** Use this option to create a new data source using the recipient list tools in Word. We explore this option in more detail in a moment.

- **Use An Existing List:** This option enables you to open an existing list created in Word or data sources created in Microsoft Access. The Select Data Source dialog box also provides options for connecting to shared data sources (on your corporate network) via a Microsoft Office Data Connection or a Microsoft SQL database server.

- **Choose From Outlook Contacts:** With this option, you select the names and addresses for the merge from your Outlook contacts. When you select the option on the Select Recipients menu, the Select Contacts dialog box will open. The Choose Profile dialog box also opens so that you can choose the Outlook profile that provides the contacts for the merge. After you select the profile, the Select Contacts dialog box opens to enable you to select an Outlook contact folder to import. If you only have one profile or you have selected a profile (Always Use This Profile), you won't be bothered by the Choose Profile dialog box.

➤ Outlook permits multiple Outlook profiles on the same computer. For more about Outlook profiles, see "Understanding Outlook profiles" in Chapter 22, "Outlook configuration and essential features."

NOTE

You can create mail merge data sources in Word, Excel, and Access (Microsoft's relational database software). You can also import data from a variety of database sources into Excel and Access. For more about Excel and external databases, see Chapter 15, "Using Excel tables and pivot tables."

Obviously, using existing lists or data sources that are shared on a network makes it easier for you to quickly access the records that you need to include in a merge. However, sometimes you must create the recipient list using the tools Word provides. Thankfully, these tools help you create, edit, and manipulate the records in the data source quickly.

Creating a recipient list

Creating a data source during a mail merge is a straightforward process. Word provides you with a form that you use to enter people's names, addresses, and other information. When you select Type New List on the Select Recipients command menu or in the Mail Merge task pane, the New Address List dialog box opens, as shown in Figure 9-7.

Word provides a default set of fields for the recipient list. The field list includes fields such as Title, First Name, Last Name, and so on. If you want to use the default fields (which also serve as the column headings in the New Address List dialog box), you can enter the name, address, and other information that you want to place in the record for the first recipient. To move forward through the field columns, use the Tab key. To back up a field column, use the Shift+Tab keys. You then create subsequent entries by selecting the New Entry button in the Address List dialog box. Each time you click New Entry, a new row is added to the address list.

If you want to modify the field list, it is important that you do so before you begin to enter field information into the address list. Select Customize Columns in the New Address List dialog box, and the Customize Address List opens, as shown in Figure 9-8.

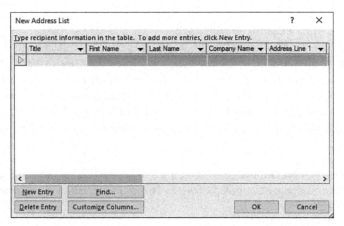

Figure 9-7   Create your records in the New Address List dialog box.

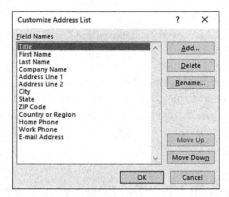

Figure 9-8   The Customize Address List dialog box

You can add, delete, or rename field names in the list. You can also use the Move Up and Move Down buttons to change the relative position of the field columns. If you want to add a field, click the Add button. The Add Field dialog box opens. Enter the name for your new field and click OK. You can use the Delete and Rename buttons as needed to modify the field list for your own particular needs. When you finish modifying the default field names, click OK to return to the New Address List dialog box.

Whether you modify the list's fields or not, enter your records as needed in the New Address List dialog box. If you want to delete a particular record, select that record and then click Delete Entry. When you finish entering your records, click the OK button on the New Address List dialog box.

The Save Address List dialog box opens. By default, your data sources are saved in the My Data Sources folder, which is a subfolder of your Documents folder. Provide a name for the data source and specify a new location for the file (if required). The file type for the new file is Microsoft Office Address Lists, which is saved with the .mdb extension (the same as Microsoft Access databases). To save the new data source, click the Save button.

Editing and manipulating a recipient list

After you create or select a recipient list for the merge, the Edit Recipient List command in the Start Mail Merge group is activated. The Mail Merge Recipients dialog box opens when you select it, as shown in Figure 9-9.

This dialog box enables you to refine the recipient list using Sort, Filter, and Find Duplicates tools. You can also access individual records in the data source and edit them when needed.

You can sort the records in the recipients list by up to three sort criteria. Select Sort to open the Filter And Sort dialog box. You can use the Sort By drop-down menu to specify the first field to sort by and then use the optional two Then By drop-down menus to specify a second and third field for the sort if necessary. Also, you can specify whether the sort should be ascending or descending using the supplied option buttons. When you are ready to perform the sort, click OK. The records in the Mail Merge Recipients dialog box sort according to your sort parameters.

NOTE

The Mail Merge Recipients dialog box also allows you to validate addresses in the address list. To do this, you need validation add-on software. Visit www.microsoft.com for more information about address validation options for Office.

If you want to preclude specific records from being included in the merge, deselect the check box for that record or records. This is a quick fix for removing a recipient from the merge but keeping the record intact in the recipient's list.

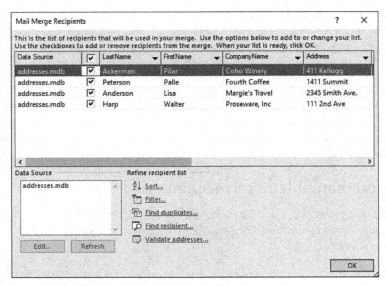

Figure 9-9   The Mail Merge Recipients dialog box

You can also filter the records in the data source. This enables you to select a subset of recipients to include in the merge based on specific criteria related to a field or fields. You can filter by up to six fields.

To open the Filter And Sort dialog box with the Filter Records tab selected, select Filter (in the Mail Merge Recipients dialog box). You then specify the field or fields by which you want to filter the data source by using the Field drop-down menus, as shown in Figure 9-10.

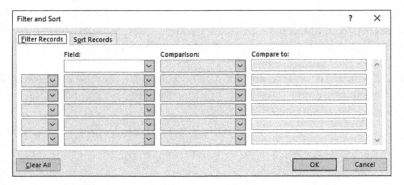

Figure 9-10   The Filter Records tab

After you select a field, you can specify the type of comparison you want to make to that field's content. You can specify a number of comparisons, including Equal To, Not Equal To, Less Than, Is Blank, and Contains. After you select the Comparison Type (such as Equal To), you type the text to be used by the comparison in the Compare To box for that particular field. For example, you might want to send letters to people on your list who have a particular ZIP Code, so you would select the Postal Code field, set the Comparison Type as Equal To, and then type the ZIP Code in the Compare To box.

You could also create a filter to filter the list for a specific state or use the Not Equal To comparison parameter to filter out people in the list who reside in a specific state. (Filtering gives you many possibilities for specifying or precluding records in the address list that meet a particular condition or conditions.)

After you set your filter parameters, click OK. The records listed in the Mail Merge Recipients dialog box are a subset of the original list, based on the criteria you set for your filter.

NOTE

You can set up conditional statements for your filters combining field criteria using AND, or you can set up a conditional OR statement in which the field criteria can be equal to a particular field or another selected field. Bottom line: You can create some elegant filters using the tools on the Filter Records tab.

The Mail Merge Recipients dialog box also gives you access to the Edit Data Source dialog box (which is similar to the New Address List dialog box discussed earlier). In the Edit Data Source box, select the current data source and then click the Edit button. Use the Edit Data Source dialog box to edit records as needed. You can also add records in the Edit Data Source dialog box using the New Entry button.

Using merge fields

When the data source is ready for the merge, the next step in the merge process revolves around inserting the appropriate merge fields into the form letter or other merge document. The field codes are inserted using the commands in the Write & Insert Fields group on the ribbon's Mailings tab.

If you are creating form letters, envelopes, or mailing labels, one of the most often used set of field codes is the Address Block. The Address Block combines the name, company name, and address information, including the state and ZIP Code.

To insert the Address Block in your document (typically three lines below the date in a letter), position the insertion point appropriately and then click the Address Block command. The Insert Address Block dialog box opens, as shown in Figure 9-11.

CHAPTER 9

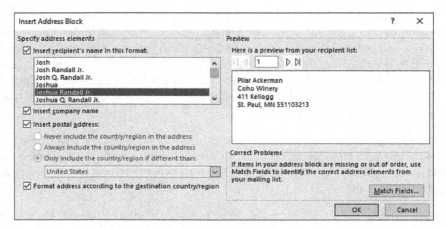

Figure 9-11   The Insert Address Block dialog box

The Insert Address Block dialog box provides you with different formats for inserting the recipient's name and address information. Choose one of the formats listed. You can also specify whether the Company Name field is included in the address block and whether to include the country/region in the address.

When you finish configuring the address block, click OK to insert it into the merge document. The merge code <<AddressBlock>> is placed at the insertion point.

Another useful merge command is the Greeting Line command. It inserts a salutation such as Dear or To and enables you to specify how the name field data is included with the greeting. Also, you can control the punctuation used after the greeting (comma, colon, or none). As with the Address Block, the Greeting Line has its own dialog box.

Be advised that the Address Block and Greeting Line are configured to use the default field names that Word supplies you when you create a recipients list (in Word). If your data source originated in another application, such as Microsoft Access or an external SQL database, you must match the field names that you used there to the typical Word merge fields that specify information such as the recipient's name or address.

Click the Match Fields button in the Address Block or Greeting Line dialog box. This opens the Match Fields dialog box (see Figure 9-12). You can also open the Match Fields dialog box using the Match Fields command in the Write & Insert Fields group.

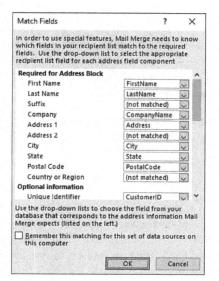

Figure 9-12   The Match Fields dialog box

The Word mail merge fields are listed on the left side of the Match Fields dialog box. You use the drop-down menus to specify the matching field from your data source. Each drop-down menu shows all the field names for your recipients list that need to be reconciled with the field names that Word uses. For example, if you used the field name Address for the street number and street in your data source, you match it to the Address 1 Word field. After you match all the fields, you close the Match Fields dialog box by clicking OK.

TIP

You can use the Preview pane in the Insert Address Block dialog box to preview all records in your recipient list. This enables you to catch any records that have blank address fields or other typos.

You can also insert individual field codes into a merge document if required. Place the insertion point in the merge document where you want to insert the field code. Select the Insert Merge Field command on the Mailings tab and select a merge field from the list provided. Remember that merge field codes can relate to any data. For example, you can set up a data source that includes information such as the names of your clients' spouses or their favorite sports and then insert that information into an appropriately crafted merge letter. This enables you to personalize each of the form letters or other merge documents that you create.

CHAPTER 9

Using merge rules

One other merge tool that can help you personalize your merge documents and control the content of the documents created during the merge is the Rules command, found in the Write & Insert Fields group. With this command, you can take advantage of several rules that control the content of merged documents during the actual merge process.

When you click the Rules command, the list of rules appears. The following rules, which are special fields, are provided on the list:

- **Ask:** This field prompts you so that you can enter text during the merge. When you create an Ask field, you create a bookmark that can include a default response; the field appears as an empty bookmark in the merge document.

- **Fill-In:** This field prompts you to enter text placed in your document (replacing the field code) after completing the merge. The Fill-In field can contain default text if you want. You provide prompt text for the field (that is, the field prompts you for the text to be entered), and you have the option to provide default fill-in text.

- **If...Then...Else:** This field enables you to enter two different text blocks into the merged documents, depending on whether a condition is met. For example, suppose you have an actual storefront in a particular state for your business. In that case, this field can insert the store's location (and address) when the recipient's state matches the If statement.

  TIP

  You can also reconcile your field names to the Word field names via the Match Fields command in the Write & Insert Fields group. This command opens the Match Fields dialog box. If you consistently use data sources that utilize the same field names, select the Remember This Matching For This Set Of Data Sources On This Computer check box so that you won't have to match the fields each time you do a merge.

- **Merge Record #:** You use this field to provide a true count of the number of records in the data file even when you use fields such as Skip Record If to merge certain recipients into the same letter or other merged document.

- **Merge Sequence #:** This field counts the actual number of merged documents that result from your merge.

- **Next Record:** This field has Word insert the next data record into the current merged document without starting a new page. This field is used by default when you create mailing labels during a merge.

- **Next Record If:** This field enables you to set a conditional statement; if the statement is met, the next record is merged into the current document without beginning a new document. This can be useful when more than one recipient in your list works at the same company. You can send a single letter to all the recipients who meet the If condition of working at that particular company.

- **Set Bookmark:** This field can control the text referred to by a bookmark, such as the bookmark created by the Ask field. You can also use the Set Bookmark field with a conditional statement such as the If...Then...Else field.

- **Skip Record If:** You use this field to set a conditional statement so that recipients who meet the condition are not included in the merge.

TIP

You can highlight the fields you placed in the merge document when you preview the merge results by selecting the Highlight Merge Fields command in the Write & Insert Fields group. Click the command again to turn off the highlighting.

Some of these special fields are useful to you, and some you might not need. Experimenting with these fields, particularly Fill-In and If...Then...Else, definitely makes sense because they can give you added capability to personalize the letters that result from your merge.

Previewing merge results

When you have your merge document, recipient list, and merge field codes squared away, you can preview the merge results. Select the Preview Results command in the Preview Results group.

You can then use the Next Record and Previous Record buttons to preview each of the resulting merged documents. You can also use the Find Recipient command to open the Find Entry dialog box. You can then search for information in all the merge fields or a specific field. To toggle off the Preview Results feature, click Preview Results.

The Check For Errors command is another tool that you can use to check the merge results (which can simulate the merge or complete the merge and report errors). When you select Check For Errors, the Checking And Reporting Errors dialog box opens, as shown in Figure 9-13.

The dialog box provides three options:

- **Simulate The Merge And Report Errors In A New Document:** This option performs the merge and displays a message box detailing whether errors occurred during the merge. When you click OK, you return to your merge document.

- **Complete The Merge, Pausing To Report Each Error As It Occurs:** This option pauses the merge each time an error is detected and then creates a merged document.

CHAPTER 9

- **Complete The Merge Without Pausing. Report Errors In A New Document:**
This option completes the merge and details any errors in the newly created merged document.

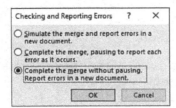

Figure 9-13   The Checking And Reporting Errors dialog box

Each of these options provides feedback regarding whether an issue arose with the merge. They are also useful in saving paper because the merge doesn't go directly to the printer.

Completing the merge

If you chose either of the Complete The Merge options in the Checking And Reporting Errors dialog box (the second and third options), you essentially complete the merge. You can save the resulting merged document and then print the document as needed (or, if the merge process has errors, you can correct the errors and run the merge again).

You're not required to check the merge for errors, so you can complete the merge using the Finish & Merge command in the Finish group (it is the only command in this group). Select Finish & Merge and then select one of the following from the list provided:

- **Edit Individual Documents:** This creates a new merged document. This is probably the best choice; it gives you an opportunity to look through the results of the merge before printing.

- **Print Documents:** This sends the merge results to your printer.

- **Send Email Messages:** If you performed an email merge, this option sends the resulting emails through your Outlook email client.

After you make your selection, the Merge to New Document dialog box will open. You can choose to merge all records, the current record or specifica a range of records (by number). Once you have selected the appropriate option button, you are finished. You have completed the merge process, and your merge letters will appear on your screen or go directly to your default printer (depending on whether you merged to a new document or directly to the printer).

Creating merged envelopes and labels

The procedure for creating envelopes and mailing labels is much the same as the process for creating form letters. You can use the Mail Merge Wizard, or you can cycle through the commands on the Mailings tab of the ribbon as you complete each step (Start Mail Merge, Select Recipients, and so on).

For merged envelopes, a crucial step is selecting the appropriate envelope type. When you select Envelopes in either the Start Mail Merge list or the wizard's task pane, the Envelope Options dialog box opens. This dialog box enables you to select the envelope size and the fonts for the delivery and return addresses. Figure 9-14 shows the Envelope Options dialog box.

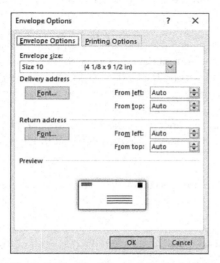

Figure 9-14   The Envelope Options dialog box

The dialog box also provides a Printing Options tab where you can specify the feed method and the orientation of the envelope in the printer. You can also select the printer tray that contains the envelopes.

After you select the envelope type, click OK to close the Envelope Options dialog box; the envelope then appears in the Word workspace. You can select or create your recipient list and insert the merge fields onto the envelope.

When you select labels for your merge document, the Label Options dialog box enables you to select the label vendor and product number and to specify the tray for the labels. Labels are a bit tricky when inserting your merge fields (after you create or select your data source). Insert the merge field or fields (in most cases, you will probably use the Address Block only) onto the first label.

Here is the important step in getting the labels to work: Click the Update Labels command in the Write & Insert Fields group. This places the field code you entered on the first label, such as the Address Block, on all the labels. Note that each label (other than the first label) is automatically assigned the Next Record field, which keeps the labels on the same page when you complete the merge.

Understanding Word fields

The mail merge process provides a good look at some of the possibilities that can be accomplished using fields. Merge fields pull data from a recipient list and place the data in the merged documents. You can use other fields, such as the Skip Record If field, to preclude certain recipients in your list from being included in the merge (based on a condition).

Word provides various other field types that you can use to enhance your documents and build online forms. For example, when you insert the current date into a document using the Date and Time dialog box, you have the option of selecting the Update Automatically check box. This option means that Word inserts a date field into your document, and the field is updated (to the current date) each time you open the document. Page numbering in your document is also controlled by a field when you insert the page number using the Page Number command on the ribbon's Insert tab. So, you are using fields even in simple documents, although you might not be aware of it.

You can insert field codes into a document via the Field dialog box. To open this dialog box, access the ribbon's Insert tab. Then select the Quick Parts command (in the Text group) and select Field on the Quick Parts menu. Figure 9-15 shows the Field dialog box.

Many fields are available in the Field Names list, particularly when the Categories selection is set to All. You might want to concentrate on certain categories of fields that enable you to easily input information related to dates, document information, and user information. Many of these informational fields are best placed in the header or footer of a document and are particularly useful when users on a network share a document. The fields can serve a housekeeping function by specifying where the document is stored (the path) and which user saved the document in its current form.

For example, when you select the Document Information category, the available fields in the Field Names box include Author, FileName, LastSavedBy, NumPages, and other fields. These fields enable you to stamp a document with information that was stamped on the document at its creation (such as the author and the file name). Also, documents can be stamped with information that can change during the document's life (such as who last saved the document and the number of pages currently in the document).

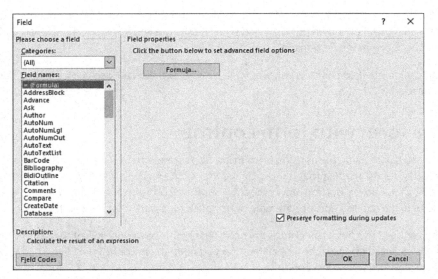

Figure 9-15   The Field dialog box

TIP

You can format field codes as if they are text. For example, select a field code such as the Address Block and then make it bold. The resulting merged information appears in bold in the merged documents.

You can view the field code for a selected field in the Field dialog box. Select a field and then click the Field Codes button. The field's code displays on the right of the dialog box. Click Hide Codes to return to the default field view.

TIP

If you are placing fields in a header or footer related to a document's properties, remember that the Document Info command on the Header & Footer Tools Design tab provides easy access to fields such as Author, Status, and Keywords.

To insert a field into a document, select the field in the Field Names list (in the Field dialog box) and then click OK. The field is inserted into the document at the insertion point.

When you insert the field, the results of the field (such as the date, page number, or file name) appear in the document. To view the field codes (which help you manage the fields), you can press Alt+F9. To toggle back to the field results, press Alt+F9 again.

You can also change Word's options, so that field codes are shown in a document: Select File to open the Backstage view and then select Options. In the Word Options window, select Advanced. In the Show Document Content area, select the Show Field Codes Instead Of Their

Values check box. You can also specify how fields should be shaded in the document using the Field Shading drop-down menu (which is just below the Show Field Codes Instead Of Their Values check box in the Options list).

You can delete field codes as you would any Word text. You can also copy, cut, and paste fields as needed.

Building a form with form controls

You can build online forms using form fields, also referred to as form controls. The control is a placeholder for the text that is input by the user of the form. Form controls can consist of text fields, check boxes, or drop-down menus. Your form controls can also include help text, which is useful in getting the appropriate type of response for a particular field on the form.

The various form fields or controls are accessed via the Developer tab of the ribbon. This tab is not included on the ribbon by default, so you need to enable it. Select File to go to Word's Backstage and then click Options.

In the Word Options window, select Customize Ribbon in the Customize Ribbon list (on the right of the window). Select Developer in the Main Tab list. Then click OK. This puts the Developer tab on the ribbon.

To create a form that any number of people can use (which is particularly useful in a setting where you work on a network), you need to create a template. Open a new blank document and then save the document in the Save As dialog box; be sure to change the Save As Type setting to Word Template.

When the new template is ready to go, you can insert the various form fields that you want to use on the form. Follow these steps:

1. Select the ribbon's Developer tab. In the Controls group, select Design Mode.

2. The Controls group provides all the control fields you need (the controls are the commands on the left of the Controls group). To view the name of a control, hover the mouse over that particular control. When you are ready click a control to insert it. The controls are as follows:

    - **Rich Text:** Provides a text block control and is typically used for text entry that you do not want changed or accessed.

    - **Plain Text:** Provides a text block control.

    - **Picture Content:** Enables the user to select an image to insert into the form.

    - **Building Block Gallery:** Enables the user to select text blocks from a building block gallery.

- **Check Box:** Provides a check box for user response.

- **Combo Box:** Enables the user to select a response from a drop-down menu or type in a text response.

- **Drop-down menu:** Provides a list of responses for the user.

- **Date Picker:** Enables the user to select a date from an interactive calendar.

- **Repeating Section:** This is a new control type designed to repeat multiple instances of content (including control content and field information). To take advantage of this control (which is an advanced feature), you must build an XML script that provides the repeating information to the Repeating Section control.

- **Legacy Forms:** Supplies a list of legacy Word form controls such as the legacy Checkbox Form Field.

- **ActiveX Controls:** Supplies ActiveX control possibilities such as the Option and Toggle buttons.

3. Insert all your form fields, as needed, to complete the form.

4. Save the document as a new template (change the Save As Type setting to Word Template in the Save As dialog box).

NOTE

By default, field codes (that is, their result) are shaded with a gray background when you select the field text.

TIP

When designing your form layout, you might want to scratch it out on a piece of paper before creating it in Word. Remember that using various drop-down menus and check boxes on the form require the form to have an easy-to-use layout. Also, you might want to use a table to position the various form fields on the page.

After you insert all the form controls on the template page (or pages), you must go back and set the properties for each of the controls (although you can set the properties for each field as you insert them). For example, if you inserted a Drop-Down List field, you must provide the list of responses that the field provides when selected by the user. Select the field control and then click the Properties command in the Controls group. The Content Control Properties dialog box opens, as shown in Figure 9-16.

In the Content Control Properties dialog box, you can add an optional title and tag name for the control. You can lock the control using the Content Control Cannot Be Deleted and

CHAPTER 9

Contents Cannot Be Edited check boxes. To remove the default value (Choose An Item), select it in the Drop-Down List Properties. Then use the Add button to add the responses you want to include in the drop-down menu.

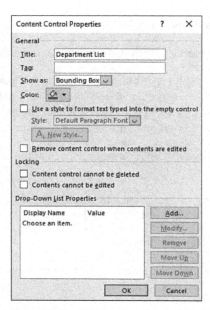

Figure 9-16   The Content Control Properties dialog box

You can change the order of the responses using the Move Up and Move Down buttons. After you edit the control's properties to suit your needs, click OK. You can also modify an existing property by selecting it in the list and then selecting the Modify button (a Remove button is also available).

When you have the controls inserted and configured, restrict the editing on the template so that users cannot change it (other than allowing user response) when it is in use. Select the Restrict Editing command in the Protect group. The Restrict Formatting And Editing task pane opens. In the Editing Restrictions area of the task pane, select the Allow Only This Type Of Editing in the Document check box. Then select Filling In Forms from the drop-down menu and click Yes, Start Enforcing Protection to protect the template. You must enter a password (twice) in the Start Enforcing Protection dialog box. Save the template, and it is ready for use.

Creating special documents

Options for large documents   257

Creating a table of contents   258

Working with captions and tables of figures   266

Generating an index   271

Working with citations and bibliographies   274

Tracking document changes   280

Building a better "big" document   287

Creating a master document   290

Word provides several features and tools that are designed for creating complex and specialized documents. For example, if you create a large document that requires a table of contents, Word has you covered. Word also enables you to easily divide a large document into different sections; each section can then have its own formatting, including page-layout attributes such as margins and page orientation.

In this chapter, we explore how to create documents that consist of more than just a couple of pages. We look at creating a table of contents, adding sections to a document, and working with a table of figures. We also discuss how to create cross-references, indexes, citations, bibliographies, footnotes, and endnotes and how to track the changes made in a document by multiple authors.

Options for large documents

Word offers a number of features that make it easier for you to work with larger, more complex documents. Examples of this include the use of bookmarks to navigate to specific spots in the document quickly, and you can also add nonprinting comments to the document to help you remember the status of a particular page or the need to revise particular content.

Large documents can also be divided into a master document where its different parts are kept in separate files. The master document feature also provides a set of special commands when you view the document in the Outline view. Master documents make it easy for you to stay organized and better edit large documents. Also, a master document can source files from different authors, making it an excellent way for multiple users to collaborate on a single, complex document.

TIP

When you work with larger documents, you typically use sections to break the document into different parts so that each section can have its own headers, footers, and page-numbering scheme. Sections are discussed in Chapter 8, "Working with tables, columns, and sections."

When you are collaborating with other authors and editors, you can take advantage of the Track Changes feature. Each person's changes are tracked in the document, and you can accept or reject these changes as needed. You can even compare different versions of the same document. Let's begin our discussion of Word and larger documents by exploring how to create a table of contents for a document divided into chapters or parts.

Creating a table of contents

If you want to make it easy for the reader of a large document to find specific parts or chapters, you need to include a table of contents (TOC). Creating a TOC in Word relies on the use of specific styles that reflect the organizational structure of your document. For example, you can use Word's built-in heading styles (Heading 1, Heading 2, Heading 3, and so forth; see Figure 10-1) to format the different levels of headings in the document. You also have the option of creating your own series of headings and using those to specify different levels in your table of contents. Whether you use built-in styles or create your own, you have to remember to use the styles consistently to format the various headings that you will use to specify the parts and levels of your document.

A good example is a document that is divided into parts and then further subdivided into chapters (each part contains several chapters). If you use Word's heading styles to format the different division levels in the document, you might use Heading 1 for the parts (Part I, Part II, and so on) and Heading 2 for the chapter titles. By assigning these built-in styles (or your own) to the different headings, you can generate a table of contents that shows two levels: parts and chapters. This process works because Word can recognize a particular heading level by the style you've assigned to it.

When you create the TOC, the page numbers generated depend on the location of the headings formatted with the styles you have specified for the different levels of the table of contents. If you edit the document and move any of the headings, you need to update the table of contents to reflect the new page numbers. You can quickly regenerate an existing table of contents by selecting the Update Table button at the top of your generated table of contents or by using the Update Table command in the Table Of Contents group. We discuss options for updating a table of contents later in this chapter in the "Adding entries and updating the TOC" section.

➤ For more about styles, "Understanding styles" in Chapter 7, "Enhancing Word documents."

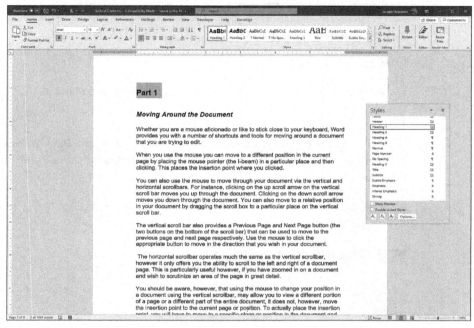

Figure 10-1   Assign styles to your document headings.

The first step when creating a TOC is to use styles (either built-in or your own) to mark and format the various heading levels in the document. You can quickly format the different headings in the document using the built-in Word Heading styles on the ribbon's Home tab in the Styles gallery. You can also mark the headings for the different TOC levels using the Add Text command in the Table Of Contents group.

Place the insertion point on a heading in the document and then select the Add Text command. Select Level 1, Level 2, or Level 3 to mark the level of the current heading. The heading will also be formatted using the built-in heading style. Level 1 is equivalent to Heading 1; Level 2 is equivalent to Heading 2; and...well, you get the picture. After you have assigned the headings the appropriate style (for the TOC), you can generate the table of contents.

Creating a table of contents with built-in styles

If you use Word's built-in styles (Heading 1, Heading 2, and so on), you can quickly insert a table of contents into the document. However, before you do so, I recommend creating a blank page at the beginning of your document for your table of contents. Creating a new section (a section break with a new page) is an even better idea. That way, you can assign different headers and footers to the table of contents section of the document and use other headers and footers for the remainder of the document.

To insert the table of contents, follow these steps:

1. Park the insertion point where you want to insert the table of contents.

2. Select the ribbon's References tab.

3. In the Table Of Contents group, select the Table Of Contents command.

    ### TIP

    You can assign the built-in Word styles to your headings using the Quick Styles in the Styles group or by opening the Styles window and assigning the Quick Styles from the window.

4. From the Table Of Contents gallery, choose one of the three built-in TOC styles provided to format the different levels of the TOC, as shown in Figure 10-2.

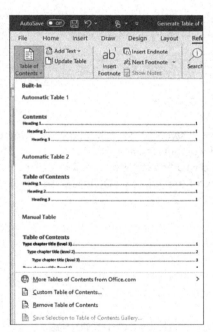

Figure 10-2   Select a TOC style from the gallery.

The table of contents is inserted into the document at the insertion point. The various levels of the table of contents are formatted by the TOC style that you selected in the Table Of Contents gallery. When you select the table of contents (click within the table of contents area), a table toolbar appears in the top-left part of the table. On the left part of the toolbar is a button that provides access to the built-in table of contents styles and a command that enables you to remove the table of contents. On the right part of the toolbar is a button that enables you to update the table (Update Table) if you have edited the document or added other items to the table of contents using your TOC styles.

Creating a table of contents with your own styles

The alternative to creating a TOC based on Word's built-in Quick Styles (the standard heading styles) is to create your own styles and use them to format your document headings and to specify the different heading levels for the table of contents. As with generating a table of contents with built-in styles, the first step is to assign the appropriate level style to each heading in the document.

The trick with using your own styles is that you need to let Word know that these styles replace the heading quick styles that it normally uses to generate the table of contents. You do this in the Table Of Contents dialog box.

Park your insertion point where you want to insert the table of contents and then select the Table Of Contents command. In the Command gallery, select Custom Table Of Contents, which opens the Table Of Contents dialog box with the Table Of Contents tab selected, as shown in Figure 10-3.

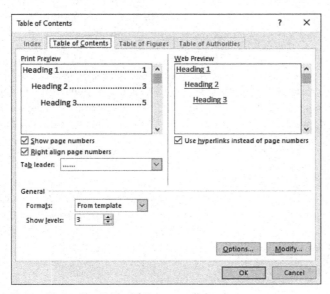

Figure 10-3   The Table Of Contents dialog box

The Table Of Contents tab gives you a preview of the table of contents hierarchy for Word's built-in heading styles (by default). It also gives you access to several options, such as whether to use page numbers in the table of contents and the tab leader's style. Also, you can set the number of levels for the table of contents using the Show Levels spin box.

To force Word to recognize your styles as the TOC levels, you must open the Table Of Contents Options dialog box; click the Options button. Figure 10-4 shows the Table Of Contents Options dialog box.

Inside OUT

Using a table of contents to move around a document

When you create a table of contents, all the entries it contains are actually linked to the headings (styles) that you used to generate the TOC, which means that the headings listed in the TOC can be used as hyperlinks to navigate the document quickly. This is particularly useful if the document will be used or shared electronically via OneDrive or a corporate network rather than printed and shared via hard copies.

When you are creating the TOC, open the Table Of Contents dialog box and make sure the Use Hyperlinks Instead Of Page Numbers check box is selected (it is the default setting, but it doesn't hurt to check). Then go ahead and generate your TOC as detailed in this chapter. You can then use the TOC to navigate the document. To move to a particular page in a document, press and hold the Ctrl key and then select a heading in the TOC; you will then be taken to that heading.

Even though you specified hyperlinks rather than page numbers when you selected the Use Hyperlinks Instead Of Page Numbers check box, the TOC will include the page numbers for each heading that appears in the TOC. Even if you must provide the TOC to someone in hard copy, you can still generate your TOC using the hyperlinks option.

By default, Heading 1 is marked as TOC Level 1, Heading 2 is marked as TOC Level 2, and so on. Individually select the numbers in the TOC level boxes for the default headings and delete them. This removes the check mark for each of the built-in headings. To specify one of your styles as a TOC hierarchical level, type the level number (1, 2, 3, and so on) into the appropriate style's TOC level box. After you have assigned the various TOC levels to your styles, click OK to return to the Table Of Contents dialog box. Click OK, and the table of contents (based on your styles) is inserted into the document.

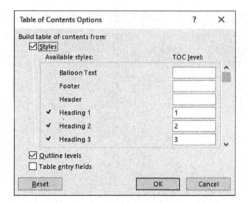

Figure 10-4   The Table Of Contents Options dialog box

Adding entries and updating the TOC

You can add entries to the table of contents even after you have inserted the TOC into the document. This is useful if you missed a heading when assigning styles to the TOC levels and, as a result, the heading was not included in the table of contents.

Select the heading and then click the Add Text command in the Table Of Contents group. On the Add Text list, select the TOC level to assign to the selected heading (Level 1, Level 2, and so on). Note that the default is Do Not Show In Table Of Contents.

Now that you have marked a new entry for the table of contents using the Add Text command, you need to update the TOC. Select the Update Table command in the Table Of Contents group (or the Update Table button that appears at the top of your selected TOC). The Update Table Of Contents dialog box opens, as shown in Figure 10-5.

Select the Update Entire Table option button. Then click OK to close the dialog box. The table of contents is updated, and any headings you added to the TOC using the Add Text command are included in it.

If you need to delete a table of contents, you can select the table of contents and then press Delete. You can also delete the TOC from the Table Of Contents (command) gallery. Select Remove Table Of Contents.

CHAPTER 10

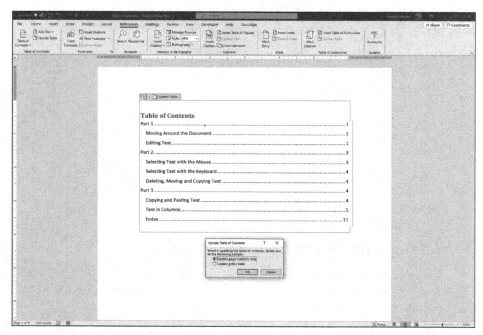

Figure 10-5   The Update Table Of Contents dialog box

Building a TOC with field codes

Another option for building a table of contents in a document uses the TC field code. This method identifies the heading and the TOC level for the heading using the TC field, which is placed to the right of the selected text. Because the code is nonprinting, its appearance in the document just serves as a marker. To view the TC field codes as you insert them in the document, click the Show/Hide command on the ribbon's Home tab (in the Paragraph group).

CAUTION

If the heading you are adding to the TOC using the Add Text command is assigned a different style than the other headings at that level, it is not reformatted with that level's assigned style. Assign the style to the heading and then update the table instead of using the Add Text command.

You can insert the TC field via the Field dialog box (as you can other field codes), but you must use some switches (switches are field codes that modify a field code such as turning it on or off) and edit the field so that it provides the TOC-level information for the entry. Marking items for the table of contents with the TC field is much easier using the Mark Table Of Contents Entry dialog box because it enables you to select the TOC entry level.

➤ Fields are also discussed in Chapter 9, "Managing mailings and forms."

Select the text that you want to mark for the table of contents. Press Shift+Alt+O. The Mark Table Of Contents Entry dialog box opens, as shown in Figure 10-6.

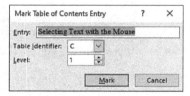

Figure 10-6   The Mark Table Of Contents Entry dialog box

The text you select appears in the Entry box. The Table Identifier box is set to C by default and can remain as is. Use the Level spin box to specify the level for the entry. Then click Mark. Repeat the process as needed to mark all the headings with the TC field and the appropriate TOC level. Click Close to close the Mark Table Of Contents Entry dialog box.

To generate the table of contents, select the Table Of Contents command on the References tab and select Custom Table Of Contents. Doing so opens the Table Of Contents dialog box.

On the Table Of Contents tab, click the Options button. In the Table Of Contents Options dialog box, clear the Outline Level check box, and select the Table Entry Fields check box (because your TOC is based on field codes instead of styles). Click OK, and then click OK again to close the two dialog boxes. The TOC is inserted into the document.

Obviously, using styles to designate the TOC level for headings in your document is much more straightforward than using the TC field; however, you might want to generate two different TOCs in the same document. The Word Table Of Contents feature enables you to create only one TOC per document, but you can generate a second TOC in the document if you know how to mark TOC entries with the TC field (and a couple of other things that I discuss later).

The procedure for creating two TOCs in the same document is straightforward. Create the first TOC in the document using styles, and then insert the TOC using the Table Of Contents command (as you would for a single table of contents). One TOC down, one to go.

Inserting the second TOC is a little trickier. Mark all the entries for the second TOC using the TC field (via the Mark Table Of Contents Entry dialog box). Then place the insertion point where you want to insert the second TOC into the document.

Now you need to insert a TOC field code at the insertion point, which generates the second table of contents (using the entries marked with the TC code). Select the Quick Parts command (on the ribbon's Insert tab) and then select Field. The Field dialog box opens.

CHAPTER 10

In the Categories box, select Index And Tables. Then in the Field Names box, select the TOC field. You must edit the TOC field code with a switch, so select the Field Codes button at the bottom of the dialog box. Then click Options.

In the Switches list, select the \f switch and click Add To Field. Click in the Field codes box and type **C**. (Remember that C was the table identifier designated in the Mark Table Of Contents Entry dialog box.) Figure 10-7 shows the Field Options dialog box with the edited field code.

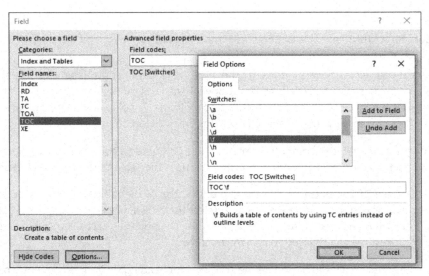

Figure 10-7   The Field Options dialog box

Click OK to return to the Field dialog box. Click OK to close the Field dialog box. When you return to the document, the second table of contents appears at the insertion point.

Working with captions and tables of figures

Business-related reports, articles for scholarly publications and other professional documents often contain tables, images, and other figures that provide supporting material for the document's narrative. For example, a chart detailing quarterly sales data typically accompanies text related to how the sales for the quarter went. You can easily add captions to your document figures and even generate a table of figures, giving the reader of the document a reference for finding particular figures in the document.

Inserting a caption

To add a caption to an image or table, select the image or table and then select the Insert Caption command on the References tab, or you can right-click the item (such as a photo) and select Insert Caption from the shortcut menu that appears. The Caption dialog box opens, as shown in Figure 10-8.

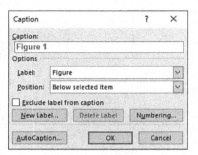

Figure 10-8   The Caption dialog box

The figure numbers are assigned automatically and sequentially to each subsequent figure. You can include additional text for the caption by typing it in the Caption text box. In the Options area of the dialog box, you can specify the label type for the figure: Figure, Table, or Equation. You can also use the Position drop-down menu to specify the position for the caption and modify the caption numbering for your figures, if needed. Select the Numbering button in the Caption dialog box to access the Caption Numbering dialog box. This enables you to change the format for the numbering, and you can include the chapter number with the figure number by selecting the Include Chapter Number check box. You must specify the style that you used for the heading that starts each chapter.

> ### TIP
>
> If you want to place several figure objects, such as Excel charts, into a document, you can use the AutoCaption command to automatically add a caption when you insert a particular figure type. The figure types include Excel charts, PowerPoint slides, and Word tables.
>
> After you have configured the caption settings for the figure, click OK to insert the caption in the document.

Inserting a table of figures

When you add a caption to a figure, you are assigning that figure the figure style. This means that once you have assigned a caption to each figure, you can easily insert a table of figures into your document.

Park the insertion point where you want to insert the table of figures in the document. On the ribbon's References tab, select Insert Table Of Figures to open the Table Of Figures dialog box, as shown in Figure 10-9.

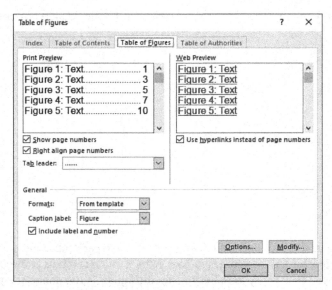

Figure 10-9   The Table Of Figures dialog box

You control whether page numbers are included in the table and the type of dot leader that separates the figure caption from the page number. The most important setting in the Table Of Figures dialog box is the Caption Label setting. Its options are None, Equation, Figure, and Table. If you are building a table of figures for items that you assigned the Figure Caption Label, make sure that it is selected in the Caption Label drop-down menu.

When you are ready to generate the table of figures, click OK. The table of figures is inserted into the document. If you add figures (with captions) to the document, you can easily update the table of figures.

Select the table of figures, and then select the Update Table command in the Captions group. You also can right-click the table and then select Update Field on the shortcut menu. Both of these possibilities open the Update Table Of Figures dialog box. Select the Update Entire Table option button and then click OK. The table updates to include additional figures you have added to the document.

TIP

Like the Table Of Contents dialog box, the Table Of Figures dialog box also provides a Use Hyperlinks Instead Of Page Numbers check box. This means that if you generate the table of figures with this check box selected, you can actually use the figure links included in the Table Of Figures to navigate the document. Press the Ctrl key and then select a figure listed in the Table Of Figures to move to that point in the document.

Using cross-references

Complex documents often require you to provide readers with the capability to quickly reference other information in the document that is pertinent to the text they are currently reading. This is where cross-references are essential. Cross-references are notations in the document that tell the reader where to find additional information on a particular subject matter. Cross-references are essentially navigation mileposts within the document that make it easy for the reader to follow the information trail related to a particular topic referenced more than once in the document.

Word's cross-referencing capability is extremely flexible. You can create cross-references associated with a heading, figure, table, or bookmark. Any bookmarked text can serve as a cross-reference. The cross-reference can give you page number information or can reference a particular table or figure number.

The great thing about cross-references is that they react to changes in the document. For example, if you move a figure noted by a cross-reference to another location in the document and renumber it, the cross-reference updates to provide the correct figure number. If text is rearranged in the document and headings associated with cross-references move, the cross-references update to provide the correct page numbers for the cited headings.

Creating a cross-reference is really a two-step process. First, you supply the anchor for the cross-reference. As already mentioned, this can be a table, an equation, or a figure that has been assigned a caption. Other possibilities are as follows:

- **Numbered Item:** Text in the document that has been numbered using the Numbering command.

- **Heading:** Text headings that have been assigned one of Word's built-in heading styles.

- **Bookmark:** Any text that has been assigned a bookmark. (We discuss bookmarks later in this chapter.)

- **Footnote:** Any footnote that you have placed in the document.

- **Endnote:** Any endnote that you have placed in the document.

CAUTION

If you want to create cross-references for tables, figures, or equations, you must use the Caption tool to assign captions to your tables, equations, or figures. The caption provides the cross-reference with the information needed to locate the figure or table and specify the figure or table number.

To create a cross-reference, place the insertion point in the document where you want to insert the cross-reference. Type the introductory text for the cross-reference, such as "For more information, see page."

Select the ribbon's References tab and then click the Cross-Reference command in the Captions group, which opens the Cross-Reference dialog box.

Select the Reference type for the cross-reference (such as Heading, Bookmark, Figure, and so on). The items available in the list box reflect the reference type you selected. For example, if you select Heading as the reference type, all the headings (that have been assigned Heading Quick Styles) in your document appear in the For Which Headings box, as shown in Figure 10-10.

After you select the reference type and the item in the document that you want to be connected to the cross-reference (such as a heading or bookmark), you need to determine the content of the cross-reference itself. For example, you can use a heading as the reference anchor and select Page Number in the Insert Reference To drop-down menu. This inserts the page number for the referenced heading into the document as your cross-reference.

Each reference type has choices for what you insert into the document as the cross-reference. A figure reference type can provide the entire caption, the label and number, or the page number for a figure. A bookmark used as a cross-reference can include the bookmark text, the page number of the bookmark, or even the paragraph number. After you select your options for the cross-reference in the Cross-Reference dialog box, click Insert. You add additional cross-references as needed using the Cross-Reference dialog box. When you are finished, click the Close button on the Cross-Reference dialog box.

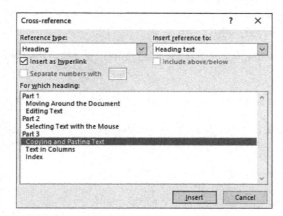

Figure 10-10   The Cross-Reference dialog box

To follow a cross-reference (go to the referenced text or heading) that you inserted as a hyperlink (the default), place the mouse pointer on the cross-reference text. A Ctrl + Click To Follow Link message box appears. Hold down the Ctrl key and click the cross-reference; you will "jump" to the location of the cross-reference in your document.

Generating an index

An index provides a list of important terms, keywords, and various content references from a document and provides a reference to the page number where each of these terms or keywords appear in the document. Generating an index in Word is similar to creating a table of contents or a table of figures. First, you need to mark the index entries and then generate the index.

TIP

To view the field codes placed in a document when you insert cross-references, press Alt+F9. Press Alt+F9 again to hide the cross-reference fields.

The commands that you will use to create your index are found in the Index group on the ribbon's References tab. As already mentioned, the first step in creating the index is to mark the various index entries throughout the document.

NOTE

Indexes are meant to contain key terms and major concepts in the document so that the reader of the document can quickly locate that information in the document; don't commit overkill when marking text entries for the index, and don't completely skimp on entries for the index. It is a *Goldilocks and the Three Bears* dilemma: The index needs to be "just right."

Marking index entries

Start at the beginning of your document and select the first text entry for the index; then select Mark Entry (in the Index group on the ribbon) to open the Mark Index Entry dialog box. The selected text appears in the Mark Index Entry dialog box's main entry box, as shown in Figure 10-11. You don't have to use the default text in the main entry box; you can type over the text to revise the main entry.

If you want to create a subentry to accompany the main entry in the index, type the text in the Subentry field. For example, if your index entry is footnotes, but the index actually points to a passage that discusses converting footnotes to endnotes, you can add the subentry of "converting to endnotes." The index entry in the index then contains "footnotes" followed by an indented "converting to endnotes" on the next line (which would also include the page number of the entry).

Figure 10-11   The Mark Index Entry dialog box

By default, the index entry includes the page number (the page where your index entry actually resides in the document). You can also specify a page range for the index entry by selecting the Page Range option button and supplying the name of a bookmark you created that includes the page range you want to assign to the index entry.

➤ **Bookmarks are discussed later in this chapter in the "Building a better 'big' document" section.**

The Mark Index Entry dialog box also provides an option for creating a cross-reference for the index entry. Suppose the main entry is "data source," and you want to include a cross-reference in the index entry that states, "See mail merge." To use the cross-reference option, select the Cross-Reference option button and enter the required text. This type of entry does not include a page number reference, but it is designed to have the reader look elsewhere in the index to locate the document information.

The Mark Index Entry dialog box also supplies two check boxes (Bold and Italic) that enable you to select formatting for the page numbers included with the index entries. After you specify the parameters for your index entry, select Mark. Because the dialog box stays open as you mark the various index entries for the document, you can mark additional entries and then click Close when you finish marking all the index entries in the document.

Inserting the index

After marking your index entries, you can insert the index. Park the insertion point in the document where you want to insert the index. You might want to start a new page or even a new section at the end of the document for the index.

To insert the index, click the Insert Index command in the Index group. The Index dialog box opens, as shown in Figure 10-12.

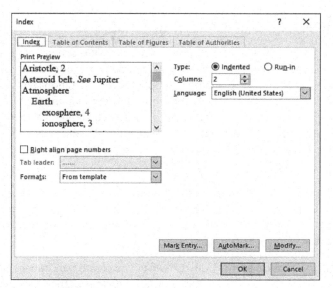

Figure 10-12   The Index dialog box

By default, the index is set up indented and in two columns. You can change the number of columns and other settings as needed using the controls on the right side of the Index dialog box. When you are ready to insert the index, select OK. The index is inserted into the document.

If you modify your document (move pages, delete pages, or insert additional pages) and mark additional entries for the index, you need to update the index in your document. Select the Update Index command in the Index group to update the index.

TIP

If you want to go beyond the main entry and subentry levels and add a tertiary-level entry to the index, type a colon (:) after the subentry text and then enter text for the tertiary-level index information.

NOTE

Different style manuals exist for different kinds of publications. Word provides citation and bibliography formatting for 12 different sets of style guidelines, including the Modern Language Association (MLA), the American Psychological Association (APA), and the *Chicago Manual of Style*.

Working with citations and bibliographies

Suppose you are working on a journal article, a paper for conference proceedings, or some other document that requires a list of your sources at the end of the document. In that case, you can take advantage of Word's citation and bibliography features. Citations are short references to articles, papers, books, or other material that you consulted that appear directly in the text of your document. For example, if you need to cite an article you read that was written by Kim Akers in 2021, the citation in the document would appear directly after any reference that you have made to Aker's article. A format that the citation might appear in could be as follows: (Akers, 2021).

The full reference for the article, including the author's name, the article title, the publication date, and the publication in which the article appeared, will be provided in the bibliography itself. As the "keeper" of the citations, the bibliography is a comprehensive list of all the resource materials you have referenced in your document.

When you insert a citation into the document (that is, when you create the citation), you provide all the information related to the article or book, such as the title, author, date published, and so forth. When you generate the bibliography, the bibliography entries created for each of the publications cited are based on the information that you provided for each of your citations (meaning your cited references).

Before you begin to insert the citations into the document, make sure that you understand the style guidelines you use for your publications. Style guides supply the rules for citing other works in your documents. For example, many educational institutions use the MLA style guidelines in the humanity disciplines and the APA style guidelines for the social sciences. Other groups, such as many book publishers, use *Chicago Manual of Style* as a resource for their writers.

The first step in the citation-to-bibliography process is choosing the style guidelines for your citations and bibliography. All the commands you need to create citations and the bibliography are on the ribbon's References tab in the Citations & Bibliography group.

To specify the style guidelines that you want, select the Style drop-down menu and select one of the listed styles. (The default is APA.) Now you can begin to create the citations for the document.

Creating citations

Citations include all the information related to the publication you are citing in your document. Park the insertion point at the end of a sentence where you want to insert the citation, and then follow these steps:

1. Select the Insert Citation command in the Citations & Bibliography group.

2. On the Insert Citation menu, select Add New Source. The Create Source dialog box opens (see Figure 10-13).

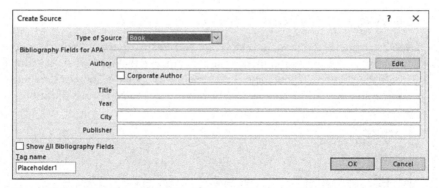

Figure 10-13   Enter the information for the publication in the Create Source dialog box.

3. Use the Type of Source drop-down menu to select the type of publication you are citing (Book, Journal Article, Report, and so on). The type of publication you select determines the number of fields of information you must fill in for a complete citation.

4. Enter the appropriate information into each of the text boxes in the Create Source dialog box. A tag name is created for the citation, based on the author's name and the year of publication.

5. When you finish entering the data for the source, click OK.

The citation is placed at the insertion point in parentheses. The actual appearance of the citation depends on the style you are using. For example, the APA style includes the author's last name followed by the year of publication in the citation. The MLA style uses only the author's last name for the citation.

Repeat the insert-citation process as needed to create all the citations for the document. When a citation has been created, it appears on the Insert Citation menu and can be quickly inserted into the document by selecting the Insert Citation command and then selecting the citation. Remember that the citation is inserted into the document at the insertion point.

If you need to edit a citation, click the citation in the document (if there are multiple occurrences of the citation in the document, any instance will do). A drop-down arrow appears to the right of the citation. Select the drop-down arrow and then select Edit Source. The Edit Source dialog box opens; it is identical to the Create Source dialog box. Edit the citation as needed and then click OK to return to the document. Any changes you have made to the source are updated in the citations you already inserted into the document.

NOTE

Any reference cited in your document really needs to be listed in your bibliography. The reverse is also true; any reference listed in your bibliography needs to be appropriately cited in your document as a citation.

Managing citations

You can manage the citation sources that you create using the Source Manager. The Source Manager provides a master list of citations compiled by Word (as an XML document) as you create the citations in your various documents. To open the Source Manager, select Manage Sources in the Citations & Bibliography group. Figure 10-14 shows the Source Manager.

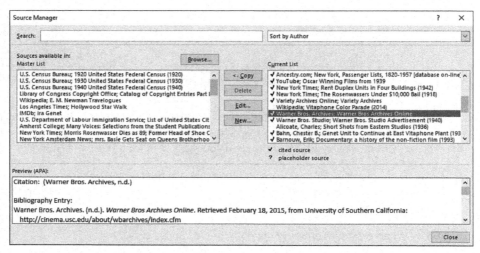

Figure 10-14   The Source Manager dialog box

The Source Manager provides two different lists. In the left pane is the master list, which is a compilation of all citations that you created. In the right pane are the citations in the current document. You can select a citation in either the master list or the current list and copy it to the other list. For example, if the master list contains a citation you want to include in the current list, select the citation and click Copy.

If you have a large number of sources in your lists, you can quickly filter the lists (the Master List and Current List) simultaneously using the Search box. Type a keyword or keywords into the Search box, and the lists filter using your terms. Delete the search terms in the Search box to refresh the lists. You can also use the Sort box on the top-right of the Source Manager dialog box. A drop-down menu enables you to sort your sources by such things as author, title, and year.

The Source Manager also gives you the tools to delete, edit, or create a new source. To delete a source, select the source (in the Master List or the Current List) and then select the Delete button. If you need to edit an existing source, select the source in the Source Manager and click the Edit button. This opens the Edit Source dialog box.

The New button in the Source Manager opens the Create Source dialog box. If you want, you can open the Source Manager and create all the citation sources for your document before you enter any of the citations into your document. When the sources are ready to go, you can quickly add citations using the Insert Citation command, which provides a list of all the sources you have previously created for the document.

TIP

You can save an inserted bibliography that you modified or one that you created from scratch to the Bibliography gallery, which is one of the Building Block galleries. Use the Save Selection To Bibliography Gallery command in the Bibliography command's gallery.

Inserting the bibliography

After you insert your citations into your document, you can use the citation sources (that you already created) to insert a bibliography into the document. As with a table of contents or table of figures, you insert the new bibliography on a new blank page or (even better) in a new document section, particularly if you want to have different headers or footers for the portion of the document that contains the bibliography.

Creating the bibliography is straightforward: Place the insertion point where you want to insert the bibliography. Select the Bibliography command in the Citations & Bibliography group. The Bibliography gallery opens (see Figure 10-15).

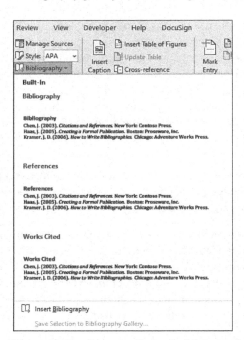

Figure 10-15   Select a style for the bibliography from the gallery.

CHAPTER 10

The gallery provides you with built-in bibliography styles. Select one of the styles: Bibliography, References, or Works Cited. The bibliography is inserted into your document using the selected style. If you don't want to use any of the built-in styles, you can insert a more generic bibliography (without a title) by selecting Insert Bibliography (in the Bibliography gallery). If you don't like the look of the bibliography style that you have inserted, select the Undo command on the Quick Access Toolbar. If you want to delete the bibliography, select it and then click the Delete key.

Inserting footnotes and endnotes

Footnotes and endnotes serve as explanatory additions to the text in a document. Similar to citations, both footnotes and endnotes can be used to reference published information that you consulted as you created your own work. Obviously, footnotes appear at the bottom of the page (in the footer area) and are included at the bottom of the same page where you inserted the footnote reference number.

As you insert footnotes or endnotes into a document, they are numbered sequentially. If you delete a footnote or endnote, the remaining footnotes or endnotes are renumbered automatically. Also, if you add footnotes or endnotes to the document, the existing footnotes or endnotes are renumbered as needed.

Whether you use footnotes or endnotes depends on the type of document you are creating and also (somewhat) on the style manual you are using as the guide for your document formatting and overall structure. Remember that each discipline, such as the sciences versus the humanities, typically requires that a specific style manual be used for a professional paper in that field. However, if you have started out with the wrong style manual, the great thing about footnotes and endnotes is that footnotes can easily be converted to endnotes, and (vice versa) endnotes can be converted to footnotes. So, if you start out using footnotes and determine that you should have been using endnotes, you can quickly remedy the problem.

TIP

To view the text for the footnote or endnote nearest to the insertion point, select the Show Notes command in the Footnotes group. It takes you either to the footer area to see the next footnote or to the last page of the document to view the current endnote.

The commands used to insert a footnote or an endnote are in the Footnotes group on the ribbon's References tab. To insert a footnote or endnote, place the insertion point where you want to place the footnote or endnote reference number in the document. To insert a footnote or an endnote, click the Insert Footnote or Insert Endnote command, respectively. Doing so places the note number in the text and moves the insertion point to the appropriate place in the document to enter the note text.

When you insert a new footnote, your insertion point moves to the footer area of the current page. Type the text for the footnote. When you insert a new endnote, the insertion point moves to the last page of the current document. Enter the text for the endnote.

You can navigate from footnote to footnote (or endnote to endnote) using the Next Footnote command in the Footnotes group; its menu provides Next Footnote, Previous Footnote, Next Endnote, and Previous Endnote.

If you need to modify the number format or other settings related to your footnotes or endnotes, you can do this in the Footnote And Endnote dialog box (see Figure 10-16). To open the dialog box, click the Footnote And Endnote dialog box launcher on the Footnotes group.

The Footnote And Endnote dialog box also enables you to convert your footnotes to endnotes and vice versa. Select the Convert button in the Footnote And Endnote dialog box. The Convert Notes dialog box opens and provides three options:

- **Convert All Footnotes To Endnotes:** Your footnotes become endnotes.

- **Convert All Endnotes To Footnotes:** Your endnotes become footnotes.

- **Swap Footnotes And Endnotes:** Any footnotes are converted to endnotes, and any endnotes are converted to footnotes.

Figure 10-16   The Footnote And Endnote dialog box

Select the appropriate option button and click OK, which returns you to the Footnote And Endnote dialog box; you can then close the Footnote And Endnote dialog box.

Tracking document changes

If you work in an environment where you create and edit Word documents that are a collaborative effort, such as departmental reports, employee handbooks, or marketing materials, you can track the changes made by each of the collaborators working on the document. Each author's or editor's changes are tagged with the individual's user name, so it is easy to identify who made particular changes to the document and when. Once all the participants have made their changes, you can review the document and determine which edits you will accept and which you will reject.

Word provides you with different views when you work in the Track Changes mode. The Simple Markup view, which is the default view for Track Changes, removes a lot of the clutter (good clutter in the form of editing events) from the document as you work.

Figure 10-17 shows a document in the Simple Markup view. A vertical line in the left margin denotes the location of an edit in the document. Comments inserted in the document (via the New Comment command in the Comments group) are represented by user name (and picture if available) and the comment in the right margin (when the Show Comments command is active in the Comments group). You can choose to reply to the comment (to the originator of the comment), or you can choose to resolve the comment. The Simple Markup view removes all the insertions and deletions that cluttered the document page when Track Changes was turned on in previous versions of Microsoft Word.

TIP

If you are working in the Simple Markup view and want to pare the screen down even more by hiding the comments in the document, deselect the Show Comments command in the Comments group. Each comment will now be represented by a comment icon. Select a comment icon to view the comment.

You can switch from Simple Markup view to All Markup view (the view that was the standard for Track Changes in previous versions of Word) with one click of the mouse. Click a vertical edit mark in the left margin, and the edit (and other edits on the page) appears as an inline edit, such as the edits shown in Figure 10-18. The text associated with the edit is also selected. Any nearby comments also appear.

Word allows for real-time collaborative editing of a document involving multiple users. Each time a user edits a shared document (shared on a network or via OneDrive), the corrections are inserted into the document (you may have to save your document to see the changes). Comments can also be exchanged between users. This "chat" allows users editing the same document to have a dialogue related to any changes made to the document. This dialogue between users occurs in real time. Comments can be inserted and deleted using the commands provided in the Comments group (on the Review tab).

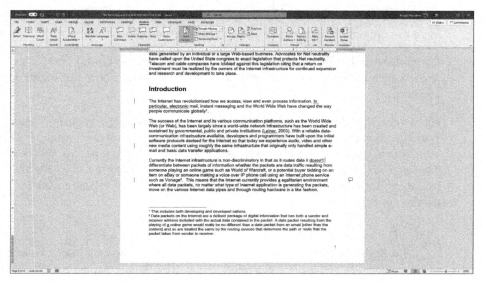

Figure 10-17   Simple Markup view

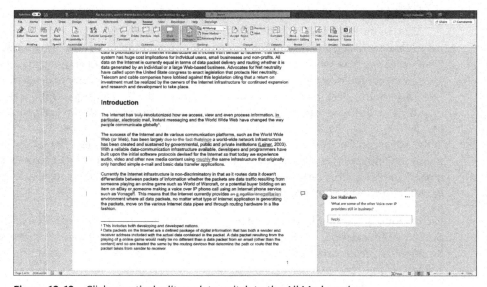

Figure 10-18   Click a vertical edit mark to switch to the All Markup view.

A document in the Track Changes mode can start to look pretty confusing in the All Markup view, particularly if a lot of editing has taken place. You can view a simple list of changes made to a document via the Reviewing Pane. The Reviewing Pane command is in the Tracking group.

The Reviewing Pane can be displayed as either a vertical or horizontal pane by selecting one of these two options on the Reviewing Pane command's drop-down menu.

Once the Reviewing Pane is open in the Word window, you can quickly move to a particular revision or comment (in the document) by clicking on that revision in the Reviewing Pane's Revisions list.

You will find that all the commands related to the Track Changes feature are located in the Tracking group on the ribbon's Review tab. Before you begin tracking changes in the document, you might want to peruse and even change the various settings related to the tracking options. You can select or deselect markup options in the Show Markup drop-down menu. You can control what is shown (such as comments or formatting) and whether balloons are used to show revisions or comments.

TIP

The Reviewing Pane can be opened to provide you with an easy-to-peruse list of your revisions and comments, even when you are in the Simple Markup view. The Reviewing Pane also provides an Update button that allows you to update the document revisions and comments when you are working with multiple editors in real time.

All these options are also provided in the Track Changes Options dialog box. Click the dialog box launcher on the bottom-right corner of the Tracking group to open the Track Changes dialog box. This dialog box allows you to specify what is shown in the document and how balloons are viewed (when you are in the Track Changes mode). If you want control over more options related to the appearance and color of deletions or insertions, select the Advanced Options button (in the Track Changes Options dialog box) to open the Advanced Track Changes Options dialog box shown in Figure 10-19.

In the Advanced Track Changes Options dialog box, you can configure different options related to how editing changes, such as deletions and insertions, are formatted and colored in the document. The Advanced Track Changes Options dialog box is divided into category areas, including Markup, Moves, Formatting, and Balloons.

Each grouping, such as Markup, uses formatting attributes and color to specify a particular type of change. For example, the Markup group includes insertions, deletions, and changed lines. By default, insertions are formatted using an underline, whereas deletions are formatted with a strikethrough.

You can determine whether changes that do not remove or insert text, such as moves and formatting, are tracked (using the appropriate check box). This dialog box also provides settings related to balloon size and margin.

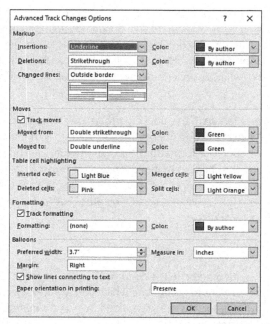

Figure 10-19   The Advanced Track Changes Options dialog box

You can change color settings for the various markup items, such as insertions or deletions. However, because the point of this feature is to differentiate the changes made to the document by different individuals working on the document, I do not recommend changing any of the color settings for items that have the By Author selection by default. This includes items such as insertions, deletions, and formatting.

Options for viewing changes

When you are ready to begin tracking the changes in a document, select the Track Changes command in the Tracking group and then select Track Changes. As you edit, changes are marked in the document. When you share the document, any changes by your collaborators are also marked in the document.

CAUTION

Unless you have some compelling reason to make a change, in most cases, you can use the default formatting and colors provided by the Advanced Track Changes Options dialog box.

As already discussed, the new default view for Track Changes is Simple Markup. To toggle between Simple Markup and All Markup, just click one of the vertical edit marks in the document's left margin. The Display For Review drop-down menu in the Tracking group also provides other possibilities for changing the view when Track Changes is enabled. One possibility, No Markup, hides all editing marks from the document and shows you the document with all the editing changes that have been made; changes are displayed as regular text as if you had accepted each change.

CHAPTER 10

Another possibility provided by the Display For Review drop-down menu is Original view. When you select Original, the original version of the document (the document before editing) is displayed. If you attempt to edit the document while in Original view, the display immediately changes to Original: Show Markup view. This view shows you all the edits and comments in the document (the same view provided by All Markup if no changes have been accepted or rejected since editing began).

The Show Markup menu (select Show Markup in the Tracking group) gives you quick access to a list of items that control what is shown in the document when All Markup is the selected view, such as comments, insertions, and deletions, or formatting. You can use the Specific People selection on the menu to show or hide the changes made by certain reviewers (that's what Word calls your collaborators) in the document; point at Specific People to see a list of all the reviewers of the document. If you want to hide changes made by other authors, deselect the Other Authors command on the Show Markup menu.

Reviewing changes

When you have all the reviewers' changes marked in the document, you can review the document and determine which changes you want to accept and which you want to reject. The commands related to reviewing the document, such as the Accept and Reject commands, are in the Changes group on the ribbon's Review tab.

To aid you in reviewing the various edits made throughout the document, you may want to open the Reviewing pane in a vertical or horizontal orientation. Select the Reviewing Pane command in the Tracking group, and then select Reviewing Pane Vertical or Reviewing Pane Horizontal. Figure 10-20 shows the Vertical Reviewing Pane.

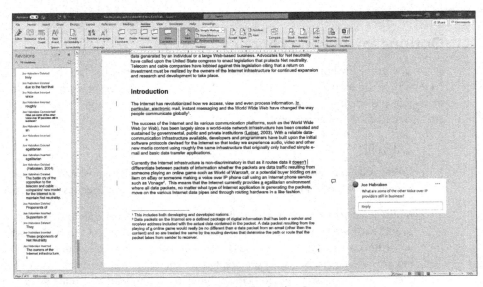

Figure 10-20   Document with changes and the Reviewing Pane

To begin the process of reviewing the document changes, go to the top of the document (Ctrl+Home) and then click the Next command in the Changes group. You are taken to the first change in the document. At this point, you can take advantage of the Accept and Reject commands and the choices on their menus.

The Accept and Reject commands enable you to accept or reject a change and then move to the next change. Just accept or reject the change or accept or reject all changes.

After you have accepted (or rejected) changes in the document, you can save the final version of the document. It makes sense to use Save As and save the document under a new file name detailing that the document review has taken place.

Comparing documents

You might want to reconcile the text in two different drafts of the same document or combine revisions from multiple authors (in two different documents) into a single, revised document. This is particularly useful if you did not circulate a single copy of the document with the Track Changes feature enabled among the various authors involved in the project. The Compare command has its own Compare group on the ribbon's Review tab.

NOTE

Ink is an option on the Show Markup menu. It refers to pen markup made to a document on a tablet PC, touchscreen, or smartphone.

To compare two versions of a document, select the Compare command and then select Compare on the Compare menu. Doing so opens the Compare Documents dialog box (see Figure 10-21). To view all the settings available in this dialog box, click More.

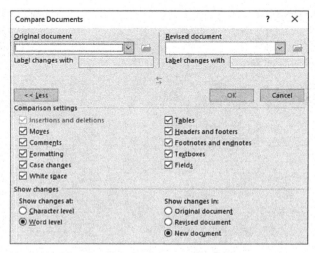

Figure 10-21   The Compare Documents dialog box

Open the original document on the left side of the dialog box and open the revised version of the document on the right side of the dialog box. The Label Changes With boxes enable you to specify the author name used to label the changes found between the documents when the comparison is made.

You can select the various comparison settings in the Comparison Settings pane (select More). This enables you to select specific actions for comparison, such as moves, comments, formatting, and so forth.

NOTE

You can control the type of changes and the level of access that reviewers have to a document. Use the Restrict Formatting and Editing pane (select Restrict Editing in the Protect group) to limit formatting and editing restrictions.

You also have control over how Word displays the differences in the two documents. For example, you can choose to show the changes in the original document, the revised document, or a new one (the latter being both the best option and the default).

After you specify the documents for comparison and set the various parameters in the Compare Documents dialog box, click the OK button. A document opens (a new document, if you went with the default setting) that has automatically marked changes to the original document based on the revised version you specified. The Vertical Reviewing Pane also opens, detailing the changes that have been marked in the document. You can now review the changes in the document as if you had the Track Changes feature enabled during the entire editing process. Figure 10-22 shows the results of a comparison between two different versions of the same document.

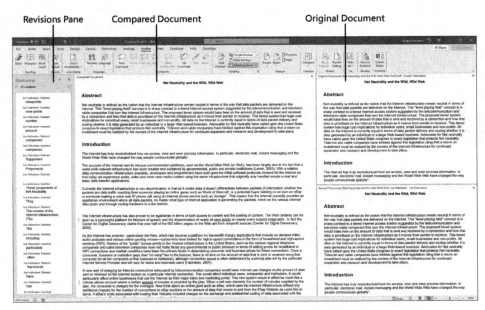

Revisions Pane   Compared Document   Original Document

Figure 10-22   Review the changes resulting from the comparison of two versions of the same document.

The Compared Document pane provides the results of the comparison between the original document and the revised document. The original and revised documents are also shown in their own panes in the Word application window. As you scroll through the compared document, you move through the original and revised documents at the same time. The summary of revisions made appears in the Reviewing pane on the left of the Word window. You can choose to accept or reject changes as you would any other document that has been edited by multiple authors using Track Changes.

NOTE

Documents that you share with other users on your OneDrive (or SharePoint site) allow them to edit the document in Word or use the Word Web app. You can view a list of users currently editing a document by selecting the author's icon on the Word status bar. If you have Track Changes turned off, Word highlights (in green) edits made by other authors.

The Compare command in the Compare group also provides the Combine command. This command opens the Combine Documents dialog box, which is structured the same as the Compare Documents dialog box. Use the Combine command and the Combine Documents dialog box when you want to quickly reconcile the changes that have been marked in two different versions of the same document. A new document is created, and you still have the opportunity to accept or reject changes made to the document (which are shown as inline edits in the new document created). The major difference between Compare and Combine is appearance. Compare creates a new document and also shows the original and revised versions of the document. Combine provides a new document only. Both scenarios, however, enable you to fine-tune any edits made to the original document.

Building a better "big" document

Working on a large, complex document can be a daunting task; tools and features in Word make it easier to navigate, comment on, and build a bigger document both when you are the sole author and when you are collaborating with multiple authors.

TIP

Much of the information that we work with on a daily basis is web content. Referencing a web page in a Word document is a common occurrence. To insert a hyperlink into a Word document, open your web browser and navigate to the page addressed in the hyperlink. Select Hyperlink on the Insert menu. The address for the page is in the Address box of the Insert Hyperlink dialog box. Provide the text you want to display in the document (for the hyperlink), and then click OK to insert the hyperlink.

Creating bookmarks

Bookmarks can be used to mark the location of specific text blocks or other items in a document. You can use bookmarks to generate cross-references in a document and to create the page run for an index entry that encompasses multiple pages. Bookmarks are also a good way to navigate a large document because they point to a specific place in the document; you can easily "jump" to any bookmark in the document. For example, when editing a long document, you might want to put a bookmark at the point in the document where you stopped editing for the day. When no longer needed, bookmarks can also be quickly deleted.

The Bookmark command is in the Links group on the ribbon's Insert tab. To create a bookmark, simply select text in the document or park the insertion point at a particular place in the document, and then click Bookmark. The Bookmark dialog box opens, as shown in Figure 10-23.

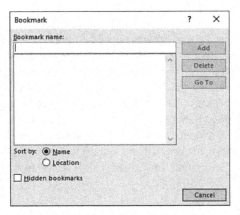

Figure 10-23   The Bookmark dialog box

Type a name for the new bookmark (no spaces are allowed). Then click the Add button to add the new bookmark to the list.

The Bookmark dialog box enables you to specify how the bookmark list is ordered; it can be sorted by name or location. You can delete bookmarks in the Bookmark dialog box (select a bookmark and click Delete), and you can use the Go To button to go to a selected bookmark.

After you have inserted some bookmarks into a document (or even just a single bookmark), you can move to a specific bookmark by using the Go To tab of the Find And Replace dialog box. To open the Find dialog box with the Go To tab selected, select Find on the ribbon's Home tab and then select Go To. You can open the Find dialog box with the Go To tab selected by pressing Ctrl+G on the keyboard.

On the Go To tab, select Bookmark in the Go To What list. Then select a specific bookmark from the Enter Bookmark Name drop-down menu. Select the Go To button to move to the selected bookmark. Close the Find And Replace dialog box when you have finished using your bookmarks to navigate the document.

Inserting comments

Earlier in this chapter, we discussed the fact that the Word Comment feature enables you to use an inserted document comment as a platform for communication among multiple authors editing the same document. Comments are not reserved for multiauthor documents, and you can insert nonprinting comments into your document that you use as reminders. For example, you might insert a comment such as "Finish this chapter" to remind yourself to complete a particular portion of the document. Comments left for other users editing a document are an extremely useful way to have a real-time discussion about changes made to the document.

The Comments group is on the ribbon's Review tab. To insert a new comment, park the insertion point where you want to place the comment and then select the New Comment command (the New Comment command is also on the Insert tab in the Comments group). A new comment balloon opens. Enter the text for the comment. The new comment is marked with your username, initials, and timestamp.

NOTE

Using comments is a great way to communicate with other authors working on the same document. With Word now available as a web app and on multiple devices (PCs and tablets), collaboration with coworkers has become even more important as users take advantage of Word's capabilities on multiple computing devices.

In the Print Layout view, comments appear as comment balloons. In the Draft view, a comment appears with pink highlighting on the document text where the comment was inserted. You can view a comment by placing the mouse pointer on that particular comment. A preview box opens, showing the comment's author, the date and time the comment was inserted, and the comment text. You can view all the comments in the document as a list in the Reviewing pane; select Reviewing Pane in the Tracking group. You can also move from comment to comment using the Go To tab of the Find And Replace dialog box (Find and then Go To). Select Comment in the Go To What list and then use the Enter Reviewer's Name drop-down menu to go to a comment made by a specific reviewer (click Previous or Next to move to a comment).

TIP

You can delete comments from the Reviewing pane. Right-click a comment to open the shortcut menu, and then select Delete Comment. You can also delete a comment by right-clicking the comment itself (in the document) and then selecting Delete Comment from the shortcut menu.

The Comments group also provides two commands for moving to comments in the document: Previous and Next. The Delete command enables you to delete a selected comment, all comments shown, or all the comments in a document, as needed.

Creating a master document

There might be occasions when you are working on a very large document, and you decide it is easier to organize the document by keeping chapters or parts in separate Word document files. Or you might be involved in a situation where you are collaborating with multiple authors who are each responsible for specific parts of a larger document. In both circumstances, it makes sense for you to take advantage of Word's Master Document feature. The Master Document feature enables you to insert links to other documents into the Master Document. These links can be chapters or other document parts that you have created as separate files, or they might be Word documents that colleagues and collaborators are writing. In essence, the Master Document feature has one great and noble purpose: It enables you to create a master document outline of the entire document, even while the various parts of the document are still being created. When the various authors complete the linked subdocuments that make up the master document, your master document is also complete. It can then be printed and distributed, or it can be saved as a PDF file and made available to anyone who needs a copy.

> TIP
>
> **Use a new blank document for the master document so that you have complete flexibility in inserting and rearranging the subdocuments that link to the master.**
>
> **The Master Document feature provides an outline view of the entire document that allows you to expand and collapse the subdocuments using the Outlining tools. You can insert new subdocuments as links to other document files or create a new subdocument for the master document from scratch directly in the outline.**

You can create global items, such as page numbering, for the master document and then apply them to the various linked subdocuments that make up the master document. (Keep in mind that all these subdocuments are separate files linked by the master document.) When you generate the table of contents for a master document, the "master" table of contents includes all the TOC headings in the various linked subdocuments. And when you are working with a master document in Word in Print Layout or Draft view, it ends up looking like any other Word document, although it is a series of links to the various subdocuments.

Working in Outline view

As already mentioned, the master document is an outline of linked subdocuments. You work with a master document in Outline view. This allows you to view the linked subdocuments and use the various Outline tools for arranging and manipulating the subdocument links in the master document outline. Figure 10-24 shows a master document that contains three linked subdocuments. The Show First Line Only check box is selected in the Outline Tools group so that all three subdocuments are on the screen. Normally, expanded subdocuments show all the pages in the subdocument.

Figure 10-24   A master document with linked subdocuments

To begin the process of creating a master document, open an existing document or a new document. If you are using an existing document as a master document, it can contain text entries and other objects. Be advised that any content in the master document (before creating the subdocument outline) is part of the "assembled" content that is realized when you link the subdocuments into the master document outline. So, the master document can be a "chapter" that is part of the larger master document you are creating; the master doesn't necessarily have to be a new blank document.

When you have the document open (new or existing) that serves as the master document, switch to Outline view; then select Outline on the ribbon's View tab. Outline view (which appears on the ribbon as an Outlining tab) provides commands (in the Outline Tools group) that enable you to promote and demote items in the outline to different levels. You can also select levels by using the Level drop-down menu. Tools such as Move Up, Move Down, Expand, and Collapse allow you to move through the outline and expand or collapse outline parts, respectively.

CHAPTER 10

After you are in Outline view, you also need to be aware of the commands in the Master Document group on the Outlining tab. When working in Outline view on your master document, make sure to select the Show Document command in the Master Document group. This "activates" the other Master Document tools. Now you are ready to create or insert the subdocuments that make up the master document.

Creating subdocuments from scratch

Creating new subdocuments from scratch is just a matter of using the Create command in the Master Document group. This adds each new subdocument that you create to the master document outline. Each time you add a new subdocument to the master document outline, a new blank Word document (the subdocument) is also created in the folder where you have stored the master document. For example, let's say I have a master document saved to My Documents (on my computer's hard drive), and I create a new subdocument in the outline titled "Chapter 1." When I save the changes that I have made to the master document, a new blank Word document is created in My Documents named "Chapter 1."

Suppose you are working in the cloud (OneDrive or OneDrive for Business) or on a network where you can easily share files with other users. In that case, the subdocuments that are automatically created as you build the master document outline can be shared with other users. These other users can then add the content to the subdocument, which is then available when you open the master document.

To create a new subdocument (from scratch) in the master document, place the insertion point in the outline where you want to insert the blank subdocument. Make sure that the outline level at the insertion point is set to one of the heading levels (1–9); it cannot be set to Body Text. To set the heading level, select the Outline Level drop-down menu (in the Outline Tools group) and specify the level (the levels 1–9 in the Outline Level list correspond to Word's built-in heading styles 1–9). Make sure the Show Document command is activated in the Master Document command group; then select the Create command. A new subdocument (it's a rectangle with an Expand button) appears in the master document outline, as shown in Figure 10-25.

NOTE

Outline view uses the built-in Word heading styles to denote the different levels in the outline. For example, Level 1 in the level list is really the Heading 1 style. Regular text in the outline uses the Body Text designation, which is the Normal style.

You can repeat the process as needed to add other subdocuments to the master document outline. Make sure that you type a heading for the new subdocument (which also serves as the file name for the new subdocument that is saved when you save the modified master document).

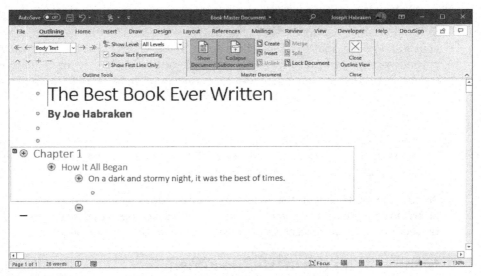

Figure 10-25   A new subdocument in the master document outline

You can enter the contents for a particular subdocument directly into the master document outline if you want. This includes text, pictures, and any other content that you would insert into a "regular" Word document.

When you save the master document, all the subdocuments that you created in the outline are saved as separate files using the subdocument heading as the file name. The fact that each subdocument exists as a separate Word document makes it easy for you to assign parts of a master document to coworkers or colleagues. It also makes it easy for you to concentrate on a particular part of the master document. For example, you can work on Chapter 1 by opening the Chapter 1 document and adding content as needed. The next time you open the master document, the content you added to the Chapter 1 document file appears in the master document outline.

Inserting existing document files into a master document outline

You have an alternative to creating empty subdocuments in the master document outline. You (and your collaborators) can create the various Word documents that will be the subdocuments in the master document before you create the master document outline. This enables each collaborator to concentrate on the chapter or part of the master document they need to create. When all the subdocuments are saved as Word document files, you can easily build the master document outline that links all that content.

To insert an existing Word document file into a master document outline as a subdocument, switch to Outline view and make sure that you have selected the Show Document command in

CHAPTER 10

the Master Document group. Place the insertion point in the outline where you want to insert the subdocument. You don't have to change the outline level for the line (to a heading level) as you must do when creating a new subdocument in the outline from scratch (as discussed in the previous section). However, you might want the same heading level for each subdocument that you insert, so the document titles are at a consistent level in the outline. (This is particularly true if you want to drag an entire subdocument section to a new position in the master document outline.)

To insert the subdocument link into the master document outline, select the Insert command on the Master Document group. The Insert Subdocument dialog box opens. You can repeat the process to insert other subdocuments as needed.

Because the subdocuments that make up the master document are separate files, they can be edited and re-edited (separately) as needed. When you open the master document file, all revised subdocument content is shown in the master document outline.

Manipulating the master document

You can fine-tune your master document using the other tools provided in the Master Document group on the Outlining tab. For example, if you want to unlink a subdocument from the original file—that is, you don't want to make changes to the subdocument itself—select a particular subdocument in the outline, and then select Unlink. The subdocument content is copied into the master document. Any changes made to the "unlinked" subdocument file (from that point on) will not be included in the master document because the subdocument file is no longer linked, or talking to, the master document.

You can use the Merge and Split commands to either merge two subdocuments in the outline or split a subdocument at a particular place into two subdocuments. If you want to protect the actual files that make up the subdocuments, you can use the Lock Document command. This enables you to make changes to the master document (such as styles, headers, footers—you name it) and not have them propagate back to the original subdocuments.

When you finish using the Outlining tools related to constructing the master document, click Close Outline View. This returns you to either the Print Layout or Draft view mode. You will find that when you are working in these other Word views, the master document looks no different than any other document you create or edit in Word. This is true even though the master document consists of linked content held in multiple Word document files rather than a typical, single-file Word document.

PART III

Excel

CHAPTER 11

Essential Excel features 297

CHAPTER 12

Worksheet formatting and management . . .345

CHAPTER 13

**Getting the most from formulas
and functions** 383

CHAPTER 14

Enhancing worksheets with charts 423

CHAPTER 15

Using Excel tables and pivot tables 461

CHAPTER 16

Validating and analyzing worksheet data . . .503

Essential Excel features

Introducing Excel   297

Navigating the Excel workspace   299

Creating workbooks and worksheets   303

Managing Excel workbooks   307

Entering data in a worksheet   317

Copying, moving, and deleting cell contents   327

Editing cell content   333

Viewing worksheets   334

Printing worksheets   336

Whether you create simple worksheets to track your small business income or home budget, or you do complex statistical analyses of migrating bird populations, Microsoft Excel gives you all the tools and features you need to assemble your data, calculate results, and then analyze those results. Excel continues to be the gold standard for spreadsheet software. This latest version of Excel builds on the features and tools provided by earlier editions of this powerful spreadsheet application and offers improvements and new features.

In this chapter, we take a look at some new Excel enhancements—some are subtle, and others are potential game-changers. (The new Stock Images library is a welcomed addition.) We also look at the process of building Excel worksheets, including entering data. In addition, we examine how to best navigate the Excel workspace and work with and manage Excel worksheets.

Introducing Excel

The latest version of Excel continues to be a number-crunching powerhouse and also provides some new and intriguing enhancements. Excel now provides you with access to stock images (from Microsoft's stock image library) and also includes 3D models that you can use to visually enhance your worksheets. We discuss the stock images and 3D models in Chapter 4, "Using and creating graphics."

Another new "visual" feature is the ability to use hex color codes to specify colors in the Excel application. This allows you to match the color formatting of a worksheet (including charts) with other related personal or company documents, so that all the worksheets and Excel objects (such as fill colors) are uniform. Because this feature is also available in Word and PowerPoint, it allows you to package information from the various Microsoft applications with consistent and matching colors. To take advantage of Hex color codes, use the Custom tab of the Colors dialog box (which is used to format the colors for worksheet cells and other Excel items such as charts); it provides a Hex box where you can enter the Hex code. For example, the hex code for navy blue is #000080 and can be entered in the Hex Code field. If you need to find a hex code for a particular color, just search the web using the color name.

Another new Excel feature relates to enhancing your worksheets with real-time data connections. Excel has always had capabilities to pull data from a variety of database sources, including web data. A new feature—linked data types—makes it even easier for you to pull data directly from reputable online data sources. A number of different data types are available, such as Stocks and Currencies, that access data from sources such as Bing and Wolfram (an extensive mathematics and research data resource). The Data Types group, which can be found on the Data tab of the Excel ribbon, provides you with the tools to format simple text entries that can then access online data. You can use the data for a variety of purposes and include the data in the Excel charts and tables you create. Figure 11-1 shows a simple worksheet that provides examples of some of the new data types, including the initial input, the result when the data type is assigned to the input, and the data that is accessed using the data type.

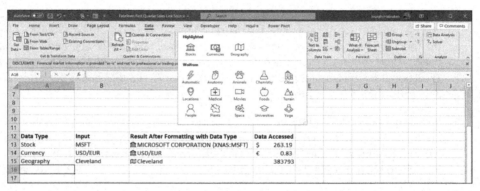

Figure 11-1   The new Data Types access online databases.

NOTE

Excel has always provided options for getting external data into your worksheets. (We discuss these possibilities in Chapter 15, "Using Excel tables and pivot tables.") Some of the options for connecting to external databases are a little more laborious than others. The new Linked Data Types feature makes it very easy to pull data from Bing and other sources. This is particularly true if you are building a worksheet that needs to include stock or currency data. When you use the linked data types, you are basically quickly formatting text entries (for example, a stock name such as MSFT). You are then provided with a real-time connection to a data source that is updated whenever you open the worksheet. Tracking the value of different currencies or a list of corporate stocks has never been easier.

Other Excel enhancements include the ability to duplicate conditional formatting rules quickly. Conditional formatting is discussed in Chapter 12, "Worksheet formatting and management," in the "Using conditional formatting" section.

This latest version of Excel also offers a new and noteworthy function: XLOOKUP. The new fuction is discussed in Chapter 13, "Getting the most from formulas and functions." This function allows you to create a table of information that can then be accessed by entering the XLOOKUP function in a worksheet cell or cells. The XLOOKUP function is easier to configure and use when compared to the older (and slightly more temperamental) VLOOKUP and HLOOKUP functions.

Excel has an additional new enhancement that is worth noting. You can now quickly view workbook statistics such as the number of cells holding data in a sheet, the number of sheets in the workbook, and the number of formulas and external connections in the workbook. These statistics can be useful in constructing a sound Excel workbook. Let's dig into the basics of Excel. We will look at the various new possibilities as we happen upon them in the chapters devoted to Excel.

Navigating the Excel workspace

The Home screen opens and supplies a list of templates and recently opened Excel workbooks when you start Excel. You can open a new blank workbook based on the Blank Workbook template, or you can open a more specialized workbook based on one of the many online templates provided by Excel. Or, you can open an existing workbook listed on the Home page under the Recent heading. Once an Excel workbook is created (or opened, if you are using an existing file), you are ready to take advantage of all the tools and features provided by Excel.

TIP

If you haven't signed in to Office using your Microsoft account (such as Outlook.com) or your Office 365 ID (or both), you can do so at the top right of the Home screen. You can also sign in from the New and Open screens if you have navigated to those areas of the opening screen. Signing in to Excel (and Office) makes your OneDrive and/or OneDrive for Business (Office 365 subscription) available as a place to save Excel files and retrieve existing files.

Figure 11-2 shows the Excel window and a new blank Excel workbook. As with the other Office applications, the tools and features you use to build and then enhance your Excel workbook are found on the ribbon and its various tabs.

When you open a new Excel workbook (using the Blank Workbook template), you are provided one sheet (Sheet1) in the workbook. Although on first inspection, one sheet might not seem like much room to work, a single Excel sheet has 16,384 columns and 1,048,576 rows, which means a single sheet has a lot of room for your data and calculations. You also can create a nearly

CHAPTER 11

endless number of sheets, so I would not worry about running out of space as you work in this powerful application.

Figure 11-2   A blank Excel workbook with one sheet tab

The Excel ribbon

The ribbon sits at the top of the Excel application window and provides access to the commands and tools you use as you work on your Excel worksheet. The ribbon Display Options button, which is the icon just to the right of your user name on the right side of the Excel window, enables you to auto-hide the ribbon, show just the ribbon tabs (their names), or show the tabs and commands all the time. A short description of the Excel ribbon tabs follows.

- **Home:** This tab provides the Clipboard group and groups that are associated with formatting and editing the worksheet data. The tab provides font, paragraph, and number formatting, Also, it provides access to formatting features such as conditional formatting, table formatting, and a gallery of cell styles. The Editing group provides quick access to functions such as AutoSum and provides the Fill, Sort & Filter, and Find & Select commands. The Home tab also provides access to the Analyze Data tool, which can help you format and arrange your data more efficiently and suggest specific chart types to visualize your data.

- **Insert:** This tab enables you to insert objects into an Excel worksheet, including pivot tables, illustrations (including pictures, shapes, icons, and SmartArt), and charts. An Add-ins group allows you to enhance your installation with add-ins such as Bing Maps; you will find that some add-ins are free while others are not. The Insert tab also provides access to features such as sparklines, filters, and the Link command. The Insert tab provides access to the sheet header and footer as well. Figure 11-3 shows the ribbon's Insert tab.

Figure 11-3   The ribbon's Insert tab

- **Page Layout:** This tab enables you to select a theme for your sheet and manipulate the margins, orientation, and paper size. The Page Setup group also enables you to place page breaks in a worksheet and select a background image for the sheet. Other commands on this tab enable you to scale the worksheet for printing and select sheet options such as gridlines and headings. The Arrange group helps you manipulate and group multiple objects on a worksheet.

- **Formulas:** This tab provides easy access to the function library by function type. Excel now provides a more vertically oriented, compact function library than its predecessors, but how commands found on ribbon tabs are arranged in your Office applications, such as Excel, will be a function of your screen size and device. This tab also provides the Defined Names group, which allows you to define names for cells and cell ranges in the worksheet. Commands are provided for auditing formulas, including Trace Precedents and Evaluation Formula. The Watch Window command helps you monitor specific cells (their results) as you add or manipulate the data in the worksheet.

- **Data:** This tab makes it easy for you to import external data from other applications or the web into Excel. Other commands available on this tab enable you to sort and filter data and specify data validation settings. The What-If Analysis command enables you to access tools for data analysis, such as Scenario Manager and Goal Seek. This ribbon tab is also home to the new Data Types group.

- **Review:** This tab provides proofing tools such as the Spelling feature and enables you to manage comments added to cells in your worksheet. Comments allow you to collaborate with coworkers in real time as you work on a shared Excel workbook. Commands are also available that enable you to protect a worksheet or the entire workbook. Commands related to sharing a workbook are also provided.

- **View:** This tab provides access to the various workbook views and also enables you to zoom in and out on the current worksheet. Other commands, such as Freeze Panes and View Side By Side, give you options for viewing a worksheet or multiple workbooks.

- **Help:** This tab provides access to the Excel Help feature. It also provides access to Excel support and feedback, as well as the Microsoft community.

- **Analysis:** This tab provides you with the Analyze Data tool, which can analyze and comment on a selected range of cells in your Excel worksheet. The Analyze Data tool provides you with help visualizing relationships in the data by providing potential chart types. This tool also allows you to ask questions about the data.

NOTE

You will find that Excel (like Microsoft Word) now provides you with two types of text annotations: comments and notes. Comments allow you to communicate with collaborators who have access to an Excel worksheet that you have shared on your OneDrive (or other cloud location). A new comment added to a sheet allows you to start a conversation with collaborators, and the group can communicate in real time. Notes have been available in Excel for many years and are not unlike a sticky note in that they can be used as reminders or contain other information related to your worksheet data.

You should be familiar with some other areas of the Excel workspace. Just above the ribbon is the Search box, which provides you with the ability to search for help and information (related to your current worksheet) by typing in keywords. On the far right of the Excel window are the Share and Comments buttons. The Share button allows you to share your current workbook if you have saved it to OneDrive (or a SharePoint site). The Comments command allows you to view the comments in the current worksheet.

Moving to the left of the screen, you see the Name box (just below the ribbon). The Name box shows the address of the currently selected cell in the worksheet. The Name box also shows the name of a range when a named range is selected (we talk about naming ranges in Chapter 12. To the right of the Name box is the formula bar, which does a few different things. As you enter information into a cell, it appears in the formula bar. The formula bar shows information that has been entered into the currently selected cell. You can also click in the formula bar to place the insertion point and edit the cell entry. When you work with formulas or functions, the result of the formula or function is shown in the cell that contains it. To view the formula or function, select the cell; the formula bar shows you the formula or function as it was entered.

At the bottom of the Excel application window, to the left of the vertical scrollbar, is the Sheet1 tab. Just to the right of the tab is the New Sheet command. Use it to add sheets to the current workbook. Individual sheets are selected by clicking their tabs. You can rename a sheet by double-clicking the tab and typing a new name.

The Excel status bar is located at the bottom of the Excel application window (just below the horizontal scrollbar). On the far right of the status bar are the View shortcuts and the Zoom slider. You can customize the status bar by right-clicking it and then selecting the various options from the shortcut menu that appears.

Moving around a worksheet

Moving around a worksheet is really just a matter of moving the mouse (or your finger, in the case of a touchscreen device) and "pointing out" the cell that you want to move to or select. If you are using a device with a keyboard, you can speed up your data entry by using keyboard shortcuts to move around the worksheet. Obviously, the arrow keys move you one cell in the direction specified by the key, but other options for navigating the cells in a sheet exist as well. Table 11-1 provides some of the Excel keyboard shortcuts for moving around a worksheet.

Table 11-1   Using the keyboard to move in a worksheet

Key Combination	Result
Tab	Moves one cell to the right
Shift+Tab	Moves one cell to the left
Ctrl+Right Arrow	Moves right to the last occupied cell in the current row (before a blank cell)
Ctrl+Left Arrow	Moves left to the first occupied cell in the current row (before a blank cell)
Ctrl+Up Arrow	Moves to the topmost occupied cell in a column (before a blank cell)
Ctrl+Down Arrow	Moves to the last occupied cell in a column (before a blank cell)
Ctrl+End	Moves to the first empty cell below the bottommost right occupied cell in the sheet
Ctrl+Home	Moves to cell A1 in the worksheet
Enter	Enters data into the cell and moves down one cell

The mouse also gives you other possibilities for interacting with the worksheet cells. You can double-click in a cell to place the insertion point and edit the data directly in the cell. You can use the mouse to zoom in or out on the current worksheet: Hold down the Ctrl key and then use the mouse wheel to zoom in or out as needed. You will also find that as you work in Excel, selecting multiple cells (called "a range," but we will get to that later in our discussion of Excel) is best accomplished with the mouse. This includes noncontiguous worksheet cells.

Creating workbooks and worksheets

Excel provides you with more than one way to start a new worksheet; one option is to use the blank workbook template and build a new workbook from scratch. An alternative to building a workbook from scratch is building a workbook based on one of the many workbook templates provided by Excel and the template library at Office.com.

If you are already working on a workbook in Excel and you would like to open a new workbook, you can quickly access the New page in the Excel Backstage. Select File and then New. The New page, shown in Figure 11-4, is all about creating a new workbook.

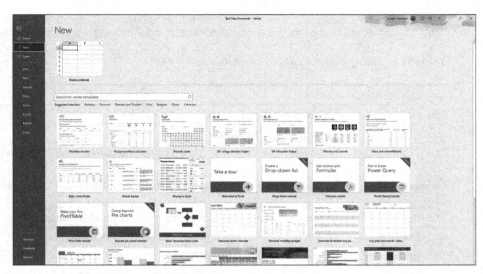

Figure 11-4   The New page in the Backstage

To create a new blank workbook, you simply have to select the Blank workbook template; then just wait a moment, and you will be provided a new workbook with a single worksheet. This single worksheet will have a lot of blank columns and rows. It's all up to you how you arrange your data on the blank sheet. The alternative to using the blank workbook is to take advantage of an Excel template. Templates provide a little more guidance in terms of taking advantage of the geography of the worksheet and typically use placeholder text or graphic elements to help corral your data in an appropriate way. We discuss the Office.com templates in the next section.

Using Office.com templates

Office.com provides you with different types of Excel templates; you can download budgets, calendars, invoices, plans, and schedules. To view the templates available in one of the template groups, select a group such as Invoices. The number of templates available in a particular group depends on the group you have selected. Each group provides several possibilities. In some cases, you might find more templates of a particular type than you need.

You can preview the templates by selecting a template in the list; the preview appears in the Preview pane of the Available Templates window. When you are ready to create a new workbook based on a particular template, make sure that the template is selected, and then click Create. Figure 11-5 shows a new workbook based on an invoice template downloaded from Office.com.

The template you select will provide the formatting, the placeholder text, and the specific formulas and functions that will be present in your new workbook. The Invoice With Finance Charge template shown in Figure 11-5 creates a new workbook with one worksheet, named Finance Charge.

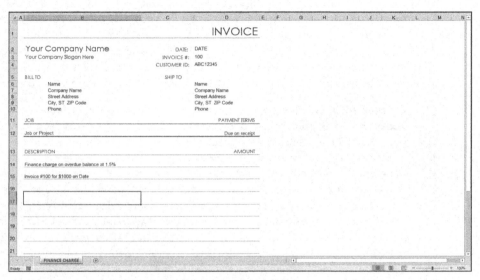

Figure 11-5   A new workbook based on an invoice template

Other templates, such as the Personal Budget template, create multiple worksheets in the workbook. The Personal Budget template provides a Summary sheet that details your monthly income, expenses, savings balance, and cash balance. This sheet also visualizes your data in two different charts and does calculations for you to let you know if you are a saver or a spender. The other sheets provided in the Personal Budget template allow you to enter your monthly income, monthly expenses, and monthly savings. The Drop-Down Menu, Summary sheet totals are linked from each of the details sheets, such as monthly income and monthly expenses.

Some of the templates not only create multiple worksheets, but in the case of the Personal Budget template, they also can include ready-made charts that allow you to visualize your data. The great part about templates is that even if you don't find a template that completely fits your needs, you can modify the worksheets a template provides. You can also add worksheets to any workbook, as discussed in the next section.

Inside OUT

Use Excel templates to explore how best to arrange data in a worksheet.

Not all of us are accountants (or play one on television), so trying to be an Excel maven right out of the gate can be a bit daunting. Unless you have prior experience setting up a worksheet so that it is readable and printable, you will find that just setting up a sheet's overall geography can be as much of a challenge as selecting the right formula or chart. Spending some time working with the different templates that Microsoft provides for Excel can help you look at a lot of different ways to arrange information on a sheet.

Other possibilities for helping you get the most out of Excel can be found in accounting books (even if they are old); corporate reports (they make the data look good even if it's not); or any other online or print resource that has a lot of numbers, formulas, and other information laid out on a page in a spreadsheet format. You can also use the Analyze Data tool on the ribbon's Home tab to help you sort out your data and create a worksheet that makes sense visually. I suggest that simply designed Excel worksheets will make it easier for other people to read and check your work. So, don't cram your worksheets with information. Also, remember that Excel allows you to work with many, many different worksheets in the same workbook. You don't have to put all the information on one worksheet. Just keep it simple. Make sure your data is correct and your formulas work, and you will be fine.

Inserting and rearranging worksheets

You can insert new worksheets into any workbook as needed. If you add more worksheets than you need, you can easily delete them. You can also name, rename, copy, and move worksheets. You determine the order of worksheets (or *sheets*, as they are also referred to) in a workbook.

You can insert a new worksheet into a workbook in a couple of ways. You can quickly insert a new sheet using the New Sheet button, which is located just to the right of the sheet tabs (at the bottom of the Excel window). You can also insert a new sheet using the Insert command in the Cells group on the ribbon's Home tab. To name a new sheet, double-click the sheet tab and type the new name.

You can also reorder the sheets in a workbook. Grab the sheet tab and then drag the worksheet to a new location in the sheet hierarchy. Rearranging the worksheets in a workbook is also accomplished in the Move Or Copy dialog box, shown in Figure 11-6.

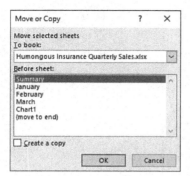

Figure 11-6   Rearrange worksheets using the Move Or Copy dialog box.

To open the Move Or Copy dialog box, right-click a sheet tab and then select Move Or Copy. You can move the selected sheet before any of the listed sheets in the workbook. You can also use the Move Or Copy dialog box to create a copy of a worksheet by selecting the Create A Copy check box.

The Move Or Copy dialog box enables you to move or copy the currently selected sheet or sheets to another workbook. The other workbook needs to be currently active in Excel, so you need to open it before accessing the Move Or Copy dialog box. Use the To Book drop-down menu to specify the workbook that accepts the move or copy operation, and then click OK.

To rename a sheet, right-click the worksheet tab and then select Rename from the shortcut menu. The current name is selected (such as Sheet 1, Sheet 2, and so on). Type the new name for the sheet.

To delete a worksheet from the shortcut menu, right-click any worksheet tab and then select Delete. If the worksheet contains data, you get a warning box alerting you to the fact that data might exist on the sheet you are deleting; click the Delete button in the warning box to continue. Be careful when deleting worksheets in a workbook: The Undo command on the Quick Access Toolbar can't undo a sheet deletion.

> TIP
>
> **To change a sheet name, double-click a worksheet tab to select the current name, and then type the new name.**

Managing Excel workbooks

The first time you save a new workbook, Excel opens the Save This File dialog box. All you have to do is type a file name for the new workbook and select the location you want to use for saving the file. Figure 11-7 shows the Save This File dialog box.

CHAPTER 11

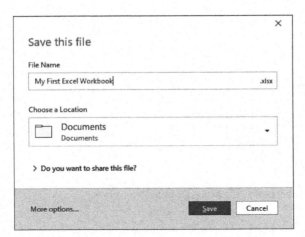

Figure 11-7 Specify the workbook name and location for your new Excel workbook.

If you want to access more options for saving the new Excel file, you can select the More Options link in the Save This dialog box, which opens the Save As page in the Backstage. The Save As page shows the various places where you can save the new Excel workbook. Figure 11-8 shows the Save As page.

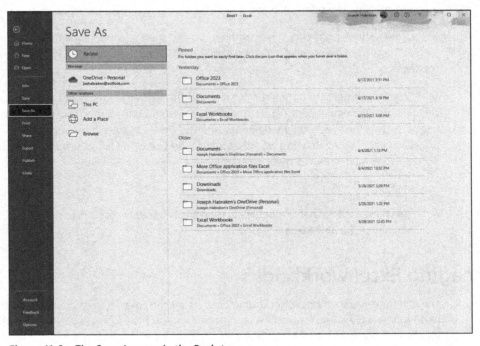

Figure 11-8 The Save As page in the Backstage

Locations (or places) provided on the Save As page include This PC and any optional places such as your OneDrive or a SharePoint site (if you have signed in to either of these remote locations). If your OneDrive is not shown, use the Add A Place command to add it; you can use this option to add SharePoint sites as well. To locate other locations, including network drives, use the Browse button.

Your job on the Save As Page is to locate a place for your new Excel workbook. When you select a recent folder or the Browse button, the Save As dialog box opens. After you have navigated to the folder location for the new workbook, provide a file name for the file and then click Save.

When you save an Excel workbook, it is saved in the .xlsx (XML file type) default file format. You can save your workbook in other file formats, including Excel 97-2003 Workbook, Single File Web Page, and Excel Template. The Save As Type drop-down menu shows the different file types. If you have already saved a file and want to save it in another format, use the Save As command in the Backstage.

TIP

It might seem like saving a new workbook can be a rather circuitous process considering you have to go through the Save This File dialog box and possibly the Save As page in the Backstage. If you would prefer to jump directly to the Save As dialog box (and avoid the Backstage) when you save a workbook for the first time, you need to change the Excel Save options. In the Backstage, click Options in the Excel Options window, and then click Save. In the Save Workbooks settings, select the Don't Show The Backstage When Opening Or Saving Files With Keyboard Shortcuts check box.

➤ For more about Excel and other Office application file types, see Chapter 3, "Managing and sharing Office files."

Another Backstage page that provides you with workbook management tools is the Backstage Info page. This page provides access to the workbook protection settings (Protect Workbook) and privacy and compatibility settings (Check For Issues); all these settings can be an issue if you are going to Share (Publish) this workbook with other users. The Info page provides access to the different versions of your workbook that the Autosave feature has created. Figure 11-9 shows the Backstage Info view.

CHAPTER 11

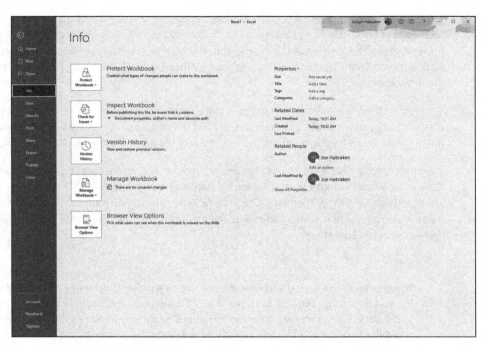

Figure 11-9   Backstage Info view

Excel was designed to promote collaboration. Two important aspects of sharing a workbook with other users relate to controlling what kind of changes people can make to your workbook and determining whether the workbook is compatible with other versions of Excel that your collaborators might be using. Let's look at workbook protection more closely and then cover inspecting a workbook that you want to share.

Protecting workbooks and worksheets

You can configure the workbook to limit the changes made by other users you share the file with. You can make the workbook read-only (meaning no changes allowed), or you can restrict permissions by individual users. The Protect Workbook command in the Info window provides these possibilities:

- **Always Open Read-Only:** This option negates other readers of a shared document from accidentally making changes to the file. This setting requires readers to opt-in for editing rights to the workbook.

- **Encrypt With Password:** The file is encrypted and protected with a password. When you select this option, you are required to enter a password for the workbook. Only users with the password can open the workbook.

- **Protect Current Sheet:** This option opens the Protect Sheet dialog box, which enables you to password-protect the sheet or specify individual sheet-related capabilities, such as Format Cells, Insert Hyperlinks, and Delete Columns. You also can configure interaction with locked cells in this dialog box. We discuss locked cells and sheet protection in more detail shortly.

- **Protect Workbook Structure:** You can use this option to keep users from changing the number of sheets in the workbook. This means that worksheets cannot be deleted or added.

- **Restrict Access:** This option enables you to give unrestricted or restricted access to the workbook (using a checklist). If you connect to a Digital Rights Management (DRM) server through your employer or institution, rights can be assigned to collaborators based on different permission levels that are based on user authentication (if you don't use a DRM, this option will not be available).

- **Add A Digital Signature:** You can digitally sign a file to prove its authenticity. Signing a file digitally requires that you obtain a digital certificate from a certificate authority (you can locate a digital certificate authority on the web).

- **Mark As Final:** This command marks the file as final and makes it read-only. All editing commands for the file are disabled. This feature is primarily designed to keep users from inadvertently making changes to a file (because a user can change Mark As Final in the Backstage).

You can see that the Info window provides some protection schemes that are all-or-nothing propositions, such as Mark As Final And Encrypt With Password. Instead of protecting an entire workbook, you can choose to protect only certain cells on a sheet (before you share it with other users). For example, you might want to lock cells that contain formulas and functions so that the person doing the data entry does not accidentally overwrite or delete the worksheet formulas or functions. Let's look at how you lock cells in a sheet.

Locking cells

Locking cells in a sheet is a two-step process. You must first select and lock the cells. Then you must turn on protection for the entire worksheet to make the lock go into effect.

Select the cells in the worksheet that you want to lock. These can be cells containing formulas, functions, or column and row labels (or names, Social Security numbers, or anything you want to protect and don't want the cells' content to be deleted or edited). If you need to select non-contiguous cells, hold down the Ctrl key and then click a cell to include it in the selected range of cells.

On the Home tab, select the Format command in the Cells group. Then select Format Cells (this command is at the very end of the Format menu). This opens the Format Cells dialog box. Select the Protection tab in the dialog box. The Locked check box should already be selected by default, as shown in Figure 11-10.

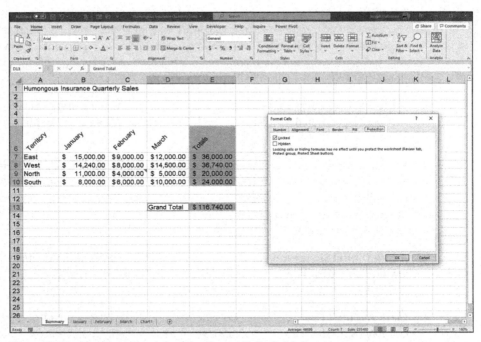

Figure 11-10   The Protection tab of the Format Cells dialog box

TIP

If you want to cut a step out of the cell locking process and avoid opening the Format Cells dialog box, select Format, Lock Cell in the Format gallery. This also toggles on the Lock Cell attribute (for the selected cells only). You can then protect the sheet to complete the cell locking process.

To close the Format Cells dialog box, click OK. Now you need to protect the sheet. Select the Format tab (in the Cells group on the Home tab) and then select the Protect Sheet command under the Protection heading. The Protect Sheet dialog box opens, as shown in Figure 11-11.

Figure 11-11   The Protect Sheet dialog box

You can enter a password to protect the sheet, if you want. You can also select other options related to what users can do to the worksheet, such as formatting cells, columns, or rows and inserting hyperlinks. To protect the locked cells on the sheet and allow data entry in other cells, you need not change any settings in the Protect Sheet dialog box. Even the password is optional. Click OK to close the dialog box.

TIP

A Protect group is available on the Excel ribbon's Review tab. This group provides commands such as Protect Sheet and Protect Workbook. This group also provides the Allow Edit Ranges option. To quickly unprotect a protected worksheet, select the Unprotect Sheet command in the Protect group on the Review tab.

When you (yes, you) or another user attempts to enter data into the locked cells on the worksheet, a message box opens to let you know that the cell is protected and is read-only. No data entry is allowed in the cell.

Specifying edit ranges

There is actually another way to protect cells in a sheet. When you use the previously described cell-lock approach, you are actually specifying the cells that are unavailable for editing or deletion. You can approach cell protection by specifying the range of cells that other users can edit. This method is a little easier to configure than the method discussed for locking cells but be advised that specifying edit ranges is primarily designed for use in network environments where workbooks are often shared by multiple collaborators and coworkers. In fact, it is really designed for situations in which you use Excel on a Microsoft Windows Server network. Because network users are listed in a global catalog provided by the Active Directory (which is a catalog of all the objects on the network, including users, computers, and networks), setting permissions for specific users or groups related to ranges that you password-protect is easy. This method certainly is not restricted to corporate networks, though, because you can specify users who have been set up on your local computer.

To specify the ranges that users can edit, you will provide these ranges in the Allow Users To Edit Ranges dialog box. Each range can be protected by a different password so that you can provide access to some cells to certain users and other cells to other users. This provides a little more fine-tuning in terms of cell access than the method we looked at involving locking cells and then protecting the sheet. In the Protect group on the ribbon's Review tab, select the Allow Edit Ranges command, which opens the Allow Users To Edit Ranges dialog box, shown in Figure 11-12.

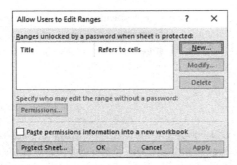

Figure 11-12 The Allow Users To Edit Ranges dialog box

To specify an editable range, click the New button. This opens the New Range dialog box. Provide a title for the range. Click the Refers To Cells box and select any cell addresses already listed. (Typically, this will be the cell address of the cell that is currently selected in the sheet.) Now you can use your mouse and select the range of cells in the worksheet that will make up the new edit range.

You can select contiguous cells or noncontiguous cells, as needed.

TIP

Whenever you are working with passwords, you need to make sure you record the passwords and keep them in a safe place. Forgotten passwords don't do anyone any good, particularly when you have work to do.

After specifying the range in the New Range dialog box, provide a password in the Range Password text box. You can also specify permissions related to the password-protected range. Select the permissions in the New Range dialog box, and the Permissions dialog box for the range opens.

You can use the Add button to open the Select Users Or Groups dialog box. You can then add users or groups to the list provided in the Users Or Groups dialog box. User accounts or groups added to the list can be local computer accounts (users with whom you share your computer and have an account in your Windows 10 settings). Also, these can be user accounts and groups that are housed on your network server, such as a domain controller in a Microsoft Windows Server network. Typically, we are talking about users who are in the same network domain and who may also have access to various SharePoint sites or OneDrive for business.

After specifying users and groups, click OK to return to the Permissions dialog box for the range. You can select a group or username in the Permissions dialog box and then specify whether you allow or deny access to the range without a password. The default setting is Allow, so you should change this—the whole point of this process is to password-protect a specific range.

When you have specified the individual permissions for each user or group, click OK to return to the New Range dialog box. You can click OK to close the dialog box. A Confirm Password dialog box opens, requiring that you re-enter the password you set for the range. Enter the password and then click OK to return to the Allow Users To Edit Ranges dialog box. The new range appears in the range list. You can repeat the process to add other ranges to the Allow Users To Edit Ranges dialog box. When you finish adding the ranges, click OK to close the dialog box.

For editing ranges to work, you still need to lock all the cells in the worksheet and then protect the sheet. Use the Sheet Selector button (the box just to the left of column A and above row 1) to select the entire worksheet. Then select the Format command on the Home tab and select Lock Cell on the menu provided. All the cells on the sheet are now locked.

Navigate to the Review tab of the ribbon and select Protect Sheet. When the Protect Sheet dialog box opens, the Protect Worksheet And Contents Of Locked Cells check box is selected, which should stay selected. However, you can also specify a password that can be used to unprotect the sheet (which can be useful if you want to allow a coworker complete access to the cells in a protected sheet). Other settings in this dialog box enable you to set exceptions to your sheet protection, such as allowing users to select locked cells, insert columns, or delete rows. You can select any of these exceptions via the appropriate check box. This dialog box also allows you to specify a password that will unprotect the sheet (definitely recommended). When you have finished fine-tuning your settings, click OK to protect the sheet.

So, let's say that you share the workbook with other users. When they attempt to access locked cells on the sheet, they are greeted by a message box letting them know that the cell is locked and is read-only. When the user attempts to enter data in a cell that is in one of the edit ranges that you specified, the Unlock Range dialog box opens. The user needs to provide the password that unlocks the range. Formatting a sheet with edit ranges provides other users with access to cells in the sheet so that they can enter data. Cells that contain formulas or functions are protected from accidental deletion or editing. Even the cells in the edit ranges are secure and require a user to enter the password to access the edit range cells.

Preparing a workbook for sharing

The Check For Issues button in the Backstage Info window (from the Excel application window select File) provides commands that enable you to check a workbook for hidden or personal information and for any accessibility or compatibility issues with the workbook. When you select the Inspect Document command, the Document Inspector opens, as shown in Figure 11-13.

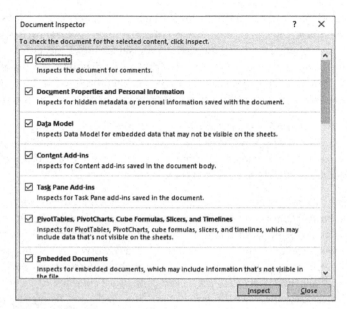

Figure 11-13   The Document Inspector

The primary job of the Document Inspector is to scour your workbook for any personal or sensitive information that you might not have realized the workbook contains. This includes information that you might have placed in comments or the headers and footers of the worksheets. The Document Inspector also checks for hidden items such as rows, columns, and sheets. When you select Inspect in the Document Inspector dialog box, an inspection runs on the workbook.

When the inspection has completed, a list of results appears in the Document Inspector. For example, personal information might have been included in the workbook properties, and this is flagged as a possible problem. Personal information includes the author's name and other seemingly innocuous information, such as the printer properties for your printer. Headers and footers are other problematic areas (at least in the Inspector's mind) because they might include information that you do not want to share with others. This means if the workbook contains any headers or footers, they will be flagged as potential problems. The Document Inspector will even document whether you have task pane or content add-ins installed in Excel and if you have any embedded objects or links to other files in the workbook.

The Document Inspector does provide remedies for these issues, but they are pretty much the equivalent of blowing up your entire backyard to get rid of a few hungry moles. For example, if headers and footers are present, the Document Inspector's solution is Remove All, meaning that all the information in the header or footer area is removed. The same goes for information in the document properties.

Instead of going with the nuclear option that the Document Inspector provides, you might want to use the information in the Document Inspector as a checklist of things you need to examine before you share the document.

CAUTION

Use the Inspect Document tool prior to protecting workbook cells or allowing edit ranges. The Inspector won't run if you have protected cells in any of the workbook's sheets. You can unprotect the sheet in the Backstage using the Unprotect command on the Protect Workbook box. After running the Inspect Document tool, remember to turn the workbook protection on before you distribute the file to coworkers or colleagues.

Recovering unsaved workbooks

The options provided by the Manage Workbook area of the Info window relate to autosaved draft copies of your workbook that were not saved when they were closed. For example, your power might have gone out before changes that you made to a workbook were saved.

A list of any auto-recovered workbook files will be listed just to the right of the Manage Workbook command button. Just click the link for one of the auto-recovered files to open it. All the auto-recovered workbooks (if there are any) will be time stamped, so you know when that particular version was created. Be advised that when you save and exit the current workbook, the various autosave versions of the workbook are deleted. You need to use these versions during your current editing session before you save the version you are now working on if you want to access them.

TIP

If you want to recover other unsaved workbooks that may be available on your computer, click the Manage Workbook button and then click Recover Unsaved Workbooks. This opens the Open dialog box, and any draft versions of the current workbook (or other workbooks) are listed. The drafts are listed because Excel (and other Office applications such as Word or PowerPoint) automatically search for draft copies using Unsaved Files as the keyword in the Open dialog box's Search box. Once you locate these unsaved files, either in the Open dialog box or listed in the Manage Workbook area of the Info page, you can then save or delete these files. You can use the Save As command to change the file name so that you can keep the draft as well as the original version of the file.

Entering data in a worksheet

Entering data in a worksheet is just a matter of accessing a particular cell and then entering the information you want in that cell. Unlike Word, where you primarily enter text, Excel allows you to enter an array of different types of information. So, your worksheet entries will typically include text, numbers, dates, times, formulas, and functions. In terms of the raw data that you enter in a worksheet (excluding the insertion of formulas or functions), you are really working with two distinct types of information: labels and values.

A label contains descriptive information, such as a person's name, a place, a thing, or a time designation, such as the day of the week or month of the year. A label has no numerical significance in Excel; labels provide context for the values in the worksheet. Now, don't get me wrong—dates can have numerical significance and can be used in formulas and functions. For example, you can subtract today's date from the date of an upcoming holiday, such as Labor Day or Thanksgiving, and compute how many days remain until that particular holiday. Social Security numbers, on the other hand, are numbers, but they are descriptors and do not have numerical significance. We don't add or subtract Social Security numbers.

A value is data that does have numerical significance. Values can be numbers, dates, and times. Values can be acted upon by formulas and functions. A value could be the monthly payment you have made on an automobile or the water levels you have measured over the course of the year on a nearby lake. Values are the fuel that drive Excel's number-crunching engine and allow you to do everything in Excel from simple math to complex analysis; without the data (values), Excel pretty much sits and stares back at you.

Entering labels

As already mentioned, text entries in the worksheet serve a descriptive purpose; they are labels. Text can be used as row and column headings and can describe particular cells. In fact, as soon as you press one of the letters of the alphabet, Excel aligns the text entry on the left side of the cell. Excel knows the basic difference between labels and values.

When you type a label into a particular cell, you need to seal the deal by pressing Enter on the keyboard, navigating to another cell (using the arrow keys or Tab), or selecting Enter (the check mark) in the formula bar. Any of these actions enters the information into the cell.

> **TIP**
>
> **If you find that a text entry is cut off when you enter data in the next cell to the right, all you have to do is widen the column by dragging the column border to accommodate the entry in the cell. You can also double-click the columns border (at the top of the worksheet) to let Excel widen the column to accommodate the longest entry in that column.**

In some situations, you might want to enter numbers but have them "seen" by Excel as text entries. You can select the cells that contain the numerical labels and format the cells as text before entering the actual numbers. Follow these steps:

1. Select the cells that contain the numbers that serve as labels.

2. On the Home tab, select the General command in the Number group.

3. In the Number format gallery that appears, scroll to the bottom and select Text.

4. Enter the numbers (including leading zeros) in the formatted cells.

5. The numbers entered into these text-formatted cells are left-aligned in the cells (the same as any text entry). The next chapter has more about formatting cells.

➤ **For more about formatting cells, see Chapter 12.**

Entering values

As already mentioned, values provide the data to be used in an Excel calculation performed by a formula or function (a function is just a built-in formula). You can enter values using the 0–9 keys on the keyboard or the numeric keypad. You are not required to enter commas, dollar signs, or percentage signs in the cell when you enter a value. Formatting the value can come afterward, using the number formats Excel provides. You are required to place the decimal point in the correct place, however.

Excel right-aligns values in the worksheet cells. Make sure that you check any values that you enter into your cells. Typing mistakes make up most of the errors typically found in a worksheet. Although a misspelled label might be embarrassing, an erroneous formula or function result due to incorrect data entry can be damaging to your credibility and business.

CHAPTER 11

Inside OUT

Check your Excel data input before taking your show on the road.

In my professional life, I have sat through many, many presentations, both from colleagues and information technology vendors, that relied heavily on Excel data to prove a particular point. These presentations also typically consist of wonderful-looking Excel worksheets and charts that have been inserted into a PowerPoint presentation and are then projected onto a giant screen in a packed meeting room. In most cases, I sit and nod my head in agreement with the number-crunching expertise of the presenter and clutch my hard copy of the presenter's PowerPoint slides for later reference.

Typically, I will leave the event feeling I have learned something. There have been times, however, where I have seen presentations like this completely blow up. On one occasion, I raised my hand and pointed out that a formula in a worksheet was not designed correctly by the presenter, so Excel was generating an erroneous answer. This incorrect answer was reflected in all the presenter's beautiful Excel charts, which were, in effect, meaningless. I have also been at events where attendees pointed out data error entries and other problems with an Excel worksheet or chart. Remember that just because Excel is doing the math and generating the charts, you shouldn't put your work on a giant screen in front of several hundred people unless you have carefully checked your data input and your subsequent use of formulas and functions. Don't let your presentation become one long user error.

Dates and times that you enter into an Excel workbook can have numerical significance. Excel sees a date as a number that reflects the number of days that have elapsed since January 1, 1900. Even though you won't see this number (Excel displays your entry as a normal date), the number is used whenever you use the date in a calculation. Times are also considered values. Time is computed as a percentage of 24 hours. To you, 10:45 a.m. might be time for a coffee break, but to Excel, it is the decimal value of .4479.

You can enter a date into a cell using more than one date shorthand or format. For example, you can use the MM/DD/YY or MM-DD-YY format. You can also enter a date in the format MONTH DAY, YEAR, such as August 9, 2011. If you need to specify a year earlier than 2000, include the entire year, such as 1954 instead of 54. It probably makes sense to always use a four-digit year for your dates to negate any misunderstanding related to the century you are referring to.

Dates that you enter have the default date format applied to them. You can change the formatting for dates via the Number tab of the Format Cells dialog box, which can be opened using the dialog box launcher on the Font group on the ribbon's Home tab. Chapter 12 discusses formatting cell entries.

TIP

To insert the current date into a cell, press Ctrl+; (semicolon).

TIP

If you enter a value, particularly a date, and the entry is shown as #####, you need to widen the column to accommodate the value.

The format for entering time is HH:MM. You can specify a.m. or p.m. with a or p (following the time), respectively. You can also enter time using the 24-hour international time format.

Using AutoComplete

AutoComplete can take some of the drudgery out of entering the same label multiple times in a worksheet column. Excel keeps a list of all the labels that you enter in a worksheet column. For example, suppose you have a worksheet tracking sales in Europe, and you are entering country names, such as Germany, Italy, and so on, multiple times into a particular column in the worksheet. After you enter Germany the first time, it becomes part of the AutoComplete list for that column. The next time you enter the letter G into a cell in that column, Excel completes the entry as Germany.

AutoComplete works with text entries and entries that contain a combination of text and numbers. Depending on the similarities of labels in a particular column, you might have to type several characters before Excel provides you with the correct match. When the AutoComplete entry appears in the cell, press Enter.

TIP

To quickly access the AutoComplete list in the current cell, press Alt+Down Arrow.

You can also choose to select an AutoComplete entry from a drop-down menu. All the entries available for a particular column appear in the list. Right-click a cell and then select the Pick From Drop-Down List on the shortcut menu that appears. A drop-down menu of AutoComplete entries appears, as shown in Figure 11-14.

Select an entry from the list. The entry is entered in the cell. Using the list enables you to see the available entries, which can be particularly useful in large worksheets that contain many different labels in a particular column.

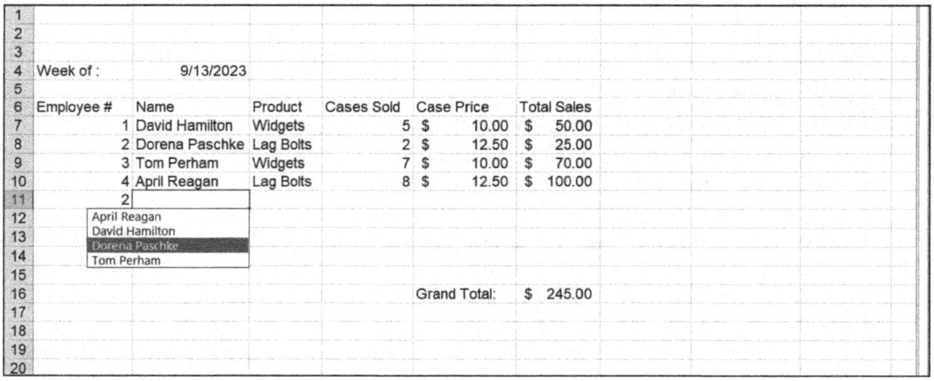

1						
2						
3						
4	Week of :		9/13/2023			
5						
6	Employee #	Name	Product	Cases Sold	Case Price	Total Sales
7	1	David Hamilton	Widgets	5	$ 10.00	$ 50.00
8	2	Dorena Paschke	Lag Bolts	2	$ 12.50	$ 25.00
9	3	Tom Perham	Widgets	7	$ 10.00	$ 70.00
10	4	April Reagan	Lag Bolts	8	$ 12.50	$ 100.00
11	2					
12		April Reagan				
13		David Hamilton				
14		Dorena Paschke				
		Tom Perham				
15						
16					Grand Total:	$ 245.00
17						
18						
19						
20						

Figure 11-14   AutoComplete drop-down menu

Filling and entering series

The capability to automatically fill cells with information is a useful and time-saving trick that can help you avoid data entry drudgery and decrease the possibility of data entry errors in your worksheets. A couple of different techniques help in filling cells with information. You can use the Fill handle, which allows you to create a series quickly, or you can use the Fill command in the Editing group of the Home tab. The Fill command can be used to enter value series where you can specify the type of series (such as linear or growth) and provide the step value for the series. The step value serves as either the amount by which the value in each subsequent cell is increased (in a linear series) or the multiple used to increase each subsequent entry in the series (in a growth series). Data series can also be created where the step value provides the increment for specifying each subsequent date in the series.

Another feature related to filling data into worksheet cells is the Flash Fill tool. It is used primarily to separate into multiple columns text information that has been lumped together in a column. For example, if you have to fix a poorly designed worksheet where first and last names have been combined in a single column, the Flash Fill feature helps you "type" the first names into a new column as soon as it recognizes the "entry" pattern for the information. Let's start our discussion of entering series into a worksheet with a discussion of the Fill handle and work our way toward the Flash Fill tool.

Using the Fill handle

The Fill handle can help you quickly create series for days of the week and months of the year. It can also provide a series for labels that contain a number. For example, suppose I divided my sales territory into regions specified as Region 1, Region 2, and so on. In that case, all I would have to do is enter the Region 1 label in a cell and then use the Fill handle to drag the rest of the series into other adjacent cells, as needed. The Fill handle can create a series in a column or a row.

The Fill handle is the small black box in the lower-right corner of a selected cell's border. The mouse pointer becomes a small + symbol when you are on the Fill handle. To use the Fill handle, drag it in the direction you want the fill to take place. For instance, if you are filling cells in a column, you can drag down or up (probably down); if you are filling cells in a row, you can drag to the right or left.

Follow these steps to create a fill series, such as the days of the week or months of the year:

1. Enter the first item in the series, such as **Monday** or **January**.

2. Grab the Fill handle and drag in the appropriate direction to extend the series. ScreenTips appear as you drag across the cells, showing a preview of each item that will be placed in each subsequent cell.

3. Release the mouse to enter the series items.

4. When you release the mouse, the series items appear in the cells. The AutoFill Options button appears, as shown in Figure 11-15.

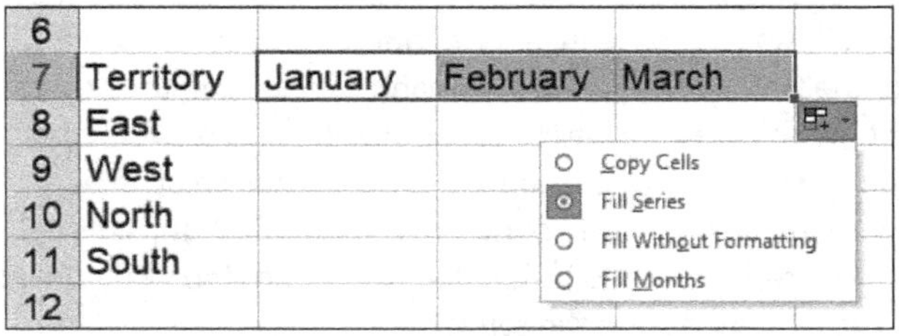

Figure 11-15   A filled month series and the AutoFill options

The AutoFill Options menu (accessed when you select the AutoFill Options button) provides a series of options related to dragging the Fill handle. Although we are using the Fill handle to extend a series, you can see from Figure 11-15 that other options are possible. These options vary depending on whether you are using the Fill handle to copy an item (such as a formula, a function, or even a heading) or creating a series, as discussed here. The possibilities provided by the AutoFill Options menu can include the following:

- **Copy Cells:** The Fill handle might have created a series when you wanted to copy the entry in a cell to other cells using the Fill handle. Select this option to copy rather than fill.

- **Fill Series:** If the Fill handle has copied the entry in the cell, you can select this option to get an extended series.

- **Fill Without Formatting:** This option creates a series but does not include any formatting that has been applied to the cell that you "extended" using the Fill handle.

You can also use the Fill handle to extend numerical series, date series, and even text series (where a number is included with a text entry, such as Region 1). When you use the Fill handle to extend a date series, the AutoFill Options menu provides other options, such as Fill Days, Fill Weekdays, Fill Months (as shown in Figure 11-15), and Fill Years. So no matter what type of date series you are trying to create from a source date, the Fill handle can create the series for you.

TIP

When you copy formulas and functions to multiple cells in a column or row, you can use the Fill handle rather than copy and paste.

The Fill handle can also be used to copy a cell's content, including formulas for functions, to a range of cells. Remember that if you don't get the result you seek, you might have to consult the AutoFill Options menu and then select the option that provides the needed fill or copy.

NOTE

If you are attempting to fill cells with a series that is already contained in the worksheet, you can select Flash Fill in the AutoFill options to enter the existing data.

In the case of numerical series, you can extend any series as long as Excel knows what the step is between the numbers in the series. The step is the incremental difference between the numbers in the series, so when you enter 2 in a cell and then 4 in the cell below it, you tip off Excel that the step is 2. Select both cells containing the first two numbers in the series, and then drag the Fill handle on the second number to create the series as needed.

The Fill handle can create a series, and it can quickly copy items to multiple cells. However, it does have a limitation in terms of copying a cell's content in more than one direction (such as down and then to the right). You can only copy down or up in a single column or to the right or left in a single row. If you need to copy into multiple columns or rows, you have to extend the series in one direction and then extend the series a second time in the second direction. This makes more sense when you attempt to copy formulas or functions to cells in a range that encompasses multiple columns or rows.

> ➤ **For more about copying formulas and functions, see the "Copying and moving formulas and functions" section in Chapter 13, "Getting the most from formulas and functions."**

Creating custom fill lists

You can also create custom fill lists and then apply them using the Fill handle. For example, you might have a group of employee names or location names that you always enter in the same order in different worksheets. When you create the custom fill list, all you have to do is enter the first item in the list in a cell and then use the Fill handle to extend the rest of the custom fill list into the required cells.

NOTE

The Fill command (in the Editing group on the Home tab) also provides a menu of commands for filling down, right, up, or left. You can use these commands to copy information from a cell to a group of selected cells.

A custom list can consist of text entries or text mixed with numbers. Therefore, custom lists are reserved for a series of labels. You can create a custom fill list from a range of cells that already exist in a worksheet, or you can create a custom list by typing in the entries for the list manually. Custom fill lists are created in the Custom Lists dialog box, shown in Figure 11-16. To open the Custom Lists dialog box, go to the Backstage (select File) and then select Options to open the Excel Options window. In the Options window, select Advanced, scroll down to the General Options, and select Edit Custom Lists.

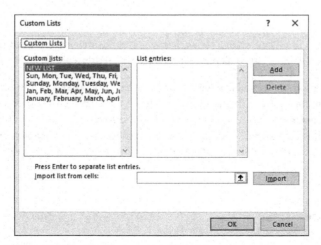

Figure 11-16 The Custom Lists dialog box

The Custom Lists dialog box provides more than one possibility for creating a custom list. If you want to import a selected range of cells into a custom list, you can specify the range by selecting the Shrink button to the left of the Import button. This gives you access to the worksheet. Select the range, and then click the Expand button to re-enter the Custom Lists dialog box. You can then click the Import button. The new list is placed in the Custom Lists pane, and the entries in the list are shown in the List Entries pane.

If you want to create the custom list from scratch, select New List in the Custom Lists pane and then click Add. You can then type the entries in the List Entries pane. Press Enter after each entry. When you are ready to add the list, click the Add button in the Custom Lists dialog box.

You can now use the custom list or lists that you created in your worksheets. Type the first entry in a custom list in a cell, and then use the Fill handle to extend the range. The new range consists of the entries you placed in the custom list.

TIP

To delete a custom list that you have created, select the list and then click the Delete button in the Custom Lists dialog box.

Creating custom series

Another option for creating a series (a series of values, including dates) in a worksheet is to take advantage of the Series dialog box. The Series dialog box gives you complete control over the series you want to create, including the step value (the increment between each subsequent cell and the cell before it) and the stop value. You can also create different types of series:

- **Linear:** This series type uses the starting value provided in the worksheet and then uses the step value to create a linear progression.

- **Growth:** This series type uses the starting value provided in the worksheet and then multiplies each value in the series by the step value to enter each subsequent value in the range. Therefore, this type of series is really a geometric progression.

- **Date:** This series type enables you to specify a date unit, such as Day, Weekday, Month, or Year. The step value is then added to each subsequent date in the series.

- **AutoFill:** This type of series mimics the use of the Fill handle. You don't have to enter a step value for this type of series.

Enter the start value for the series you want to create in a cell in the worksheet. You can then select the cell and the range of cells that will be filled by the information you enter into the Series dialog box. To open the Series dialog box, select the Fill command on the Home tab and then select Series. Figure 11-17 shows the Series dialog box.

CHAPTER 11

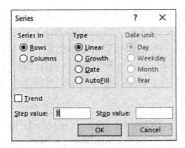

Figure 11-17   The Series dialog box

Select the appropriate option to specify whether the series appears in rows or columns. Select the type of series you want to create, such as linear, growth, or date. Enter the step value for the series in the Step Value box. If you did not select the cells you want to fill using the series, you can enter a step value for the series. This specifies the end of the series and also dictates the number of cells the series fills. When you are ready to create the series, click OK.

Using Flash Fill

When you copy data from other sources—particularly from the web—and try to "shoehorn" it into Excel using the Paste command, you can end up with columns of information that need to be further divided into additional columns. For example, you might have a list of people (from the web or in a PDF) where the first and last names are listed in the same column. You want to break out the first and last names into separate columns (which allows you to sort the data by last name more easily). The Flash Fill feature is designed to recognize data entry patterns in your worksheet and fill in the rest of the data for you.

As an example, to break first names out of a column (let's call it the Name column) where first names and last names are combined, you would create a new column named "First Name." Then type the first name of the first person listed in the Name column. Drop down one cell by pressing Enter and begin to type the name of the second person. You won't get the entire name typed in before the Flash Fill feature kicks in as shown in Figure 11-18.

	Employee	First Name	Name	Product	Cases Sold	Case Price	Total Sales
8							
9	Employee	First Name	Name	Product	Cases Sold	Case Price	Total Sales
10	1	David	David Hamilton	Widgets	5	$ 10.00	$ 50.00
11	2	Dorena	Dorena Paschke	Lag Bolts	2	$ 12.50	$ 25.00
12	3	Tom	Tom Perham	Widgets	7	$ 10.00	$ 70.00
13	4	April	April Reagan	Lag Bolts	8	$ 12.50	$ 100.00
14							
15							
16							
17							
18							Grand Total: 245
19							

Figure 11-18   Flash Fill inserts the data for you.

The Flash Fill feature automatically recognizes that you are typing the first names found in the Name column, and it will fill the rest of the first names into your new First Name column. So, as soon as the Flash Fill first names appear in your column (as you are typing), press Enter to allow Flash Fill to complete your entries. To complete this scenario, you could then create a new Last Name column and use Flash Fill to enter all the last names into a column. You would then have a worksheet where the first names and last names are in separate columns. (Don't forget to delete the old and now unneeded Name column.)

The Flash Fill feature isn't limited to recognizing patterns in text entries that use a space as the divider (such as in the case of a name). You can also use it in other instances. For example, if you had a long list of Social Security numbers in a column, you could create a "last fours" column that shows only the last four digits of the Social Security number. Just start the new column and type the first couple of "last fours," and Flash Fill takes care of the rest. Flash Fill needs to merely discern a pattern in existing data to automatically fill entries for you. Suppose you aren't consistent in the way you enter information into a worksheet. In that case, the Flash Fill feature probably won't be able to determine the data you are trying to "fill" in a particular column or row.

TIP

If the Flash Fill feature doesn't seem to be working, provide a couple of examples of how Excel should break the data out of a particular column into the new column. Then select the Format command on the ribbon's Home tab and select Flash Fill. This might nudge Excel into recognizing the pattern that you want it to use when flash filling cells adjacent to the original entries.

Copying, moving, and deleting cell contents

We have already covered how to use the Fill handle to copy data (both labels and values) from one cell to a range of cells (or from a range to a range). You can also use the Copy command in the Clipboard group to copy a cell's content to another cell. Cell ranges (a group of cells) can be copied and then pasted, and a single cell's content can be pasted to a range of cells. Also, you can move cell data using cut and paste, or you can drag and drop cells or cell ranges in new locations on a sheet.

Copy-and-paste and cut-and-paste are pretty familiar to even the most novice Office user, and it is a very straightforward process to select a cell or cells and then use the Copy or Cut command to place the cell or cell contents onto the Clipboard. Where it can get confusing is based on the different options provided by the Paste command. It provides you with more options than simply taking the cell (or cells) content and pasting it into a new location. Paste options allow you to simply paste the formatting of the source cells or paste the results of a formula rather than the formula itself. These different Paste command possibilities can be used to paste information on the current worksheet, the current workbook (meaning from worksheet to worksheet), or even from workbook to workbook. Let's take a look at what the Paste command has to offer.

TIP

You can use Ctrl+C to copy, Ctrl+X to cut, and Ctrl+V to paste. When you use Ctrl+V, the Paste icon appears below the pasted items, enabling you to adjust the type of paste you make.

Select a cell or range of cells to be copied. Then select Copy or Cut as needed from the Clipboard group on the ribbon's Home tab. When you select the Paste command, a gallery of different paste options appears, as shown in Figure 11-19.

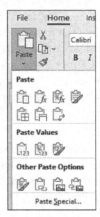

Figure 11-19 The Paste gallery

The Paste gallery divides the different paste options into categories. Each of the options found in the categories provides a ScreenTip when you place the mouse on a specific option icon. The options available depend on what you have copied to the Clipboard. Obviously, the option you select depends on the results you require. The Paste gallery categories follow:

- **Paste:** This category provides, from left to right, the following options: Paste, Formulas, Formulas And Number Formatting, and Keep Source Formatting. The Paste option pastes the contents, but they are formatted according to the formatting that has been applied to the new location. If you want to keep the original formatting, use the Keep Source Formatting option. If you are pasting formulas or functions, take advantage of the Formulas option; if you want to keep the original formatting that was applied to the cells containing the formulas, use the Formulas And Number Formatting option. A second row of Paste options include No Borders, Keep Source Column Widths, and Transpose (which would allow you to transpose a column to a row or vice versa).

- **Paste Values:** If you want to paste the values calculated by a formula or function, you can use the options provided in this category instead of pasting the formula or function itself. Options are provided to paste the value only (Value), the value and its number formatting

(Values And Number Formatting), and the value and the cell formatting (Values And Source Formatting).

- **Other Paste Options:** You can paste the formatting of the select cell (or cell range) using the Formatting option. If you want to link the copied data to the destination cell or cells, use the Paste Link option. Linked data updates automatically when you change the values (such as the results of a formula or function) in the source cell or cells.

When you select one of the options and paste the cell or range into a worksheet, the Paste Options button appears just below the pasted content. You can access the same options that were available in the Paste gallery from this button. The cell or range that you originally copied still has a marquee (that sparkly rectangle thing) denoting that the cell or cells have been copied to the Clipboard. Press Esc to get rid of the marquee.

You can access the Clipboard to view cells or cell ranges that have been copied or cut to it. This enables you to reuse items on the Clipboard. For example, you can paste any of the items on the Clipboard, so if you have cut and then pasted a range, you can paste that same range again from the Clipboard to the current worksheet or another worksheet in the workbook.

To view the contents of the Clipboard, select the Clipboard launcher at the bottom right of the Clipboard group on the ribbon's Home tab. The Clipboard appears as a pane on the left side of the Excel workspace.

The Office Clipboard can hold up to 24 items, which makes it easy to paste data from worksheet to worksheet or even to another Excel workbook. When you place the mouse on an item stored in the Clipboard, a drop-down menu arrow appears. You can use the menu to paste the item. You can also remove it from the Clipboard by selecting Delete on the drop-down menu. You can paste all the items on the Clipboard using the Paste All command. If you want to remove all the current items on the Clipboard, click the Clear All button.

Using the Paste Special dialog box

The Paste gallery provides several possibilities in terms of how copied or cut content (in a cell or range) is then pasted to a new location. The Paste Special dialog box provides more options than the Paste gallery. Many of the options provided in the Paste Special dialog box relate to pasting cells (that have been copied or cut) from one worksheet to another worksheet, or cells from one workbook to another. Because worksheets can be formatted differently, the options in the Paste Special dialog box are designed to enable you to fine-tune what is pasted and how it affects the worksheet where the cells will be pasted. To open the Paste Special dialog box (after you copy or cut a cell range), select Paste and then Paste Special. Figure 11-20 shows the Paste Special dialog box.

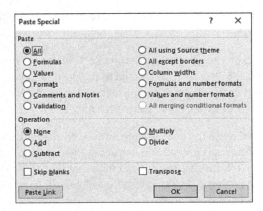

Figure 11-20   The Paste Special dialog box

Most of the options provided in the Paste area of the Paste Special dialog box have names that give you a good idea of what they do. Some of the options paste the contents of the cell or range in the worksheet. For example, Values converts formula and function results to the actual value calculated when the cells are pasted. The Formats option pastes the cell formatting. The Formulas option pastes the formulas or functions in the range but does not include any of the formatting provided by the source range. Some of the other options paste only formatting or other attributes. For example, the Formats option pastes only the cell formatting found in the range and any formatting that has been applied to the text or values found in the cells. Another example is the Column Width option, which pastes only the column width from the source range.

Using the Paste Special Operation options

The Paste Special dialog box goes beyond the various options you might need for pasting cells and cell ranges into a worksheet. The Operation options enable you to perform an operation on a selected range of cells based on a value supplied in the copied cell. You don't actually paste a cell or range of cells for the operation to take place; the Paste Special dialog box uses the originally copied value to adjust the values in a second range of cells. You can add, subtract, multiply, or divide the values in the range.

For example, you might have a list of products in a worksheet that is accompanied by a range of prices for the products. If your supplier raises your cost for each item by 2 percent, you can multiply the values in the range of prices by 1.02 to raise your prices by 2 percent. So, for lack of a better name, we can call the cell containing the 1.02 the *adjustment value*. The cells that are adjusted using the adjustment value can be referred to as the *adjusted range*.

> ### TIP
> The Skip Blanks check box in the Paste Special dialog box enables you to skip blank cells when pasting ranges in your worksheet.

To use the Operation option, enter a value in a cell that serves as the adjustment value. Then copy the cell to the Clipboard using the Copy command (Ctrl+C). The marquee appears around the cell. Now select the range of cells that you want to adjust. The marquee remains around the copied adjustment value even though the range of cells to be adjusted is currently selected. Select Paste and then Paste Special to open the Paste Special dialog box. In the Operation options area of the Paste Special dialog box, select the operation that you want to take place (such as Add, Subtract, Multiply, or Divide) and then click OK. The selected range (the adjusted range) adjusts according to the operation you chose and the adjustment value you originally copied to the Clipboard.

Transposing a cell range

The Paste Special dialog box can also be used to transpose a range of cells that are currently in a row to a column, or vice versa. This is particularly useful if you want to change the column headings that you have placed in the top row of your worksheet into row headings. To transpose a range of cells, you typically use the Cut command (because you are moving the cells) and then the Paste Special dialog box, which provides the Transpose option.

Select the range of cells that you want to transpose, and then select Cut on the Home tab. The marquee marks the range of cells that have been cut. Click in a cell that is the first cell in the range where you transpose the cut range. Make sure that there are empty cells below (if you are transposing a row to a column) or to the right (if you are transposing a column to a row) of the cell that you selected after cutting the range to be transposed. Then open the Paste Special dialog box by selecting Paste, Paste Special.

In the Paste Special dialog box, select the Transpose check box and then click OK. The range of cut cells is transposed to the new location.

Moving cells and ranges

For moving cell content from one place to another in a worksheet, you can use Cut and Paste if you choose; however, dragging and dropping is much easier. You can drag cell content to a new location and drag the contents of a range of cells to a new location. If you drag and drop a range onto a cell or cells that already contain data, the data is replaced by the data in the range you are moving.

Select a cell or cell range to be moved, and then drag the border of the selected cell or cells to the new location. To insert the range between existing cells in a worksheet, hold down the Shift key as you drag. You can also move the data to another worksheet in the current workbook. To move the data to a different worksheet, press the Alt key and drag the selection to the worksheet's tab. You're switched to that sheet, where you can drop your selection at the appropriate location in the worksheet.

TIP

If you want to copy a range using drag-and-drop, hold down the Ctrl key as you drag a copy of the range to a new location.

Clearing and deleting cells

You will find that when you explore the possibilities for removing entered data on a worksheet, the cell and its contents are actually two associated but different entities. You can quickly remove a cell's content (or a group of cells in a selected range) by pressing the Delete key. You can also use the Clear command to clear the contents of a cell, but it also gives you some options for clearing formatting that was applied to a cell (or range of cells) or comments that have been added to a cell. The Clear command is in the Editing group on the Home tab (its icon is an eraser). The Clear gallery provides the following options:

- **Clear All:** This option clears formatting, content, and comments.

- **Clear Formats:** This option clears the formatting that has been applied to the cell, including font, alignment, and number formatting. This option also clears any conditional formatting or cell styles that have been applied to the cell or cells.

- **Clear Contents:** This option clears the contents of a cell or range of cells (much like the Delete key).

- **Clear Comments and Notes:** A comment can be added to a cell and is best used as a way to communicate information to coworkers when you are working on the same shared workbook. An inserted comment is posted to everyone you have shared the workbook with, and a comment has a reply box making it easier for a collaborator to respond to a comment you have inserted in the shared workbook. Notes are best used as reminders or questions you might have related to the data in a particular cell. (Notes do not have the reply box found with comments.) You can remove a comment or note from a cell or a selected range of cells by using this option on the Clear menu.

- **Clear Hyperlinks:** This option removes a hyperlink from the selected cell or range of cells.

- **Remove Hyperlinks:** This option deletes a hyperlink from a cell or cells and removes the formatting.

Clearing cell content is relatively foolproof: You select the cell or a range of cells and then use the Delete key or one of the options on the Clear command's menu to get rid of that data. If you want to actually remove cells from the worksheet, you need to determine how you want the cells around the deleted cells to be repositioned. Remove cells only if you want the other cells in the worksheet to shift to new positions. Otherwise, just delete the data in the cells or type new data into the cells.

To remove cells from a worksheet, select the cell or cell range and then select the Delete command in the Cells group of the ribbon's Home tab. The Delete command provides a gallery that enables you to delete cells, rows, columns, or an entire worksheet. To open the Delete dialog box, select Delete Cells. Figure 11-21 shows the Delete dialog box.

Figure 11-21   The Delete dialog box

The Delete dialog box enables you to select whether the remaining cells shift left or up to fill the space left by the deleted cells. You can also choose to delete the entire row or column by selecting the appropriate option. When you are ready to delete the cells, click the OK button. The cells are removed from the worksheet, and the remaining cells move to fill the gap left by the deleted cells.

➤ **For information on inserting cells into a worksheet, see the "Inserting cells" section in Chapter 12.**

Editing cell content

Accurately entering information into the cells of your Excel worksheet is extremely important, particularly in the case of values. A worksheet boasting the most complex functions Excel can offer still calculates incorrect results if you have made an error when entering the data onto the worksheet.

While entering text or values in a cell, you can edit your work if you make a mistake. As you enter data, you can quickly back up and delete a typo using the Backspace key. If you've already entered the data and moved on to another cell before noticing that it is incorrect, you have a couple of options.

If the data entered is really a mess, click the cell and retype the entire entry. When you press Enter or move to another cell, your new entry replaces the original data in the cell.

If the data contains only a one- or two-character mistake, you might want to edit the entry. Double-click the cell with the error; the insertion point appears on the far right of the cell. You can use the mouse or the keyboard to move the insertion point and correct the errors in the entry. Several keystrokes that are useful when editing data directly in the cell follow:

● **Right- or left-arrow key:** Moves one character to the right or left, respectively

● **Home:** Moves to the beginning of the entry

- **End:** Moves to the end of the entry

- **Delete:** Deletes the character to the right of the insertion point

After editing the data in the cell, press Enter or click the Enter button on the formula bar to enter the changes to the data. You can also edit your cell data in the formula bar. Select a cell to edit and then use the mouse to place the insertion point in the formula bar. The various movement keystrokes just listed also work in the formula bar. When you have finished editing the cell, click the Enter button in the formula bar or move to another cell.

TIP

You can also check for typos using the Spelling feature. Select the Spelling command on the Review tab or press F7 to open it.

Viewing worksheets

Excel provides different workbook views and makes it easy for you to zoom in and out on the current worksheet. Changing the view has no effect on how your worksheet looks when printed (unless you have hidden rows or columns, which are discussed in Chapter 12). The ribbon's View tab, shown in Figure 11-22, provides the Sheet View, Workbook Views, Show, and Zoom groups, which enable you to manipulate the basic view of the current worksheet and the Excel window.

The View tab provides other commands for manipulating the worksheet and viewing multiple workbooks. Chapter 12 discusses the various commands found in the Window group.

Figure 11-22   The ribbon's View tab

The Sheet View group is a new addition to Excel and is designed to create custom views of worksheet data that can be viewed by coworkers you have shared the workbook with. So, a workbook must be shared for the Sheet View group commands to be active. These custom worksheet views provide another tool for analyzing data and are created using the filter tools found on the Data tab of the Excel ribbon. We will discuss how to create a custom sheet view in Chapter 15 in the section "Creating custom sheet views."

The Workbook Views group gives you different views of the current worksheet. The Normal view, which is the default view, provides the basic landscape that we use to enter values, labels, formulas, and functions in the worksheet. Because we spend most of our time working in the Normal view, we aren't always cognizant of where the page breaks are located in the worksheet and how the worksheet translates to the printed page.

To get a better idea of the overall layout of the worksheet and to view any page breaks in the worksheet, select the Page Layout command. The amount of information that you can place on one Excel page is based on the default paper size and page orientation that is configured for Excel. In most cases, in the United States, the paper size is letter (8.5×11 inches), and the orientation is portrait. Page breaks are automatically placed in the worksheet when you exceed the usable space on any page. Figure 11-23 shows a worksheet that has a page break that places the two columns on the far right of the worksheet on a second page.

After you have an indication of the overall layout of the sheet, particularly in the case of the page breaks, you can attempt to remedy any issues before you print the worksheet. For example, the worksheet shown in Figure 11-23 would print on two pages, essentially orphaning the last two columns of the worksheet. You have options related to this problem. If the cell range that is pushed onto the second page (or any number of pages) is fairly small (such as a column or two or a row or two), you can have Excel scale the worksheet to fit on one page when you print the worksheet (discussed in the next section). However, doing so reduces the font size on the printout, and you don't want to end up with a printed page that requires a magnifying glass to read.

After you use Page Layout view to look at your worksheet, dashed lines appear on the worksheet in Normal view. These are the page breaks present in the worksheet.

Another option is to adjust the page orientation or the paper size, perhaps even the margins. For example, a worksheet with a lot of columns might print on one page if you switch the orientation from portrait to landscape using the Orientation command on the Page Setup tab (discussed in the next section of this chapter).

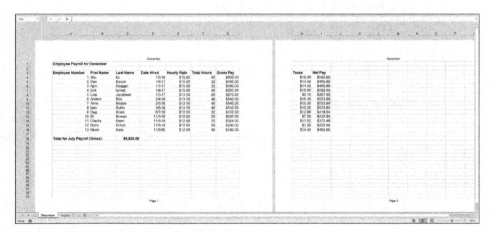

Figure 11-23   The Page Layout view

The Workbook Views group also provides a possibility for adjusting a page break or breaks: You can use the Page Break Preview command. When you select Page Break Preview, Excel zooms out on the worksheet and shows the page breaks as dashed lines. The Welcome to Page Break Preview dialog box also appears, letting you know that you can drag page breaks to a new position in the worksheet as needed. Click any of the page breaks and drag to a new location.

TIP

You can also use the View shortcut icons on the status bar to switch between Normal view, Page Layout view, and Page Break Preview.

When you are working in Normal view, Page Layout view, or Page Break Preview, you can use the Zoom slider on the status bar to change the zoom level. You can also take advantage of the commands in the Zoom group on the View tab. To open the Zoom dialog box, select the Zoom command. The Zoom dialog box enables you to set a specific magnification from a range of options, including 200%, 75%, and 25%. You can choose to fit the current selection (a selected range) on the screen using the Fit Selection option. If you want to set a custom zoom level, use the Custom box in the Zoom dialog box.

You can quickly zoom to 100% using the 100% command. If you want to focus on a particular range of cells, you can zoom to a certain selection. Select the range and then select the Zoom To Selection command. You can then use the Zoom slider as needed to zoom in or out on the current selection.

TIP

You can also use the mouse wheel to zoom in and out on your worksheet. Simply hold down the Ctrl key as you use the mouse wheel. Rolling the mouse wheel away from you zooms in; rolling the mouse wheel toward you zooms out.

To finish our discussion of the View tab, let's take a quick look at the Show group. This group enables you to remove items from the Excel workspace, such as the formula bar, the row and column headings, and the gridlines from the worksheet. This group provides four check boxes that toggle the feature on or off; these commands are Ruler, Gridlines, Formula Bar, and Headings. The Ruler command is inactive in Normal view and is available only in Page Layout view. This makes sense because Page Layout view shows you how your worksheet will appear on the printed page. You can use the ruler to align objects such as charts and images on a worksheet.

Printing worksheets

As you enter information in a worksheet, you really don't need to worry about the actual layout of the sheet until you need to print. Printing in Excel is really a two-step process. First, you will find that the Page Layout tab of the ribbon provides all the commands you need to adjust the overall layout of the sheet, including page orientation, margins, and page sizes. You can also scale the sheet and insert page breaks into the worksheet as needed.

After you have adjusted the various page layout settings using the Page Layout tab, you can move on to the second half of the tasks related to printing and open the Backstage Print page. The Print page enables you to specify the printer for the printout and also configure other print settings, such as what is to be printed, how many copies should be printed, and how the printouts should be collated. Let's look at the Page Layout command and then the Print page options.

Using the Page Layout commands

The ribbon's Page Layout tab provides several groups of commands that relate to getting the worksheet ready to print. The Page Setup, Scale To Fit, and Sheet Options groups enable you to control the size and orientation of the worksheet pages, scale the worksheet data to fit on a page, and include gridlines or headings in the printout, respectively. The Page Layout tab, shown in Figure 11-24, also includes the Themes group and the Arrange group; Chapter 12 discusses themes.

Figure 11-24   The Page Layout tab of the ribbon

The Page Setup group on the Page Layout tab provides important commands in configuring the page settings for the worksheet. Commands are provided for everything from setting the margins to specifying print titles consisting of row or column headings that are repeated on each printout page. The commands provided in the Page Setup group are as follows:

- **Margins:** The Margin command provides three different margin settings in a gallery: Normal (top and bottom .75 inch, left and right .7 inch), Wide (top, bottom, left, and right 1 inch), and Narrow (top and bottom .75 inch, left and right .25 inch). You can also access the Margins tab of the Page Setup dialog box by selecting Custom Margins.

- **Orientation:** This command enables you to switch from portrait to landscape, or vice versa.

- **Size:** This command provides a gallery of page sizes, such as Letter, Legal, Executive, and A4 through A6 (sizes provided may vary by printer). Select More Paper Sizes to open the Page tab of the Page Setup dialog box. You can use the Paper Size drop-down menu to select other page sizes available on the default printer.

- **Print Area:** This command enables you to set a print area based on a selected range in the worksheet. You can also use this command to clear a print area that you have previously set.

- **Breaks:** This command provides a menu of commands that enable you to insert a page break, remove a page break, or reset all the page breaks in the worksheet.

- **Background:** This command enables you to select an image that is used as a background for the worksheet.

- **Print Titles:** This command opens the Sheet tab of the Page Setup dialog box. Print titles are column or row headings that you want repeated on each page of the printout. This is an extremely useful feature when you are working with large worksheets that span multiple pages.

The Scale To Fit group on the Page Layout tab enables you to scale the worksheet by width, height, or scale. By default, the scale is set to 100%, and you can decrease or increase the scale as needed to either shrink or expand the size of the worksheet. The Width command shrinks the width of the worksheet on a page or pages. The default width is set to Automatic, so the width of the actual sheet determines the number of pages that will be used. If you want to shrink a worksheet with a minimal number of columns outside the first page, you can select 1 on the Width menu to shrink the worksheet to fit on one page (by width). You can specify from one to nine pages on the Width menu.

The Height command also provides a menu of page number selections, from 1 to 9. It is best used when you have a worksheet with many rows and want to make a few errant rows fit onto a page.

Both the Width and the Height menus provide a More Pages selection that opens the Page tab of the Page Setup dialog box, as shown in Figure 11-25. You can use the Fit To option and the accompanying spin boxes for width and height to scale the worksheet to a specific number of pages wide and a specific number of pages tall.

TIP

You can remove a page break in the Page Break Preview by dragging the page break off the worksheet.

The page tab of the Page Setup dialog box also provides an Adjust To option that enables you to scale the worksheet as a percentage of its normal size. This is the same setting as the Scale setting found in the Scale To Fit group on the Page Layout tab.

The Sheet Options group on the Page Layout tab provides check boxes related to gridlines and headings. If you want the gridlines on the worksheet to print, select the Print check box under Gridlines. You can also have the column and row headings print by selecting the Print check box under Headings.

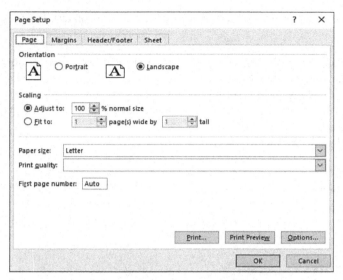

Figure 11-25 The Page tab of the Page Setup dialog box

Setting a print area

You do not always have to print an entire worksheet; instead, you can easily tell Excel what part of the worksheet you want to print by selecting the print area yourself. If the area you select is too large to fit on one page, no problem—Excel breaks it into multiple pages. Print areas are useful when you want to print only a portion of a worksheet.

To set a print area, select the range in the sheet that serves as the print area. Select the Print Area command and then select Set Print Area. The print area is denoted by a dashed-line frame. When you open the Print page in the Backstage, only the print area is previewed. You can also clear a print area, if needed. Select the Print Area command and then select Clear Print Area.

Inserting page breaks

Excel determines the page breaks in the worksheet to be printed based on the paper size, the margins, and the print area (if one has been selected). Excel does not do any thinking when it places page breaks in your worksheet. It places them where they are needed, even if it breaks up the continuity of the data that you have entered in the sheet's columns and rows. You can insert your own page breaks into the worksheet to make the pages more presentable, more understandable, and break information in logical places. You can insert page breaks into the worksheet in Normal view, Page Layout view, or Page Break Preview.

To insert a page break to the left of a column, select the column in the worksheet (click the column's heading). Select the Breaks command and then select Insert Page Break. You can also insert a page break, specifying a row as the break position. The page break is inserted above the selected row.

You can specify that a page break is inserted above and to the left of a cell in the worksheet, meaning that you get two page breaks: One along the row and one along the column. This can be useful when you are working with a large worksheet that might contain various sections, such as four quarters of data positioned on the worksheet into obvious quadrants. All you have to do is select the cell that is below and to the right of where you want the page breaks to be inserted, select Breaks, and then select Insert Page Break.

After inserting page breaks, take the time to peruse your worksheet in Page Layout view or Page Break Preview (particularly if you want to adjust the location of page breaks). You can also use the Backstage Print page to preview the printout of the worksheet. If you want to start over and remove the page breaks that you have inserted in the worksheet, select the Breaks command and then select Reset All Page Breaks.

Setting print titles

If you have a multiple-page worksheet and have either many rows or many columns, it makes sense to set print titles for the worksheet. Print titles enable you to specify a row or rows where you have entered column names or headings and repeat these on each sheet of the printout. You can also specify column(s) that contain row headings and then repeat these headings on each printout page.

To access the Sheet tab of the Page Setup dialog box, select the Print Titles command. In the Print Titles area of the Sheet tab is a Rows To Repeat At Top box and a Columns To Repeat At Left box. To specify rows to repeat, click the Shrink button on the right of the Rows To Repeat At Top box. The dialog box rolls up (that is, shrinks). Select the row or rows to be repeated using the mouse. Click the Expand button on the dialog box to return to the Sheet tab. If you need to also include columns as print titles, click the Shrink button to the right of the Columns To Repeat At Left box and repeat the process by selecting the columns that you want to print. When you have completed the process, click OK to close the Page Setup dialog box.

> TIP
>
> **You can access the Page Setup dialog box by selecting the dialog box launcher on the Page Setup, Scale To Fit, or Sheet Options groups.**

Working on the print page

When you have the Page Layout settings the way you want them, you can access the Backstage Print page to finalize settings for your sheet printout (you can actually print multiple sheets in a particular workbook). Select File on the ribbon to access the Backstage, and then select Print. Figure 11-26 shows the Excel Print page.

The Print page gives you a preview of your printout. You can use the page indicators on the left of the preview to move through the pages of the printout. You can also use the Zoom To Page command to zoom in and out on the current page.

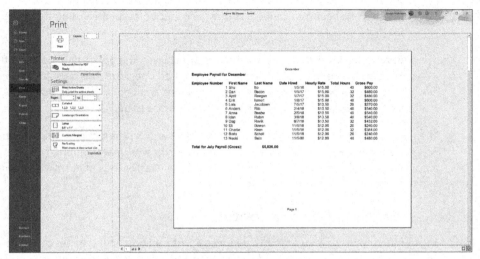

Figure 11-26   The Backstage Print page

The Print page enables you to set the number of copies you want to print and to choose the printer for the printout. Also, you can adjust printer properties for the selected printer. The Settings area of the preview window enables you to control options related to the printout, including what is actually printed and how the printout and settings relate to page size, margins, and scaling. The options provided on the Print page follow:

- **Print Active Sheets:** By default, this menu is set to Print Active Sheets; it determines what you print. You can also choose to print the entire workbook (all the sheets in the workbook) or only a selection in the current worksheet. To print only certain pages, enter the page numbers of the pages you want to print in the Pages boxes.

- **Print One Sided:** Again, this is the default setting for this menu. You can also choose to print on both sides of the paper. Two settings for two-sided printing are supplied; one is for flipping pages on the long edge, and the other is for flipping pages on the short edge.

- **Orientation:** This menu enables you to switch between portrait and landscape orientation.

- **Page Size:** The Page Size menu is set to the page size you specified on the Page Layout tab of the ruler. You can change the page size via this menu. Letter is the default.

- **Custom Margins:** This drop-down menu enables you to change the margin settings that you might have set via the Margins command on the Page Layout tab. You can choose from margins provided in the gallery or select Custom Margins to access the Margins tab of the Page Setup dialog box. You can use the spin boxes as needed to set the margins for the worksheet. You can also specify a header or footer area using the appropriate spin box.

- **Custom Scaling:** You can scale the worksheet using the options provided on this menu. You can choose to have the entire sheet print on one page (this is useful when the sheet has a page break between most of the columns and one or two "straggler" columns) or choose to fit all the columns or all the rows on one page.

There is also a Page Setup link at the bottom of the various print options. This link opens the Page Setup dialog box. Before we end our discussion of worksheet printing (which is just a matter of clicking the Print button on the Print page), we need to look at how to specify headers and footers for your worksheet printouts.

Inserting headers and footers

Headers and footers are used to place repeating information on the pages of your printout. For example, you might use a header to include a name for the worksheet and perhaps include the date or your name at the top of each page of the printout. Footers are ideal for the page numbering you want on each page of the printout. To open the Page Setup dialog box from the Backstage's Print page, click Page Setup just below the Scaling menu. To access the header/footer information for the worksheet, select the Header/Footer tab.

The Header/Footer tab provides a preview of the current header and footer (which means there is probably not a header or footer). The tab also provides check boxes that enable you to determine whether there are different headers and footers for odd and even pages and whether the first page is different (in terms of headers and footers) from the rest of the printout.

To specify a header for the worksheet, click the Custom Header button. This opens the Header dialog box, shown in Figure 11-27. You can specify a header for the left, center, and right sections of the worksheet.

For example, you might want to place your name in the left section of the header, the title of the worksheet in the center, and perhaps a draft number or the date in the right section. Enter the text for a header section. You can then select the text and use the Format Text button to open the Font dialog box and format the selected text.

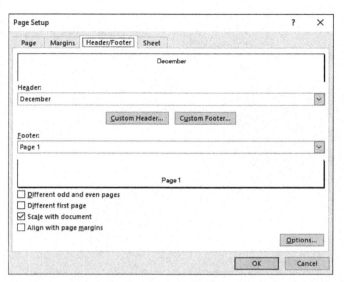

Figure 11-27   The Header/Footer tab of the Page Setup dialog box

Several buttons are provided to insert information into the header, such as the page number, date, file path, and sheet name. You can even insert and format a picture such as a logo into the header. When you have the information for the various sections of the header, click OK to return to the Header/Footer tab. A preview of the header is provided.

If you want to include a footer, click the Custom Footer button. The Footer dialog box opens. The Footer dialog box is basically a replica of the Header dialog box and gives you the same three section panes and tools. Enter the footer information as needed in the three footer sections, and then click OK to return to the Header/Footer tab of the Page Setup dialog box. When you have finished specifying the options for the header and/or footer, click OK to return to the Print page.

The header and/or footer information appears in the preview provided by the Print page. When you are ready to print your worksheet, click the Print button.

Worksheet formatting and management

Formatting text entries   345

Formatting values   349

Adding comments to notes and cells   354

Using themes   357

Formatting cells using borders and color   357

Using cell styles and the Format Painter   360

Using conditional formatting   363

Manipulating cells and cell content   369

Working with columns and rows   373

Working with worksheets   375

Naming ranges   378

Adding images and graphics to worksheets   381

Entering the data into an Excel sheet is only the first step, and you will certainly need to include labels (text), values, formulas, and functions in your worksheet. Formatting entries in cells so that certain information is highlighted or certain cells are emphasized can also be important. Creating a sheet with visual appeal and a sensible layout can help make all those columns and rows of information easier for others to understand.

In this chapter, we look at formatting cell entries. We look at how to format text labels, including wrapping text in a cell or joined cells, and how to work with the formatting of values, such as numbers and dates. Coverage is provided on manipulating cells and cell entries as well as columns, rows, and entire sheets. We also discuss how to add graphics to Excel sheets for more visual appeal.

Formatting text entries

Formatting text entries (or *labels*, as we like to call them in Excel worksheets) can be as simple as assigning different font settings or assigning alignment attributes to a cell or a range of cells. Formatting text in Excel isn't really that much different from formatting text in Word or PowerPoint. You can easily add bold or italic to the contents of a cell or cells using commands on the ribbon. You can also change the font and font size used by a range as needed.

Excel also provides some cell-formatting features that are a little "flashier" than your basic font-formatting attributes, such as bold, italic, and underline. For example, the Orientation command enables you to rotate text in a cell or cell range. This can be particularly useful when you want to create eye-catching row or column headings but want to do it without greatly increasing the row or column size.

The ribbon's Home tab provides all the commands for the basic formatting attributes. The Font group provides you with the ability to change the font and font size and to select font attributes, such as bold, italic, underline, and font color. The Font group also includes the Border and Fill Color commands, which we discuss later in the chapter.

The Alignment group contains the vertical alignment commands—Top Align, Middle Align, and Bottom Align—that enable you to control the vertical alignment of text in a cell. The horizontal alignment tools are also present in this group—Align Text Left, Center, and Align Text Right—as are the Decrease Indent and Increase Indent commands.

To format labels in a cell or cell range, select the cells that are to be formatted. Then select the attributes that you want to apply to the text labels by using the commands in the Font and Alignment groups.

NOTE

The ribbon's Home tab is very similar in Excel, Word, and PowerPoint. The Home tab always provides the Clipboard group and a new Undo group. Also on the Home tab are the Font and other command groups, such as Paragraph (in Word and PowerPoint) or Alignment (in Excel), that are related to formatting or aligning the text in cells. If you are trying to change the basic "look" of items in one of the 365 applications, the Home tab is the place to go.

TIP

You can also use keyboard shortcuts to format cells, such as Ctrl+B for bold, Ctrl+I for italic, Ctrl+U for single underline, and Ctrl+5 for strikethrough.

Accessing the Format Cells dialog box

Font and alignment attributes can also be controlled via the Format Cells dialog box. Because all the information that we put into a worksheet is placed in cells, it makes sense that all the various formatting attributes we assign to sheet labels would be considered cell formatting.

To format the text in a cell or cell range, select the range and then open the Format Cells dialog box, as shown in Figure 12-1. You can open the Format Cells dialog box by selecting the dialog box launcher in the Font, Alignment, or Number group. The group from which you launch the dialog box dictates the tab selected. For example, if you launch the Format Cells dialog box from the Font group, the Font tab is selected when the dialog box opens.

Inside OUT

Don't apply too much formatting.

The discussion in this section primarily focuses on the formatting of text entries. Remember that Excel is different than Word or PowerPoint in that people seem to be somewhat intimidated by rows and columns of numbers. You can use formatting to make your text entries stand out but don't overdo, or you might make your worksheet even more difficult to understand.

Having said that about text entries, you know that you can also apply any of the font formatting and alignment settings to values (numbers) in your sheets to make them stand out or otherwise be differentiated from the surrounding data. This can be very useful on a large crowded worksheet, but it can also be overused.

So, please remember that Excel aligns values on the right of the cell and text entries on the left by default. If you do format values in a sheet, make sure that the sheet remains readable and that it is still apparent what is a value (numbers, including the results of formulas and functions) and what is a label (text) on the sheet.

In terms of formatting values on a sheet, conditional formatting is a very useful tool that I highly recommend as a way to show how your numerical values measure up to different conditional criteria. Conditional formatting allows you to format values (including the results of formulas) based on whether a particular value meets a specific condition. We discuss conditional formatting later in this chapter.

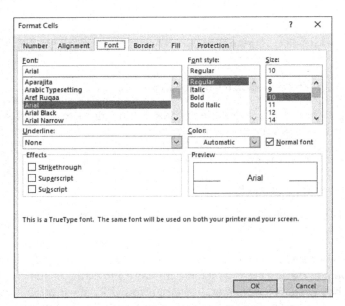

Figure 12-1 The Font tab of the Format Cells dialog box

You can also open the dialog box from the Format command in the Cells group; select Format, then Format Cells. Figure 12-1 shows the Font tab of the Format Cells dialog box.

The Font tab of the Format Cells dialog box provides you with access to the same font attributes provided by the commands in the Font group. The Font tab, however, provides you with some additional font attributes, such as the accounting underline styles (such as the single and double accounting styles) and provides you with effects, such as strikethrough, superscript, and subscript.

Although font formatting is meant to make your sheet look "better," too much font formatting can be distracting. You might want to limit yourself to only a font type or two and only use bold, italic, and other formatting attributes, such as font color, when you are sure that they truly enhance the sheet.

Changing text orientation

You can change the orientation of text in a range of cells by using the Orientation command in the Home tab's Alignment group. This is useful in cases where your labels must conform to very narrow columns or in cases where you want to align labels on the diagonal so that they are readily noticeable. Also, orientation is useful if you just want to add a little bit of design drama to the top of the sheet.

Select the cell range that you want to format with the Orientation command. Then select Orientation in the Alignment group. The orientation possibilities are as follows:

- **Angle Counterclockwise:** Tilts the text upward on the diagonal in a counterclockwise direction, as shown in Figure 12-2.

- **Angle Clockwise:** Tilts the text on the diagonal clockwise.

- **Vertical Text:** Aligns the text vertically in the cells, expanding the row height as needed to accommodate the longest entry in the row.

- **Rotate Text Up:** Rotates the text up vertically.

- **Rotate Text Down:** Rotates the text down vertically.

- **Format Cell Alignment:** Opens the Format Cells dialog box with the Alignment tab selected.

The options provided by the Orientation command are limited to five different orientations for the text. If you want to create a custom rotation, you can do so on the Alignment tab of the Format Cells dialog box. Drag the Orientation Degree dial to specify the orientation for the text visually. Alternatively, you can determine the orientation by specifying the actual degrees of the angle to be used using the Degrees spin box. Positive angle values give you a text-up rotation, and negative angle values give you a text-down rotation. When you finish setting the orientation on the Alignment tab, click OK to close the Format Cells dialog box.

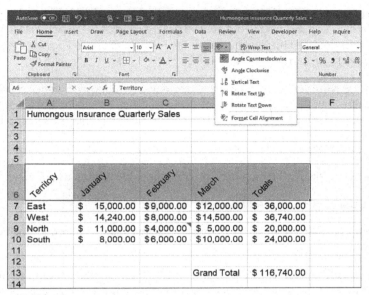

Figure 12-2   Rotate text labels using the Orientation command.

Formatting values

The various number formats provided by Excel for the numerical values in your sheets are extremely useful for differentiating the different types of values present. You want to make it easy for anyone viewing the sheet to be able to quickly distinguish between the different types of data in a sheet, such as currency, percentages, and dates. Obviously, you can format values as you format text in a sheet with settings, such as bold and italic or a font color; however, assigning actual numeric formatting to a value (such as currency or percentages) gives that value or range of values immediate meaning.

Although you can enter numbers with formatting as you type, such as $20.50 or 2,300 (Excel automatically recognizes this number formatting), it is much easier to enter the values and then format them after the fact. When I am working in Excel, I try to concentrate on entering my data first and foremost and then take advantage of Excel's different possibilities for formatting the values in your sheet. Proof your values before and after you format them to make sure everything has been entered correctly.

The shortest path for formatting numbers is to take advantage of the commands in the Number group on the ribbon's Home tab. This group provides commands related to specific number formats, such as the percent style, and it provides you with the ability to increase or decrease the decimal places in cell values. It also provides a gallery with access to several number formats. The Number group commands are as follows:

- **Number Format:** Provides 11 different numeric formats, such as Number, Currency, Fraction, Scientific, and Text, on the drop-down gallery, which is set to General by default. It also provides access to the Number tab of the Format Cells dialog box via the More Number Formats command.

- **Accounting Number Format:** Provides different accounting or currency formats. The default is U.S. dollars. This command also includes other international accounting formats, such as British pounds, the Chinese yuan (People's Republic of China), and the euro.

- **Percent Style:** Displays the number as a percentage.

- **Comma Style:** Displays the number with commas as the thousands separator.

- **Increase Decimal:** Increases the number of decimal places.

- **Decrease Decimal:** Decreases the number of decimal places and rounds the number as needed.

The Number Format command's gallery provides the greatest number of options in terms of formatting values in a sheet. Additional numeric formats are available in Excel in the Format Cells dialog box. You can use the More Number Formats command at the bottom of the Number Format gallery or the dialog box launcher at the bottom of the Number group to open the Format Cells dialog box. The Number tab is selected in the dialog box. This tab provides a Category list of different number formats, as shown in Figure 12-3.

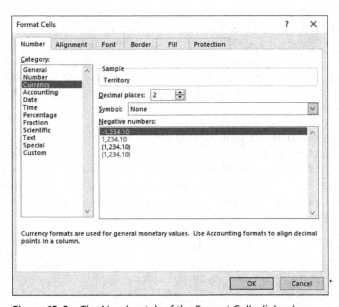

Figure 12-3   The Number tab of the Format Cells dialog box

Using the Format Cells dialog box

The Number tab of the Format Cells dialog box provides several categories of number formats. Table 12-1 provides a list of the different number formats provided on the Number tab of the Format Cells dialog box and a short description of each.

Table 12-1   Excel number formats

Number Format	Example	Description
General	10.6	No specific number format. This is the default number format.
Number	3,400.50	This format provides two decimal places with a decimal point as a separator. Negative numbers are shown in red.
Currency	$3,400.50	The default currency format, including the default symbol ($ for U.S.). Negative values are shown in red.
Accounting	$3,400.50	Aligns currency symbols and decimal points for vertical values (in a column).
Date	11/7/2010	The default date format is the month, day, and year separated by a slash.
Time	10:30:45 PM	The default time format is hour, minutes, and seconds separated by a colon; AM or PM is also designated.
Percentage	99.50%	The default percentage format has two decimal places.
Fraction	½	The default fraction format provides for up to one digit on either side of the solidus (or fraction slash, as the slash dividing the two numbers is also referred to).
Scientific	3.40E+03	The default scientific format has two decimal places and can be used to display extremely large numbers.
Text	123456	Use the text format to format numbers as text.
Special	44240	This format is designed to display ZIP Codes, phone numbers, and Social Security numbers correctly so that you don't have to enter any special characters, such as hyphens or parentheses.
Custom	00.0%	Use this format to create custom number formats. You can edit any of the existing codes as you create your own custom formats.

Several of the number formats enable you to control the number of decimal places used by the format and also how negative numbers to which a particular format is assigned appear in the sheet. Some formats also enable you to include or exclude the thousands separator—the comma. A sample of how the selected number format looks in your sheet is provided on the right of the Number tab. After selecting a format (or designing your own format using the Custom category), click OK. The format is assigned to the selected cell range in the sheet.

CHAPTER 12

Creating custom number formats

Although there are probably more than enough built-in number formats for most Excel users, you might find yourself in a situation where you really need to create a custom format. To create a custom format, select the Custom category on the Number tab, as shown in Figure 12-4.

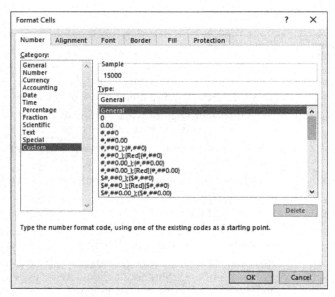

Figure 12-4   Creating a custom number format

If you want to base your number format on an existing format, select that format; then click Custom to view the codes for that format. You can then edit the existing number format and create your custom form in the Type box. As you specify the custom format, a sample is provided above the Type box. Probably the best way to learn to create your own formats is to look at the format codes that have been created for the different numerical formats provided by Excel.

The rules for creating custom formats are straightforward. Each custom format can consist of up to four sections. The sections are divided by semicolons. Each section has a specific purpose in terms of the state of the value to be formatted. The first section serves as the format for the number if it is positive, the second section provides the formatting if the number is negative, the third section provides the formatting for zero values, and the fourth section provides the formatting for text. So, a custom format would follow the pattern of POSITIVE; NEGATIVE; ZERO; TEXT. A sample numeric format code with all four sections might look something like this:

`#,##0.00;[Red] -#,##0.00;0.00;[Blue]"Replace with Value"`

The number sign (#) serves as a digit placeholder, and the zeros in the code pad the format with zeros when necessary to fill the format. The commas serve as thousand separators. The color codes, [Red] and [Blue], dictate the colors for those sections of the custom format. Note that the second section, which is used for negative numbers, also includes a hyphen (-) that serves as a minus sign.

> ## NOTE
>
> **The text-formatting section of a custom number format might seem counterintuitive because we are talking about formatting numbers. You can use this section of the format code to let users who enter data in the sheet know that they can't put text entries in cells formatted with the format. For example, you could set up the text section of the format as ;[Blue]"Replace with Value" so that any text entered is replaced with the text "Replace with Value" in blue. So, it is a way to give a heads-up to anyone who might be doing data entry for you on a shared Excel workbook.**
>
> **Your custom format does not necessarily need to include all four sections. For example, you could create a custom format that includes only two sections, such as:**
>
> #,##0.00;[Red] -#,##0.00;0.00
>
> **This specifies how to format the values when they are either positive (the first section) or negative (the second section).**

After you have determined the number of sections you are going to create in the custom format, you can enter the codes that supply the formatting guidelines for each section. The codes that you use in the custom formats are straightforward. We have already looked at how you use the number sign (#) and zeros in a custom format. Table 12-2 provides a list of some of the other codes you can use in your custom formats and examples of how the codes would be used.

Table 12-2   Excel custom format codes

Code	Example	Usage
#	#,###	Digit placeholder; this particular example provides for no decimal places but does insert a comma at the thousands mark. The number of #'s placed in the code for your format does not limit the number of characters you can type in a cell formatted with the code.
0	#,##0.00	Digit placeholder; used to pad format.
?	#0.0?	Digit placeholder; does not display the insignificant zeros but can be used to add spaces on either side of the decimal point to align numbers in a column by the decimal point.
.	#,##0.00	Specifies the decimal place in the code.
%	0.000%	Percentage; formats the number as a percentage (meaning Excel multiplies the number by 100). This example includes three decimal places.

_	#,##0.00_	Space; creates a space in the format that is the width of one character.
""	#,##0.00 "Profit"	Quotation marks; used to include text in codes (with or without numbers). In this case, a positive number format includes the text "Profit."
$	$###.##	Currency; designates that the numerical format following the $ code should be formatted as U.S. currency. Other codes that display without quotation marks include the /, &, -, and =.
m, d, y	m/dd/yy	Date; displays the current month (1–12) without leading zeros. The day would be displayed as two digits with leading zeros, as would the year.
h, m	hh:mm	Time; displays the hour and minutes as a double-digit number.

Table 12-2 provides only a subset of the different codes that you can use to create custom formats. As already mentioned earlier in this section, you can modify any of the format codes provided in the Format Cells dialog box to meet your needs. Just select a code such as a currency code and then click Custom to view the code and modify it as needed. Using the provided format codes as the starting point for your own custom number formats provides you with the basic design for custom formats for currency, dates, fractions, or scientific notation.

Adding comments and notes to cells

Excel has two different ways for you to embed text information in a cell or cells of your worksheet: comments and notes. Comments allow you to add queries or explanatory text related to a cell or cells that can then be easily read by anyone you have shared your workbook with. So, comments are for collaboration on shared workbooks and are actually threaded for real-time communication and supply a reply box that can easily be used by collaborators. Inserted comments are readily accessible to anyone sharing the workbook.

Notes are designed to serve more as an electronic sticky note or annotation, which you can use for brief notations and reminders that are primarily designed for your own use. Unlike comments, notes do not have a reply box, nor are they threaded (in a conversation). So, comments are best used when a workbook is shared with others. Notes allow you to insert your own thoughts related to a cell or range of cells. Let's take a look at inserting comments. We can then take a look at how to add and delete notes.

Inserting a Comment

As already mentioned, comments are designed for you to communicate with collaborators who are working on the same shared Excel workbook. To share a workbook, you or one of your coworkers must first save it to a cloud storage destination such as a OneDrive or SharePoint site. Once the file is shared (by you or including you), you can insert a comment as needed.

To add a comment to a cell, click the cell to select it. You can also select a range of cells and assign the comment to the range. There are three possibilities for inserting a comment:

- Select the ribbon's Insert tab and then select the Comment command in the Comments group.

- Select the ribbon's Review tab and then Select New Comment in the Comments group.

- Right-click the selected cell or selected cell range and select New Comment from the shortcut menu. Figure 12-5 shows a new Comment box.

Enter the text for the comment (see Figure 12-5) and then click the Post button on the bottom of the comment box; the new comment will be sent to everyone with whom the workbook has been shared. A Reply box appears at the bottom of the comment and can be used to make an additional post.

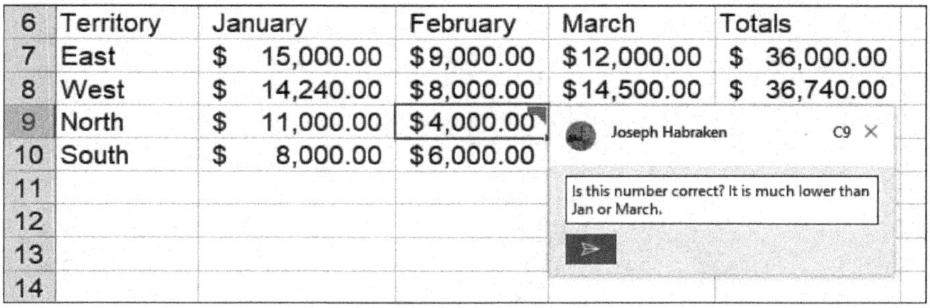

6	Territory	January	February	March	Totals
7	East	$ 15,000.00	$9,000.00	$12,000.00	$ 36,000.00
8	West	$ 14,240.00	$8,000.00	$14,500.00	$ 36,740.00
9	North	$ 11,000.00	$4,000.00		
10	South	$ 8,000.00	$6,000.00		
11					
12					
13					
14					

Joseph Habraken   C9 ✕

Is this number correct? It is much lower than Jan or March.

Figure 12-5   A new comment box

Viewing and deleting comments

The Comment group on the ribbon's Review tab provides a set of tools for working with comments. For example, select the cell containing a comment and then click the Delete button to remove the comment and its thread. However, jumping around the worksheet (or worksheets) in a workbook to find new comments or replies to already existing comments puts you into a bit of a whack-a-mole situation. You can use the Previous Comment and Next Comment commands in the Comments group to move from comment to comment. However, there is an even better solution related to working with a large number of comments.

Once you have more than one comment in a workbook, it makes sense to use the Comments pane to view all the comments (including responses) in the shared workbook. Select the Show Comments command in the Comments group. The Comments pane opens. Comments in the workbook will be listed in order based on the posted date and time.

TIP

You can edit a comment that you have inserted into a shared workbook. Go to the ribbon's Review tab and then select the Show Comments command to open the Comments pane. Any comment that you originated (including your responses to collaborator's inserted comments) can be edited. Click Edit (in the lower-right corner of the comment box). Type the edited version of the comment and then click Save.

Deleting comments in the Comments pane is just a matter of clicking a comment and then selecting Delete. If you want to delete an entire thread, select the original comment in the thread and then select the ellipsis in the upper-right corner of the comment (in the Comments pane). Select Delete Thread to remove the comment and all associated comments.

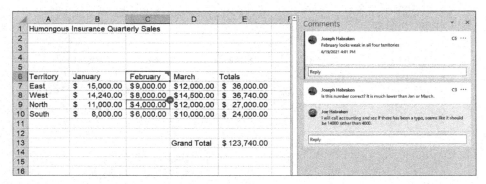

Figure 12-6   The Excel Comments pane

Inserting and deleting notes

The notes feature is another possibility for annotating cells in your worksheets. Notes are really designed as an electronic scratchpad that allows you to insert your ideas and thoughts inline with a cell or cell range in a worksheet. Notes can be inserted into a workbook that has been shared or that has not been shared. This is mainly because notes are designed for you, not your collaborators (whereas comments are designed for collaboration).

To insert a note, right-click a cell (or selected cell range) in your worksheet and then select New Note. A yellow note will appear next to the selected cell or range. Your Microsoft 365 user name will appear at the top of the note. Type the text for the note and then click outside the note. A red triangle will appear in the upper-right corner of a cell that contains a note.

When you no longer need a note and want to delete it, right-click on the cell that contains the note and select Delete Note from the shortcut menu that appears. You can also use the Delete command in the Comments group for deleting notes. (Sure, it's confusing, but it works.) Select a cell containing a note and then click Delete. If necessary, you can undo the deletion by selecting Undo on the Quick Access Toolbar.

Using themes

Themes provide a way for you to apply cell formatting and create a uniform-looking sheet. A theme is a collection of colors, fonts, and text effects. Themes are consistent across the Office applications, such as Excel, Word, and PowerPoint. This enables you to create a group of related Office application files (document, workbook, and presentation) that have the same overall look.

The Themes gallery is accessed using the Themes command, which is available in the Themes group on the ribbon's Page Layout tab. The Themes group also houses the Colors, Fonts, and Effects commands. To preview a theme, place the mouse on that theme in the gallery. When you have found the theme that you want to use for the sheet, select it.

As already mentioned, a theme controls the colors, fonts, and effects (formatting settings) when you apply it to a sheet. You can change these theme attributes using the Colors, Fonts, and Effects commands. If you adjust any of these theme attributes and want to save the result as a new theme, access the Themes gallery and then save the theme using the Save Current Theme command. You can then browse for saved themes using the Browse for Themes command.

You can also create custom theme colors and theme fonts. To create custom theme colors, select Customize Colors in the Colors gallery. This opens the Create New Theme Colors dialog box, which enables you to set the theme background color, accent colors, and hyperlink colors. In the case of theme fonts, select Customize Fonts in the Fonts gallery, and the Create New Theme Fonts dialog box opens, enabling you to specify the heading and the body font for your custom theme. The theme feature is pretty consistent across the Office applications (particularly Excel, Word, and PowerPoint). If you are interested in reading more about working with themes, see Chapter 18, "Advanced presentation formatting, themes, and masters," in the PowerPoint section of this book.

Formatting cells using borders and color

The overall design of a worksheet is often dictated by accounting or data analysis principles or your personal Excel best practices. For example, data is sometimes arranged in columns and rows so that formulas or functions can be strategically placed to do calculations on the data, either at the bottom of the sheet or the right of the sheet. In the best of circumstances, you end up with worksheets that are laid out so well that it is easy to interpret the sheet's results. However, in some cases, you might have to doctor up a sheet so that it is more readable and easier to understand. You will find that cell borders, cell backgrounds, or fill colors can be used to highlight certain information on your sheet and make your results more understandable. For example, you can use borders and colors to highlight certain areas of the sheet and draw attention to specific cells or a range of cells.

CHAPTER 12

Cell formatting can make a sheet look more visually appealing, but it can also emphasize cells or cell ranges, making it easier for anyone perusing the sheet to have a more immediate understanding of how the results shown in the sheet relate to the data that is used in the calculations. Borders can be used to group certain cells or highlight individual cells, and you can use cell fill color to emphasize or group cells using color. The Borders command and the Fill Color command are both housed in the Font group on the ribbon's Home tab.

Adding cell borders

The Borders command provides a gallery of different border types, such as Bottom Border, Top Border, All Borders, and so on. Figure 12-7 shows the Borders gallery, which includes the Draw Borders tools at the bottom.

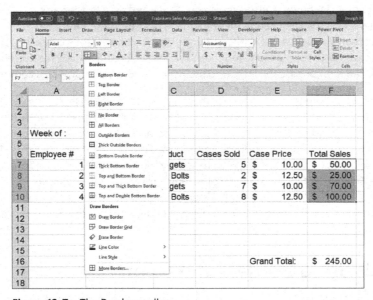

Figure 12-7   The Borders gallery

Select the cell or cell range to which you want to apply the border and then select a border from the Borders gallery (click the arrow to the right of the Borders command). The Borders gallery provides single- and double-line border formats as well as thick border formats.

You can also draw the border for a cell range. The Draw Borders area of the Borders gallery provides a drawing tool—Draw Border—and it also provides the Line Color and Line Style menus, which enable you to select the color for the border line and the line style, such as a single line, dashed line, double line, or thick line.

To draw the border using the default line settings, select the Draw Border command and then use the pen mouse pointer to select the cells you want to format. You can select the attributes for the line using the Line Color and Line Style menus. When you have finished working with the border drawing tool, press the Esc key or click the Draw Border Line command to turn off the feature (this is the Borders command in the Font group).

For maximum control over the borders you want to place on a selected range of cells, you can use the Border tab of the Format Cells dialog box. To access the dialog box, select More Borders in the Borders gallery. Figure 12-8 shows the Border tab of the Format Cells dialog box.

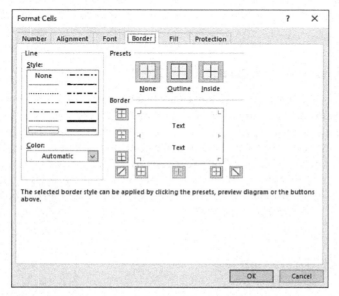

Figure 12-8   The Border tab of the Format Cells dialog box

The Border tab provides you with border presets as well as all the tools you need to create your own custom borders. You can use the Style box to select the line for the style and use the Color drop-down palette to specify the color for the line. You can use the various Border buttons provided adjacent to the border preview diagram to specify the borders you want to apply to the cells. You can also click inside the preview diagram to place the borders. When you have completed specifying the options for your custom borders, click OK. The borders are applied to the selected cell range in the sheet.

NOTE

The Draw Border Grid option in the Borders gallery enables you to draw both internal and external borders on a cell range.

Using background colors

Backgrounds or cell fill colors provide you with an excellent way to add color to your sheets. The fill colors available are based on the current theme you have selected for your worksheet. You can quickly add a background color to a selected cell or cell range using the Fill Color command in the Font group.

Select the range of cells to which you want to add a fill color. Then select the drop-down arrow for the Fill Color command. The Color palette gives you access to the current theme colors and provides standard colors you can apply to your cell range. If you want to select a custom color, you can click More Colors; this opens the Colors dialog box, where you can specify a custom color for the range.

Using cell styles and the Format Painter

An easy way to apply cell formatting to a range of cells that includes font, border, and fill settings is to take advantage of the cell styles provided by Excel. These cell styles are more than just ways of adding color and formatting to a sheet, however. Excel provides specific cell styles for helping you denote cells that need to be checked or results that should be considered bad or good. Other cell styles are provided specifically for headings and results, and there are also cell styles provided for number formatting. The Cell Styles are provided in the Styles group of the Home tab. The default styles include Normal, Bad, and Good; select the More button to open Cell Styles gallery, which is shown in Figure 12-9.

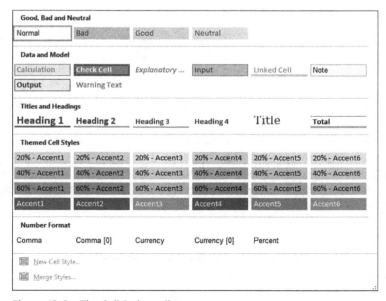

Figure 12-9   The Cell Styles gallery

You'll find a number of useful cell styles in the Cell Styles gallery, including the Bad, Good, and Neutral categories of styles as well as heading and themed cell styles. The themed cell styles are based on the current sheet's theme.

The Cell Styles gallery is designed as a set of samples. As already mentioned, cell formatting can be used to differentiate cells that contain particular content; therefore, the cell styles provided are really to get you thinking about the possibilities for showing information more clearly in a sheet by using cell styles. You can use the cell styles provided, but this feature becomes even more useful (and particular to your purposes) if you create your own cell styles.

Creating a cell style

You can create a cell style by example. Format a cell or range of cells with font and cell attributes (such as font settings and border and fill settings); you can also specify number formatting for the style by formatting the contents of the cell (or the cell range) with the different number formats provided in the Number group or the Number Format gallery.

When you are ready to create the cell style, select the Cell Styles command and then select New Cell Style in the Cell Styles gallery. The Style dialog box opens, as shown in Figure 12-10.

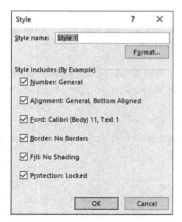

Figure 12-10   The Style dialog box

By default, the style includes the Number, Alignment, Font, Border, Fill, and any Protection settings assigned to the cell. If you provided all these attributes, you can leave all the check boxes enabled. If there is a particular attribute you do not want to include in the cell style, clear the appropriate check box.

If you want to fine-tune any of the attributes you have set for the cell style (your examples), click the Format button. This opens the Format Cells dialog box. Although we have discussed most of the tabs provided by this dialog box, the following list provides a quick review:

- **Number:** This tab is where you set the number format for the values that use the style. The formats include Number, Currency, Date, Time, and Percentage.

- **Alignment:** This tab enables you to specify the Horizontal and Vertical alignment of the cell content. You can also rotate text using the Orientation dial.

- **Font:** This tab provides all the font attributes, such as Font, Font Style, Size, Underline, and Color.

- **Border:** Use this tab to specify a border for the cell style, including Line Style and Color.

- **Fill:** Select from many background colors and fill effects provided. You can also specify custom colors.

- **Protection:** You can lock cells that contain formulas or functions or data that you do not want others to be able to edit. Locking cells does not protect areas of the sheet until you choose to protect the sheet.

> ➤ **For more information on locking cells and protecting sheets, see "Protecting workbooks and worksheets," in Chapter 11, "Essential Excel features."**

When you have finished working with the various cell attributes for the style in the Format Cells dialog box, click OK to return to the Styles dialog box. Make sure you provide a name for the style in the Style Name text box. When you click OK, the new cell style is created and is placed in the Custom category area in the Cell Styles gallery. You can now access your new cell style as needed by selecting the Cell Styles command and then selecting your style from the gallery.

Using the Format Painter

You can also copy the cell formatting from one cell to another cell—or to a range of cells—using the Format Painter. This is useful in cases in which you just want to have consistent formatting in a sheet but don't want to have to deal with cell styles.

Select a cell that has the formatting that you want to copy. Click the Format Painter command in the Clipboard group. You can then click a single cell to paste the format, or you can click and drag to format an entire range of cells. If you want to copy the formatting to multiple noncontiguous ranges or from a sheet to two or more other sheets, double-click the Format Painter. You can paste the format as many times as needed. When you have finished working with the Format Painter, click the Format Painter command to toggle it off.

Using conditional formatting

Thus far, our approach to cell formatting has related to the "look" of the cells in the worksheet; we want the sheet to look good and also have the formatting be purposeful, so it helps make the worksheet easier to read. Another cell formatting feature provided by Excel is conditional formatting. Conditional formatting is a more dynamic way of formatting cells, based on whether a cell's content meets a particular condition (or conditions).

Conditional formatting uses formatting attributes, such as fonts, borders, and fill colors, to "point out" cells in a sheet that meet certain conditions. For example, if you want to format all the monthly sales totals in a sheet that fall below a certain amount, you use conditional formatting. The cells that meet the condition you set could be formatted with any of the cell-formatting attributes we have discussed thus far.

In the example we are discussing, a condition could state that all monthly sales figures that fall below 2,500 are then formatted in red with a blue border. Both the condition that you set and the formatting that is applied when the condition is met are completely up to you. Just make sure you select cell-formatting attributes for the conditional formatting that stand out from the other cells' format you have used in the worksheet. You are also not limited by the number of conditions that you can apply to a cell. The conditional formatting can be based on an unlimited set of conditions. Obviously, conditional formatting is an excellent tool to apply to cells that contain the results of formulas or functions.

When you select the Conditional Formatting command in the Styles group, the Conditional Formatting gallery opens. It provides you with several options related to applying conditional formatting to the selected range of cells in the sheet. Figure 12-11 shows the Conditional Formatting gallery.

Figure 12-11   The Conditional Formatting gallery

You will find that the conditional formatting feature provides you with more than just the ability to apply a condition or conditions to a cell range. Let's look at each of the options provided in the Conditional Formatting gallery and the possibilities they present.

Using highlight cell rules

When you select Highlight Cells Rules, you are provided with a list of conditions or rules such as Greater Than, Less Than, Between, and Duplicate Values. For example, if you select the Greater Than rule, the Greater Than dialog box opens.

To take advantage of this "prepackaged rule," specify a value on the left side of the dialog box that serves as the condition. You can type a value in the box, or you can click the Collapse button and specify a value by selecting a cell in the sheet. When you return to the Greater Than dialog box (after specifying a cell in the sheet), you can fine-tune the formatting that is used by selecting the formatting drop-down arrow. A series of formatting attributes are supplied by default for the rule. You can specify a custom format for the rule by selecting Custom Format. This opens the Format Cells dialog box, which provides you with control over all the cell-formatting attributes applied by the rule. Figure 12-12 shows the Greater Than dialog box containing a condition and format. The Net Pay column is formatted by this conditional formatting.

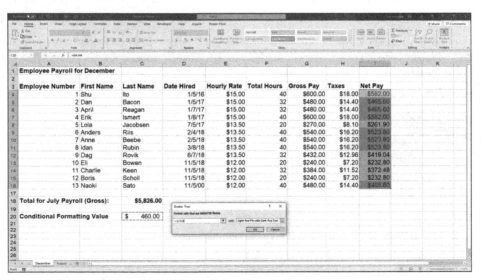

Figure 12-12   The Greater Than dialog box and the affected cell range

When you are ready to apply the rule to the selected range, click OK. The conditional formatting is applied to the cells that meet the conditions of the rule. You can apply additional rules to the range of cells as needed. Remember, you are not limited to the number of conditions that you apply to a cell or a range of cells. However, make sure you keep track of the formatting that each rule applies to the range so that if a particular cell (or cells) meets more than one condition that is applied, you can tell by the formatting that the cell meets multiple conditions.

TIP

To clear the conditional formatting rules from a range, select Conditional Formatting, Clear Rules, and then Clear Rules From Selected Cells. You can also clear all the rules on a sheet by selecting Clear Rules From Entire Sheet.

Using top/bottom rules

The top/bottom rules enable you to quickly apply conditional formatting to cells in a range that fall into the top or bottom 10 items and the top or bottom 10 percent of the values in the range. You are not locked into the top or bottom 10 values in your range when you use the top or bottom 10 items rules. The dialog box for each of these rules provides spin boxes that enable you to specify the number of items that are used by the rule. For example, if you want to see the bottom five items in the selected range, you can change the 10 in the Bottom 10 Items dialog box to 5 by using the spin box (or by selecting the 10 and typing 5).

Also, two rules are available in the top/bottom rules based on the average of the values in your selected range: Above Average and Below Average. You don't need to worry about calculating the highest 10 values or computing the average. The rule takes care of the computation, and based on that computation, the rule applies the conditional formatting.

To apply one of the top/bottom rules, select Top/Bottom Rules in the Conditional Formatting gallery and then select one of the rules provided. When you select a rule such as Above Average, a dialog box specific to that rule appears. Select the formatting for the condition and then click OK.

Using data bars

If you like to visually compare data in a range of cells without resorting to a chart or sparklines, you can take advantage of the data bars provided in the Conditional Formatting gallery. The data bars are actually bar charts that are placed in the cells of the selected range. This enables you to quickly see how the various values in the range compare with each other. Figure 12-13 shows a range of values that are formatted with data bars.

CHAPTER 12

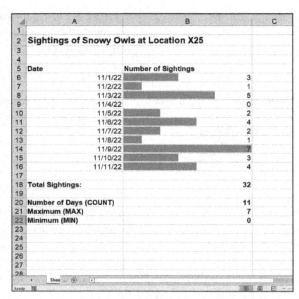

Figure 12-13   Data bars enable you to visually compare values in a range.

NOTE

Sparklines are mini-charts placed inline with a row or column of values (so they look similar to the data bars feature). Sparklines offer you another easy way to add visual information to a worksheet without creating a full-blown chart. Sparklines and charts are discussed in Chapter 14, "Enhancing worksheets with charts."

When you select Data Bars in the Conditional Formatting gallery, you can choose from bars that use a gradient fill or a solid fill. The data bars might skew the concept of how you think about conditional formatting, but they do provide you with another option for quickly comparing sheet values.

Using color scales

Another possibility provided by the Conditional Formatting gallery is the color scale. Each color scale consists of a set of either two or three colors.

When you apply a three-color scale to a range of cells—such as the Green-Yellow-Red color scale—you separate the values into three subsets based on the values in the cell. The top third is formatted with the first color (green), the middle third with the second color (yellow), and the bottom third with the third color (red). As already mentioned, there are also two-color scales, which divide the values into top and bottom halves, using the two colors provided.

As with data bars, the color scales are used for relative comparison of the values in the cell range. They enable you to see by color the cells that fall in the same tier within the range. Six preset three-color scales and six preset two-color scales are available. Each scale uses a different set of colors.

Using icon sets

The Conditional Formatting gallery also provides you with icon sets that can be used to format the values in a selected range. The icon sets are somewhat similar to the color scales in that the icons are in groups that enable you to differentiate where the values in the range fall in relation to each other.

When you select Icon Sets in the Conditional Formatting gallery, you are provided different categories of icon sets, such as Directional, Indicators, and Ratings. The number of icons in the set you select specifies how the values in the range are grouped. An icon set containing five icons formats the values in the range based on five groupings of the values (highest to lowest). A three-icon set groups the values in three different groupings (thirds).

Creating and copying conditional formatting rules

You are not limited to the rules provided by the rule categories, such as highlighting Cells Rules or Data Bars, listed in the Conditional Formatting gallery. You can create your own highlight cells rules, top/bottom rules, or other rule types as needed.

New rules are created in the New Formatting Rule dialog box. You can open this dialog box by selecting New Rule in the Conditional Formatting gallery, or you can select More Rules when you have accessed a rule category, such as Highlight Cells Rules or Color Scales. Figure 12-14 shows the New Formatting Rule dialog box.

> ### TIP
>
> You can manage the rules you create in the Conditional Formatting Rules Manager dialog box; select Manage Rules in the Conditional Formatting gallery. You can edit existing rules, delete rules, and create new rules from this dialog box.
>
> Creating a new rule is a two-part process. First, you select the rule type in the Select A Rule Type list. For example, if you want to create a rule that formats cells in the sheet that contain values that fall between two values, you choose Format Only Cells That Contain in the Select A Rule Type list.

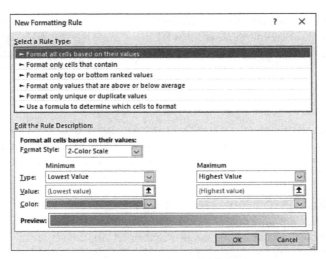

Figure 12-14   The New Formatting Rule dialog box

You then select a condition for the new rule. For example, you might set the condition as Between. The rule also needs to know what two values specify the range that cell values would have to fall between to satisfy the rule. You can do this in two ways: You can type the two values (the low and high values for the range) in the dialog box. The other possibility is to specify two cell addresses that contain the values that specify the range of values to be used by the rule.

As already mentioned, you can also create other rule types, such as top or bottom rules or above or below average rules. To create a top or bottom rule, select Format Only Top Or Bottom Ranked Values in the Select Rule Type list. You can then specify whether you want to format the top or bottom of the values and specify the number of values you want the rule to format. The default number is 10, but you can specify any number you want. In the case of the above or below average rules, all you have to specify is whether the rule formats values above or below the average.

The second part of the process of creating a new rule is specifying the formatting that applies to cells in the range that meet the condition of the rule. The New Formatting Rule dialog box provides a preview of the formatting for the new rule. However, it starts out as No Format Set, meaning you have to specify the formatting before the rule is ready to go.

Click the Format button in the New Formatting Rule dialog box, which opens the Format Cells dialog box. Use the tabs on the dialog box to specify the formatting for the new rule. You can work with any of the cell-formatting attributes, including font, border, and fill. When you click OK in the Format Cells dialog box, you return to the New Formatting Rule dialog box. Click OK, and your rule is applied to the selected range.

You can also copy conditional formatting from a cell and apply it to another cell or a range of cells. If you want to copy the conditional formatting only, select the cell with the conditional formatting and then select Copy in the Clipboard group. Select the cell or cell range that you want to format with the conditional formatting and then select Paste to open the Paste Gallery; select the Formatting option in the Other Paste Options. The conditional formatting and any other formatting that was applied to the source cell will be applied to the destination cell or cells.

TIP

You can use the Format Painter to copy and paste conditional formatting. Select the cell that contains the conditional formatting and then click the Format Painter. Select a single cell to paste the conditional formatting in that cell or click and drag to apply the conditional formatting to range of cells. The conditional formatting will be copied to the destination cell or range of cells. You can also use the Format Painter to "paint" conditional formatting to individual, nonadjacent cells by double-clicking the Format Painter icon.

Manipulating cells and cell content

As you enter data in Excel, you might find that you need to add cells to the worksheet to accommodate the information you need to include in the sheet. You might also find that there are occasions when you want to add long text entries or explanatory text and want the information to span several cells and to wrap in the cells as text would in a paragraph. The solutions to these various minor issues are easy to come by in Excel.

You can easily insert cells and join cells, if necessary, and then wrap text in a cell or joined cells as needed. In cases where you have entered repeating labels or values into your sheet and find that you need to change either the text entries or the values, Excel also has you covered with the Replace feature, which shares the Find And Replace dialog box with the Find feature.

Inserting cells

You can insert single or multiple cells into a sheet. Inserting cells causes the data in the adjacent cells to shift down a row or over a column (to the right) to create a space for the new cells.

The number of cells inserted depends on the number of cells you select before inserting the new cells. To insert cells into a sheet, follow these steps:

1. Select the cell range where you want the new cells to be inserted. Excel inserts the same number of cells as you select.

2. Select the Insert command on the Home tab and then select Insert Cells. The Insert dialog box opens, as shown in Figure 12-15.

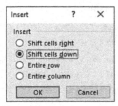

Figure 12-15   The Insert dialog box

3. The Insert dialog box provides you with options for how the current cells are affected by the insertion of the new cell. Select Shift Cells Right or Shift Cells Down. If you want to insert an entire row or column, select the appropriate option.

4. Click OK. Excel inserts the cells and shifts the adjacent cells according to the option you specified in the Insert dialog box.

Inserting cells is useful if you have inadvertently mismatched data in your cells as you have entered it. For example, you might have entered an employee's name and then entered a portion of another employee's data. If you insert the required number of cells, you can fix the input problem by quickly adding the new data and editing the mismatched data without deleting a lot of information or inserting new rows or other information. You can even move the incorrect data to its appropriate location by dragging the information to the new cells.

Merging cells and wrapping text

You can merge cells on a worksheet. This can be particularly useful when you want to add a large heading to a sheet or need to add a paragraph or two of explanatory text and want it to appear directly on the sheet. You can merge cells that are contiguous in a particular row (from left to right), or you can merge cells that are contiguous in a column (from top to bottom). You can also merge cells that are contiguous and span more than one row or column.

Excel provides you with options for merging cells. Select the cells you want to merge and then select the Merge & Center command in the Alignment group. The Merge & Center command provides four different options:

- **Merge & Center:** This option merges the cells and centers the content (such as a large heading) across the newly merged cells.

- **Merge Across:** Use this option to merge all the cells in a selected row or rows.

- **Merge Cells:** Use this option to merge contiguous selected cells in a single column or row or in multiple columns or rows. This option does not center the content across the merged cells.

- **Unmerge Cells:** This option enables you to unmerge cells that you have merged. All you have to do is select the merged cells and then use this option to put the cells back in their unmerged condition.

When you have the cells merged, you can take advantage of the various alignment commands in the Alignment group to align the text in the merged cells as needed.

If you are working with a large text block, you can wrap the text within the merged cells. As you type text, even in merged cells, the text consists of a single line that bleeds over into the cells to the right of the merged cells. As soon as you enter other data in the cells to the right of the merged cells, your large text entry is truncated (as is any entry that is too large for a cell). To wrap the text within the merged cell, select the merged cell and then select the Wrap Text command in the Alignment group. The text wraps in the merged cell, filling the cell much like a text box. The width of the cell that was created by merging the multiple cells dictates the number of times your text needs to wrap.

TIP

You can find merged cells using the Find feature. Use the Format option provided by Find to search for merged cells.

Finding and replacing cell items

Sheets can become quite large (there are a lot of columns and rows that can be filled), so there might be occasions when you want to find specific cell content, and the easiest way to find it quickly is using the Find And Replace feature. The Find And Replace feature is also useful in situations where you have entered a particular label or value into the sheet and find that you have consistently entered it incorrectly. A great way to change multiple occurrences of a label or value is using Excel's Replace feature; you can locate data in the sheet and replace it with new data as needed.

The Find And Replace feature can do more than just find text strings or values in cells and replace them with other information; it can also be used to search for cell formatting and optionally replace that formatting with formatting that you specify. To open the Find And Replace dialog box with the Find tab or the Replace tab active, select the Find & Select command in the Editing group and then select either Find or Replace. Figure 12-16 shows the Replace tab of the Find And Replace dialog box with the options expanded.

The Find and Replace tabs function similarly. The only real difference is that the Replace tab also provides a Replace With box, enabling you to specify the content or formatting that will be used to replace the item or formatting that is to be found in the worksheet. If you want to match the capitalization of your entry in the Find What box, select the Match Case check box. If you want to locate cells that contain exactly what you have entered into the Find What text box, select the Match Entire Cell Contents check box.

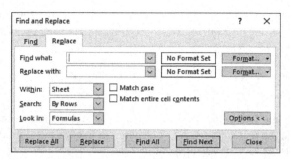

Figure 12-16   The Find And Replace dialog box

You can use wildcards in the Find What box to aid in your searches. You can use the question mark (?) as a wildcard for a single character. The asterisk (*) can serve as a wildcard for any number of characters. Enter text in the Find What box (on either the Find or Replace tab) and then use the Format button to specify any formatting that you might want to include in the search. The Format button (to the right of the Find What box) opens the Find Format dialog box and provides you with access to all the cell-formatting possibilities.

If you want to provide the formatting by example (the format to be found), click the Format button's drop-down arrow and then select Choose Format From Cell. The mouse pointer becomes an Eyedropper tool. Click it in a cell that contains the formatting you want to find. You will be returned to the Find And Replace dialog box. After you specify formatting using either the Find Format dialog box or the Eyedropper tool, the format is previewed in the box to the right of the Find What box.

Because we are talking about finding formatting and then replacing it, you also need to specify the format to be used as the replacement. This is accomplished by providing a format to the right of the Replace With box. Select Format to open the Replace Format dialog box. You can specify the formatting using the tabs in this dialog box. You also can specify the "replacement" format using the Eyedropper tool. Select the Format drop-down arrow, and then select Choose Format From Cell. Click a cell that contains the format you want to use.

TIP

You don't have to include a search string if you are searching for formatting only. Just specify the formatting and then run the search. You can also specify formatting only as part of the replace options for a find-and-replace operation.

So, let's look at what happens after you set up a search using the Find tab. When you are ready to conduct your search, you can use the Find Next button to find the next occurrence of the search string (or formatting). Click the Find Next button as needed to cycle through the found cells that match your search criteria. If you want to find all the cells that contain your search string, click the Find All button. A list of all the cells found by the search will be listed at the bottom of the Find And Replace dialog box. The sheet, cell address, and value found are supplied in the list. To navigate to a particular cell (that was found), click the cell reference in the list.

When you are working on the Replace tab, you can replace each subsequent occurrence of the found string or formatting using the Replace button. If you have set up your find-and-replace operation carefully and are sure that items will be replaced correctly, click Replace All and take care of all the replacements in one fell swoop.

The Go To feature is also accessed via the Find & Select menu, and specific items that you can go to are specified on the Find & Select menu, such as formulas, comments, and conditional formatting. This provides a quick way to select occurrences of specific items or formatting in the sheet. For example, if you select Formulas, the formulas in the sheet are selected.

Working with columns and rows

Manipulating columns and rows in your sheets is very straightforward. You can easily change the column width for a column or columns and adjust row heights. You can also insert or delete columns and rows as needed. Inserting or deleting columns or rows doesn't change the number of columns or rows in the sheet; the number of columns or rows in a sheet is fixed. When you delete columns or rows, you remove them from their current position, but they aren't removed from the sheet.

You can also hide columns and rows in the sheet. This is particularly useful in cases when you have data in the sheet that you do not want prying eyes to see or information that you do not want to include in a printout. For example, you might want to print an employee list but do not want to include the columns that list employee salaries.

Changing column width and row height

You have probably noticed that the default column width is not all that wide; it is 8.43 characters (64 pixels), to be exact, and it doesn't readily accommodate long text entries or values that have been formatted as currency or other long numeric formats. You might have found entries in certain cells that have been changed to ########. This lets you know that you need to adjust the column width so that it can accommodate the entry and its formatting.

> TIP
>
> The Format command also provides an AutoFit Row Height and an AutoFit Column Width option.
>
> To adjust a column's width, position the mouse pointer on the column's right border. The mouse becomes a sizing tool. Drag the column border to the desired width. You can also change a column's width using AutoFit, which adjusts the column width to accommodate the widest entry within the column; to use AutoFit, double-click the sizing tool on the column border. The column immediately adjusts to its widest entry.

If you want to adjust several columns at once, select the columns. Place the mouse on any of the column borders and drag to increase or decrease the width. Each selected column is adjusted to the width you select. You can also double-click to use AutoFit to adjust the width of the selected columns.

If you want to specify a more precise column width for a column or a number of selected columns, select the Format command (in the Cells group on the Home tab) and then select Column Width. The Column Width dialog box opens. Specify the width in the Column Width text box and then click OK.

You can also adjust row heights, if you want, using the mouse; just drag the bottom border of a row to adjust the height. However, your row heights automatically adjust to any font size changes that you make to data held in a particular row. Row heights also adjust if you wrap text entries within them. You may need to adjust column widths in your sheets far more often than row heights.

You can adjust row heights using the Row Height dialog box. Select the Format command and then choose Row Height. Adjust the row height in the Row Height text box by typing a new value (the default is 15) and then click OK.

TIP

You can also access the Insert and the Delete commands from the shortcut menu. Right-click the selected columns or rows and then select Insert or Delete, as needed.

Inserting columns and rows

You can insert a single column or row or multiple columns or rows as needed. To insert a single column, click in the column that is to the right of where you want the new column to be inserted. Click the Insert command in the Cells group and then select Insert Sheet Columns. The new column is inserted to the left of the currently selected cell (and its column).

For inserting a single row, click in a cell in the row that you want to insert the new row below. Click the Insert command and select Insert Sheet Rows. The new row is inserted below the current row.

To insert multiple columns or rows, select the number of columns or rows you want to insert. In the case of columns, drag over the column headings; for rows, drag over the row numbers. Then use Insert Sheet Columns or Insert Sheet Rows to insert the columns or rows specified. New columns are placed to the left of the selected columns, and the selected columns are pushed to the right. The new rows are placed below the currently selected rows.

Deleting columns and rows

You can also delete a column or row from the sheet. In either case, select the column or row you want to remove by clicking the appropriate column or row heading (drag to select multiple columns or rows).

Select the Delete command in the Cells group and then select Delete Sheet Columns or Delete Sheet Rows, as needed. The columns or rows are removed from the sheet. Remember that any data that is included in the columns or rows is also deleted. It makes sense to ensure you have laid out your sheet in a way that is appropriate to your needs from the get-go. This saves you a lot of time dragging information around on the sheet and possibly negates the need to insert (or delete) a lot of columns or rows in the sheet.

Hiding columns and rows

As already mentioned, there may be occasions when you want to hide certain columns or rows in a sheet, both on the screen and when you print the sheet. Hiding columns or rows is straightforward, and the process is easy to reverse.

In the case of columns, select the columns you want to hide. Select the Format command and then point at the Hide & Unhide option. Select Hide Columns, and the columns are hidden.

The same process can be used for rows. Select the rows and then select Format, Hide & Unhide and then Hide Rows. The rows are hidden.

Reversing the process is just a matter of accessing the Hide & Unhide options provided by the Format command. Select Unhide Columns to get your columns back and Unhide Rows to see those hidden rows.

Working with worksheets

We had the opportunity to look at the various views that can be used when you are examining a sheet in Chapter 11. There are also some additional tricks related to viewing sheets that can help you when working with large sheets that contain many columns or rows or in cases where you want to see two disparate parts of the same large sheet simultaneously. As with columns and rows, you can also hide sheets if needed.

➤ For more information about viewing Excel worksheets, see the "Viewing worksheets," section in Chapter 11.

Freezing rows and columns

Adding or viewing the data can be problematic in a large worksheet containing many columns, rows, or both. Because the column labels or row labels are not visible when you scroll down or to the right, determining what you should type into a certain cell can be a mystery. For example, you

CHAPTER 12

might be entering employee information, and the employee names are in the first and second columns of the sheet. If you scroll any distance to the right (when you have a number of columns of data to work with), the names provided are no longer visible in the Excel workspace. This makes it difficult to add new data or even determine what the data in a particular cell represents.

You can freeze your column and row labels so that they remain on the screen no matter how far you scroll to the right or scroll down in the sheet. The Freeze Panes command is in the Zoom group on the ribbon's View tab. The Freeze Panes command enables you to freeze panes (both column and row labels), freeze the top row (the column labels), or freeze the first column (the row labels).

The Freeze Top Row and the Freeze First Column options on the Freeze Panes gallery are self-explanatory and require nothing from you other than just choosing one of these options after selecting the Freeze Panes drop-down arrow.

If you want to use the Freeze Panes option, you need to specify the rows and columns you want to freeze. This is accomplished by selecting the cell that is below the row you want to freeze, and to the right of the column you want to freeze.

Figure 12-17 shows a sheet where the Freeze Panes command has been used to freeze columns A through C and rows 1 through 5 (1–4 are unimportant; we are mainly concerned with freezing row 5, which contains the headings for the columns). Notice that cell D6 was selected before the panes were frozen. This is because cell D6 is one cell below the last row to be frozen and one cell to the right of the last column to be frozen.

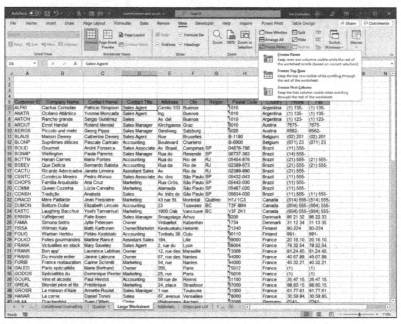

Figure 12-17   Freeze panes to keep column or row labels on the screen when you scroll.

When you have identified the cell you want to use to specify the rows and columns to freeze, select the cell. A vertical "freeze" borderline is placed between the frozen columns and the other "active" columns. A horizontal borderline is placed between the frozen rows and the active rows.

Then all you have to do is select Freeze Panes to freeze the specified row and column in place. Now you can scroll down or to the right in the sheet, and the row and column labels should stay on the screen as you scroll. When you finish working with the frozen panes, you can easily remove them. Select the Freeze Panes drop-down arrow and then select Unfreeze Panes.

Splitting worksheets

Another useful trick for dealing with large sheets is the Split command. You can split the current worksheet window into multiple panes. Doing so enables you to view different parts of the same large worksheet in different panes simultaneously. This is useful for looking at data or the results of calculations that are typically quite distant in the geography of a large sheet.

To split the current sheet into multiple panes, select the cell where you want the split to occur. When you specify a cell, the split appears below the selected cell or to the right of the selected cell. After specifying the cell, select the Split command on the View tab. You can use the mouse to drag the split to a new location as needed.

You can also manually place splits in a sheet. A horizontal split box sits just above the vertical scrollbar. Drag the horizontal split box onto the sheet to create a horizontal split. There is also a vertical split box just to the left of the horizontal scrollbar. Drag the vertical split box onto the sheet to create a vertical split.

After you have your horizontal/vertical splits on the Excel screen, you can scroll within each of the independent panes to locate certain parts of your sheet. When you have finished working with the split panes, select the Split command to remove all the splits from the sheet window.

Hiding worksheets

We have already discussed hiding worksheet columns and rows, but you can also hide an entire sheet in your Excel workbook. This enables you to hide sensitive information as you work on the other sheets in the workbook.

The sheet you want to hide should be the active sheet. If it isn't, click the sheet's tab to make it the active sheet. Select the Format command on the Home tab, and then point at the Hide & Unhide option. Select Hide Sheet to hide the current sheet. Other sheets in the workbook will still be available. You can hide other sheets in the workbook by repeating the process.

CHAPTER 12

TIP

You can hide an entire open workbook via the ribbon's View tab. Use the Hide command to hide a workbook window and then use Unhide to unhide it. When you need to work on a sheet that you have hidden, you are only a few mouse clicks away from unhiding it (yes, *unhiding* sounds wrong; I guess Microsoft didn't want to make *found* the opposite of *hidden*). Select Format and then point at the Hide & Unhide option. Select Unhide Sheet. The Unhide dialog box opens. The Unhide dialog box lists the sheets that you have hidden in the current workbook. Select the sheet you want to unhide and then click OK.

Naming ranges

When you enter values in an Excel worksheet, you typically use the worksheet geography to visually organize that information. For example, if you are entering values for employee sales, the sales values typically go into a column that has the "Sales" heading. The Sales column would probably be adjacent to a column that provides the employee names (matching each employee with the appropriate sales figure).

So, data (values) on a worksheet are usually arranged in a table format, and related values are typically located in the same column or row and make up a range of contiguous cells. You use ranges of values in calculations, so it makes sense to simplify the process of identifying a range of cells by giving the range a name. You can then use this range name in calculations, such as total company sales, or compute the average, mean, maximum, or minimum for the sales range.

For example, the Sales range discussed in the previous paragraph could be given the name "Sales." The range name could then be used directly in formulas or functions as a substitute for the range itself, which is specified by the beginning and ending cell addresses in the range. Range names can be quite useful, and remembering a range name is a lot easier than remembering the cell range in terms of the cell addresses.

You can use range names in calculations (in both your own formulas and Excel functions) to create charts and to move to a particular place in a sheet using the Go To feature (press Ctrl+G to open the Go To dialog box).

Creating a range name for a selected range of cells is easy. There are some rules related to naming ranges, however. You are limited to 255 characters for a range name. You cannot use spaces. You also cannot use most of the symbols on the keyboard. The underscore and the period are allowed, however. The name has to start with a letter, underscore, or backslash.

You can use alphanumeric characters (A to Z and 0 to 9), so range names can consist of a combination of numbers and letters. You cannot, however, name a range C, c, R, or r (meaning the name of the range is "c" or "r"). These single letters are reserved for selection shortcuts. You can use the underscore in the place of a space where you want to create range names that describe the cell range, such as `gross_income` or `taxable_income`. (These two types of income are the same if you don't have any `tax_shelters`.)

There is more than one way to create range names. You can select a range of values and then define the name, or you can have Excel generate range names for the selected values using the column or row headings as the range names. To specify a range name for a selected range of cells, select the cell range and then click the Define Name command in the Defined Names group of the ribbon's Formulas tab. The New Name dialog box opens, as shown in Figure 12-18.

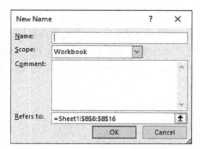

Figure 12-18   Create a range name for a selected range of cells.

Provide a name for the range in the Name text box. By default, the scope of the range name is at the workbook level, meaning you can specify this range anywhere in the workbook using the range name. You can change the scope to a specific sheet in the workbook. Select the Scope drop-down menu and select a sheet from the provided list.

You can also enter optional comments related to the range and its name in the Comment text box. Before you create the new name, take a moment to check the range specified in the Refers To text box. You can adjust the range if it is incorrect by selecting the Collapse button. You can reselect the range in the sheet and then click the Expand button to return to the New Name dialog box. Click OK to create the range name.

Creating range names from selections

You can also create range names based on the column labels or row labels that you have created in the worksheet. For example, suppose you have several columns of numbers, such as sales figures for different regions by month (January, February, March). In that case, you can quickly create a range name for each of the columns using the column labels. To create range names from row or column labels, select the ranges (either in columns or rows) and make sure that you include the row or column containing the descriptive labels for the range. Then click the Create From Selection command in the Define Names groups. The Create Names From Selection dialog box opens, as shown in Figure 12-19.

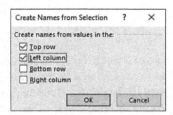

Figure 12-19   The Create Names From Selection dialog box

Select the location of the labels that you want to use as the range names using the check boxes provided: Top Row, Left Column, Bottom Row, or Right Column. If the labels are in the top row of the selected range and the values are arranged in columns, select Top Row. If the labels are in the first column (the left column) and the values are arranged in rows, select Left Column. When you are ready to generate the range names, click OK.

Managing range names

You can view and manage your range names in the Name Manager. The Name Manager enables you to create new range names, edit existing range names, and delete range names that you no longer want.

To open the Name Manager, select the Name Manager command in the Defined Names group. Figure 12-20 shows the Name Manager.

All the range names in the current workbook are listed in the Name Manager. You can filter the list using the Filter drop-down button on the right side of the dialog box. You can filter by scope (sheet or workbook) and filter for names that contain errors.

If you find that you need to edit a particular range name, select the name in the list and then click the Edit button. This opens the Edit Name dialog box, which enables you to modify the name, comments, or the range for that particular name.

To create a new range name, select the New dialog box. This opens the New Name dialog box. Specify a name, a cell range, and optional comments for the new range name. When you click OK to create the new name, you return to the Name Manager.

You can also delete range names from the Name Manager. Select a name in the list and then click the Delete button. You are asked if you are sure you want to delete the name. Click OK. The name is removed from the list.

Remember that the main reason you create range names is to use them as a way to specify a range of values in a formula that you design or an Excel function that you use. Range names can be quickly inserted into a formula or function via the Use in Formula command, which provides a list of your range names.

> ➤ **For more information about using range names in formulas and functions, see "Using range names in formulas and functions" in Chapter 13.**

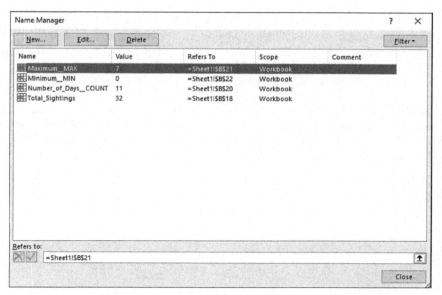

Figure 12-20   The Name Manager

Adding images and graphics to worksheets

You can add pictures, clip art, shapes, icons, and SmartArt graphics to your Excel worksheets just as easily as you can add these items to Word documents or PowerPoint presentation slides. For example, you can quickly insert a company logo graphic or insert a picture of the salamander species that is the subject of a population study you have detailed in your Excel sheet.

The Insert tab provides the Illustrations group, which enables you to insert your digital photos (Pictures), clip art and other online images (Online Pictures), shapes (Shapes), and SmartArt graphics (Insert A SmartArt Graphic). Pictures can be useful if the image directly relates to the subject matter of the sheet. Clip art is less useful, and overly cute clip art can diminish the impact of the facts and figures that you have included in the sheet. Office.com provides you with more than just clip art, however, and also houses a large number of royalty-free photos in the online clip art and photo library (accessed using the Online Pictures command).

SmartArt graphics provide you with the possibility of creating illustrative graphics that can help make sense out of the information in the sheet. For example, if you create a sales report that details the quarterly sales of your sales force by region, you can include an organizational chart showing the report structure for the regions. You can do this by creating an organizational chart using one of the SmartArt graphics provided in the Hierarchy category.

➤ For an overview of using images and graphics in the Office applications, see Chapter 4, "Using and creating graphics."

Obviously, the graphic type that you use most often in Excel will be a chart based on the data in a sheet. Other graphical possibilities that help provide meaning to data visually are sparklines and conditional formatting graphical options, such as data bars, color scales, and icon sets.

➤ **For information on adding charts to your Excel worksheets, see Chapter 14.**

Excel is different from Word and PowerPoint in that Excel worksheets must be designed and formatted so that they can provide a meaningful snapshot of often complex numerical information. Use graphical elements such as pictures and graphics sparingly and only when they are an aid to understanding the data provided in the sheet.

Getting the most from formulas and functions

Performing calculations in Excel worksheets   383

Relative versus absolute referencing   385

Creating and editing formulas   389

Working with Excel functions   392

Entering a function in a cell   393

Using range names in formulas and functions   399

Referencing cells or ranges on other worksheets   402

Copying and moving formulas and functions   404

Choosing the right function   405

Proofing your formulas and functions   417

Excel's real power lies in its ability to do calculations. We enter values into Excel because we want to have those values acted upon by formulas or functions. Excel is all about answers, and the answers are provided by the various formulas and functions that you place in your worksheet. Whether you are a biologist using statistical functions to enumerate a population study of snowy egrets in the Hudson River valley or a financial maven tracking investment, Excel provides all the tools you need to do the math.

In this chapter, we look at the basics of building simple formulas and taking advantage of Excel's huge library of built-in formulas—functions—to do calculations. We explore a number of different function categories, including statistical, logical, date, and financial functions. We also discuss the best practices for entering, copying, moving, and proofing your formulas and functions.

Performing calculations in Excel worksheets

Excel provides you with two different ways to do calculation in your worksheets: formulas and functions. Formulas are do-it-yourself math. You specify the cells to be referenced in the calculation, and you also provide the operators, which determine what kinds of calculations actually take place. Formulas are best reserved for simple calculations, such as subtraction, multiplication, and division. Figure 13-1 shows a subtraction formula that subtracts the payment to the instructor (G10) from the Tuition Total for that class (D10).

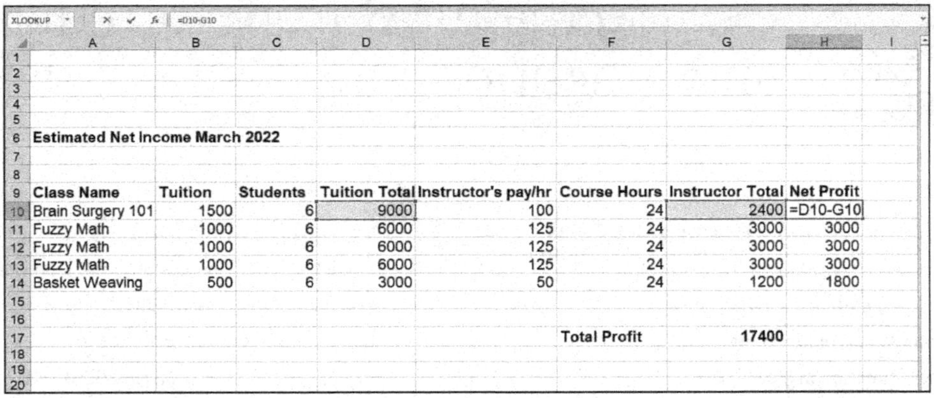

	A	B	C	D	E	F	G	H
6	Estimated Net Income March 2022							
9	Class Name	Tuition	Students	Tuition Total	Instructor's pay/hr	Course Hours	Instructor Total	Net Profit
10	Brain Surgery 101	1500	6	9000	100	24	2400	=D10-G10
11	Fuzzy Math	1000	6	6000	125	24	3000	3000
12	Fuzzy Math	1000	6	6000	125	24	3000	3000
13	Fuzzy Math	1000	6	6000	125	24	3000	3000
14	Basket Weaving	500	6	3000	50	24	1200	1800
17						Total Profit	17400	

Figure 13-1 A subtraction formula

NOTE

You can show the formulas and/or functions in a sheet by selecting the Show Formulas command. The command is found in the Formula Auditing group on the ribbon's Formulas tab.

Note that the formula (=D10-G10) is shown in H10 in Figure 3-1 and in the formula bar. When you place the insertion point in the formula bar, the cells involved in the formula are selected using a different color for each cell address included in the formula.

Functions, on the other hand, are built-in formulas provided by Excel. The Excel Function Library is huge; it provides nearly 500 functions, grouped into categories that include date and time functions, engineering functions, financial functions, math and trigonometry functions, statistical functions, and even text functions. Figure 13-2 shows the PMT function, which is an Excel function used to determine the periodic payment on a loan that has a fixed interest rate.

Note that the function is designated by the function name (PMT). The cells that are to be acted on by the function are B11 (the interest rate), C11 (the term: 60 months), and D11 (the actual cost of the car or the principal). Note that the only operator you see in the function is the /. This is because the annual interest rate needs to be divided by 12 so that you are calculating the monthly payment.

Creating your own formulas is best reserved for situations where Excel doesn't provide you with a function that will do the same job. As already mentioned, most of the formulas that you need to create take care of simple math problems that are used to subtract or divide values (or results from other formulas or functions). Developing an awareness of what the Excel functions can do in terms of complex calculations is time better spent than attempting to create your own elaborate formulas. You will find that there is, in most cases, an Excel function for whatever you are trying to calculate.

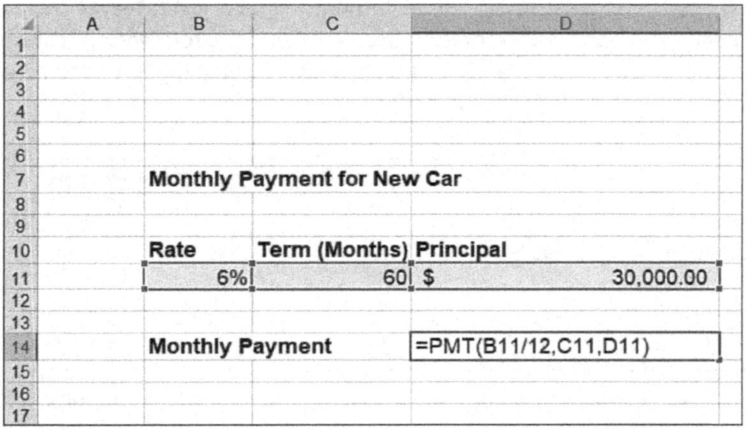

Figure 13-2 The PMT function

Relative versus absolute referencing

Understanding how Excel references cells in your worksheets when you specify them in a formula or function is fundamental to the overall understanding of how best to use formulas and functions in your sheets. If you are ever going to copy a formula or function in a sheet (and you will need to and want to), you need to understand how both relative referencing and absolute referencing work in Excel.

When you create a formula or function and designate cell references, Excel uses a form of referencing called *relative referencing*. When you copy a formula or a function from one cell to another cell, the cell references in the formula or function are rewritten to adjust to its new location. For example, Figure 13-3 shows a simple worksheet that uses the SUM function to add the January through March sales totals for each of the regions designated in column A. The SUM function was entered once in cell E4 and then copied (using the Fill handle) to cells E5, E6, and E7.

Note that as the function was copied down into the other total cells, the function adjusted to its new location and specifies the correct range of cells to be acted on by the function. This is because of relative referencing. Although you specified a range of cells to be summed in cell E4, what Excel saw was that it was to take the three cells to the left of the cell containing the function (E4) and add them together.

> ## NOTE
>
> When you select a cell containing a formula or function and place the insertion point in the formula bar, the range finder highlights the cells referenced in the formula or function.

When you copy the function down to cells E5 through E7, Excel just takes the three cells to the left of the function and adds them together. This is what relative referencing is all about and why it is so easy to copy a formula and function in a worksheet and get the correct answer (or answers).

	A	B	C	D	E
1	Quarter 1 (Sales in Millions)				
2					
3	Region	January	February	March	Total
4	East	50	67	45	=SUM(B4:D4)
5	West	56	45	98	=SUM(B5:D5)
6	South	78	77	55	=SUM(B6:D6)
7	North	89	62	72	=SUM(B7:D7)
8					
9					

Figure 13-3   Relative referencing enables you to quickly copy a function to multiple cells.

In some situations, you need to override Excel's relative referencing so that a formula or function does not change all the cell references when you copy it to a new location. This is where *absolute referencing* comes in. Suppose that you have a worksheet that computes the commission made on sales by each of your salespeople. The commission rate is specified in one cell. Figure 13-4 shows the simple multiplication formula that was created to multiply the total sales (in column B) by the commission percentage, which is located in cell B17. The formula was entered in cell C11 and then copied to cells C12 through C14.

XLOOKUP	▾	×	✓	ƒx	=B11*B17	
	A		B		C	
1						
2						
3						
4						
5	December Sales Commission					
6						
7						
8						
9						
10	Name		Total Sales		Commission	
11	Luis Alverca		4200		=B11*B17	
12	Mary Kay Andersen		3400		=B12*B17	
13	Cristina Potra		2700		=B13*B17	
14	Jeff Price		5400		=B14*B17	
15						
16						
17	Commission Percentage		0.1			
18						

Figure 13-4   Absolute referencing is used to override relative referencing.

Note that the commission percentage (B17) is specified in the formula as B17. This is because you want the commission formula (you created) to always (absolutely) reference cell B17 even when you copy the formula to other cells. Note that cell B11 (which is the total sales for John Smith) is included in the formula in C11 as a relative reference (no dollar signs are used on B11 to "lock" the column or row designation).

As the formula is copied down, B11 is adjusted to the new location and is automatically changed in each subsequent cell, first to B12, then B13, and then B14. If cell B17 was not designated in the formula as an absolute reference, as soon as the formula was copied from C11 to C12, the formula would no longer work. That is because the formula would attempt to adjust the relative reference for B17 to B18. B18 is empty (it contains no value), so that would result in no calculated value in C12 (you multiply something by a null value, and you get null).

NOTE

In Figure 13-4, I used my own formula with the asterisk serving as the multiplication symbol (=B11*B17). However, I could have used the Excel multiplication function =PRODUCT(B11,B17). In most cases, I would suggest you go with available functions rather than designing your own formulas. If you set up the function correctly, they always (okay, at least most of the time) provide you with the right answer.

Inside OUT

Be patient when working with calculations in Excel.

If you are an accountant, engineer, mathematician, astronaut, or any of the other millions and millions of math-capable people out there in the world, you can probably ignore this sidebar. For all of you who were liberal arts majors or just thought knowing a lot of math was going to slow you down, you might want to read on. Excel's ability to help walk you through the use of any of its built-in functions has become increasingly effective with each new version of Excel. Recent additions to the Office application, such as the Tell Me box (at the top center of an Office application's window) and the Smart Lookup features, have made the Office applications much more helpful in all sorts of situations. Not only are the Office applications such as Excel more helpful now, Excel has always been pretty good in terms of walking you through the process of setting up a function. For example, the Insert Function dialog box has been around for a long time and can help you search for a function. Also, the Function Arguments dialog helps you to specify the information that a function requires to return a valid result. We work with both items in this chapter.

There are also some other things that you can do to feel more comfortable when using Excel functions:

- Use the web as a resource. There are many blogs, YouTube videos, and other resources on the web for fine-tuning your knowledge of a particular Excel function (or any feature for that matter). A good place to start your web journey related to Excel functions Microsoft's support site for Office at *https://support.office.com*, where you can search for Excel functions. The search returns two very useful links. One is a list of all Excel functions by category (such as Database functions, Financial functions, and Statistical functions). A link to Excel functions by name (alphabetical) is also provided and can be very useful. Each of these lists provides a short description of each function.

- Ask your colleagues if they have ever created a worksheet like the one you are tasked to do. Seeing examples of how other Excel users place their data and functions on a worksheet can be helpful even if you don't adopt their approach.

- Make sure you take advantage of Excel's formula auditing tools. These tools include error checking and formula evaluation, and they also allow you to toggle between the actual function and the value that it returns. We discuss these tools later in the chapter.

Once you are comfortable with a particular function, it might make sense to use range names in the function so that you don't have to deal with the nuances of absolute references. We discuss using range names in formulas and functions later in this chapter.

To specify a cell reference as absolute, add a $ (dollar sign) before the column letter and before the row number that make up the cell address (such as our example of an absolute reference: B17). The easiest way to add the dollar signs to an absolute reference is to press F4 after you have specified the cell address in a formula or function.

In our example, we looked at a single cell as an absolute reference. You can also have the situation where you only designate the column or row in a cell address as absolute rather than making both the column and row designation absolute. Remember that cell references are two parts: column designation and row designation. So, you can make a reference in a formula or function where only the column is absolute, and the row reference is still relative. This is referred to as a *mixed reference*.

Let's look at an example, using the PMT function as the function we want to copy in a worksheet. Figure 13-5 shows the PMT function as it was originally written in cell C7. A row of car amounts (principals) are listed in row 5, and different interest rates are listed in column B. Only one term (the number of monthly payments) is listed in cell C14.

When the function is copied across the columns, you always want the function to look for the rates in column B. So, column B is designated as absolute in the function ($B). You also want the function to continue to look in row 5 for a principal when it is copied down, so row 5 is designated as absolute in the function ($5). Finally, the term in C14 must always (absolutely) be referred to by the function, no matter where you copy it. So, it is designated as an absolute (C14). Thus, we have mixed references and one absolute reference in the same function.

Using absolute references and mixed references can be a little tricky. If you enter a formula or a function with incorrect absolute or mixed referencing, Excel typically lets you know. For example, if you neglect to make column B absolute in the example in Figure 13-5, as soon as you copy the function to the next column, you get the message #NUM in the cells. This is because there is a numerical error in the function. All you have to do is fix the function and then recopy it to the other cells in the sheet to fix the problem. Excel also offers a number of other tools for correcting formulas and functions, including the ability to trace precedents and dependents and do error checking on formulas and functions. We look at some of these tools later in this chapter.

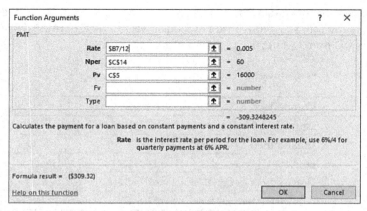

Figure 13-5   Mixed references can be used in cell addresses.

Creating and editing formulas

Creating formulas in Excel is really straightforward. You specify the cell addresses of the values that you want in the formula, and then the values in the formula (specified by cell addresses) are then acted on by the operator or operators that you specify in the formula. When you begin a new formula in a cell, you start the formula's notation with the = sign. This lets Excel know that you are entering a formula. You can then specify the cell addresses for the formula and the required operators. For example, you might enter the following formula:

=B6–C6

You are specifying that Excel should take the value in C6 and subtract it from the value in B6. The result is returned in the cell where you entered the formula. Table 13-1 shows some of the common arithmetic operators used in Excel formulas.

Table 13-1 Arithmetic operators

Operator	Performs	Example
+	Addition	=A1+B1
−	Subtraction	=A1-B1
*	Multiplication	=A1*C12
/	Division	=A1/B3
^	Exponentiation	=A1^2

Excel also provides other operators that are referred to as comparison operators. These operators can compare two cells and return one of two logical values: TRUE or FALSE. Table 13-2 provides a list of comparison operators.

Table 13-2 Comparison operators

Operator	Comparison	Example
=	Equal	=A1=B1
>	Greater than	=A1>B1
<	Less than	=A1<C12
>=	Greater than or equal to	=A1>=B3
<=	Less than or equal to	=A1<=2

Obviously, after you know what operator or operators you are going to use, the rest of the formula typically consists of the cell addresses that are to be acted on by the formula. The values in those referenced cell addresses are referred to as *operands*. Operands in a formula can consist of a cell range, single-cell addresses, constants (values, dates, or text you enter as part of the formula), or range names.

Understanding operator precedence

An important part of creating formulas relates to operator precedence. In the simplest terms, operator precedence means that certain operations in a formula take precedence over (or take place before) other operations in a formula. For example, in the formula =B2+B3*C2, the multiplication of B3*C2 takes precedence, so B3 is multiplied by C2, and then B2 is added to that result. The order of operator precedence is as follows:

1. Parentheses ()

2. Exponent ^

3. Multiplication *, Division /

4. Addition +, Subtraction -

5. Equal to =, Less than <, Greater than >

In the case of the formula =B2+B3*C2, if you want the formula to add B2+B3 before multiplying the result by C2, you would have to write the formula as

=(B2+B3)*C2

Operations enclosed in parentheses take precedence over operations that are not in parentheses.

Entering formulas

You can enter formulas in one of two ways: by typing the entire formula, including the cell addresses, or by typing the formula operators and selecting the cell references. Because many of the errors found in Excel typically relate to incorrectly entered information, it makes sense to point to the cells or cell ranges that are included in a formula. This makes it less likely for an incorrect cell address or range to be placed in the formula. Follow these steps to enter a formula:

1. Select the cell that will hold the formula. Type = to begin the formula.

2. Click the first cell that will be referenced in the formula. The cell address is entered in the formula in the formula bar.

3. Enter the appropriate arithmetic operator after the cell address of the value to indicate the operation you want to perform.

4. Click the next cell that will be referenced in the formula.

5. Repeat steps 3 and 4, if necessary. You can also enter constants into the formula as needed.

6. When the formula is complete, click the Enter button on the formula bar or press Enter. The formula is entered in the current cell.

After the formula has been entered into the cell, the result of the formula appears in the cell. When you select the cell, you can view the formula in the formula bar. If you click in the formula bar, the range finder highlights the cells that you specified in the formula.

TIP
If you are entering a formula and want to get rid of it and start again, press the ESC key.

Editing formulas

Editing formulas in Excel is straightforward. You can edit a formula in the formula bar or directly in the cell. To edit the formula in the formula bar, select the cell containing the formula; then place the insertion point into the formula (in the formula bar) and edit as needed. As soon as you place the insertion point in the formula bar, the range finder highlights the cells referenced in the formula.

CHAPTER 13

You can use the arrow keys to move within the formula bar. To go to the beginning of the formula in the formula bar, press the Home key; the End key takes you to the end of the formula. You can also do in-cell editing: Double-click a cell to place the insertion point into the contents of the cell, such as a formula.

When you need to edit a cell reference (or references) in a formula, it is probably easiest to do this in the formula bar. Select the cell address in the formula that you want to change. You can type the changes required; however, it is more foolproof to click the cell, so that cell's address is inserted into the formula, replacing the selected cell reference. When you have finished editing the formula, click the Enter button in the formula bar or press the Enter key.

> ➤ **For more information about editing a cell's content, see "Entering data in a worksheet," in Chapter 11, "Essential Excel features."**

Working with Excel functions

Formulas provide you with a way to do simple arithmetic and some logical expressions, but most of the heavy lifting you do in terms of calculations in Excel is accomplished using functions. Functions can do everything from adding a range of numbers, counting the number of entries in a range, and providing you with the return on an investment when you have a constant interest rate and consistent monthly deposits. And you can bank on the fact that my previous statement doesn't even scratch the surface of possibilities in terms of the different kinds of functions that Excel provides.

Functions consist of two parts: the function name and the cell addresses that are to be acted upon. These cell ranges or individual cell addresses are also referred to as the function's *arguments* because the function uses them to arrive at an answer. One of the most common functions used is the SUM function, which is also referred to as the AutoSum function because Excel has provided an AutoSum command in just about every version of Excel that I can remember. It is designed to quickly add a range of numbers. So, the SUM function might look like this in a worksheet:

```
=SUM(B4:D4)
```

where the argument is the range of cells B4 to D4, which will be added by the SUM function. The SUM function can also add cells that are not in a contiguous range using the syntax =SUM(B3, C6, D12). Individual cell addresses serve as the arguments in the function and are separated by commas. The number of arguments (or cell addresses) that can be placed in the SUM function is endless, meaning that many functions do not control the number of legal arguments specified in the function.

Some functions do not have any arguments. For example, the =NOW() function, which is a date function, returns the current date and time formatted as a date and time. It does not require an argument in the parentheses to work.

The number of arguments allowed in Excel functions can vary, and some functions allow optional arguments. For example, the FV function, which calculates the future value of an investment that has a constant interest rate and the same payment amount over the investment period, allows for an optional present value of the investment if you have rolled the money over into a new money market account, certificate of deposit, or other investment instrument. Figure 13-6 shows a simple future value worksheet that includes an optional present value (the initial investment on the worksheet).

Figure 13-6 shows the Function Arguments dialog box, which is used to build a function in the current cell. The Future Value function (FV) requires that a Rate (the interest rate divided by the number of payments in a year), the Nper (the total number of payment periods in the investment), and the Pmt (the actual payment) be supplied for the function to work. It also allows for an optional PV (or Present Value) to be included.

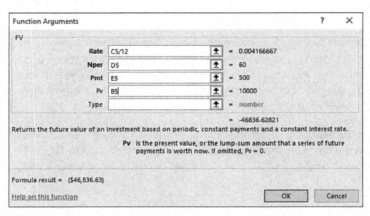

Figure 13-6   Supplying a Future Value function with arguments

Entering a function in a cell

Excel provides different methods for inserting a function into your worksheet. You can enter a function (as you can a formula) by typing an equal sign (=) followed by the name of the function. The cell references for the function are then provided within the parentheses that follow the function name.

Typing functions can be just as fraught with potential errors as typing formulas. Because the actual entry of items into an Excel sheet can result in errors, Excel provides you better ways for inserting functions. There are two methods for inserting functions—the Insert Function dialog box and the category commands provided in the Function Library. Both avenues get you to the same place—the Function Arguments dialog box. The Function Arguments dialog box enables you to specify the arguments to be used by the function. This can require that you specify a range of cells or individual cell addresses. Because the Function Arguments dialog box provides separate input boxes for the required arguments for the function, you can use the mouse to easily specify the arguments directly on the worksheet. This can greatly cut down on the possibility of specifying the wrong range or cell address in the function.

Although using the Function Arguments dialog box is relatively straightforward, some of the more commonly used functions, such as SUM, AVERAGE, and other statistical functions such as MAX (maximum) and MIN (minimum), can be inserted in a more direct way via the AutoSum command. Let's look at AutoSum, and then we can return to our discussion of inserting functions using the Function Arguments dialog box.

Using AutoSum

As already mentioned, the SUM function is probably the most-used function in Excel. We are always adding things together, such as the total number of employees, the total number of widgets in our inventory, or the total amount of money in our bank account.

You can insert the SUM function into a worksheet using the AutoSum command on the ribbon's Home tab or the AutoSum command in the Function Library group of the ribbon's Formulas tab. Select the cell where you want to place the SUM function. Typically, you choose a cell that is at the bottom of a column of values or the end of a row of data. This makes it easy for AutoSum to figure out the range of cells that it should include in the SUM function.

When you select the AutoSum command, AutoSum inserts =SUM and selects the range of cells to be included in the function. The range is also specified in the function. Figure 13-7 shows the SUM function inserted by the AutoSum command and the range of cells that is included in the function.

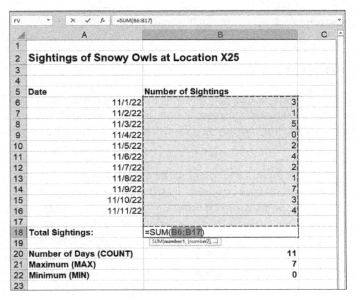

Figure 13-7   AutoSum attempts to select the range of cells to be added.

Note that the range of cells is specified as B6:B17. The beginning and end of the range are separated by a colon (:). AutoSum does not always select the correct range of cells. When you insert the SUM function using AutoSum in a cell that is at the bottom of a column and the end of a row, AutoSum selects the cells in the column. Blank cells within a range stop AutoSum from selecting the entire cell range you might want to specify in the function. You can change the range selected as needed. Use the mouse to extend or reduce the selection marquee or select an entirely new range of cells. After you have the correct range specified, click the Enter button in the formula bar or press the Enter key. The SUM function is placed in the cell and returns a result.

You can also insert other statistical functions from the AutoSum drop-down menu. These functions include Average (AVERAGE), Count Numbers (COUNT), Maximum (MAX), and Minimum (MIN). To enter one of these functions, such as AVERAGE, select the cell that contains the function and then select the drop-down menu for the AutoSum command on the Home tab or the Formulas tab. The function is entered in the cell. The function attempts to select a range. However, success depends on where you are placing the function and how the values you want to be acted on are arranged in the worksheet. Use the mouse if you need to specify the range for the function and then press Enter. The result of the function appears in the cell.

> **TIP**
>
> The Count Numbers (or COUNT) function does not count blank cells or cells containing text. If you want to count values, use COUNT. If you want to count cells that contain text entries use the COUNTA function.

Using the status bar statistical functions

Because we are talking about some of the statistical functions, such as Average (AVERAGE), Count Numbers (COUNT), Maximum (MAX), and Minimum (MIN), and how to insert them, I want to take a short side trip and discuss the statistical counters (or auto-calculate fields) that are provided by the Excel status bar. When you select a range of cells, the status bar can automatically calculate such things as the average, count, minimum, maximum, and sum for the range. The result is shown in the status bar (not in the sheet).

To activate one of these statistical counters, such as Average, Count, or Sum, right-click the status bar to open the Customize Status Bar menu. Select a statistical function such as AVERAGE, COUNT, or MIN (you can enable as many of these statistical counters as you want).

Now when you select a range of cells in the sheet, the results of the enabled statistical functions appear on the status bar. These status bar statistical functions provide you with a quick statistical summary of any selected cell range.

Using the Insert Function dialog box

The Insert Function dialog box can be accessed via the AutoSum drop-down menu; select the AutoSum drop-down arrow on the Home tab of the ribbon and then select More Functions. You can also access the Insert Function dialog box from the Insert Function command on the ribbon's Formulas tab. In either case, the Insert Function dialog box opens, as shown in Figure 13-8.

TIP

If you need more help with a particular function, select the function in the list and then click Help On This Function to open the Excel Help window.

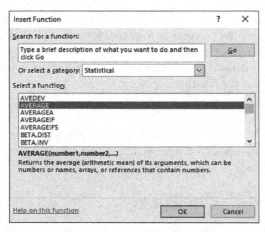

Figure 13-8   The Insert Function dialog box

The Insert Function dialog box is designed to help you find a function in cases where you have a good idea of the worksheet calculation but aren't sure which function to use or can't remember the name of a function that you use only occasionally. To search for a particular function, type a brief description of what you want to do in the Search for a Function box and then click Go. For example, you could type investment value, and Excel would list financial functions (among other functions) that help you calculate the present or future value of an investment.

If you want to see functions that you have recently used, you can use the Or Select A Category drop-down menu to view the most recently used functions. You can also peruse the functions by category, such as Financial, Date & Time, Statistical, Logical, and so on, by selecting a particular category of functions via the drop-down menu.

When you select a function in the Select A Function list box, the syntax for the function appears below the function list. A definition of the function is also provided.

After you have located the function that you want to place in the worksheet, make sure that the function is selected and then click OK. The Function Arguments dialog box opens. Provide the various arguments for the function, as required, and then click OK. This places the function in the worksheet and returns your result.

Using the Function Library

Another alternative for inserting a function into a sheet is to use the function category commands that are provided in the Function Library group on the ribbon's Formulas tab. The Function Library group also provides access to the Recently Used command, which lists recently used functions as well as the Insert Function command and the AutoSum command, which has a drop-down menu that includes other statistical functions, such as AVERAGE and MIN.

Each of the Function Library categories provides access to an entire category of functions. For example, selecting the Financial command lists Financial functions in alphabetical order. Figure 13-9 shows the ribbon's Formulas tab.

Figure 13-9   The ribbon's Formulas tab

The Formulas tab provides more than just access to the Function Library. It also provides commands that are related to range names, auditing formulas and functions, and determining when and how results should be calculated in the worksheet. The command groups on the Formulas tab are as follows:

- **Function Library:** This group provides function category commands that enable you to specify a function to be inserted into a worksheet. Commands include Insert Function, AutoSum, and Recently Used. Category commands, such as Financial, Logical, Text, and so on, enable you to access specific lists of commands by category. The More Functions command provides access to additional function categories, such as Statistical, Engineering, and Cube.

- **Defined Names:** This group provides the commands for creating, accessing, and managing range names. Using range names in formulas and functions is discussed in the next section of this chapter.

➤ **For more information about creating range names, see the "Naming ranges" section in Chapter 12.**

- **Formula Auditing:** This group provides tools that enable you to check formulas and functions for errors. It also enables you to show the formula and functions in a worksheet (rather than their results) and activate the Watch Window, which is used to monitor the values in certain cells as changes are made to the values in the worksheet. Proofing your formulas and functions is discussed later in this chapter.

CHAPTER 13

- **Calculation:** This group enables you to immediately calculate the results in a sheet (Excel automatically calculates results by default) and also change calculation options such as switching from automatic calculations to manual.

NOTE

If the Euro Currency Tools have been added to your Excel installation, the Formulas tab will also include a Solutions group that is used for Euro conversion and formatting. Add-ins are added to Excel (add-ins such as Power Pivot and the Solver) via the Excel Options dialog box. Configuring Office add-ins is discussed in Chapter 2 in the Add-ins section.

To take advantage of the Function Library, select a function category to view the functions in that category. Place the mouse on a function (in a category list). A ScreenTip appears that provides you with a brief description of the function. For example, Figure 13-10 shows the Logical gallery (opened by selecting Logical in the Function Library) with the ScreenTip for the IF function.

Figure 13-10   The Logical gallery and the ScreenTip for the IF function

After you locate the function that you want to insert into the worksheet, select the function in the gallery. The Function Arguments dialog box opens, as shown in Figure 13-11.

The Function Arguments dialog box lists both the required (and in some cases optional) arguments for a function. In Figure 13-11, the IF function is shown, which requires that a logical test be provided along with a value if true and a value if false. The logical test can include cell addresses, operators, and a constant, if needed. The value if true can be a calculation, a cell address, or a text string. When you include text strings in functions, you need to place quotation marks around the text.

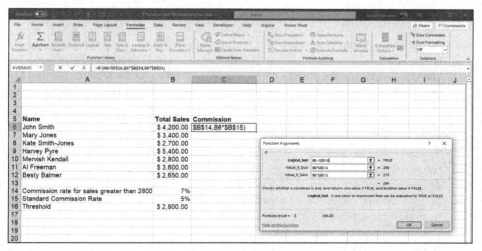

Figure 13-11   The Function Arguments dialog box for the IF function and the accompanying sheet

In the sheet shown in Figure 13-11, the function is inserted in cell C6 and is copied down, so the commission for each salesperson is calculated. The logical test requires that the total sales for a salesperson be greater than cell B16 (which holds the value of 2,800.00). If the logical test is true (if total sales exceed B16), then the commission rate is calculated by multiplying the total sales by cell B14 (7%). A salesperson selling more than the threshold amount gets a higher commission because the commission is figured at the higher rate (7%). If the value is false, the total sales are multiplied by the standard commission rate in cell B15 (5%).

After you have provided the various arguments required by the function, you can click OK. This closes the Function Arguments dialog box; the function is placed in the worksheet and provides you with a result.

Using range names in formulas and functions

Range names can be used in both your formulas and functions to reference cell ranges. Because range names can be more descriptive than the actual cell range that they represent, they can provide you with a more meaningful way (if you use descriptive name ranges) to specify the arguments in a formula or function.

Using range names for cells that provide constants or other arguments for a formula or function can also negate the need to use absolute referencing in the formula or function. The range name is, in effect, an absolute reference of a specific cell or cell range because of the range name itself. This can be particularly useful in cases when you are building formulas or functions that pull data from multiple sheets in the same workbook or even other workbooks that are shared by colleagues. The range names help you differentiate arguments and can also cut down on the possibility of incorrectly specified cell addresses or ranges in a formula or function. And it always makes sense to cut down on potential user entry errors when working in Excel.

All the range names you create can be accessed via the Use In Formula drop-down menu. The Use In Formula command is housed in the Defined Names group on the ribbon's Formulas tab. The Use In Formula drop-down menu is available when you are typing a formula or function into a cell from the keyboard or inserting a function using the Function Arguments dialog box.

Inserting a range name into a formula

You can insert range names into your formulas as you create them. Begin the formula by typing the equal sign (=); specify any cell addresses to be included in the formula by clicking that cell or selecting the cell range. Add operators as needed to the formula. When you want to specify an argument by range name, select the Use In Formula command and select the range name from the list provided. Figure 13-12 shows a formula being created in cell C12. The Commission Percentage range name, which is the range name for cell F18 (the commission percentage value), is pasted into the formula.

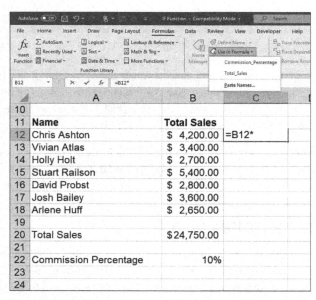

Figure 13-12   Insert range names into a formula.

When you have pasted the range name into the formula, you can then complete the formula as needed (in the case of Figure 13-12, I just need to insert the range name for the Commission Percentage and then press Enter). If you need to paste additional range names into the formula, repeat the process using the Use In Formula command. Press Enter when you have finished creating the formula.

Inserting a range name into a function

Range names can also be inserted into the functions that you use in your worksheets. First, create your range names as we have discussed, and then you can select the function you want to use from the Function Library category commands or the Insert Function dialog box. Specify the range names to be used by the function in the appropriate argument box in the Function Arguments dialog box. For example, let's say you are using the PMT function to figure out monthly payments at different interest rates and principals. You want to insert the term (Nper) into the Function Arguments dialog box but don't want to have to use absolute referencing, so you specify the cell using an already defined range name.

Figure 13-13 shows the Function Arguments dialog box for the PMT function and the Use In Formula range name list. The Nper box in the Function Arguments dialog box is the "target" for the pasted range name. The Term Range Name refers to cell C14 in the worksheet. If a range name was not used to specify the value in C14, you would have to specify the term in the Functions Arguments dialog box as an absolute reference C14. This is because the function will be copied to a range of cells to compute the monthly payment at the different interest rates on the sheet.

When you are inserting range names into the Function Arguments dialog box (or directly into a formula or function in a cell), you can insert the range name from the Use In Formula range name list or the Paste Name dialog box. The Paste Name dialog box also allows you to view range names available in the current workbook. To open the Paste Name dialog box, select the Use In Formula command and then select Paste Name.

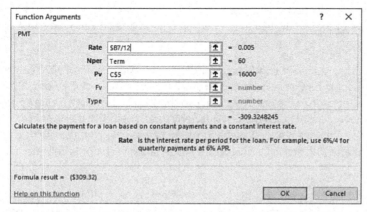

Figure 13-13   Insert range names into the Function Arguments dialog box.

The Paste Name dialog box is useful in cases where you have created a large number of range names for the sheets in your workbook. A long list of range names in the Use In Formula range name list can make it hard to find the range name you want. The Paste Name dialog box, on the other hand, allows you to scroll up and down through the Paste Name list. Selecting a range name in the Paste Name dialog box also does not immediately insert the range into the function (as does the Use In Formula range name list). The Paste Name dialog box requires you to click OK after specifying the range name to be pasted.

Referencing cells or ranges on other worksheets

When you work in situations where data that spans more than one sheet in an Excel workbook must be summarized, you need to include cell references in a formula or function that consist of cell addresses or ranges that are not on the current worksheet (the worksheet that contains the formula or function). For example, you might have created a different worksheet for each quarter of the year that details your sales figures or expenditures, and you want to have a worksheet in the workbook that provides summary information for all four quarters.

Here is the syntax for a cell reference on a worksheet that is in the same workbook as the sheet you are working on:

```
'sheet name'!cell address
```

The single quotation marks are required for the sheet name reference only if the sheet's name contains spaces.

The best way to specify a cell address on another sheet in the same workbook, or a range of cells in the same workbook, is to select the cell or range of cells as you create a formula or function that includes this information as an argument. By pointing out the arguments (rather than trying to type in the cell addresses) contained on the other worksheet or worksheets, you don't have to worry about the syntax related to how you refer to a cell on another sheet; Excel takes care of that for you.

For example, let's say you want to add your quarterly sales totals, each of which is on a separate quarterly worksheet in an Excel workbook. All you have to do is select the AutoSum command to insert the SUM function in the cell. Now, you can show Excel the cells that are to be added. Click the worksheet tab that holds the first quarterly total. Then click the cell containing that total. The first cell reference is added to the function. Before navigating to the next worksheet, type a comma (,) after the first cell address entry to separate each of the cell references in the function.

Go to the next worksheet and select the total for the next quarter; then type a comma. As you build the function, the cell references appear on the formula bar. Repeat the process as needed, separating each cell reference with a comma. After specifying the last cell reference to be included in the function, press Enter (do not include a comma after the last entry). The SUM function returns the sum of the four-quarter totals.

You can also insert cell addresses that specify cells on other worksheets into the Function Arguments dialog box, which is used to build functions. Select the appropriate argument box in the Function Arguments dialog box and then navigate to the worksheet that contains the cell or cell range. Select the cell or range, and it is added to the Function Arguments dialog box.

Figure 13-14 shows a function and a formula that reference cell addresses on other worksheets in the workbook. Specifying these addresses using the point-and-click method is much easier than trying to type the cell references into the formula or function.

TIP

To view two open workbooks side by side, select the View Side By Side command on the ribbon's View tab.

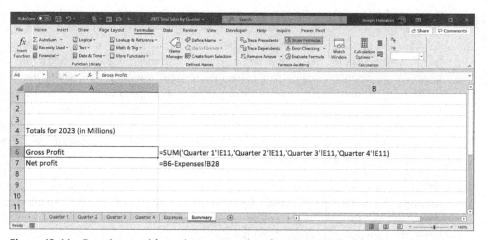

Figure 13-14   Functions and formulas can contain references to cell addresses outside the current worksheet.

You can also reference cell addresses that are in other workbooks (meaning a separate Excel file). The syntax for cell addresses referenced in other Excel workbook formulas or functions is as follows:

`'[workbook name]sheet name'!cell address`

This is the syntax used when the other workbook is open. The syntax for a closed workbook is a little more involved:

`'drive letter:\folder\[workbook name]sheet name'!cell address`

The easiest way to reference cells or ranges in other workbooks is to open all the workbooks involved. You can then switch between the workbooks to specify the cell addresses used in a formula or function in much the same way that you can move from worksheet to worksheet in a single workbook and then select the cells to be used as operands or arguments. Please believe me when I say that it is much easier to point to a value using the mouse or your finger—whether it is in the same workbook or a different workbook—rather than trying to type the cell references into your formula or function.

TIP

Another way to reference cell ranges on other sheets in a workbook (sheets other than the one where you are inserting a formula or function) is to use range names to specify the ranges. A range name can basically be a description of the location in terms of the sheet that it is on. This may make it easier for you to visualize a formula or function that calculates a result using cell ranges from several sheets in a workbook.

Copying and moving formulas and functions

Copying and moving formulas and functions is straightforward as long as you remember the fact that Excel uses relative referencing by default. This makes it easy to copy a formula or function that acts on rows or columns that are similar to the row or column where you first inserted the formula or function. For example, if you have several rows of values that contain the same number of cells, you can use the SUM function to total the first row and then drag the SUM function down using the fill handle to copy it so that it totals each subsequent row in the worksheet. The cell references in the function change relative to its position because of relative referencing. This way, you get the correct total for each row.

You can copy formulas or functions using the fill handle (when appropriate), and you can also use the Copy and Paste commands. Remember that copying a formula or function can be tricky if you have not specified any absolute references, which basically lock the address of certain values in the formula or function. If you get an error value such as #NUM, Excel's relative referencing is wreaking havoc with your copied formula or function.

➤ **For more about relative and absolute referencing, see "Relative versus absolute referencing," in this chapter.**

Moving a formula or function can be accomplished by dragging the formula or function (that is, the cell containing the formula or function) to a new location on the worksheet. You can also use Cut and Paste as needed. Even if you move a formula or function, it still returns the original results, meaning it continues to reference the cell addresses originally specified when you built the formula or function.

Choosing the right function

Excel functions provide you with ready-made formulas for just about any type of calculation you want to undertake. Statistical, Financial, and Math & Trig are all examples of function categories that supply functions that perform calculations. Statistical functions, such as COUNT and AVERAGE, are designed for doing statistical analysis. Financial functions, such as PMT and FV, compute the monthly payment on a car or house and the return on an investment, respectively. Math & Trig functions, such as SINE and COS, return the sine and cosine of an angle, respectively (sorry for dredging up any potential trigonometry nightmares).

There are also functions that do not actually do what we typically think of as calculations. For example, the lookup functions are designed to look up information in a table and then return that information into a second table called the lookup table. Until recently, there have only been two LOOKUP functions: HLOOKUP and VLOOKUP. XLOOKUP is a new "flavor" of LOOKUP function that is actually easier to set up and use than the popular VLOOKUP function or the INDEX MATCH function (which also can return information from a table to a destination table). We will discuss how to use XLOOKUP in the upcoming section, "Lookup & Reference functions."

Another example of a function that does not actually compute a particular value (such as the SUM or PRODUCT) functions) is the logical function IF. IF provides you with the ability to set up a conditional statement and then perform one action if the condition is true and another action if the condition is false. And I haven't even mentioned the text functions, which are designed to manipulate text strings in your worksheets.

It goes without saying (but obviously, I am going to say it anyway) that there are a lot of different possibilities in Excel functions. Just take a tour of the possibilities by perusing through the different function categories provided in the Function Library. An exhaustive listing of Excel functions and their uses is beyond the scope of this book. However, the information that follows is designed to provide you with some help in understanding how to best take advantage of some of the most often used functions in your worksheets.

Financial functions

The financial functions provide you with the ability to do all sorts of different financial calculations; there are depreciation functions, financial functions (related to securities), and investment and annuity functions. Many of these functions are related to financial and accounting principles that require a solid knowledge base to use them correctly. However, there are other simpler financial functions that just about anyone can take advantage of. For example, you can easily calculate the monthly payments on loans, compute the present value of an investment, and determine the future value of an investment.

When you are working with financial functions, you need to have some basic terminology under your belt, particularly if you want to take advantage of some of the financial functions that enable you to compute the return on a simple investment or the periodic payment on a loan.

For example, to compute the current value of an investment, you need to know the Rate, Nper, and the Pmt.

The rate is the interest rate you will pay or get on an investment, and Excel will ask for the rate when you are setting up a financial function, such as PV (Present Value) in the Function Arguments dialog box. We have all at the very least had an interest-bearing checking account that is tied to a particular interest rate or made some other type of investment that accrued at a specific rate. The rate supplied to you for both investments and loans is typically the APR, or the annual percentage rate. This means that when you provide the rate for a financial function such as PV, you need to divide the annual interest rate by the number of payments you make each year to provide the function with the interest rate per period.

Another piece of information that you need to supply to a financial function such as PV is the total number of payment periods in the investment, or Nper; the Nper is based on the number of payments you make annually. So, if you make monthly payments on the investment for five years, the Nper is 60 (5*12).

The PV function also needs to know how much the payment was each period. For PV to work, the payment must be the same for each period during the life of the investment. Figure 13-15 shows a simple worksheet that uses PV to compute the value of a five-year investment.

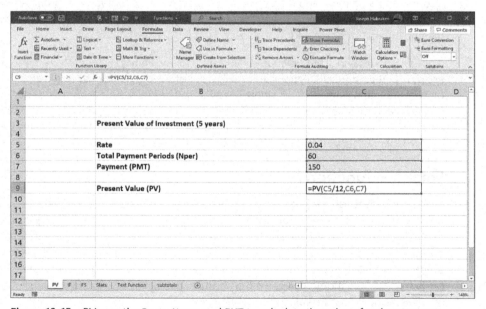

Figure 13-15   PV uses the Rate, Nper, and PMT to calculate the value of an investment.

If you understand one financial function, such as PV, you can probably work your way through similar functions, such as FV (Future Value), NPER (number of payment periods for a loan), and

PMT (loan payment), because they use similar arguments (such as the Nper and Rate) when you build them. For example, the syntax for the PMT function is

```
=PMT(Rate, NPER, PV)
```

When using the PMT function or any other financial function that includes the Rate (interest rate), remember that it needs to be divided by the number of payments you make in a year. For monthly payments, you would divide the rate by 12; for quarterly payments, you would divide by 4. Most loans that we deal with in our personal lives, such as car loans and mortgages, have 12 payments per year. That means when you use PMT to figure out a monthly auto or home loan payment, the rate would be divided by 12.

Logical functions

Logical functions enable you to evaluate conditional statements. The IF function is probably the most used of the logical functions and provides you with the ability to include other formulas or functions as part of the true or false answer that is derived from your conditional statement. The syntax for the IF function is as follows:

```
=IF(logical_test, value_if_true,value_if_false)
```

The logical test can use operators such as less than (<), greater than (>), and equal to (=). The value_if_true or the value_if_false can consist of values, formulas, functions, or text strings. If you use text strings as the true or false values, the text must be enclosed within quotation marks, such as "text".

In terms of providing an example to illustrate the use of the IF function, let's say that you have total sales figures for your sales personnel, and you want to calculate the commission for each salesperson. You have two commission rates: a low commission rate and a high commission rate. Any salesperson selling more than $28,000.00 of merchandise receives a high commission rate. Those who fall below $28,000.00 receive the lower commission rate. A breakdown of the IF function just described would be as follows:

```
Logical_test: total sales > $28,000.00
Value_if_true: total sales*High Commission Rate
Value_if_false: total sales*Low Commission Rate
```

Figure 13-16 shows a sample worksheet that uses the IF function. The cells containing the low commission rate, high commission rate, and the threshold (B14, B15, and B16) have all been named using the row labels to the left. Therefore, the range names have been used in the Function Arguments dialog box (which negates the need to use any absolute references, if you want to copy the function to other cells).

CHAPTER 13

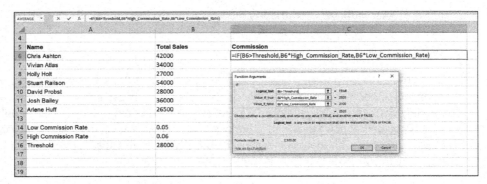

Figure 13-16   The IF function

When you have finished entering the arguments for the IF function in the Function Arguments dialog box, click OK. You can then drag the fill handle down and copy the function to the other commission cells that are associated with each employee.

Another Excel logical function that is similar to IF and named IFS can be very useful in situations where you want to create an IF statement with multiple (more than two) conditions. This is great because the IF function is really limited to two conditions: one true and one false. Before the addition of the new IFS function, if you wanted to create an IF statement with more than two conditions, you had to nest an IF statement (or multiple IF statements) inside an IF statement to increase the number of conditions. The syntax for an IF statement nested inside an IF function would be IF(logical test 1, value_if_true1, IF(logical test 2, value_if_true2, value_if_false2)). Note that this nesting of the IF inside the IF only provides you with three conditions. The more conditions you have, the messier it gets when you nest multiple IF statements inside an IF inside an IF.

The IFS function makes it much easier to take advantage of multiple conditions in a worksheet. For example, using our commission scenario discussed in relation to the IF statement, let's say that we have four conditions based on the total sales of a group of individuals, as shown here:

```
Test 1: total sales < $29,000.00, Value if True=0
Test 2: total sales <$35,000.00, Value_if_true: total sales*Basic Commission Rate
Test 3: total sales <$43,000.00, Value_if_true: total sales*Medium Commission Rate
Test 4: total sales <$55,000.00, Value_if_true: total sales*High Commission Rate
```

The IFS function is actually easier to use than you would think. The Function Arguments dialog box allows you to create each of your logical tests and the value if the test is true. Figure 13-17 shows a worksheet that uses IFS to compute the commission to be paid to each individual based on a sliding scale related to their total sales.

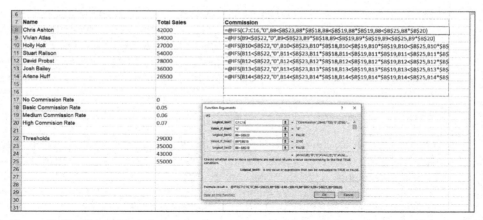

Figure 13-17   The IFS function makes it easy to create a formula that contains multiple conditions.

Note that because there were a number of thresholds to reach the different commission rate levels, the commission rates and thresholds had to be entered into the value as absolute references, which allowed the IFS function created in cell C8 to be copied down to the cell range of C9 to C14.

Statistical functions

The statistical functions provide you with often-used functions, such as SUM, AVERAGE, COUNT, MAX, and MIN. There are more complex statistical functions, such as CORREL (correlate changes in compared variables), CHISQ.TEST (test how actual data compares to a random distribution), and FREQUENCY (used to analyze a series of values and group them in frequency ranges). So, whether you use basic statistical functions or perform fairly heavy-duty statistical analysis, the Excel statistical functions provide you with all the analysis functions you need. Figure 13-18 shows the COUNT, MAX, and MIN for a range of values.

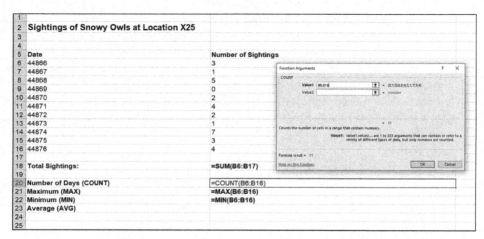

Figure 13-18   Many of the statistical functions calculate a result on a range of cells.

Note that when you use the Show Formulas command on the Formulas tab to see the formulas rather than the results, the dates are changed to numerical values. The syntax is pretty consistent for the relatively simple statistical functions, such as AVERAGE and MAX, and some of the more esoteric statistical analysis functions, such as MEDIAN (computes the median for a range of cells) and STDEV.P (calculates the standard deviation of a range of values). The syntax for the AVERAGE function follows:

```
=AVERAGE(cell range)
```

The AVERAGE, COUNT (Count Numbers), MAX, and MIN functions can be quickly inserted into a function using the menu provided by the AutoSum command on the Formulas tab and the AutoSum command on the Home tab. For example, to insert the AVERAGE function, select AutoSUM and then AVERAGE. Use the mouse to specify the range for the function to act on and then press Enter or click the Enter button on the formula bar.

TIP

You can access all the statistical functions by selecting the More Functions command and then pointing at statistical.

Lookup & Reference functions

The Lookup & Reference functions provide a number of different functions, including the following:

- HYPERLINK (enables you to specify a link to a local or remote file)

- TRANSPOSE (converts a vertical range to a horizontal range, or vice versa)

- LOOKUP functions (Historically, there have been two LOOKUP functions: VLOOKUP and HLOOKUP.)

VLOOKUP (which stands for vertical Lookup) is designed to do a vertical lookup from columns of information and returns a value from an array (which is just another word for a multicolumn lookup table) based on the search criterion. For example, you can create a four-column array that contains employees' last names in the first column, their first names in the second column, their departments in the third column, and the phone extension of each employee in the fourth column. It is this fourth column that serves as the information that VLOOKUP inserts into the worksheet. HLOOKUP (designed to lookup data in a horizontal table) is similar to VLOOKUP but operates in rows rather than columns, meaning the table array would be oriented in rows of information.

So, now that I've described VLOOKUP and HLOOKUP, I want to try and sell you on the newest LOOKUP function XLOOKUP, because I think it is easier to set up and easier to troubleshoot. XLOOKUP was introduced in October of 2019 as a replacement for VLOOKUP. XLOOKUP can also return values from a table of information, but it is much easier to set up, and because of the way the function works, it won't necessarily be disrupted when you add or remove rows and columns in your worksheet (which was definitely a potential danger with VLOOKUP). XLOOKUP can also be used for a horizontal lookup, which allows you to use the function when data is oriented horizontally. Let's take a closer look at how to use XLOOKUP.

XLOOKUP uses a lookup value that is contained in a lookup array that resides in a data table. Other corresponding data also resides in the table that contains the lookup array. It is this corresponding data that you want to copy to a new table using the XLOOKUP function. Let's look at a simple example of how you can use the XLOOKUP function.

CAUTION

When you set up your worksheet for XLOOKUP, **make sure that the lookup and return arrays are the same length. So, if the lookup array contains 20 records (rows), the return array must also have 20 rows. If these two columns are not equal in terms of cells in each column, the** XLOOKUP **function will return #VALUE! error message, which is a general error message letting you know that something is wrong with the way you set up the function and that it is not referencing cells correctly.**

Let's say you want to create a worksheet where you can type an employee name and have the employee's phone extension "appear" next to their name in an extension column. The XLOOKUP function is ideal for this situation, but first, we need to have a few things in place before XLOOKUP can do its magic. Place the XLOOKUP function in the Extension column of the sheet (directly to the right of the employee name column); the function (placed in the column to the right of the employee name column) then automatically looks up the phone extension based on the information in the employee name column. Figure 13-19 shows an XLOOKUP function that looks up the phone extension for each employee as his or her name is entered in the first column of the Function Results table. The lookup array containing the employee names is situated in column D to the right of the function results. The return array is in column F and contains the extension numbers for each of the employees.

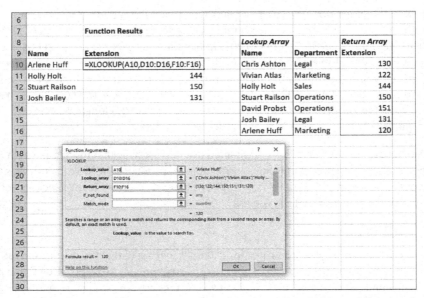

Figure 13-19 XLOOKUP can look up information in an array and insert it into a cell.

The syntax for XLOOKUP is as follows:

```
=XLOOKUP S(lookup_value, lookup_array, return_array, [if_not_found], [match_mode],
[search_mode])
```

Only the first three elements of the XLOOKUP function are required: the lookup value, the lookup array, and the return array. When you use the XLOOKUP function, it probably makes sense to create range names for the lookup array and the return array. Using range names prevents you from providing an erroneous range for either of the arrays, particularly in cases where you are using the function to comb through very large data tables. Also, keep in mind that the function can be used to lookup values that have numerical significance, such as sales figures, population studies—you name it. XLOOKUP has you covered.

If you look back at the syntax for XLOOKUP, you will find that there are also three optional elements of the function: [if_not_found], [match_mode], and [search_mode]. The [if_not_found] option allows you to specify text that will be entered when a valid match is not found by the XLOOKUP function. The [match_mode] option allows you to specify the type of match made by the function using a set of switches as follows:

- **0:** This is the default switch and requires an exact match. No match returns the text entry #N/A.

- **-1:** Requires an exact match, but if a match is not found, it returns the next smaller item (meaning you are working with values—numerical data).

- **1:** Requires an exact match, but if a match is not found, it returns the next larger item.

- **Wildcards:** You can use wildcard characters such as * and ? for your search.

You can also specify a search mode in the XLOOKUP function. This is another optional mode that allows you to search in a particular direction in a data table. The switches used for this option are as follows:

- **1:** This is the default switch for the search mode and begins the search, starting with the first item in the return array.

- **-1:** This switch can be used so that the search is reversed and begins with the last item in the return array.

- **2:** This switch performs a binary search (a binary search is designed to find a match in an ordered list) on a lookup array that has been sorted in ascending order.

- **-2:** This switch is the opposite of the 2 switch; it performs a binary search on an array that is sorted in descending order.

Although this is not an exhaustive study of XLOOKUP, I hope that you see some of this powerful function's possibilities for use in your Excel worksheets. If you are working with large data tables and/or data downloaded from a SQL or other database, I think you will find that XLOOKUP can help you pare down the data using the functions' capabilities, particularly the possibilities provided by the match ([match_mode]) and search ([search_mode]).

CAUTION

XLOOKUP is available to users who have access to a Microsoft 365 subscription. So, if you are using an earlier version of Office (such as Office 2019 or earlier) you don't have access to the function. Also, this means that if you do have a Microsoft 365 subscription and share an Excel workbook that uses XLOOKUP with someone who has an older version of Office, there is no backward compatibility, so it won't work for them. If backward compatibility is important to you, use VLOOKUP rather than XLOOKUP. The syntax for VLOOKUP is

```
=VLOOKUP(Lookup_value,Table_array,Col_index_num)
```

The Lookup_value is the cell that contains the information that the function uses to look up the information in the table array. So, the Table_array is the range or range name that specifies the table that contains the information. The Col_index_num tells VLOOKUP which of the columns in the Table_array should be placed in the cell that contains the VLOOKUP function.

CHAPTER 13

Date & Time functions

Excel views dates and times as values. Dates are based on the starting point of January 1, 1900. So, if you enter this date in a worksheet and then format the date as a general number, the value shown is 1.

Time is also perceived by Excel as a value. Times are seen as a fractional part of a day. For example, 12:00 p.m. is equivalent to 0.5, whereas 9:00 a.m. would be 0.375.

You don't typically have to convert dates or times to their actual value equivalents. The fact that dates and times are seen as numerical values means that you can include dates and times in your formulas and functions. Excel provides you with date and time functions that enable you to quickly place the date and/or time into your worksheet or to calculate values related to date or time entries. For example, the NETWORKDAYS function can return the number of workdays between two dates as long as you also supply the number of holidays that fall between the two dates. The NETWORKDAYS function uses the following syntax:

```
=NETWORKDAYS(Start_date, End_date, Holidays)
```

The start and end dates are the beginning and end dates for the time span. The holidays are also specific dates of when the holidays actually fall. The holidays (if there are more than one) can be entered as a range into the function. The NETWORKDAYS function is an excellent way to determine how many working days there are during a particular project cycle.

The date and time functions are accessed via the gallery provided by the Date & Time command on the Formulas tab. Two simple-to-use functions that place the current date into a worksheet are NOW and TODAY. NOW enters the current date and the time. The TODAY function enters the current date only.

These two functions are dynamic, so they change to the current date and/or time when you open the workbook. If you want a static date on a worksheet that serves as a timestamp of when you started the worksheet, enter the date and/or time manually.

Text functions

You might find it odd that Excel also provides a number of functions designed to work with cells containing text entries or labels. As we discussed at the outset of the Excel section of this book, Excel knows when you have entered text in cells, and it knows when you enter numbers—values—into cells. It automatically left-aligns text and right-aligns values because it knows which is which. The text functions provided by Excel enable you to split text entries in cells, combine text entries, manipulate the case of text, and convert numbers to text.

If you want to join text entries in two or more columns into a single column, you can take advantage of the CONCATENATE function. You can join the text from 255 different text strings into a single text string (in a single cell) using this function. The syntax for the CONCATENATE function is as follows:

```
= CONCATENATE (text1, text2, ... text255)
```

To insert cell addresses in the text boxes provided in the CONCATENATE function's Function Arguments dialog box, click in an argument box (such as Text1) and then click the cell you want to reference. Repeat this process, placing the text string cell addresses in subsequent argument boxes. As already mentioned, you can specify 255 cell addresses.

You can also type text in the argument boxes in the CONCATENATE function's Function Arguments dialog box. This enables you to add a text string to the text concatenated by the function that does not exist in a cell in the worksheet. This text must be placed between quotation marks. For example, if you are combining information, and you need to include a space between text strings (such as the combination of first and last names shown in Figure 13-20), you can insert a space (it must be surrounded by quotation marks) in a text box that is between the text entries that are combined (such as first and last names).

Other useful text functions relate to problems you might have with information that you import into Excel, such as imported text that contains extra spaces or unprintable characters. The TRIM function can be used to remove extra spaces. If you want to remove any unprintable characters from imported text, use the CLEAN function. The TRIM and CLEAN functions make a copy of the text contained in the cell or cell ranges specified in the function (TRIM or CLEAN). So, you end up with multiple copies of the text string in your worksheet (the before and after). You can't delete the original text with too many spaces (or in the case of the CLEAN function, the unprintable characters) because the function no longer has the original text to reference and provide you with the result.

You can convert the result of either the TRIM or CLEAN function to a value using Copy and Paste and then discard the original text that was imported. This leaves you with the trimmed or cleaned result.

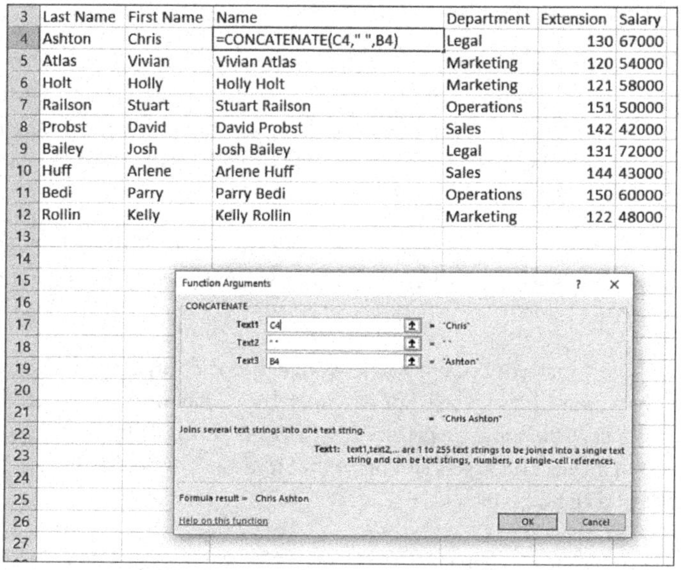

Figure 13-20   Use the CONCATENATE function to combine text strings.

Select the cell containing the TRIM or CLEAN function and then click Copy in the Clipboard group. Then select Paste. In the Paste gallery, select the Values option. Now when you select the cell or cells that originally contained the TRIM or CLEAN function, you find that the function has been converted to a text string. You can go ahead and delete the original, imported text.

TIP

Another easy way to join or concatenate text from multiple cells is to set up your own formula using the following syntax:

```
cell address&" "&cell address
```

The ampersand (&) serves as the operator in the formula.

Other function categories

Excel also contains other function categories than those we have discussed thus far. As already mentioned, nearly 500 functions are available in Excel. Many of the function categories relate to specific disciplines such as accounting, finance, statistical analysis, and engineering. When you select the More Functions command, several function categories are listed, such as Statistical, Engineering, and so on. We have already discussed the statistical functions. The list that follows provides a description of the other function categories found in the More Functions gallery:

- **Math & Trig:** This group provides a combination of useful mathematical and trigonometric functions. Functions such as COS (cosine), SIN (sine), and TAN (tangent) are used in computations related to a right-angled triangle. Another useful math function is ROUND, which enables you to specify the number of decimal places that a range of cell values should be rounded to. There are also the EVEN and ODD functions, which can be used to round values to even or odd numbers, respectively.

- **Engineering:** Excel provides a number of functions that are useful for engineering-related applications. For example, there is CONVERT, which converts measurements from one system to another (such as miles to kilometers). Another conversion function provided in this category is the BIN2HEX function, which can be used to convert binary numbers to hexadecimal.

- **Cube:** The cube functions are used to interact with external data that is derived from an analysis services cube. The data is served up from a Microsoft SQL Server that provides the analysis services.

- **Information:** These functions enable you to derive information concerning a cell, such as the content or formatting of a cell. For example, the ISERR function returns TRUE if an error exists in a cell (meaning an incorrectly designed formula or function) or FALSE if there is no error in a cell. ISBLANK is similar in that it returns either TRUE or FALSE based on whether or not a cell is blank.

- **Compatibility:** This category consists of functions that were native to earlier versions of Excel (many were native to Excel 2007) but have been replaced by new functions in the current version of Excel. You would use the compatibility functions only in cases where you share your workbooks with coworkers or colleagues who still use earlier versions of Excel, such as Excel 2007. You can determine the Excel version of a Compatibility function by reading the function description in the Insert Function dialog box.

Remember, you are not required to use every type of function provided by Excel. Make sure that you test functions that are new to you. Use sample data that enables you to easily determine whether you are getting the appropriate result when you plug the data into the function.

Proofing your formulas and functions

Just because a formula or function returns a value doesn't necessarily mean that it's correct. Making sure that your formulas and functions are providing the correct results in your worksheets is incredibly fundamental, though many Excel users assume that if Excel came up with that answer, it has to be right. Fortunately, Excel provides tools that can help you proof your formulas and functions.

There can be different causes for formulas or functions to return an incorrect value. For example, you might have made a syntax error in actually creating the formula or function. You might not have included the appropriate operators for a formula, or perhaps you did not provide a function's arguments in the correct order. This is why it makes sense to build functions using the Functions Argument dialog box rather than trying to type a function into a cell.

Errors can also result from incorrect cell references. You have the syntax for the formula or the function correct, but you did not reference the correct cells or range of cells.

Although Excel provides error messages when a formula or function cannot calculate a return because of an obvious reason, the error messages will not save you when a formula or function contains an error that still allows it to return an answer—albeit an incorrect answer.

Excel provides a number of different error messages that can help you proof a problem formula or function. Other tools, such as the ability to view formulas in the worksheet and the fact you can also trace the cells related to a particular problem formula or function, can also help you fix issues related to calculations.

Common error messages

Excel seems to have an endless supply of error messages, and it does have your back when a formula or function contains an egregious error. Excel flags the problem formula or function with a specific error message. Some of the most common error messages are provided in Table 13-3.

CHAPTER 13

Table 13-3   Common error messages

Error Message	Description
#REF	A cell referenced in the formula or function cannot be found. This can be the result of an incorrect range name or specifying a range that no longer exists.
#NAME?	Excel does not recognize text included in a formula or function, such as a range name. This can be a syntax error (an incorrectly spelled function name) or a problem with a range name specified in the function.
#DIV/0!	The formula or function is attempting to divide by 0. This is typically due to an incorrectly referenced cell in the formula or function (a cell that does not contain a value).
#VALUE	An incorrect argument is present in the formula or function. This can be caused by referring to both text and value entries in the same formula or function. You can't add words to numbers.

These errors can often be easily corrected by carefully examining your formula or function. In the case of the #NAME? function, check whether you have misspelled the function name or have missing parentheses in a function. The #DIV/0! error can occur if you have copied a formula or function and have not taken into account cell referencing in the formula or function. You might have to use an absolute reference so that the cell you are dividing by is always referenced in the formula or function.

When an error message appears in a cell, a smart tag is provided for the error. When you select the smart tag, the menu provided identifies the error type and also provides you with access to help on the error. Other options provided enable you to view the calculation steps for the formula or function, and there's an option to edit the function in the formula bar.

> **TIP**
>
> You can configure the Error Checking settings such as background error checking and the error-checking rules that are enabled in the Excel Options window. Select File and then click Options in the Backstage. Select Formulas to view the error-checking settings.

The Circular Reference Warning is an error message that you want to definitely pay attention to. When you attempt to create a formula or function that includes the formula or function within the range of cells that the formula or function acts on, you have a circular reference.

If you suspect that circular references are contained in workbooks that have been created by coworkers or colleagues, you can check them using the Circular References command in the Error Checking gallery. Any circular references in the worksheet are listed. The Circular References check is just one of the possibilities provided by the Formula Auditing command group found on the ribbon's Formulas tab. Let's look at some of the other tools.

Using the auditing tools

One of the easiest auditing tools to use is the Show Formulas command. It shows you all the formulas and functions in a worksheet rather than their results. This allows you to peruse your formulas and functions for any possible issues that need to be addressed but were not of a nature that resulted in an error message being placed in the cell where the formula or function resides.

Two other extremely useful formula-auditing commands are Trace Precedents and Trace Dependents. To display the cells that are referenced by a particular formula or function—the precedents—select a formula or function in the worksheet and then select the Trace Precedents command. Blue arrows are drawn from the precedents for the currently selected function or formula, as shown in Figure 13-21.

You can repeat the command as needed to view the precedents for other formulas or functions on the sheet simultaneously. When you want to remove the arrows from the worksheet, select the Remove Arrows command or one of its subcommands: Remove Precedent Arrows or Remove Dependent Arrows.

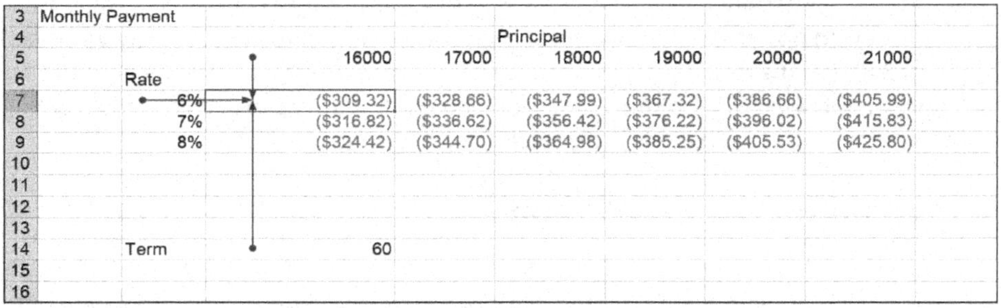

	Monthly Payment			Principal					
3	Monthly Payment								
4				Principal					
5			16000	17000	18000	19000	20000	21000	
6	Rate								
7	6%		($309.32)	($328.66)	($347.99)	($367.32)	($386.66)	($405.99)	
8	7%		($316.82)	($336.62)	($356.42)	($376.22)	($396.02)	($415.83)	
9	8%		($324.42)	($344.70)	($364.98)	($385.25)	($405.53)	($425.80)	
10									
11									
12									
13									
14	Term		60						
15									
16									

Figure 13-21   Trace precedents for a formula or function.

You can also trace the dependents for a particular value or range of cells. Select the cell or range of cells and then select the Trace Dependents command. Trace arrows are drawn from the cell or cell range to any formulas or functions that depend on that value or values.

When an error message is shown in a cell, you can use the Trace Error command to show the cells or cell range involved in the bad formula or function. Select the cell containing the error message, select the Error Checking drop-down arrow, and select Trace Error. The precedents for the cell are shown.

Another useful auditing command is the Error Checking command. It can be used when a cell contains an error message. The Error Checking command (in the Formula Auditing group) opens the Error Checking dialog box, as shown in Figure 13-22.

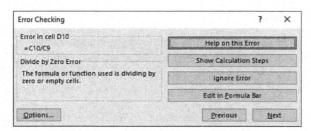

Figure 13-22   The Error Checking dialog box

The Error Checking dialog box enables you to access help in the Excel Help window related to the type of error present in the cell. It also enables you to show the calculation steps and evaluate the formula. When you select Show Calculation Steps, the Evaluate Formula dialog box opens. Select Evaluate to begin evaluating the formula or function. You can also step in and out on the different portions of the formula or function until you find the portion of the formula or function that is causing the error.

The Error Checking dialog box can also act as a sort of spell checker for errors. After you have dealt with one error in a worksheet, you can click Next in the Error Checking dialog box and proceed to the next error found in the sheet. After you have repaired that error (perhaps by viewing the calculation steps), you can then proceed to the next error and so on until you have dealt with any and all cells in the worksheet that contain errors.

Using the Watch Window

Although it is not an auditing tool per se, the Watch Window can be a useful tool in monitoring certain cells in a worksheet in terms of how the entering of worksheet data or the editing of worksheet data affects those cells. The Watch Window can be particularly useful in cases where you have formulas or functions that are dependent on cell addresses or ranges that span multiple worksheets in a workbook. For example, you might have a summary worksheet that summarizes data from other worksheets in the workbook that provide detailed information for each quarter of your fiscal year.

> ### TIP
>
> **You might want to name cells that you plan to watch in the Watch Window. A descriptive range name makes it easier to differentiate the multiple cell references that end up in the Watch Window. You can't enter a cell or cell range in the Watch Window by range name. Already named cells and ranges appear in the Name column.**

To open the Watch Window, select the Watch Window command in the Formula Auditing group. Figure 13-23 shows the Watch Window. The Watch Window floats on top of your worksheets and remains in view even when you switch worksheets in a workbook. In fact, the Watch Window is also visible even when you switch to a different Excel workbook. Therefore, the

Watch Window is also useful when you have cells in other workbooks that provide precedents to the cell that you have included in the Watch Window.

To add a cell to the Watch Window, navigate to the sheet that contains the cell or a cell range and then select Add Watch in the Watch Window. The Add Watch dialog box opens. Select the cell or cell range, and the reference is added to the Add Watch dialog box. When you click Add and return to the Watch Window, the cell reference is listed. It supplies the book, sheet, name, cell, and the current value of the cell as well as any formula or functions that reside in the cell. You can add additional cells to the Watch Window as needed.

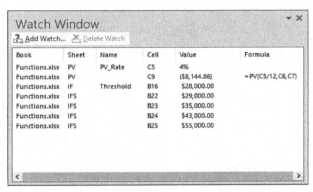

Figure 13-23   Keep an eye on specific workbook cells in the Watch Window.

Any changes you make to cells that are precedents for the cell or cells you are watching in the Watch Window are reflected in the Watch Window. For example, if you entered data on a worksheet for first-quarter sales and you are watching the yearly total SUM function on a summary sheet, the cell's value in the Watch Window reflects any data additions or changes.

To remove references from the Watch Window, select a listed reference and click the Delete Watch command. When you are finished using the Watch Window, click its Close button. Even if you close the Watch Window, it retains the list of cell addresses that you have added to it.

CHAPTER 13

Enhancing worksheets with charts

Understanding Excel charts   423

Creating charts   435

Modifying a chart   441

Working with chart elements   444

Creating a combination chart   454

There is little doubt that Excel's many tools and features allow you to create complex and meaningful worksheets that serve all sorts of purposes—from basic accounting to statistical analysis to complete mathematical mania. Excel has evolved far beyond the early spreadsheet programs that were first available for the personal computer. However, Excel still uses the same classic spreadsheet geography of columns and rows of numbers used by these earlier programs. All those cells containing values, labels, formulas, and functions can be quite difficult for many people to readily understand. Providing a way to visualize all that data in a worksheet is where Excel charts come in. Charts provide you with the ability to take a visual snapshot of worksheet data and represent it as a graphic. Charts can greatly enhance the understanding of worksheet data and how that data is related.

In this chapter, we look at how to create charts in Excel. We also discuss what type of charts to use in particular situations and how you can modify and manipulate charts and chart elements. Other chart types discussed include histogram and Pareto charts. We also look at sparklines and take advantage of the new Recommended Charts command, which helps you select an appropriate chart type to accompany your sheet data.

Understanding Excel charts

Excel charts provide a pictorial representation of worksheet data. Charts not only provide a way for people to better grasp trends or relationships in the worksheet data, but they can also add visual impact to your Excel worksheets. Charts are objects (just like a photo or a SmartArt graphic) that can be included anywhere on a worksheet. Charts can also be created on their own worksheet in a workbook. This is particularly useful for charts that contain a lot of detail and don't fit particularly well on a large worksheet that already contains all the data used to create the chart.

Chart terminology

Working with charts is pretty straightforward. It does not hurt, however, to have a handle on some of the terminology you will run across when creating charts; a list of basic chart terms follows:

- **Chart area:** The area inside the object frame that contains the chart, the axes, data point labels, legend, chart title, and other chart elements.

- **Plot area:** The area of the chart between the chart axes. This is where the data points are plotted.

- **Data series:** Related data points are referred to as a data series. Typically, a data series corresponds to a particular row or column of values in your worksheet (depending on how you have arranged your data in the worksheet). Each data series in a chart has its own pattern or color. Single-line charts or pie charts are examples of charts that have only one data series. In bar charts, particularly in cases where you are comparing entities over time (such as the performance of sales regions over time), multiple data series are present on the chart (one series for each region).

- **Categories:** Categories reflect the number of elements in a series. For example, on a chart that charts regional sales totals, the x-axis consists of the names of the regions, which are the categories for the chart.

- **Axis:** A two-dimensional chart, such as a line chart, has an x-axis (horizontal) and a y-axis (vertical). The x-axis contains the data series and categories in the chart. If you have more than one category, the x-axis often contains labels that define what each category represents. The y-axis reflects the values of the bars, lines, or plot points. In a three-dimensional chart, the z-axis represents the vertical plane, and the x-axis (distance) and y-axis (width) represent the two sides on the floor of the chart.

- **Legend:** The legend provides the key for how color-coding or patterns have been used to differentiate the different elements in a data series on the chart. For example, a pie chart uses a different color to show the various categories that appear as parts of the pie.

- **Data labels:** Labels that appear on the chart denoting the value of the data points used to create the chart.

- **Gridlines:** Gridlines help visualize the value of a particular data point on the chart. Gridlines are typically used along the y-axis (where the value data points originate), but you can also include gridlines for the x-axis, which can be useful in situations where you have created a combination chart.

- **Background:** The background consists of the space behind and below the chart area. For example, the chart wall is the area directly behind the plot area and any gridlines shown on the chart. The chart floor is the bottommost part of the chart area.

Figure 14-1 shows a line chart embedded in a worksheet. This line chart contains one data series: the measured lake level for each month of the year. The x-axis consists of the labels associated with the data points: in this case, the months of the year, January through December. The y-axis consists of the scale for the values represented by the chart: in this case, a scale in feet. The x-axis lists the categories for the chart—each month is a specific category.

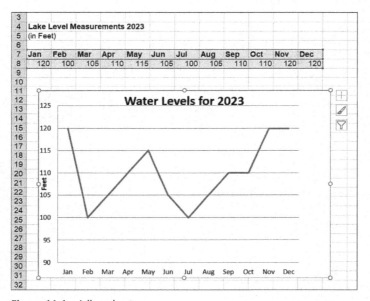

Figure 14-1   A line chart

Notice that when a chart is selected in a worksheet (as it is in Figure 14-1), the contextual Chart Tools appear on the ribbon and consist of Chart Design and Format tabs. We will explore the specific commands and tools provided by the Chart Tools as the chapter progresses.

Charts can also be created that have multiple data series. Figure 14-2 shows a bar chart that has four data series—one data series for each of the sales region's monthly totals. The chart in Figure 14-2 also includes a legend that shows the color coding for the different data series (each region's sales) displayed on the chart.

You can build combination charts in Excel so that you can visualize the data series in a worksheet in a unique way that enables you to emphasize or differentiate the various sets of data points. Figure 14-3 shows a combination chart that includes both a line chart and a column chart.

CHAPTER 14

The columns in the chart in Figure 14-3 show the sales for four regions—East, West, South, and North—over a three-month period (January through March). Total sales are also included in the chart and have been formatted as a line chart that shows the growth of overall sales during the three-month period. Using a combination chart enables you to emphasize more than one set of data points by combining two different chart types.

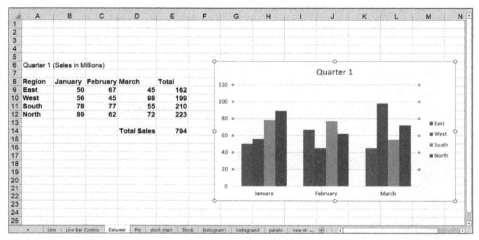

Figure 14-2   A column chart with multiple data series

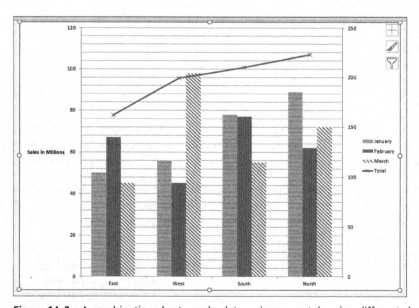

Figure 14-3   A combination chart graphs data series separately using different chart types.

Using different chart types

Excel provides you with many different chart types. It is important that you develop an understanding of the purpose of each chart type and then use the appropriate chart type when charting your data. Using a chart type that isn't designed for your purpose doesn't really enhance anyone's understanding of the worksheet data and might actually misrepresent what is going on with the data.

For example, a line chart would do an excellent job of showing the change over time of the sales figures for a particular product or company. However, place that same data in a bar chart, and the changes are less obvious. Finally, throw that same data into a pie chart, which is completely wrong for showing change over time, and suddenly, the sales figures (even poor sales figures) look relatively the same. This is not to say that people deliberately choose the wrong chart type to hide the true nature of worksheet data and any associated trends. However, because Excel offers so many different (and flashy) chart types, it is possible to inadvertently select the wrong type of chart for a particular situation. Let's look at several commonly used chart types that Excel provides.

Column chart/bar chart

The column/bar chart is probably one of the most commonly used business chart types. These types of charts work very well in showing how different data series or groups of data points compare. Figure 14-4 shows a bar chart that displays the total sales for each salesperson listed in the worksheet.

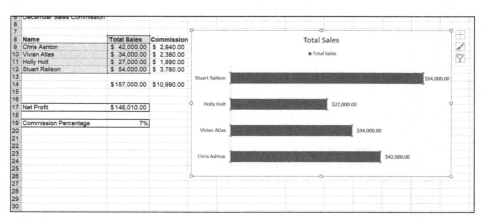

Figure 14-4   A bar chart comparing total sales

Column and bar charts make it relatively easy to quickly discern the highs and lows in terms of the data points charted. Column or bar charts are often used to show the relative success of salespeople or franchise locations or can even be used to compare the number of goals made during a season by a group of individual hockey players. If you have totals you want to compare, column and bar charts are the route to go. Obviously, the tallest column in a column chart shows the highest data point; in a bar chart, it is the longest horizontal bar.

Line chart

Line charts are perfect for showing change over time. Line charts are straightforward two-axis charts, with numerical values plotted on the y-axis in relation to labels provided on the x-axis that describe what is actually being measured. Line charts are often used to depict business growth or business decline.

For example, you might plot the monthly profits of your small company over the past 12 months. The y-axis consists of the net profits for each month, and the x-axis consists of the months of the year, January through December. Line charts work very well when you want to discern the highs and lows in productivity or value. Line charts are not particularly good if you want to compare the relative success of one data series against another data series. Figure 14-5 shows a line chart that provides a separate line for each region's sales data points from January, February, and March.

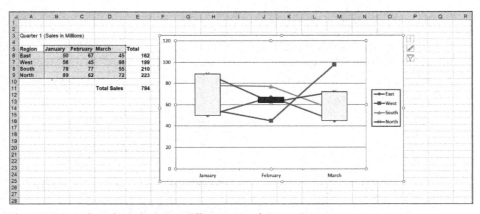

Figure 14-5   A line chart depicting different sets of data points

Although the line chart makes it easy to track the changes over time for each of the regions in terms of their sales figures for the January through March timeframe, the lines do not provide a good way to compare the overall performance of each region. This is accomplished better by using a column/bar chart.

Pie chart

Pie charts enable you to show how the various parts relate to the whole. For example, you might be trying to keep track of your monthly expenses. A pie chart would enable you to visually represent the relative size of each of your monthly expenses as compared with your total expenses.

Pie charts are great for showing how costs, sales, or other data series for a group of categories relate to each other. Figure 14-6 shows a pie chart that has a single data series: the individual values for the total sales for different regions.

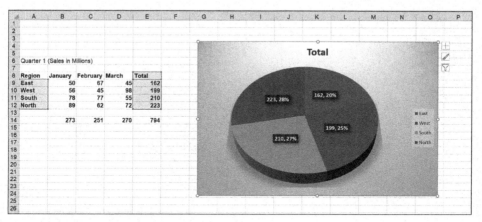

Figure 14-6   Pie charts show how the parts relate to the whole.

Pie charts can support only one data series and differ from other chart types, such as bar charts and line charts, which can show multiple data series on the same chart. If you need to show multiple data series in a pie chart–like format, you can use a doughnut chart.

In the case of the pie chart shown in Figure 14-6, it is clear that the South (the light green pie piece on the lower left) realized the most sales when compared to the other "sales" regions (West has the second-highest sales total, followed by North and East). Pie charts showing percentages make it even easier to determine the percentage of a particular item plotted on the chart in reference to the whole (meaning 100% of sales).

Area chart

Area charts enable you to show trends using cumulative totals over time. These types of charts emphasize the general direction of the data series up or down and show the magnitude of change. Area charts are somewhat similar to line charts; however, area charts show not only trends over time but can also show how data series shown in the chart relate to the whole and each other. This enables you to view trends related to each data series and to compare data series. Figure 14-7 shows an area chart that tracks sales from different regions over 12 months of the year (January through December).

The chart uses the 3D area chart type, which uses three axes—x, y, and z—to provide the vertical, horizontal, and depth aspects for the chart. The 3D area chart shows the trends for the sales in each region and provides for a comparison of the regions. The 3D layout, however, can be problematic if you have a set of data points that have much smaller or larger values than the other data sets depicted in the chart. If this is the case, it makes sense to go with a line chart that depicts each data series using a separate line rather than trying to use the area chart.

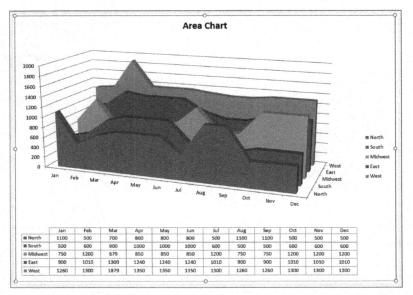

	Jan	Feb	Mar	Apr	May	Jun	Jul	Aug	Sep	Oct	Nov	Dec
North	1100	500	700	800	800	800	500	1100	1100	500	500	500
South	500	600	900	1000	1000	1000	600	500	500	600	600	600
Midwest	750	1200	679	850	850	850	1200	750	750	1200	1200	1200
East	900	1010	1300	1240	1240	1240	1010	900	900	1010	1010	1010
West	1260	1300	1879	1350	1350	1350	1300	1260	1260	1300	1300	1300

Figure 14-7   Area charts show trends and enable a comparison of data points.

X Y (scatter) chart

Scatter charts enable you to determine whether the data points in a series fall on the chart in a pattern called a cluster. Scatter charts are used to see whether there is a correlation between values. One set of values is plotted on the x-axis, and the other set of values is plotted along the y-axis. Figure 14-8 shows a scatter chart.

The scatter chart in Figure 14-8 plots the owl count against the temperature taken each day the count was conducted. Let's say you want to see whether there is a correlation between owl activity and temperature. You could plot the daily count versus the daily temperature, as shown in this chart.

Because scatter charts are meant to determine the correlation between two different sets of values, you typically need a large number of data points to get a discernable pattern on the chart. Remember that both the x-axis and y-axis on a scatter chart consist of values. If you have a situation where only one set of data is values, you will use a line chart rather than a scatter chart.

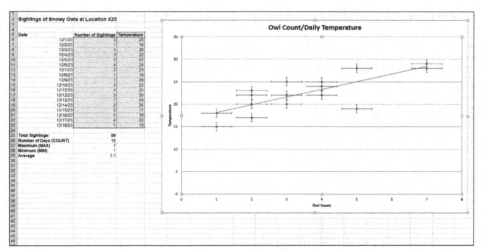

Figure 14-8   Scatter charts enable you to see the relationship between associated data series.

Stock chart

Stock charts (also known as box plots, box and whiskers plots, and candlestick plots) are particularly useful when you are tracking a particular stock that is in your stock portfolio or that you are considering making part of your portfolio. Stock charts can be created using three different data series, four different data series, or five different data series—all of which are related to the price of the stock. For example, the three-data-series stock chart uses the daily high, low, and close value of the stock. The four-data-series stock chart uses the open, high, low, and close price for the stock.

Figure 14-9 shows a stock chart tracking Microsoft stock in June of 2021. Stock charts not only show you the range of a stock's price on a particular day, but the chart can also show trends over the timeframe that you have charted. The trendline added to the Stock Chart is based on the daily closing price.

> ### NOTE
>
> Finding stock information—such as the daily open, high, low, and close values of a particular stock—on the web is pretty easy. You can get it directly from Bing or use sites such as the MSN Money Central website, Yahoo Finance, or Google Finance.

> ### NOTE
>
> Scatter charts use Cartesian coordinates (two different sets of values) to create the points that appear in the chart plane. René Descartes (yes, Descartes, the philosopher and mathematician) came up with the Cartesian coordinate system in the seventeenth century. Remember this the next time you get a Descartes question during trivia night.

The stock chart can be used for data types other than stock prices. You can use it in any situation where you have a particular data point that fluctuates during a specific time frame. For example, you might want to chart data related to the daily change in water temperature of a vernal pool that you are using for a salamander population study.

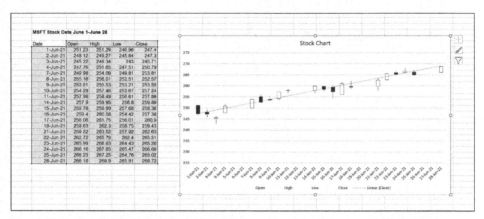

Figure 14-9   Stock charts provide trends while tracking multiple fluctuating data points.

Other chart types

We have already looked at the stock chart provided in the Other Charts command's drop-down gallery. Four other chart types are provided in this gallery. The list that follows provides a brief description of each chart type:

- **Surface chart:** This type of chart is designed to group related values by color or pattern. A 3D surface chart looks a lot like a relief or topographic map and can be used to determine how one variable can be affected by two other variables. Surface charts are created using an x-axis data series, a y-axis data series, and a z-axis data series. There must also be a z-axis value for each x-axis and y-axis pair. So, basically, the surface chart shows how the z-axis data is affected by two variables: the x-axis data and the y-axis data.

- **Doughnut chart:** This chart type is actually considered a type of pie chart and is designed to show how the parts compare with the whole, much like a pie chart. A doughnut chart, however, can include more than one data series, which a pie chart cannot. You can use a doughnut to compare the sales of different regions over a specific timeframe or show your monthly expenses for more than one month for comparison.

- **Bubble chart:** This chart type is similar to a scatter chart and is found in the Pie & Scatter chart category. It does differ from a scatter chart in that a scatter chart can use only two sets of variables (one for the x-axis and one for the y-axis); a bubble chart can work with three sets of values. The third value set determines the size of the bubbles. Thus, the bubble chart shows related x and y data in clusters and shows the relative value of each z-axis data point as a gradation of bubble sizes.

- **Radar chart:** This chart type can plot multiple data sets. The values from each category are plotted along a separate axis line that radiates out from the chart's center point. The scale for each data set to be included on the chart must be the same. Radar charts can be used to show business performance measurements or compare safety features on different automobiles. These charts work best with a limited number of categories so that each data set is discernable on the chart.

TIP

This discussion of charts focuses on the default chart types (and variants) provided by Excel. The Excel Analysis Toolpak provides you with additional chart types and data analysis tools, so it makes sense for you (or your IT support) to install the Toolpak. If you add the Developer tab to your ribbon (using the Excel Options window), you can quickly add or remove Excel Add-ins via the commands shown in the Add-ins group.

Before we end this overview of Excel chart types, let's take a look at a couple other chart types that you may not be aware of and that will give you some additional possibilities as far as your chart repertoire goes. Additional charts that you might find very useful are the histogram, Pareto, waterfall, and sunburst charts.

Histogram charts look like a bar chart but are actually designed to show the distribution of data where the chart's horizontal axes are data ranges—known as bins—you define for the chart. By default, Excel creates a histogram chart from a column of data that uses three bins with the bin ranges determined by Excel based on the data range you selected for the chart (this would be based on a column of data that provides a range of values). Figure 14-10 shows a histogram that summarizes a column of greenhouse gas emissions data from the Maine Department of Environmental Protection. The number of bins for the chart was configured using the Format Axis pane options.

A Pareto chart, which is kind of a histogram on steroids (named after Vilfredo Pareto, a nineteenth-century philosopher and economist—definitely another answer for trivia night)—is a compound chart that summarizes data in a bar chart by the frequency of occurrence (of a particular variable). The chart will go from high-occurrence to low-occurrence from left to right. This ranking of individual components in a process allows you to determine inefficiency. For example, you might have a manufacturing setting where you have listed how much time the items you are manufacturing spend at a particular point in the process. Let's say that you make a complex item that needs gaskets inserted, some soldering, and a couple of other steps; a Pareto chart could be used to visualize points in the process that are not that efficient and could benefit from new manufacturing equipment or additional staff.

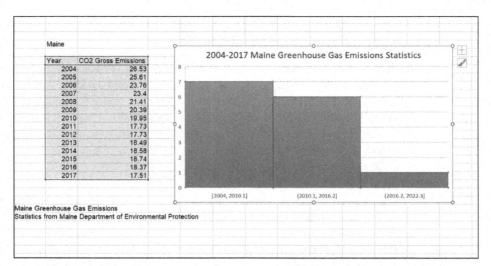

Figure 14-10   A histogram chart

A waterfall chart is designed to help you visualize how a value changes over time. The change to the value can be positive or negative. Waterfall charts work very well for visualizing home budgets (think about how your net income goes up and down over time because of fluctuating expenses. Waterfall charts also work well for tracking net profit for a small business or net gain from a particular investment.

Sunburst charts can be used to graph hierarchical data in Excel. Hierarchical data is ranked data, meaning the data falls into a series where each data point is ranked in terms of its relative value to the other data points in the hierarchy. For example, when you are looking at your monthly bills, the individual items in the group can be arranged from low to high or high to low (in terms of the amount of each bill). Your monthly bills can also be placed into groups or subsets based on the type of service or item related to the bill. For example, we all pay different bills that can be grouped as utilities, insurance, or food. Hierarchical data sets that have natural groupings are perfect for creating sunburst charts. The sunburst chart shown in Figure 14-11 visualizes data from a home video library.

The sunburst chart in Figure 14-11 is built from data that includes the film name, genre, sub-genre, and the rating of each film (on a scale of 1 to 10). Each film is represented by a "ray" in the sunburst. Each film's rating is reflected in the thickness of the ray. The film title is shown on the innermost part of the ray and is followed (outward) by the genre and subgenre of the film.

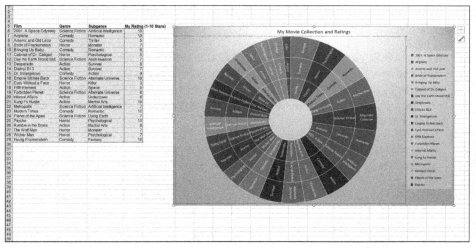

Figure 14-11   A sunburst chart

Although each chart type has a specific purpose and requires that the appropriate data be supplied in your Excel worksheet, creating charts in Excel is straightforward. (In fact, Excel can help you choose the correct chart type.) After you have created a particular chart type, the commands and tools available for changing the design and formatting of the chart and chart elements are a consistent proposition, no matter what chart type you have created. Let's look at how to create a chart and then look at the options Excel provides for modifying the chart and chart elements.

TIP

The sunburst chart is not the only Excel chart that can help you visualize hierarchical data. There is also the treemap chart, which represents your data in boxes and rectangles. The Relative width of the box that represents each item in the chart is related to whatever numerical value you have assigned to a particular data point.

Creating charts

Charts reflect the data in a worksheet, so you need to make sure the values and labels in the worksheet provide the information in a way that makes it relatively easy to create a chart. You should arrange the worksheet data in a consistent manner, either horizontally in rows or vertically in columns. Also, avoid empty cells, rows, or columns within the areas of the worksheet that serve as the data series for your chart or charts.

Although a chart is based on the values in your worksheet, your sheet labels provide the categories and information used as axes titles and legend information. It makes sense to make row

CHAPTER 14

and column headings (your labels) very descriptive yet short enough to fit well on the chart as chart elements.

When building a worksheet that includes a chart, place the data on the sheet so that the sheet can also easily accommodate an inserted chart below or to the right of the data range. This enables you to easily view or print the worksheet data and the accompanying chart. Charts with a large amount of detail and those derived from large worksheets would probably best be created on their own worksheet.

Excel provides you with different ways to insert a chart into a worksheet as an object. You can also choose to move a chart from the sheet containing the data to its own sheet. Let's take a look at how you insert a chart into a sheet and then look at two new features for creating a chart: recommended charts and the Quick Analysis gallery.

Inserting a chart from the ribbon

Inserting a new chart into the current sheet is a two-step process: Specify the data you want to chart and then select the chart type to insert. Therefore, select the range to be charted. If you are not selecting a contiguous range for the chart, select the first range of cells to be included in the chart and then hold down the Ctrl key to select other cells or ranges for the chart.

TIP

ScreenTips can be accessed for any of the chart types that are provided by the chart type command's gallery. These ScreenTips provide a brief explanation of the chart type.

To choose the chart type, switch to the ribbon's Insert tab. The Charts group provides commands for specific chart types, including Insert Column Chart, Insert Line Chart, and Insert Pie or Doughnut Chart. Select the drop-down arrow to the right of any of these chart commands to select a chart subtype. For example, when you select the Insert Pie or Doughnut Chart command, you can select from three different subtypes: 2D Pie, 3D Pie, and Doughnut. After you make a selection, the chart is inserted into the current sheet.

If you like to be able to peruse all the chart types (in a list) before inserting a chart, you can open the Insert Chart dialog box from any of the chart type commands (you can also click the dialog box launcher at the bottom of the Charts group to open the Insert Chart dialog box). In the case of the Insert Pie or Doughnut Chart gallery, select More Pie Charts. The Insert Chart dialog box (shown in Figure 14-12) provides a list of all the chart types and also provides a gallery of subtypes for the current chart type (in Figure 14-12, it's a pie chart and its subtypes). After selecting a chart type and/or subtype in the Insert Chart dialog box, click OK to insert the chart.

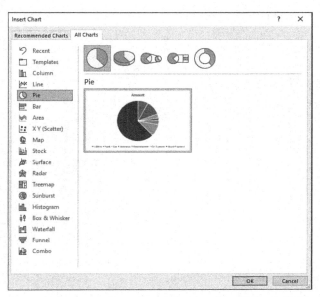

Figure 14-12   The Insert Chart dialog box lists all the available chart types.

Selecting a recommended chart

The Recommended Charts feature helps you determine the best chart type for your data, and it can be particularly useful in situations where you aren't quite sure what type of chart would best represent the data in the sheet.

To view recommended charts for your data, select the cell range for the chart and then navigate to the Insert tab. Select the Recommended Charts command in the Charts group. The Insert Chart dialog box opens with the Recommended Charts tab selected, as shown in Figure 14-13.

The recommended charts for your data are listed on the left of the Recommended Charts tab. To see a preview of a particular chart type, select the chart thumbnail. The chart preview also provides a definition of each recommended chart type under the chart preview (on the right of the Recommended Charts tab). To insert one of the recommended charts, select the chart thumbnail and then click OK.

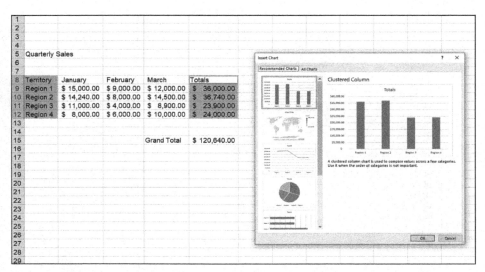

Figure 14-13   Excel provides you with a list of recommended charts for your sheet data.

Inserting charts with the Quick Analysis gallery

Another option for inserting a chart into your worksheet is the Quick Analysis gallery. The Quick Analysis gallery provides quick access to conditional formatting settings, charts, statistical functions, table settings, and even sparklines. Think of the Quick Analysis gallery as a way to quickly access different analysis features from one location (the Quick Analysis gallery), negating the need to switch to the ribbon's Home tab, Insert tab, or Formulas tab—you get the picture; the Quick Analysis gallery is quick.

To insert a chart using the Quick Analysis gallery, select the cell range for the chart. The Quick Analysis button appears at the very bottom right of the selected range. Click the button, and the gallery opens; select Charts to view the Quick Analysis charting options. Figure 14-14 shows selected data and the Charts options provided in the Quick Analysis gallery.

The Quick Analysis gallery provides recommended charts for the selected data range. You can select one of the options provided to insert that chart type. If you want to access the Recommended Charts tab of the Insert Chart dialog box, select the More Charts option. The Recommended Charts tab provides the same chart type options that are available in the Quick Analysis gallery. However, the Recommended Charts tab does allow you to preview each of the recommended chart types before inserting one of them into the sheet. Whether you select one of the recommended charts from the Quick Analysis gallery or the Recommended Charts tab of the Insert Chart dialog box, your chart still ends up as an object on the current worksheet.

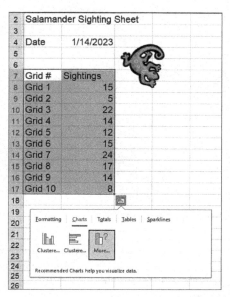

Figure 14-14 The Quick Analysis gallery provides recommended chart types.

Tools for quickly customizing a chart

The chart is selected when you insert a new chart into the current sheet. Three very useful tools that allow you to quickly customize the chart are available next to the chart's right border: Chart Elements, Chart Styles, and Chart Filters. Here is what they do:

- **Chart Elements:** Click the Chart Elements button to open the Chart Elements list. This list (which appears on the left side of the chart) allows you to select or deselect the chart elements to be shown in the current chart. The chart elements listed depend on the type of chart (and chart subtype) you selected when you inserted the chart.

- **Chart Styles:** Click the Chart Styles button to open a Chart Styles gallery for the current chart type. The Chart Styles gallery provides you with a number of different chart styles, as shown in Figure 14-15. Select a particular style to see how it affects the chart. You can also select from a number of color schemes by selecting Color in the Chart Styles gallery.

- **Chart Filters:** Click the Chart Filters button if you want to filter the chart in place. The Filters gallery provides you with a list of the data series and categories in the current chart. You can select a particular series or category to view the portion of the chart that relates to that data. You can also deselect series or categories to see how this changes the chart when that series or category is removed. When you have finished filtering the data, you can reselect all the series and categories and then click Apply to put the chart back into its original condition.

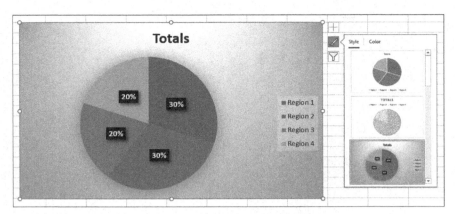

Figure 14-15   Quickly select from a list of chart styles and colors.

When you have finished working with one of the quick format tools, you can switch to one of the other tools (for example, from the Chart Styles gallery to the Chart Filters feature) by selecting a different tool button. If you want to shut down the gallery for one of the tools, reselect the tool button. If you have finished manipulating the chart using these tools and want to return to the sheet, click outside the chart to deselect it.

Moving, copying, or deleting a chart

When a chart is selected in a sheet, the Chart Tools are available on the ribbon. If you want to move the chart to its own chart sheet (rather than as an object in the current worksheet), select the Move Chart command on the Chart Tools, Design tab (the last command on the right). When you select the Move Chart command, the Move Chart dialog box opens.

You can move the chart to a new sheet by clicking the New Sheet option button in the Move Chart dialog box. You can also specify the name for the new sheet by typing the name in the text box to the right of the New Sheet option button. The Move Chart dialog box also provides an Object In option button. You can use this option to move the selected chart to any of the other sheets in your current Excel workbook.

Select the Object In drop-down menu and then select the worksheet that will be home to the chart object. When you are ready to move the chart (to a new sheet or a different worksheet), click OK.

Chart objects (on a sheet) can be treated like any other object you place on an Excel worksheet, such as a picture, stock image, or SmartArt graphic. You can use Copy and Paste to make copies of the chart and Cut and Paste to move the chart. You can also remove unwanted charts. To remove an embedded chart in a worksheet, select the chart and then press the Delete key. If you want to delete a chart that is on its own sheet (a chart sheet), right-click the worksheet's name tab and then select Delete. The sheet is removed from the workbook.

CAUTION

When you delete a chart object on a worksheet, you can use Undo to get it back. When you delete a chart sheet in a workbook, Undo does not bring back the deleted sheet.

Modifying a chart

After you have the chart embedded on the current worksheet (along with the worksheet data the chart uses) or have added a chart to its own new sheet, you can modify the chart's design, layout, and format. Select the chart, and the Chart Tools become available on the ribbon.

The Chart Tools are divided between two Chart tabs: Chart Design and Format. The Chart Design tab provides commands that enable you to manipulate the various chart elements (such as the chart title, data labels, and trendlines) and change the chart layout or colors. The Chart Styles gallery on the Chart Design tab allows you to select from a number of chart styles for the current chart type. Other commands provided on this tab include the Switch Row/Column and Change Chart Type commands. The Design tab also provides the Move Chart command, which allows you to move an embedded chart to its own sheet or any other sheet in the workbook.

The (Chart) Format tab provides the command groups that you would find for modifying other graphic object types, such as text boxes or pictures. These groups include the Insert Shapes, Shape Styles, and the WordArt Styles groups. The Arrange group provides commands for arranging objects on the sheet (remember that a chart is just another object type).

There is also a Size group on the far right of the Format tab that you can use to change the height and width of the chart. If you go all the way down to the other end of the Format tab, the Current Selection group (on the far left) provides you with the ability to select a particular chart area and then apply the various formatting commands available to that area (such as the whole chart, the chart title, or a particular data series).

➤ **For an overview on working with and formatting objects such as images and SmartArt graphics in the Office applications, see Chapter 4, "Using and creating graphics."**

In terms of modifying a chart (rather than just another object on a sheet), you will probably spend more time fine-tuning the chart elements and chart display using the commands on the Chart Tools, Design tab. Let's take a look at how some of these commands are actually applied to a chart.

Changing chart type or chart data

As already discussed, the Chart Tools, Design tab enables you to modify the chart type, manipulate the data used by the chart, and select a layout or style for the chart. If you find that you have created a chart that doesn't provide a proper picture of the data you selected to include in the chart, you might want to rethink the chart type you have selected. You might also need to change how the chart is looking at your data (in rows instead of columns), or you might even need to change the data selection the chart is using.

Changing the chart type doesn't mean that you necessarily have to switch to a completely different chart type, such as a line to bar. Instead, you can fine-tune the chart type you have currently selected by going with a different chart subtype. For example, you might be using the 3D pie chart type but want to switch to the exploded pie in 3D to better differentiate the parts of the pie.

To change the chart type, select the Change Chart Type command in the Type group. The Change Chart Type dialog box opens. This dialog box is the same as the Insert Chart dialog box. Select a chart type and/or subtype as needed to change the chart type of the currently selected chart. To apply the change in type or subtype, click OK.

Another command that can be useful in cases where a chart doesn't look quite right is the Switch Row/Column command. This command can be used in cases where the chart has based the x-axis or y-axis on column data rather than row data, and you want to swap the data on the x-axis with the y-axis, or vice versa.

This command can also be used to manipulate a single axis, such as the x-axis, when you have labels at the top of your data columns and labels for each data row. A bar chart, by default, charts the column labels along the x-axis. However, if you want the x-axis to show you data related to the row columns, such as the names of your salespeople or regions or the fruits and vegetables that you ate last week, you can use the Switch Rows/Columns command to switch the label data shown on the x-axis and the legend.

In cases where you have selected an incomplete or incorrect data range for a chart, you can modify the data selection used by the chart using the Select Data command. Click the Select Data command, and the Select Data Source dialog box opens, as shown in Figure 14-16.

TIP

Right-click a chart and then select Change Chart Type to open the Change Chart Type dialog box.

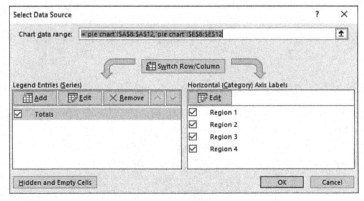

Figure 14-16   The Select Data Source dialog box.

To change the data range for the chart, select the current data range in the Chart Data Range text box and then use the Shrink button to access the worksheet data. Select the range to be used by the chart and return to the dialog box.

You can also use the Switch Row/Column button in the Select Data Source dialog box to swap the series or axis data. Using the Switch Row/Column command in the Select Data Source dialog box might make more sense to you because you see how the series and axis labels are swapped rather than how the chart itself is changed. You can add entries, such as legend entries, to the Select Data Source dialog box. You can also edit and remove labels as needed.

The Select Data Source dialog box also makes it easy to deal with hidden or empty cells that fall within the data range being used by the chart. Click the Hidden And Empty Cells button to open the Hidden And Empty Cells Settings dialog box. By default, empty cells are shown as gaps in the chart. You can also choose to have empty cells shown as zero or have the chart connect data points with a line so that gaps are effectively ignored. As for hidden rows or columns that fall into the chart data source range, you can choose to ignore the hidden data or click the Show Data In Hidden Rows And Columns option button to include this data in the chart. When you finish working in the Hidden and Empty Cell Settings dialog box, click OK to return to the Select Data Source dialog box. To close the Select Data Source dialog box and return to the chart, click OK.

Selecting chart layouts and styles

Each chart type has a number of different chart layouts available. A chart layout provides specific chart elements, such as title, legend, and data labels. You can use a chart layout (also referred to as a *quick layout*) to quickly add needed chart elements to a chart, and then you can further modify the layout as necessary.

The various layouts for the currently selected chart can be accessed for a specific chart type by using the Quick Layout button, which is located on the Design tab's Chart Layouts group. Figure 14-17 shows the Quick Layout gallery for a pie chart.

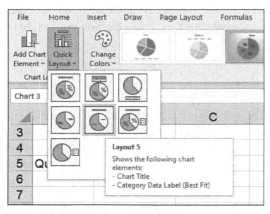

Figure 14-17   The Quick Layout gallery

You have to select a layout based on the thumbnail provided. Place the mouse on a layout thumbnail, and it is previewed on the chart. The layouts differ in the chart elements that they provide, such as the legend and axis titles, and in the position of these elements on the chart. Some layouts also provide data labels and data tables; data tables are particularly useful when you place a chart on its own sheet. Because the data for the chart is in the data table, you don't have to switch back and forth between the chart sheet and the sheet where the data is held.

You can also control chart elements using the Add Chart Element command. This command provides a list of elements supported by the current chart type. You can add or remove elements and specify where a chart element should appear on the chart.

You can also modify the chart using one of the chart styles provided in the Chart Styles gallery. Figure 14-18 shows the Chart Styles gallery and the chart styles available for a bar chart. These styles affect the data series and the background of the chart (such as the back wall, floor, and so on). Color schemes for a particular style can be controlled using the Change Colors command (also in the Chart Styles group).

Figure 14-18   The Chart Styles gallery

When working with the Change Colors gallery, you can select one of the multicolor color schemes for your chart, or you can select from a large number of monochromatic color schemes. Monochromatic color schemes, particularly the grayscale schemes, can be used to make the chart information more readable on a printout. The grayscale color schemes, obviously, serve you well if you are going to print a chart on a grayscale printer such as a laser printer.

TIP

Remember that you can select any chart element, including data points, data series, and the chart title or legend, using the selection drop-down menu in the Current Selection group on the Chart Tools, Format tab.

Working with chart elements

Although we think of a chart as a single object, it is actually made up of a number of different elements, and many of these elements can be manipulated individually. Elements on a chart that contain text, such as the chart title and axes titles, can be moved, sized, and formatted in place. We discussed the Quick Layout gallery in the previous section and how it provides different chart layouts. Each layout can include a different mix of chart elements and arrangements in the chart frame.

You can select a chart element (including the chart area) using the Current Selection group's drop-down menu. The Current Selection group is on the far left of the Chart Tools, Format tab. The Current Selection group also provides the Format Selection command. This command opens the Format task pane for the currently selected chart element. For example, if you select Legend in the Current Selection drop-down menu, the Format Legend task pane opens when you select the Format Selection command.

Individual chart elements are manipulated using the Add Chart Element command on the Chart Tools, Design tab. Adding and removing chart elements from a chart can also be accomplished using the Chart Elements button (the Plus symbol button) immediately to the right of a selected chart. Figure 14-19 shows the Add Chart Element gallery and the Chart Elements quick access pane.

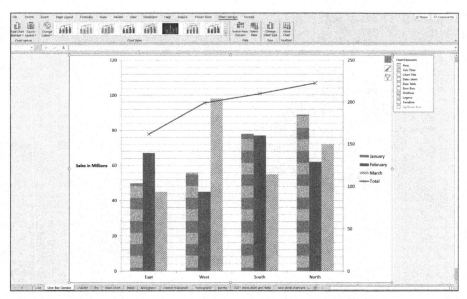

Figure 14-19   The Add Chart Element gallery and the Chart Elements pane

Both the Add Chart Element gallery and the Chart Elements quick access pane enable you to add (or remove) the elements on the currently selected chart, including data labels, error bars, gridlines, and the legend. The Add Chart Element gallery lists the different chart elements (such as Axes and Legend), and when you select an *active* chart element in the Add Chart Element gallery, you are provided with a submenu of choices. (I use the term *active* because some elements are grayed out or inactive depending on the chart type you are working with.) So, let's say that you want to add data labels to a bar chart, such as the chart shown in Figure 14-19. Select Data Labels in the Add Chart Element gallery; the choices provided on the Data Label submenu are related to the placement of the data labels in reference to the bars on the chart and include Center, Inside End, Inside Base, and Outside End.

The Chart Elements quick access pane is much simpler than the Add Chart Element gallery because it enables you to add or remove an element by toggling a particular chart element on or off using the appropriate check box. For example, if you want to add data labels to the current chart, select the Data Labels check box in the Chart Elements quick access pane to place the data labels in the outside end position.

If you need more control over a particular chart element, you can open the element's formatting pane. Figure 14-20 shows the Format Data Labels task pane. You can open a format task pane for a particular chart element using the Add Chart Element command; select Add Chart Element, then point at the chart element you want to format. On the submenu for the chart element, select the More (name of element) Options command. You can also double-click a chart element in the chart frame to open the associated format task pane.

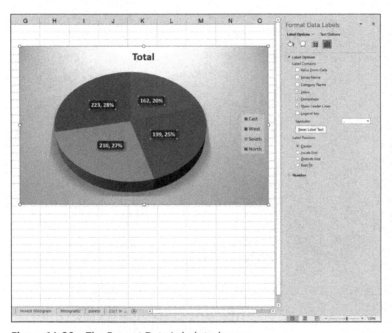

Figure 14-20   The Format Data Labels task pane

The options provided by various chart element format task panes are relatively consistent. There are options specific to the element. You can control settings such as Fill and Line, Effects, and Size & Properties. Other options for elements relate to what an element contains and its position within the chart frame. For example, data labels have both check boxes for what each label should contain, such as Series Name, Value, and/or Legend Key. Other options relate to the position of the label, such as Center, Inside End, and Outside End.

Although chart elements are a special kind of object that live inside the chart's plot area (or frame), both the Fill & Line and Effects formatting options for chart elements are similar to those that you find when formatting a shape, a SmartArt graphic, or other graphic element.

Chart elements such as data labels and titles also have text options associated with them. These options include text fill and text outline settings. You can also switch between the various chart elements from within the current element's task pane. Select the Options drop-down menu for the current element and select another element to format. For example, you can quickly switch between the Format Axis settings to the settings for the chart title. The discussion that follows provides information on manipulating specific chart elements, starting with titles and data labels.

TIP

You can format text elements in a chart, such as a label or text in the legend, as you would any text in any of the Office applications. Select the text and use the formatting options provided by the mini toolbar or the text-formatting commands on the ribbon's Home tab.

Modifying titles and data labels

Chart titles provide descriptive text for the chart and other elements, such as the axes. Editing the chart title text or other text-based elements such as the axis titles can be done by placing the insertion point in the text box that serves as a particular chart element (such as the title). You can then edit the text as needed.

Data labels are different from the other text boxes on the chart in that the values shown for the data labels are derived from the worksheet data that you used to create the chart. There-fore, you cannot edit a data label in situ. The value changes only if you edit the worksheet data related to the chart.

To change the position of a chart title or axis title, you can drag the selected title object to a new position on the chart. You can take advantage of the commands in the Add Chart Element gal-lery to specify a position for an element, such as the chart title or axis title. You can also position data labels using the Data Labels commands in the Add Chart Element gallery and access the Format Data Labels task pane.

Working with the legend and data points

The legend for the chart is the color or pattern key for the data series represented on the chart. You can move and size the legend on the chart as needed. The Legend command in the Add Chart Elements gallery provides different legend positions and gives you the option of turning the legend on or off.

You can access additional formatting options for the legend by opening the Format Legend task pane. You can open the task pane for the Add Chart Element gallery by double-clicking the legend's frame. The Format Legend task pane enables you to control the fill, border color, and effects for the legend as well as the position of the legend.

The Format Legend task pane does not provide you with control over the color scheme used to differentiate the data series on the chart. Colors are automatically assigned to the different data series based on the chart type (and theme you are using for your Excel worksheet). You can change the color scheme for the chart, which changes the legend colors as well, using the Change Colors command on the Chart Tools, Design tab.

If you want complete control over the way the legend looks, you can replace the default colors for the data series on the chart. The fastest way to do this is to right-click on the data series, such as a column in a column chart or a pie slice in a pie chart. A shortcut formatting toolbar appears along with a chart-oriented shortcut menu that you can use to access commands such as Select Data, Add Data Labels, and Format Data Series. The formatting toolbar allows you to access both the Fill and Outline for the currently selected chart element. Select a new fill color using the Fill Color palette. You can also use this shortcut toolbar to change the outline color for the data series.

If you want even more control over the fill color or the border on the data series, you can double-click a data series such as a column or pie slice to open the Format Data Series task pane, as shown in Figure 14-21). You can access the fill, border, and color options for the currently selected data series by clicking on the Fill And Line icon at the top of the Format Data Series pane. The Format Data Series pane also provides you access to Effects setting for the currently selected data series. Once the Format Data Series task pane is open, you can quickly select other data series in the chart using the Series Options drop-down menu, which is near the top of the task pane. The Series Options drop-down menu also allows you to select other chart elements (other than the Data Series) including the Chart Axes, Chart Area, Chart Title, and the Plot Area.

Figure 14-21   The Format Data Point task pane.

Opening the Format Data Series task pane allows you to select gradient or pattern fills and manipulate the border for the data series. Any format changes you make to a data series are reflected in the chart's legend.

TIP

The formatting attributes for a chart element that relate to how the data is portrayed in the chart are found in the Format task pane for a particular element by clicking the Options button that looks like an Excel column chart.

Manipulating axes and gridlines

If you are working with a chart type that shows the vertical and horizontal axes in the chart area, such as a line chart or a bar chart, you can manipulate the scale on the value axis. Double-click the axis frame (you might have to select it before you can double-click it, just so you can see it) to open the Format task pane for the axis. Axis options allow you to set the bounds for the axis and also the minimum and maximum for the axis. You can also specify the major and minor units for the axis.

TIP

If you are going to use different patterns, textures, or gradients to differentiate data points on a chart, make sure that each data point can be readily identified—meaning don't select patterns for the different data points that are hard to tell apart.

In the case of a value axis (such as the primary vertical or y-axis on many line and column charts), you can choose to display the axis using numbers represented in the thousands, millions, or billions. You can also choose to show the axis with a log 10–based scale. This is also known as a *logarithmic scale* because it uses a specific quantity to create the scale on the axis. In the case of the log 10–based scale, the scale would consist of 1, 10, 100, 1,000, and so on. This type of scale is extremely useful in cases where you have data that encompasses a very large range of values.

Gridlines make it easier for you to determine the values associated with a particular data point on a chart, particularly in cases where you have not included data labels. Depending on the chart layout that you select for your chart via the Chart Layouts gallery, your chart might already contain the major gridlines, which are placed perpendicular to the value axis on your chart.

Because this is the y-axis in many chart types, the primary horizontal gridlines serve as reference points for the value units placed on the y-axis itself. The easiest way to access the gridline settings for a selected chart is to select the Add Chart Element command and then point at Gridlines in the Add Chart Element gallery. Gridline options allow you to either turn on or off (with a series of checkboxes) different chart gridlines, including the following: primary major vertical, primary major horizontal, primary minor vertical, and primary minor horizontal. If necessary,

CHAPTER 14

you can access the Format Gridlines task pane to format the fill and shadow settings for the specified gridlines.

Adding trendlines, drop lines, and bars to a chart

You can add additional elements to your charts, such as trendlines, drop lines, and error bars. A trendline provides the overall slope or trend of the data points and is based on the relationship between each set of x and y values shown on a chart. Figure 14-22 shows a linear trendline that has been added to a stock chart (which is also known as a candlestick or box plot). The trendline is based on the close value for the stock shown. The trendline provides an overall analysis of how the stock has done over the timeframe shown on the chart.

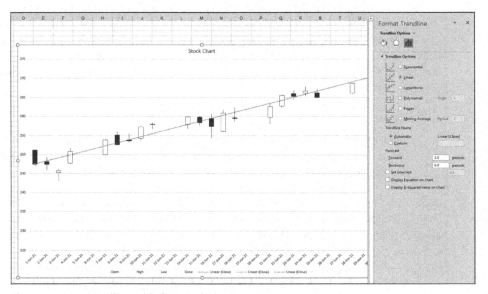

Figure 14-22   Trendline added to stock chart

You can add trendlines to many Excel 2D chart types, including line, column, bar, area, stock, scatter, and bubble charts (you can't add a trendline to a 3D chart). Excel provides some different trendline types via the Trendline command in the Add Chart Element gallery (select Add Chart Element and then point at Trendline). The trendline types include Linear, Exponential, Linear Forecast, and Moving Average.

Additional types of trendlines can be accessed in the Format Trendline task pane (shown in Figure 14-22). The type of trendline that you use depends on the type of data you are working with and the type of analysis you want to make with the trendline. The trendline possibilities are as follows:

- **Exponential:** This type of trendline provides a best-fit curve that is best used in cases where the data points rise or fall in constantly increasing rates and then level off. For example, an exponential trendline could be used to analyze production data for a factory that has rapid growth in its production rate until it reaches maximum capacity and levels off.

- **Linear:** This type of trendline creates a best-fit straight line based on the data points in the series that you have specified for the trendline. This type of trendline is best used in cases where you want to see whether your data points are trending up or down; this trendline can be useful for a quick look at trends in sales figures.

- **Logarithmic:** This trendline type provides a best-fit curved line that projects future data trends when the data used to create the chart changes dramatically (either up or down) but then levels out again. Logarithmic trendlines are best for showing long-range trends where the percent change is reflected in the trendline rather than the absolute change (in values).

- **Polynomial:** This trendline type is basically a way to do linear regression on data that fluctuates greatly and where there is not necessarily a true linear relationship between the x and y variables.

- **Power:** This trendline is a curved line that can be used to show the relationship between two sets of values (x and y) when there is an increase or decrease at a specific rate.

- **Moving Average:** This trendline averages the data points found in two periods and draws a trendline based on the averages. You can specify the period for a moving average trendline by formatting the trendline in the Format Trendline task pane.

NOTE

When you are using trendlines on your charts, you are performing linear regression, which analyzes the relationship between data points on your chart's x- and y-axes. The validity of a trendline is measured by determining the square of the correlation coefficient R, which is a fractional number between 0 and 1. The closer R^2 is to 1, the greater the correlation between the x and y variables—meaning as x changes, y also changes somewhat consistently.

The settings for any of the available trendline types can be fine-tuned in the Format Trendline task pane. You can open the Format Trendline task pane by double-clicking a trendline in the chart or by selecting Trendline then More Trendline Options in the Add Chart Element gallery.

You can also change other formatting options related to a trendline in the Format Trendline task pane. You can change both the line formatting and the effects settings (shadow, glow, and so on).

Using drop lines and high-low lines

Drop lines are lines that extend from the data points on the chart down to the horizontal or x-axis. The drop lines are used to make the chart easier to read, and they enable you to more easily determine the x-axis attributes of the data points used to create the chart. You can use drop lines on line and area charts. To add drop lines to a chart, select Lines and then Drop Lines in the Add Chart Element gallery.

You can also add high-low lines to your 2D charts. The high-low line extends from the highest to the lowest value in each chart category. For example, you might create a line chart that com-pares your actual monthly expenses (one data series for the chart) with a budget (another data series on the chart) that you create. The high-low lines connect the high value in each category (say you have categories such as food, utilities, entertainment, rent, and so on) with the mini-mum value in each category.

You can format your drop lines or high-low lines by double-clicking one on the chart. This opens the Format Drop Lines pane or the Format High-Low Lines task pane, respectively. These task panes provide you with control over line and effect formatting.

Adding error bars and up/down bars to a chart

You can also add error bars and up/down bars to your charts. Error bars are used to reflect uncertainty or variability in the data that has been charted and can help show the potential amount of error relative to the data points in a chart data series. Error bars can be used in 2D area, bar, column, line, scatter, and bubble charts.

The error bars are created on the chart based on an error amount. You can quickly create error bars that use the standard error, percentage, or standard deviation as the error amount. Select Add Chart Element, point at Error Bars, and then select one of the error bar types. Figure 14-23 shows standard error bars on a scatter chart. The figure also shows the Format Error Bars task pane.

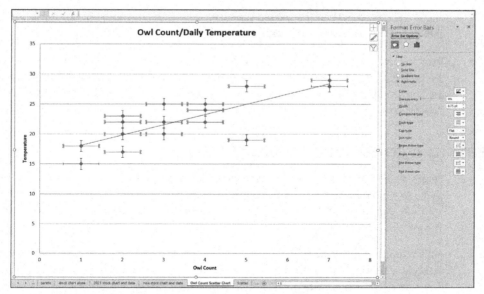

Figure 14-23   A scatter chart with error bars and the Format Error Bars task pane

If you want to specify an error amount or change other settings related to the error bars on your chart, double-click an error bar to open the Format Error Bars task pane. The task pane allows you to specify the direction of the error bar as well as the end style. More importantly, you can set the error amount from the standard error to one of the following:

- **Fixed Value:** You can specify a fixed amount as the error value.

- **Percentage:** A percentage can be specified as the error value.

- **Standard Deviation:** Excel computes the standard deviation for the chart data and uses it as the error amount for the error bars.

- **Standard Error:** Excel uses the standard error equation to compute the standard error for the chart data.

- **Custom:** You can specify the positive error value and the negative error value for the error bars. When you select Custom in the Format Error Bars dialog box, you must then specify the error values by clicking Specify Value. The error values (positive and negative) can be based on data ranges in the worksheet, or you can specify them as a series of values separated by commas.

Up/down bars are used to show the difference between the first and the last data series on the chart. For example, if you are comparing two data series, you get an up bar when the data point in the first series is less than the second series. You get a down bar when a data point for the first series is greater than the second series. You can take advantage of up/down bars in 2D line charts that use multiple data series.

To assign up/down bars to your chart, select Add Chart Element, point at Up/Down Bars, and then select Up/Down Bars. You can format the fill and the effect settings for up/down bars in the Format Up (or Down) Bars task pane. Double-click any up or down bar in the chart to open the task pane.

Creating a combination chart

Before we end our discussion of Excel charts, we should look at how you create a combination chart. A combination chart combines two or more chart types in a single chart. Excel provides premade combination charts such as pie of pie and bar of pie charts. A pie of pie chart is shown in Figure 14-24.

A pie of pie chart (or a bar of pie chart) enables you to separate out certain data points into the secondary chart, meaning the second pie. This can be extremely useful when you have a situation where a few large data points dominate the pie chart, and you would like to make smaller slices of the pie more visible by moving data points that represent smaller values to the secondary pie.

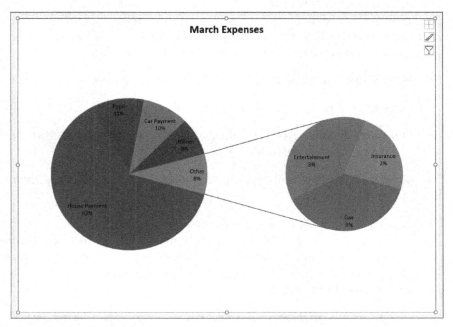

Figure 14-24   Pie of pie chart

Working with a pie of pie chart

Because pie charts enable you to specify only a single data series, how the different data points end up in the primary and the secondary plot or pie depends on how you have the data series arranged in a column or row in your worksheet. By default, Excel uses the last third of the data points listed in the chart data range to create the secondary chart. Remember that this is the default setting for a pie of pie chart, and you do have options regarding how the data series is split between the two charts in the combination chart. If you want to go with the default, you can arrange your data in the worksheet so that it is sorted from high to low based on the values you chart (use the Sort & Filter command on the Home tab to quickly sort ascending or descending as needed). This means that the lower values, which typically make up the smallest slices on the pie, are placed at the bottom of your values and therefore appear in the secondary pie when you are creating a pie of pie chart.

You can fine-tune the pie of pie chart by specifying whether a data point (pie piece) is shown on the primary pie or the secondary pie. You can also change other settings, such as the gap between the two plots and the second plot size in the Format Data Point task pane. Double-click a pie piece (data point) in either the first plot (large pie) or the second plot (small pie) to open the Format Data Point task pane.

You can determine how to split the series by position value or percentage value using the Split Series drop-down menu. You can also specify where a data point (pie piece) belongs using the Point Belongs To drop-down menu. As with other chart elements, the Format Data Point task pane also allows you to control the fill and effects settings for the data point.

Creating a custom combination chart

You are certainly not limited to the combination chart types that Excel provides, such as the pie of pie; charts are created by virtue of the fact that you supply a data series of values for them. If you have more than one data series in a chart, you can apply different chart types to the different data series, creating a combination chart that combines two or more of the different chart types supplied by Excel. This means that you can combine a line chart and a bar chart in the same combination chart or even have a combination chart that combines multiple chart types such as a line, bar, and pie. The possibilities are dictated by your data and your need for showing the relationships between the various data series visually.

For example, you can easily create a column and line chart combination. Let's say that you have sales figures for each of your sales regions (East, West, South, and North) for the months of January, February, and March. It certainly is not difficult to calculate the quarter total for each region using the SUM function and to include this information in the worksheet.

You could then create a chart that places the sales figures for each region using the region names as the category names along the x-axis. The months (January through March) would serve as the data series for the chart (along with the values associated with the sales for each month by region), so the legend would supply the color coding for each of the data point values by month.

The totals data series (the total sales for each region) would also be included on the chart. This data series could then be formatted as a line chart, providing you with a column chart that provides a comparison of the monthly sales of each region and a line chart that provides a look at the trend of your total sales for the quarter.

To create a combination chart, select all the data you want to include in the chart, including the data series that serves as the secondary plot. Select the Insert tab, and then use the chart type commands to insert the chart that serves as the primary plot or chart.

Now you need to select the series that you want to convert to a secondary chart. Use the drop-down menu in the Current Selection group (on the Chart Format tab) to select the data series that provides the values for the secondary plot. To change the data series to another chart type, you can select the data series and then select Change Chart Type, or you can right-click the selected data series and select Change Series Chart Type from the shortcut menu. Both options open the Change Chart Type dialog box, as shown in Figure 14-25.

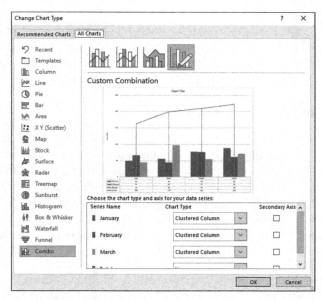

Figure 14-25   Change the chart type for a data series to create a custom combination chart.

Select the Chart Type drop-down menu for the selected series. For example, Figure 14-25 shows a clustered column chart; I've changed the Totals series to Line. This created a custom line and column combination. After you have made your changes in the Change Chart Type dialog box, click OK. Your original chart is now a combination chart.

NOTE

The Format Data Series task pane can also be used to set a number of options related to the data in a chart. In the case of pie charts, you can set the pie explosion percentage and the size of a secondary plot.

You can create a number of different combination charts, including column/line, column/area, and even pie/area. Remember that each data series can be formatted separately, meaning that the attributes of each of the charts—the primary and secondary plots—can be modified as needed. This includes applying data labels to the different series and using things such as drop lines and other descriptive chart elements (axis titles and gridlines, for example) to make the chart readily meaningful.

Using sparklines

Another Excel tool for visualizing data in a worksheet are sparklines. Sparklines are small charts that are embedded in sheet cells; sparklines can be inserted in rows or columns. You can position sparklines so that they appear at the bottom of a column of values or the end of a row of values (including formula or function results). This enables you to place the sparklines directly inline with the data they visually represent. Sparklines are not meant to replace full-blown charts in Excel but can be used to accompany data series in the worksheet.

A sparkline can these forms: Line, Column, or Win/Loss chart. Sparklines can be inserted in a single cell or multiple cells (for multiple rows or columns of data). You can also insert a sparkline for a row or column of values and then drag the sparkline's fill handle to copy the sparkline to other rows or columns as you would an Excel formula or function. When you change the data in a row or column that has an associated sparkline, the sparkline chart is immediately updated.

Creating sparklines

As already mentioned, three different types of sparklines can be inserted in a worksheet: Line, Column, and Win/Loss.

- **Line:** A Line sparkline can be used to show a trend in the data.

- **Column:** A Column sparkline enables you to visually compare different data points.

- **Win/Loss:** Win/Loss sparklines can be used to show the win/loss trend over time for your investments or the performance of your favorite sports team.

You can insert a sparkline in a cell or a range of cells. The different types of sparklines are available in the Sparklines group on the ribbon's Insert tab. To insert a sparkline, follow these steps:

1. Select the cell or cell range where you want to insert the sparkline.

2. Select the sparkline type that you want to insert from the Sparklines group. The Create Sparklines dialog box opens, as shown in Figure 14-26.

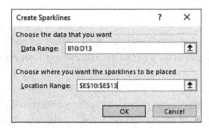

Figure 14-26 The Create Sparklines dialog box

3. The Create Sparklines dialog box requires that you specify a data range and a location range. To specify the data range, click the Shrink button and then select the cells that contain the values that are used to create the sparklines. Do not include cells containing labels as you would for an Excel chart.

4. If you selected the cell range where the sparklines were to be inserted, a location range is already shown in the Location Range text box. If you need to specify the range or edit the current range, click the Shrink button and select the location range. This range will automatically be specified as an absolute reference.

5. After the data range and the location range have been selected for the sparklines, click OK. The sparklines appear in the location range cells. Figure 14-27 shows a range of cells containing sparklines that use values arranged in rows.

When you select a sparkline in a range, the other sparklines in that range (meaning the cells in the range) are also selected. As with a number of other features in Excel, a specific set of contextual sparkline tools is provided when a cell containing a sparkline is selected. Let's look at the Sparkline Tools, Design tab's commands.

	Territory	January	February	March	
8					
9	Territory	January	February	March	
10	Region 1	$ 15,000.00	$ 9,000.00	$ 12,000.00	
11	Region 2	$ 14,240.00	$ 8,000.00	$ 14,500.00	
12	Region 3	$ 11,000.00	$ 4,000.00	$ 12,000.00	
13	Region 4	$ 8,000.00	$ 6,000.00	$ 10,000.00	
14					

Figure 14-27 Sparklines in a sheet

Modifying sparklines

The Sparkline Tools, Design tab provides a number of different options for modifying and enhancing the sparklines that you inserted into a worksheet. You can change the type of sparkline you have inserted after the fact, and you can change the style assigned to the sparklines. The command groups provided by the Sparkline Tools, Design tab are as follows:

- **Sparkline:** This group contains the Edit Data command. This command enables you to edit the group and data location for all the sparklines in a specific group. The Edit Single Sparkline's Data command enables you to edit a specific cell containing a sparkline without editing the values used by the other sparklines in the group. The Hidden And Empty Cells command enables you to specify whether hidden and empty cells should be treated as gaps or zeros and whether the data should be shown that is included in any hidden rows or columns within the data range for the sparkline.

- **Type:** You can change the type of sparkline you have inserted using the Line, Column, and Win/Loss commands provided by this group.

- **Show:** You can highlight certain data points in the sparklines, including the high point, low point, and negative points. You can also specify that markers are shown on the sparklines, which indicates the number of data points used to create the sparkline.

- **Style:** The Style gallery provides you with a number of different sparkline styles for each sparkline type: Line, Column, or Win/Loss. The Sparkline Color and Marker Color commands are also provided to enable you to select your own colors for the sparklines and the markers you are including on the sparklines (selected via the Show group), respectively.

- **Group:** This group provides commands that can be used to group or ungroup sparklines. The Clear command is provided to enable you to clear the selected sparklines or selected sparkline groups. The Axis command enables you to modify the horizontal and vertical axis options. You can change the horizontal axis type as well as specify minimum and maximum values for the vertical axis.

Sparklines offer you with another possibility for providing a visual representation of the data in a worksheet. Although sparklines do not provide the detail you find in a full-blown Excel chart, they can be useful in doing quick comparisons of a range of data values or to show a trend in those values.

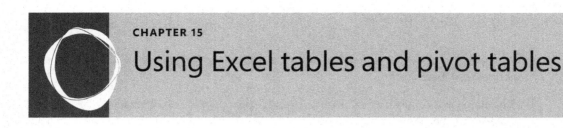

Using Excel tables and pivot tables

Excel and databases   461

Defining a table range   463

Creating a table using styles   464

Using the table design tools   465

Sorting table data   467

Filtering table data   470

Using the data form   479

Creating outlines and subtotals   480

Working with external data   484

Connecting to other data sources   488

Working with pivot tables   494

Although we primarily think of Excel as a number cruncher, it also provides several tools and features for working with collections of information, which we refer to as databases. Excel enables you to view and manipulate data records and field information in a database table. You can also sort records in your table, filter the records, and import or connect to external data sources.

In this chapter, we look at Excel's database capabilities, including a number of different table-manipulation tools and data tools. We also look at how to group and ungroup ranges in a table and create subtotals in a table. We wrap up the chapter with a discussion of pivot tables, which provide you with a dynamic way to view and analyze worksheet data.

Excel and databases

A database is a collection of organized information. The basic container used to hold data in a database is the table, and complex databases can consist of many associated tables. Excel allows you to interact with and manipulate tables by using a number of different tools. You can create your own tables in Excel or import data into a table, or connect to data provided by other databases external to Excel. The fact that database information is held in discrete tables means that you can interact with database information that lives in a number of different database platforms, including Microsoft Access, the web, and server-based database systems such as those provided by Microsoft SQL Server. Excel tables can also be shared via a SharePoint Services server.

Just the thought of working with a database might intimidate you, but a data table looks much like any other Excel worksheet, with the data arranged in columns and rows. Tables are not that difficult to work with, though it is important that you structure the table correctly for you to take advantage of the commands and tools provided on the ribbon's Data tab. This means that a table must have the data arranged in records and fields. So, let's define what a field is and then talk about database records.

Each column in the table is a field. Each field holds a discrete piece of information, such as an employee's name, phone number, or department. The very first row in the table consists of field names or headings, which define what is contained in each field. The fields actually serve as the columns in the table, and the field headings play an important role when you are filtering data in the table.

Each row in the table is a record. A record is all the information related to a particular person, place, or thing. The record comprises the field entries made for it. For example, if you have a table of employees, each record in the table is the record for a different employee.

Inside OUT

Structure Excel tables like tables in a relational database using primary keys that uniquely identify each record in the table.

Tables you create in Excel are referred to as *flat-file databases* because you cannot set up relationships between associated tables in Excel, such as an employee table with an employee sales table. Relational databases created in Microsoft Access use related tables to create the structure and data relationships for the database. Tables in a relational database will each contain a primary key, which is a field (such as an employee number or invoice number) that uniquely identifies each record in the table.

So, it probably makes sense to structure your Excel tables as you would structure a table in a relational database (even if the data did not come from or will not go to a relational database) with a column designating a primary key that uniquely identifies each record in the table. For a group of employees, the unique identifier could be their social security numbers. If you are putting together a table of products that you create and sell but don't have SKU or product numbers, just assign a unique number to each product. You can actually create the ID column field and then assign numbers (using the series feature) for each of the products by typing the first number in the sequence and then using the Fill handle to assign the rest.

You might be wondering why you would want to tackle database tables in Excel when there is more powerful relational database software such as Microsoft Access. The best answer is that when you're looking at individual tables, Excel provides a number of tools that enable you to view the data in different ways using sort and filter commands. Excel's ability to perform calculations also enables you to use formulas, functions, and other Excel features such as charts to quickly go beyond the data analysis that you could do within an actual database software application. Therefore, don't think of Excel as a database-creation application as much as an analysis engine that can be used after the database has been created. Also, remember that your Excel (database) tables really don't look any different than the other worksheets you create in Excel. The information still appears in columns and rows. So, you can use everything you already know about Excel to work with data in tables.

Defining a table range

To define a table in Excel, you use the Format As Table command on the ribbon's Home tab. Before you can define the table, you need to create the table or import it from a source external to Excel. We look at working with external data later in the chapter, so let's concentrate on issues related to creating your own table directly in Excel.

TIP

You might want to include a key field in your table. This provides a field column that contains a unique identifier for each record in the table, such as employee number or invoice number. You can then use the key field to quickly sort your records back into the original order. You can use the fill handle to quickly create a series and assign unique numbers in the key field column as needed.

Before you start entering data into a table, you might want to take a moment and do a little planning first. It makes sense to determine the fields that you want to include in the table and that make up each record. You also need to determine the purpose of the table; is it truly a data repository, or is it a way to list some data and then manipulate it? If you are building the table for analysis purposes, you don't necessarily have to include all the information that you have collected for the database as you would if you were building a table that serves primarily as an information resource.

For example, if you are working with employee salary data or sales information for your sales force and want to be able to filter and sort the data to get a better picture of performance, do you need to include extraneous information in the table, such as the employee's phone number or the names of a particular salesperson's children? Therefore, the first thing you need to decide is what fields to include in the table. After the fields are entered in the top row of the table, you can enter each of the records that make up the table.

NOTE

When you scroll down through a large table in Excel, the field headings remain on the screen as you move down through the records in the table.

CHAPTER 15

After you have the table in an Excel worksheet, defining the table range is very straightforward. Follow these steps:

1. Select the cell range for the table, including the field names in the top row of the table.

2. Select the ribbon's Insert tab and then click the Table command in the Tables group. The Create Table dialog box opens, as shown in Figure 15-1.

3. Make sure the range specified in the Create Table dialog box encompasses your entire table range. You can modify the range by clicking the Shrink button (at the right of the box that contains the cell range) and then selecting a new range for the table.

4. Click OK. The range is now defined as a table.

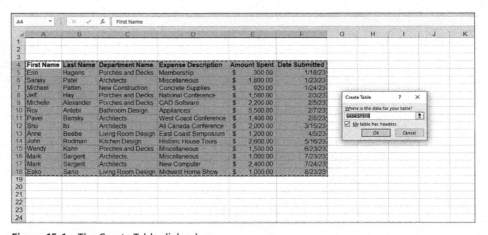

Figure 15-1   The Create Table dialog box

As soon as you close the Create Table dialog box, the table is formatted with the default table style, and drop-down menus appear on each field heading in the table. These are the AutoFilters for each field in the table. The AutoFilters enable you to sort and filter the records in the table by each field.

Creating a table using styles

You can also create your database table by selecting a table style in the Table Styles gallery. This enables you to specify your table range and pick a table style—all pretty much at the same time.

Select the cell range for the table. Then select the Format As Table command in the Styles group on the ribbon's Home tab. The Table Styles gallery appears, as shown in Figure 15-2.

Select one of the table styles in the gallery. When you select the style, the Table Styles gallery closes, and the Format As Table dialog box opens. Make sure that the data range for the table is correct, and then click OK. The table is created and assigned the table style you selected.

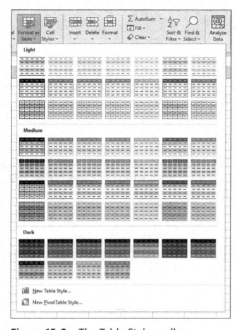

Figure 15-2   The Table Styles gallery

Database tables do not necessarily need to be discrete tables on their own Excel worksheets. You can also create tables by selecting a subset range of any existing worksheet that is arranged in the appropriate table format of field columns and record rows. Think of the table feature as a way to access the data analysis tools on the Data tab of the ribbon and then use them as a way to analyze and order your data.

You can also define multiple tables within a single worksheet, which enables you to group data in such a way that you can do some meaningful manipulations of the information by using the commands on the Data tab.

Using the Table Design Tools

After the table range has been specified, you can take advantage of the Table Design Tools to change the table style and other options related to the table style. You can also refresh data that comes from an external source, export the table to a SharePoint list, or convert the table back to a normal worksheet range. Figure 15-3 shows the Table Design tab. It is another example of Excel's (and the 365 applications') contextual tool sets.

Figure 15-3   The Table Design tab

Basic commands related to the table style and table options are available to you whether the data is external or internal to Excel. The commands available in the External Table Data group are limited to the Export command if you are working with a table created in Excel. The Table Design tab command groups are as follows:

- **Properties:** This group provides the table name (which you can edit as needed) and also the Resize Table command. You can resize the table to include more or fewer rows and columns if required, meaning you are changing the table range.

- **Tools:** This group provides you with the ability to create a pivot table from the current table (we discuss pivot tables later in the chapter). The Remove Duplicates command is also provided to enable you to specify a column that contains duplicate entries and delete them. This group also provides the Convert To Range command, which converts the table data range back to a regular worksheet data range.

- **External Table Data:** This group provides the Export command, which can be used to export your Excel table to a SharePoint list. Other commands in the group relate to external table data and enable you to refresh the data, view the data properties, and unlink from the external data source.

- **Table Style Options:** This group provides a series of check boxes that enable you to fine-tune the table. For example, you can include or preclude a header row or a total row. The Banded Rows formatting can also be turned on or off. You can also choose to format the first column or last column in the table and add banded columns to the table.

- **Table Styles:** This group provides access to the Table Styles gallery. Place the mouse on a style in the gallery to preview that particular style on your table. The More button enables you to view the entire gallery. Click a style to assign it to the current table.

Although the Table Design tab becomes active when you select a cell or cell range that falls in the table range, the real meat-and-potatoes commands (or tempeh and sweet potatoes for vegans) of table manipulation are provided by the AutoFilters placed on each of the table field headings and the various commands provided on the ribbon's Data tab. Two of the most fundamental manipulations of table records are sorting and filtering and can be accomplished using the AutoFilters on a table's column field headings.

Sorting table data

Sorting by the fields in a table enables you to quickly place the records in the table based on your sort criteria. You can sort data by using the Sort commands on a field's AutoFilter menu or by selecting one of the Sort commands in the Sort & Filter group on the ribbon's Data tab. To quickly sort the table by a particular field, select that field's AutoFilter arrow, as shown in Figure 15-4.

TIP

If you don't see the AutoFilter arrows on the table field headings, select a cell within the table range and then select the Filter command on the ribbon's Data tab.

You can then select Sort A To Z (Ascending) or Sort Z To A (Descending) as needed on the Auto-Filter menu. The records in the table are sorted by the field you selected in the direction you selected (ascending or descending). You can also use the Sort commands in the Sort & Filter group. Click in the field column that you want to use as the sort field. Then select either the Sort A To Z or Sort Z To A command. The table records are sorted by the field you specified.

You can also sort by multiple fields in the table. For example, assume that you have a table where the last name field column is followed by the first name field column. You can select any two cells in these two field columns and then select either the Sort A To Z or Sort Z To A command in the Sort & Filter group to sort the table by the last name field followed by the first name field.

This enables you to sort out all the Smiths and Jones that appear in your table. In terms of a more generic application of this multiple field sorting, Excel sorts by the first selected field column (starting on the left) and then moves to the right, sorting by each subsequent field column that has been selected.

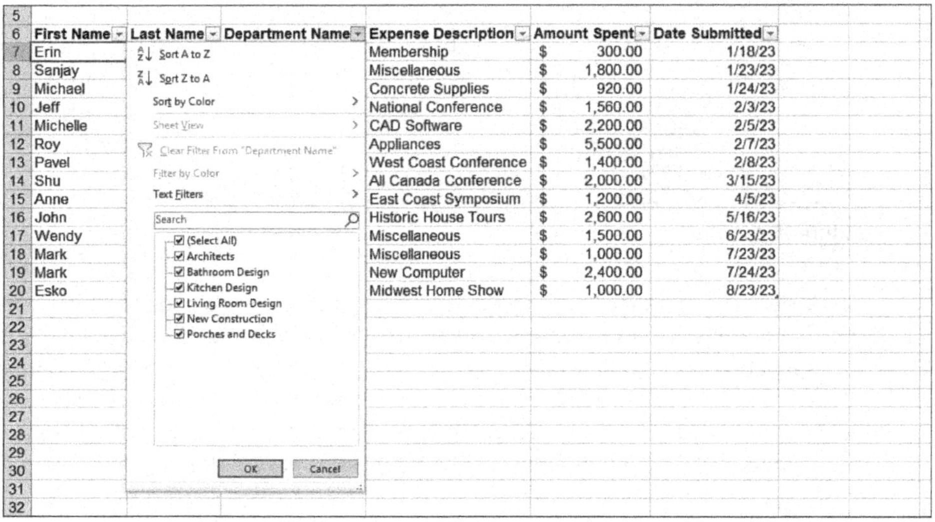

Figure 15-4   The AutoFilter menu for the Department Name table field

How Excel sorts data

When Excel sorts the records in a table, it follows rules for how the data is actually sorted. Numbers appear first in a sort list and, in the case of an ascending sort (A to Z), are sorted from the smallest (negative numbers qualify as smaller numbers) to the largest. Numbers (or values) include dates, which Excel perceives as values. Keep in mind that Excel looks at the content of the cell, not the formatting of the content. Therefore, even a date that appears as December 1, 2021, is still a number to Excel.

In the case of text entries, the field column data is sorted by punctuation and special characters such as #, &, *, and so on (in the order you find them on the keyboard), followed by the letters of the alphabet (A through Z). Text with numbers would follow regular text entries when you perform a sort. If you have a field column that contains numbers, text, and text with numbers, the ascending sort would use this sort order: numbers, followed by text, and then numbers with text.

Using the Sort dialog box

In cases where you cannot conveniently sort by multiple fields because of the location of the fields in the table, and you would like more control over the number of levels in the sort, you can use the Sort dialog box. The Sort dialog box enables you to specify 64 levels for your sort.

To open the Sort dialog box, go to the ribbon's Data tab, then select Sort in the Sort & Filter group. Figure 15-5 shows the Sort dialog box.

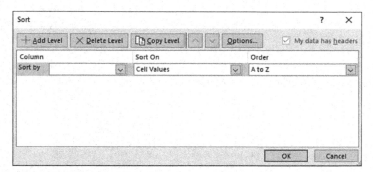

Figure 15-5   The Sort dialog box

The first sort level is available when you open the Sort dialog box; specify the first field name in the first level's Sort By drop-down menu, which lists all the fields in the table. By default, sort levels sort on the values that are in the field column you have specified in the primary sort level (or *key*, as sort levels are also known). You can choose to sort by values, cell color, font color, or cell icon. The cell and font color can be specified by cell attributes that you have manually assigned to cells. These attributes can also be the result of conditional formatting. This includes the possibility of the field column's cells containing cell icons that have been inserted into cells that have met conditional formatting criteria that you have assigned to the table cells.

➤ **For information on using conditional formatting, including icon sets, see "Using conditional formatting" in Chapter 12, "Worksheet formatting and management."**

After you have specified what column should be sorted and what the sort should be performed on (values, cell colors, and so on), you can specify the order of the sort level. For cells containing text, this is Sort A To Z or Sort Z To A, and for numerical values, it is Smallest To Largest or Largest To Smallest. Dates are Oldest To Newest or Newest To Oldest.

TIP

You can also open the Sort dialog box from the ribbon's Home tab. Select Sort & Filter in the Editing group and then select Custom Sort.

You can also create custom sort lists to determine the sort order. Select Custom List in the Order drop-down menu and then create the custom list in the Custom Lists dialog box. Custom lists were discussed in Chapter 11, "Essential Excel features," in reference to creating custom series, but the lists can also be used to determine the sort order of information in a field column.

After you have specified the parameters for the first sort level, click the Add Level button to add another level to the Sort dialog box. Configure the level by going through the same steps you used to configure the first level. You can also delete levels if needed, and you can copy levels to hasten the configuration process for field columns that are similar in content and how you want them to be sorted.

You can also change the sort options related to the case of text entries and the orientation of the sort. By default, the case of the text is ignored during sorting, and Excel assumes that you have placed your fields in columns and your records in rows. When you click the Options button in the Sort dialog box, the Sort Options dialog box opens. The Sort Options dialog box is extremely simple. It provides the Case Sensitive check box, which you can select to specify that case be considered during the sort. Uppercase text is sorted before lowercase text when this check box is enabled.

A sort typically takes place from top to bottom, meaning the rows are rearranged according to the sort parameters. This is why Sort Top To Bottom is the default option selected in the Sort Options dialog box. If you have a situation where you want to sort the columns instead of the rows, you can switch the sort to Sort Left To Right (this would be useful in cases where you want to sort a worksheet arranged in columns rather than rows, like a database table is arranged). Click OK to close the Sort Options dialog box.

After you have specified your sort levels and the information for each level, you can run the sort. Click OK, and the sort takes place in the table.

CHAPTER 15

Filtering table data

Sorting allows you to arrange the records in the table in a particular order; filtering enables you to view subsets of the table records based on specific criteria. One option for filtering the data in the table is to use the AutoFilter lists on each of the table field headings. AutoFilter enables you to quickly filter the table in place.

When you select the AutoFilter arrow for a particular field, the AutoFilter menu provides a list of all that field's entries. By default, all the values are selected, meaning there is no filtering currently applied to the table based on that field. Figure 15-6 shows the AutoFilter list for a table field (a date field, which provides the months of the year in the filter list).

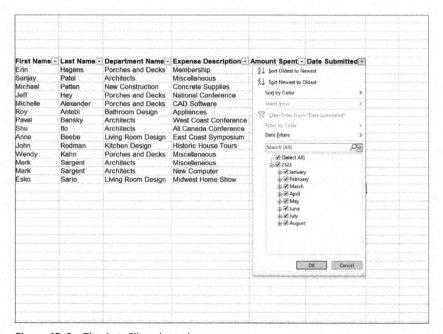

Figure 15-6   The AutoFilter drop-down menu

The most straightforward method of filtering the table by a specific field is to deselect the Select All check box in the field list and then select the field value you want to use to filter the table. You can select more than one value in the field data list (each value or label will have its own check box in the field list). Remember that the purpose of the filter is to show a subset of the table records, so you can specify multiple criteria for a single field (just choose more than one check box as needed). When you are ready to run the filter based on actual field values, click OK. The table records will be filtered based on your selection or selections in the AutoFilter list.

AutoFilter enables you to filter by more than one field, so you can create filters based on criteria for more than one field in the table. Simply use the AutoFilter drop-down menu to specify the filter criteria for each field that you want to include in the filter. The field or fields you have used to filter the table will have a small filter icon (it looks like a funnel) on the AutoFilter drop-down arrow. This serves as a reminder as to which fields in the table have been used to filter the data.

You can clear a filter that is specific to a field. Select the AutoFilter drop-down arrow and then select Clear Filter From "*Field Name*" on the AutoFilter menu. Any other filters applied to the table remain in force. If you want to clear all the filters you have applied to the table, select the Clear command in the Sort & Filter group.

Using the AutoFilter Search box

Each of the AutoFilter drop-down menus for your field columns contains its own Search box (just above the field value list). The Search box can be used to quickly search for data that appears in that field. This can be particularly useful when you are working with a database table that has a large number of records. The list of field values for each field, obviously, is as numerous as the number of records in the table, so having a Search box that can be used to find a specific field value quickly can really speed up the filtering of the table.

Select a field's AutoFilter arrow to access the AutoFilter menu. Click in the Search box. As you begin to type your search entry, matches appear in the results list as you enter each character for a number (value) or text entry. Continue to type the search parameter string until you have the desired results listed. For example, to view all the people with the last name of *Smith*, you might need to type `smi` to view just the Smiths and not any Smythes. The data found by the search in that field column is listed below the Search box, and the check boxes for matches to your search string are selected. To run the AutoFilter based on the search results, click OK. If you need to fine-tune the search string, do so and then run the filter.

Creating custom AutoFilters

So far, we have looked at filtering tables as an all-or-nothing proposition. Either the records completely met the field parameters that were set via the AutoFilter menu on a field or fields, or the records didn't. You can also create custom AutoFilters that provide you with the ability to filter your data based on conditional statements. These conditional statements enable you to filter the table records for a range of field values or text entries rather than an exact match to a single criterion.

The AutoFilter menu provides number, date, and text filters that are designed to help you create more complex filters for each of these specific data types. For example, when working with a field column that contains numbers (values), you can specify filter criteria based on conditional statements such as equals, does not equal, is greater than, between, and so on. For text entries in a field column, you can also create conditional statements such as equals, begins with, ends with, and contains. In the case of dates, you can use conditional statements such as equals, before, and after, and you can also choose from a wide variety of data filters such as tomorrow, yesterday, next week, next quarter, and year to date. Figure 15-7 shows the different data filters provided for a field column that contains dates.

Figure 15-7   Custom AutoFilters such as date filters enable you to filter by a data type quickly.

As already mentioned, each data type filter, such as those for numbers or for text, enables you to quickly create a custom AutoFilter based on a conditional statement that you select from a list. For example, if you want to see employee expense records that fall into a certain data range, you could select the Between filter on the Date Filters list. This opens the Custom AutoFilter dialog box, as shown in Figure 15-8.

Because you selected the Between filter (for a date filter), the Custom AutoFilter dialog box has automatically entered two criteria for the filter: Is After Or Equal To and Is Before Or Equal To. All you have to do is specify the two dates that provide the beginning and end of the data range that you want the filter to use. The Custom AutoFilter dialog box even provides Calendar icons, so you can insert the dates directly from a particular calendar month (as shown in Figure 15-8).

Creating a Custom AutoFilter for a number field, such as a salary field, is every bit as straightforward as working with date fields. Selecting a Between filter for a number field allows you to select Is Greater Than Or Equal To in the Custom AutoFilter dialog box as the start point for a numerical range and Is Less Than Or Equal To as the end point.

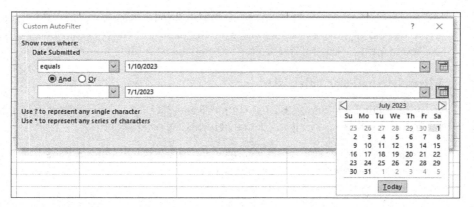

Figure 15-8   Creating a date range AutoFilter in the Custom AutoFilter dialog box

When you use the Custom AutoFilter dialog box, you can modify the filter criteria by using the criteria drop-down menus. You specify the values, dates, or text entries for the AutoFilter by using the field content drop-down menus, which are to the right of the criteria lists. You can specify the specific value or text entry that should be used by the AutoFilter for each criteria by selecting a field column entry in the drop-down menu. You can also type in filter parameters and use the question mark (?) to represent single characters and the asterisk (*) to represent a series of characters. These two wildcards are most useful in situations where you are working with a field that contains text entries.

When you are ready to run the AutoFilter, click OK. The table is filtered based on the criteria set for the field's custom AutoFilter. You can apply custom AutoFilters to multiple field columns to filter by more than one field in the table. For example, you could do a custom AutoFilter that will filter a Department Name field by specific departments using the And operator. You could then run a Between AutoFilter on a Salary field column to see who (which employees) in the specified departments (specified by the department filter) made a salary that fell in the range specified by the custom AutoFilter applied to the Salary field.

If you want to create a custom AutoFilter that isn't listed in the set of filters provided for a particular field, you can open the Custom AutoFilter dialog box and set up your filter from scratch. Select Custom Filter at the bottom of any of the different data type (numbers, text, or dates) filter lists. The Custom AutoFilter dialog box opens, and you can set the filter operators and criteria as you require.

TIP

You can quickly filter a number field using the Top 10 number filter. The Top 10 AutoFilter enables you to quickly show the top or bottom items in a field column (10 is the default number, but you can change it) based on the values in the field or a percent. For example, you could find the top 10 sales representatives based on the percent of sales.

CHAPTER 15

You can clear custom AutoFilters in the same way that the quick AutoFilters are cleared: by using the field's AutoFilter menu. If you want to clear all the custom AutoFilters that you have applied to a table, click the Clear command on the Sort & Filter group.

Filtering tables with slicers

Another option for filtering table data is the slicer. A slicer is similar to a filter in that it filters a table in place and shows only the data that meets the slicer's criteria.

To create a slicer for a table, select any cell in the defined table area. Click the Table Tools Design tab to access the Insert Slicer command, which is in the Tools group. When you select Insert Slicer, the Insert Slicers dialog box opens, as shown in Figure 15-9.

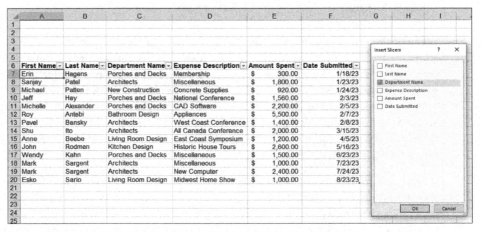

Figure 15-9 Specify the fields to be used by the slicer to filter the table.

The Insert Slicers dialog box lists the fields (column headings) available in the table. You can select one field in the Insert Slicers dialog box to create a slicer that filters by that one field, or you can specify more than one field and build a separate slicer for each field selected. Each slicer you create can only be related to one field in the table.

After selecting the fields in the Insert Slicers dialog box, click OK. A slicer is created for each selected field. The slicer for a particular field lists all the data entries that appeared in that particular field column. Click one of the specific field entries to filter the table by that entry.

Figure 15-10 shows a slicer that was created to filter a table by the Department Name field. The figure also shows the results of selecting Porches And Decks in the Department slicer.

A slicer is an easily accessible sheet object and can be moved and arranged on the worksheet just as any other object (such as a chart) can. When a slicer is selected, the Slicer tab appears on the ribbon (see Figure 15-10).

NOTE

Slicers were introduced in Excel 2013 as a way to filter pivot tables; the latest version of the slicer feature provides you with another way to quickly filter your Excel data tables.

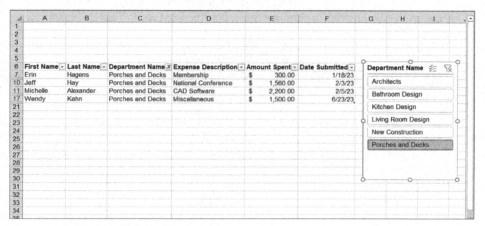

Figure 15-10   A slicer filtered table

You can change the style for the slicer by selecting one of the styles in the Slicer Styles gallery. You can also change the slicer settings by selecting the Slicer Settings command in the Slicer group. This opens the Slicer Settings dialog box.

By default, a slicer filters the data and also sorts the data in ascending order (A to Z). You can change the sorting direction to descending by clicking the Descending option button in the Slicer Settings dialog box. By default, a slicer also visually indicates items that contain no data; you can change this setting by selecting the Hide Items With No Data check box. When you have finished modifying the settings in the Slicer Settings dialog box, click OK to return to the current Excel worksheet.

Creating advanced filters

The custom AutoFilters (and the slicers) do have limitations in terms of the number of fields you can use to filter a particular table. The fact that each AutoFilter also has to be configured using its own Custom AutoFilter dialog box makes AutoFilters rather cumbersome. Also, AutoFilters are best used for comparisons, which can be limiting in terms of filtering your table data. An alternative to AutoFilters (and the slicers) is to set up your table for advanced filtering.

Advanced filters enable you to filter a database by as many fields as you want. Advanced filters use a criteria range to set the filter criteria (which we get to in a moment). Advanced filters can filter the table in place, or they can copy the results of the advanced filter—the filtered records—to a specified range on the current worksheet.

CHAPTER 15

Before you can create an advanced filter, you need to create a criteria range for the table. The criteria range consists of an exact duplicate of the field headings found in the table. The criteria range also consists of at least one empty row below the copied field headings. If you are going to use multiple criteria for a particular field, you need multiple blank rows below the field headings you designate as the criteria range. It is in the cells directly below each of the field heading copies that you place the filter parameters for the advanced filter.

First, copy the row that contains the field headings for the table. You can then paste these headings somewhere onto the worksheet so that there is at least one empty row below the copied field names. It makes sense, however, to have multiple empty rows available for multiple criteria for a single field.

You can place the copied field headings above or below the database table; it's up to you. Just make sure that there is a clear separation between the table and the criteria range that you specify when you run the advanced filter. Figure 15-11 shows a database table (A4:F18) and an accompanying criteria range (A20:F21).

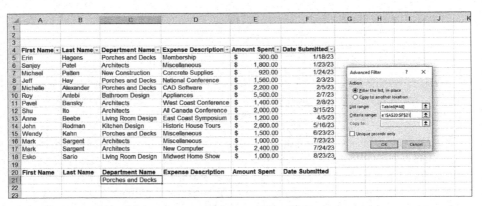

Figure 15-11   A table, criteria range, and Advanced Filter dialog box

In this case, the criteria range consists of the cells containing the copied field headings and the row below the copied field headings. A criterion, **Porches and Decks**, has been typed below the Department Name field heading in the criteria range. The Advanced Filter dialog box is configured to filter the table in place. Both the List Range (the table range) and the Criteria Range are specified in the Advanced Filter dialog box.

It is the criteria that you place below the field names included in the criteria range that enable you to filter the table records. For example, in Figure 15-11, when OK is selected in the Advanced Filter dialog box, the table is filtered to show only the records that have "Porches and Decks" specified in the Department Name field column. This example shows only a single criterion, but you can specify multiple criteria and use a different operator, such as greater than (>) or less than (<), as part of the criteria.

In cases where you have criteria for more than one field column in the same criteria range row, you are creating an And statement. The advanced filter bases its results on the first criteria *and* the second criteria (and additional criteria if included). In cases where you are specifying multiple criteria for a single field column, you are creating an Or statement.

Although advanced filters might look like more trouble than they are worth, they are the only way to filter a table using a number and variety of criteria. Advanced filters can be used to copy records from a large table to a table that includes only a subset of records based on the filter. This makes it easier to work with subsets of the records provided by the table.

After you have copied the field headings for the advanced filter to an area that can serve as a criteria range, you are ready to create the advanced filter. Follow these steps:

1. Enter criteria for the advanced filter under the Criteria Range field headings as needed. You can enter filter criteria for more than one field (type the criteria below the field name), or you can enter multiple criteria for a single field: Type the multiple criteria in the required number of cells below the field name.

2. Click in the database table you are filtering. Because you have defined this range as a table, it is automatically specified as the List Range in the Advanced Filter dialog box.

3. Select the Advanced command in the Sort & Filter group. The Advanced Filter dialog box opens.

4. Set the action for the filter. You can filter the list in place or copy the results of the filter to another location on the worksheet. If you are going to copy the results to another location, make sure you give yourself plenty of open space (meaning empty cells) for the copied results.

5. The List Range is the range for the table. If you performed step 2, the range shown in the List Range box should reflect the range for the table. If not, click in the worksheet and select the range for the table.

6. Click in the Criteria Range box. Select the field headings and the number of rows below the field heading you have copied to provide the criteria range. If you are specifying criteria only in the row below the copied field headings, you only need to specify the field heading row and the row below it. If you are specifying multiple criteria for a single field (or fields), make sure each row that contains a criterion statement is included in the criteria range.

7. (Optional) If you select the Copy To Another Location option button as the action for the filter, you need to specify where the filter should place its results. All you really need to do is click in the blank cell that serves as the upper-left limit for the filter results. The results then spill over into other cells as needed.

8. When you are ready to run the filter, click OK.

TIP

You can use the question mark (?) and the asterisk (*) as wildcards when building filters for text fields. In cases where you want a filter criterion to find a specific occurrence of a specific text string when it is not part of a larger text string, use the following format:

```
="=text string"
```

TIP

If you want the results of the advanced filter to show only unique records, select the Unique Records Only check box in the Advanced Filter dialog box.

The results of the advanced filter appear in the table if you filtered the table in place. If you chose to have the filter results copied to another area of the worksheet, the results appear there. If you filtered the table in place, you can clear the advanced filter by selecting the Clear command in the Sort & Filter group.

Each time you change the criteria in the criteria range, you need to rerun the filter. Select Advanced in the Sort & Filter group and make sure the List Range and Criteria Range are correct for the filter you want to run. Then click OK to run the filter.

Creating custom sheet views

You can see that the sorting and filter features provided by Excel allow you to create different subsets or custom "views" of your data. In the past, you could save different iterations of the same Excel worksheet as separate files, but that really negates the power of sharing a single cloud-based Excel file with a group of collaborators. So, the Excel ribbon's View tab now provides a new command group named Sheet View. The purpose of the Sheet View tools, such as Keep and New, is to create custom worksheet views. These different views of the same shared worksheet can be viewed by you and viewed by your collaborators who also have share access to the cloud-stored Excel workbook.

Before you can take advantage of the Sheet View commands, the workbook that contains the data table must stored on your OneDrive or other cloud storage platform, such as a SharePoint site. The workbook can then be shared with coworkers and collaborators.

Creating a new sheet view is a two-step process: sort and/or filter the table as needed and then save the sorted/filtered table as a sheet view. To begin the process, use the Sort & Filter group commands (on the Data tab) to get the desired view of the table. For example, let's say I have a table that shows recent expenses for a list of employees. (including costs for travel, hardware/software, and memberships). A field is included in the table that identifies the department affiliation for each employee. I want to see the purchases made by the members of the Porches and Decks department.

First, select the Filter command in the Sort & Filter group and then use the drop-down filter menu for Department Name and select Porches And Decks. The filter used provides a subset of the original table. To save the currently filtered table as a sheet view, go to the View tab and select New in the Sheet View group. Note that the column headings and row numbers are shaded as soon as you create the view. Now you can either keep the view or exit it. To save the view, select the Keep command in the Sheet View group. If you don't want to keep the sheet view, select Exit.

All the sheet views you keep for a particular worksheet can be accessed by selecting the Options command in the Sheet View. The Sheet View Options dialog box will open, as shown in Figure 15-12. The default naming convention for Sheet View is View#, where each view is numbered sequentially. You can rename sheet views as needed, and you can also duplicate and delete them.

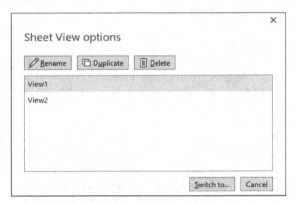

Figure 15-12   The Sheet View Options dialog box allows you to name and manage your sheet views.

Using the data form

Entering records into a very large table can be both time-consuming and a little hard on the eyes as you add more and more rows. An alternative way to enter table data one record at a time that has been around in Excel for years is the data form. However, when Excel 2007 adopted the new ribbon-based user interface that we now use in the 365 applications, the data form lost its place as one of the readily accessible data tools on the Data menu. The form is not available via a command on the ribbon's Data tab. This also holds true in the current version of Excel, so if you want to take advantage of the data form to enter or find records in your database table, you need to add the Form command to the Excel Quick Access Toolbar. As I already mentioned, the form can be quite useful when you are working with extremely large tables, and you just want to deal with one record at a time. All your table fields will be listed in the form, which makes data entry easy. The data form also provides a find feature (you can search both forward and backward in the table) and allows you to delete records as needed.

The form provides you with the ability to view, edit, and add records to the table individually. It also enables you to quickly search the database table to find records.

You can quickly add the Form command to the Excel Quick Access Toolbar from the Excel Options window. Follow these steps:

1. Select the Customize Quick Access Toolbar menu and then select More Commands. The Excel Options window opens with the Quick Access Toolbar settings selected.

2. In the Customize Quick Access Toolbar pane of the Options window, select Choose Commands From and then select All Commands.

3. Scroll down through the commands listed in the Command pane and select Form.

4. Click the Add button to add the Form command to the Quick Access Toolbar. Then click OK to return to the Excel window.

Now you can open the form as needed when you are working with a table. Click in a record (a row in a table) and then click the Form command on the Quick Access Toolbar. The record opens in the Form window. You can edit a record or delete a record from the Form window. You can also enter new records to the table by selecting New. The new record is inserted at the bottom of the table.

If you want to find a particular record or records, click the Criteria button. Enter criteria in a field or fields and then click the Find Next button. The first record that meets your criteria is shown in the Form window. You can click the Find Next button to move to the next record that matches your criteria. When you have finished working with the form, select Close.

Creating outlines and subtotals

The ribbon's Data tab also provides an Outline group that provides the Group, Ungroup, and Subtotal commands. The Group command enables you to create outline groups in a worksheet. The groups can then be individually expanded or collapsed, so you can hide information at a particular outline level and view only a summary of the data (such as sales totals by regions or salary data by department) rather than each individual row of data.

The purpose of an outline is to take advantage of a hierarchy that is already present in the worksheet. If you think about a text outline, it is made up of different levels of information, such as primary levels, secondary levels, and so on. In Excel, the hierarchy is based on logical groupings of information. Typically, the key to grouping several rows of information is that they are tied together by a summary row. This row can be above or below the detail rows, but it has to be in the same place for you to create an outline. For example, you might have a sales sheet that shows the monthly sales figures for each of your regions for an entire year. At the end of each quarter, a summary row provides a total for each region's sales for that quarter. Figure 15-13 shows a worksheet that has been formatted as an outline using the Group command.

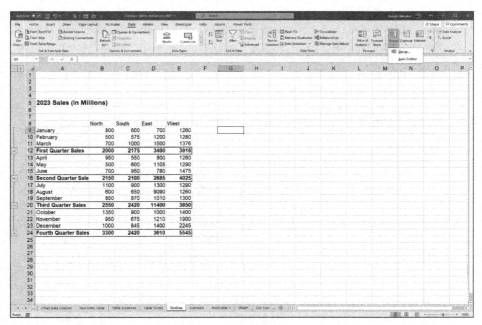

Figure 15-13   You can group related data into outlines.

Note that each group in the outline has a button on the left that can be used to collapse the grouped rows. You can collapse a particular quarter group and view the summary row for only that particular group. You can click the control for a collapsed group and expand the group to show all the data in a particular group. Level numbers are also provided at the top of the worksheet area just above the row numbers and to the left of the column letters. You can use these buttons to collapse the outline to level 1 or to expand the outline to level 2, as needed.

To create an outline, you have two choices: You can create the outline manually, or you can allow Excel to create an auto outline. If you are working with a range of cells that has been formatted as a table, you can't use the auto outline possibility. So, you might want to use the Convert To Range command on the Table Tools, Design tab to convert the table back to a regular worksheet. It definitely makes sense to try the auto outline scenario first because Excel is good at recognizing the groupings in a worksheet.

Select the worksheet, click the Group command, and then select Auto Outline. If auto outline doesn't group the data in the worksheet as you anticipated, you can go the manual outline route. If you need to clear the outline grouping provided by auto outline, select the Ungroup command and then select Clear Outline.

To manually create the outline, select the worksheet data and then click the Group command. Select Group, and the Group dialog box opens. This dialog box provides you with two options: Rows and Columns. Click the appropriate option button for grouping the data and then click OK. The worksheet is converted to an outline. If you don't get a proper outline, you can clear the current outline and then rearrange the data as needed so that it can be placed in an outline. Remember, it is all about establishing a hierarchy that is consistent throughout the worksheet.

Another possibility provided by the Outline group is the Subtotal command. The Subtotal command is easier to work with than the Group command because it automatically inserts subtotal rows for you in the worksheet and can also provide summary data. The trick with subtotals is that you need to have a data column that provides a way to group associated rows of data.

TIP

You can also collapse or expand the detail in your outline groups by using the Show Detail and Hide Detail commands in the Outline group, respectively.

For example, an employee list that includes a Department column could be sorted by department, grouping all the employees in the worksheet in their respective departments. You can then have the Subtotal command act on other column data; for example, if a Salary column is also included in the worksheet, the Subtotal could group the employees by department and then provide a salary subtotal for each department. So, to use the Subtotal command to both group data rows and provide subtotals based on those groupings, you need one column of information that can provide the grouping and another column of information that provides the values that are used to compute the subtotals for each group.

To apply the Subtotal command to a worksheet, sort the rows by the column data that provides the logical grouping of the row data. For example, the data in the sheet has been sorted by Department. Then click the Subtotal command. The Subtotal dialog box opens, as shown in Figure 15-14.

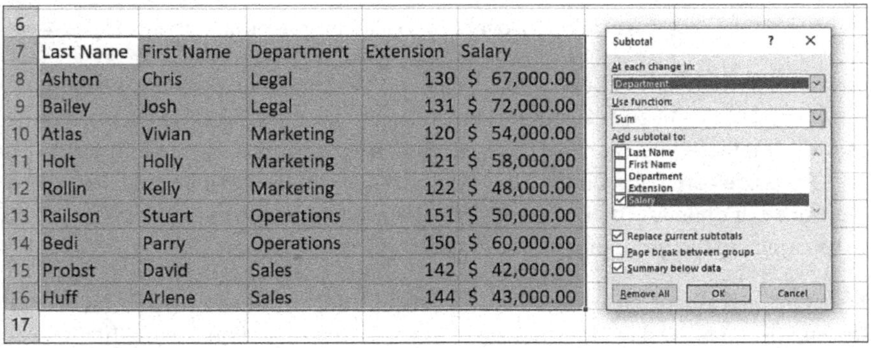

Figure 15-14   A data sheet and the Subtotal dialog box

Use the At Each Change In drop-down menu to specify the column title (or field name) that serves as the grouping mechanism for the rows in the column (this would be the column that you used to sort the worksheet). In the Use Function drop-down menu, select the function that you want to use for the subtotal rows in the worksheet. The default is SUM, but you can also use other statistical functions such as COUNT, AVERAGE, and MAX.

NOTE

You can't use the Subtotal command on a worksheet range that has been formatted as a table.

In the Add Subtotal To box, select the check box for the column that contains the values you want to use in the subtotal calculation. This is a column that contains numerical values.

Other check boxes provided in the Subtotal dialog box enable you to replace any current subtotals in the worksheet or place page breaks between the groups, which can be useful on large worksheets that are then printed. A check box is also provided that includes a summary, including a grand total below the worksheet data. When you are ready to add the subtotals and groupings to the worksheet, click OK. Figure 15-15 shows a worksheet that has been grouped by department.

The Subtotal command placed a subtotal for each department in the Salary column. A grand total has also been placed at the bottom of the worksheet range. Controls are also provided that enable you to expand and collapse the different levels created in the worksheet by the Subtotal command, creating an outline in the worksheet.

	Last Name	First Name	Department	Extension	Salary
6					
7	Last Name	First Name	Department	Extension	Salary
8	Ashton	Chris	Legal	130	$ 67,000.00
9	Bailey	Josh	Legal	131	$ 72,000.00
10			**Legal Total**		$ 139,000.00
11	Atlas	Vivian	Marketing	120	$ 54,000.00
12	Holt	Holly	Marketing	121	$ 58,000.00
13	Rollin	Kelly	Marketing	122	$ 48,000.00
14			**Marketing Total**		$ 160,000.00
15	Railson	Stuart	Operations	151	$ 50,000.00
16	Bedi	Parry	Operations	150	$ 60,000.00
17			**Operations Total**		$ 110,000.00
18	Probst	David	Sales	142	$ 42,000.00
19	Huff	Arlene	Sales	144	$ 43,000.00
20			**Sales Total**		$ 85,000.00
21			**Grand Total**		$ 494,000.00
22					
23					

Figure 15-15   A worksheet configured with subtotals

Working with external data

Excel provides you with a number of options for getting external data into a worksheet. After you import data from another source or connect to a data source such as a database server, you can then use Excel's wide variety of capabilities to work with the data. The fact that Excel is an extremely powerful number cruncher means that you can probably perform calculations and data analysis that would be extremely time-consuming or very labor-intensive in another software application, such as Microsoft Access.

Excel makes it easy to import data from other applications or database servers. The Get & Transform Data group commands on the Data tab enable you to import data from Access, web tables (on websites), text files, and other database sources, such as a Microsoft SQL Server. Let's look at the possibilities.

Importing data from Access

Access is a powerful desktop relational database application, and it can also be used as the front-end client for databases hosted by a database server, such as a server running Microsoft SQL Server. Whether Access is installed on your computer will depend on the applications provided by your Microsoft 365 subscription or your Perpetual Office purchase. You actually do not need Access, however, to import an Access table into Excel.

Access uses the table as the data container for its database records. Most Access databases (of any complexity) contain a number of related data tables.

Even though each database contains multiple tables, it is not that difficult to specify a table in the Access database and import it into Excel. Follow these steps:

1. Select the cell in the current worksheet (an empty worksheet would be a good idea) that serves as the upper-left corner of the imported table data.

2. Select Get Data, then point at From Database on the Get Data menu.

3. Select From Microsoft Access Database on the Get Data menu; the Import Data dialog box will open. (It looks a lot like the Open dialog box that the 365 apps use to open files.) Navigate to the folder or the network drive that contains the Access database and then select it.

4. Select Import in the Import Data dialog box. The Navigator window will open, as shown in Figure 15-16.

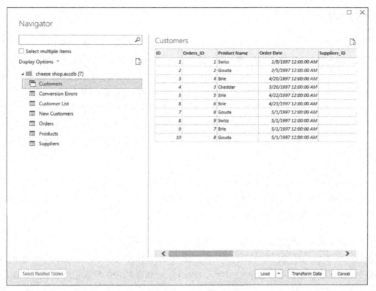

Figure 15-16   The Navigator is used to select database tables for import into Excel.

5. The Navigator lists the tables and the queries in the Access database (queries look like tables and consist of columns and rows of data that has been pulled from tables in the database); select a specific table or tables (use the Select Multiple Items check box to allow the selection of multiple items). A preview of the selected table (or the first table selected in multiple selections) will appear on the right side of the Navigator.

6. Select Load; the Access table (or tables) will be loaded on the current worksheet. The Queries & Connections pane will also open in the Excel window application and list the table or tables to which you are now connected. (The Queries & Connections pane will list them as queries.)

7. Since the Access table (or tables) is imported as an Excel table, it will be formatted as a table including the AutoFilters drop-down arrows on every column heading . You can use the AutoFilters to sort or filter the data as you require. You can also use any of the Table Tools, Design commands to change the look of the table. The table you have imported is linked to the Excel worksheet, so changes made to the Access database are reflected in the worksheet when you update the link between the external data and Excel. To refresh a link to an Access database or other external databases, select the Refresh All command on the Data tab. You can use the Refresh All command to refresh all the links to external data or refresh the external data on the current worksheet by selecting Refresh.

Importing a web table

You can also import data from any table that appears on a web page. The From Web tool that is used to select a web table that is then linked to an Excel worksheet is actually quite good at identifying table data on websites. You can import data from a table on the web that is static, meaning the data in the table is not updated. You can also import data from a table that is dynamic, meaning the data is updated in the table over time. For example, you might want to include stock data that is published in a table on the web, and that is periodically updated. Because Excel imports the external data as a link, the linked data can be refreshed in the Excel worksheet.

When you create a link to a web table, you must specify the site that contains the table. So, you might want to use your web browser to navigate to the website. You can then select the website's URL and copy it so that you can paste it into the From Web window's URL (address) box.

Once you have the URL copied and you are ready to go, select the From Web command in the Get & Transform Data group on the ribbon's Data tab. In the From Web dialog box, paste (or type) the URL and select OK. The Navigator dialog box will open. (Yes, this is the same Navigator dialog box you used for getting data from an Access database in the previous section.) Depending on the size of the data table you are attempting to connect to, it might take a few moments for Excel to connect to the website. Once the connection is made, the Navigator window will open and list the content that Excel was able to identify on the web page you specified. Excel is very good at telling the difference between information in paragraphs and information arranged in rows and columns. Paragraphs of text will be identified in the Navigator as Document. Because you are looking for data, use the left side of the Navigator window to select any tables that were available on the website. For example, if you pasted the URL for a web page that contained a single table (meaning one set of data in columns and rows), that table of data will be designated as Table 0.

To open the connected data table, select the table in the Navigator's list (on the left side of the Navigator window). A preview of the table will be provided on the right side of the Navigator window. If the preview of the web-based data table shows that the data is in an appropriate table format (columns and rows), you can load the data into the current Excel worksheet. Select the Load button. It might take a moment for the data to appear in the worksheet. The Queries & Connections pane will also open as the data is loaded into Excel, and it will show the loaded table as a connection.

Web table data imported into Excel is automatically formatted as a table. This means that you can filter and sort the data as you would any data table in Excel. You can also take advantage of many of the commands on the Data tab to manipulate the data, and you can add formulas and functions to the data for calculations or create a chart based on the data.

Importing text files

We deal with a lot of data in both our work and personal lives. At work, data is typically shared on a network. Also, most of the database management software that we interface with is usually provided by a specialized server. The same goes for personal information that we gather from our online banking websites or an app we use on our phones to track our stock portfolio. Some of these database tools—again, both at work and home—are very good at sharing information with other software packages and tools; others are not.

So, you will find that there are situations in which you will need to download data that has very little formatting, so a tool, such as Excel, can actually digest it. For example, when I want to do some number crunching on my bank account, I have to download my latest transactions and deposits as a delimited text file. I then have to import the information into Excel to work with it. Delimited text files, unfortunately, are not all uniform. Every data service that you download text files from seems to put its own spin on how a delimited text file is formatted.

That means even though these text files can then be imported into Excel, you will still need to tell Excel what type of delimited text file it is dealing with. This is because there are tab-delimited text files, comma-delimited text files, and other text files that use other characters to delimit their fields and records. The delimiter is basically the special character (or a space or a tab) that separates each field and each record in the text file.

To import a text file into Excel, select the From Text/CSV command in the Get & Transform Data group. The Import Data dialog box opens. Locate and select the text file you want to import and then click Open. The Import Preview window will open, as shown in Figure 15-17.

Excel actually analyzes the text file and tries to determine the delimiter and provide a preview of what the data will look like in Excel columns and rows, meaning a table. Excel also attempts to detect the data type. Figure 15-17 shows the preview of how a Comma-Separated File (CSV) will appear.

Figure 15-17   The Import Preview window

If the preview of the data import looks weird, you can change the delimiter using the Delimiter drop-down menu; it provides you with choices such as tab, semicolon, comma, and so on. You can also change the data type detected. By default, Excel uses the first 200 rows of the data to determine the data type. You can change this setting using the Data Type Detection drop-down menu.

When you are ready to import the text file, select Load. The Queries & Connections pane will open, showing the new data connection. The text file will be placed in the current Excel work-sheet at A1 (you can move it on the sheet as necessary). As with any imported data, you can sort and filter immediately since it is automatically imported as a table. You can also manipulate the table data using the various Excel commands and functions.

Connecting to other data sources

You can connect Excel to a number of other data sources, including hosted data services such as Windows Azure Marketplace, which is a data services subscription service hosted by Microsoft. The different data sources to which you can connect are listed on the Get Data gallery, which is accessed by selecting the Get Data command in the Get & Transform Data group. Figure 15-18 shows the Get Data gallery with the From Database subgallery selected.

External data sources can include Microsoft SQL Server databases. Typically, these are databases available to you when you work at a corporation or institution that uses Active Directory on Windows Server to handle user and computer authentication and also uses SQL Server to man-age databases.

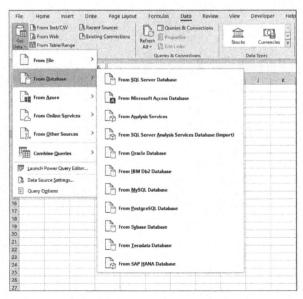

Figure 15-18   The Get Data gallery and the From Database subgallery

SQL Server is a powerful network database platform. Suppose you do a lot of work with information in a corporate or another large institution environment. In that case, chances are that you work with data that is stored on a SQL server or one of Microsoft's database platform competitors, such as Oracle. As already mentioned, Excel can be used to connect to a SQL server and work with the data on the server. As with any other data connection that you make between an external data source and Excel, once you have the data in Excel, it can be analyzed and manipulated as needed.

Even if you don't work for a "Microsoft shop" that deploys Microsoft's various server varieties, you can take advantage of external data sources available on the web, which are powered by Microsoft SQL Server, such as Microsoft's Azure Marketplace (Microsoft provides a subscription for access to Azure Marketplace). In fact, the Get Data gallery provides a From Azure option, allowing you to quickly connect Excel to an Azure database.

To connect to an external data source via the Get Data gallery, you will need to log on to the database server that hosts the information and import a data table. This means that you will need to know the server name and have logon credentials for the server. For example, let's say you want to access a SQL Server deployed by your company. In some cases, you might be able to log on using Windows authentication, or you can log on using a username and password specifically for the SQL Server. When you select a particular database or other source using the Get Data gallery, the Queries & Connection window will open in Excel. For example, in the case of a SQL server connection, you supply the Server name in the Server box, and you can also supply the Database name for the connection, but this is optional. Once this information is entered, select OK to continue, and the SQL Server database window will open.

The SQL Server database window is where you provide your credentials (username and password). You can use your current Windows credentials, the credential for the database itself, or another Microsoft account. Once you have entered this information, select Connect. The Connection Navigator window will open and allow you to choose the table or tables you want to connect to in the remote database. Once you have selected the table or tables, select the Load button. It may take a few moments for the data to load, but the selected table (or tables) will be connected to the current worksheet as a table. You can sort, filter, and otherwise manipulate the data in the table as you would any other Excel table.

NOTE

Microsoft Azure is a cloud services website hosted by Microsoft. You can access a number of free data sources on the Azure site and import them into Excel for subsequent analysis (in tables or pivot tables). All you need to sign up for an Azure account is a Windows Live account (such as Outlook.com). You can then sign up for a free account at *https://azure.microsoft.com/en-us/*.

Using Microsoft Query

Although you will find that the various possibilities provided by the Get Data gallery allows you to directly connect to a number of different database server platforms, there may be some occasions when you want to connect to a database source and run a query to select the data you import into Excel. A query is really a question that you pose to a database. Queries enable you to extract data from more than one related table by specifying the field information that is to be included in the query. For example, you could design the query to extract data related to specific products that you sell from a products table and also extract data from a suppliers table that provides information about the suppliers that provide you with your products. For queries to work, there needs to be a relationship between the tables that you use in the query. There-fore, you should have some familiarity with the database itself and how it is structured before you attempt to create queries in Excel to access information in the database.

Microsoft Query enables you to connect to common data sources such as Access and Excel files and also dBASE files. (dBASE was one of the first PC-based relational databases.) You can also create queries to access data in a SQL Server database. After you create a query, you can then use it in the future; the query can be used in other Excel worksheets, and it can be modified as necessary. The data sources that you identify during the process of creating the query are also available in the future. This makes it easy to reconnect to a particular database or database server from Excel. When you create a new query, you must identify or create a data source for the query first. You can then create the query.

Creating a data source

Creating a data source establishes a connection to the database you use when you create your query. To open the Choose Data Source dialog box, select Get Data, then From Other Sources, and finally From Microsoft Query. The Choose Data Source dialog box opens. The Databases tab of the Choose Data Source dialog box provides you with four options for database sources: New Data Source, Access Connection, dBASE Files, Excel Files, and MS Access Database. The Choose Data Source dialog box is designed to allow you to create a query for a new data source, such as dBase or Microsoft Access. So, to begin the process of creating the new query, select New Data Source, and then click OK. The Create New Data Source dialog box opens. The Create New Data Source dialog box walks you through the steps in creating the new data source.

The first step you must perform in the Create New Data Source dialog box is to enter a descrip-tive name for the data source. Create a name for the source that makes it apparent what data-base platform you are accessing and the database you will use in the query. After you have named the data source, select a driver for the type of database you want to access. You can choose a driver for a large number of different database types, including those already men-tioned in this section, such as dBASE, Access, and SQL.

NOTE

ODBC stands for Open Database Connectivity and is a standard (supported by Microsoft) for accessing different database file types and platforms. It is ODBC that allows Microsoft Query to connect to different types of databases. Figure 15-19 shows the Create New Data Source dialog box and the list of database types.

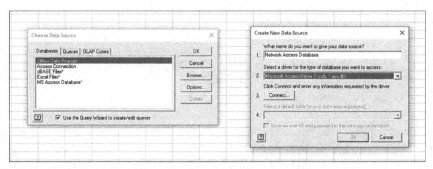

Figure 15-19   Select the driver type for the data source.

After you have selected the driver for the data source, click the Connect button. What happens next depends on the driver you selected for the database. If you selected a driver for a database file type, such as Access, dBASE, or Paradox, you need to specify the location of the file on your computer or network.

If you selected a database type that is a hosted database service using server technology such as SQL, you have to log on to the server. For example, if you selected SQL Server as the driver type, when you click the Connect button in the Create New Data Source dialog box, the SQL Server Login dialog box opens. Provide your log-in credentials in the SQL Server Login dialog box and then click OK to connect to the server. A SQL server can be the home for more than one database, so you may have to click the Options button to specify the database for your connection.

Creating the query

After you have connected to your database, which can be your own Access database or a remote database on a SQL server, the Query Wizard opens, as shown in Figure 15-20.

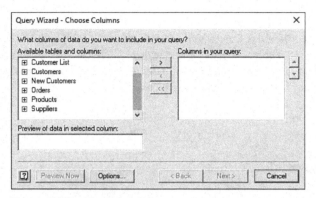

Figure 15-20   The Query Wizard

On the left of the Query Wizard dialog box is a list of the tables in the database. Expand a table and then choose specific fields that you want to serve as the columns in your query; select a field and then click the Add button to add it to the columns in your query list. You can use fields from multiple tables if required. However, it is important that a relationship exists between the tables in the database.

If you attempt to create a query using fields from multiple tables that are not related, the Query Wizard requires that you create the joins between the tables. This would require that a key field in a table also exist as the foreign key in a second table for you to be able to create the relationship. This discussion is a little beyond the scope of this book, so I would say that if you are going to work with database tables in Excel, you should spend some time working with the databases in their native applications (such as Access) to make sure you understand how relational databases work.

After you have specified the columns for your query, click Next. On the next screen, you can specify that the data be filtered by a particular field or fields, which establishes the row in the table that is created by the query. Set the filters for the query (if required) and then click Next. On the next screen, you can specify that the data be sorted by a field or fields. After specifying the sort fields and sort order, click Next.

The final Query Wizard screen enables you to save your query so that it is available in the future in the Choose Data Source dialog box on the Query tab. Select Save Query and then use the Save As dialog box to name and save the query. You then return to the Query Wizard's Finish screen; click Finish. The Import Data dialog box opens, as shown in Figure 15-21.

You can import the data as a table or as a pivot table report (or as a pivot chart). The data can be imported into the current worksheet or a new worksheet. Specify the various options in the Import Data dialog box and then click OK. The data is imported into an Excel table. You can manipulate the data as you do any Excel data, including sorting and filtering.

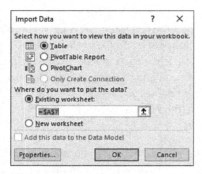

Figure 15-21   The Import Data dialog box

Viewing and refreshing connections

If you are working with external data in Excel tables, you might want to view the connections for your Excel workbook. You can also refresh connections to take advantage of the fact that when the data source is updated, this information is also available in Excel after the link to the source has been refreshed.

To view the connections for the current Excel workbook, select the Queries & Connections command in the Queries & Connections group on the ribbon's Data tab. The Queries & Connections pane opens on the right side of the Excel application window, as shown in Figure 15-22.

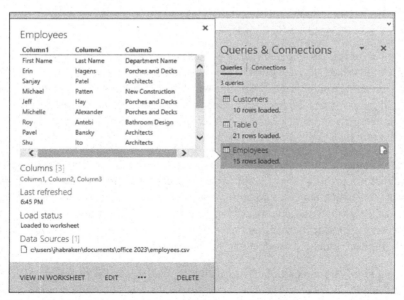

Figure 15-22   The Queries & Connections pane with preview

You can preview a query or connection in the Queries & Connections pane by placing the mouse on that particular connection. To refresh or remove a listed query or connection, right-click on the connection in the Queries & Connections pane and then select Refresh or Delete, as needed. You can also set properties related to a particular connection, such as the refresh properties for the source; right-click on the connection and then select Properties to open the connection's Properties dialog box. The Usage tab enables you to specify refresh-related settings and also some formatting and drill-through (the number of records to retrieve) settings for OLAP (Online Analytical Processing) databases.

Another tool that you can access from the Queries & Connections pane is the Power Query Editor, which allows you to remove columns or rows from the query/connection and merge or append queries that you have created. All the ins and outs of the Power Query editor are beyond the scope of this chapter. However, the Power Query Editor interface is fairly user-friendly, and if you have already been working with queries and database connections in Excel, it should provide you with another possibility (definitely an advanced possibility) for viewing, refreshing, and fine-tuning your work with external database sources. You can access the Power Query Editor by double-clicking on a query listed in the Queries & Connections pane.

Working with pivot tables

Pivot tables enable you to analyze and summarize table data. You can use an Excel pivot table to create a report for a table that you created in a worksheet, and you can also create a pivot table from data that you import into an Excel worksheet, such as an Access database table or a table from another data source. A pivot table can even be used to analyze data that you imported into Excel using Microsoft Query.

An Excel pivot table is called a pivot table because it enables you to arrange table data in a cross-tabulated report. You can pivot or rearrange the information in the pivot table to analyze the data it contains. You not only determine which table fields are used as row and column headings in the pivot table, but you also specify fields that contain the values you want to analyze and summarize using the pivot table. Pivot tables can also specify fields that serve as filters for the data that is summarized in the pivot table.

To take advantage of what a pivot table can do with table data, you need a source table that has certain attributes. The table you specify as the data source for the pivot table needs to contain at least one field (meaning a column of data in the table) that contains repeating data. For example, you might have a table that shows the weekly sales for your sales force. A column in the table lists the product names that have been sold. Because your salespeople sell the same products, there are repeated product names in the Product column.

Another requirement for a pivot table is that the source table contains at least one field that consists of values. You need numerical data if the pivot table is going to provide you with summary information, such as subtotals and totals. Figure 15-23 shows a simple table that benefits from analysis using a pivot table.

Figure 15-23 shows the source table on the left of the worksheet, and the pivot table is directly to the right of the source table. The pivot table Fields list (the task pane on the right side of the Excel window) provides the fields section (a list of the fields in the source table) and the areas section, which provides the different areas of the pivot table.

The row labels for the pivot table, which are contained in the Row Labels section of the pivot table task pane, are the Region entries followed by the Name column. The regions can then be expanded or collapsed to show or hide the name of the sales representatives in the region, respectively.

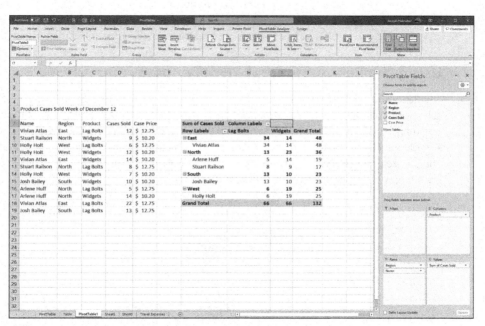

Figure 15-23   Pivot tables enable you to analyze table data.

The column labels, which have been added to the Column Labels area, consist of the products listed in the source table's Product field. The Total field has been added to the Values area section. The fields placed in the Values area are automatically acted on by the pivot table, and by default, sums are provided for the values. The subtotals provided by the pivot table enable you to see how each salesperson did on each product item, and the pivot table can also be collapsed by region to view the region subtotals only.

You can quickly rearrange the field information that you have placed into the various areas of the PivotTable task pane to quickly pivot the data shown in the pivot table. You can also remove fields or add fields—whatever it takes to enable you to see the data in the pivot table as you require.

Excel provides you with two options for creating a new pivot table. You can create a pivot table from scratch (which we discuss in detail in a moment), or you can insert a recommended pivot table. Using the recommended pivot tables is a good way to get familiar with how pivot tables are structured and how they can be used to create different "views" of the same data. Let's take a look at how to insert a recommended pivot table and then look at inserting your own pivot table.

NOTE

Specifying row labels, column labels, and values is straightforward. However, specifying a report filter can be a little confusing. Think of the report filter as a field or fields that you want to use to see a subset of the data. For example, if you have sales representatives' names set as your row labels, you could then use a grouping field such as region to quickly filter the data by including the region field in the Report Filter area. Slicers also enable you to filter data, so you might find slicers even more useful than filters.

Using the Recommended PivotTables command

The Recommended PivotTables command is in the Insert tab's Tables group. Although you can specify the data source for a recommended pivot table, the Recommended PivotTables command works best (and fastest) when you are on a sheet that contains a table and you have already selected the table range that you want to use as the data source for the pivot table. Then all you have to do is select Recommended PivotTables. This opens the Recommended PivotTables dialog box, as shown in Figure 15-24.

Figure 15-24   Quickly insert a pivot table based on a selected table using the Recommended PivotTables command.

The Recommended PivotTables dialog box provides a list of recommended pivot tables on the left. Select one of the thumbnails to preview it. When you have found the recommended pivot table that you want to insert, click OK. The pivot table is inserted into a new sheet. The PivotTable Fields task pane also opens to the right of the new pivot table. You can manipulate an inserted recommended pivot table as you would a pivot table you create from scratch, which is our next subject.

Creating a pivot table

You can also create a new pivot table using the Create PivotTable dialog box, which is opened using the PivotTable command on the ribbon's Insert tab. You can insert a pivot table on the current worksheet or on a new worksheet.

The pivot table can use a table on a worksheet in the current Excel workbook as the data source, or you can connect to an external data source. The real nuts-and-bolts portion of the pivot table–creation process relates to the field placement in the pivot table. You need to determine the fields that serve as rows headings, column headings, and values to be acted on by the pivot table. The great thing about the pivot table is that you can quickly rearrange the field placement and look at the data in a number of different ways.

It makes sense to get your table in shape before you create the pivot table, although you can edit a table and update the associated pivot table (or pivot tables—yes, you can have multiple pivot tables for a single data source). If you are going to use an external data source, use the Get & Transform Data commands on the Data tab to connect to the data source. This enables you to spend some time looking over the data before you create the pivot table.

You can create a pivot table from any data source connection, even data connections in other workbooks. However, I think it is easier to create the pivot table based on a table (external data or something you have input in Excel) that you can see on a worksheet in the current workbook. To insert a pivot table, follow these steps:

1. On the ribbon's Insert tab, select pivot table. The Create PivotTable dialog box opens, as shown in Figure 15-25.

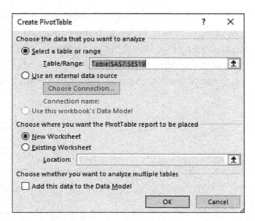

Figure 15-25   Specify the table range and the pivot table location in the Create PivotTable
dialog box.

2.   To create the pivot table from a table or range on the current worksheet or in the current
workbook, click the Table/Range box and then select the range. If you are going to use
an external data source, click the Use an External Data Source option button and then
click the Choose Connection button. In the Existing Connections dialog box, select a data
source and then click Open.

3.   After you have specified the range for the pivot table or specified a connection, select
either the New Worksheet or Existing Worksheet option button to specify where the pivot
table is created. In the case of the Existing Worksheet option, also specify a location for
the pivot table. All you need to do is select the cell that serves as the upper-left corner for
the pivot table.

4.   Click OK, and the new pivot table's blank frame is inserted into the current worksheet
or a new worksheet. The PivotTable Fields task pane also opens on the right of the Excel
window, as shown in Figure 15-26.

5.   The PivotTable Fields task pane is used to specify the data source table fields that are used
in the pivot table. Select the fields you want to add to the pivot table report. You can drag
the field names to the different report areas, or you can click in an area and then select
the check box next to a field. As you specify the fields for the pivot table, the pivot table
begins to appear on the sheet.

CHAPTER 15

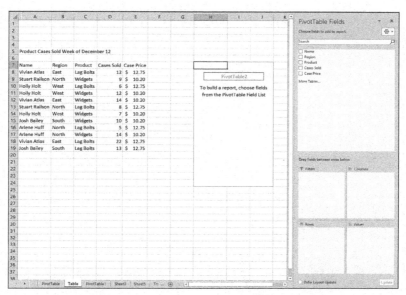

Figure 15-26   The pivot table placeholder and the PivotTable Fields task pane

Remember that a pivot table is meant to provide you with a dynamic report. If the field arrangement that you have specified for the pivot table isn't working, or you want to rearrange the fields, you can do so in the PivotTable Fields task pane. When you have finished working with the fields, you can close the PivotTable Fields task pane.

The pivot table contains Expand and Shrink buttons as well as drop-down menus for the column and row labels. You can use the field drop-down menus to sort or filter the data in the pivot table. Figure 15-27 shows the list provided for the row labels.

The list enables you to change the sort order of the selected field and also to select the field value (or values) that you want to use to filter the pivot table. You can use the Select Field drop-down menu to toggle between the fields that serve as row or column labels as needed.

CHAPTER 15

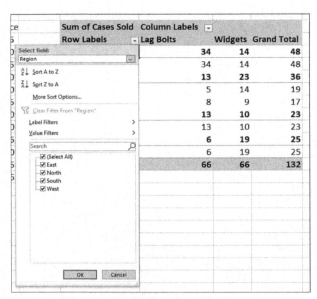

Figure 15-27   A row field's drop-down menu

Working with the pivot table tools

When you select a cell in the pivot table, PivotTable Analyze and Design tabs become available on the ribbon. The PivotTable Analyze tab enables you to specify pivot table and field settings and to specify how values are summarized and are shown. The Design tab is dedicated to the layout of the pivot table and enables you to apply styles to it.

The PivotTable Analyze tab

The PivotTable Analyze tab enables you to manipulate the fields in the table and also filter the data in the pivot table; for example, you can insert a slicer for the pivot table. You can use the Expand Entire Field or Collapse Entire Field command in the Active Field group to expand or collapse the currently selected field or fields as needed.

The Group commands allow you to group a selection of fields and then ungroup them if needed. The Filter group contains the Insert Slicer and Insert Timeline command. We look at inserting slicers in a moment. The Insert Timeline command is interesting in that it allows you to filter the data in a pivot table so that only the data that falls within the date range you have specified on the Timeline slicers shows in the pivot table. Figure 15-28 shows a pivot table and a Timeline slicer for that pivot table. Selecting a date range on the Timeline slicer hides the data that does not fall within that time range.

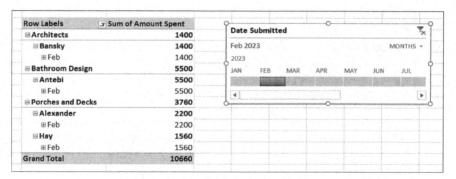

Figure 15-28   A Timeline slicer allows you to filter pivot table data.

The Analyze tab also provides the Data group, which supplies you with commands that enable you to refresh the data source for the pivot table or to change the data source. The Actions group provides commands that allow you to clear or move the pivot table and to select elements of the table such as values and labels.

If you need to access the PivotTable Fields task pane (or Field List, as it is also known), select the Show command in the Show group and select Field List. The Show command also provides access to the Buttons command and the Field Headers command. The Buttons command allows you to toggle the Expand and Collapse buttons in a pivot table on or off. The Field Headers button toggles the field headers on or off.

The Design tab

The PivotTable Tools, Design tab enables you to manipulate the layout of your calculated fields and to also assign styles to the pivot table. The Layout group provides the Subtotals, Grand Totals, Report Layout, and Blank Rows commands.

The Subtotals command enables you to hide the subtotals or to specify that the subtotals appear at the bottom (the default) or top of a group in the pivot table. The Grand Totals command enables you to turn the grand totals off or on for rows and columns or specify that grand totals are shown only for the rows or columns in the pivot table. The Report Layout command enables you to choose from a number of different formats for the pivot table, such as Compact, Outline, and Tabular. The Blank Rows command is used to insert or remove blank lines after each item in the pivot table.

The PivotTable Styles gallery provides a number of different styles that can be applied to the pivot table. If you apply a particular style, you can then use the PivotTable Style Options check boxes to hide or show elements such as row headers, column headers, or banded rows and columns.

Using slicers

We already addressed slicers earlier in this chapter when we applied slicers to a table. You can also use slicers to filter the data in a pivot table. A slicer is an easily accessible workspace object that resides on the sheet with the pivot table. You can select and deselect items on the slider to quickly filter the pivot table using different data parameters.

You can create multiple slicers for a pivot table. For example, you could create a slicer that filters row data and a slicer that filters column data. To create a new slicer, select the Insert Slicer command on the PivotTable Tools, Analyze tab. The Insert Slicers dialog box opens and shows all the fields available to your pivot table.

A slicer can filter the data in the pivot table by only a single field. However, you can create multiple slicers by selecting more than one field in the Insert Slicers dialog box. After selecting a field (for a single slicer) or multiple fields (for multiple slicers), click OK. The new slicer (or slicers) appears on the current worksheet. The slicer lists the field values in the field that you selected in the Insert Slicers dialog box. Select a particular field value to filter the pivot table by that value. To remove the filter, click the remove filter icon in the upper-right corner of the slicer's frame.

When you have a slicer selected, the Slicer Tools, Options tab becomes available on the ribbon. You can use the styles available and the size settings to format the slicer. If you have multiple pivot tables on a worksheet, you can associate the slicer with those pivot tables. This enables you to filter more than one pivot table using a single slicer. Select the PivotTable Connections command, and the PivotTable Connections dialog box opens. Select the pivot tables listed in the dialog box that you want to associate with the slicer. Then click OK to close the dialog box.

> ## NOTE
>
> **Slicers can also be used to filter data in a pivot chart. A pivot chart is a visualization of PivotTable data and can be quickly created via the PivotChart command on the pivot table Tools, Analyze tab.**

Slicers can be moved on the worksheet as needed, and you can also delete a slicer that you no longer need. Make sure that the slicer is selected, and then press Delete on the keyboard.

Validating and analyzing worksheet data

Taking advantage of data validation   503

Performing a what-if analysis   510

Using Goal Seek, Solver, and Forecast Sheet   518

Excel provides you with powerful capabilities for manipulating, analyzing, and visualizing worksheet data. However, even the most elegant charts and data analysis won't mean much if you have incorrectly entered data in a worksheet.

In this chapter, we look at Excel's data validation features. You can create data validation rules that will cut down on the possibility of data being entered into a worksheet incorrectly.

We also discuss Excel's tools for analyzing worksheet data. We look at the data table feature and the Scenario Manager, which both provide you with the ability to do a what-if analysis of your worksheet data. Coverage is also provided of Goal Seek and Solver, both of which enable you to derive values based on a predefined goal. We finish with a discussion of the Forecast Sheet feature, which allows you to take historical time-based data and create a forecast.

Taking advantage of data validation

Even a worksheet containing the best-built formulas and the most advanced Excel functions can still end up providing you with invalid results for the various sheet calculations. This is because people can make mistakes when entering the data into the worksheet. No matter how well designed the worksheet is, incorrect values in cells still render invalid results when they are acted upon by formulas and functions.

A strategy for greatly reducing the possibility of an invalid data entry in a cell or cell range is to use data validation rules. Data validation simply means that the data entered into a cell range that has a validation rule applied to it must meet the criteria specified by the validation rule. For example, the validation criteria for a data validation rule might specify that only a date can be entered into the cell range to which you have applied the rule. This means that only entries in a date format can be entered in the cells. You can even take the validation rule further and specify a range of valid dates, which means that any dates outside the range required by the rule will be invalid. You can also create validation rules that control the number of characters that can be entered into the cells in a particular range. For example, you might create a validation rule for a cell range where a U.S. state must be entered, and you want the state to always be entered using the two-character state abbreviation. The validation rule can limit the text length in the cell range to two text characters (such as IN or ME).

A validation rule can do more than limit entries to a specific length, however. You also can create a validation rule that allows only entries from a list of values that has been entered in a range elsewhere on the sheet. For example, if you have sales regions such as north, south, east, and west, you can specify in the validation rule that only these entries are valid in the Region column. The rule wouldn't negate someone entering the wrong region in a cell, but it greatly limits (by virtue of the validation list) what can be entered into the cells "controlled" by the validation rule.

Data validation rules can help you when you are inputting data into a worksheet that you use only occasionally or a large worksheet where it might be difficult to concentrate on what needs to be input into a particular range of cells. The validation rule can provide an input message that clearly tells you what a valid entry would be for each cell in the range. When incorrect data is entered into a cell in a range governed by a validation rule, the validation rule can also provide an "incorrect data" message that alerts you to the incorrect entry and provides help on the data that can be entered into the cell.

NOTE

You can create validation rules for any worksheet. This includes ranges in a worksheet that is formatted as a table. When creating rules in a table, you only need to select a field column heading when creating the rule, and the rule will then be applied to all the cells in that particular column under that particular field column heading.

Data validation can also be extremely useful when you design a worksheet used by coworkers, colleagues, or subordinates. Creating data validation rules can help ensure that whoever ends up entering information into the worksheet does it correctly.

Specifying validation criteria

Creating a validation rule is straightforward. You specify the criteria for the rule, and then you have the option of also providing an input message and an error alert for the rule. The Data Validation command is in the Data Tools group on the ribbon's Data tab.

To create a new data validation rule, select the cell range to which you will apply the rule. On the ribbon's Data tab, select the Data Validation command and then select Data Validation. The Data Validation dialog box opens.

The criterion for the validation rule is specified on the Settings tab. The Allow drop-down menu provides the following options:

- **Any Value:** The default setting has no restrictions. So, why is it even available? You can create a validation rule that doesn't restrict data input but provides an input message to coach users to place certain data in a range of cells. Using this criterion does not restrict users from entering whatever they want in the cell, however.

- **Whole Number:** Select this setting to restrict the data entry to numerical values with no decimals.

- **Decimal:** This setting restricts data entry to numerical values but allows decimals.

- **List:** This setting restricts the data entry to the entries you specified in a list you created elsewhere on the worksheet or workbook. Only the items in your list are considered valid entries in the cell range.

- **Date:** This setting allows only calendar dates to be entered into the cell range validated by the rule.

- **Time:** This setting restricts the data entry to time values.

- **Text Length:** This setting enables you to restrict the entry of text in the cell range by a specific number of characters.

- **Custom:** This setting enables you to use a formula (or function) as the criterion for data validation. For example, you might have a total budget for a project of $5,000.00. You can specify that the sum of the range of individual expenses entered in the cell range does not exceed 5,000; this would look something like =SUM(range of cells)<=5000. The cell range in the parentheses must be specified as absolute references for this scenario to work. You can also use other functions, such as the IF function, to validate whether an entry is true or false based on the condition set up in the IF function. Create the formula or function in a cell in the worksheet and then specify the cell's address when you specify the custom criterion.

Select the Allow criterion that you want to use for the validation rule. If you select Whole Number, Decimal, Date, or Time, you have the option of setting up a conditional statement for the rule. Using the Data drop-down menu, you can select from a number of different inequality statements, including Between, Not Between, Equal To, Less Than, and the like.

For example, if you select Between, you need to provide the starting and ending value for the allowed range of data entries. Figure 16-1 shows the Data Validation dialog box with the Settings tab selected.

In Figure 16-1, the Allow setting is configured as Date. The Data option has been set to Between, which requires that a start date and end date be specified for the allowed data range.

When you use inequality statements such as Between or Greater Than, you can specify the date, time, or numerical value by typing the value in the text boxes provided at the bottom of the Data Validation dialog box. For example, you could type the start date and end date for the allowed range.

CHAPTER 16

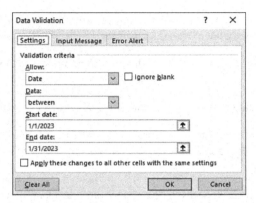

Figure 16-1   The Settings tab of the Data Validation dialog box

There is an alternative for providing the start and stop values of an allowed range when you use Between or another inequality expression such as Greater Than. You can specify the start and stop values for the allowed range by specifying cell addresses in the worksheet that provide the values. For example, you might put the start date and end date in cells in the worksheet and then specify these values by entering the appropriate cell addresses in the Start Date and End Date text boxes.

> **TIP**
>
> You can use the =TRIM function to keep users from inadvertently adding leading or trailing spaces to text entries in a cell. This is useful when entering employee numbers (which, like Social Security numbers, are not values) or other identifying information into a cell range. The Custom criterion formula would be =cell range =TRIM (cell range). Both references to the cell range must be made absolute references for this to work.

Configuring input messages and error alerts

After configuring the validation criteria for the data validation rule, you can configure an optional input message and error alert for the rule. The input message is specified on the Input Message tab of the Data Validation dialog box.

The input message is made up of a title and an input message. Figure 16-2 shows the Input Message tab of the Data Validation dialog box.

The input message is designed so that it appears when the user clicks a cell that has been assigned the data validation rule. The more specific you are when entering the input message, the easier it is for users to comply with the validation rule as they enter data.

You can also configure an error alert for the validation rule. The purpose of the error alert is to give the user some sort of direction in terms of correcting the entry of invalid data. Figure 16-3 shows the Error Alert tab of the Data Validation dialog box.

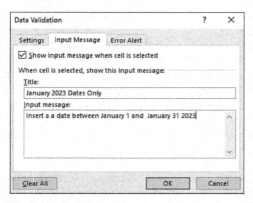

Figure 16-2   Enter an input message for the validation rule.

Figure 16-3   Create an error alert for the validation rule.

Error alerts can be configured to provide different levels of protection in terms of whether invalid data is even allowed to be entered into the cell. Three different error alert styles are provided, as follows:

- **Stop:** This error message style provides an error message box that enables the user to retry or cancel the entry. Data that violates the rule cannot be entered into the cell range that has been assigned this rule.

- **Warning:** This error message style provides a warning box. The user has the option to continue by selecting Yes. This means that incorrect data can be entered in the cell range.

The user is also provided the option of selecting No or Cancel in the warning box, which removes the entry from the cell.

- **Information:** This error message style provides an informational box. Incorrect data can be entered in the cell, and all the user has to do is click OK in the message box. The user can retry the entry by clicking Cancel.

Using the Stop error message style makes sense when it is imperative that data entered in a cell range be completely valid as dictated by the validation rule. You can use the Warning and Information styles when you want to suggest how data be entered in a cell range, but it isn't crucial that data be entered in a form other than that dictated by the validation rule.

When you have completed configuring the validation rule, click OK to close the Data Validation dialog box. You can now enter data into the range governed by the validation rule.

If you decide you want to remove a validation rule from a cell range, select the range and then select the Data Validation command to open the Data Validation dialog box. You can clear the rule by selecting Clear All on any of the dialog box tabs.

Circling invalid data

If you create validation rules that use the Warning and Information error message styles, users can potentially insert invalid data into the range where you have applied the validation rule. Users can also use the Clipboard to paste information into a cell, bypassing a validation rule.

You can circle the invalid data that appears in a cell range where a validation rule has been applied. Figure 16-4 shows invalid data that has been circled in a worksheet.

	A	B	C	D	E
1					
2	January 2023 Expenses				
3					
4	Date	Amount Spent	Purpose of Expense	State	
5	1/7/2023	$ 240.00	Client Dinner	ME	
6	1/9/2023	$ 2,500.00	Flight to San Diego	CA	
7	1/12/2023	$ 600.00	Hotel	CA	
8	2/2/2023	$ 300.00	Rental Car	CA	
9	Jan 7th 2023	$ 50.00	Client Breakfast	ME	
10		$ 12.50	Breakfast	MA	
11					
12					

Figure 16-4   Circle invalid data in a worksheet.

To circle invalid data, select the Data Validation command and then select Circle Invalid Data. Any cells that contain invalid data and are governed by a validation rule are circled. You can correct the cell entries as needed. To remove the validation circles from the worksheet, select the Data Validation command and then select Clear Validation Circles.

You can also do error checking related to your validation rules via the Error Checking command in the Formula Auditing command group on the Formulas tab. The Error Checking dialog box flags validation errors as you use it to move through a worksheet. More about the auditing tools is discussed in Chapter 13, "Getting the most from formulas and functions."

Inside OUT

Better data practices mean better results.

Given that we are so busy in our work lives, you might wonder if data validation is all that important or useful. You might think you are careful enough when entering data and double-checking your work. Setting up validation rules can also be time-consuming, particularly if you inherited worksheets from a former "revered" coworker who didn't really know Excel all that well. And now you are a little afraid to retrofit these somewhat dodgy worksheets with validation rules.

Throughout the Excel section of this book, I have tried to emphasize a key point: It does matter how "nice" your worksheets look or whether they were created years ago by a legendary employee (of whom you can never speak ill). If they contain erroneous data, they are meaningless. You have probably heard the saying: "garbage in, garbage out." So here are some tips for incorporating data validation into your Excel repertoire:

- **Use validation rules that help enter data:** Validation rules can be built that allow you to pull valid entries from a drop-down box and can be designed to limit the type of data (dates versus text, for instance) that can be entered in the cell.

- **Templates with validation:** Create your own worksheet templates that already have all input cells (cells where you or someone else enters data) configured with validation rules. If you do the same type of report periodically (weekly or monthly) you can open the template and complete a new worksheet without having to create the validation rules on the fly.

- **Break large worksheets into associated worksheets:** A single Excel sheet has a lot of geography (meaning cells) associated with it, but you certainly don't have to use it all. Don't build a monster worksheet when you can break that data into subsets and work with smaller associated tables that are linked by formulas and functions.

➤ For information on error checking, see "Using the auditing tools," in Chapter 13.

CHAPTER 16

Performing a what-if analysis

Excel provides you with the ability to perform a what-if analysis on worksheet data. An analysis of the data in a worksheet can really be approached in one of two different ways: manipulating values to affect outcomes or specifying an outcome such as a required net profit and allowing Excel to determine the values required to give you the desired outcome.

As already mentioned, the first possibility for conducting a what-if analysis consists of using varying key values in a worksheet, which enables you to see how these changes to the key values affect the result of a particular formula or function. For example, you might want to analyze how different variable costs, such as marketing and supplies, affect your net profits.

There are two different ways to perform a what-if analysis where you specify changes to key values to affect the results of formulas or functions (meaning the outcomes). A data table enables you to vary one or two input values. The changes in input are then reflected in the results of formulas or functions also included in the table.

The other possibility for performing a what-if analysis where key values are varied to provide different calculated outcomes is to use a scenario. Scenarios enable you to create different versions of the same worksheet where certain values in the worksheet are changed. Each scenario then provides a different outcome. For example, you might be selling your house, and the only fluid variables are the sales price that you get and the real estate broker's fee. You can create different scenarios that show different sales prices and broker's fees to see the different possible profits you might make on the sale of your home.

The other approach to analyzing data is to specify an outcome and then work backward (sort of a reverse what-if analysis) to see what key values must be in the worksheet to get the desired outcome. For example, you might want to save $200 a month in an IRA. You can do a worksheet that shows your monthly income and fixed monthly expenses (such as your mortgage). You can also include expenses that are not fixed, such as entertainment and travel. And you can allow Excel to determine how much you can spend on these variable costs and still sock away the desired amount of money in your retirement fund each month.

Two different tools enable you to start with an outcome value (the result of a formula or function) and then work backward to determine the key values to get the desired results. Goal Seek enables you to determine the value that you need in an input cell to get a desired result. The other tool is the Solver add-in, which can be used to help you find an optimum value in relation to limitations that are provided by the values in other cells in the worksheet, such as the fixed and variable expenses that we discussed in relation to specifying a monthly contribution to your IRA account.

The Goal Seek tool is limited to determining one key value. Solver can help you determine the value for more than one variable based on a desired result.

Let's look at working with data tables and the Scenario Manager to determine how changes in values affect outcomes. We can then look at how you can work backward from a particular outcome and determine the values necessary to reach your specified goal.

Creating a data table

Creating a data table is a straightforward way to vary one or two values involved in a worksheet calculation (or calculations) and then view the results based on the changes that were made to the value (or values). Data tables are a quick way to see how a single varied input cell affects calculations performed by formulas or functions. If you are going to tackle multiple variables for a what-if analysis, it probably makes more sense to use the Scenario Manager, which we discuss in the next section. Therefore, the discussion that follows looks at how to create a one-value data table.

The data table is really an addition to your worksheet. The first thing you need to do is create the worksheet containing the values, formulas, and functions that will provide you with the results.

For example, let's say that you want to see how different automobile values (ranging from $14,000 to $25,000) affect your monthly payment when you have a four-year loan (48 months) with a fixed interest rate of 6%. You can use the PMT function to quickly calculate the monthly payment at $14,000 by using the Functions Arguments dialog box to specify the cell location for the Rate (divided by 12 for monthly payments); Nper (the term in months); and Pv (the present value or cost of the car).

When you have your simple worksheet complete, and it is returning results from the formulas or functions you placed in the worksheet, you can build the data table as an accessory to the worksheet. Placement of the data table isn't really crucial, but the layout of the data table certainly is. Figure 16-5 shows a simple car loan worksheet that uses the PMT function in cell D9.

The leftmost column of the data table is where you can place a range of values that serve as the values that replace the original input cell in your worksheet. In our example, the input cell is the principal for the loan, which is in cell D6 of the worksheet. The values in the data table that you use to replace the input value are in the range C15:C20.

Leave a blank cell between the first value in the leftmost column of the data table and the heading for that column. In Figure 16-5, the blank cell is C14.

	A	B	C	D	E
1					
2					
3					
4			Monthly Car Payment at Different Terms		
5					
6			Principal (Loan amount)	$ 14,000.00	
7			Interest Rate	6%	
8			Term (4 years)	48	
9			Monthly Payment	($328.79)	
10					
11			Data Table		
12					
13			Principals	Monthly Payment	
14				($328.79)	
15			$ 15,000.00	($352.28)	
16			$ 17,000.00	($399.25)	
17			$ 19,000.00	($446.22)	
18			$ 21,000.00	($493.19)	
19			$ 23,000.00	($540.16)	
20			$ 25,000.00	($587.13)	
21					
22					

Figure 16-5 Create a data table for your what-if analysis.

The top row of the data table is where you reference any formulas or functions in your worksheet that you want to calculate different results based on the range of possibilities provided in the first column of the data table. In our example, the worksheet contains only one function in cell D9. You reference this function in the top row of the data table (row 14) by typing an equal sign in cell D14 and then clicking cell D9. This places =D9 in cell D14 and is basically a pointer to cell D9, which contains the PMT function. (This function is used to calculate the periodic payment on a principal with a fixed interest rate and term.)

After you have the data table set up, you can have Excel work its magic and calculate the different monthly payments for each of the principal values that you have input in the data table. Select the empty cell above your range of different principals (input values). Make sure that the selection range includes all the cells to the right of the input values, including the cell that references the function (or functions) back in the worksheet. In the example shown in Figure 16-6, the data table range would be C14:D20. To open the Data Table dialog box, select the cells in the data table, select the What-If Analysis command on the Data tab (in the Forecast group), and then select Data Table (see Figure 16-6).

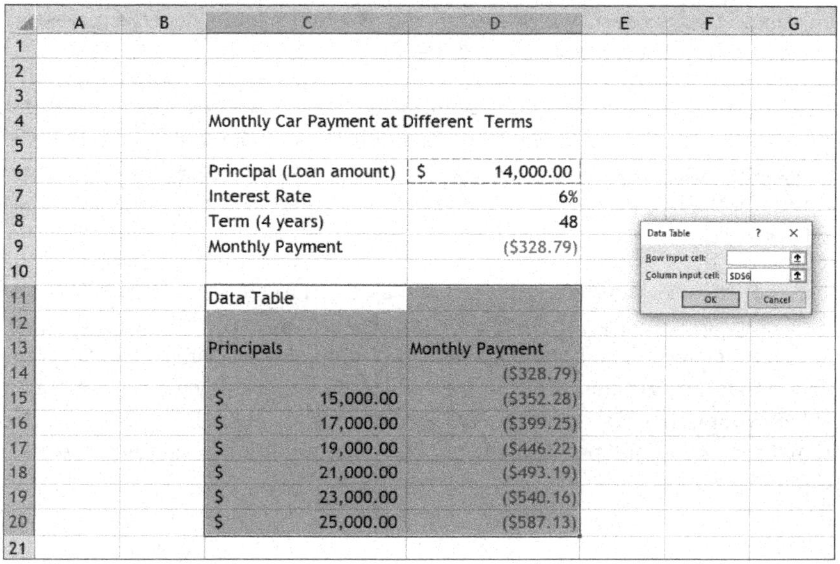

Figure 16-6   The data table and the Data Table dialog box

In the Data Table dialog box, you specify the row input cell and/or the column input cell. When you are using only one variable for the data table, as we have in the example provided here, only the Column Input Cell needs to be specified. This would be cell D6, where the principal for the loan was specified in the worksheet.

After specifying the input cell addresses, click OK. The values appear in the data table. After you get a feel for the general layout of a data table, you can use it with worksheets that contain more than one formula or function. The great thing about a data table is it provides you with a whole range of possible values based on the varied input values.

> **NOTE**
>
> Think of the data as a cross-tabulated report. The range of different values is placed in the first column of the table and, in the case of a two-variable input table, also in the first row. The results in the table then relate to the formulas or functions that act on the variable data ranges.

Creating scenarios

The Scenario Manager enables you to create different scenarios or models of the possible results in a worksheet when different values are placed in key cells. For example, you might be selling your house and want to calculate different scenarios related to your profit. Two key values related to calculating your net profit that might be variable are the real estate broker's commission and the actual sales price of the home.

You can put your data (and appropriate formulas and/or functions) in a worksheet that provides baseline calculations. For example, in the case of the home sale, you would create a worksheet that calculates your net profit on the sale based on your costs related to the sale and a specific sales price for the house. The worksheet can be structured to provide the most realistic calculation of the net profit.

You can then create different scenarios that enable you to see how changes in the sales price and brokerage fees (let's say you are talking to different agents who charge different percentages) affect the amount of money you walk away with at closing. For example, you could create a scenario that provides the best-case scenario where you are paying the lowest brokerage fee but selling your house for the highest possible price. You might also create a worst-case scenario that shows your net profit when you sell your house for a lower sale price and pay a higher brokerage fee.

NOTE

You can specify up to 32 changing cells for a scenario, meaning you can vary the values in 32 different cells in a worksheet for your what-if analysis. This provides you with a lot of possible combinations for any analysis you create.

Each scenario created provides you with a different potential outcome. When you create scenarios, you can vary some data values in a worksheet to view different potential outcomes for the formulas and functions that are affected by the changing cells you specify for the worksheet's scenarios.

To create scenarios for a worksheet, build a worksheet as you would any other worksheet. Enter your data, formulas, and functions. When you are ready to begin the scenario creation process, select the What-If Analysis command on the Data tab and then select Scenario Manager—the Scenario Manager dialog box opens. Click the Add button to create a new scenario. The Add Scenario dialog box opens, as shown in Figure 16-7.

Enter a name for the scenario in the Scenario Name text box. Use a descriptive name for the scenario because you might create multiple scenarios for the worksheet. For example, you might name the scenario "best case" if you will provide values for the changing cells that are optimum values. You might also name the scenario "most likely" or "reality" if you provide values for the changing cells that are extremely realistic.

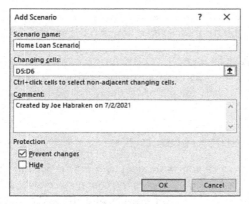

Figure 16-7   The Add Scenario dialog box

The most important aspect of creating the new scenario is to specify the cells in the worksheet that serve as the changing cells for the scenario. The changing cells are those in the worksheet that can be varied. In our home sale example, the sales price of the house and the broker's fee are both considered values that could be changed, so the cells in the worksheet that contain these values would be listed in the Changing Cells text box.

TIP

If you are working with many changing cells for your scenario, you might want to name those cells and then specify the Changing Cells addresses using the cell names rather than the cell addresses. This helps you keep the different values you're working with straight as you specify the different values for each scenario.

Select the changing cells as needed. To select a contiguous range, drag with the mouse. You can select noncontiguous cells by selecting the first cell and then holding down the Ctrl key as you select other cells. Cell addresses inserted into the Changing Cells text box are specified as absolute references.

When you have provided the name and the changing cells (and added optional comments), click OK. The Scenario Values dialog box opens, as shown in Figure 16-8.

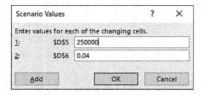

Figure 16-8   The Scenario Values dialog box

Enter a value for each of the changing cells that you specified in the Add Scenario dialog box in the Scenario Values dialog box. When you have completed entering the values, click OK.

The Add Scenario dialog box opens; create your next scenario for the worksheet. This cycle continues (Add Scenario dialog box to the Scenario Values dialog box) as you create each additional scenario. When you finish creating all the scenarios for the worksheet, click Cancel to close the Add Scenario dialog box.

Viewing scenarios and creating reports

You can view the scenarios that you create for your worksheet by using the Scenario Manager. The Scenario Manager not only enables you to quickly plug the changing cells values into your worksheet based on each scenario that you created, but you can also add additional scenarios or edit or delete existing scenarios.

To open the Scenario Manager, select the What-If Analysis command and then select Scenario Manager. The Scenario Manager lists all the scenarios that you have created for the worksheet, as shown in Figure 16-9.

Figure 16-9   The Scenario Manager dialog box

To view the results of a particular scenario in your worksheet, select the scenario in the Scenarios list and then click the Show button. The results of formulas and functions in the worksheet are recalculated based on the values for changing cells specified in the scenario. You can select any of the scenarios and quickly view the outcomes provided by that specific scenario.

The Scenario Manager dialog box allows you to view the results provided by each scenario and manage your scenarios (such as edit or delete scenarios). Also, you can create reports or summaries of the scenarios that you have created for a worksheet.

The summary of the worksheet scenarios that you have built can take the form of a scenario summary that lists each scenario and the changing values provided by the scenario. Summary information includes the results of formulas or functions in the worksheet that were affected by the changing cells specified for the scenarios. Figure 16-10 shows a scenario summary for a home purchase worksheet that had three different scenarios. The scenarios provide a Most Likely case that is based on the home's price and the current interest rate. The two other scenarios, Best Case and Worst Case, looked at a lower price and interest rate and a higher price and interest rate, respectively.

	A	B	C	D	E	F	G	H
1								
2		Scenario Summary						
3				Current Values:	Most Likely	Best Case	Worst Case	
5		Changing Cells:						
6			D5	$ 300,000.00	$ 300,000.00	$ 250,000.00	$ 350,000.00	
7			D6	6%	6%	4%	7%	
8		Result Cells:						
9			D8	($1,798.65)	($1,798.65)	($1,193.54)	($2,328.56)	
10		Notes: Current Values column represents values of changing cells at						
11		time Scenario Summary Report was created.						
12								

Figure 16-10   A scenario summary for a worksheet with multiple scenarios

The summary lists the changing cells and specifies how result cells were affected by the changing cells in each scenario. The result cells are the cell addresses for the cells that contain the formulas or functions affected by the changing cells.

Your scenario summary can also take the form of a PivotTable report. The PivotTable report enables you to sort and filter the data provided in the report as you would data in any Excel PivotTable. The PivotTable report can be useful when you have a large number of different changing cells in your worksheet scenarios, and the changing cells affect a number of different cells containing the results of formulas or functions.

➤ For information on using PivotTables, see Chapter 15, "Using Excel tables and pivot tables."

To create a new scenario summary from the Scenario Manager dialog box, click the Summary button. The Scenario Summary dialog box opens, as shown in Figure 16-11.

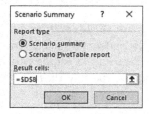

Figure 16-11   The Scenario Summary dialog box

Select the report type: Scenario Summary or Scenario PivotTable Report. In the Result Cells text box, specify the cells that contain results (formulas and functions) that are affected by changing cells in your scenarios. When you click OK, the report is created on a new worksheet.

NOTE

Suppose multiple copies of a particular worksheet exist (in different workbooks), and different users have created scenarios for that worksheet. In that case, you can merge the scenarios into a single worksheet using the Merge command in the Scenario Manager dialog box.

Using Goal Seek, Solver, and Forecast Sheet

As mentioned earlier in this chapter, Excel also provides two additional analysis tools: Goal Seek and Solver. Goal Seek is designed to work backward from a desired outcome, and it will determine the value that is required for a particular input cell to get a specific result in a dependent formula or function. Goal Seek is designed to help you determine the value of only one input cell involved in the calculation, so although it can be extremely useful, it is also fairly limited.

Solver, which is an Excel add-in, provides you with the ability to find the required value for a number of input cells involved in a predetermined calculation result. Therefore, Solver can be used in situations where you want to determine the value for more than one input cell involved in the calculation result provided by a dependent formula or function.

Working with Goal Seek

To use Goal Seek, create your worksheet, including the formula or function that is dependent on the input value that Goal Seek determines for you. For example, let's say that you put together a worksheet that uses the FV (Future Value) financial function to determine how much you need to put into an investment account each month over a 10-year period to end up with $20,000 in the account when you are getting a 3% annual interest rate.

The FV function uses the format =FV(Rate, NPER, PMT), where the Rate is the interest rate, the NPER is the total number of payments, and PMT is the payment made each period. You want Goal Seek to determine the PMT because you already know the interest rate (3%) and the number of payments, which is 120 (12 monthly payments × 10 years).

➤ **For more information on financial functions, see, "Financial functions," in Chapter 13.**

After you have your worksheet set up, all you need to do is give Goal Seek three pieces of information: the cell address, the desired goal amount for the dependent formula or function, and the changing cell address for which Goal Seek determines the value. Select the What-If Analysis command and then select Goal Seek. The Goal Seek dialog box opens, as shown in Figure 16-12.

Specify the Set Cell address, which is the cell containing the formula or function. Enter the desired goal for the value in the To Value text box. Specify the address of the cell for which Goal Seek determines a value in the By Changing Cell text box. Click OK, and Goal Seek determines the changing cell value and shows your goal value in the cell containing the formula or function.

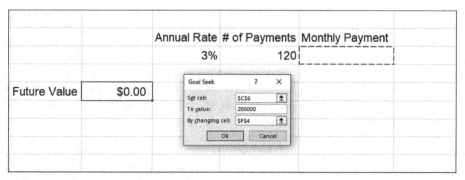

Figure 16-12   The Goal Seek dialog box and accompanying worksheet

The target value and found value (in the changing cell) are inserted into the worksheet. The Goal Seek Status dialog box opens, letting you know that Goal Seek found a solution. Click OK to close the Goal Seek Status dialog box.

In some cases, Goal Seek might not be able to find a value that provides you with the goal that you have specified. You can use the Goal Seek Status dialog box to step through the calculations to see where the problem might be or why Goal Seek could not arrive at a solution. If you are using Goal Seek in relatively simple worksheets that do not use a long chain of calculations to arrive at a particular specified goal, Goal Seek can provide a solution in most cases.

Working with Solver

If you need to determine the values for multiple adjustable or changing cells based on a desired result, you can take advantage of Solver. Solver not only provides for multiple changing cells, but it also enables you to set constraints on the value that a changing cell can have to satisfy the desired outcome. This means that you could specify a value that a particular changing cell must be above or below when Solver determines the value for that cell based on the outcome value. Solver is an optimization tool (as is Goal Seek) and enables you to find the best solution in a worksheet with obvious constraints on certain values. This can be useful for optimizing sales or production or finding the best mix of variable values related to a particular outcome.

Before you take advantage of Solver, which is an Excel add-in, you need to enable it. (If it already appears in the Analyze group of the ribbon's Data tab, it is already installed.) Open the Excel Options window in the Backstage by selecting Options. In the Excel Options window, select Add-Ins. At the bottom of the Add-Ins settings, select Excel Add-ins in the Manage drop-down menu, and click Go. The Add-Ins dialog box opens, listing a selection of available add-ins, which includes Solver. Select the Solver Add-in check box and then click OK. Solver is added to an Analysis group available on the ribbon's Data tab.

As with the other analysis tools we have discussed, such as scenarios and Goal Seek, you build your worksheet including the formulas and functions required. When you configure Solver, you can then put values in the cells that serve as the variable or changing cells.

As already mentioned, Solver enables you to place constraints on the values allowed in a changing cell. For example, you might be looking at how you want to allocate your small business's monthly budget dollars based on the total budget and certain limitations you have set for budget line items, such as marketing or travel. Let's say that you would rather see more money go toward marketing in a particular month, so you are setting a ceiling on travel (which is also a changing cell). You can place the constraint amounts directly on the worksheet (in an area near the monthly budget worksheet that you have created), or you can specify the constraint amount when you specify the constraint in the Add Constraint dialog box (which is accessed via Solver).

Placing the constraint amounts on the worksheet itself means that you can always go back and change those amounts and then rerun Solver to see how changed constraints have affected the changing cell values that Solver used to adhere to your specified outcome. Solver can save its findings as scenarios, which you can then open as needed using the Scenario Manager.

The first step in the process of using the Solver is to input your worksheet data. Enter your data as you would any other sheet and place all your formulas and functions so that they return a result. Let's say that you want to figure out an FV (Future Value) investment puzzle. You want to know what combinations of interest rates, number of payments, and the monthly payment will net you a total of $35,000. The only constraints related to this Solver problem are you cannot afford a monthly payment to this investment fund that is more than $350. You also cannot find an interest rate greater than 7%. You are placing no constraints on the number of payments it takes to get to $35,000. Figure 16-13 shows the initial sheet set up for the Solver and the Solver Parameters dialog box.

To configure Solver, click the Solver command in the Analyze group. The Solver Parameters dialog box opens, as shown in Figure 16-13.

Figure 16-13 The Solver Parameters dialog box

Click in the Set Objective text box and then click the cell that provides the outcome for Solver to use to calculate the values of changing cells. If you want to maximize the set objective (such as maximize your profits), click the Max option button in the To area of the dialog box. You can also click the Min option button to minimize the value. If you want the set objective to be a specific amount, click the Value Of option button and specify the value for Solver to use as a goal. In our FV example, we want the Solver to figure out the variables required to build up a $35,000 investment. So, in this case, the Value Of option is selected and **-35000** is entered in the text box to the right of the To: option button. (It is entered as **-35000** because Excel "sees" the investment return as a payment, which is displayed as a negative number.) Once the value is specified at the top of the dialog box, you can then specify variable cells and the constraints for the variable cells.

In the By Changing Variable Cells text box, specify the cells that Solver can change as it attempts to reach your set objective. You can select a range of cells or select multiple noncontiguous cells by holding down the Ctrl key as you select each cell. After you have the variable cells specified, you can set any constraints that should be applied to changing cells as Solver works to set values for your specified goal. To add a constraint, click the Add button. The Add Constraint dialog box opens. Specify the changing cell's address in the Cell Reference text box; you can then specify that the cell reference is less than or equal to, equal to, or adheres to another constraint parameter provided by the drop-down menu.

In the Constraint text box, specify the value that should be used to constrain the changing cell. You can type the value in the Constraint text box or specify a cell address in the worksheet that contains the constraint value. For example, Figure 16-14 shows a constraint that specifies that the value in changing cell F5 must be less than or equal to a constraint value specified in cell D8. In our example, there are actually two changing values that are constrained by a value entered in the worksheet. The D5 annual rate is constrained by a maximum of 7% (cell D9), and the Monthly Payment is also constrained by a maximum of $350.00 (cell D8).

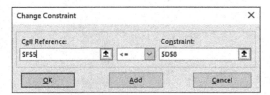

Figure 16-14   Create a Solver constraint in the Change Constraint dialog box.

You can add as many constraints as needed. All the constraints are listed in the Subject To The Constraints list in the Solver Parameters dialog box. Your constraints can be changed and deleted as needed using the Change and Delete buttons, respectively.

If you are working with some functions that use payments (which are considered negative numbers) or you want Solver to be able to make certain variables negative numbers, deselect the Make Unconstrained Variables Non-Negative option. Solver also provides you with different solving algorithms, such as the GRG Nonlinear, LOM Simplex, and Evolutionary Engines. For most financial and statistical functions, you can use the GRG Nonlinear default setting.

When you are ready to run Solver, click the Solve button. The Solver Results dialog box opens as shown in Figure 16-15 and lets you know whether Solver was able to find a solution. In the case of our investment sheet, Solver came up with a monthly payment of $304.95 (which is below the budgeted $350). However, we would have to get a 7% interest rate, and it will take around 88 payments to reach our goal of $35,000.

The Solver Results dialog box also provides you with the ability to run a report based on the answer, sensitivity, or limits of the Solver's work, and you have the option to save the provided solution as a scenario.

By default, the Solver solution replaces your original data (and any results from formulas or functions) in your worksheet. If you're not satisfied with the Solver results or you just want to start from scratch, you can select the Restore Original Values option button. To close the Solver Results dialog box, click OK.

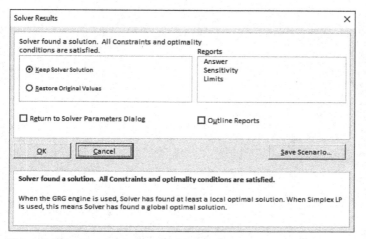

Figure 16-15   The Solver Results dialog box

Creating a Forecast Sheet

Another useful forecasting feature provided by Excel is the Forecast Sheet. The Forecast Sheet shares the Forecast group with the What-if Analysis command on the Data tab of the ribbon. The Forecast Sheet feature is easy to set up and will return a forecast based on historical time-based values. For example, you might have monthly revenue figures for your small business from the past couple of years, and you would like to create a forecast of what things might look like in the coming years.

To create a Forecast Sheet, enter (or copy and paste) your time-based values in a worksheet (such as your gross sales or net profit for each month of a particular time period). Remember, the more data you input, the better the forecast. For example, you could create a two-column worksheet in which the first column (on the left) provides a series of dates (say, a range of months over a two-year period). The second column (on the right) would contain the net profit or total sales (or whatever you are measuring) associated with a particular month.

Once you have your data input in a worksheet, you are ready to create the Forecast Sheet. Select the Forecast Sheet command, and the Create Forecast Worksheet dialog box opens, as shown in Figure 16-16.

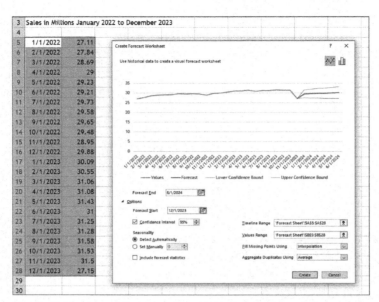

Figure 16-16   Create The Forecast Worksheet dialog box

In the Create Forecast Worksheet dialog box, you can choose between a line chart or column chart to visualize your forecast. You can also specify the Forecast End and the Forecast Start (the default is the month or timeframe that flows the time stamp on your last data point). If you did not select the time or values range in the worksheet, you can do that in the Create Forecast Worksheet dialog box using the Timeline Range and Values Range boxes, respectively. When you are ready to create your forecast, select Create. A new datasheet and chart will be created, as shown in Figure 16-17.

The data that is placed in the new worksheet is a duplicate of your original data along with the forecasted data for the next six months (in the future), which is the default for the Forecast Sheet tool. The forecasted data is actually provided in a forecast set, a lower confidence-bound set, and an upper confidence-bound set. The chart is a visualization that combines your original data and the forecasted data. Note that the chart in Figure 16-17 has three different lines for the forecasted data, showing you the three different datasets that the Forecast Sheet tool came up with based on your original dataset.

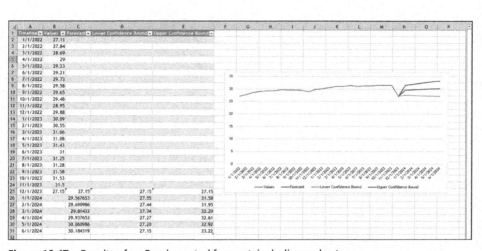

Timeline	Values	Forecast	Lower Confidence Bound	Upper Confidence Bound
1/1/2022	27.11			
2/1/2022	27.84			
3/1/2022	28.69			
4/1/2022	29			
5/1/2022	29.23			
6/1/2022	29.21			
7/1/2022	29.73			
8/1/2022	29.58			
9/1/2022	29.65			
10/1/2022	29.48			
11/1/2022	28.95			
12/1/2022	29.88			
1/1/2023	30.09			
2/1/2023	30.55			
3/1/2023	31.06			
4/1/2023	31.08			
5/1/2023	31.43			
6/1/2023	31			
7/1/2023	31.25			
8/1/2023	31.28			
9/1/2023	31.58			
10/1/2023	31.53			
11/1/2023	31.5			
12/1/2023	27.15	27.15	27.15	27.15
1/1/2024		29.567653	27.55	31.58
2/1/2024		29.690986	27.44	31.95
3/1/2024		29.81432	27.34	32.29
4/1/2024		29.937653	27.27	32.61
5/1/2024		30.060986	27.20	32.92
6/1/2024		30.184319	27.15	33.22

Figure 16-17   Results of an Excel-created forecast, including a chart

PART IV

PowerPoint

CHAPTER 17

Essential PowerPoint features 529

CHAPTER 18

Advanced presentation formatting, themes, and masters 555

CHAPTER 19

Better slides with pictures, objects, and SmartArt 585

CHAPTER 20

Enhancing slides with animation, transitions, and multimedia 611

CHAPTER 21

Delivering a presentation and creating support materials 641

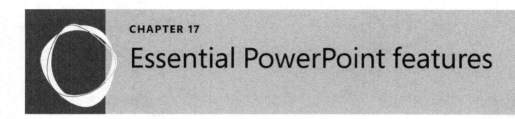

Essential PowerPoint features

PowerPoint   529

Options for creating a new presentation   530

Creating a template   537

Inserting new slides   540

Modifying a slide's layout   543

Working with slides in different views   543

Opening a new presentation window   548

Rearranging and deleting slides   549

Modifying bulleted lists   549

Using numbered lists   551

Viewing a presentation during editing   552

Microsoft PowerPoint is the standard "visual aid" software application for providing informative presentations. Whether you are giving a presentation at an important business meeting or showing pictures of your latest vacation to family and friends, PowerPoint provides an easy-to-use yet powerful presentation platform. PowerPoint is not only a powerful tool for presenting "live," but it's also useful at demonstration tables and kiosks for playing self-running presentations. It even allows you to share a presentation easily and show PowerPoint presentations via the web.

In this chapter, we look at the essential tools and features of this powerful presentation application. As you get familiar with the PowerPoint interface and workspace, we also look at the basics of constructing a PowerPoint presentation, including the options for creating a new presentation. In addition, we spend time looking at how to best create and manipulate your presentation slides.

PowerPoint

Microsoft PowerPoint builds on the changes and functional improvements made to early iterations of this powerful presentation software. As a member of the Microsoft 365 application suite, PowerPoint continues to be upgraded over time, as are the other 365 applications such as Word and Excel. Recent improvements to PowerPoint include the addition of a free stock image library (from Microsoft) and the ability to hide the current slide in the Presenter view.

When you open the PowerPoint application window (see Figure 17-1), you are greeted by the Start screen. The Home page of the Start screen provides you with a list of PowerPoint templates, and you can start a new presentation by selecting one of the templates (including the Blank Presentation template), and the Home tab provides a list of recently opened presentations under the Recent heading. You can also access presentations under the Pinned and Shared with Me headings. If you have a lengthy Recent list of presentations, use the Search box to find a presentation or presentations using keywords.

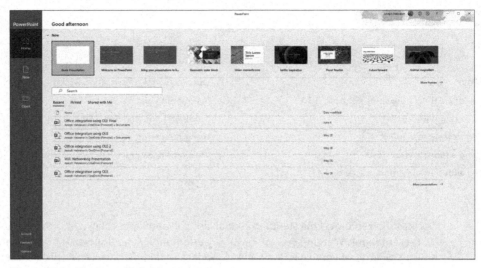

Figure 17-1 The PowerPoint Start screen

The Start screen also provides New and Open tabs. The New tab provides a more extensive listing of PowerPoint templates and a search box that can be used for searching Microsoft online for more templates and themes. (We will differentiate between a template and theme later in this chapter.) You will find that templates are available for basic presentations and specific types of presentations, such as a business or education presentation. The Start screen also provides an Open tab, which provides a list of recently opened presentations. The Open tab enables you to locate PowerPoint files in other locations, such as your OneDrive or PC. Let's take a look at the options for creating a new presentation. This will also allow us to look at the differences between a template and a theme and discuss how you save your presentation file.

Options for creating a new presentation

PowerPoint provides you with two very similar launch pads for starting your new presentations or opening existing presentations. We have already talked about the Start screen, which is available when you start the PowerPoint application. If you are working in PowerPoint and want to start a new presentation, the process is a little different, and you will go to the PowerPoint Backstage to create a new file. You will find that the Start screen and Backstage are similar in terms of accessing presentation templates or themes.

To access the New page from the PowerPoint application window, select File on the ribbon and then select New. Figure 17-2 shows the New page. The New page provides access to many templates and themes. The Search box can be used to find additional online templates and/or themes. When browsing the templates and themes, it can be difficult to differentiate between the two.

A template is a presentation blueprint that provides a presentation theme (defined in the next paragraph), individual slides with specific slide layouts, and, in a number of cases, placeholder text and other design objects already on the individual slides. Templates provide the greatest amount of handholding when placing content on the presentation slides and determining the type of information that should be available on each slide.

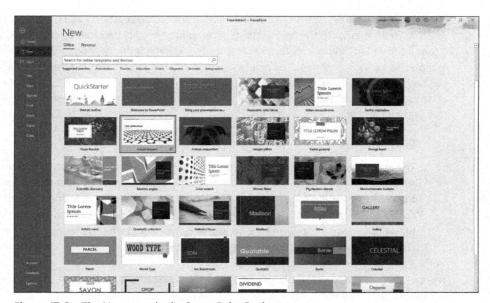

Figure 17-2   The New page in the PowerPoint Backstage

You can also create a new presentation based on a theme. A theme provides the font family, color scheme, and (typically) design elements for the slides in the presentation. PowerPoint now offers variations (variants) for many of the themes provided, expanding the color schemes available.

You can also create new presentations based on an existing presentation. This option opens a copy of an existing presentation, including the theme, slide layout, and slide content from the presentation. You can then edit the presentation copy as needed to create a new presentation. To open a copy of a presentation from the File tab, select Open. This will take you to the Open page; right-click any of the listed presentations and select Open A Copy. A copy of the presentation opens in the PowerPoint window and allows you to specify the file's name when you save it for the first time.

Creating a new blank presentation allows you to start from scratch. Both the Start screen and the New page provide access to the Blank Presentation template. Creating a presentation using the Blank Presentation template gives you the most control over the presentation's design elements and the layout of individual slides (all items we discuss in this part of this book).

Let's take a more detailed look at the options for creating a new presentation. We start the discussion with a look at templates.

Using templates

PowerPoint draws a fine line between what constitutes a template and what constitutes a theme (we talk about themes in the next section). A template typically provides an overall "look" for a presentation (including screen colors and fonts, meaning a theme) and includes placeholder text on several sample slides. A template also typically includes design elements on slides, which can be edited as needed. For example, a sample company logo on the master slide of the template can be replaced with your own logo. A template provides a prepackaged presentation that you edit and add to, making it your own.

CAUTION

The PowerPoint Start screen and the Backstage's New page primarily provide you with simple templates that include a theme and a standard group of content slides. Some of the choices on these pages are themes rather than templates. Themes provide uniform colors and fonts for slides in a presentation but do not provide you with sample slides, placeholder text, or design elements as a template would. Themes found on the Start or New pages include Ion, Organic, Depth, and Slice.

You can search for online templates using the Search box on either the Start screen's New tab or the Backstage's New page. You also can create your own templates and then use them as starting material to create new presentations; we talk about creating a template in a moment. When searching for other templates available online, click in the Search box and then type your search criteria.

NOTE

If you do a PowerPoint template search on your computer using the File Manager (search for `*.potx`), you will find that a few PowerPoint templates are installed on your computer in the `Program Files\Microsoft Office\root\Templates\1033` folder. (They are put there during the Office installation process, and the numbered folder at the end of the path—in this case—1033) will vary depending on the language you are installing. These installed templates (which don't show up on the Start screen or the New page) include QuizShow, Pitchbook, Contemporary Photo Album, and Training.

The template search results (in either the Start screen's New tab or the Backstage's New page) show all the online templates and themes that match your search criteria. Some templates provide all the slides that you need for your presentation; all you have to do is customize them for your purpose. Other templates provide a few sample slides and the overall look for a presentation.

TIP

You can also download presentation templates directly from the Office website at *https://templates.office.com* website. When you download a template using Microsoft Edge (or another web browser such as Firefox), move the template from your default download folder to your `AppData\Roaming\Microsoft\Templates` folder for easier access via the Start or New page in the PowerPoint Backstage. To view hidden folders in Windows, open the File Explorer and then select View, Options. In the Folder Options dialog box, select View, Show Hidden Files, Folders And Drives.

When you locate a presentation template in the search results that you may want to use, click the template's sample picture. A larger sample page will open for the template. Additional information, such as the template provider and a description of the template, is typically provided on the right side of the template sample, as shown in Figure 17-3. The sample template in the figure is a retail pitch deck, which provides several slides (a deck) that include graphics and charts for your data.

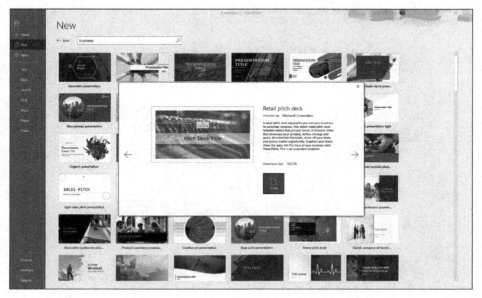

Figure 17-3   You can preview a template on the Start screen or New page.

CHAPTER 17

TIP

If you find a presentation template during a search that you like but aren't going to use immediately, you can pin it to the Template/Theme list that is provided on the Start screen and the Backstage's New page. This makes it easy for you to use the template later without searching for it again. Select the pin in the upper-right corner of the template sample.

When you preview a particular template, you will find that navigation arrows on the left and right of the presentation sample allow you to move through the list of templates and themes listed by your search (either to the left or right as needed). So, if you don't like a particular template, you can skim through the other templates provided in the search results. If you don't want to use the current template, select the Close button (X) to return to the search results.

When you do find the template you want to use and have opened its preview window, click the Create button. This opens a new presentation in PowerPoint based on the template.

Figure 17-4 shows a new presentation based on the pitch deck template (we discussed earlier). Note that the overall look (the theme) for the template sets up the presentation as a number of sample slides containing placeholder text and sample objects. You can edit the slides and their content to modify and complete your presentation. You can also insert additional slides and add objects to those slides if needed.

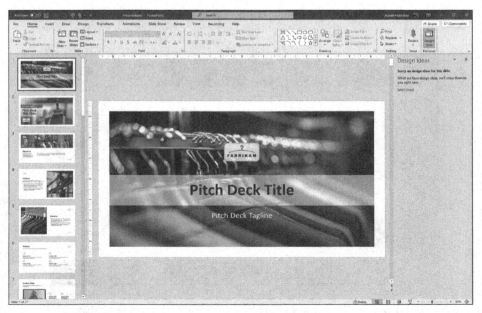

Figure 17-4   Modify the slides provided by the template.

Using a theme to create a new presentation

A theme is a collection of colors, fonts, and text effects. Many of the possibilities provided on the New page are actually themes rather than templates.

To preview a theme, select the theme's sample picture. A sample image is provided for the theme's title slide, as is a description of the theme. Some of the themes provided have color and font variants. (Variants provide variations for the theme.). These variants can be selected via the PowerPoint ribbon's Design tab once you have opened a template or theme. When you are ready to use a selected theme, select Create. A new title slide opens in the PowerPoint workspace using the theme you selected. As with the templates available, themes will occasionally also provide sample slides that you can modify for your own purposes.

> ### TIP
>
> **You can also find templates at Microsoft's template library (*https://templates.office.com*). The templates (and themes) are arranged in popular categories such as budgets, resumes, brochures, cover letters, and newsletters. This collection of templates and themes provides possibilities for all the 365 applications, such as Word, Excel, and PowerPoint. A Search box is provided near the top of the web page, so you can focus the search engine on PowerPoint by providing the application name when using the Search tool.**

➤ For a discussion on changing themes in a presentation, see "Working with themes," later in this chapter.

Creating a presentation from an existing presentation

You can create a presentation based on any existing presentation. This enables you to make a copy of the existing presentation and then edit it to create a whole new presentation.

If you have just started PowerPoint and are on the Start screen, you can quickly open a copy of any of the presentations listed under Recent. The same goes if you are in PowerPoint and navigate to the Open page of the Backstage. In either case, right-click a listed presentation and then select Open A Copy. A copy of the presentation opens in the PowerPoint workspace. Make sure you save this "new" presentation, which hasn't been named yet because it is a copy.

If the presentation isn't in your Recent list, you can still open a copy. If you are on the Start screen, select Open, Browse, which will open the Open dialog box. If you are in the Backstage, select Open, Browse, which also opens the Open dialog box.

Locate the presentation file you want to copy and then select it. Click the Open button's drop-down arrow and then click Open As Copy. A copy of the presentation opens in the PowerPoint window. Note, however, that this copy is a little different from the copy we made by right-clicking a presentation in the Recent list. This copy (opened using the Open dialog box) is named, Copy (1) `file name` (where `file name` is the original name of the file). So, if you want to give the presentation a new name (to get rid of Copy in the name), you must use the Save As command; select File, and then select Save As. In the Save As dialog box, provide a new name for the "copied" presentation and a new location if necessary.

Inserting slides from the Reuse Slides task pane

We have already looked at how to open a copy of an existing presentation. PowerPoint also makes it easy for you to insert slides from an existing presentation into your current presentation. The Reuse Slides task pane enables you to use any or all slides in an existing presentation. The Reuse Slides task pane is opened using the Reuse Slides command at the bottom of the New Slide gallery. To insert existing slides into your current presentation, follow these steps:

1. On the ribbon's Home tab, select the New Slide command and then select Reuse Slides. The Reuse Slides task pane opens on the right side of the PowerPoint application window. Title slides from recently opened presentations will appear in the Reuse Slides pane; presentations are sourced from your Documents folder, OneDrive folder, email attachments, and SharePoint sites. If one of the presentations listed provides the slides you want to reuse, select the Choose Content link below the slide title to open all the slides in the presentation.

2. If the presentation that contains the slides you want to reuse isn't listed, you can use the search box at the top of the Reuse Slides pane to find it. You can also select Browse (below the search box), which opens the Choose Content dialog box.

3. In the Choose Content dialog box, locate the PowerPoint presentation that will supply the slides to be reused and then select Choose Content. The slides in the presentation are listed in the Reuse Slides task pane, as shown in Figure 17-5.

4. To add a slide from the Reuse Slides task pane to the current presentation, select a slide. By default, it is formatted using the theme that has been set for the current presentation. Add other slides as needed to build the new presentation.

5. When you have finished working with the Reuse Slides task pane, select its Close button.

TIP

Reused slides are inserted into a presentation with their source formatting. If you do not want to keep the original formatting for a slide (or slides) that you insert using the Reuse Slides task pane, clear the Use Source Formatting check box at the top of the task pane.

The Reuse Slides task pane closes. You can now insert new slides or modify the slides that you "copied" using the Reuse Slides task pane.

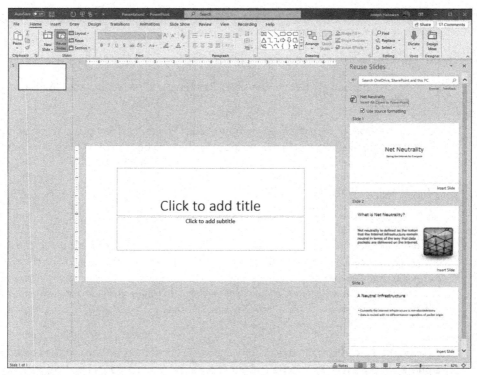

Figure 17-5   Use the Reuse Slides task pane to insert slides from an existing presentation.

TIP

You can also quickly add slides from an opened presentation to the Reuse Slides pane from the Slide Sorter View. Select a slide or slides (use the mouse to drag and select multiple slides) and then right-click one of the selected slides. On the shortcut menu, select Reuse Slides. The slides will be added to the Reuse Slides pane.

Creating a template

You can create your own templates from your PowerPoint presentations. These templates can include custom logos, special design elements, and even custom color combinations and fonts (themes). You can share templates with coworkers, which can be useful if you want to create consistent-looking presentations for your small business or club. Templates can be fairly bare-boned (with little or no slide content), or they can include any number of slides containing text, pictures, and other objects.

You can save any presentation as a template. To create your own template from the current presentation, follow these steps:

1. Select File to open the PowerPoint Backstage, and then select Save A Copy.

2. To save the copy (which will be saved as a template), select Browse. The Save As dialog box opens.

3. In the Save As Type drop-down menu, select PowerPoint Template. When you select the template file type, the folder location defaults to your Custom Office Templates folder (Users*Username*\Documents\Custom Office Templates).

4. Specify a name for the template.

5. Click Save.

The new template is saved to your Custom Office Templates folder. Before you can access your custom template (or templates) from the Start screen or the Backstage's New page, you need to set the default personal templates location in the PowerPoint Options window. Because your new template was saved to the custom template folder (in your Documents folder), you use the location syntax C:\Users*Username*\Documents\Custom Office Templates, where *Username* is the log-in name you use for Windows.

To open the PowerPoint Options window, select File and then Options. In the PowerPoint Options window, select Save. In the Default personal templates location box, enter **C:\Users\ *Username*\Documents\Custom Office Templates**, as shown in Figure 17-6. Then click OK to close the PowerPoint Options window.

Now you can access your own template or templates from the Start screen or the New page. A Personal category now appears on the Start screen or the New page (just to the right of the Featured heading). To view your custom templates, select Personal. Thumbnails of your templates are previewed. Select the custom template you want to use for a new presentation. You can use the navigation buttons to see a few more images of the template (as you could with any template available on the Start screen or New page). Select Create to open a new presentation based on the template.

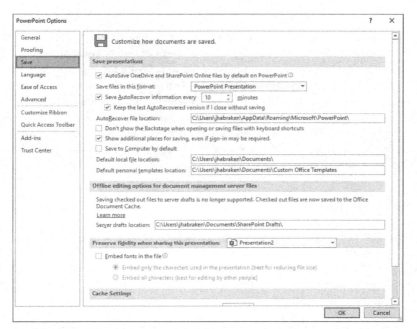

Figure 17-6 Specify the default location for your custom PowerPoint templates.

Inside OUT

Creating presentations that have visual impact but still show restraint

Chapters 17–21 focus on PowerPoint, and as you read through or consult these chapters, I think you will find that PowerPoint provides a lot of bells and whistles that you can apply to your presentations. This chapter discusses some of the basic PowerPoint features that affect the way your presentation slides look, including text and bulleted list formatting. This chapter also introduces themes, which control the color, font, and other formatting options for your presentation slides.

As we move through subsequent chapters in the PowerPoint section of the book, we will discuss many features and commands (more advanced possibilities with each chapter) that relate to both the look of individual slides in a presentation and the overall presentation itself. Our approach to the material allows you to accumulate features; however, that does not mean you have to use all of them when you design a new presentation. Although you can build a presentation with transitions, slide animations, embedded videos, and other media files, the focus of any presentation should be to help you impart information to your audience. A presentation that literally explodes off the screen with effects might impress the audience, but does it inform the audience?

I am not saying that your slide presentations should consist entirely of static slides that impart information but aren't visually interesting; I am just suggesting that you show some restraint when designing your presentations. I realize that you probably have coworkers or colleagues who think Prezi (and other presentation software of the same ilk) is the only way to build a modern presentation and that PowerPoint just isn't flashy enough anymore. Good, useful information in a presentation can be just as compelling as the most frenetic presentation. Concentrate on creating presentations that have a beginning, middle, and end, and respect the needs of your audience.

Inserting new slides

When you create a new presentation using a template (even the Blank Presentation template) or a theme, you are almost always provided with a title slide. The title slide contains two text boxes: one for the title and one for a subtitle. All the text on your slides resides in text boxes or table boxes (all objects appear on a slide in their own frames, for easy manipulation). To enter text on a slide, such as the title text box, click in the text box and type your text.

After you fill in the text box (or boxes) on a slide, you are probably ready to insert another slide into the presentation. Select the layout for the new slide. The New Slide command is in the Slide group, which resides on the ribbon's Home tab. Other slide-related commands, such as the Layout, Reset, and Section commands, are also in the Slides group.

When you select the New Slide command, a gallery of slide layouts is provided for common slide types, such as Title Slide, Title and Content, and Blank. Figure 17-10 shows the Slide gallery. The slides available in the gallery are based on the currently selected presentation theme (which is listed at the top of the gallery).

To insert a particular slide layout type, select it in the gallery. The new slide opens in the Slide pane and is added to the list of thumbnails. You can click in the provided text boxes, such as the slide title, and add text as needed. Most of the slide layouts include a content area that can contain text or other objects, such as a table, picture, or SmartArt.

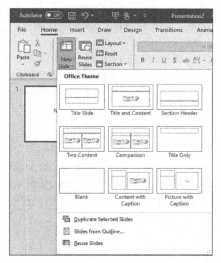

Figure 17-7   Insert a new slide into the presentation.

Entering text

Each new slide has at least a title text box (unless you insert a blank slide) and a content area box. If you want the content area of a new slide to contain text (instead of other content, such as a table or a picture), select the Click To Add Text placeholder and type the text for the slide. The default formatting for content text is a bulleted list.

PowerPoint provides an alternative to entering text on each slide in the Slide pane. You can switch to Outline view and enter slide text in an outline format. You can also add new slides when you are working in Outline view. To switch to Outline view, click the ribbon's View tab and then select Outline View (in the Presentation Views group).

Each slide in the presentation is represented in the outline as a primary heading. The text used is the title text for the slide. To add text to a slide (such as a bulleted list below a slide heading), click below the heading (in the outline) and then enter the text. Each time you press Enter, you add another item to the bulleted list. You can switch from the secondary level of the outline (the bulleted or numbered list level) by pressing Shift+Tab. This places you at the primary level in the outline, and each new heading that you type creates a new slide.

You can switch back to the secondary outline level to add text items to a slide by pressing Tab. Multiple levels are available in each slide, so you can press Tab as needed and then enter text at that level of the outline.

The whole point of Outline view is to make it easier for you to concentrate on the text and the sequencing of your text as you build a presentation with a clear beginning, middle, and end (Aristotle came up with this concept, not me). You can easily rearrange the text on your slides using Outline view. For example, you can drag an entire bulleted list from one slide to another in Outline view. You can also move items around in Outline view as needed to organize the presentation. When you want to return to Normal view, select Normal on the View tab or click the Normal icon on the right side of the PowerPoint status bar.

Inserting slides from a Word outline

Another option for creating new slides in a presentation is to base them on an outline that you typed in Microsoft Word. This option quickly creates new slides that contain slide titles and accompanying slide text based on the text in the outline. You can insert as many slides as the outline provides.

> **NOTE**
>
> **Creating an outline of your presentation in Word enables you to concentrate on the text in the presentation and makes it easy to arrange your thoughts. You can add pictures and other objects after you insert the outline into PowerPoint.**

To insert a Word outline into PowerPoint as presentation slides, select the New Slide command on the Home tab and then select Slides From Outline. The Insert Outline dialog box opens.

Select the Word outline document and then click Insert. The new slides (based on the outline) are inserted into the current presentation. You can edit the new slides as you would any other slide, including adding objects to the slides as needed.

Inserting other object content

If you want an object other than text in a slide's content pane, you can use the icons provided in the content pane of a newly inserted slide to select the type of object to insert. We discuss working with tables, graphics, and media such as sound and movies in subsequent chapters, but let's walk through the basics of inserting an object.

On a new slide, select an object icon, such as Picture. The Insert Picture dialog box opens, as shown in Figure 17-8. Note that the Windows default library for pictures is Pictures. When you open the Insert Picture dialog box, the Open command appears at the bottom right of the dialog box. As soon as you select a picture, the command changes to Insert.

To insert one of your pictures, select a picture in the Insert Picture dialog box and then click Insert. The picture is placed on the slide. The process for inserting other object types is fairly similar to that of inserting a picture: You specify the object type to be inserted, PowerPoint gives you a dialog box for choosing the specific item, and you insert it onto the slide.

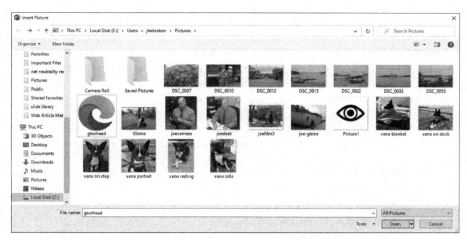

Figure 17-8   The Insert Picture dialog box

Modifying a slide's layout

You might find that you need to modify the initial layout you selected for a slide. For example, you might want to make a slide that has a title text box and a single content pane into a slide with two content panes. You can then have one pane with bulleted text and another pane with an object such as a picture. You can change the layout for any slide in the presentation. You can modify the layout even if you have already entered text or other objects on the slide.

Select the thumbnail for the slide you want to modify (or select multiple slide thumbnails in the navigation pane if you want to modify several slides). Select the Layout command in the slides group. The Layout gallery opens. The Layout gallery is similar to the New Slide gallery. Select a new layout from the gallery. The new layout then is applied to the currently selected slide or slides. You might have to rearrange some of your slide content when you apply a new layout. This typically only requires a little resizing and some movement of elements on the slide.

Working with slides in different views

PowerPoint can display your presentation in different views. These views are available in the Presentation Views group on the ribbon's View tab, and each view is designed for a particular purpose. For example, Normal view is designed to build your presentation and provides you with the Slide pane, enabling you to insert text and other objects onto the current slide. Each slide is also represented by a thumbnail on the left side of the PowerPoint window, which makes it easy to select a specific slide in the presentation (or several slides at once). By contrast, the Notes Page view concentrates on the speaker's notes that you are creating for your presentation and de-emphasizes the actual slides.

Slide Sorter view is useful in arranging and rearranging your presentation slides. This view provides thumbnails of all the slides in the presentation and is designed for arranging your presentation slides into the proper order. Although you can create sections in your presentations in any view, the Slide Sorter view makes it easy to create sections and then arrange slides within these sections, which represent the different "parts" of the presentation. The views provided on the ribbon's View tab (in the Presentation Views group) follow:

- **Normal:** This is the default view, which includes the Slide pane, the Notes pane, and a navigation pane that includes thumbnails of all the slides in the presentation.

- **Outline View:** This view enables you to view the slides in an outline format that concentrates on the text on each slide. You can add new slides directly to the outline and add slide text at different levels in the outline. Tab and Shift+Tab are used to move up and down a level in the outline, respectively.

- **Slide Sorter View:** This view shows all the slides as thumbnails so that you can easily rearrange them by dragging slides to new positions in the presentation. Figure 17-9 shows the Slide Sorter view.

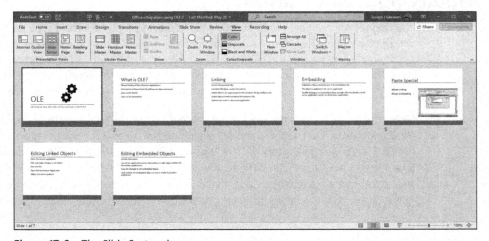

Figure 17-9   The Slide Sorter view

- **Notes Page View:** This view enables you to see the current slide and its accompanying notes page. This view is designed to enter and review the speaker notes you are creating to go with each slide in the presentation.

- **Reading View:** This view plays the presentation as a slideshow. However, it shows the slideshow so that it fits within the current PowerPoint window, even when the window is not maximized. This means you can quickly view slide designs, animations, and transitions without running a slide show in the full-screen mode. You can return to the previous view (from the Reading view) by pressing the Esc key.

You can switch between these different views as needed using the commands in the Presentation Views group. Some of these views also have icons in the PowerPoint status bar. Icons are provided on the right side of the taskbar for the Normal, Slide Sorter, and Reading views. An icon is also provided for the Slide Show command.

Another possible view of a presentation is as a slideshow. This view isn't available on the View tab; it is an option in the PowerPoint status bar (the icon just before the Zoom slider). We talk more about the different possibilities and views when you run your slideshow in Chapter 21, "Delivering a presentation and creating support materials."

You have options in switching views in the PowerPoint workspace. You can take advantage of the View shortcuts on the PowerPoint status bar. Icons are provided on the right side of the taskbar for the Normal, Slide Sorter, Reading, and Slide Show views. The Slide Show icon plays the slideshow beginning with the current slide.

CAUTION

You can't edit the slide content when you are in Slide Sorter or Notes Page view; however, just double-click a slide in either view to return to Normal view and edit away!

Zooming in and out

As you work on the content of individual slides, you might want to zoom in or out on a slide. You also might find it useful to be able to zoom in and out as you work with your slides in Slide Sorter view. You can use the Zoom slider to zoom in and out on presentation slides or slide content when you are in Normal, Slide Sorter, or Notes Page view.

You can also change the zoom level using the commands in the Zoom group on the View tab of the ribbon. When you select Zoom, the Zoom dialog box opens, as shown in Figure 17-10.

Figure 17-10 The Zoom dialog box

You can select any of the available presets in the Zoom dialog box by clicking the appropriate option button. You can also use the Percent spin box to specify an actual percentage. The Zoom group provides the Fit to Window command as well. Select this command in either Normal view or Slide Sorter view; the zoom percentage adjusts so that the slide or slides fill the window.

CHAPTER 17

Rulers, gridlines, and guides

PowerPoint provides visual guides that help you better arrange objects on your slides. These different guide tools include rulers, gridlines, guides, and smart guides. Let's start our discussion with smart guides.

Smart guides are guides that appear automatically when you move an object on a slide (a text box, picture, chart, or any object). The smart guides tell you when objects on the slide are level or when they are spaced evenly. The best way to experience the smart guides is to place some objects on a slide and then drag them around to see what happens. The ribbon's View tab also provides additional commands that help you work with object placement. The Show group provides the Ruler, Gridlines, and Guides commands.

To view the horizontal and vertical rulers, select the Ruler check box. When the rulers (horizontal and vertical) are placed in the workspace, the horizontal and vertical positions of the mouse pointer are shown as tick marks on the horizontal and vertical rulers as you move the mouse around the slide.

If you want more help in aligning objects on the slide, you can turn on the gridlines by selecting the Gridlines check box. The gridlines are nonprinting horizontal and vertical lines.

For even more precision, you can turn on the guides. When you select the Guides check box, horizontal and vertical guidelines appear on the slide. You can move either of these guidelines as needed on the slide's surface. You can then use either guide to help you more accurately align objects on the slide. Clearing any of these command check boxes removes those particular items from the workspace.

If you want to specify settings related to the gridlines and the guides—including the smart guides—you can open the Grid And Guides dialog box. Select the dialog box launcher at the bottom of the Show group. Figure 17-11 shows the Grid And Guides dialog box.

Figure 17-11   The Grid And Guides dialog box

By default, the Snap Objects To Grid option is disabled. When you enable the Snap To feature, objects are "snapped" to the nearest intersection of the grid as you drag the object. If you are using Snap To, you might also want to select the Display Grid On Screen check box so that you can see the grid as you align objects. You can also change the default spacing for the grid using the Spacing box and enable the Display Drawing Guides On Screen option, which places vertical and horizontal guides that intersect at the middle of the slide.

The check box for the Display Smart Guides When Shapes Are Aligned feature is also in the Grid and Guides dialog box. It is enabled by default, and I can see no real reason why you would want to disable it. When you have finished working in the Grid And Guides dialog box, click OK.

Color/grayscale commands

By default, your presentation slides are shown in color. The Color command is selected (by default) in the Color/Grayscale group. You can view your presentation in grayscale or black and white and then customize how the various colors are translated to grayscale or black and white. This translation can be done on an object-by-object basis, so you have complete control over how a particular object, such as a clip art image or table, looks in grayscale or black and white. The purpose of these commands is to control how a printout of your presentation looks when you print in black and white, such as when you use a laser printer. This is useful when you want to provide your audience with grayscale or black-and-white handouts.

To view the slides in grayscale or black and white, select either the Grayscale command or the Black And White command. When you switch to Grayscale or Black And White view, the ribbon shows the Grayscale or Black And White tab. These tabs provide a series of commands that enable you to change the grayscale or black-and-white characteristics of a selected object on the slide.

NOTE

If you still create black-and-white overhead projector transparencies from your presentation slides, the grayscale and black-and-white possibilities are useful.

The commands provided on the Grayscale or Black And White tabs are extremely straightforward. For example, if you want an object to be rendered to grayscale or black-and-white automatically (based on its actual color), select the object and then select the Automatic command. The other commands provide more definitive options for the grayscale or black-and-white rendering of an object.

For example, when you select an object and then select the Black command, the object is black when printed on a black-and-white printer. You can select multiple objects and then assign the same grayscale or black-and-white attribute to several objects at once.

Select the Back To Color View command when you finish working with the Grayscale or Black And White commands. This returns you to the ribbon's Home tab rather than the View tab.

Opening a new presentation window

You can open a second window that shows the current presentation; this enables you to view a presentation in two different views at the same time. For example, one window could use the Normal view, and the other could use the Slide Sorter view. This enables you to manipulate the same presentation in different ways pretty much at the same time.

You could cut and paste or copy and paste an object from slides in one of the windows to the other window. Changes that you make to the presentation in either window are reflected in both windows.

To open a second presentation window, select the ribbon's View tab and then select the New Window command. A second window containing the current presentation opens on the Windows desktop. To arrange the two open presentation windows side by side, select the Arrange All command. Figure 17-12 shows two windows containing the same presentation. Normal view is used in the left window, and Slide Sorter view is used in the right window.

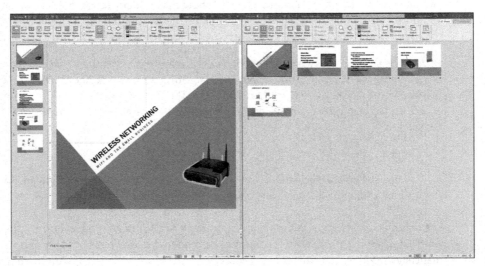

Figure 17-12   You can open multiple windows containing the same presentation.

You can close either window at any time. When you close one of the windows, maximize the remaining window so that PowerPoint takes full advantage of the space available on the Windows desktop.

TIP

If you don't want an object to be included in a black-and-white printout of the slide, select the object and then select the Don't Show command.

Rearranging and deleting slides

When you have a few slides in a presentation, you might want to rearrange them. You can reorder slides in Normal view and Outline view by dragging slide thumbnails and outline headings to new locations in the presentation, respectively. I prefer Slide Sorter view. Depending on the size of the presentation, you might be able to view many, if not all, the slides in the presentation when you are in Slide Sorter view; this makes rearranging the slide order easy.

Select Slide Sorter on the View shortcuts or Slide Sorter on the View tab to switch to Slide Sorter view. Drag the slide to its new location; a vertical line shows the position of the slide as you drag it in the presentation. If you need to drag the slide to a location that is not in Slide Sorter view, drag the slide down to scroll through the other slides in the presentation.

You can also copy a slide in Slide Sorter view as easily as you can move a slide. Simply hold down the Ctrl key while you drag the slide. When you release the mouse, PowerPoint inserts a copy of the selected slide into the presentation.

As already mentioned, the slide thumbnails found in Normal view can also be dragged to new locations as needed. Drag up or down in the navigation pane to scroll up or down in the slides list. Release the mouse when you reach the position in the presentation where you want to place the slide.

You can delete a slide (or slides) easily by selecting it in either the Slides/Outline pane tabs or Slide Sorter view. Press the Delete key to delete the selected slide or slides.

NOTE

The Slides tab in Normal view works best for moving slides when you have only a few slides in a presentation. If you have many slides, you might want to switch to Slide Sorter view.

Modifying bulleted lists

Most of the slide layouts in the New Slide gallery provide a title text box and other object placeholders. For example, there are layouts for a title and content, a title and two contents, a title and a caption, and so on. Because the bulleted list is such an important mainstay of a PowerPoint presentation, the object boxes enable you to begin entering text in a bulleted list immediately. This makes the object content box a text box. Each time you press Enter, you can create a new bulleted item in the list.

Because presentations are really a collection of topics and points you want to bring to your audience's attention, most of your presentation slides will probably contain bulleted lists (and perhaps numbered lists). Again, by default, typing in any content box or text box provided by the New Slide gallery produces a bulleted list.

You can control the bullet formatting of your bulleted lists using the Bullets gallery. The gallery enables you to change the bullets used in the list. If you want even more control over the bullets for the list, you can access the Bullets And Numbering dialog box.

You can change the bullet options before you begin typing your bulleted list, or you can modify an existing bulleted list. To modify a bulleted list already on a slide, select the bulleted text. Select the Bullets command arrow to access the Bullets gallery. You can preview any of the bullet formats provided in the gallery by placing the mouse on that bullet type.

When you are ready to assign a new bullet format to the slide, select one of the bullet styles provided in the gallery. To specify a custom bullet shape for a bulleted list, you need to access the Bullets And Numbering dialog box. Select the Bullets command arrow and then select Bullets And Numbering in the Bullets gallery. The Bullets And Numbering dialog box opens with the Bulleted tab selected, as shown in Figure 17-13.

You can select any of the bullet shapes provided on the Bulleted tab. You can also customize the bullets by using a picture as a bullet or by selecting a new symbol to be used as a bullet. Select the Picture button in the Bullets And Numbering dialog box if you want to specify a picture as the bullet shape. The Insert Pictures dialog box opens. You can use any pictures on your computer, Office.com pictures, or pictures stored online, including on Flickr and your OneDrive. If you use a picture on your computer, use the Browse button to locate the picture and then insert it.

To search for a picture (or clip art) on Office.com, use the Search Office.com search box. You can also search the web for pictures using the Bing search box. In either case, the Insert Picture dialog box lists pictures that match your search. Select an image and then click Insert. The picture is assigned to your bulleted list as the bullet.

You can also specify a new bullet type using any of the many symbols that are installed with the fonts on your computer. In the Bullets And Numbering dialog box, click the Customize button. The Symbol dialog box opens, as shown in Figure 17-14.

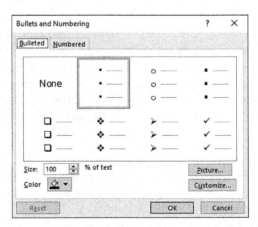

Figure 17-13   The Bullets And Numbering dialog box

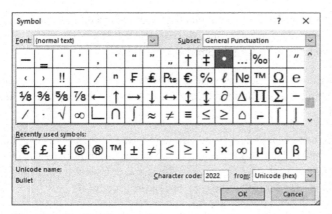

Figure 17-14   The Symbol dialog box

You can use the Font drop-down menu to select different font symbol sets. Some of the most interesting symbols are found in the Wingdings and Webdings font sets, but all the font families you have available provide symbols.

NOTE

If you insert a text box from the ribbon's Insert tab and want to type a bulleted list, you need to turn on bulleting by selecting the Bullets command on the Home tab.

To select a particular symbol, select it in the list provided. Then click OK to return to the Bullets And Numbering dialog box. The new bullet symbol is added to the list of bullets provided on the Bulleted tab. You can change the size or color of the new bullet symbol (which is selected) by using the Size spin box or the Color drop-down menu, respectively.

Select OK to return to the current slide when you have finished making modifications to the new bullet symbol. The new bullet is applied to your selected bulleted list.

TIP

You can insert your own pictures as bullets. You don't have to do anything special to the picture. Select the Picture button in the Bullets And Numbering dialog box, and click the Browse button to locate your picture. You also can "create" bullets from the Office.com clip art and photos you have stored elsewhere.

Using numbered lists

Because your presentation might also provide step-by-step procedures or a sequence of topics, you can use numbered lists on your presentation slides. Numbered lists operate pretty much like bulleted lists when creating a new list or modifying an existing list. If you have inserted a new slide with a default bulleted list, you can switch from bullets to numbering by selecting the Numbering command in the Paragraph group. You can also select an existing list and change it to numbering by selecting the Numbering command.

If you want to select a different numbering style (the default is the Arabic system; that is, 1, 2, 3, and so on), select the Numbering command arrow; the Numbering gallery opens. Select a number style from the gallery.

You can modify the size and color settings for a numbered list and specify the number with which to start the list in the Bullets And Numbering dialog box. Changing the start number for a numbered list is useful if you have two associated slides and you want the list on the second slide to pick up where the numbering on the previous slide's list left off.

To open the Bullets And Numbering dialog box, select the Numbering command arrow and then select Bullets And Numbering in the Numbering gallery. The Numbered tab is selected when the Bullets And Numbering dialog box opens. You can choose from any of the numbering styles provided on the tab; they are the same styles provided in the Numbering style gallery.

If you want to change the starting number for the numbered list, use the Start At spin box to specify the "start at" number. You can also change the size or color of the numbering by using the Size spin box or the Color drop-down menu, respectively. When you have finished modifying the numbering settings, click OK. You return to your slide, and the new settings are applied to the numbered list.

Viewing a presentation during editing

As you begin to build your slide presentation, check to see how your slides look when displayed in a slideshow. The Slide Show tab of the ribbon provides commands that enable you to view your presentation as a slideshow; these commands are in the Start Slide Show group. The From Beginning and From Current Slide commands can be used to start the slideshow from the first slide or the currently selected slide, respectively. Figure 17-15 shows the ribbon's Slide Show tab. The Start Slide Show commands are on the far left of the tab.

Figure 17-15   The Slide Show tab of the ribbon

TIP

The Captions & Subtitles group on the Slide Show tab is a fairly recent addition to the PowerPoint ribbon. This group allows you to include captions and subtitles with your presentation. An external microphone is a requirement if you plan to use the subtitles feature. (A headset microphone typically provides good results.) You also need a solid Internet connection to use the Captions & Subtitles features because PowerPoint is using a cloud-based speech service to generate the subtitles (as you speak). If you give your presentation with a mic and a good Internet connection, you should get good results. The Captions & Subtitles settings (found using the Subtitle Settings drop-down menu) allow you to set the position for the subtitles (Bottom, Top, Below Slide, and Above Slide). You can also choose from a huge list of languages to set the spoken language and the subtitle language.

What happens when you select either the From Beginning command or the From Current Slide command depends on whether you have multiple monitors on your computer. If you have multiple monitors on your computer, PowerPoint shows your presentation in Presenter view.

Presenter view is enabled by default and gives you a view of the current slide, the next slide, and any notes associated with the current slide on your primary monitor. The other monitor only shows the current slide in the Slide Show view. Other presenter tools available in Presenter view include pen and pointer tools and a Zoom feature. Presenter view is designed to help you give a presentation. It provides on-screen notes (instead of requiring you to print out your notes), and it shows you the next slide (before your audience sees it). This view also provides a timer that enables you to see the current slide's elapsed time on the screen (the timer is also associated with slide timings, which we discuss in Chapter 21).

If you don't have multiple monitors on your computer, selecting the From Beginning command or the Current Slide command shows your presentation's first slide or current slide (depending on the command you selected) in a full-screen slideshow view. You can advance to the next slide by clicking the mouse. You can also press the Page Down key, the right-arrow key, or the down-arrow key to navigate to the next slide in the slideshow.

TIP

Even if you don't have multiple monitors, you can open your presentation in Presenter view. Press Alt+F5 (you don't have to be on the View tab), and the presentation opens.

If you want to back up a slide, press the Page Up key (you can use the up-arrow and left-arrow keys as well). You can also back up a slide by right-clicking the mouse and selecting Previous from the shortcut menu that appears.

When you finish viewing the slideshow, you can end it and return to the PowerPoint workspace; press the Esc key, or right-click the mouse and select End Show to return to the slide that was last viewed in the slideshow.

TIP

You can also start the slideshow from the current slide by clicking the Slide Show button in the View shortcuts on the PowerPoint status bar.

This short discussion of previewing a slideshow as you begin to piece together your presentation is provided to get you in the habit of previewing your slides in slideshow format. We look at issues and PowerPoint features related to planning and preparing a professional presentation in Chapter 21.

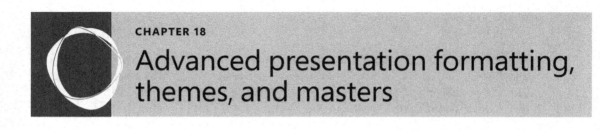

Advanced presentation formatting, themes, and masters

Working with text boxes and formatting   555

Arranging text in tables   566

Working with themes   570

Using headers and footers   576

Understanding masters   577

Altering and creating master slides   579

Creating layout masters   581

Using slide sections   582

Creating PowerPoint presentations that are both informative and visually appealing means you must walk a fine line between the actual purpose of your presentation and its overall design. To get your message across, you must create slides that are both easy to read and understand. PowerPoint slides are meant to hit the high points related to your subject matter and provide a guide to both you and the audience as you walk them through the information.

However, even the most informative and easy-to-understand presentation can be plagued by visually unappealing slides that are not uniform in fonts, colors, and design elements. In this chapter, we look at options for formatting slide text and arranging text in both text boxes and tables.

We discuss the possibilities for manipulating slide color and other attributes using themes and background styles. We also look at the possibilities for inserting repeating information or elements in slides using headers and footers. Our look at overall design considerations and repeating objects also includes a discussion of slide masters. We end the chapter with a discussion of presentation sections, which can help you manage and arrange the slides in a presentation into subgroups of information. The section feature is particularly useful when you are trying to organize a presentation containing many slides.

Working with text boxes and formatting

Most of the text found on your presentation slides will be held in a frame called a text box (although tables can also hold text, as can other objects such as SmartArt). When you insert a new slide into a presentation, you are provided several layout options for that slide. The new slide can use such layouts as Title And Content or Two Content. To add text to a text content box, place the insertion point in a title or content box (both are default text content boxes) with placeholder text and then enter the text. The default for content boxes is a bulleted list.

To edit existing text in a text box, select the current text or place the insertion point and then edit the text. You will only need to create a new text box when you want to place text on the slide in a position other than what is provided by the default text box or text boxes on the slide (which are provided by the slide layout you select).

Inserting a text box

Text boxes are "drawn" onto a slide using the Text Box command in the Text group of the ribbon's Insert tab. Not only do you have control over the format of the text within the box, including the text direction and special text effects, but you also have options for formatting the text box itself, including outside borders and fill color.

To create a new text box on a slide, follow these steps:

1. Select the Text Box command on the Insert menu.

2. Place the mouse pointer on the page and then drag diagonally to create the text box.

3. Release the mouse button, and the insertion point appears in the text box.

Figure 18-1 shows a new text box on a presentation slide (to the right of two pictures). To enter text in a text box, click inside the box and type the required text.

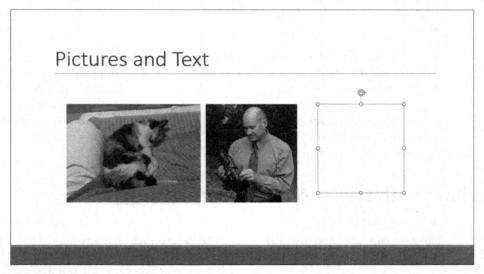

Figure 18-1   A new text box

You can type the text and then format the text after the fact, or you can immediately take advantage of the various font- and paragraph-formatting tools provided on the Home tab to apply basic formatting attributes before you type. These attributes include options such as Bold, Italic, Bulleted Lists, or Numbered Lists.

NOTE

You can add text to nearly any inserted shape. Select the shape and then select the Text Box command on the Drawing Tools Format tab.

In the next section, you see that the possibilities for formatting the text in the text box are not limited to the various font and paragraph commands on the Home tab. Other tools that allow you to add text effects and WordArt styles to your text are provided by the Drawing Tools.

Basic text formatting

The standard formatting commands for both the font and paragraph attributes of the text in a text box are provided in the Font and Paragraph groups on the Home tab, respectivley. The Font group provides control over the font type, size, color, and other attributes such as bold, italic, and underline. The Paragraph group enables you to change the horizontal alignment of the text, create bulleted and numbered lists, change the line spacing, and indent text. Figure 18-2 shows the Home tab, including the Font and Paragraph groups.

NOTE

When you insert a text box onto a slide, the font used will depend on the template/ theme that was used for creating the presentation. If the default font for the template is Century Gothic, then your text box will use the Century Gothic font. Presentations created using PowerPoint's blank template will use the Calibri font for inserted text boxes.

Figure 18-2   The ribbon's Home tab

Changing font attributes

To change the font attributes of selected text, select the text attribute by clicking the appropriate command (or commands) in the Font group. If you find that you want to remove the text formatting that you have applied to text in a text box, select the Clear All Formatting command to remove all the formatting from the selected text.

NOTE

You can select text in a text box and change font and paragraph attributes, or you can select the text box itself (the frame) and then change attributes for all the text in the text box.

You can also access additional font attributes such as Strikethrough, Superscript, and Small Caps by using the Font dialog box. To open the Font dialog box, select the dialog box launcher on the Font group.

The Font dialog box offers you control over some of the same font attributes available in the Font group on the Home tab. It also, however, offers additional font-formatting possibilities, such as Strikethrough, Superscript, Subscript, and Small Caps.

Changing paragraph attributes

Paragraph attributes include settings such as Paragraph Alignment (Left, Center, Right, and Justify), Indents, Columns, Bulleted Lists, Numbered Lists, and Line Spacing. You can assign any of these paragraph settings to selected text (including an entire selected text box). You can also select a specific command, such as Numbered List, and then type the new text as needed.

The Paragraph group offers three additional commands that go beyond the typical paragraph formatting. These commands are as follows:

- **Text Direction:** This command provides a gallery of text orientations, including Horizontal, Rotate All Text 90°, and Stacked. Hover the mouse over a text direction setting in the gallery to preview that setting on the currently selected text box.

  TIP

  You can copy and paste text formats using the Format Painter on the Home tab.

- **Align Text:** This command provides a gallery of settings that change the text's alignment within the text box. Settings provided for Align Text are Top, Middle, and Bottom. You can access more alignment settings by selecting More Options; this opens the Format Shape task pane, which provides a larger list of alignment possibilities in the Vertical alignment drop-down menu.

- **Convert To SmartArt:** This command provides a gallery of SmartArt shapes. You can convert the text box to any of the shapes provided. Place the mouse pointer on a SmartArt shape in the gallery to preview the shape on the currently selected text box.

➤ We discuss SmartArt in more detail in Chapter 19, "Better slides with pictures, icons, and SmartArt."

You can also access the more basic paragraph settings for selected text or a text box via the Paragraph dialog box. Select the dialog box launcher in the Paragraph group. The Paragraph dialog box provides more precise setting possibilities for indents and line spacing, including spin boxes for Before and After, which enable you to set the amount of white space before and after a text line, respectively. The Paragraph dialog box also provides access to the Tabs dialog box, which you can use to set tab stops for a selected text box.

➤ Setting tabs in PowerPoint, both in the Tabs dialog box and directly on the ruler, is similar to creating tab settings in Word. See the "Working with tabs" section of Chapter 6, "Essential Word features."

Formatting a text box with the Shape Format tools

So far, in our discussion related to text boxes, we have looked at the basic text and paragraph settings found on the Home tab of the ribbon. There are other options for formatting a text box and its contents that go way beyond these basic settings. When you select a text box on a slide, the Shape Format tab appears on the ribbon. Select Shape Format, and the various shape formatting command groups are made available. These commands are used to format a PowerPoint object that you add to a slide, which includes shapes and text boxes. The Shape Format tab and its various command groups are shown in Figure 18-3.

Figure 18-3   The Shape Format tab

The commands directly associated with the changes you can make to the text box and the text within the text box are primarily housed in the Shape Styles and WordArt Styles command groups. The Shape Styles commands are used to apply formatting to the text box. The WordArt Styles group enables you to apply special text effects and control the text fill and outline.

Selecting quick styles and shape attributes

Shape styles (or *quick styles*, as they are also referred to) are sets of formatting attributes that affect the Text Box Border, Font Color (and Bullet Color if applicable), and Text Box Background (Fill) Color. Taking advantage of shape styles (quick styles) allows you to assign a grouping of formatting attributes to a text box designed to go together (kind of like a dress shirt that comes with a matching tie). The shape styles are housed in the Shape Styles gallery. You can use the scroll arrows to scroll through the styles provided or click the More button to view the entire gallery.

The fills (text box background) and styles provided are based on the current theme. You can view additional theme fills by selecting Other Theme Fills at the bottom of the gallery. These fills do not provide changes in the font color. You can change the font color by using the Font Color command on the Home tab.

Shape fill, outline, and effects

The alternative to selecting one of the quick styles is to manually change the shape fill, outline, and effects. The Shape Fill, Shape Outline, and Shape Effects commands are also available in the Shape Styles group (make sure the Shape Format tab is selected on the ribbon).

To change the text box fill (or the fill used by other shapes), select the Shape Fill command and select a color from the Theme colors provided. You can also choose from Standard colors or select More Fill Colors to choose a color from the Colors dialog box. Standard colors can be selected on the Standard tab of the Colors dialog box. If you want to select a Custom color or specify a color by its RGB (Red, Green, and Blue) number, you can use the Custom tab of the Colors dialog box. This dialog box also allows you two additional ways to specify a color. You can use a color hexadecimal number or an HSL (Hue, Saturation, Lightness) number.

PowerPoint also provides the Eyedropper tool, which you can use to copy a color from an object on a slide and then apply it as the color for the shape fill or the shape outline. For example, you might have a picture on a slide and want to "steal" a color from the picture and apply it to the fill for your text box or shape. To use the Eyedropper tool, follow these steps:

1.   Select the shape on your slide (such as a text box) and then select Shape Fill (or Shape Outline) on the ribbon.

2.   In the Shape Fill (or Shape Outline) gallery, select Eyedropper.

3.   Move the Eyedropper (the mouse pointer) to the object that contains the color you want to use. When you click the color, the text box is formatted with that color.

The Eyedropper tool also works when you apply a text fill or text outline color to the text in a text box (which we discuss in the next section).

The Shape Fill command provides more options for a text box background than just colors. You can select Picture to specify a picture as the background; all you have to do is specify the picture file in the Insert Picture dialog box. When the picture appears in the text box, you can use the Picture Tools to customize the image so that it works well as a background for the accompanying text in the text box.

> ➤ **Editing pictures in the Office applications, including PowerPoint, is discussed in Chapter 4, "Using and creating graphics."**

The Shape Fill command does not limit you to color and pictures as a text box background. You are also provided with gradients and textures. When you select the Gradient command, a gallery of gradients appears. Point at a gradient to preview it on the text box.

Textures are also an option as the fill for the text box. Select Texture on the Shape Fill menu, and a gallery of textures appears. Preview a texture or textures by moving the mouse over the possibilities in the gallery.

After you have selected a fill for the text box, you can use the Shape Outline command to specify the color for the text box border. You can select from theme or standard colors, or you can use the Color dialog box to specify a custom color. The Shape Outline command also enables you to specify the weight for the text box border and the dash style for the line. The default is a solid line.

TIP

You can assign quick styles to text boxes and other shapes (any object, really) from the Quick Styles command on the Home tab.

To put the finishing touches on the text box, you can add an effect using the Shape Effects command. This command provides a number of different effects that are grouped in galleries under a particular effect category. These categories include Preset, Shadow, Reflection, Glow, and 3D Rotation. Select any of the specific shape effects in the category galleries to preview the effect on the text box.

Fine-tuning shape formatting

The Shape Styles group commands take care of most of the possibilities in formatting the appearance of a text box (or any other shape you insert onto a slide). If you want to fine-tune the format settings for a text box or other object, you can use the Format Shape task pane. To open the Format Shape task pane, select the dialog box launcher on the bottom right of the Shape Styles group. Figure 18-4 shows the Format Shape task pane with the Fill And Line options expanded in the task pane.

The Format Shape task pane provides options for both the shape and the text in the shape. Let's look at the shape options first. We then look at the text options in the next section.

The Fill and Line options are available in the task pane when the Fill & Line icon is selected below the Shape Options heading. To access the various Fill or Line settings, click Fill or Line to expand that node in the task pane. The Fill settings (when expanded) provide a variety of possibilities, including Solid Fill, Gradient Fill, Pattern Fill, and Slide Background Fill (the text box picks up the fill color from the slide). When you select a Fill option, you can select from Preset Gradients or manually set the gradient's Type, Direction, and Angle. Color, Position, Transparency, and Brightness settings are also available as Fill options.

The Line settings enable you to specify the line type (Solid or Gradient) and the line color. Other settings include line Transparency, Width, Compound Type, Dash Type, Cap Type, and Join Type.

Figure 18-4   The Format Shape task pane

When you select the Effects icon at the top of the Format Shape task pane, you can access all the different shape effect possibilities. Most of these effects, such as Shadow, Reflection, and Glow, provide access to several presets and allow you to set custom sizes, colors, and the transparency level. The full list of Effects settings is as follows:

- **Shadow:** This shape effect can be used to specify a shadow type for the text box using a gallery of presets. Additional settings, including Transparency, Size, Blur, Angle, and Distance, enable you to fine-tune the overall look and size of the shadow.

- **Reflection:** Another of the shape effects; select a preset from the provided gallery. You can then fine-tune the reflection using the Transparency, Size, Distance, and Blur settings.

- **Glow:** This effect adds a glow to the edges of the shape. You can select from a number of presets and then fine-tune the Color, Size, and Transparency of the glow.

- **Soft Edges:** This effect can be specified by selecting from several presets (that are based on point size, 1 through 100). You can also fine-tune the size of the soft edges if needed. You can then control the Color, Size, and Transparency of the glow and the size of the soft edges.

- **3D Format:** You can specify a 3D bevel effect for the text box (or other shape) based on the Bevel, Depth, Contour, Material, and Lighting settings for the object. Galleries are provided by both Top bevel and Bottom bevel. You control the Depth and Contour by selecting a color and adjusting the setting using the accompanying spin box.

- **3D Rotation:** This shape effect allows you to rotate a 3D version of the text box or shape by selecting from a gallery of presets. You can then customize the rotation axes by specifying the X, Y, and Z settings using the provided spin boxes or a direction button such as Left, Right, Up, or Down. You can also choose to keep the text flat in the 3D object.

Manipulating the 3D options for a particular shape can be trial and error at best. You might need to take advantage of the Reset button that both of these rather complex formatting options provide for your convenience. After specifying the Format Shape dialog box settings, select Close to return to the PowerPoint workspace.

Using WordArt styles and text settings

The Shape Format tab provides you with special settings for the text contained in a text box or other shape. You can assign WordArt styles to the text, which are special text effects that go way beyond the regular text-formatting possibilities provided on the ribbon's Home tab.

The WordArt styles provide a gallery of different effect styles that can be directly assigned to the text. You can also set your own text fill, outline, and effects if you want. The Format Shape task pane also provides even more granular settings for text settings, including the fill, outline, and effect for the text and the text alignment and direction.

To take advantage of the WordArt Styles gallery, select the WordArt Styles drop-down arrow on the Drawing Tools Format tab. You can then scroll through the possibilities provided in the gallery. If you want to see the entire gallery, click the More button.

To preview a style in the gallery, place the mouse on a style, and it will be applied to the text in the text box. Once you find the style you want to use, select it, and it will be assigned to the text in the text box (or other shape). You can clear a previously assigned WordArt style from the text by using the Clear WordArt option in the WordArt Styles gallery.

Text fill, outline, and effects

If you don't want to use a WordArt style provided in the gallery, you can customize the text by assigning your own fill, outline, and effects settings to the text. The Text Fill command enables you to apply a text color, picture, gradient, or texture to the text in the text box. You can select a color from the colors provided or select More Fill Colors to access the Color dialog box. You can also use the Eyedropper tool to copy a color from any object in the Slide pane.

You can also use a picture as the fill for text in a text box; select Picture and then specify and insert the picture file from the Insert Picture dialog box. You might wonder why you would want to use a picture to provide the fill for text, given that you won't actually see the entire picture. Think of this possibility in terms of the colors provided by the picture rather than the picture itself.

Assigning the background colors to the text using the Text Fill command would enable you to match the text nicely with the accompanying picture on the same slide. Both would use the same color palette, making you look like a design guru. The text fill can also consist of a gradient or texture. Either of these possibilities can be selected from the Text Fill command.

CHAPTER 18

In terms of the text outline, you can use the Text Outline command to select from a variety of colors, or you can use a color you select from the Color dialog box (use the More Outline Colors setting). The Text Outline command also enables you to set the weight and dash style used by the text outline color you select.

The Text Effects command enables you to select from the effects galleries, including Shadow, Reflection, Glow, and Transform. Select a category such as Transform and then preview the possibilities provided in a specific gallery by mousing over a choice or choices. Figure 18-5 shows the Transform gallery provided by the Text Effects command.

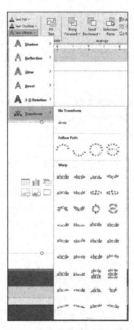

Figure 18-5   Use the Text Effects command to assign special effects to your text.

Although the various text effects are certainly more exciting than what we typically think of as text formatting, I suggest that you use these possibilities judiciously. Cramming a slide with text with different effects applied to it might be hard to read or just jarring in terms of design sensibility. Use the effects to best effect, which means use them sparingly and appropriately. The effects should add to the slide's appeal, not take away from its ability to communicate.

Setting text effects in the Format Shape task pane

You can configure and fine-tune text effect settings in the Format Shape task pane (just as you can fine-tune the other shape settings). Select the dialog box launcher on the WordArt Styles group to open the Format Shape task pane with the Text Options selected.

Figure 18-6 shows the Format Shape task pane with the Text Effects icon selected. As with the Shape Options we discussed in the previous section, expand one of the settings groups, such as Shadow, Reflection, or Glow, and then change the settings as needed. The Text Effect settings (Shadow through 3D Rotation) work exactly the same as the effect settings we discussed for formatting shapes (see the list in the previous section).

The Format Shape task pane also provides you with access to other text settings (not just the text effects). To access the Text Fill or Text Outline settings, select the Text Fill & Outline icon at the top of the Format Shape task pane. You can then expand the Text Fill or Text Outline settings in the task pane.

The Text Fill settings can consist of No Fill, Solid Fill, Gradient, Picture, Texture, or Pattern. When working with the Solid Fill option, you can select a Color and Transparency level for the text. The Gradient option provides you with the ability to set the Color, Direction, Type, and Angle of the gradient. You can then use the Gradient Stops slider to set the stops for the gradient. The Picture or Texture Fill option enables you to select from provided textures or use a picture or clip art as the fill for the text. The last of the fill options, the Pattern Fill, enables you to select a Pattern as well as Foreground and Background colors.

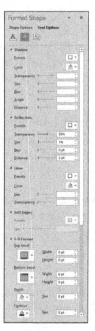

Figure 18-6   The Text Effects in the Format Shape task pane

TIP

You can move the Format Shape task pane anywhere in the PowerPoint application; grab it by its top (the top of the task pane) and drag it to a new location anywhere on the Windows desktop. You can also drag any of the task pane borders to expand its size (both height and width). To place the task pane back in its original position, drag it against the right side of the PowerPoint window until it "snaps" back into place.

The Text Outline (meaning the text border) can be a Solid Line or a Gradient Line (or No Line). When you select the Gradient Line option, you can set the Preset Colors, Type (Linear, Radial, Rectangular, or Path), the Gradient Stops for the gradient, and the Brightness and Transparency of the gradient.

You can also access the Text Box settings in the Format task pane. These settings allow you to control the vertical alignment and direction of the text. You can also specify margins for the text box (or other shape containing text) and determine if the text should wrap in the shape. After you have modified the Format Shape task pane settings, you can close it by clicking the Close button.

Arranging text in tables

Another option (other than a text box) for placing text on a slide is the table. A table can be very useful when you want to display numerical information in an easy-to-read format or want to arrange information in columns or rows. The intersection of a table column and row is referred to as a cell.

The easiest way to create a table on a slide is to create a new slide that uses the Title and Content layout (or use any slide with a content option); insert the new slide using the New Slide command on the Home tab. In the content area of the slide, select the Insert Table icon. The Insert Table dialog box opens.

Specify the number of columns and rows for the new table using the spin boxes provided. When you are ready to place the table on the slide, click OK in the dialog box. The table is placed on the current slide.

Inserting a table on an existing slide

You can also insert a table onto an existing slide. This allows you to include a table on a slide where you already have content and don't want to change the slide's layout.

To insert the table, switch to the ribbon's Insert tab and then select the Table command; you can select the columns and rows for the table by using the table grid provided by the Table command. When you release the mouse, the table is placed on the slide. You can drag the table to the appropriate position on the slide as needed. You can also use any of the sizing handles to size the table so that it is appropriate for your purposes.

Formatting a table

After you have the table on the slide, you can enter text into the cells provided by the table. The easiest way to move forward (left to right) from cell to cell in the table is to use the Tab key. Shift+Tab moves you backward (from right to left) from cell to cell. As you type text in a cell and exceed the width of the column, the text wraps, and the cell height increases to accommodate your entered text. You can widen a column by dragging the border on the column.

PowerPoint also provides specific tools for working with both the layout and design of a table. When you select a table (as an object) or place the insertion point in a cell, the Table Design and Layout tabs become available on the ribbon.

> ### TIP
>
> **You can also draw a new table on a slide. Select the Table command on the Insert tab and then select Draw Table. You can then use the mouse to draw the outside borders of the table and the interior row and column borders. If the columns and rows are uneven, use the Distribute Columns or Distribute Rows commands on the Table Tools, Layout tab as needed.**

The Layout commands appear on the Layout tab (select Layout just to the right of the Table Design tab command). These tools range from commands that enable you to insert columns and rows, merge and split cells, and change the text alignment in a cell or cells. The Design commands control the table's overall look by providing table styles and commands that enable you to configure the table's shading, border, and effects.

Table layout commands

The Layout tab houses several command groups that enable you to manipulate your rows, columns, and cells and work with the text alignment within the cell. Figure 18-7 shows the Table Tools, Layout commands.

Figure 18-7   The Table Tools, Layout tab commands.

The Layout command groups are as follows:

- **Table:** This group provides the Select and View Gridlines commands. The Select command allows you to select the table, the current column, or the current row.

- **Rows & Columns:** These commands enable you to delete and insert rows and columns into the table. The Delete command enables you to delete the selected columns, selected rows, or the entire table. In terms of inserted elements into the table, you can insert rows above or below a selected row or rows, and you can also insert columns to the left or right of the selected column or columns. If you select multiple rows or columns, that is the number of new rows or columns that will be inserted into the table.

- **Merge:** You can select cells and then merge them into a single, larger cell using the Merge Cells command. Use the Split Cells command if you want to split a cell (a regular cell or a merged cell) into two or more cells. You specify the number of columns and rows created when a cell is split by using the Split Cells dialog box.

- **Cell Size:** You can change the width or height of the current row or column (or selected rows or columns) by using the Width and Height spin boxes, respectively. If you want to distribute the columns or rows in the table evenly, use the Distribute Columns command or Distribute Rows command, respectively. Using both commands makes all the cells in the table the same size.

- **Alignment:** This group provides commands such as the Align Left and the Center commands that can be used to specify the horizontal alignment of the text within a cell or cells. If you want to specify the vertical alignment of text in a cell or cells, use the Align Top, Center Vertically, or Align Bottom commands. This group also provides commands for specifying the text direction in a cell or cells and internal cell margins for a cell or cells.

- **Table Size:** This group contains the Height and Width spin boxes, which can be used to adjust the size of the table. If you want the height and width ratio to remain the same when you change the height or width of the table, select the Lock Aspect Ratio check box.

- **Arrange:** This group helps you arrange objects such as tables (and text boxes, shapes, and even pictures) on a slide. You can lay items using the Bring Forward or Send Backward commands. There are also commands for alignment (Align) and grouping objects (Group).

Many of the command options provided on the Layout tab can be used on an individual cell or a group of selected cells. The easiest way to select entire columns or rows is to place the mouse at either the top of a column or on the left of a row until the mouse pointer becomes an arrow. Then use the arrow to drag and select multiple columns or rows as needed.

Table Design commands

The Table Design tab provides commands that enable you to quickly format the table, including its shading and borders. Commands are also available that enable you to apply quick styles and other WordArt formatting to the text within the table cells.

The first set of commands resides on the Design tab's left end in the Table Style Options group. Because tables often contain headings in the top row or can contain important information in the first column, the Table Style Options group provides check box commands that enable you to emphasize certain rows and columns in the table.

For example, you can emphasize your column headings (which appear in the first row) by selecting the Header Row check box. If you are planning on having totals or other summary information in the last row of the table, you can use the Total Row check box to emphasize the last row of the table. The colors used by the Table Style Options command are based on the table style currently assigned to your table.

You can choose an alternative table style by selecting a style from the Table Styles gallery. You can scroll through the table styles available in the gallery, or you can click the More button to view the entire gallery, as shown in Figure 18-8.

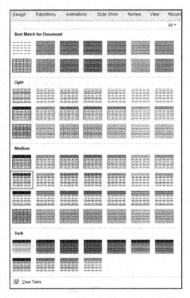

Figure 18-8   The Table Styles gallery

In cases where you want to specify shading for the table that is not available in one of the table styles provided in the gallery, you can use the Shading command to select a color, picture, gradient, or texture for the fill. You can specify the external and internal borders for the table using the Borders command and its accompanying gallery. You can even specify Diagonal Down and Diagonal Up borders for table cells.

If you would like to add 3D effects to table cells, the Effects command enables you to select bevels, shadows, and reflections for a cell or cells. The effect choices are similar to the effect possibilities discussed earlier in the chapter when we looked at the Drawing Tools shape effects provided in the WordArt Styles group. And as with text in a text box, you can choose to format the text in your table with WordArt Styles or specify text fill, lines, and effects using the commands available in the WordArt Styles group.

Working with themes

PowerPoint pioneered the concept of the theme, which is best described as a unified collection of font, color, and design attributes that can be applied to all the slides in a presentation. This provides an overall look of uniformity for the slides in the presentation, even when the slides use different layouts or contain different types of objects. PowerPoint provides a variety of different themes, and you can modify these themes to create your own custom themes.

You already know that you can base a new presentation on a template or a theme. (We talked about this in Chapter 17.) Because each template has its own theme, you assign the template's theme to your new presentation (and get some sample slides and object placeholders in the bargain).

When you base your new presentation on a theme, you get a title slide and all the theme's attributes, such as the slide background, fonts, and other design elements. Therefore, whether you use a template or a theme to initiate a new presentation (on the Start screen or the New page), the theme actually dictates the colors, fonts, effects, and the background style for your presentation slides.

> NOTE
>
> In PowerPoint, a theme controls the slide colors (including the background), the fonts, and the effects. It also controls the layout of the title and content areas on a slide. Therefore, a theme also affects the overall layout of each slide.

> TIP
>
> When selecting a template or theme for a new presentation, try to keep the purpose of your presentation in mind. If you are giving a presentation on major cost-cutting measures that must be enacted at your company, you want to use slide colors, fonts, and design elements that match the tone of the presentation. You probably don't want to use a theme such as the Black Tie theme because it uses a lot of black and muted grays, which makes it seem like you are presenting at a wake (and people are going to be depressed enough when you talk about cost savings).

Remember that the presentation theme you select also controls the position and orientation of the title and content boxes on the slides, controlling the layout for each slide. Suppose a particular theme doesn't provide slide layouts that you find appropriate for the type of content you are presenting. In that case, you can go with another theme or adjust how the theme affects the different layout masters for the presentation. We discuss the slide master and the layout masters later in this chapter.

> ➤ Presentation templates are discussed in Chapter 17, "Essential PowerPoint features."

Applying themes

When you create a new presentation using a template, a theme, or an existing presentation—more than likely, that existing presentation also had a theme applied to it—you are assigning a theme to your slides. Selecting a theme that you can live with at the outset of the presentation creation process negates you from having to do a lot of work rearranging objects on your slides because you have changed to a radically different theme (radically different from your "starting" theme).

Different themes have different layout restrictions, and you don't want to go back and rearrange text and other content boxes when they are adjusted by the layouts provided by a new theme. I'm not saying that you should never change a presentation's theme; I just want you to be mindful that there might be consequences.

A theme can be applied to your current presentation by selecting a theme in the Themes gallery. The Themes gallery is on the ribbon's Design tab in the Themes group. To preview a theme on the current presentation, place the mouse on a particular theme. When you have found the theme that you want to use for the presentation, select it. It is applied to all the slides in the presentation.

Working with themes is not an all-or-nothing proposition. If you don't like the color scheme or design elements of an existing theme, you have options for modifying a theme. A quick fix when you don't like the color scheme or background of a theme is to apply a variant of that theme. (We discuss theme variants in the next section.)

You also have the option of modifying the colors, fonts, effects, and background settings for a theme (and any of its variants). Changes you make to a theme or one of its variants can be saved as a custom theme. So, read on as we discuss theme variants, colors, fonts, effects, and background styles.

Applying theme variants

PowerPoint makes it easy for you to apply different color schemes and backgrounds to your presentation slides using themes. Each specific theme also has variants, which are variations on the selected theme. Variants of a theme are accessed via the Variants gallery, as shown in Figure 18-9; it provides variations of the current theme (in most cases, different color schemes and backgrounds). To see how the variation looks on the current slide, place the mouse on the variant in the Variants gallery to get a preview.

You can expand the Variants gallery by clicking the More button on the right side of the gallery. When you locate the variant you want to use, select it. As mentioned in the previous section, you can select a theme variant and then modify the colors, fonts, and effects as needed.

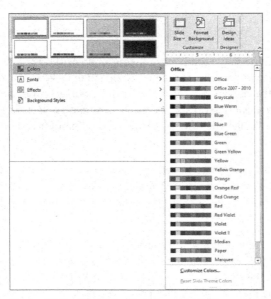

Figure 18-9   The Variants gallery and Colors gallery

Theme colors

Each theme and theme variant has a color scheme. As already mentioned, you can adjust the colors for the current theme by selecting a variant. You can also adjust the color set using the Colors command, which can be opened from the Variants gallery. Click the More button in the Variants gallery to access the Colors gallery (refer to Figure 18-9). This gallery provides some built-in color schemes. You can preview the colors on the current slide by placing the mouse on one of the theme color sets.

If you want to create your own theme colors, you can do so in the Create New Theme Colors dialog box (see Figure 18-10). To open this dialog box, select Customize Colors in the Colors gallery. Use the various color drop-down menu palettes to select the specific colors for the theme color set. When selecting a color, you can use theme colors or standard colors. To access more colors (more than the theme and standard colors), select More Colors, and the Color dialog box opens.

When you have selected the colors for the new theme colors, type a name in the Name text box. When you click Save, the color theme is added to the Colors gallery under the Custom heading.

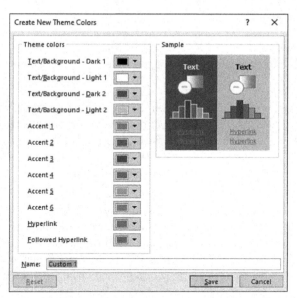

Figure 18-10   Use the Create New Theme Colors dialog box to create your own color sets.

Theme fonts

You can also adjust the fonts used by the current theme (or theme variant). Expand the Variants gallery and then select the Fonts command. A gallery of different font sets opens. Each font set provides the appropriate font sizes for the different title and text boxes that appear on your different slide layouts.

If you want to create your own theme fonts, you can select Customize Fonts in the Fonts gallery, and the Create New Theme Fonts dialog box opens. Use the Heading Font and Body Font drop-down menus to specify the heading and body fonts, respectively. A sample of your font selection is provided in the dialog box.

Enter a name for the new theme fonts and then select Save. The new theme fonts appear on the Fonts gallery under the Custom heading.

TIP

If you want to delete custom theme colors or custom theme fonts that you have created, right-click them in their respective gallery (Colors or Fonts gallery) and then select Delete from the shortcut menu.

Theme effects

Theme effects can also be modified for the current theme or variant by selecting built-in effects from the Effects gallery. Expand the Variants gallery and then select the Effects command; the Effects gallery appears.

You won't see dramatic changes to your slides when you change the theme effects. Think of the effects as theme design refinements. You can't create your own effects sets, but you can save effects changes that you have made to the current theme by creating a custom theme (which we talk about in a moment).

Theme backgrounds

PowerPoint makes it easy for you to fine-tune the background style for the selected theme or theme variant. In earlier versions of PowerPoint, background formatting and presentation design elements were typically dealt with on the presentation's slide master (which we talk about later in this chapter); however, this also meant that all the slides had the same background. PowerPoint provides options for changing the background on all the slides (or specific slides) in the presentation.

You can apply a new background style to the current theme or variant via the Background Styles gallery. Expand the Variants gallery and then select Background Styles. Select a background style from the gallery. The background style is applied to the slides in the presentation.

You can also format the background manually using the Format Background task pane. You can open the Format Background task pane by selecting Format Background in the Background Styles gallery or by selecting the Format Background command in the Customize group on the ribbon's Design tab.

Figure 18-11 shows the Format Background task pane with the Solid Fill option selected. You can select from a number of fill options. These options are as follows:

- **Solid Fill:** This option allows you to specify a Fill Color and Transparency.

- **Gradient Fill:** You can select from some Preset Gradients and create a custom gradient where you control gradient attributes, such as the Type, Direction, Color, and Position of the gradient.

- **Picture Or Texture Fill:** This option allows you to specify a picture or texture as the background fill. You can insert your own picture or a picture from Office.com for the background, and you can tile the picture as a texture if you want. You can also set the offset and scale axes for the gradient and specify the alignment.

TIP

If you want to hide background graphics provided by a theme on a particular slide, select the Hide Background Graphics check box in the Format Background task pane when that slide is selected in the Slide list.

- **Pattern Fill:** You can specify a pattern as the background fill for your slides. You also control the foreground and background color from the pattern.

Figure 18-11   The Format Background task pane

You can apply your background settings to the current slide (which is done automatically as soon as you change any of the background settings), or you can apply the new background to all your slides by clicking the Apply To All button. If you want to "throw out" the background changes you have made (so that they aren't applied to either the current slide or any of the slides in the presentation), click the Reset Background button. When you have finished working with the Format Background task pane, you can select Close to close it.

Creating a custom theme

We have already looked at options for saving custom color sets and font sets. You can also save all the modifications that you make to a theme as a custom theme. This includes changes you have made to colors, fonts, and background styles. You can then access your custom themes for future use.

To create a custom theme, change theme elements (colors, fonts, and background settings) in an existing theme or a variant and select Save Current Theme. The Save Current Theme dialog box opens. By default, your custom themes are saved to `Users\User Name\AppData\Roaming\Microsoft\Templates\Document Themes`. Make sure that you save your theme to this folder so you can easily access it (and other custom themes that you create) from the Themes gallery.

Enter a name for the custom theme and then select Save. Now when you access the Themes gallery, your new custom theme appears under the Custom heading. You can also open saved themes using the Browse For Themes option in the Themes gallery. This is useful if you didn't save a theme to the default folder, and the theme is not listed in the Themes gallery.

Using headers and footers

Each slide in your presentation will be unique in terms of the slide's content. There will be occasions when you want to add repeating information to every slide in the presentation. In PowerPoint, repeating information placed on your slides is housed in the footer, which means the repeating information will appear at the bottom of each slide. For example, you might want to include the date and a slide number at the bottom of every slide. You also have the option of placing additional information in the footer, such as your name. The footer information can appear on specific slides, or it can appear on all the slides in the presentation. (We'll discuss how to do that in a moment.) If you choose to include the information on all the slides, there is a setting to keep the footer information off the title slide (which is pretty common practice).

Although headers are not available for your slides (see the Header And Footer dialog box in Figure 18-12), you do have the option of creating both headers and footers for your note pages and handouts. All the settings related to headers and footers are located in the Header And Footer dialog box. A tab is provided for slides, and a tab is provided for notes and handouts.

To open the Header And Footer dialog box, navigate to the ribbon's Insert tab. Then select Header & Footer in the Text group. Figure 18-12 shows the Header And Footer dialog box with the Slide tab selected. You can also open the Header And Footer dialog box by selecting either the Data & Time or Slide Number commands in the Text group.

On the Header And Footer dialog box's Slide tab, you can specify that the date and time are included in the footer and whether the date should be updated automatically. A check box is also provided for the slide number, which places a slide number in the footer. If you also want to include additional footer information, such as your name, select the Footer check box and then enter the text into the Footer text box provided.

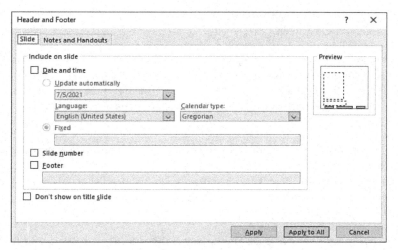

Figure 18-12   The Header And Footer dialog box

> **TIP**
>
> **If you are annoyed by the fact that the footer is used exclusively for repeating informa-tion on your slides, you can actually create a new Slide Master for your presentation. Then you can move some of the footer elements (such as the date) up into the Header area of the slide. We discuss how to edit or create additional Slide Masters in the next section.**

If you want to apply the footer settings to the current slide only (or a group of selected slides in the Slide Sorter or on the Slide tab), click the Apply button. If you want to apply the footer set-tings to all the slides in the presentation, click the Apply To All button. If you apply the footer settings to all slides, you might want to take advantage of the Don't Show On Title Slide check box because footer information is typically not included on the presentation's title slide.

➤ Headers and footers can also be set for your presentation notes and handouts. For infor-mation on working with the notes and handout masters, see the "Working with notes and handout masters" section of Chapter 21, "Delivering a presentation and creating support materials.

Understanding masters

When you assign a theme to a presentation or add footers to the presentation slides, you are manipulating the master slide for the presentation. The master slide isn't actually a slide but is the design blueprint for all the slides in the presentation, including the background fill, colors, fonts, and effects provided by the current theme. The master slide also provides the positioning and the size of the content placeholders—the title text box and the bulleted list text box—which are present on most slides.

Whatever you do to the master slide is inherited by all the slides in the presentation (that use the master slide for their formatting). For example, if you place a graphic of your company logo on the slide master, the logo appears on all the slides in the presentation. If you change the background style for the master slide, the background style changes on all the presentation slides.

This ability to modify the master slide goes beyond broad changes, such as applying a background style or placing an image on the master slide. If you change the bullet character or change the indents for the different levels of the default bulleted list in the bulleted list placeholder on the master slide, these changes propagate to all slides in the presentation, including slides you add to the presentation.

To view the slide master for your presentation, select the ribbon's View tab. Select the Slide Master command in the Master Views command group. The slide master and its accompanying layout masters appear in the PowerPoint application window. Select the slide master (the first and largest thumbnail) in the master list, and the slide master appears in the Slide pane, as shown in Figure 18-13.

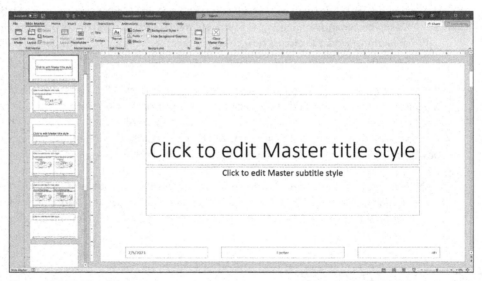

Figure 18-13   The slide masters

In the Slide pane, all the layout masters for the presentation (based on the template and theme) are listed as thumbnails to the left of the slide master, appearing below the thumbnail for the slide master (it is the larger thumbnail at the top of the thumbnail list). Note that a dotted line connects each of the layout masters with the slide master. The layout masters provide the different slide layouts you access when you use the Insert Slide command or the Layout command on the ribbon's Home tab. Every slide you insert into your presentation is associated with one of the layout masters. If you place the mouse on a layout master, the name of the layout master appears, as well as a list of the slides that have been assigned that layout master.

The various slide layout masters inherit any changes that you make on the master slide. The dotted connection line that runs from the master slide to the layout masters illustrates that thematic changes (colors, fonts, and so on) propagate to the layout masters. The opposite is not true, however. If you make changes directly on a layout master, these changes do not propagate back to the slide master. So, if you want a unified, consistent look for a presentation, you should edit the master slide only. You might be tempted to edit individual layout masters to suit a particular purpose, but it is probably a better idea to create a new layout master that is specific to your purpose. This creates your special layout without changing any of the provided default layouts. The next section discusses altering and creating master slides and is followed by a section that discusses working with layout masters.

Altering and creating master slides

When you are in the Master view, the Slide Master tab appears on the ribbon. The Slide Master tab provides different command groups related to modifying and/or creating master slides and layout masters. These command groups are as follows:

- **Edit Master:** This group enables you to insert a new slide master or layout master. Commands are also provided for deleting and renaming masters.

- **Master Layout:** This group enables you to specify the master slide layout's default placeholders (title, text, date, and so on) via the Master Layout command. By default, all placeholders are present on a master slide. The Insert Placeholder command is used to insert placeholders on layout masters, and check boxes are also provided in this group, including a title and footers on layout masters.

- **Edit Theme:** This group provides access to the Themes gallery.

- **Background:** This group provides access to the Colors, Fonts, and Effects commands, which can be used to modify the theme on a master slide. If you want to change the background style on a master slide or layout master, you can use the Background Style command. A check box is also provided to hide background graphics that you might have inserted onto the slide master.

- **Size:** You can change the default slide size from Standard (4:3) to Widescreen (16:9), or vice versa (depending on the original size setting). This command also allows you to access the Slide Size dialog box, which you can use to create a custom slide size and control the orientation of slides, notes, and handouts.

You can change the slide master as you require using the various group commands provided by the Slide Master tab. This includes rearranging and sizing the content placeholders on the master slide. You also have control over any of the theme-related settings (colors, fonts, and effects) and background styles for the slide master using the Edit Theme and/or Background group commands.

When altering the slide master, you should be aware of a couple of things. If you radically change the location of the title or content placeholders provided on the master slide or move the footer content boxes to another location on the slide, this can negatively affect the layout masters. For example, if you move the default title placeholder down on the master slide, it might overlay other content placeholders that are on individual layout masters. This means slides based on particular placeholders might look really messed up because of changes made to the slide master.

When you feel that you need a slide master with a dramatically different look, it makes better sense to create a new slide master. You can then apply the new slide master to only the slides that require this different look.

To create a new slide master, select the Insert Slide Master command in the Edit Master group. The new slide master is inserted into the Slide Master pane. A default set of layout masters is also created and associated with the new slide master. You can modify the new slide master as needed. Creating a second slide master is the easiest way to employ two different themes in the same presentation. The first slide master can be formatted with one theme, and the second slide master can be formatted with a second theme.

When you use two or more slide masters, the number of layouts available for a new slide multiplies. (In the case of two slide masters, the number of available layouts doubles.) You can quickly view the various layouts in the New Slide gallery, which you open via the New Slide command on the Home tab (when you are working in Normal view). Note that two different sets of slide layouts are provided; the set at the top (the default slide master) has been assigned a theme, and the second set (a new slide master) has not been assigned a theme. Note that the "added" master slide provides slide layouts categorized under the Custom Design heading in the New Slide gallery.

TIP

When you are in Master view, you can delete a slide master by selecting it and then selecting the Delete command in the Edit Master group.

The changes that you make to your second slide master are not limited to theme formatting. As with any other slide master, you can add graphics and rearrange the content placeholders on the slide master as needed.

When you are in Master view, you can check which slides have been assigned a particular slide master or a particular layout master. Place the mouse on the slide master or the layout master, and a message box appears, detailing which slides are associated with the master.

If you create additional slide masters and then don't use them, you can delete them from the Slide Master pane. By default, new slide masters are preserved in the Slide Master pane, whether you use them. This isn't a bad thing; it just keeps your added slide masters as part of the presentation regardless of whether you use them. If you are uneasy about having slide masters that you do not use still hanging around, deselect the Preserve command after you create a new slide master. If you don't use the slide master, it is not preserved.

Creating layout masters

You also can create new layout masters. You can create a new layout master for the default slide master, or you can create a new layout master for a slide master you have added to the presentation.

Creating your own layout masters enables you to specify layouts for special slides. This negates the need for radically changing the layout of individual slides in the presentation. You can probably create a new layout faster than you can edit an existing slide in the presentation.

When you create a new layout master, it is associated with the presentation's master slide. However, if you have more than one master slide in your presentation, you must select the thumbnail of the appropriate slide master before you create the new layout master. This will ensure that the new layout master is associated with the correct slide master.

To insert the new layout master, select the Insert Layout command in the Edit Master group. The new layout master appears in the Slide pane and is added as a thumbnail to the list of masters on the left of the screen. By default, a title placeholder and footers are added to the layout master. You can remove the title or the footers by deselecting the Title or Footers check boxes in the Master Layout group.

To add placeholders to the new layout master, select the Insert Placeholder command in the Master Layout group. A number of different placeholder types are provided by the Insert Placeholder command.

You can add a number of different placeholder types to the layout master, including Text, Picture, and Chart. Then when you use the layout master to create a new slide, the content specified on the layout master is provided in the new slide.

TIP

You can change the background style for a layout master. This change does not affect the other layout masters associated with the slide master.

For example, to place a content box on the layout master, select Content in the Insert Place-holder gallery. You then use the mouse to draw the content placeholder box. You can size the placeholder and arrange it on the layout master as needed. Arranging and sizing placeholders is no different from working with content boxes on a regular slide—it is all mouse work.

As mentioned at the beginning of our discussion on the slide master and layout masters, I think it is better to create custom slide masters and layout masters rather than radically chang-ing the default slide master and its associated layout masters. In most cases, radically different slide designs and layouts are used minimally in a presentation. Therefore, create your own masters for these exceptions, and rely on the default masters for the more typical slides in your presentation.

TIP

When you have finished working in the master view, select the Close Master View com-mand to return to your presentation.

Using slide sections

A great way to organize a presentation with a large number of slides is to break it into parts using sections. Slide sections do not affect the layout or look of your slides, but they *do* pro-vide you with an organizational tool for grouping associated slides in a presentation. Having the slides in a presentation grouped by sections makes it easy for you to arrange large parts of your presentation without dragging individual slides around. This is particularly useful when you fine-tune the overall sequence of slides in your presentation and try to hit those beginning, middle, and end sweet spots. Sections can be collapsed, which enables you to focus on the sec-tion itself. This makes it even easier to move a section within the presentation.

The best view to work in when you are creating and rearranging sections is the Slide Sorter. You can switch to the Slide Sorter by using the Slide Sorter button on the PowerPoint status bar or by switching to the View tab on the ribbon and then selecting Slide Sorter.

The Section command is on the ribbon's Home tab in the Slides group. The easiest way to create a new section is to select the first slide that appears in the section. Select Section, Add Section. A new section is placed between the selected slide and the slides that precede the selected slide in the presentation. You can then navigate to the next slide that starts a new section in the presen-tation and create a new section at that point. Repeat the process until you have grouped all the slides in the presentation into specific sections.

When you insert the section into the presentation, the section is listed as "Untitled Section." If you select the section, you can then rename it by clicking the Section command and then selecting Rename Section. The Rename Section dialog box opens. Type a name for the section and select Rename.

You can rename any section that you create and rename the Default Section if it is created automatically. If you are working on a ribbon tab other than the Home tab, right-click a section and then select Rename Section to access the Rename Section dialog box. This forgoes the necessity of switching back to the Home tab.

NOTE

If you create a new section in the presentation in a place other than the very beginning of the presentation, the slides that precede the new section are automatically placed in a section titled "Default Section."

When you have the presentation divided into sections, you can easily rearrange the presentation. Each section has a collapse/expand button on the left side of the section bar. You can collapse a section or sections as needed. If you want to collapse all the sections in the presentation, right-click any section and then select Collapse All from the shortcut menu provided. Figure 18-14 shows a presentation with four sections; two of the sections have been collapsed, and two expanded sections show thumbnails of the slides in those sections.

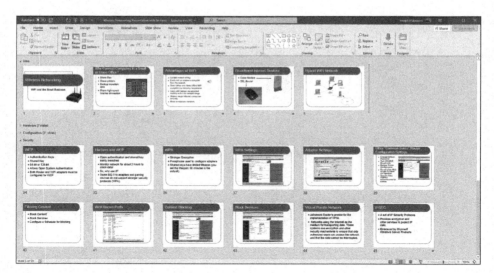

Figure 18-14   Collapsed sections in the Slide Sorter

You can drag a section to a new position in the presentation to rearrange the presentation as needed. The number of slides in a collapsed presentation will be noted to the right of the section title.

You can also copy all the slides in a section and paste the entire section into another presentation. Select a section and then select Copy on the Home tab. You can then open an existing presentation or start a new presentation and paste the slides into it. You can also cut and paste slide sections from one presentation to another.

Sections provide markers in your presentation that make it easy to jump to a particular part of the presentation when you are running a slideshow.

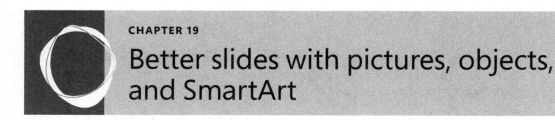

Better slides with pictures, objects, and SmartArt

Using graphics to enhance slides   585

Inserting a picture   587

Adding stock images to slides   589

Creating a photo album   591

Working with shapes   593

Inserting icons   595

Using SmartArt graphics   596

Adding charts to slides   602

Working with slide objects   606

Adding hyperlinks to slides   608

Using PowerPoint Designer   609

PowerPoint presentations tell a story. Whether you provide coworkers an update on the company's quarterly sales or share your latest vacation photos and experiences with your travel club, a presentation needs to be succinct and complete (with a beginning, middle, and end). Much of the information can be shared as text, but images and other graphics can greatly enhance the audience's understanding of the presented information. Clip art, pictures, and SmartArt can also make slides more visually interesting and appealing.

This chapter looks at adding graphics such as clip art, pictures, and SmartArt to your PowerPoint slides. We explore how graphics can serve as informational objects, such as pictures and charts, and how objects such as icons and SmartArt can be used as design elements on your slides. We also discuss working with object layers and how to group related objects. Our discussion includes adding hyperlinks to slides, accessing external information on the web, and pointing to information on a presentation slide. We end the chapter with a discussion of the PowerPoint Designer. This design tool can help you create more professional slide layouts. PowerPoint Designer actually detects the pictures, charts, and other graphic elements on a slide, and it suggests different layouts for the current slide.

Using graphics to enhance slides

The graphics you place on your PowerPoint slides can be informational in nature or just serve as design elements (or both). A chart or picture can often be more effective than text when getting a particular idea or concept across. For example, a chart of recent sales figures gives the audience a better feel for recent sales trends than a table of numbers. Graphics can also add visual interest to your slides. PowerPoint now provides access (as does Excel and Word) to a stock images library that negates the need to use clip art and images sourced from the web. The stock image library is a searchable resource that allows you to add images to your slides that match the theme of a slide (or the entire presentation). For example, if you are giving a presentation at a town meeting related to the need for a new playground, you can search *playground* in the stock images window. You can then select from a number of playground-related images for your slide or slides. The stock images also include icons, stickers, videos, and illustrations for your use.

PowerPoint enables you to insert different visual objects onto a slide. Several of the possibilities are as follows:

- **Picture:** You can insert your own digital pictures from your computer or your OneDrive directly onto your presentation slides. PowerPoint supports a number of digital picture file formats (including jpg, bmp, png, and tiff). PowerPoint also provides tools that enable you to modify inserted pictures. You can crop, correct, and add effects to your images.

- **Stock Images:** This possibility allows you to access stock images provided by Microsoft. The files located by the default Bing search are licensed under the Creative Commons licensing rules, which we discuss in more detail in the "Adding online images to slides" section later in this chapter.

- **Screenshot:** You can capture a screenshot of any open window using the Screenshot command. You can then add these screenshots directly to a slide. This is extremely useful when you want to include a screenshot of another application window (such as Excel) on a presentation slide.

- **Shapes:** You can insert many different shapes into your slides (or into the master slide) to add visual appeal. PowerPoint provides a Shapes gallery that has an enormous number of shapes, including lines, rectangles, block arrows, flow charts, banners, and callouts.

- **Icons:** The icons library is made up of emoji-like black and white images that can be used to enhance slides and help visually tell your story on a particular slide or slides. The icons are broken down into categories such as Analytics, Travel, Vehicles, and Medical.

- **3D Models:** 3D models are available in an online library (additional libraries can be stored locally on your computer) that provides you with 3D images that can be rotated on any axis. The 3D model library is broken down into categories such as Animated, Animals, Tools, Anatomy, and Avatars. Think of these images as just another way to add interest and information to a presentation slide.

- **SmartArt:** SmartArt gives you access to all sorts of diagrams that enable you to create block diagrams, flow charts, organizational charts, and even pyramid diagrams. If you've ever had to place an inverted pyramid on a slide and tried to draw it in another software package or construct it from shapes, you understand how useful SmartArt can be.

- **Charts:** You can add column, line, pie, bar, and other chart types to your PowerPoint slides. The chart data is entered into an Excel worksheet, making it easy to provide the information that makes the chart a reality. You can edit the chart data at any time.

➤ **You can also link Excel worksheet data and Excel charts to PowerPoint slides. See Appendix A, "Office application integration," for more information.**

PowerPoint provides additional objects that can also be considered graphics or design elements. For example, you can insert WordArt text boxes. These special text boxes add interesting text elements to a slide. You can also add equations to your slides. PowerPoint provides a gallery of equations, including the area of a circle, the binomial theorem (one of my favorites), and the Pythagorean theorem (okay, this is my favorite). You can also insert new equations that you create.

> ➤ **Video and sound can enhance your slides. For more about adding video and sound to your PowerPoint presentations, see Chapter 20, "Enhancing slides with animation, transitions, and multimedia."**

There is more than one way to insert a graphic such as a picture or shape into your slides. When you insert a new slide into a presentation, it will provide content area icons for inserting objects such as a chart, SmartArt, a picture, or icon. When you select one of these content options, the graphic is inserted onto the slide, replacing the content frame.

You can also insert items such as pictures and shapes as objects within their own frames. The ribbon's Insert tab, shown in Figure 19-1, provides the commands for inserting the various graphic object types into your slides.

Figure 19-1 The ribbon's Insert tab

After you insert a visual on a slide, contextual tools that relate to the particular graphic type appear on the ribbon. For example, the Picture Tools, Format tab appears on the ribbon when you insert a picture. When you insert a SmartArt graphic, the SmartArt tools become available on the ribbon.

Inserting a picture

You can quickly insert a picture file that you have stored on your computer using the Pictures command in the Images group. PowerPoint supports several popular picture file formats, including Windows Bitmap (.bmp), Graphics Interchange Format (.gif), Joint Photographic Expert Group (.jpg), Portable Network Graphics (.png), and Tagged Image File Format (.tiff).

To open the Insert Picture dialog box, select the Pictures command on the Insert tab and then select This Device. If you are working with a new slide that contains content placeholders, you can also open the Insert Picture dialog box by selecting the Pictures icon in the content placeholder. Figure 19-2 shows the Insert Picture dialog box.

The default location for the Insert Picture dialog box is the Pictures library. If you need to navigate to another location on your computer or computer network, you can do so using the location pane on the left the Insert Picture dialog box. When you have located the picture you want to insert, select the picture and then click Insert (or double-click the picture). The picture is inserted into the current slide.

When the picture is selected on the slide, the Picture Format tab appears on the ribbon.

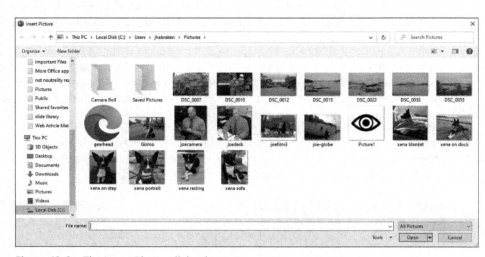

Figure 19-2   The Insert Picture dialog box

The Picture Tools enable you to adjust the picture (such as brightness and contrast), select a picture style, arrange multiple pictures on the page, and crop and size the selected picture. The Picture Tools groups are as follows:

- **Remove Background:** This command enables you to remove the background from the picture. When you select the Remove Background command, the Background Removal tab appears on the ribbon. You can mark areas to keep in the picture or mark areas to remove from the picture. Figure 19-3 shows a picture with the background to be removed and the ribbon's Background Removal commands, which are used to fine-tune the removal of the picture's background.

- **Adjust:** This group provides commands that enable you to adjust the sharpness, brightness, and contrast and to make color corrections to the picture, including its saturation and tone. You can also add artistic effects to the picture and reset the picture settings if needed.

- **Picture Styles:** Picture styles provide you with different frame formats, which include frame shapes and frame border styles. You can preview a style on the selected picture by placing the mouse on any of the styles in the gallery.

- **Accessibility:** This group contains the Alt Text command, which allows you to enter the alternative text for an image or other object such as SmartArt. The alt text is then read out loud by screen reader software.

- **Arrange:** This group lets you layer multiple images (using commands such as Bring Forward and Send Backward). It also enables you to group graphics and align images (left, center, right, top-middle, bottom) and allows you to rotate and flip pictures.

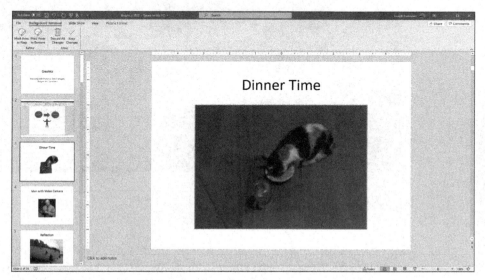

Figure 19-3   Remove the background from a picture

- **Size:** This group provides Height and Width spinner boxes for sizing a picture. You can also use the Crop command to crop the image as needed.

When you finish manipulating the picture, click outside the picture frame to deselect it. The picture tools are also removed from the ribbon.

➤ For more information on working with pictures and other graphics in the Office applications, see Chapter 4, "Using and creating graphics."

Adding stock images to slides

PowerPoint and the other Microsoft 365 applications provide access to a huge Stock Photos library. The new Microsoft stock photo library gives you access to many free stock images. You will find that the library also contains fee-based images that you can use if you pay for them. To open the Stock Images library, select Pictures in the Insert tab's Images group and then select Stock Images from the Insert Picture From gallery. You can also open the Stock Images library

Stock Images window by clicking the Stock Images icon in a new slide's content area. Figure 19-4 shows the Online Pictures window.

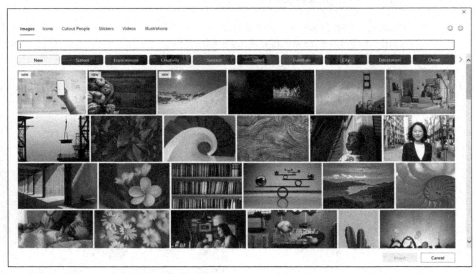

Figure 19-4   The Online Pictures window

TIP

PowerPoint also provides you with the ability to search for online pictures using the Online Pictures in the Insert Picture From gallery dialog box. Images you locate in an image search might have licensing restrictions (in terms of use), so track down the licensing terms for an image if you are going to use it for any "professional purpose." You can read more about Creative Commons and content licensing at *http: //creativecommons.org/licenses/*. Again, I suggest you take advantage of the stock images rather than rooting around on the web for pictures that might have use restrictions.

You can insert an image or images by selecting the appropriate thumbnails in the Stock Image window. A Search box is provided at the top of the window to search for images using keywords. Categories of image types are also provided, such as Sunset, Environment, Creativity, and Speed, and can be used to browse for a particular image type. After making your selection(s), select the Insert button, and the image(s) will be inserted onto the current slide. The Picture Format tab of the ribbon provides all the commands you need to adjust, style, and arrange pictures on the slide.

TIP

If you want an image to repeat on every slide (say, for a logo), place the image on the presentation's master slide. Slide Masters are discussed in Chapter 18, "Advanced presentation formatting, themes, and masters."

Creating a photo album

If you have a bunch of digital photos that you want to get onto PowerPoint slides with a minimal amount of hassle, you can create a PowerPoint photo album. The Photo Album tool is perfect for quickly placing your digital vacation photos on a series of slides. The Photo Album command is on the Insert tab in the Images group.

When you use the Photo Album command, a new presentation is created, including a title slide for the presentation. Different picture layouts enable you to specify the number of pictures placed on each slide on the album. You also have control over the frame shape for each picture inserted into the photo album, and you can assign a theme to the photo album. All these settings are housed in the Photo Album dialog box, so you can specify the pictures for the album and then quickly create the entire album without manipulating individual slides or pictures.

You can use the Photo Album command even if you are currently in the middle of another presentation. Because a new presentation is created for the photo album, the slides in the current presentation are not disturbed.

To create a new photo album, select Photo Album on the Insert tab and then select New Photo Album. The Photo Album dialog box opens. The first step in the process of creating the photo album is to specify the pictures to include in the album. Select the File/Disk command, and the Insert New Pictures dialog box opens. This dialog box opens to the Pictures library by default. Next, locate the pictures that you want to use for the photo album. It makes sense to select as many of the pictures as you can at this point. Select the first picture and then select subsequent picture files while holding down the Ctrl key. To select a series of pictures, select the first picture series, and then select the last picture in the series with Shift+click. This selects all the pictures in the series. After you have selected the pictures, click the Insert button in the dialog box.

You are returned to the Photo Album dialog box, and you can now manipulate the picture order in the album, choose picture options, and specify the layout for the album.

If you need to change the order of the pictures in the album, select a picture and then use the Move Up or Move Down buttons to change the position of the picture in the album list. If you decide that you don't want a particular picture in the album, select the file name and then click the Remove button.

TIP

If you need to add pictures to the photo album that are in a different location than the pictures already inserted, select File/Disk and use the Insert New Pictures dialog box to locate and add the pictures to the Photo Album dialog box.

CHAPTER 19

Adjusting picture settings

The Photo Album dialog box also provides a series of buttons that enable you to adjust settings for each individual picture. You can use the Rotate Left button or the Rotate Right button to rotate the currently selected picture 90 degrees to either the left or right, respectively. You can also adjust the contrast or brightness of the selected picture up or down using the appropriate buttons. You can adjust other picture options as well, such as selecting to have all the pictures changed to black and white.

If you want to include a text box on each slide that is created in the photo album, select New Text Box. The text box is added to the Pictures in Album list. The text box appears on each slide; after the photo album is created, you can add text to the text box to describe the picture on the slide or provide ancillary information related to each picture.

Configuring album layout settings

By default, each picture listed in the Photo Album dialog box is placed on a separate slide and fitted to the slide, so you don't have to worry about the potentially different sizes of the pictures you want to add to the photo album. The Fit to Slide option does not enable you to select the frame shape for the inserted pictures.

The Picture Layout drop-down menu (in the Photo Album dialog box) does give you other options for how the pictures appear on the slides. The One Picture, Two Pictures, and Four Pictures options place the specified number of pictures on each slide. These settings also enable you to specify the frame shape for the picture by selecting a shape from the Frame Shape drop-down menu. A number of frame shapes are available, including Rounded Rectangle, Simple Frame, White, Center Shadow Rectangle, and Soft Edge Rectangle.

If you want to include a title text box on each slide, you can select the layout of one picture with a title picture. Options for two and four pictures with a title are also included in the Picture Layout drop-down menu. Selecting any of the options that include a title also enables you to specify the frame shape for the pictures. Both the number of slides you specify in the layout and the frame shape you select are previewed in the Album Layout area of the Photo Album dialog box.

> ### CAUTION
>
> If you aren't familiar with the frame shapes and presentation themes available in PowerPoint, you might want to wait and adjust these settings on the photo album after creating the album. You can then take advantage of the Themes gallery and the Pictures Style gallery, which provide visual examples of the built-in themes and styles available.

You also have the option of specifying a theme for the new photo album presentation. Click the Browse button next to the Theme box. This opens the Choose Theme dialog box. The Choose Theme dialog box opens to the default Office themes folder, and the themes are listed by name. You can't view a preview of the theme, but if you have a good feel for the overall look and layout of a particular theme (or themes), you can select a theme and then click Open to apply it to the new photo album. This returns you to the Photo Album dialog box. When you have all your settings squared away for the new photo album, select Create. The photo album opens in the PowerPoint workspace with the title slide selected.

Because the photo album is no different from any other PowerPoint presentation, you can modify presentation settings such as the theme for the presentation. You can also edit each slide in the presentation, which is required if you specified that a text box or title box be included on each slide when you configured the settings for the photo album in the Photo Album dialog box.

If you want to add photos to the photo album or change any of the settings related to the photo album, you can do so in the Edit Photo Album dialog box. Select the Photo Album command and then select Edit Photo Album. The Edit Photo Album dialog box provides all the settings that were available in the Photo Album dialog box. You can insert additional pictures, modify picture settings, or change the picture layout and frame shape as needed.

When you have finished making changes to the album settings, click the Update button to return to the photo album. Remember that the photo album is a new presentation, so click the Save button on the Quick Access Toolbar and specify a name and location for the photo album in the Save As dialog box.

Working with shapes

You can add shapes to your slides as design elements and also use them as interesting text boxes (many of the shapes can contain text). When you work with shapes, remember that less is always better, so don't crowd your slides with a lot of rectangles and circles. Proper slide design relates to balance, and emphasis is not on the quantity of shapes and other graphic elements crammed on each slide.

To insert a shape, select the Shapes command on the ribbon's Insert tab. The Shapes gallery appears, as shown in Figure 19-5.

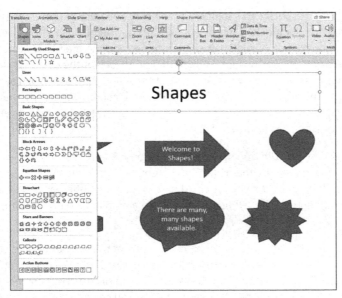

Figure 19-5   The Shapes gallery and a slide with inserted shapes

The shapes provided in the gallery are divided into categories, including lines, rectangles, block arrows, and callouts, just to name a few. When you have located the shape that you want to use, click it. A drawing tool replaces the mouse pointer. Drag the slide to draw the shape. You can size and position the shape on the page as needed.

When the newly inserted shape is selected, the Shape Format tab becomes available on the ribbon. This tab provides an Insert Shapes and Shape Style command groups, as well as WordArt Styles, Accessbility, Arrange, and Size groups. (This is similar to the tools available when a picture is selected on a slide.) The Shape Styles group provides a Shapes Style gallery, and you also can change the shape fill, outline, and effects as needed using the appropriate command in the Shape Style group.

If you want to place text in a shape, select the Text Box command in the Insert Shapes group and then click the shape to place the insertion point. You can type your text as needed. You can then use the WordArt Style gallery to format the text. You configure individual WordArt text settings using the Text Fill, Text Outline, and Text Effects commands.

> ➤ For more details on working with shapes and the drawing tools, see the "Using shapes and the 365 drawing tools" section in Chapter 4.

Inserting icons

Another possibility for adding images to your presentation slides is the Icons command. The Icons command is in the Illustrations group of the ribbon's Insert tab. The numerous icons provided in the Insert Icons window are SVG (scalable vector graphic) files. The SVG file format provides you with images that can be rotated, colored, or sized without any loss of image quality.

To open the Insert Icons (see Figure 19-6) window, select Icons (in the Illustrations group) on the Insert tab.

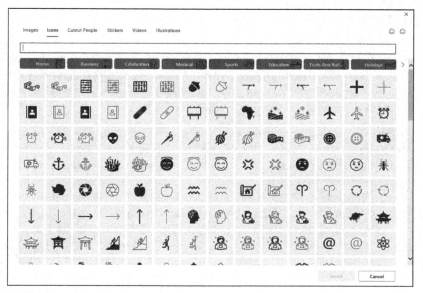

Figure 19-6   The Insert Icons window

The Insert Icons window provides a number of categories of icon types on the left side of the window. The Icons themselves are listed in subgroups based on the listed categories. You can scroll through the various categories using the scrollbar or jump to a particular icon category by clicking the category in the Category list.

To insert an icon, select the icon in the Insert Icons window. You can actually select multiple icons; make sure that a check mark appears on the top right of the icon image when you select it. Once you have selected the icon or icons to be inserted, select the Insert button.

As already mentioned, Icons can be easily moved and sized, as can shapes and SmartArt graphics. To manipulate the color of an icon, you can use the Graphics Styles or the Graphics Fill and Graphics Outline commands on the Graphic Tools Format tab (which appears when you select an icon). You can also rotate and crop icons, and you can use the Group command to group any number of selected icons.

Inside OUT

Use icons to create custom bullets.

For those of you who have worked with different releases of the 365 application suite, you have probably noticed that, over time, different sources of clip art and other images for your use in the applications have come and gone. At one time, Office.com was the key resource for finding usable images for your PowerPoint presentation slides. Flickr was even considered a valid resource at one time, and you could link your Flickr account to your Office installation. However, times change as do software applications. This latest edition of Microsoft Office now provides a new image class—the icon.

Microsoft promotes the icons as a way to add some whimsy and fun to your presentations, documents, and even your Outlook email. You will have to decide how many icons on a slide is just too much whimsy and fun. This is not to say that the icons won't serve you well as graphic elements on your presentation slides, but remember, less is probably better than more.

Using icons to create interesting bullets for your bulleted lists is something I can really get behind. The process for creating icon bullets is very straightforward. When you are in a bulleted list on a slide, select the Bullets drop-down arrow and select Bullets And Numbering. This will open the Bullets And Numbering dialog box. Select the Picture button, and an Insert Pictures window will open. Select From Icons, which opens the Insert Icons dialog box. Locate the icon you want to use and then click Insert. The bullets in the bulleted list will be replaced by the icon you selected in the Insert Icons dialog box.

Using SmartArt graphics

SmartArt graphics provide different diagram types that you can use to visually illustrate information on a slide. However, SmartArt isn't just a series of design elements or shapes. You can use SmartArt to show relationships between text entries, producing slides that make important concepts easy for your audience to understand. Bottom line: SmartArt graphics look professional and are impressive additions to your slides in both visual and informational terms.

PowerPoint provides different types or categories of SmartArt, with each type having a particular purpose. For example, the Cycle category creates diagrams that represent sequential cycles or a process that takes place in a circular flow. Figure 19-7 shows a cyclical diagram on a slide in Slide Show view, which not only gives the audience a picture of an overall process, but it gives you the outline for your talking points related to that particular slide.

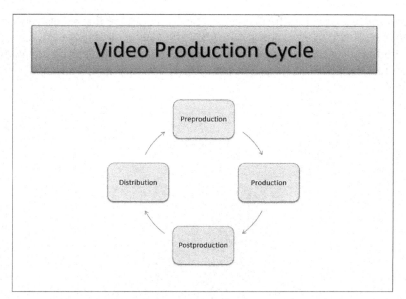

Figure 19-7   A cyclical SmartArt graphic

As already mentioned, SmartArt graphics come in many categories. Because SmartArt is designed to enable you to communicate visually, each SmartArt type or category offers Smart-Art slanted toward a particular purpose. The following list describes the SmartArt categories:

- **List:** The SmartArt lists enable you to go beyond the typical PowerPoint bulleted list, and they better show the relationship of items in a list. You can arrange text in both vertical and horizontal lists that include shapes to emphasize the text. The List SmartArt graphics can also provide insight into the relative importance of the list items or the sequence in which the listed items occur.

- **Process:** This group of SmartArt graphics shows a progression of items. It can provide the sequential steps in a task or process and give a visual representation of linear workflow or display how parts of an information sequence relate to the whole.

- **Cycle:** This category provides graphics related to the process cycle and the circular flow of events or steps. Some diagrams emphasize the steps in the process cycle; others enable you to better describe the overall process and the relationship of the various segments.

- **Hierarchy:** These SmartArt graphics provide you with diagrams such as the classic organizational chart in a branching tree format and enable you to emphasize the hierarchical relationship of items in a diagram. There is even a Picture Organization Chart SmartArt graphic that makes it easy to construct an organizational chart with photos of the people listed in the chart. Other diagrams in this category help you show how items in the diagram build upon each other.

- **Relationship:** This category provides relationship diagrams that enable you to show the hierarchy of related items and illustrate how concepts or ideas relate to a central theme. This group includes the basic Venn and radial Venn diagrams. Venn diagrams show the possible or logical relationship between different items. Figure 19-8 shows an example of a basic Venn diagram.

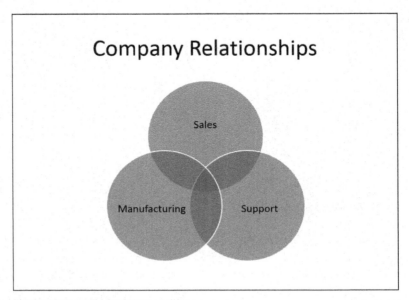

Figure 19-8   A SmartArt Venn diagram

- **Matrix:** The matrix SmartArt graphics are designed to show the relationship of different items or quadrants to the whole. These graphics enable you to create affinity diagrams, which are designed to organize information based on natural relationships. A cycle matrix is included that shows how items are related to a central cyclical process. A good example of this is the basic communication process, which requires listening, interpreting, and responding.

- **Pyramid:** This group provides both a basic pyramid and an inverted pyramid. Pyramids show both hierarchical relationships and the proportional importance of items in the hierarchy.

- **Picture:** This group pulls together all the SmartArt graphics from the other categories that help you incorporate pictures into the diagram. These possibilities include the continuous picture list, the captioned pictures diagram (which provides multiple levels of pictures), and the hexagon cluster (which provides a grouping of clustered images with minimal accompanying text).

- **Office.com:** This group provides some additional SmartArt Graphics, including converging text diagrams, interconnected block process diagrams, and interconnected rings. Interconnected rings provide you with a starting point for creating a Venn diagram showing the overlapping relationship between three different items or terms.

You can add a SmartArt graphic to a slide and then enter the accompanying text and pictures, or you can format existing text on a slide, such as a bulleted list, with any of the SmartArt graphics in the SmartArt Graphic gallery. When you insert a SmartArt graphic on a slide or convert existing text to a SmartArt graphic, you are provided with the SmartArt Tools, which include both a Design tab and a Format tab. Even after you insert a SmartArt graphic onto a slide, you can enhance the graphic's layout, style, and overall formatting (including the text that the SmartArt graphic contains).

Inserting a SmartArt graphic

You can insert a new SmartArt graphic on a slide via the Insert SmartArt Graphic icon in a slide content box, or you can select the SmartArt command on the ribbon's Insert tab. In both cases, the Choose A SmartArt Graphic dialog box opens, as shown in Figure 19-9.

NOTE

You can add animation schemes to your SmartArt graphics to create slides with even more visual impact. See Chapter 20 for more information.

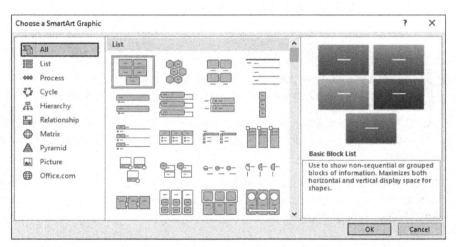

Figure 19-9   The Choose A SmartArt Graphic dialog box

The graphic categories are located on the left side of the dialog box. By default, All is selected. Select the category of SmartArt graphic you want to create. The graphics in the category are listed.

To preview an individual SmartArt graphic, select the graphic; a preview and description of the graphic appears on the right side of the dialog box.

When you have located the diagram that you want to use, make sure that the graphic is selected and then click OK. The SmartArt graphic is placed in the current slide.

You can enter the text for the diagram directly on the diagram parts itself (such as the item boxes in a cyclical diagram). Just select any of the [TEXT] placeholders in the diagram and type the required text. You can also add the text for the diagram using the Text pane that accompanies the SmartArt graphic (to the left of the slide). Replace the [TEXT] placeholders in the list with your text. You can collapse the Text pane by clicking the pane's Close button, and you can then expand it when needed by using the Expand button on the left side of the graphic. Remember that diagrams visually communicate an idea, process, or relationship, so the diagram should not require much text; in fact, your text entries should be considered the labels for the diagram parts—that's it.

Converting text to a SmartArt graphic

You can convert existing text in a text box to a SmartArt graphic. This enables you to quickly convert a bulleted list on a slide (or other text) into an appropriate diagram. To convert text to a SmartArt graphic, follow these steps:

1. Select the text box that contains the text you want to convert. This can be any text box on a slide, including bulleted and numbered lists.

2. On the Home tab, select the Convert To SmartArt command in the Paragraph group. The SmartArt gallery opens, providing a subset of the available SmartArt graphics.

3. Select a graphic from the gallery or access more graphics by selecting More SmartArt Graphics and selecting a graphic. This opens the Choose A SmartArt Graphic dialog box.

4. If you select a diagram in the gallery, the text in the text box is immediately converted. To do the conversion from the Choose A SmartArt Graphic dialog box, select a graphic and then click OK.

The existing text is placed in the text placeholders on the SmartArt diagram. The diagram replaces the original text box. You can edit the text as needed on the diagram or use the SmartArt's accompanying text pane.

Using the SmartArt tools

Whether you create a SmartArt graphic from scratch or convert existing text to a SmartArt graphic, the SmartArt Design and Format tabs appear on the ribbon when the SmartArt is selected. Let's take a look at these SmartArt-related tools.

The SmartArt Design tab

The SmartArt Design tab provides commands that enable you to manipulate the number and position of individual graphics in the diagram and to change the layout and style of the Smart-Art graphic. The command groups on the Design tab are as follows:

- **Create Graphic:** This group enables you to add elements (shapes) to the diagram and change the positioning of the shape. For example, if you have a box list graphic, you can add another shape (a box) before or after the currently selected shape by using the Add Shape command. You can also reorder the shapes in the list using the Reorder Up and Reorder Down commands and change the positioning of the diagram from right to left (or vice versa) using the Right To Left command. The commands available in this group depend on the type of SmartArt graphic you inserted into the slide.

- **Layouts:** The layouts available in the Layouts gallery are specific for the type of SmartArt graphic you placed in the slide. For example, if you inserted a basic cycle diagram into the slide, you can change the layout from the Basic Cycle to the Block Cycle or Radio Cycle by selecting a new layout in the Layouts gallery. More layouts are provided in the Choose A SmartArt Graphic dialog box, which is also accessible from the Layouts gallery.

- **SmartArt Styles:** This command group provides the Change Colors command, which specifies a new color scheme for the SmartArt graphic. The schemes available are specific to the type of diagram you placed in the slide. You can also change the style for the diagram by selecting one of the styles from the SmartArt Styles gallery. These styles are specific to the type of diagram that you inserted and include 3D possibilities.

- **Reset:** If you don't like your changes to the SmartArt graphic, you can select the Reset Graphic command. The Convert command enables you to convert the SmartArt graphic to text or convert the diagram to a group of shapes.

When you have finished working with the Design tab commands, deselect the SmartArt graphic's frame. This will remove the SmartArt Tools from the ribbon, and now, you can move on to your next task.

The SmartArt Format tab

When a SmartArt graphic is selected on a slide, you also have access to the SmartArt Format tab. This tab provides commands related to the formatting of the SmartArt graphic frame (not the individual items) and the text within the various shapes that populate the diagram.

You can use Shape Fill, Shape Outline, and Shape Effects to format the SmartArt graphic's out-side frame. This enables you to select a fill color for the SmartArt background (this does not fill the individual shapes in the diagram) and format the SmartArt graphic with different effects such as the Shadow, Reflection, and 3D Rotation settings.

The WordArt Styles gallery and the Text Fill, Text Outline, and Text Effects commands in the WordArt Styles group can be used to change the formatting of the text that has been entered on the various shapes in the diagram. When you use these commands to format the text, it is a one-size-fits-all scenario. All the text on the various shapes that make up the diagram are for-matted in the same manner.

➤ **For more information related to working with SmartArt graphics, see the "Working with SmartArt graphics" section of Chapter 4.**

Adding charts to slides

Charts can be inserted into slides to represent important data visually. Because many people do not immediately relate to tables full of numbers, an accompanying chart gives your audience a better understanding of everything from sales trends to population figures to quarterly earn-ings. Charts digest all those numbers, providing a much more meaningful pictorial view of the information.

When you insert a chart, you use an Excel worksheet to enter the data for that chart. You also use the Excel chart feature, so many of the considerations that go into creating a chart in Excel are applicable when you insert one into a PowerPoint slide.

You also have tools for working with charts on your PowerPoint slides. The Chart Tools contex-tual ribbon addition provides three tabs of commands: Design, Layout, and Format.

➤ **Charts are covered in detail in the Excel section of this book. See Chapter 14, "Enhancing worksheets with charts."**

Inserting a chart onto a slide

You can insert a chart using the Chart command on the ribbon's Insert tab, or you can select the Insert Chart icon in a content box. Both scenarios open the Insert Chart dialog box, shown in Figure 19-10.

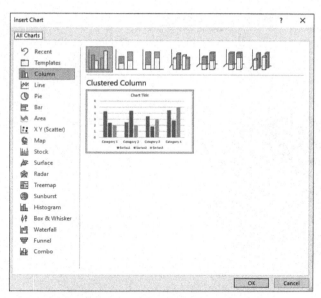

Figure 19-10   The Insert Chart dialog box

The chart types are listed on the left side of the Insert Chart dialog box. Select a particular chart type, such as Column or Pie. Note that each chart type also provides different formats. For example, the column chart type can be inserted into different formats, including a clustered column, stacked column, and clustered cylinder. The pie chart formats include a 3D pie and an exploded pie. Select the format type for the selected chart type (chart types are along the top of the dialog box), and then click OK.

The chart is inserted into the slide, and a worksheet window opens, containing generic labels and data points for the chart. At this point, the chart doesn't reflect your data or text labels. You need to modify the labels (text entries) and the numerical data on the worksheet. When you do so, the chart immediately reflects the new data. Click in the appropriate cells on the worksheet and enter your text labels and data as needed. If you need to add more data points than those provided, you can drag the data range border (the lower-right corner) to extend the data range and enter more labels and numerical information. Figure 19-11 shows a pie chart on a Power-Point slide and the data used to create the chart.

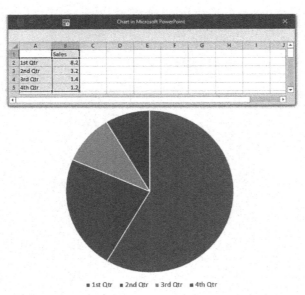

Figure 19-11   An inserted chart and the associated data sheet

If you find the datasheet that is used by default in PowerPoint to create charts a little limiting, you can quickly acess all Excel's commands and features. This provides you many more tools as you enter data or otherwise modify the sheet related to your chart. Click the Edit Data In Microsoft Excel icon at the top of the worksheet.

When you finish editing the data on the Excel worksheet, you can close it. You don't need to save the worksheet; the data that you entered in the sheet remains linked to the chart on the PowerPoint slide. If you do need to reopen the worksheet, you can do so by selecting the Edit Data command on the Chart Design tab (when the chart is selected on the slide).

CAUTION

You must enter your data and text labels within the data range provided on the work-sheet to reflect the modifications you make in the chart. The bottom line is that you want to type over the sample data. If this doesn't work for the chart you have in mind, enter your data in Excel and then create your Chart in Excel. You can then easily copy and paste the chart onto a PowerPoint slide.

Modifying and formatting a chart

When the chart is selected on a slide, the Chart Tools are available on the ribbon. You can use the various tools to modify the chart layout and style. You can also edit the chart title, legend, and data labels and format the chart's frame and text using the shape styles and WordArt styles. Although the chart is based on data that was entered in a separate worksheet (separate, in that it was really created in Excel), the chart itself behaves like any other object that you place on a slide, such as SmartArt or a picture. You can size and move the chart on the slide as needed.

To make any substantive changes to the chart, you can rely on the Chart tools. The various commands provided by this contextual ribbon addition are divided between two tabs: Chart Design and Format.

The Design tab provides commands related to the chart's type and layout and allows you to edit the data used to create the chart. The Change Chart Type command enables you to change the current chart to another type. If you then need to edit the data for the chart, select the Edit Data command. This tab also provides a Quick Layouts gallery, which enables you to adjust the overall layout of the chart. Each chart type has specific layouts available.

The Add Chart Element command also makes it easy to fine-tune your chart's layout by adding various chart elements. You can change the style of the chart by taking advantage of the Chart Styles gallery.

The Format tab grants access to Shape styles to modify the frame of the chart; you can also change the fill, outline, and effects for the chart frame. When you select text objects on the chart, such as the title or legend, you can take advantage of the WordArt Styles gallery and the other text settings on this tab. This tab also enables you to add shapes to the chart and arrange objects in the frame.

PowerPoint provides inline command buttons that enable you to manipulate chart elements, change the chart style, and filter the data sets on your chart. These commands are the very chart tools that you will find when you work with charts in Excel.

When the chart frame is selected, these command buttons appear on the right side of the slide. When you select one of these commands, a pane opens on the left of the slide, giving you various choices (related to the command you selected). Figure 19-12 shows the Style/Color pane, which is opened by selecting the Style/Color command (it looks like a paintbrush).

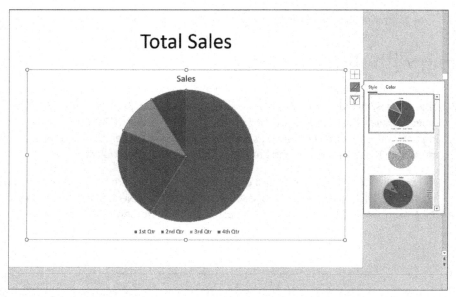

Figure 19-12   Inline chart commands enable you to quickly manipulate a chart.

CHAPTER 19

More information on these three commands follows:

- **Chart Elements:** This command pane provides a list of the chart elements available for the chart, including the chart title, data labels, and legend. You can select and deselect these elements as needed.

- **Chart Styles:** When Chart Styles is selected, the command pane houses several chart styles for the current chart type. When you select Color, you see different color schemes you can apply to the chart.

- **Chart Filters:** You can quickly filter the chart by values or names using this command. When Values is selected in the command pane, you can select or deselect series and/or categories (depending on the complexity of the chart) to view the chart with only a subset of the data represented. Mouse over the categories list (categories are the y-axis values for the chart) to see only the values represented on the chart. When you select Names in the Filter pane, you can control whether the chart shows series and categories names. After making a change on either the Values or Names tab of the pane, click the Apply button.

Creating and formatting a chart is really only half of the equation when it comes to visualizing data using charts. You must also select a chart type that visualizes your data appropriately. This means choosing the right chart type for the situation. If you are showing the relationship of parts to a whole, such as how your individual monthly expenses relate to your total monthly expenses, use a pie chart. If you want to show change over time, such as changes in your retirement account, use a line chart. Make sure that you understand how the chart type you pick translates the numerical data into a visual representation. Select the wrong chart type for the situation, and the chart is really just a useless picture on a slide.

➤ **For more about choosing the right chart type, see Chapter 14.**

Working with slide objects

An object can be anything you place on the slide. In this chapter, we looked at a number of object types, including pictures, stock images, shapes, and Smart Art. Text boxes qualify as objects as well. Resizing and rotating objects is straightforward. To resize an object, drag the sizing handles on the object's frame as needed. If you want to maintain an object's height/width ratio, drag the lower-right sizing handle diagonally to size the object.

You can also easily rotate a selected object, such as a shape. When you select the object, the rotation handle (the green dot) appears at the top of the object. Place the mouse on the handle; drag the rotation handle to rotate the object when the Rotation icon appears.

PowerPoint makes it simple to position multiple objects and even deal with layered objects on a slide. If you need to be accurate in placing items on a slide, you might want to take advantage of the ruler, gridlines, or guides. You can turn on any of these items by using the commands in the Show group on the Ruler's View tab. By default, objects are snapped to the grid. If you are placing objects close together, you can also have objects snap to other objects. You can specify the grid and guide settings by selecting the dialog box launcher on the Show group. This opens the Grid And Guides dialog box, which provides the snap, grid, and guide settings for the presentation.

Grouping objects

Grouping objects enables you to fine-tune the positioning of any number of objects on a slide. You might have already placed the objects exactly the way you want them in terms of their positioning to each other. You then might need to adjust the overall positioning of all the objects in relation to the top or bottom of the slide or the slide title.

You can group the objects on the slide and then move them as a group. Select all the objects on the slide by using the mouse to drag a selection box around the objects. You can also click to select an object and then hold down the Ctrl key to select subsequent objects as needed.

When the objects are selected, click the Format tab of the drawing tools. Use the Group command in the Arrange group to group the objects. A frame appears around the grouped objects. You can now position or rotate the grouped objects as if they were a single object. If you need to ungroup the objects, select the group's frame, select Group, and then select Ungroup. The objects become individual items with their own frames.

Layering objects

In some cases, you might end up with fairly complex slides that contain many objects. You might have even deliberately layered objects on a slide. For instance, you might be using a combination of shapes, text boxes, and pictures to build a custom logo or other layered item. Or you might overlap adjacent objects using layering to provide additional visual interest.

You can use the Bring Forward command to bring an object forward in the stack (one object) or to bring it to the front of the stack (so that it is on top). The Send Backward command enables you to send a selected object backward (one layer) or to send it to the bottom of the object pile using the Send To Back option. When you have the objects layered correctly, select the entire stack (drag the mouse around the object stack). You can then group the layered objects using the Group command. This enables you to move the stack without messing up the layers.

NOTE

When you align two or more objects on a slide (vertically or horizontally), smart guides appear automatically. This enables you to align objects in relation to each other without using the gridlines or guides.

CHAPTER 19

Adding hyperlinks to slides

You can add hyperlinks to your PowerPoint slides. Hyperlinks enable you to jump to external information such as web pages or files on your computer or a network. For example, you could use a hyperlink to open an Excel worksheet that is associated with a chart that you have copied and pasted into a slide. Hyperlinks can also jump to a bookmark, which can point to a slide in the current presentation. This is useful when you anticipate that a slide shown later in the presentation will elicit requests from the audience to see the earlier slide. You can be ready for the question by placing a hyperlink to the slide on the current slide.

Hyperlinks (or Links) are added to a text box on a slide using the Insert Hyperlink dialog box, shown in Figure 19-13. You open the Insert Hyperlinks dialog box using the Link command (in the Links group) on the Insert tab.

By default, the Existing File Or Web Page setting is selected in the Link To box. This setting enables you to create a link to a file on your computer or a web page. By default, the contents of the Documents folder are displayed in the Insert Hyperlink dialog box. If the link you are creating is to an existing file, you can select any document in the folder or navigate to another folder to specify an existing file. You can also select Recent Files to view a list of files you have recently opened. This provides another option for specifying an existing file as the destination for the hyperlink.

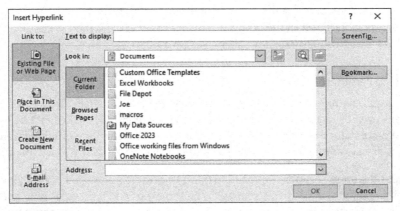

Figure 19-13   Insert a hyperlink into the current slide.

If you want to create a hyperlink to a web page, you can type the URL for the site in the Address box. If you select Browsed Pages, you are provided with a list of recently browsed web pages. You can select from this list to specify the web address for the hyperlink.

As another alternative to typing the hyperlink, open Microsoft Edge or your default web browser and navigate to the website. Copy the URL for the website. When you return to PowerPoint, paste the address of the website into the Address box.

When you want to specify a slide as the destination for the hyperlink, select Place In This Document in the Link To box. A list of slides in the presentation appears in the Insert Hyperlink dialog box. Select the appropriate slide in the list.

Before you click OK, which closes the Insert Hyperlink dialog box and creates your hyperlink on the slide, you need to take care of one more task. Enter the text that you want to display on the slide when the hyperlink is inserted. The text can be any text you choose; it won't affect the hyperlink's ability to navigate to the destination. For example, the hyperlink text displayed on the slide does not have to be the URL for the website the hyperlink takes you to. When you have finished configuring the hyperlink, click OK to return to the slide.

NOTE

You can create a ScreenTip for the hyperlink. Select ScreenTip in the Insert Hyperlink dialog box, and then specify the ScreenTip text in the Set Hyperlink Screen Tip dialog box.

The hyperlink isn't active on the slide when you are in Normal view. You need to run the slide in a slide show to test your hyperlink. Click the Slide Show shortcut on the right side of the PowerPoint status bar. The slide show begins from the current slide, which is the slide that contains the hyperlink to be tested. If the hyperlink is to a website, your web browser opens and navigates to the site. If you selected a file as the destination, the application in which the file was created opens and loads the file. And if you specified a slide in the presentation as the hyperlink destination, you are taken to that slide in the slide show. You can press Esc to return to the PowerPoint workspace.

Using PowerPoint Designer

Designing PowerPoint slides that have great visual impact is pretty much the hope of everyone who has ever typed a bulleted list on a slide. Some individuals have an innate design sense, and others have taken a design course or two. PowerPoint has a tool—PowerPoint Designer—that can help you create slides that look both professional and visually appealing. So, put your beret on, and we will take a look at this powerful slide design tool.

The PowerPoint Designer works in the background as you create and edit your presentation slides. When you are stuck on a slide's design or just aren't coming up with any inspiration, you can call on the Designer to provide you with some design ideas related to the current slide.

NOTE

The first time you select the Design Ideas command to open the Designer, you might have to enable it to search for design ideas for you. Just select Turn On to open the Design Ideas pane. You only have to do this on first use; you will be good to go in the future.

To take advantage of the Designer, build a slide. Type a bulleted list and add graphic elements, such as icons. As you work, the Designer will activate (if it has any suggestions), and the Design Ideas pane will open.

Figure 19-14 shows a slide that consists of one bulleted list, a slide title, and three random icons. Yet, the Designer was able to come up with several possible layouts, fill schemes, and font schemes for the content. Compare the original slide in Figure 19-14 with the Designer's options provided in the Design Ideas pane.

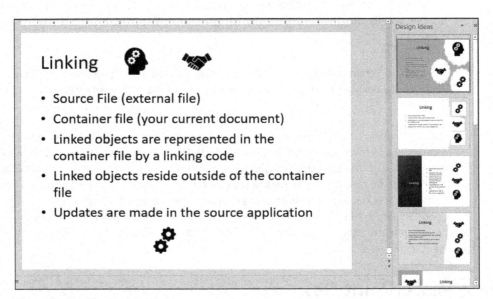

Figure 19-14   The Design Ideas pane

When you use the Designer's layouts, don't consider them to be the final word on your slide's design. You can select one of the design ideas and then modify it to suit your own taste and needs. Think of the design ideas as the starting point for a great slide rather than the endpoint. The best thing about the Designer is that it provides you with alternatives in terms of a slide's overall look. And hopefully, the Designer's help will fuel your own creative abilities and build better slides.

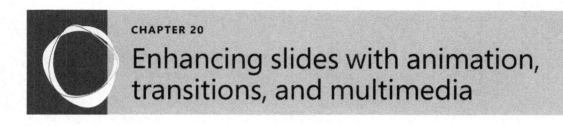

Enhancing slides with animation, transitions, and multimedia

Animations versus transitions   611

Assigning animation to a slide object   614

Advanced animation techniques   622

Managing slide animations   628

Adding transitions to slides   630

Adding sound to a slide   634

Editing sound options   635

Adding video to a slide   636

As Microsoft PowerPoint has evolved over the years in terms of the enhancements that you can apply to your presentation slides, people have come to expect flashier and more graphically rich presentations. Whether you regularly give PowerPoint presentations as part of your profession or just use PowerPoint for your travel club or to show family pictures, your audience expects a visually compelling slideshow. You can't just click through a static series of slides without any special effects or multimedia.

This chapter looks at animation effects, including how you can apply them to slide objects and customize these animations. We also discuss the use of slide transitions, including two transitions, Morph and Zoom, that go way beyond what you would typically expect from a slide transition. We will conclude our discussion of enhancing your presentations with how to add sound and video to your slides.

Animations versus transitions

Before we dive into working with animation effects and slide transitions, we need to discuss how they differ and how each affects a slide and its contents. Animations are special effects that are added to an object or objects on the slide. Animations can be applied to text boxes, pictures, SmartArt graphics—any object type you can add to a slide.

Animations are designed to emphasize objects on a slide and control the entrance or exit of objects as the slide is viewed during the slideshow. Animations affect objects such as clip art and SmartArt a little differently than text boxes. For example, if you assign an animation to a clip art object such as the Fly In animation, the clip art will fly onto the slide when you click the mouse or after a delay timer expires. (We talk more about setting timers for animations later in this chapter, in the section "Setting timings for animations.")

When a text box includes bulleted lists or text in paragraphs, each paragraph is animated by the animation effect. If you have a text box that includes four items in a bulleted list, each item in the list is considered a separate paragraph. By default, you must click the mouse four times to get the entire bulleted list to appear on the slide. Each bulleted item flies in separately upon each subsequent click of the mouse.

You are not limited to one animation per slide: You can apply an animation effect to each object on a slide if you choose. You can also apply multiple animations to a particular object. For example, you could apply an entrance effect for a bulleted list and then assign a secondary animation to the bulleted list that emphasizes each item in the list.

When you assign animation effects to objects, a number is placed to the left of the object to show that an effect has been applied. The number also tells you the sequence in which the effects are applied to the objects when you run the slideshow. Figure 20-1 shows a slide with multiple objects. An animation effect has been applied to the title text box, and it is the first effect in the animation sequence (so, it is assigned the number 1). Animation effects have also been applied to the bulleted list (with each item numbered on the left as a separate animation). An animation effect also has been applied to the WiFi router icon to the right of the bulleted list.

NOTE

You have complete control over how and when objects assigned animation effects appear on or exit from the screen. We discuss this in detail in the sections of this chapter that cover animation effects.

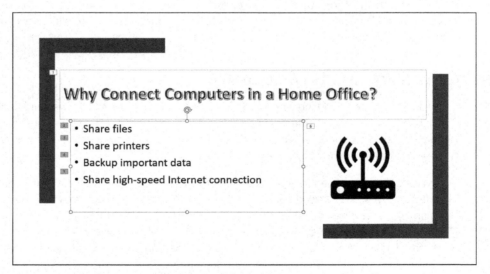

Figure 20-1   Each of the numbers on the slide represents an animation effect.

The slide also includes a bulleted list consisting of four bulleted items. An animation effect has been applied to the text box that contains the bulleted list. Notice that the individual bulleted items have been numbered in sequence from 2 through 5. Lastly, there is an icon on the right of the slide that will fly in after the bulleted list. The icon fly-in is animation effect 6.

When this slide is viewed during a slideshow, only the slide title appears when you switch to the slide. On the first click of the mouse, the title text appears. On subsequent mouse clicks (the next four clicks), the bulleted list items appear in sequence. Finally, one more click will initiate the fly-in of the wireless icon. So, to be clear, animation effects are designed to animate objects on the slide.

Transitions, which are also referred to as transition effects, are another way to add special effects to a presentation. Transitions are assigned to slides. A transition goes into effect during the slide's entrance in the slideshow. So, transitions are more of an all-or-nothing proposition. You can't have the transition effect apply to only certain objects on the slide; it is applied to the entire slide and all that it contains.

PowerPoint provides lots of different transition effects. Some of the transition effects are based on film and video transitions, which are used to switch between scenes in a film or television program; these effects include the fade, wipe, and dissolve. Other transitions, such as shred, vortex, and ripple, provide visually exciting transitions that wow your audience.

When using animation effects and transitions in your slide presentations, keep certain points in mind. The list that follows provides some tips for using special effects appropriately and judicially:

- **Less is better:** Remember that your presentation is meant to convey information, not hypnotize the audience (or give them motion sickness). You don't have to animate every object on every slide or necessarily assign transitions to every slide. Use these features sparingly to get the most bang out of them when you do use them.

- **Give the audience a rest:** There is no crime in showing slides that have no animations or transitions. After animating several slides in a row or having slide transitions for several slides in a row, put in a slide or two with no effects. This is particularly useful when you are showing a slide that contains important information. You stress the information by not dressing it up with an animation or transition.

- **Use effects to best effect:** Both the animations and transitions provide effects that can be of thematic value to your presentation. For example, if you are discussing issues related to the proper disposal of hard-copy proprietary information, what better slide transition to use than the shred transition? If you are emphasizing the spiraling value of a company's stock using a chart, why not animate that chart with the spin animation?

Be sure to think about how you use special effects such as animations and transitions when you are developing the overall design plan for your presentation. How you present the information

CHAPTER 20

can be as important as the information itself. You can take advantage of special effects to add interest to your presentation, but don't let them take over your presentation or obscure the information you want to provide your audience.

Assigning animation to a slide object

The Animations tab of the ribbon provides all the commands related to the application and modification of animation effects. Animating an object (or objects) on a slide is an easy three-step process. Select an object on the slide, select an animation from the Animation gallery, and then use the Effect Options gallery to fine-tune the selected animation. Figure 20-2 shows the Animation gallery.

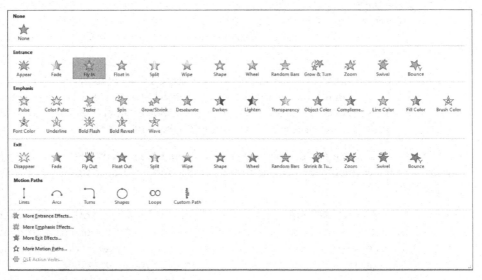

Figure 20-2   The Animation gallery

The Animation gallery groups the animation effects into four categories: Entrance, Emphasis, Exit, and Motion Paths. The first three categories—Entrance, Emphasis, and Exit—are self-explanatory. Let's look at these standard animation effects, and then we will discuss the Motion Paths category in its own section later in the chapter.

The Entrance category provides animations that dictate how the object enters the slide when the animation plays. The Emphasis group provides animations that enable you to emphasize objects such as the items in a bulleted list. For example, as you talk about a particular item in the list, you can click the mouse to emphasize the bulleted item with a pulse or spin. The Exit category provides animations that remove items from the slide. For example, if you assign an exit animation such as the Fade effect, the items in the bulleted list fade (sequentially) each time you click the mouse.

To assign an animation effect to an object or objects on a slide, follow these steps:

1. Select the object or objects on the slide. You can select multiple objects by clicking the first object and then holding down the Ctrl key as you click subsequent objects.

2. Select the Animations tab on the ribbon.

3. Place the mouse on an animation in the Animation gallery to preview the animation on the slide object. If you want to access the entire gallery, click the More button.

4. Select the animation you want to use to close the gallery and assign the animation to the slide object.

You can repeat this process as needed to apply other animation effects to other objects on the slide. When you want to preview the animation effects assigned to the objects on a slide, click the Preview button on the Animations tab. This gives you a preview of the animation effect or effects in Normal view.

Accessing additional animation effects

The Animation gallery provides only a subset of the animation effects available. You can access additional animation effects via a set of dialog boxes that open from the Animation gallery. Each animation effect type—entrance, emphasis, and exit—has a separate dialog box. For example, to open the Change Entrance Effect dialog box, shown in Figure 20-3, you would select the More Entrance Effects link on the bottom left of the Animations gallery. The Change Entrance Effect dialog box offers many different entrance effects.

Figure 20-3   The Change Entrance Effect dialog box

The entrance effects in the Change Entrance Effect dialog box are grouped into categories titled Basic, Subtle, Moderate, and Exciting.

The categories are based on the "specialness" of the effects they include. For example, the Exciting category provides more elaborate animation effects than the Basic category. Let's compare two effects. The basic entrance effect—called Fade—fades the object or object elements, such as a bulleted list, onto the slide. In contrast, the Pinwheel entrance effect in the Exciting category spins the object elements onto the slide, providing a much more exciting and elaborate entrance. It's kind of like the difference between showing up at an event in a limousine and dropping into an event from a hot air balloon. The first option is flashy, but the second option is pretty much a show stopper.

To access the dialog box for a specific effect type, you can then use the More Entrance Effects, More Emphasis Effects, and More Exit Effects commands at the bottom of the gallery to open the Change Entrance Effects dialog box, the Change Emphasis Effects dialog box, and the Change Exit Effects dialog box, respectively.

By default, each dialog box provides a preview of the effect you select, and the effect is previewed on the selected object or objects. You might want to drag the dialog box off the Slide pane so that you can see the preview of the effect on the slide. The selected effect is not assigned to the object until you click the OK button in the dialog box and return to the PowerPoint workspace.

If you want to preview the animation after you have closed the dialog box, select the Preview command on the Animations tab. You can also open the slideshow at the current slide by clicking the Slide Show button on the status bar. This enables you to view the animation as it appears during the slideshow. When you want to stop the slideshow and return to Normal view, press the Esc key on the keyboard.

Using motion paths

Another animation effect type, the Motion path, enables you to determine the pattern for a slide object's entry and its path on a slide. Motion paths can emphasize objects in much the same way you use emphasis animation effects such as the Spin and Underline effects. Motion paths can move an object in a circular, octagonal, or trapezoidal path. A vertical figure-eight motion path even moves an object in a figure-eight pattern.

However, motion paths do not necessarily have to move objects only in place on the slide. You can also use a custom motion path to relocate an object on a slide. For example, you might want to have a chart and a text box switch positions on the slide to get your audience to concentrate more closely on the chart itself. Or you might want to use a motion path to have an object interact with another object. Figure 20-4 shows a clip art image of a cow that has been assigned a custom motion path that makes the cow jump over the image of the moon.

Figure 20-4 shows the path for the clip art image with a dotted line that appears on the slide. A green triangle shows the beginning of the motion path, and a red arrow designates the end-point for the motion path.

When you are working with the standard motion paths (any of the motion paths other than the custom path), and you select and change the position or the size of the motion path, a ghosted image of the object appears at the new exit point for the path. This is useful for seeing where the object (such as a picture or clip art) ends up on the slide when the motion path runs in your slideshow. You can preview the motion path at any time by selecting the motion path and then selecting the Preview command in the Preview group (just to the left of the Animation group).

Figure 20-4 A custom motion path assigned to a clip art object

Applying a motion path

To apply a motion path to a selected object or objects, scroll through the Animation gallery until you can access the Motion Paths category area provided in the gallery. You can also open the entire gallery by clicking the More button (you still might have to scroll down to see the available motion paths).

NOTE

If you do not want to preview an effect selected in one of the Change Effects dialog boxes, clear the Preview Effect check box at the bottom of the dialog box.

On first inspection, the available motion paths in the Animation gallery might appear to be rather meager. However, the motion paths are a little different from the other animation effects available in the gallery. Although you can change some options related to the entrance, emphasis, and exit animation effects, such as the direction and whether a compound object (such as a SmartArt Venn diagram) is animated as a whole or as parts, motion paths give you more customization possibilities. For example, you can control the length of the path, the position of the path, and other path attributes, such as the shape of the path and the path direction. So, think of the motion paths available in the Animation gallery as types of motion paths that you can customize; this gives you more options than you might at first expect.

To assign a motion path to an object on a slide, select the object. Then select a motion path in the Animation gallery, such as Lines, Arcs, or Loops. If you want to access additional motion path animations, select the More Motion Paths command at the bottom left of the gallery. The Change Motion Path dialog box opens and is divided into three different categories of paths. The categories are as follows:

- **Basic:** This category provides different path shapes, including circle, hexagon, and square paths, as well as several star paths.

- **Lines_Curves:** This category provides different arc, line, and curve paths, and includes special paths such as funnel, heartbeat, and spring shapes.

- **Special:** This category provides unique paths such as bean, loop de loop, peanut, and neutron shapes. It also includes different figure-eight paths.

When you select a motion path in the Change Motion Path dialog box, it is previewed on the selected object. To assign the motion path to the object, click OK; the Change Motion Path dialog box closes.

Editing a motion path

After the path has been assigned to the object, the path itself is represented by a dotted line (when the Animations tab is selected on the ribbon, and the object is selected). A green triangle designates the beginning of the path, and the end of the path is designated by a red arrow. The path also has its own sizing handles.

Using the mouse (or other pointing device), you can change some of the motion path's attributes, such as its size and its location in relation to the object. The path's start point begins at the center of the object assigned the motion path, and the object moves through the path to the endpoint, which also occurs when the center of the object reaches the red triangle (in the case of loops and circular paths, the start point, and endpoint are the same). You can change the position of the start point and endpoint and change the relative positioning of the path itself in relation to the object.

NOTE

Fine-tuning a motion path can be a little tricky. After each change made to the motion path, use the Preview command. If you don't like a particular change, take advantage of Undo, and then give it another try.

Additional motion path settings are accessed via the Effect Options command, which is on the far right of the Animation group. The options available in the Effect Options gallery, shown in Figure 20-5 for a horizontal figure-eight effect, depend on the motion path you select. Some motion paths have alternative motion paths, such as the horizontal and vertical figure eights. You can switch between these two orientations via the Effect Options gallery.

The options typically available on the Effect Options gallery enable you to reverse the path direction and edit individual points in the path. When you select the Edit Points command, a series of point handles becomes visible on the motion path. You can drag any of these handles to change the path. For example, on a figure-eight motion path, you can stretch the size of either oval in the figure eight or change the ovals into any shape you desire.

Figure 20-5   Change the motion path options.

In the Effect Options gallery, two commands are grouped in an Origin category: Locked and Unlocked. These options do not dictate whether you can make changes to the motion path animation (such as locking the settings for a motion path). Instead, they relate to what happens when you move the motion path or the object that has been assigned the motion path.

By default, the motion path is unlocked, which means that when you move the object on the slide, the motion path moves with it. If you select Locked, the path does not move when you move the object. So, in a sense, these two options are a little counterintuitive. You would probably think that the Locked setting would keep the object and the motion path locked, but the reality is just the opposite.

The Locked and Unlocked options do not differ when you move the motion path itself. In both cases, moving the motion path does just that; it doesn't move the object on the slide that has been assigned the motion path.

Although the Effect Options gallery is rather limited in terms of the different possibilities for modifying a motion path, you can access additional options in a dialog box that is specific to the motion path you have selected. All you have to do is select the dialog box launcher under the Effect Options command. Figure 20-6 shows the Horizontal Figure 8 dialog box.

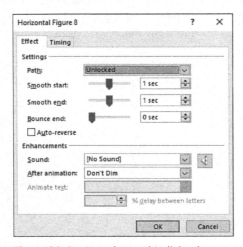

Figure 20-6   A motion path's dialog box

If you are using an animated clip art or another image, the dialog box gives you an Effect tab and a Timing tab. If you are animating an object such as a rectangle or circle that you created in PowerPoint, these objects can contain text, so you will be provided with a third tab: Text Animation. The Effect tab enables you to set the path for the animation to Locked or Unlocked (the default). You can also use the available sliders to change the animation's start, end, and bounce intervals. For example, to lengthen the duration of the start, move the Smooth Start slider bar to the right. This takes duration time away from the Smooth End setting (and the Bounce End setting, if there is a bounce at the end of the animation). By default, animations are provided for a duration of 2 seconds. You can modify the duration on the Timing tab using the Duration drop-down menu.

The Effect tab also enables you to include enhancements to the animation, such as sounds, and specify what happens after the animation ends, including settings such as Hide After Animation and Hide On Next Mouse Click (we talk more about animation and sound later in this chapter). Colors are provided in the After Animation drop-down menu to enable you to change the fill color for the object upon the completion of the animation. If you choose the same fill color as that used by the slide, the object disappears after the animation plays.

I've already mentioned that the motion path animation's duration can be set on the Timing tab of the dialog box. This tab also enables you to set the Start parameter for the animation by selecting On Click, With Previous, or After Previous. You can also set a delay for the animation or choose to have the animation repeat.

Also, the Timing tab enables you to specify the trigger for the animation. A trigger can be any object on the slide. For example, you can specify the title text box as a trigger for an animation. When you click the title on the slide, the animation plays. Triggers can also be related to playing other animations or events on the slide. For example, if you have a video or sound file on the slide, the animation can be triggered to play upon playing that other object (the video).

If you are animating an object that can (or does) contain text, you can use the Text Animation tab settings to control how the text is animated. A Group text drop-down menu allows you to group the text as a single object or by different paragraph levels. You can then choose to animate the text with the attached shape, or you can have the text load into the shape in reverse order.

When you have finished editing the settings for the motion path, click OK, which enables your new settings on the motion path animation and returns you to the Normal view.

Creating a custom motion path

You can also create a custom motion path. This is easier than it sounds and really is just a matter of recording the path of the object as you drag it with the mouse. Because most of the motion paths PowerPoint provides are designed to move an object in place, creating a custom motion path for an object enables you to dictate the object's final position on the slide after the motion effect animation plays.

To create a custom path, follow these steps:

1. Select the object to which you want to assign the custom path.

2. Navigate to the Animations tab and open the Animation gallery.

3. In the Motion Paths category of the gallery, select Custom Path.

4. Place the mouse pointer on the center of the object to which you want to assign the custom path.

5. Hold down the left mouse button; the mouse pointer becomes a drawing tool. Draw the custom path on the slide.

6. When you reach the endpoint for the custom motion path, double-click the mouse.

A preview of the custom path plays. The path itself is represented on the slide as a dotted line.

As with any motion path, you can change the settings for the path using the mouse (and the sizing handles) or the options in the Effect Options gallery. You can also access a Custom Path dialog box by selecting the dialog box launcher under the Effect Options command. As discussed in the previous section, this enables you to change the effect settings (including the addition of a sound), timing, and triggers for the custom path. You can preview any of the changes that you make to the custom path by selecting the Preview command.

Advanced animation techniques

PowerPoint gives you additional tools and options for fine-tuning animation effects. We have already looked at effect options related to motion paths; however, you can modify even simple entrance effects, particularly when you assign an animation to a bulleted list, a SmartArt graphic, or a chart that contains multiple items in a sequence.

PowerPoint also enables you to add more than one animation effect to an object. I advise restraint in terms of multiple animations on an object because you don't want to pile animation effects onto your objects. However, it wouldn't be beyond reason to add an entrance effect to an object such as a bulleted list and then also assign an emphasis effect, which enables you to revisit each bullet point on the slide as you emphasize and review important information before changing to the next slide.

PowerPoint also provides the Animation Painter, which is similar to the Format Painter (used to copy text formatting). The Animation Painter enables you to copy the animation effects assigned to an object (including any effect options that you have fine-tuned) to another object.

The Advanced Animation group provides access to the Add Animation, Animation Pane, Trigger, and Animation Painter commands. We discuss all these commands in later sections, including how to set triggers for an animation, which is considered one of the options when you set the Timing options for an effect in that effect's dialog box. You can open the dialog box associated with a selected animation using the dialog box launcher below the Effect Options command in the Animation group.

The Trigger command enables you to specify how a particular animation is triggered or started. You can specify the trigger to be the click of a particular object on the slide. For example, you can specify the title text box as a trigger for an animation. When you click the title on the slide, the animation plays. You can specify any object on the slide as the trigger for an animation. The animation does not have to be applied to the trigger object, so you can click a clip art image or picture on a slide, and this action can trigger an animation on another object. The trigger can also be set to begin an animation after reaching a particular bookmark in a sound or video object on the slide. Adding bookmarks to sound files you record in PowerPoint can be accomplished using the Add Bookmark command in the Audio Tools Playback tab.

Changing effect options

If necessary, you can modify the effect options for an animation assigned to an object, select the object and then navigate to the ribbon's Animations tab. The Effect Options command provides a gallery of options related to the animation effect type, meaning whether you have assigned an entrance, emphasis, or exit animation. The options available in the Effect Options gallery are also specific to the type of object assigned the animation. For example, text boxes have options beyond a clip art image or a SmartArt graphic assigned an animation effect. Objects that consist of multiple paragraphs, such as a text box or a SmartArt graphic that includes many shapes in the graphic, have options for animating all the object parts one by one or all at once.

To change the options for an animation effect, select the object assigned the animation. Then select the Effect Option command to access the options available for that effect and object type. Figure 20-7 shows the Effect Options gallery for a bulleted list assigned an entrance animation.

Both entrance and exit animations provide effect options that enable you to specify the direction of the object's entrance or exit, such as to the bottom, left, top, and so on. Emphasis animations have effect options that relate to the color or the level of the animation effect. For example, if you use the Fill Color animation, the effect options provided include a color palette that enables you to select the fill color for the animation. In the case of the Transparency animation, you select the level of transparency assigned to the objects in the Effect Options gallery.

As already mentioned, the type of object also has a bearing on the effect options available for a particular animation. For example, when you access the effect options for an object that has multiple parts, such as a bulleted list, you provide sequence options that enable you to determine whether the object should be animated all at once or whether the individual parts should be animated separately.

If you want to fine-tune the options for an animation, you can open the animation effects dialog box. Select the dialog box launcher below the Effect Options command. The dialog box for a particular animation type provides options related to the effect itself and supplies enhancement possibilities, such as whether to play a sound with the animation effect. The dialog box for an animation also provides a Timing tab where you can set options related to the animation's start, delay, and duration. We discuss animation sound and timing options later in the chapter.

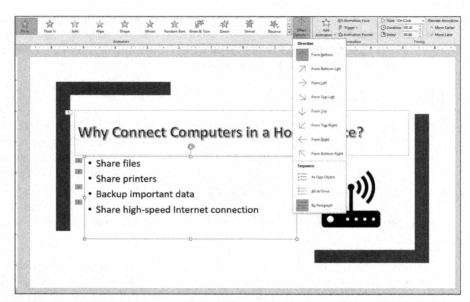

Figure 20-7   The Effect Options gallery

Because the dialog box is specific to a particular type of animation, the settings available vary in the dialog box, as do the options available for that animation type in the Effect Options gallery. For example, the dialog box for an entrance or an exit animation has options for setting the direction of the effect and provides slider bars that enable you to specify the duration of the "smooth start" or "smooth end" for the animation. In contrast, the dialog box for an emphasis animation includes options only for including a sound and timing settings related to the animation effect.

Adding additional animations

The Advanced Animation command group on the Animations tab provides you with the Add Animation command. This command opens the Add Animation gallery, which is really a duplicate of the Animation gallery provided in the Animation group. You can add any of the available animation effects to the current object. The added effect is numbered sequentially in relation to the other animations that have been already added to the slide.

The added animation occurs after the primary animation you added to the object. So, if you plan to use both an entrance and an exit animation on a particular object, make sure that the entrance animation occurs in the animation sequence before the exit animation. It makes sense to assign the entrance animation to the object via the Animation gallery and assign the exit animation—which is really the secondary animation for the object—using the Add Animation command.

NOTE

The default animation setting for text boxes is to animate the object by paragraph. This enables you to bring each item in a bulleted list separately when you use an entrance animation.

As already mentioned, the Add Animation gallery is much the same as the Animation gallery. At the bottom of the Add Animation gallery is a series of commands, such as More Entrance Effects and More Emphasis Effects. Use any of these commands to open the corresponding dialog box for that type of animation. You can then select from the larger library of animation effects (by type) provided in the specific dialog boxes.

Using the animation painter

The Animation Painter enables you to copy the animations that have been applied to an object and "paint" (or "paste," if you prefer) these animation settings onto another object or objects on a slide. This enables you to fine-tune animations on a particular object and then apply the animation or animations to other objects on the same slide or other slides in the presentation. This can be particularly useful if you want to have an overall scheme for the animations that appear throughout the presentation.

To use the Animation Painter, select an object that has been assigned the animation or animations you want to copy. Then select the Animation Painter in the Advanced Animation command group. The mouse pointer will include a paintbrush, letting you know that the Animation Painter is active, and the object's animations have been copied. Navigate to the slide containing the object to which you want to assign the animations that have been copied from another object. Then click the object to assign the animations to the object. A preview of the pasted animations plays as soon as you click the Animation Painter on the object.

One click on the Animation Painter command enables you to apply the copied animations to one object. As soon as you click that object, the Animation Painter applies the animations and then becomes inactive. You can use the Animation Painter to apply copied animations to multiple objects in the presentation by double-clicking the Animation Painter command. When you have finished assigning the animation or animations to objects in your presentation, select the Animation Painter command again to deactivate the tool.

Including sound effects with animations

You can enhance your animations by adding sound effects to them. When the animation plays, the accompanying sound also plays. PowerPoint supports many popular sound file formats, including the following:

- **Wave:** The Waveform Audio file format (.wav) stores sound as a waveform file. These files are relatively small when compared to some of the other sound file formats.

- **MIDI:** The Musical Instrument Digital Interface (MIDI) file format (.mid) contains a series of control information that can be played back on an MIDI-enabled device such as a computer.

- **MP3:** The Moving Picture Experts Group (MPEG-3) audio file format (.mp3) is a popular compressed file format.

- **WMA:** The Windows Media Audio file format (.wma) is a compressed music file format developed by Microsoft.

- **AIFF:** The Audio Interchange File Format (.aiff) is an uncompressed waveform sound file type originally used by Apple computers.

- **M4A, MP4:** PowerPoint also supports these advanced audio- and video-coding file formats. M4A and MP4 are known collectively as MPEG-4 Part 14. M4A is an audio codec, and MP4 is an audio and video container format.

To specify a sound for an animation, select the object assigned to the animation and then click the dialog box launcher under the Effect Options command. This opens a dialog box for the animation effect assigned to the object. Figure 20-8 shows the dialog box for a Fly In animation applied to a bulleted list.

Figure 20-8   The Sound drop-down menu in the Fly In dialog box

The Effect tab of the dialog box controls settings related to the direction and the start and end of the animation. More important to our discussion of sound, the Enhancements area of the Effect tab enables you to specify a sound file to be played with the animation.

The default sound setting for all animations that you have assigned to slide objects is No Sound. When you select the Sound drop-down menu, you are presented with a list of sound files that can be applied to the animation. These sounds include applause, camera, chime, and wind. Select a sound provided in the list (these sounds consist of .wav files). Click the Sound icon to set the volume level for the sound.

If you want to use a sound file other than the ones PowerPoint provides, you can access these sounds via the Other Sound option in the Sound drop-down menu. Selecting the Other Sound option opens the Add Audio dialog box. You can take advantage of any sound files that you have created or downloaded to your computer. However, to use the sound file, it must be in one of the supported file formats discussed earlier in this section.

TIP

If you have assigned multiple animations to an object, the easiest way to open the options for a specific effect is to use the Effect Options command that is available for each animation listed in the animation pane.

When you have added the sound to the animation, you can click OK to close the animation's dialog box. Click the preview button on the Animations tab to preview the animation with the assigned sound.

Setting timings for animations

You can set the timing for an animation using the commands available in the Timing group on the Animations tab. The Start command enables you to set how the animation is started. The default setting is On Click, but you can specify that the animation start with the previous animation (With Previous) or after the previous animation has ended (After Previous).

The Duration command provides a spin box that enables you to set the actual duration of the animation. You can speed up or slow down animations as you require. If you want to have the animation play automatically after a specified delay, use the Delay spin box to specify the actual time for the delay.

Although it is not included in the Timing group, the Trigger command in the Advanced Animation group also has some bearing on the mechanism for starting an animation; the Trigger command enables you to specify how a particular animation is triggered or started. You can specify the trigger on the click of a particular object on the slide. For example, you can specify the title text box as a trigger for an animation. When you click the title on the slide, the animation plays. You can specify any object on the slide as the trigger for an animation. The animation does not have to be applied to the trigger object, so you can click a clip art image or picture on a slide and use that to trigger an animation on another object (such as a bulleted list).

Also, you can set the timing settings for an animation in the animation's dialog box on the Timing tab. Figure 20-10 shows the Timing tab of the Fly In animation's dialog box.

On the Timing tab, you can set the animation's Start, Delay, and Duration settings. The dialog box also enables you to configure the animation to repeat using the Repeat drop-down menu. If you want the animation to rewind when it finishes playing (which is useful if you have used an animation such as a motion path that moves an object on the slide), you can check the Rewind When Done Playing check box. You can also set the trigger options for the animation via the Triggers drop-down command provided on the Timing tab. You can specify any object on the slide as the trigger for the animation.

When you finish setting the timing-related settings for the animation in the dialog box, click OK to return to the PowerPoint workspace. Take advantage of the Preview command to preview the settings you have configured for the animation.

Figure 20-9   The Timing tab of the Fly In dialog box

Managing slide animations

The Animation pane is an extremely useful tool for managing, reordering, and fine-tuning the animations that you have assigned to the slide objects on a particular slide. The Animation pane lists all the animations that have been assigned to objects on the current slide. To open the Animation pane, select the Animation Pane command in the Advanced Animation group. Figure 20-10 shows a presentation in Normal view with the Animation pane present on the right side of the PowerPoint workspace.

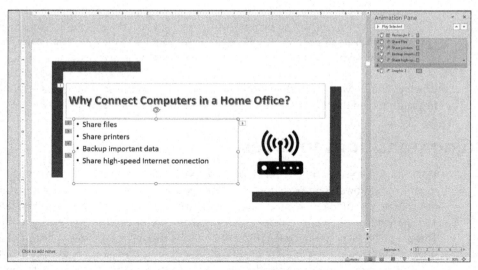

Figure 20-10   Slide with assigned animations and the Animation pane

You can use the Animation pane to accomplish a variety of animation-management tasks, including reordering, deleting, and modifying animations. To reorder the animations in the Animation pane, you have a couple of options. You can select an animation and then move it up or down in the Animation pane using the Move Earlier or Move Later arrow at the bottom of the Animation pane. You can also drag an animation to a new position in the Animation pane to reorder the sequence of the animations. Also, you can set the action for when an animation should begin, and you can access effect options and timing settings by clicking the drop-down arrow next to a selected animation.

The bottom of the Animation pane provides delay and duration information for the animation (delay is on the left, and duration on the right—both in seconds). You can use the Seconds drop-down button to zoom in or out on the advanced timeline information to the right of each of the animations. This gives you the relative timing of the animation as it compares to the other animations placed on the slide.

If you want to delete an animation from the slide, select the animation in the Animation pane and then either press the Delete key on the keyboard or select Remove from the drop-down menu to the right of the animation. This drop-down menu also enables you to set the animation's start and access the animation's timing settings.

The Animation pane is particularly useful in sorting out multiple animations that you added to an object. For example, you might have assigned both an entrance and an exit animation to an object. Both these animations are listed separately in the Animation pane. This makes it easy to access the dialog box for an animation by selecting the drop-down menu next to the animation and then selecting Effect Options.

CHAPTER 20

TIP

You can also reorder animations on a slide without using the Animation pane. Use the Reorder Animation commands on the Animations tab.

When you finish working with the Animation pane, you can close it using its Close button, which frees up more of the PowerPoint workspace for working with your slides in Normal view.

Adding transitions to slides

Transitions give you another effect type to add visual interest and perhaps even a little excitement to your PowerPoint presentations. When you show a slideshow of a presentation that does not contain any slide transitions, you are doing what is called a *straight cut* in film terminology. The change from the current slide to the next slide is abrupt and can be jarring to the audience. There is no visual buffer between the content of the two adjacent slides. A transition is a special effect that provides a visual shift between slides rather than an abrupt cut or switch. The transition between the slides is triggered when you navigate from the current slide to the next slide (either by a click of the mouse or based on a timing), and that next slide has been configured with the transition. So, if you want a transition between slide A and slide B, you assign the transition to slide B.

The ribbon's Transitions tab provides the command groups that enable you to select a transition, configure transition options, and configure sound and timing settings for a transition. Figure 20-11 shows the Transitions tab of the ribbon.

Figure 20-11   The ribbon's Transitions tab

The Transitions tab also provides a Preview command, making it easy for you to preview a transition assigned to a slide. The Preview command shows the transition as the changeover is made between the two slides (the current and the next slides).

PowerPoint provides several transitions, including the wipe, split, dissolve, checkerboard, and blinds transitions. The Transitions gallery groups the transitions into three categories: subtle, exciting, and dynamic content.

Before we review how to assign a transition to a slide or slides, let me say a couple of words about transitions in general. Remember that these are special effects, like the animation effects. Use them to add visual interest to the presentation, not make the audience feel like they are sitting in front of a strobe light at a 1970s disco. Also, consider the additive effect of animations and transitions. If you use a slide transition to get to a slide, is it really necessary to also load up the slide with animations? For example, if you use the Glitter transition, followed by objects on the slide configured with the Grow and Turn animation effect, you might have too much going on in terms of visual interest. That is not to say that transitions and animations can't be used together; you can do so, but you don't want to mix different types of effects randomly. Plan the look you want for the slide, considering your purpose and the presentation's topic, and then plan your use of transitions and animations appropriately.

You can assign transitions to your slides when you are working in Normal view, Outline view, or the Slide Sorter. If you want to apply the same transition to several slides, you can easily do this in Slide Sorter view by selecting multiple slides. And although the preview is obviously smaller in Slide Sorter view, you can get previews of all the selected slides and the assigned transition by selecting the Preview command.

To assign a transition to a slide, select the slide. You can then scroll through the Transition gallery (which is in the Transition To This Slide group) to select a transition. Alternatively, you can click the More button to view the entire gallery. When you place the mouse on a specific transition, it is previewed on the selected slide or slides. To assign a transition, select the transition in the gallery.

Modifying transitions

You can modify the transition after you have assigned a particular transition in the gallery to a slide. The Effect Options command provides a gallery of options related to the transition you selected. Figure 20-12 shows the Effect Options gallery for the Wipe transition.

Figure 20-12   The Effect Options gallery for a Wipe transition

The options provided in the gallery are specific to the transition. For example, the Wipe transition can be modified in terms of its direction, such as from the right, from the top, or from the bottom (refer to Figure 20-12). Other transitions have other options, which, again, depend on the transition itself. For example, the Split transition enables you to configure the split to go either in or out; you can also choose whether the split is vertical or horizontal. The Checkerboard transition can be configured to occur from the left or the top. Some transitions, such as the Honeycomb transition, have no options.

Not only do you have control over transition options (if available), but you can also control the duration of the transition and determine whether a sound plays when the transition plays. To set the duration of the transition, use the Duration spin box in the Timing group of the Transitions tab.

If you want to have a sound play with the transition, select the Sound drop-down menu in the Timing group. It provides a number of sound files, including Applause, Chime, and Voltage. If you want to use a sound that you have recorded or downloaded to your computer, you can select the Other Sound command in the Sound drop-down menu. This opens the Add Audio dialog box. Navigate to the folder that holds the sound file, and then select the appropriate file; click OK to assign the sound file to the transition.

You can also specify how the slide is advanced. By default, slides are advanced by a click of the mouse. You can specify a time in the After spin box. The slide then automatically advances based on that setting. You can clear the On Mouse Click check box in the Timing group if you plan to use the timing to advance the slide, or you can leave the option selected. Doing so enables you to advance the slide before the timing you have set. It's always good to have options.

TIP

If you want to apply a selected transition to all the slides in the presentation, select the Apply To All command on the Transitions tab.

Using the Morph transition

As I mentioned in the introduction to this chapter, PowerPoint provides the Morph transition, which is definitely not your typical transition. Typically transitions are seen as a way to add special effects to a presentation. Morph provides you with an excellent way to move from a slide to the next slide and visually show that there is an informational link between the two slides. This link is shown through the repetition of graphics (pictures, SmartArt, icons, and the like) on the slides.

The Morph transition will actually animate the transition from the first slide to the second slide by keying on the graphics shared by the two slides. For example, you might have a short list of terms or tips on a slide that you have illustrated using icons, pictures, or other images, such as the slide shown in Figure 20-13.

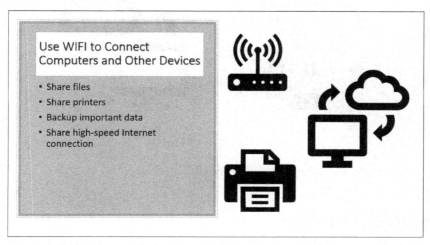

Figure 20-13   The first slide in a Morph transition scenario

The slide shown in Figure 20-13 is the slide that comes just before the slide to which you will assign the Morph transition. The next slide in the presentation (the one with the Morph transition) needs to include one or more of the graphics that are on the previous slide. The easiest way to do this is to select the thumbnail of the previous slide in the Slide pane and then select the New Slide command on the Home tab and select Duplicate Selected Slides. Now that you have a copy of the previous slide, you can edit it to include the appropriate text. You can also delete any of the graphics that you will not need. (Remember, you need at least one repeating graphic for Morph to work.) Make sure that you have also resized and moved the repeating graphics (from the previous slide). For example, Figure 20-14 repeats two of the graphics from Figure 20-13. Note that the size and placement of the network diagram and the WiFi router icon has changed. When you view the presentation as a slideshow (click the Slide Show button on the Status bar) and move from the initial slide to the slide with the Morph transition, the repeated graphic elements will morph in size, and they will move to a new location. In our example, the WiFi router icon would move from the upper middle of the previous slide to the lower left of the Morph slide. The network diagram drawing will move from the right and "grow" as it morphs to its final destination.

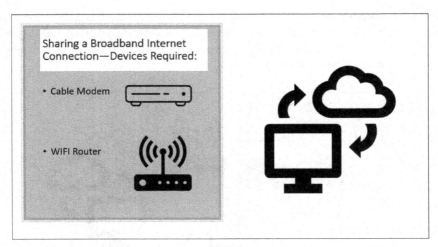

Figure 20-14   The slide formatted with the Morph transition

Adding sound to a slide

Sounds can emphasize information on slides or serve as actual content to your presentation (such as a sound clip from a famous speech). The sound can consist of a sound effect or narration. You can insert a sound clip as an object onto a slide. The sound plays when you click the image that represents the sound object during a slideshow. PowerPoint enables you to insert sound files that have been sourced in different ways. For example, you might already have sound files that you have created or downloaded to your computer. You can insert these sound files into a slide. You can also record sound, such as narration, directly to a slide by using the Record Sound utility. Office.com provides a library of prerecorded sound effects as well. When you get your sound on a slide, PowerPoint provides tools for modifying and enhancing the audio.

First, you have to get some audio onto a slide before you can take advantage of Audio Tools. The Insert tab of the ribbon includes the Media group, which provides commands for inserting video and audio onto your presentation slides. When you select the Audio command, you have two options:

- **Audio On My PC:** This command opens the Insert Audio dialog box, which enables you to insert prerecorded sound files (see the supported sound file types listed earlier in this chapter) stored on your computer.

- **Record Audio:** This command opens the Record Sound utility. This feature enables you to record narration and other sounds using the microphone on your PC.

Whether you insert an existing audio file or record new audio, you will find that both these options insert a sound icon on the slide to represent the associated sound file. You can then edit options related to the sound file using the contextual audio tools, which appear when the image representing the sound file on the slide.

Editing sound options

After adding an audio file to a slide, you have a great deal of control over both the graphic representing the sound file and the audio file embedded in the slide. When you insert the audio into the slide, it is represented by a sound icon and has a control bar that enables you to play the sound, rewind the sound, and adjust the sound volume. Figure 20-15 shows the Playback tab of the Audio tools, which becomes available on the ribbon when a sound file on a slide is selected (meaning an inserted sound file or recording).

You can replace the standard sound icon picture that is inserted into the slide. The Audio Format tab provides many of the same commands used to adjust the settings of a picture, including a Picture Styles gallery and tools for cropping and sizing the image. So, when you change the sound file's picture, you can edit the new picture's settings if you want. For example, you may want to change the picture style and adjust picture attributes such as brightness, contrast, and color.

Figure 20-15   The Playback tab

To change the default sound icon picture, select the Audio Format tab and then select the Change Picture command in the Adjust group. The Change Picture gallery provides you with several options, such as From A File, From Stock Images, and From Icons. Select one of the options, and the appropriate dialog box or window will open. For example, if you select From A File, the Insert Picture dialog box will open.

> ➤ **For detailed information on working with pictures and other graphics in the 365 applications, see Chapter 4, "Using and creating graphics."**

In terms of editing the actual sound clip, the Playback tab enables you to trim your audio clip, apply fades to the audio, and adjust how the audio clip is started during the slideshow. The Playback tab also provides a Play command, enabling you to preview any changes that you make to the audio clip.

The trim audio dialog box

If you want to trim the audio, you can select the Trim Audio command, which opens the Trim Audio dialog box. The timeline provided in the Trim Audio command has both a start marker (green) and an end marker (red).

You can trim the clip from the beginning using the start marker, allowing you to cue the audio to start at a particular point. If you want the clip to end before it plays in its entirety, you can move the end marker to establish a new end time for the marker. Spin boxes are also provided for the start and end times, and you can use them to set the starting and ending points of the clip. When you have finished working in the Trim Audio dialog box, click OK.

You can also add a fade to either the beginning or the end of the audio clip. Specify the Fade In or the Fade Out duration using the appropriate spin box. The fades enable you to put some dead air at the beginning or end of a clip so that they do not seem to start or end abruptly when you play them during your presentation.

If you want a slide animation to play when a sound object file reaches a certain point during playback, you can add a bookmark to the sound object. Play the audio file to the point where you want to place the bookmark. Then on the Audio Tools, Playback tab, select the Add Bookmark command, which places the bookmark in the sound file. If you need to remove a bookmark in a sound file, select the bookmark on the sound object's playback bar and then select the Remove Bookmark command.

Adding video to a slide

You can also add video to your PowerPoint slides. You can insert online videos, such as a YouTube videos, or you can insert videos that you have created. The possibilities include video files stored on your OneDrive (which are not really online videos—they are just stored online instead of your computer), videos from YouTube (which you can add as a service to your 365 applications, such as PowerPoint), and any online video that has a video embed code. You paste the embed code onto the slide, and the code serves as the conduit to the video content on the web.

Working with video content in PowerPoint is very straightforward, and many video file formats are supported. Inserted video can greatly enhance your presentations by providing actual examples of concepts you are presenting, and these videos can also be used as icebreakers to warm up the crowd early in your presentation. Let's take a look at inserting online video and then examine the process for inserting your own video files.

Inserting online video

The potential number of online videos you can use in your PowerPoint presentations is huge and growing every day. I'm not saying that every video you find on the web can work on your PowerPoint slides, but you can use video clips from a number of sites, including YouTube. If you get an error message when you paste an embed code into the Insert Video dialog box, you cannot use videos from that website. If you decide to use embedded web video clips in your presentation, be advised that you need to be sure you have an Internet connection on your computer when you play your presentation as a slideshow. Also, be aware of the fact that websites can be down, and video websites sometimes remove videos. So, although this is a great way to include video in your presentation, there is a chance that it might not work. Certainly, don't make it the center of your presentation.

As an added precaution make sure you have the most recent version of the Windows Media Player installed on your computer. You can get the recent Windows Media Player from *www.microsoft.com*.

To insert a video clip into the current slide, you will take advantage of the Video command on the ribbon's Insert tab (in the Media group). When you select the Video command, you open the Insert Video From gallery, which provides you with three options:

- **This Device:** This option opens the Insert Video dialog box. You can use the dialog box to browse through the files stored on your computer, including your OneDrive (which isn't really stored on your computer). A Search box in the upper-right corner of the dialog box can help you find the particular video file you want to insert onto the current slide.

- **Stock Videos:** The Stock Videos option allows you to access the Microsoft Stock Images library, which contains a number of video files that you can use on your PowerPoint slides.

- **Online Video:** This option provides you with the Online Video window, which is where you insert the URL address of an online video. You can use YouTube, SlideShare, Vimeo, and other streaming video sources. All you need to know is the URL for the video source.

Figure 20-16 shows the Insert Video dialog box.

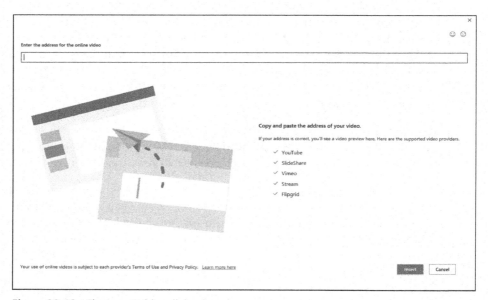

Figure 20-16   The Insert Video dialog box

TIP

You can also insert your own videos onto a slide using the Insert Video icon provided in a new slide's content area. When you select the icon, the Insert Video dialog box will open. The dialog box defaults to your Documents folder, and it also provides a Search box in the upper-right part of the dialog box, which can be used to locate the video file you want to insert.

You can insert video files from YouTube by searching YouTube directly from the Insert Video dialog box. When you run a search using the YouTube search box, your search results are listed as thumbnails in the results window. When you locate the video that you want to insert into the current slide, select the video and then select Insert. The video is inserted into the slide.

You can size the video and move it on the slide, as you require. When the video frame is selected, the Video Tools appear on the ribbon. The Format commands are similar to the Format commands provided for pictures or shapes; they enable you to change the style of the video frame, including the shape and border.

Useful commands are provided on the Format tab, in the Adjust group. You can correct the brightness and contrast of the video using the Corrections command. You can also colorize the video using the Color command. The Crop command is another useful command at the other end of the ribbon in the Size group. You can crop the video frame if you want to concentrate the viewer's attention on a particular part of the video frame when the video plays.

Another option for inserting video onto a PowerPoint slide is to use a video embed code. The embed code is really just an HTML/XML pointer to the video clip on the web. When you "activate" the embed code, the video plays on the slide. If you want to use a video embed code to insert video content onto a slide, you first need to locate the video on a website such as YouTube using your web browser. You then copy the video's embed code to the Clipboard. Different video sites provide different ways to access the video embed code for a video. In the case of YouTube videos, the embed code is accessed by clicking the Share command and then Embed (these commands are below the video). An embed code will appear. You can use the Copy command on your web browser's Edit menu or use Ctrl+C to copy the selected embed code using the keyboard.

After you copy the embed code for the video, you can open the Insert Video window and then paste the code in the From A Video Embed Code box by pressing Ctrl+V on the keyboard. You then click the Insert button (in the embed code box) to insert the video code into the slide.

When you select the video embed code box (which looks just like an inserted video box), all the commands available on the Video Tools, Format tab are available to modify the video frame (as they are for an inserted web video). When you switch to the Video Tools, Playback tab, most of the group commands are unavailable, as they are for inserted online video clips. The Playback commands are accessible only when you insert your own video files into a slide, which we talk about in the next section.

Inserting a video file

When inserting video files that are stored on your computer (or on your OneDrive), make sure your video file is in a file format that PowerPoint supports. The following file types are supported:

- **Windows Video File:** The Audio Video Interleave file type (.avi) is a commonly used video format and has been the standard for Microsoft Windows for years. It uses the Microsoft Resource Interchange file format to store compressed audio and video information.

- **Movie File:** The Moving Picture Experts Group file format (.mpg or .mpeg) has been around for years and was one of the first standards for video and audio compression.

- **Windows Media Video:** The .wmv file format provides highly compressed video and audio in a file that requires minimal space when stored on a computer.

- **Windows Media File:** Yet another Microsoft media file type, the .asf file format is used to stream video and audio over a network.

- **MP4 Video:** This collection of QuickTime video file types includes .mp4, .m4v, and .mov.

You have two options for inserting your video file into a slide. You can select the Insert Video icon in a slide content box, or you can go to the ribbon's Insert tab, select the Video command, and then select Video On My PC. If you select the Insert Video icon in a slide content box, the Insert Video dialog box opens. The Insert Video dialog box enables you to insert video files from your computer or OneDrive, directly from YouTube, or via a video embed code. To insert video from your computer, click the Browse button to the right of the From A File option, which opens the Insert Video dialog box.

If you aren't working on a slide that contains a content box (as discussed in the previous paragraph), you can still insert video files from your computer; select the Video command on the Insert tab (in the Media group), and then select Video On My PC. The Insert Video dialog box opens.

So, both the Insert Video icon in a content box and the Video command on the Ruler's Insert tab get you to the Insert Video dialog box. In the Insert Video dialog box, navigate to the folder that holds your video file. Select the file and then click Insert. The video is inserted into the slide. An accompanying control bar enables you to play the video, rewind or fast-forward the video, and change the sound level for the clip. You can size the video frame, if required, and move the video on the slide as you would with any other slide object.

CHAPTER 20

Modifying your video clips

When an inserted video file is selected on the slide, the Video Tools become available on the ribbon. As already mentioned, the Video Tools consist of two tabs: Format and Playback. The Format tab has many similarities to the Format tab of the Picture Tools and can be used to modify the frame, correct brightness/contrast issues, and change the color of the video. The tools that enable you to manipulate the video, such as trim the video or add a fade, are on the Playback tab.

You can use the Trim Video command to trim the beginning or end of the video. This enables you to specify a new start or stop point in the video so that you show only the portion of the video clip that is important to your presentation.

➤ **The Video Tools, Format tab provides commands that are similar to those found on the Picture Tools, Format tab. Check out the information in Chapter 19, "Better slides with clip art, pictures, and SmartArt," to get more insight into how to use the Format tab tools.**

TIP

If you are working with a very large video file, you can link it to the PowerPoint slide instead of embedding it. Select the Insert drop-down arrow in the Insert Video dialog box, and then select Link To File.

The Playback tab also provides the Bookmarks group. You can use the Add Bookmark command to insert bookmarks into the video object. Bookmarks in a video file can trigger animation effects that you have configured on other objects on the slide. For more about triggering animations, see "Advanced animation techniques," earlier in this chapter.

You can also set fades at both the beginning and end of the clip using the Fade In and Fade Out commands, respectively. You can specify that the video be played in full-screen mode when you play the presentation as a slideshow. Select the Play Full Screen check box in the Video Options group.

TIP

You can test any of the playback changes that you make to the video. Use the Play button as needed. If you want to get a better idea of how the changes you made will appear in the slideshow, select the Slide Show icon on the PowerPoint status bar to start a slideshow from the current slide.

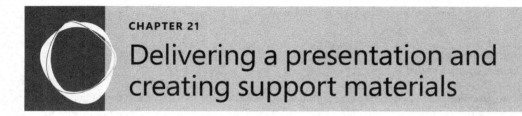

Delivering a presentation and creating support materials

Planning your presentation   641

Checking the presentation for spelling and grammar errors   642

Running through a completed presentation   644

Using the presenter view   646

Using hidden slides   648

Creating a custom slide show   649

Creating a self-running presentation   652

Creating an interactive presentation   656

Working with the notes and handout masters   659

Printing presentations, notes, and handouts   661

Exporting a presentation   663

Sharing your presentation   665

Once you have created and fine-tuned your presentation, you are ready to show it to your audience. Traditionally, the slideshow is a speaker's aid and provides the audience with important points and visuals related to the presentation. However, PowerPoint gives you other possibilities for sharing a presentation with an audience. You can create a self-running presentation, which allows individuals or small groups to view the presentation at a conference booth or in a kiosk setting.

A presentation often involves more than just the slideshow itself. Audience members may expect you to provide handouts or other supporting material related to the presentation. PowerPoint makes it easy to print handouts and speaker notes for your presentation.

In this chapter, we look at strategies for showing your presentation to others. We also discuss finalizing your presentations, creating self-running presentations, and how to create ancillary materials such as handouts.

Planning your presentation

Before we look at some of the aspects involved in getting a PowerPoint presentation finalized and ready to deliver as a slideshow, I want to say a few words about planning your presentation. This isn't related to planning the presentation outline and the content, but it is about the pre-planning involved in the delivery of the presentation.

Even if you create the most incredible PowerPoint presentation ever seen, you still need to do some planning related to the actual execution of your presentation. PowerPoint gives you a technological edge when speaking to your audience; however, it won't save you if you haven't done your homework related to your audience, the purpose of the event, and the questions your audience might pose. So, I would suggest you think about the following as you prepare to launch your presentation:

- **Audience:** You need to have a good idea of who will be in the audience when you give your presentation. This affects the level of the information you are providing—and, to some degree, the tone of the presentation—including your use of slide styles, animations, transitions, and multimedia. For example, if you are presenting a sophisticated engineering project to a neighborhood association, keep the technical aspects of the presentation simple. Likewise, consider your audience's visual literacy. A presentation using a lot of bells and whistles, such as animations and multimedia, is easier to digest for a crowd that is technically attuned to graphics and special effects.

- **Purpose:** You must have a good feel for why you are giving the presentation. If you are trying to drum up investors for a construction project, the slideshow must help sell the need for the project and make it clear to the audience that you have the expertise to execute the project. Remember that most people can remember only a few major points from even a short presentation, so hit the most important information more than once, and provide a solid conclusion that pulls together the major concepts for the audience.

- **Place:** You really need solid information about the venue where you plan to give your presentation. If you have included a lot of web hyperlinks and perhaps web videos in your presentation, but the site has no Internet connection, you will have to do a lot of dancing to make up for all that missing information. You need to be ready for anything. Always bring your own laptop. You might also want to have hard copies of the presentation ready in case no video projector is available, or the projector light bulb blows just before you take the stage. Oh, and don't count on any kind of audio system that you can use for sound during your presentation.

So, you must tailor your presentation for the audience and the venue. Your presentation also needs to have an extremely clear purpose (clear to the audience, not just you). Remember that you can hope to make only a few main points; any more than that, and the audience will be bordering on information overload. Reaffirm your main points in the conclusion of the presentation.

As both a speaker and an attendee at many educational and technical conferences, I have seen a nearly endless list of things that can go wrong with a presentation—be ready for any eventuality. Spend some time planning the delivery of your presentation and anticipating some of the potential problems you might face. Doing so will make the presentation go smoothly.

Checking the presentation for spelling and grammar errors

Making sure that your presentation slides are free of spelling and grammatical errors is important in protecting the veracity of the information in the presentation. If you have obvious spelling errors, for example, the audience will have a hard time taking you seriously. You are probably familiar with the Spelling and Grammar features in Microsoft Word and the fact that they flag spelling and grammar errors automatically: red wavy lines for spelling errors, green wavy lines for grammar errors.

PowerPoint has the same spelling- and grammar-checking capabilities as Word and the other Office applications. Grammar checking (as you type) in PowerPoint is not enabled by default, but you can enable it in the PowerPoint Options window. Select File and then, in the Backstage, select Options. The PowerPoint Options window opens. Select Proofing to access the spelling and grammar settings, as shown in Figure 21-1.

Figure 21-1   The PowerPoint Proofing options

The Mark Grammar Errors As You Type check box is at the bottom of the Proofing options; select it to enable grammar checking as you type. Most of the other Proofing settings are enabled by default. Click OK to save changes and return to the PowerPoint application window.

Do not be complacent about spelling errors and grammar problems because you think Power-Point is catching them all (it flags misspellings by default and grammar errors after you enable the feature). Run the spelling tool after you complete your presentation; also, do not forget to inspect your slides visually. Proofread your slides and check for contextual errors, such as using the word *there* when you should have used the word *their*. Because PowerPoint text usually consists of short, bulleted fragments, it is easy to make a spelling error that the Spelling feature doesn't flag.

NOTE

Use the thesaurus to find synonyms for specific words on your slides. You can also translate slide text using the Translate command in the Language group. The Language command allows you to select the proofing language used by the proofing tools, such as the Spelling feature.

➤ For more general information about the Spelling feature in Office applications, see the "Using the Editor" section of Chapter 7, "Enhancing Word documents."

Running through a completed presentation

Before you show your presentation to an audience, run through it several times, checking that the slides are in the right order and that the object animations and slide transitions work correctly (particularly where you have assigned triggers or timings to animations or transitions). Running through the presentation also enables you to practice your prepared speech as you show your slides.

The Slide Show tab of the ribbon is where you will find all the commands you need to run through your presentation. The Slide Show tab provides commands to create custom slideshows, hide slides in a presentation, and record slideshow timings for a self-running show. We discuss these possibilities later in this chapter in the section, "Creating a self-running presentation." Figure 21-2 shows the Slide Show tab.

Figure 21-2   The ribbon's Slide Show tab

The Start Slide Show group on the Slide Show tab provides two commands for starting the slideshow. The From Beginning command and the From Current Slide command operate exactly as advertised. You can use either command to fire up your slideshow, depending on whether you want to start from the beginning or with the slide you are currently editing.

After you start the slideshow (from the commands on the Slide Show tab or the Slide Show button provided in the View shortcuts on the status bar), you typically click the mouse as needed to advance through the slides. You can sit back and practice your narration if you have set timings for slides via slide transitions as the slides change automatically. (We talk more about setting slide timings later in the chapter.)

In terms of navigating the slideshow itself, PowerPoint gives you some easy-to-access tools when you are in Slide Show view. Move the mouse over the bottom-left area of the current slide to access a collection of six tools. From left to right, these tools are as follows:

- **Previous:** The Previous arrow quickly returns to the previous slide.

- **Next:** The Next arrow advances to the next slide in the presentation.

- **Pointer Gallery:** Select the Pen icon to change the mouse pointer into a laser pointer, pen, highlighter, or eraser (if you have already drawn on a slide). You can also select the color used for the pointer.

- **See All Slides View:** Available in the Slide Show window, the See All Slides View button is just to the right of the Pointer Gallery button. Click this button to get a thumbnail view of all the slides in the presentation. You can't move the slide thumbnails around in this view (as you can when you are working in Slide Sorter view), but you can quickly jump to any slide in the presentation by selecting the slide.

- **Zoom:** The Zoom tool enables you to specify an area of the slide and then zoom in on it with an additional click of the mouse.

- **Subtitles:** This tool allows you to toggle on/off the captions and subtitles for the slide show during the presentation.

- **Menu:** This tool provides a pane of helpful commands. These commands include enabling the presenter view during the show and setting the arrow and subtitle settings. A Last Viewed command makes it easy to return to the previously viewed slide, and an End Show command makes it easy for you to end the show.

You can also access these different command options from a shortcut menu that is provided when you right-click a slide. You can stop the slideshow at any time by pressing the Esc key or selecting End Show on either the shortcut menu or the Slide Show menu. A black screen appears when you proceed beyond the last slide if you run through all the slides in a presentation in Slide Show view. Click the mouse to exit the screen and return to the PowerPoint application window.

Using the presenter coach

Even if you run through your presentation a couple of times and are feeling pretty good about the slideshow, you might want to get some additional feedback on the presentation. One option is to show the presentation to a coworker or two and get feedback. If you have ruled this out as an option, there is another alternative: rehearse your presentation with Presenter Coach.

The Presenter Coach feature (which requires an Internet connection) uses artificial intelligence and other algorithms to evaluate your pacing and pitch. The Presenter Coach also listens for informal speech and inappropriate language, and it can detect when you are being too wordy. The Presenter Coach is designed to help you with your verbal presentation skills rather than critiquing your slide design or content.

To start the Presenter Coach, select the Rehearse With Coach command (in the Rehearse group of the Slide Show tab). Your presentation will load, and the Presenter Coach Welcome box will open in the lower-right corner of the presentation window.

The Welcome box contains a Show Real-Time Feedback check box (which is enabled by default) and a Start Rehearsing button. To run through the presentation under the scrutiny of the Presenter Coach, select Start Rehearsing. Speak clearly, and the coach will listen. When you have completed giving the presentation, press Esc to return to the PowerPoint window. It might take a moment or two, but a Rehearsal Report window will open. The report provides statistics, such as the total time spent to give the presentation and the number of slides rehearsed. You are also judged on filler language, repetitive language, and inclusive language. Pacing, pitch, and originality are also "judged" by the coach.

Once you have reviewed the rehearsal report, you can either congratulate yourself on your verbal skills or practice the presentation again by selecting the Rehearse Again button in the upper-right corner of the report.

Using the presenter view

You can present your slideshow using the "regular" Slide Show view that we discussed in the "Running through a completed presentation" section, or you can show your slideshow in Presenter view. Presenter view is designed with you (the presenter) in mind. It is geared toward providing the speaker with the information they need while running the slideshow. Figure 21-3 shows the Presenter view. Although Presenter view is designed to be used on multiple monitors or a monitor and a video projector, PowerPoint enables you to run Presenter view on a single computer screen. This is a great way to practice your presentation before you hook up your notebook or touchscreen device to an external monitor or a video projector.

If you happen to have two monitors connected to your computer, check the Use Presenter View check box on the Slide Show tab of the ribbon. Now when you start the slideshow, it opens with Presenter view on your primary monitor and Slide Show view on the secondary monitor. If you find that this isn't happening automatically, select the Monitor drop-down menu on the Slide Show tab (in the Monitors group) and select Primary Monitor.

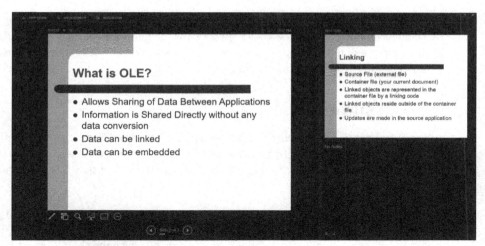

Figure 21-3   Presenter view

If you have only one monitor on your computer, you can still use the Presenter view to practice your presentation. Start the slideshow, right-click the first screen in the slideshow, and select Show Presenter View from the shortcut menu.

The Presenter view divides your computer screen into different panes. On the left of the screen, you see the current slide, and you can access the Slide Show tools (such as the Pointer gallery or the Zoom feature) and a set of navigation buttons. Above the current slide is a timer that shows the elapsed time since the current slide has been on the screen.

A ribbon sits at the top of the left side of the Presenter view screen. This ribbon provides three commands: Show Taskbar, Display Settings, and End Slide Show. The Show Taskbar command shows the Windows at the bottom of the screen and enables you to quickly switch to another application that is open on the desktop.

The Display Settings command provides a drop-down menu that can be useful when you are working with multiple monitors. The first command, Swap Presenter View And Slide Show, enables you to swap what is being shown on two monitors connected to your computer. For example, I have seen PowerPoint presentations in which the speaker had the Presenter view on the audience's "big screen" and was trying desperately to swap it with the slideshow on the presenter's laptop. The other command, Duplicate Slide Show, places the "basic" slideshow on both screens.

The End Slide Show command is self-explanatory. When you want to end the slideshow, select End Slide Show.

On the right side of Presenter view, the next slide is shown as a thumbnail. If you have notes associated with the current slide, they appear below the thumbnail of the next slide. This pane of the right side of the Presenter view screen also provides Make The Text Larger icon and Make The Text Smaller icons that allow you to zoom in and out on your notes, respectively.

Using hidden slides

At the outset of this chapter, we discussed the fact that you need to anticipate potential problems when you actually deliver your presentation. Presenter view, discussed in the previous section, can help you keep track of your slides (you always know what slide is up next), and you can also view your slide notes.

You also need to anticipate, as much as possible, what type of additional information your audience might request during your presentation. For example, if you show a chart on a slide, someone in the audience might ask you about the raw data on which the chart is based. Even though you didn't originally plan to show the data during the presentation, wouldn't it be great if you already had the data arranged in an easy-to-read table on an available slide? This is where hidden slides come in. These are slides that you prepare in anticipation of audience questions or follow-up that you might want to make on your topic if you have extra time at the end of your presentation. However, the slides are saved in the presentation but are hidden; they aren't shown when you run the presentation as a slideshow.

TIP

To unhide a slide or slides, select the slide or slides and then click the Hide Slide command a second time.

The Hide Slide command is housed on the ribbon's Slide Show tab in the Set Up group. You can hide a slide or slides when you are working in Normal view or in the Slide Sorter. To hide multiple slides, select the slides and then select the Hide Slide command.

A hidden slide is marked with a diagonal slash through the slide's number (which you can see in both Normal view and the Slide Sorter). Hidden slides are also "ghosted" in Slide Sorter view. Remember that a hidden slide still remains in the presentation; however, it is not shown during the slideshow. Figure 21-4 shows a presentation in Slide Sorter view. Slides 14, 15, and 16 are marked as hidden.

TIP

You can right-click a slide thumbnail in Normal view or in Slide Sorter view and select Hide Slide from the shortcut menu.

Hidden slides can be anywhere in the presentation; you don't necessarily have to group them. However, you might want to keep them in sequence with slides that cover similar information. If you have a lot of slides in your presentation, you can also divide the presentation into sections and create a specific section to house the hidden slides. That way, the hidden slides aren't mixed in with the rest of the slides.

To access a hidden slide during a slideshow (in either Slide Show view or Presenter view), click the See All Slides icon. Thumbnails of all your slides (including the hidden slides) appear on the screen. Hidden slides are ghosted. To open a hidden slide, select the slide. You return to either Slide Show view or Presenter view with the hidden slide displayed.

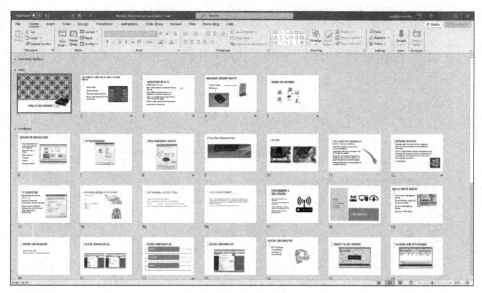

Figure 21-4   Slides in the presentation can be hidden.

If you decide to use hidden slides in your presentations, determine some sort of structure for their placement. If you have a few hidden slides, you might want to keep each hidden slide near the other slides in the presentation that it pertains or refers to. If you have a larger number of hidden slides in a presentation with a lot of slides, it might make sense to cluster all the hidden slides in a section or place them at the end of your presentation for easy access (if and when you need them). You don't want to be spending time searching for a hidden slide or slides as you deal with the question-and-answer period that typically follows a presentation.

Creating a custom slide show

The Slide Show tab has an option for creating a custom slideshow. The Custom Slide Show command enables you to take a subset of your current presentation and designate it as a custom show. This means that you can create shorter presentations from the contents of a lengthy presentation. For example, you might have given a two-hour presentation at a conference and now want to break the presentation into two one-hour custom shows that you can give as lunchtime seminars. You can create any number of custom shows from a single PowerPoint presentation.

To create a custom slideshow, select Custom Slide Show on the Slide Show tab and then select Custom Shows. The Custom Shows dialog box opens. From here, you can create new custom shows and modify existing custom shows. After you create a custom show, it appears in the Custom Shows list. To create a new custom show, click the New button. The Define Custom Show dialog box appears.

All the slides in the presentation are listed in the Slides In Presentation list. To add a slide to the custom show, select the slide and then click the Add button. You can select multiple slides (select the check box for each slide) and click Add to add multiple slides to the custom show. Slides added to the custom show are listed in the Slides In Custom Show list, as shown in Figure 21-5.

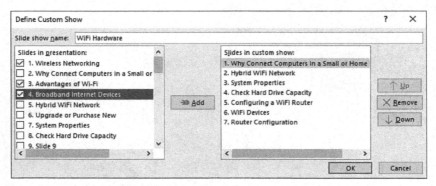

Figure 21-5   Create a custom show in the Define Custom Show dialog box.

When you have specified the slides for the custom show, click in the Slideshow Name text box and type a name for the custom show. To create the custom show and return to the Custom Shows dialog box, click OK. The new custom show is listed in the Custom Shows dialog box.

You can edit a custom show by selecting the show in the Custom Shows dialog box and then clicking Edit. This opens the Define Custom Show dialog box. You can use the Add and/or Remove buttons to add slides to the custom show or remove slides from the show. You can also use the Up and Down arrows to reorder the slides in the Slides in Custom Show list.

The Custom Shows dialog box also enables you to remove a custom show or copy a custom show. Making a copy of a custom show lets you add or remove slides from the copy and specify a new name for the copy. This provides a quick way to repurpose an existing custom show.

When you are finished working in the Custom Shows dialog box, click Close to return to the PowerPoint workspace.

TIP

You can run a custom show as a slideshow from the Custom Shows dialog box. Select the show in the Custom Shows list and then select Show.

The custom show or shows you create for a presentation are listed on the menu that is provided when you select the Custom Slide Show command. To show a custom show as a slideshow, click the custom show's name on the menu. The custom show begins to play. The custom show performs in Slide Show view the same as any other PowerPoint presentation; any settings that you assigned to the slides in the original presentation that are part of the custom show, including animations and transitions, are in force during the showing of the custom show.

Inside OUT

Add more energy to your slide presentations.

PowerPoint provides a new and more dynamic option for quickly navigating to a slide or group of slides during a presentation—Zoom. This feature places a Zoom navigation link on a slide; there are three possibilities: Summary Zoom, Section Zoom, or Slide Zoom:

- Summary Zoom allows you to create a slide or that will show the entire presentation.

- Section Zoom allows you to create a landing slide that will show all the slides in a particular section of a slide presentation.

- Slide Zoom allows you to set up a Zoom slide that will take you to a series of selected slides (or a single slide).

The Zoom feature provides you with another great option for structuring a presentation, including quickly navigating to a series of hidden slides. The Zoom feature can also be useful in creating a start slide for a presentation that makes it easier for people online or people viewing your presentation on their computers to start your presentation.

To take advantage of the Zoom feature, you really need to employ some of the best practices for organizing your PowerPoint presentation that we have discussed in this section of the book. This means you need to use sections in your presentations to group slides that contain related information. Even your hidden slides can be grouped in a section for easy access (rather than having them scattered throughout the presentation).

To create a Zoom slide, insert a new slide in your presentation or navigate to an existing slide that you will use as a navigational landing page. Select the ribbon's Insert tab and then select Zoom. On the Zoom menu, select Summary Zoom, Section Zoom, or Slide Zoom; a dialog box will open that allows you to select the slides or sections that will be accessed using the Zoom type you are creating. If you have sections in your presentation, the Summary Zoom will create a link (using a slide's thumbnail that starts a particular section) for each section. If you use the Section Zoom, you specify which section should be navigated using the Zoom link (which, again, will be represented by a thumbnail of the first slide in that section).

When you select a Zoom link while presenting your slideshow, you will be able to navigate to a single slide, a section, or the beginning of your entire presentation (depending on your Zoom link type). When you have navigated through all the slides that were specified in the Zoom link, you will be taken back to the slide that contains the Zoom link. At that point, you can continue your regular sideshow.

Creating a self-running presentation

A self-running presentation means different things to different people. For example, you might want to create a self-running slideshow that advances each slide after a specified period. However, you plan to provide the narration that accompanies the slides in person. You are configuring the slides with timings because you want to concentrate on your speech instead of changing the slides. This scenario requires that you spend time practicing the presentation so that the slides don't get ahead of you or you don't get ahead of your slides as you deliver the narrative.

Another type of self-running presentation is one that runs at a trade show booth or in a kiosk. A live speaker does not accompany this type of self-running show, so you record the narration that goes with the slides as part of the presentation. Two "viewing" options exist for this unaccompanied self-running show: You can allow a user (such as an interested customer) to browse the presentation interactively (which we discuss in the next section), or you can have the presentation run itself by looping continuously. The Set Up group on the ribbon's Slide Show tab provides the commands that help you add timing to a presentation and also record a slideshow. When you record a slideshow, the timings are set, and narration can also be recorded.

Setting up a slideshow

You can specify settings for a slideshow, including the show type, the slides shown during the slideshow, the selection of a custom show, and other options related to the slideshow, such as how the slides are advanced and whether you want to use the Presenter view (for a presentation given by a speaker). You open the Set Up Show dialog box by selecting the Set Up Slide Show command in the Set Up group. Figure 21-6 shows the Set Up Show dialog box.

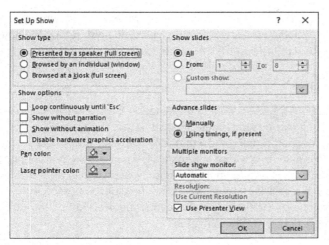

Figure 21-6   The Set Up Show dialog box

Three options are provided in the Show Type area of the dialog box: Presented By A Speaker (Full Screen), Browsed By An Individual (Window), and Browsed At A Kiosk (Full Screen). The default show type is Presented By A Speaker (Full Screen), which assumes that the presentation is designed for a speaker. If you are setting up a self-running show, there are two options. You can specify either the Browsed By An Individual (Window) option or the Browsed At A Kiosk (Full Screen) option.

Show options are also provided in the Set Up Show dialog box and allow you to loop the show continuously, turn off the animation, or turn off any animation in the presentation. When you select Browsed At A Kiosk (Full Screen) as your Show Type, the Loop Continuously Until Esc option is automatically selected. This will keep the presentation running continuously.

If you will be presenting the slides, options are provided for the pen and laser pointer color (hold down the Ctrl key and press the left mouse button during the slideshow to access the laser pointer). The Pen Color option is available only when you are setting up a show that is to be presented by a speaker. Other settings in the Set Up Show dialog box allow you to specify the slides to be shown, or you can choose from a list of custom shows. Also, you can also specify how the slides should be advanced in the presentation. The default setting is Using Timings, If Present. This option makes the best sense for self-running presentations unless you want to include action buttons on slides that allow users to interact with the presentation.

> **TIP**
>
> If you are configuring a slideshow that you plan to present, make sure that the Use Presenter View option is selected. This enables you to see your notes and the next slide in the presentation, helps you stay on top of your presentation, and reduces presentation anxiety.

CHAPTER 21

With the Set Up Show dialog box, you also can specify the monitor to use when you have multiple monitors available (including video projectors). When you finish setting the options for the slideshow, click OK to return to the PowerPoint workspace.

Rehearsing timings

If you want to set the timings for a self-running presentation that do not include narration, you can use the Rehearse Timings command on the Slide Show tab. This scenario works when you want to set the timings for a self-running show that will run in a kiosk or in a case. This scenario also works if you want the slides to advance automatically when you are presenting and narrating the slideshow. Remember, setting up the timings involves moving from slide to slide and timing the animations you set for the various objects on the slides. For example, if you configure entrance animations for objects, particularly bulleted lists, you need to step through the animation to set the appropriate timing for the animation.

TIP

If you want to stop recording, click the Close button on the Recording toolbar. You have the option to save the timings that have been made thus far.

When you are ready to rehearse the timings for the slideshow, select the Rehearse Timings command. The slideshow begins. A Recording toolbar is present in the upper left of the show window.

The toolbar includes a timing counter that times the slideshow. The Recording toolbar also provides a Next button, which works the same as a mouse click to advance to the next slide or step through an animation sequence. A Pause button enables you to pause the timer as needed. If you want to reset the timer for a particular slide and start the timing for that slide over, you can click the Repeat button on the Recording toolbar.

After you select the Rehearse Timings command, the clock is ticking, so be ready. Work through the slides as you give your narration; remember, you are setting up timings for a slideshow you will present in person. When you complete the slideshow, a message box opens and provides the total time for the slideshow. If you want to keep the slide timings for the show, click Yes; click No to dump the timings and try again.

Recording a slideshow

Also, you can record a slideshow that has the timings for the slides and animations and includes recorded narration and laser pointer actions. The Record Slide Show command enables you to record the slideshow from the beginning or from the current slide.

The recording process is similar to the process for rehearsing timings, as discussed in the previous section. The big difference is that you can record audio (meaning your narration) and record your mouse laser pointer actions as if you were giving the slideshow. The recorded show can then be played back as a self-running show. You can use the Set Up Show dialog box to configure the slideshow to loop continuously.

Select the Record Slide Show command and then select Start Recording From Beginning or Start Recording From Current Slide to start the slideshow recording. In both cases, the Record Slide Show window opens, as shown in Figure 21-7. (It is somewhat similar to the Slide Show window.)

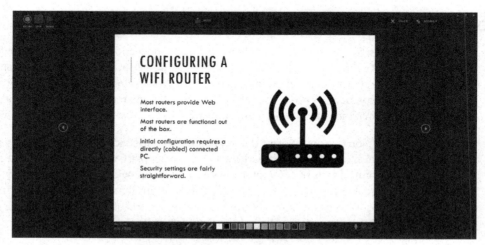

Figure 21-7   The Record Slideshow window

When you are ready to begin recording the slideshow, click the Record button on the Recording toolbar in the upper-left corner of the slideshow window. As already mentioned, you can use it to pause the recording or to restart the recording for the current slide, as needed. You can also access the presentation notes and enter them if you haven't done so already. The Settings drop-down menu in the upper-right corner also allows you to select either a microphone or video camera to record material for the slides in your presentation.

When you have finished recording the timings and adding any notes or media recordings), you will be returned to PowerPoint (the timings are saved automatically, unlike the Rehearse Timings command). The timing for each slide appears to the left and below each slide in the presentation.

You can clear the timing and/or narration for the currently selected slide or all the slides in the presentation. Select the Record Slide Show command and then point at Clear. Choose the appropriate option from the menu provided (such as Clear Timing On Current Slide). If you clear timings and/or narrations on a particular slide, you can then go back to that slide and redo the recording. With the slide selected in the Slide Sorter, select Record Slideshow and then select Start Recording From Current Slide. Click the Start Recording button in the Record Slideshow dialog box.

Record your timing and narration for the slide (including the timing for any animations on the slide). When you finish with that slide, immediately click the Close button on the Recording toolbar to return to the Slide Sorter; the new timing is shown for the slide.

To play your automated slideshow, click the From Beginning button on the Slide Show tab. The slideshow plays using the timings that you set and includes recorded narration (if you recorded the narration).

Creating an interactive presentation

If you are considering creating a slideshow for a trade show booth or some other venue where the audience for the show consists of only one or two people at a time, you might want to allow your audience to control the show instead of creating a self-running show. Obviously, turning over control to your audience is fraught with danger, but you might find that more people are likely to tune in if they can interact with it instead of just passively standing by and watching it.

You can use action buttons to place different controls on the slides, meaning that you place the action button on a slide, and a particular action takes place when it is clicked. Action buttons can perform all sorts of different actions. PowerPoint provides premade controls, including buttons that enable you to go back or forward and buttons that play a movie or a sound. You can also configure a custom action button to meet your particular needs, such as moving to a particular slide in the slideshow, running an application, or running a macro that you have recorded.

> ➤ **For more information about enabling and recording macros, see Appendix B, "Microsoft 365 macros."**

The use of action buttons on slides is certainly not limited to slideshows in which you want to give the audience interactive capabilities. You can use action buttons on slideshows that you present. They can make it convenient for you to go back to a particular slide or open another application as you show your slides.

The action buttons are found in the Shapes library provided by the Shapes gallery on the ribbon's Insert tab. Most of the Shapes gallery is devoted to different shapes that can be added to a slide as graphical elements. Action buttons look like a shape but are also designed to make a particular action happen. To insert an action button, follow these steps:

1. In Normal view, navigate to the slide that will hold the action button.

2. Select the ribbon's Insert tab.

3. Select the Shapes command in the Illustrations group. The Shapes gallery opens, as shown in Figure 21-8.

4. Select an action button from the Action Buttons section of the Shapes gallery (at the bottom of the gallery). The mouse pointer becomes a drawing tool.

5. Drag the drawing tool on the slide to create the action button shape. The Action Settings dialog box appears.

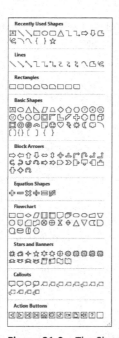

Figure 21-8   The Shapes gallery, including the Action Buttons

6. You can set up the action settings for the action button so that a mouse click or a mouse over activates them. A single action button can do one action on a mouse click and then do a second action on a mouse-over. Select the dialog box tab you want to configure based on how you want the action to be activated (the settings on the Mouse Click and Mouse Over tabs of the dialog box are the same).

7. Specify the action for the action button by using the option buttons on the dialog box tab that you selected.

8. When you finish setting the options for the action button, click OK to return to the slide in Normal view.

NOTE

Action buttons are just like any other shape or object that you place on a slide. You can move them, size them, or delete them.

To test your action button, click the Slide Show shortcut on the status bar to start the slideshow from the current slide. Click the action button to see whether you get the expected results. You can add multiple action buttons to a particular slide, if needed. If you want to set up the same action buttons on all your slides, such as Backward and Forward action buttons for navigation of the slideshow, place the action buttons on the slide master for the presentation.

➤ The slide master is discussed in Chapter 18, "Advanced presentation formatting, themes, and masters." See "Understanding masters" for more information.

Inside OUT

What happened to the Office Presentation Service and Skype?

As the Microsoft 365 applications have evolved over the last decade, features have come and gone. For example, PowerPoint has historically provided two different options for presenting web-based presentations: Skype (for Business) and the Office Presentation Service.

Skype has served as the primary conference calling and meeting software for the Microsoft 365 application suite for a number of years and was first acquired by Microsoft in 2011. Skype for Business provided real-time online meetings and was available to users of Microsoft 365 ProPlus. However, Skype for Business could not be installed as a stand-alone application; it had to be run as part of the application suite. With the introduction of Microsoft Teams, a collaborative meeting platform that also provides the ability to stream PowerPoint presentations to meeting attendees, Skype has become the latest member of the Microsft 365 application suite to be retired. Skype for Business was removed from service on July 31, 2021.

A free option for streaming live presentations via the web was the Office Presentation Service. It was available along with Skype as an option on PowerPoint's Slide Show under the Present Online command. The Office Presentation Service was retired in June 2021.

So, with Skype and the Office Presentation Service no longer available, Microsoft Teams is the go-to solution for online meetings, streaming PowerPoint presentations, and sharing files. Microsoft Teams is the newest member of your Microsoft 365 subscription (depending on your subscription type); if your 365 subscription doesn't include Microsoft Teams, it is also available as a free download. You need a Microsoft Live ID (an Outlook.com email account can serve as a Live ID) to register and download an installation of Microsoft Teams.

Working with the notes and handout masters

Although most of PowerPoint's capabilities are slanted toward creating slideshows, you can create ancillary printed materials from your presentation slides. I'm talking about notes and handouts. Notes are the script that you create to go with the slideshow. Your notes may provide only a few facts or other key points that are not included as actual slide content, or you might create detailed notes for every slide. Your choice depends on the type of presentation you are creating. For example, you might be creating training materials that include a PowerPoint presentation, and you want to include a detailed script for use by the trainers who give the presentation to your employees or clients. Or you might be assembling a presentation about a topic that you can pontificate on for hours, so you might not even need any notes.

Handouts are an ancillary product derived from your presentation slides that you can give to the audience. Handouts can make it easier for your audience to follow the presentation and perhaps use the handout as a convenient place to take notes of their own. You can even print handouts that provide every slide in the presentation. You can determine the number of slides included on each page of the handout, and you can specify a range of one to nine slides per page.

PowerPoint provides masters for both the notes and the handouts. Each master determines the header and footer information to be included in the resulting printout and can be configured to use a particular theme or background style. Their respective master also controls page setup attributes for both the notes and the handouts. You can access the master for either your handouts or your notes on the ribbon's View tab. The Handout Master and Notes Master commands are in the Master Views group.

Setting handout master options

To access the Handout Master, select the Handout Master command on the View tab. The Handout Master tab appears on the ribbon, and the Handout Master opens in the application window, as shown in Figure 21-9.

Figure 21-9   The ribbon's Handout Master tab

You can configure page settings, determine the placeholders on the Handout Master, and set a theme or background for the handouts. The Handout Master tab provides the following groups:

- **Page Setup:** This group provides commands that enable you to set up the handout orientation to either Portrait or Landscape. You can also change the slide size and the number of slides to show on each page. You can select from one to nine slides per page or provide a Slide Outline view of the slides on the page.

- **Placeholders:** This group is a set of check boxes that enable you to determine whether a header or footer appears on the page. Options are also provided for including the date and for numbering pages.

- **Edit Theme:** The choices in the Theme gallery are grayed out. Because the design of the slides printed in the handout depends on the theme you set for the presentation, you won't have access to these commands when working on the Handout Master.

- **Background:** You can fine-tune the colors, fonts, and effects for the currently assigned presentation theme, and you can specify a background for the handout pages by using the Background Styles gallery. You even have the option of hiding any background graphics that appear on the master.

- **Close:** This group provides one command: Close Master View. Click this view when you want to return to Normal view.

Inside OUT

When is the best time to distribute your presentation handouts?

Determining whether you should distribute your presentation handouts before or after the presentation is always difficult. Sometimes handouts can be a distraction, and the audience is more absorbed in reading them than watching your presentation. You have to decide what works best for you. However, here are some reasons for providing handouts before you begin the presentation:

- It is a good idea to provide the audience with paper to take notes. One of my favorite handouts is the 3 Slides Per Page handout because it places blank lines for note-taking next to each slide on the printed page.

- Handouts can help you keep your momentum when presenting. If you provide handouts of the slides, your audience can catch up using the handouts, particularly if they are distracted and/or playing with their cell phones. There is nothing worse than someone holding up his or her hand and asking you to go back to the previous slide.

- The handouts allow the audience to frame more specific questions. Audience members can jot down their notes directly next to the image of a particular slide. This allows you to quickly find the slide they are taking about in the presentation and address their questions in more specific terms.

- Your printout can be your business card. You don't always get to chat with audience members after a presentation. If an audience member wants to know more about the services or products you champion, make sure that you include your email and phone number on the title slide if they want to get in touch with you after the fact. Be advised, if the presentation is not good, you have given your email to an unhappy bunch of people. Again, decide what works best for you and the situation.

For the header and footer text, placeholder text is provided. You can select this text and then replace it as needed to insert header and footer information into the Handout Master. When you finish working with the master, select Close Master View.

Setting notes master options

To access the Notes Master from the View tab, select Notes Master. The Notes Master tab appears on the ribbon. The Notes Master tab provides the same command groups provided by the Handout Master tab.

You can use the Page Setup commands to change the page setup and also to change the page and slide orientation. The Placeholders group has a number of check boxes that enable you to determine what appears in the header and footer areas on the page, such as the date and page number.

Also, you can manipulate the slide and notes text box on the Notes Master. For example, if you want the slide to take up less space on the master, you can select the slide box and resize or move the slide as needed. You can then expand the notes area.

By default, the master text box is configured to include a five-level outline. You can select the text in the master text box and then change it using the various font and paragraph commands available on the Home tab. You can also select the Format tab of the drawing tools (which appears when you select the text box) and change any desired settings. When you finish setting the options for the notes master, click Close Master View on the Notes Master tab.

Printing presentations, notes, and handouts

You can print the slides in your presentation as needed. You can also print your speaker notes and print handouts for your audience. Printing these various items is accomplished from the

PowerPoint Backstage. To access the Backstage, select File on the ribbon. To access the Print window, select Print. The Print window opens, as shown in Figure 21-10.

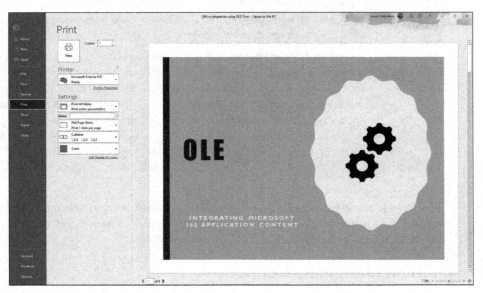

Figure 21-10   The Backstage Print window

You can specify the number of copies you want to print and specify both the printer and its properties for the print job. The Settings area of the window lists the various options related to printing your presentation slides.

By default, all slides will be printed. You can change this setting to print the current slide, or you can specify a custom range in the Slides box. For example, you can specify a range such as 1–23 or specify slides that are not in a range by using commas (for example, 2, 5, 8, and so forth). You also have the option of printing (or not printing) any hidden slides in the presentation.

By default, each slide prints on a separate sheet. Because printing one slide per page is likely the last thing you want to do, changing the Full Page Slides setting makes sense. To change this setting, click the arrow to the right of the Full Page Slides setting. The Print Layout gallery appears.

You can choose among different layouts for the printout. If you want to print your notes, select the Notes Pages layout. An Outline layout also is provided for printing the presentation as an outline.

When printing handouts, you can choose among different layouts that enable you to specify the number of slides printed on each page. You can also select special options related to the printout, such as Frame Slides (a frame prints around each slide), Scale To Fit Paper, and High Quality (which provides a printout of the highest quality your printer can produce).

After you determine the layout for the printout, you can specify whether the printout should print on one or both sides of the paper (if you have a printer that provides this option).

If you print multiple copies of the printout, you can also specify whether the print job should be collated. An orientation drop-down menu enables you to specify the orientation for the printout as well. Portrait is the default, but you can switch to landscape.

You might want to take advantage of one more option, depending on the printer you are using and whether you are going to make grayscale copies of your printout. The Color menu enables you to specify Color, Grayscale, or Pure Black And White for your printout. The Color setting is straightforward; however, there are some differences between the Grayscale and Pure Black and White settings.

There is no difference between the Grayscale and Pure Black And White settings when you print text, fill, lines, clip art, and slide backgrounds. The only differences between these two settings relate to shadows and charts. The Grayscale setting uses grayscale to print these items, whereas the Black And White setting uses black for the shadows and white for charts. In most cases, particularly when you have a laser printer that provides excellent print density, you want to go with a grayscale printout. You can always print a slide page as a test using the Grayscale setting and then apply the Pure Black And White setting to determine the best setting for your particular printer.

When you finish setting the options for your printout, click the Print button in the Print window. Your printout is then sent to your printer.

Exporting a presentation

We've already looked at different ways to show a slideshow and print the content in your PowerPoint presentation. PowerPoint also provides some other options for exporting your presentation file. For example, you can create an Adobe Acrobat (PDF) version of the slide presentation, which makes it easy to email or post your presentation on a website (a PDF also makes it easy to print the entire presentation). Other Export options include creating a video of the presentation and packaging the presentation for a CD.

The PowerPoint Export tools are accessed in the Backstage; select File and then Export. Figure 21-17 shows the Export page in the Backstage. The options available on the Export page are as follows:

- **Create PDF/XPS:** This command creates a PDF or XPS document of your slide presentation. Both file formats preserve the slide layout and formatting (including fonts and images).

- **Create A Video:** This saves your presentation as an MP4 digital video. All timings, narration, and even recorded mouse gestures (such as laser pointer or pen use) are preserved in the video version of the presentation. The video also incorporates your animations, transitions, and any inserted media, such as sound or movie files. You can save the video at different resolutions, which means you can dictate the video's file size (the lower the resolution, the lower the file size).

- **Create an Animated GIF:** As one of the newest export options, the Create an Animated GIF feature allows you to save your presentation as an animated GIF. Animated GIFs (graphics interchange format) have been around since the early days of personal computing. (GIFs were developed for CompuServe in 1987.) A GIF is an image file that contains several images in a single file, so when it is played back, the individual images provide an animated sequence. When you select Create An Animated GIF, you are provided with file size choices (Extra Large to Small). Options are also provided for setting the seconds to spend on each slide and which slides in the presentation to use for the GIF.

- **Package Presentation For CD:** If you want to give someone a complete and working copy of your presentation, or if you want to transport your presentation to another computer, you might want to package the presentation for CD. This process ensures that any linked or embedded items are packaged with the presentation content (linked or embedded items can include videos, sounds, charts from Excel—anything external to the actual PowerPoint presentation file).

- **Create Handouts:** We discussed formatting and printing handouts in the previous section. However, you can create handouts that place your slides and notes in a Word document. You can then format the handouts using Word's powerful layout and formatting features. The Word handouts are configured so that if you make any changes to the slides in the presentation, the handouts are updated to reflect those changes. You can fine-tune the colors, fonts, and effects for the currently assigned presentation theme, and you can specify a background for the handout pages by using the Background Styles gallery.

- **Change File Type:** The Change File Type option enables you to select from a number of different file formats. For example, you can save your presentation in the PowerPoint 97-2003 file format if you need to collaborate with a user of this earlier version of PowerPoint. You can also save your presentation as a PowerPoint picture presentation, with each slide in the presentation represented as a picture. An option is also provided on the Change File Type pane for saving the current presentation as a PowerPoint template.

The Export page provides a range of possibilities for transforming your presentation into a file type that you can easily share with your audience. PowerPoint also provides the Share page in the Backstage, which offers additional options for sharing presentations with collaborators. The Share page also allows you to take advantage of the cloud when publishing and presenting your presentation content. We talk about sharing in the next section.

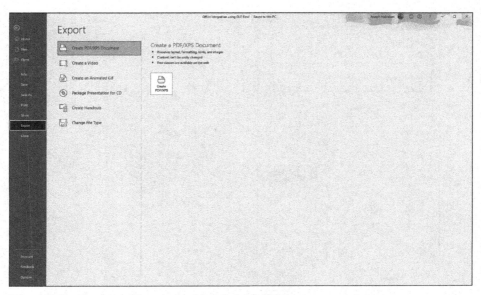

Figure 21-11   The Export Page in the PowerPoint Backstage

Sharing your presentation

You can collaborate with colleagues and coworkers as you build your PowerPoint presentations. Multiple users can edit a PowerPoint presentation in a networking environment that supports the sharing process. You can share presentations on your OneDrive or on a SharePoint server (available if you subscribe to Microsoft 365 or work at a company that hosts a SharePoint site). You can also share a presentation via email as an attachment.

If you want to make the file available to multiple collaborators and work on the same version of the file in real time, the first step is to save your presentation to your personal or business OneDrive (or business SharePoint site). You can do this using the Save As page in the PowerPoint backstage.

Once the file is available on your OneDrive, the quickest way to share the current presentation is to take advantage of the Share button in the upper-right corner of the ribbon. The Share button is always available, no matter which of the ribbon tabs you currently have selected. When you select the Share command, the Send Link dialog box opens, as shown in Figure 21-12. This dialog box allows you to share a link to the file (via recipients' email addresses) and allows you to determine the link settings.

By default, recipients are provided access to the file with editing privileges. You can clear the Allow Editing option box if you do not want to share editing privileges with colleagues who you don't need to edit the presentation,

If you select the Share button and have not saved the file to your OneDrive, you will be asked to save the file to your OneDrive. Once the file is on your OneDrive, you can then share it and send invitations for the presentation.

Figure 21-12   The Send link dialog box

You can also set the link settings for the share. Select the Anyone With The Link Can Edit box. The default setting for the share, Can Edit, allows editing, so if you want a colleague to have view-only status for the share, select the Can View option. Additional settings for the link can be accessed by selecting the Link Settings option. The additional link settings provide you with the option to set an expiration date or password for the link. When you have completed con-figuring the link settings, select Apply. The OneDrive-stored presentation will be accessible by coworkers who receive the share link for the file.

NOTE

When you select the Share command in the PowerPoint Backstage, you will be returned to the PowerPoint application window, and the Send Link dialog box will open. All set-tings related to sharing the current presentation file are set in the Send Link dialog box, including the ability to share a copy of the current presentation.

In the final analysis, even the most well-designed PowerPoint presentation is still, in many situa-tions, going to require that you get up in front of a crowd (even if you present the presentation online via a sharing platform such as Microsoft Teams). Presenting a PowerPoint slideshow to others, particularly in formal settings where you speak in front of a crowd (a crowd that some-times includes your boss), can be exhilarating and exhausting. Make sure you spend as much time practicing the presentation as you do creating and editing it. So, when you have finished sharing, printing, or presenting a slideshow to the best of your ability, please make sure to take some time to celebrate your accomplishment.

PART V

Outlook

CHAPTER 22

Outlook configuration and essential features 669

CHAPTER 23

Managing email in Outlook 701

CHAPTER 24

Using the calendar for appointments and tasks 739

CHAPTER 25

Working with contacts and planning meetings 769

CHAPTER 26

Securing and maintaining Outlook 797

Outlook configuration and essential features

Introducing Outlook   669

Outlook and email accounts   670

Configuring Outlook at first start   673

Understanding Outlook profiles   677

Understanding Outlook data files   681

Importing and exporting data   687

Navigating the Outlook workspace   689

Working with views in Outlook   692

Categorizing Outlook items   695

Searching for Outlook items   696

Printing Outlook items   698

Outlook has long been the communication hub for the Microsoft 365 application suite. The latest iteration of this popular email and contact management application is no different; it gives you the capability to communicate with others and stay organized and productive. Outlook is the tool of choice for sending and receiving emails, scheduling appointments and meetings, and keeping track of your daily tasks.

Much of this chapter is dedicated to configuring Outlook and taking advantage of its basic features. The discussion includes an overview of the Outlook application environment and information on how to organize Outlook items using categories and import/export data.

Introducing Outlook

The newest version of Microsoft Outlook builds on the features found in previous versions of this powerful personal information manager. Outlook continues to be a multifaceted communication application, enabling you to work with and manage many different types of information. Although many of us think of Outlook as our email client, it really is so much more; Outlook enables you to create and manage a number of different items, such as emails, appointments, meetings, tasks, and contacts.

Although some of the Outlook updates are on the subtle side (and we will discuss these in their proper turn throughout the Outlook section of this book), there are also some changes of note. For example, the Read Aloud command (on the Home tab of the Outlook ribbon) can read aloud a selected message. This feature allows you to sit back for a moment and listen, which is a nice respite from staring at the computer screen.

Another new feature is the Translator for Outlook, which can be activated using the Translate command on the Outlook ribbon's Home tab. The Translator can be used to translate a message into your choice of languages. The translation appears side by side with the original email and in its original language. We will explore the setup and use of the Translator in Chapter 23, "Managing email in Outlook."

A new feature that has been added to other members of the 365 application suite, including Word and Excel, is access to a huge library of stock images. These images can be used to add visual interest to your Outlook emails. The great thing about the stock images is that Microsoft curates them, so you don't have to worry about copyright or other issues related to using images you scavenge from the web. Because one of Outlook's primary duties is email management, let's begin our discussion of some of the functions and features of Outlook with a look at the different types of email accounts you can configure in this powerful email client.

TIP

As you consult the Outlook chapters in this book, you will find—as you will with all updates of the Microsoft 365 application suite—some new Outlook enhancements will be obvious to you. And you'll find that other improvements will be less transparent, under-the-hood tweaks that provide you with better application performance.

Outlook and email accounts

Outlook supports different types of email accounts. You can use Outlook as your email client on any of the following:

- An internet email account from your internet service provider

- A web-based email account such as Microsoft's Outlook.com

- A Microsoft Exchange mail account hosted by an Exchange server on your corporate network, which is now referred to as an Exchange ActiveSync account

Also, you can take advantage of Outlook email on smartphones and other "smart" devices. In fact, you can also configure Outlook to manage multiple (and different types of) email accounts at the same time on the same device. But let's take a step back for a moment and talk about how your Outlook email client actually gets configured with your email account and password.

There are really only two scenarios related to the installation and configuration of the Microsoft 365 application suite:

- One scenario assumes that your IT department (at your workplace) has installed and configured the 365 apps that you need to get your job done.

- In the other scenario—a home or small business 365 installation—you are going to install and configure your 365 installation, including Outlook.

If you work in a corporate environment, your IT folks installed your 365 suite apps and configured Outlook with your email credentials. This means you are ready to send and receive email.

If you are installing and configuring Microsoft 365 (including Outlook) on your home or small business computer, there are a couple of things you need to know about before installing the 365 suite.

First, remember that you only need to configure one email address to get Outlook up and running. You are certainly not limited to a single email address when you use Outlook. You can easily add email addresses even after configuring the initial email account when you first ran Outlook. We discuss adding (and removing) email accounts in Chapter 23.

TIP

If you are signing into a work or school installation of Outlook that has not been configured, you will need to enter your company's or institution's email address and password. This will serve as the sign-in information that Outlook needs to get up and running to send and receive email. If you also want to include an additional email account (or two), you can add those accounts once you get Outlook up and running.

Another important point related to Outlook and email accounts is that when you add an email account, you are adding a service. Outlook supports different kinds of email accounts services. There are several possibilities in terms of email account types such as Office 365, POP, and Google that can be configured in Outlook. Let's take a quick look at the different types of email accounts that Outlook can provide. We will begin our discussion with a look at Exchange Server email accounts. We can return to the process of setting up your initial email account in Outlook.

Exchange ActiveSync

No one would deny that Outlook was originally conceived as the client software for Exchange Server accounts. And Outlook really shines when you are connected to an Exchange ActiveSync Server (which is the server software that hosts the email accounts, shared calendars, and other Outlook features in a networked environment); you can easily share calendars, tasks, meetings, and all sorts of information with other Exchange users.

If you are using Outlook on a corporate network that takes advantage of Exchange ActiveSync, the network administrator typically sets up your account on your computer (this also establishes your profile for you). The name of the Exchange Server and your network username are required to complete the configuration. An Exchange network provides several email features that are not available when you use Outlook for Internet email (such as a POP3 account from your ISP). These features include the capability to redirect email replies, set message expirations, and even grant privileges to other users, who can then monitor your email, calendar, contacts, and tasks (just to name a few possibilities). If you don't work for a large corporation or institution that has its own Exchange servers, your access to Outlook email and calendar features will be determined by the Office 365 version you subscribe to. If you are subscribing to any of the Office 365 Business or Office 365 Enterprise packages, the email accounts provided as part of these subscriptions supply you with all the email and scheduling features that are available to an Exchange ActiveSync account. If you subscribe to Office 365 Personal or Office 365 home, your email account will be an Outlook.com account that does not provide all the bells and whistles associated with an Exchange ActiveSync account. This doesn't mean that you can't take advantage of most of Outlook's email and calendar features; however, some of the collaboration features Outlook provides aren't available.

Outlook.com email

You can also use Microsoft's free Outlook.com email with Microsoft Outlook. Outlook can automatically configure your Outlook.com email account; you simply need to provide the email account username and password. Setting up access to your Outlook.com email account from within Outlook is no big deal. In fact, Outlook makes it easier to add your Outlook.com and Exchange ActiveSync accounts than it does POP or IMAP email accounts, which certainly was not the case in past versions of Outlook.

Adding a personal email account to your Outlook configuration, along with an Exchange business account, actually allows you to keep your personal and professional emails sequestered in different Outlook inboxes. This allows you to work with personal email more quickly rather than opening your Outlook.com email account in a separate web browser window.

Internet email

Nearly all of us use an internet service provider (ISP) for our home or small business internet connections. The ISP also typically gives you email accounts, such as *yourname@provider-name*.com. Most providers supply you with multiple accounts, and you can configure the email account names (the domain name, such as brighthouse.com or Comcast.net, will be determined by your provider). Internet email accounts can use one of two different types of email-retrieval systems. These email types are based on the protocol used by the email server: POP3 (Post Office Protocol version 3) or IMAP (Internet Message Access Protocol). Outlook supports both mail-retrieval protocols.

POP3 has been the standard protocol for Internet email for years, and ISPs typically use POP3 on their mail servers. A POP3 email server really functions as a mail drop, meaning that your email is forwarded to the POP3 server and sits there until you connect with your email client (Outlook) and download the email to your computer. The great thing about POP3 accounts (at least, for ISPs) is that you download your email from their server. This means that you get it off their server, and they don't have to store it for you.

If you are using a POP3 account, the Post Office Protocol handles only the receive part of the send-and-receive process for your email. Your ISP also provides an SMTP (Simple Mail Transport Protocol) server. This server handles the email that you send from Outlook, over the internet, to a final destination. Typically, that destination is the POP3 server that serves as the mail drop for the person to whom you are sending the internet email.

IMAP is a protocol that allows an email client to download email from an IMAP mail server. IMAP differs from POP3 in that connecting to the server with your email client (Outlook) does not remove your email from the mail server. Instead, you receive a list of saved and new messages, which you can then open and read. However, you can delete messages from the IMAP server.

IMAP is particularly useful when you access one email account on more than one computer or another device (such as a mobile phone or other smart device). Because the email is not downloaded to the email client as POP3 email is, you can access it on the IMAP server as needed from different devices. Examples of IMAP-based email systems are Google Mail and Yahoo! Mail.

We typically interact with these email accounts using a web browser; however, Outlook's capabilities as an email manager might make it worthwhile to add your Google account (or other IMAP account) to Outlook's configuration. Obviously, having an email client such as Outlook that can access and manage internet email accounts using either POP3 or IMAP provides you with a single resource for managing multiple and different types of email accounts.

TIP

When you add a new email account to Outlook, Outlook can attempt to configure the email account settings (such as the incoming and outgoing mail servers) purely based on the email account that you provide. Sometimes this works, and sometimes it doesn't.

Configuring Outlook at first start

CHAPTER 22

When you run Outlook for the first time, it walks you through the configuration of your email account. When configuring your email account, Outlook also creates a profile that contains your email account information, the location of your data files, and the location where your emails reside. We discuss Outlook profiles in the next section, but it should be made clear that the profile created is closely associated with the first email account you create in Outlook. So, if you use Outlook primarily as an Exchange Server client, configure your Exchange email account as the initial account in Outlook. If you only use Outlook as an internet email client, configure Outlook at first start for internet email. Be advised that in most cases—particularly if you work for a corporation or institution—your Outlook configuration has already been set up for you by IT techs. So, when you start Outlook for the first time, it might take you right to your inbox.

Inside OUT

For home and small business installations, create a new Outlook.com email.

If you are configuring Outlook yourself, it might be a good idea to sign up for an Outlook.com email (which also provides you with free access to OneDrive) and use it as both your credentials for your purchase of the 365 suite and the initial installation of Outlook. Outlook.com email accounts are similar to corporate Exchange Server accounts. Because you must have an Outlook.com email for OneDrive, and you should create an Outlook.com account to purchase your Microsoft 365 software download, you might as well use the email for your Outlook configuration as well. This is particularly true because the account is required to activate your installation of Outlook and the other 365 apps. You can then add any other email accounts—such as your internet email accounts—to Outlook once it is up and running.

For those of you who are configuring your own Outlook clients, start Microsoft Outlook, and the Sign In To Set Up Office window will open, as shown in Figure 22-1. You have two options at this point: Sign In or Create Account. The Sign In option allows you to enter an existing email address. The Create Account option allows you to create an Outlook.com email account on the fly. This might seem like a good idea, but it isn't. The email account you add to the "new" installation of Outlook needs to be credentialed to activate the installation. That is why it makes sense to use the Outlook.com email that you used when you purchased your 365 subscription.

Select Sign In as your option to set up Outlook. You are taken to the Activate Office screen. Enter your email address in the box and then select Next. The next screen asks for your email password; enter the password and select Next. The email account will be added to your Outlook account information, and you can begin to send and receive emails.

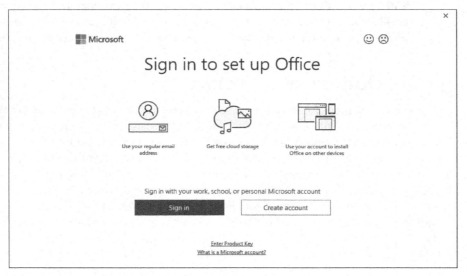

Figure 22-1   The Sign In To Set Up Office window

Adding email accounts to Outlook

After configuring an initial email account, you can begin to use Outlook. However, as you use Outlook, you might find that you want to add another email account to the Outlook configuration. To add a new email account to Outlook, select File on the ribbon. In the Backstage, select the Info page (if not already selected) and then select the Add Account button (just below your Account information).

You will be returned to the Outlook application window, and Outlook will do a quick search for any email addresses it can find on the computer. While the search is going on, the Outlook box will open, as shown in Figure 22-2.

Email address

Email address

Advanced options ⌃
☐ Let me set up my account manually

Connect

No account?   Create an Outlook.com email address to get started.

Figure 22-2   The Outlook Add Email window

Type the email address in the Email Address box, and then select Connect. A Security box will open requesting the password for the email account. Enter the password and select OK. When the process is complete, select OK to return to the Outlook application window. You will need to restart Outlook before the new email address will be added to the configuration.

In some cases, Outlook might have trouble configuring an email account. (This happens with POP accounts sometimes.) If this happens, you can manually enter the account information. Make sure that the email address is entered correctly in the Email Address box, and then click the Advanced Options link. You can then select the Let Me Set Up My Account Manually check box. Select Connect to continue. The Outlook Advanced Setup dialog box will open. This option allows you to choose the email account type and is shown in Figure 22-3.

CHAPTER 22

Figure 22-3   The Outlook Advanced Setup dialog box

The Outlook Advanced Setup window allows you to choose the type of account you want to install. The options provided are as follows:

- **Microsoft 365:** An account type provided to Office 365 subscribers. It is similar to an Exchange account in that it provides corporate Office 365 subscribers an email environment similar to those hosted on a network using Exchange Server.

- **Outlook.com:** An account type for the free Microsoft email and ID account. It is the successor to Hotmail. It functions similarly to an IMAP account, although it can be configured as either a POP or IMAP account. It also can function as an ActiveSync Exchange client for some Microsoft services.

- **Exchange:** This account type is an email account based on services provided by a Microsoft Exchange server.

- **Google:** This account type provides Google email services and is similar to an IMAP account and can be configured as a POP or IMAP email account. It can also be used to log onto other Google services.

- **POP:** The old standby for Internet email, this email type uses POP (Post Office Protocol) and SMTP (Simple Mail Transport Protocol) to move email to and from your email client respectively.

- **IMAP:** This account type uses IMAP (Internet Message Access Protocol) to access email on a server. IMAP leaves the emails on the server (as opposed to POP, which removes them) so that you can access your email from different devices.

- **Exchange 2013 or earlier:** Yes, there is some enterprise computing going on out there that is running on older versions of Exchange. This option provides legacy support for companies still running Exchange 2013 or earlier installations.

Select an account type such as POP. Figure 22-4 shows the POP Account Settings window. It requires that you supply user, server, and log-in information to configure the account.

Figure 22-4   You can manually configure your Internet email account, such as a POP account.

In the case of a POP account, you enter the incoming mail server address, connection settings, and authentication settings, as well as the SMTP server (outgoing server) in the appropriate boxes. Then you select Next. After the account has been set up, you can select Connect, and the account will be added to your Outlook configuration.

Understanding Outlook profiles

Outlook creates an Outlook profile upon initial startup when you configure an email account in Outlook. That profile is then loaded every time you start Outlook. It provides information to Outlook related to your email account (or accounts) configuration. You actually can use different types of email accounts in Outlook and have only one Outlook profile. However, multiple profiles can help sequester settings for different types of email accounts in their own related profiles.

So, if you have an email account configured in Outlook, you have an Outlook profile. An email profile comprises email accounts, data files, and information about where your email is stored. Outlook automatically creates a new profile when you run Outlook for the first time. After that, the profile is loaded every time you start Outlook.

Most users need only a single profile, even when you have configured Outlook for multiple email accounts. However, you might find it advantageous to create more than one profile for yourself. This allows you to have one profile related to your internet email account—meaning your personal email—and another profile for your Exchange email account. This is useful when you want to use Outlook on your home computer for internet email, but you can also connect to your Exchange server and network via a secure connection (such as a virtual private network connection over the internet) and check your Exchange email as well. The different profiles keep the two types of email accounts separate and sequestered. However, having more than one email account doesn't mean you have to create more than one profile in Outlook. Each email account will have its own inbox and other related mailboxes, such as folders for your sent and received emails. Remember that you have the option of creating multiple profiles, but you don't have to. If you work in a company or institution of any size, I would suggest you not worry about your Outlook profile because your IT department will have set it up along with your email account.

Creating a new profile

As already mentioned in this chapter, as soon as you configure an email account in Outlook, you also create a profile. If you need to create a new profile or manage existing profiles, you use the Mail Setup dialog box, which you access via the Windows Control Panel.

CAUTION

Be very careful working with your Outlook profile. You can view it, but don't try to change it unless you have a compelling reason. Inadvertently damaging or deleting the Outlook profile will play havoc with your Outlook configuration.

In Windows, the fastest way to get to the Control Panel, which houses the user accounts settings, is to press the Windows+R, which opens the Run box. Type **control panel** in the box and press OK. The Control Panel window will open. In the Control Panel, select User Accounts. In the User Accounts pane, select Mail (Microsoft Outlook). The Mail Setup dialog box opens, as shown in Figure 22-5.

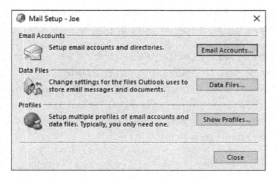

Figure 22-5   The Mail Setup dialog box

The Mail Setup dialog box enables you to manipulate Outlook settings without being in Outlook. You can create email accounts, change data file settings, and also create and manage profiles. You can't create a profile from within Outlook, so, you do it outside Outlook.

To create a new profile, follow these steps:

1. In the Mail Setup dialog box, click Show Profiles. The Mail dialog box opens with the General tab selected (it is the only tab).

2. Select Add. The New Profile dialog box opens.

3. Type a name for the new profile, and then click OK.

As soon as you click OK, the Add New Account window opens. This is the same tool that opens at Outlook's first start, as discussed in the previous section. To summarize that discussion: You can enter your name, email address, and password, and then Outlook attempts to connect with your mail server and automatically configure your account. Alternatively, you can manually configure the server settings for the account.

When you click Finish on the last screen of the Add New Account process (after configuring the email account), you return to the Mail dialog box. The dialog box lists your new profile.

Managing profiles

The Mail dialog box not only lists the profiles set up on your computer, but it also gives you the capability to manage them. If you no longer need it, select the profile and then click Remove.

You can also edit the properties of a profile. In editing the properties of a profile, you have two possibilities: the email accounts associated with the profile and the data files used to store Outlook items. Select a profile in the Mail dialog box, and then select Properties. This opens the Mail Setup dialog box for the selected profile. This is not the same as the Mail Setup dialog box shown in Figure 22-5, though they do look a lot alike. This Mail Setup dialog box is specific to one of your mail profiles and will show the name of that specific profile.

If you want to change the email account settings in the profile, click the Email Accounts button. This opens the Account Settings dialog box. This dialog box can also be accessed directly from Outlook via the Backstage Info window (select Account Settings) and provides many Outlook settings. For example, you can edit data file settings on the Data Files tab. You can also edit other settings, including the RSS feeds, calendars, and address books. Figure 22-6 shows the Account Settings dialog box with the Email tab selected.

When changing the email settings for the current profile, you can add an email account, repair an existing email account, or remove an account. You also can change the folder the account uses when new messages arrive.

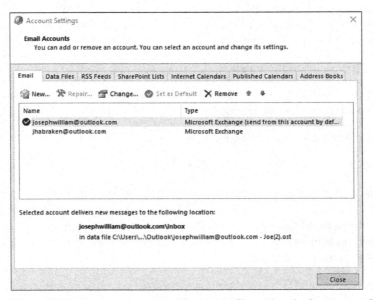

Figure 22-6   You can change email and data file settings in the Account Settings dialog box.

The Data Files tab of the Account Settings dialog box enables you to view the location of the Outlook data files associated with the current profile. We discuss managing Outlook data files in the next section, "Understanding Outlook data files." When you click Close in the Account Settings dialog box, you return to the Mail Setup dialog box. Click the Close button again, and you return to the Mail dialog box and your list of profiles.

Because you can manage both the email accounts and data files from inside Outlook, we work with these different settings in the appropriate context in other chapters found in the Outlook section of this book. However, it is important to understand that you can access profile-related setting issues via the Mail dialog box, which you reach using the Windows Control Panel. In some situations, you have to change settings related to a profile from the Mail dialog box.

For example, adding or deleting an Exchange Server account from within Outlook while Outlook is running can be a problem. (This relates to the fact that Outlook is currently using your default profile and data file to operate.) You might find that adding or deleting email accounts by accessing the Account Settings dialog box via the Control Panel is less problematic than attempting to do it from "inside" Outlook.

Loading profiles

The Mail dialog box (select Mail when you are in the User Accounts And Family Safety Control Panel window to open it) provides option buttons related to loading profiles. Look for the When Starting Microsoft Outlook, Use This Profile statement in the lower part of the Mail dialog box. You have two options:

- **Prompt For A Profile To Be Used:** If you select this option button, a Choose Profile dialog box opens when you start Outlook, enabling you to select the profile that will be loaded from a drop-down menu. This is useful if you have multiple profiles for different types of email accounts—say, internet email versus Exchange Server email. This setting is necessary when multiple users access their Outlook email accounts on the same computer. The user can select their specific profile.

- **Always Use This Profile:** Select this option if you want to specify a default profile to be loaded when Outlook starts. Use the drop-down menu to select the profile name.

Whether you need to deal with multiple profiles and profile settings depends on your particular work environment. If you are a home or small business user, you might need to create and manage Outlook profiles. In corporate network environments, particularly those that use an Exchange Server for email accounts, a network administrator takes care of email account configurations and profile settings. So even though you might feel empowered after reading this material on profiles, I recommend that you leave the profile and email settings completely alone unless you determine that you really need to create and control multiple profiles.

Understanding Outlook data files

When you work in Outlook, you manage and manipulate different types of items, such as email, appointments, contacts, and tasks. These different items have their own homes in Outlook. For example, new email messages are in the Inbox, whereas the To Do list displays tasks. You might find it odd to learn that these different Outlook items are stored in a single Outlook data file. In fact, all your Outlook items are contained in this single data file. POP accounts use a container referred to as a personal storage folder or .pst file. IMAP accounts use a storage folder, which is referred to as Offline Store files or .ost files. These storage folders are essential to Outlook's operation and your access to your emails, appointments, tasks, and meetings.

The storage folder is actually created when you create your Outlook profile and configure Outlook with a POP3 or IMAP email account. The .pst or .ost file is actually stored on your computer. Outlook stores its data differently when it serves as an Exchange Server client or for web-based email such as Outlook.com. That data file is actually kept on the Exchange mail server and made available to you when you log on to the mail server.

Let's assume that you configured the first email account on Outlook as a POP3 account. As already mentioned, when you configure the first email account for Outlook, it creates the default profile and your Outlook personal storage file, or .pst data file. By default, the profile's name is Outlook. The data file's name is *your email account*.pst, meaning that the .pst file is named after the first email account you configured in Outlook. The .pst file is often referred to as "the personal folders file."

When you consider how important the personal folders file is to Outlook and to you (in terms of all those emails that you have in Outlook), you understand that, in most cases, you should not play around with this file. That's not to say that you shouldn't back up the personal folders file, which we discuss in a moment. But you should have a compelling reason for other manipulations of the personal folders file, such as changing the file's location or renaming the file—both of which you can do.

Configuring Outlook for Microsoft Exchange Server

Configuring Outlook as an email client for Microsoft Exchange Server does not create a personal folders file. In the Exchange Server environment, your email and other items are stored on the server running Exchange Server. Outlook does create a local data file, however, so you can use your Exchange account offline. This data file has the extension .ost; it contains a copy of the items stored on the Exchange server. This file is referred to as the offline Outlook data file. Microsoft's Outlook.com email service (formerly Hotmail) also uses a data file with the .ost extension. This is because a copy of your email folders (such as emails, contacts, and the calendar) is also stored on Microsoft's server. The offline Outlook data file just provides you with a copy of your personal files.

To view the default personal folders file (.pst) or the offline Outlook data file (.ost), or both, select the Outlook ribbon's File tab to access the Outlook Backstage. Select Info and then select the Account Settings button. Select Account Settings on the menu to open the Account Settings dialog box.

The Account Settings dialog box opens to the Email tab by default. Select an email account from the Settings list, and the Outlook data file for that account (either a .pst or an .ost file) appears in the lower pane of the dialog box. You can select the Data Files tab to view the Outlook data files associated with the current Outlook profile. Figure 22-7 shows the Accounts Settings dialog box with the Data Files tab selected. Two email accounts are associated with the profile. One is an Outlook.com email (with an .ost file), and the other is an internet email account (with a .pst file).

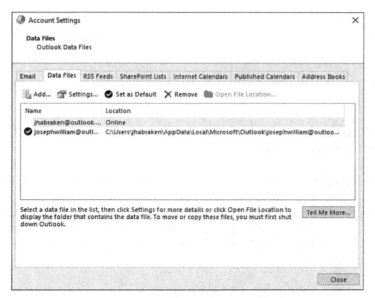

Figure 22-7   You can view the data files associated with the current profile.

The type of data files shown in the Account Settings dialog box depends on your type of configured email accounts. Any POP3 account has an associated personal folders file, and an Exchange account has an offline Outlook data file.

The Account Settings dialog box enables you to change the default data file for the Outlook profile. You can also open the file location for a selected data file. In addition, you can use the Remove command to remove an unneeded data file.

You can view the settings for a personal folders file or an offline Outlook data file. Select the data file in the list, and then select Settings on the Account Settings toolbar. This opens the Outlook Data File dialog box.

> **NOTE**
>
> Depending on how Outlook was initially configured (and by whom), your profile might not be named Outlook. The name of your personal folders file might also vary. Remember, it has the extension .pst or .ost (depending on the type of email you use), no matter what the name is.

For personal folders files, the Outlook Data File dialog box provides the alias or name of the data file and the file name and path for the data file. You have two options related to a personal folders file. You can use the Change Password button to assign a password to the Outlook data file; if you want to reduce the size of your Outlook data file (they can become quite large when

CHAPTER 22

you have a lot of Outlook items), you can take advantage of the Compact Now button. The act of compaction also removes dead space created when items are deleted.

This is useful if multiple users share the same computer. You can also use the Compact Now button to compact the data file. This reduces the size of the file.

NOTE

When you add an Outlook.com email account to Outlook, an offline Outlook data file is also created on your computer.

If you open the settings for an offline Outlook data file (.ost) associated with your Exchange Server account, the Microsoft Exchange dialog box opens. This dialog box provides four different tabs of settings. Remember that your network administrator probably configured your Exchange server account for you; I do not recommend changing any of the settings provided by the Microsoft Exchange dialog box. Consider the following explanation of the dialog box tabs to be purely informational:

- **General:** This tab specifies the name of the Exchange Server and the account mailbox name.

- **Advanced:** This tab enables you to add mailboxes that should be open when Outlook connects to the Exchange Server. You also have the option of using the cached Exchange mode (which places the .ost file on your computer) so that you can work offline. The default setting enables the cached Exchange mode.

- **Security:** This tab provides options related to encryption and user identification. By default, Outlook and Microsoft Exchange trade encrypted data. You can also choose to have user identification required at logon. The type of authentication used is another selection you can make on this tab.

- **Connection:** This tab enables you to select the connection type that you use to reconnect to Exchange when you have been working offline. You can connect to Exchange via your local area network or phone line, or via HTTP by using Outlook Anywhere.

When you close either the Outlook Data File dialog box or the Microsoft Exchange dialog box, you return to the Account Settings dialog box. Click Close to close this dialog box and return to the Outlook application window.

Creating personal folders files

Outlook gives you the capability to create new personal folders files. This can be useful if you want to create a personal folders file for a particular project and then place items from your current Outlook Inbox or other email folders into the new personal folders file. This removes the emails from your default personal folders file and cleans up your Outlook folders. It also creates an archive of the project. Obviously, if you have used earlier versions of Outlook, you are already aware of Outlook's capability to archive older emails. So, if you are good about archiving Outlook items, you might not feel a huge need to be moving things into secondary .pst files that you create. Think of the use of secondary .pst files as a potential convenience, not something that you have to do.

> ➤ Outlook enables you to archive old email messages and items. Outlook saves these items in another personal folders file. See Chapter 27, "Securing and maintaining Outlook," for more information.

You can create a new Outlook personal folders file from the Account Settings dialog box (with the Data Files tab selected) or the Outlook application window. From the Outlook window, follow these steps:

1. Select the ribbon's Home tab.

2. Select the New Items command in the New group.

3. Point at More Items and select Outlook Data File. The Create Or Open Outlook Data File dialog box opens.

4. The Data File dialog box shows the default Outlook data file and any other created data files. Type a name for a new data file in the File Name box and then click OK.

The new data file appears in the Outlook Navigation pane below your email account's Inbox and other mail folders. You can create folders in the new data file and then copy or move email messages to the data file. You can use the secondary data file to back up specific items or to group items related to a specific project that you no longer need to keep in your current inbox or other folders.

Repairing Outlook data files

Personal folders files can become damaged or corrupt. A sure sign that your default personal folders file is corrupt is that Outlook cannot open it when you start Outlook.

You can use the inbox repair tool (scanpst.exe) to try to correct problems with a personal folders file. You must exit Outlook to run the tool.

Exit Outlook and then open the Windows File Explorer. (Open it via the Taskbar icon on the Windows Desktop or select File Explorer on the Start page after right-clicking and selecting All Apps.) To locate the `scanpst.exe` program file, click the Search box to open the Search Tools in File Explorer. Make sure you select PC before you enter the search term **scanpst.exe**. The results of the search should list the `scanpst` program. Double-click `scanpst` in the search results. The Microsoft Outlook Inbox Repair Tool dialog box opens. In the Enter The Name Of The File You Want To Scan box, your Outlook .ost profile file should be listed, as shown in Figure 22-8.

If the data file you want to repair is not listed, you can enter the name of the file you want to scan or use the Browse button to locate the file. The default folder for your personal folders file is Documents\Outlook Files. If you browse for it and can't find it, search for an .ost file type. Once you have the correct file name in the Microsoft Outlook Inbox Repair Tool dialog box, you can click the Start button. The Inbox Repair tool checks the file, and a message box opens, letting you know the level of the problems identified during the scan.

You can have the Inbox Repair tool make a backup copy of the file before repairing it. This is the default setting and a good idea, particularly if the repair process further damages an already corrupted file. The Inbox Repair tool places the backup copy in your Outlook Files folder with the extension .bak.

Click the Repair button, and the Inbox Repair tool attempts to repair the file. When the process is complete, the Repair Complete message appears; click OK to close it. You can now open Outlook with the repaired .pst file.

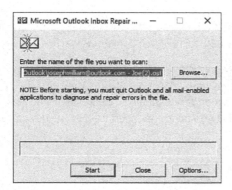

Figure 22-8   Use the Inbox Repair tool on damaged personal folders files.

If the Inbox Repair tool recovered folders and items, a Lost And Found folder in your folder list (in the Navigation pane) displays. At this point, you should probably create a new Outlook personal files folder (using the method we discussed in the previous section). Drag the items in the Lost and Found folder to the new .pst file. You can also drag additional items to the new personal folders file and then make the new .pst file the default personal folders file for Outlook by using the Accounts Settings dialog box (accessed via the Backstage). Restart Outlook, and it loads the new .pst file. You can delete the old personal folders file using the Account Settings dialog box.

Importing and exporting data

You can import and export information to and from Outlook. The types of information that can be imported include mail account settings, internet email, addresses, calendars (.ics and .vcs), and Outlook personal folders files (.pst). For example, you might be migrating from another personal information manager or email client to Outlook and want to import your address book or contacts list; Outlook can import this type of information in a number of different file formats, including comma-separated values (.csv) and vCards (.vcf).

> TIP
>
> **You can quickly import your entire contact list or specific groups of contacts from Google Mail to Outlook. Select Contacts in the Gmail window and then click the More button. On the More menu, click Export. You need to export the contacts to a CSV file (the actual export file type in Gmail is Outlook CSV) for import into Outlook or another application. When you have the CSV file, you can import it into Outlook using the Import And Export Wizard.**

You might also need to export data from Outlook to another application. You can export Outlook data to Excel and Access, potentially in several different file types, including comma-separated values, tab-separated files, and Outlook data files (.pst).

The Backstage Open window handles both the import and export of data. This is where you can access the Open Calendar command to open a calendar file and access the Import And Export Wizard, which takes care of both the import and export of a number of different data types.

Importing data

To import data into Outlook, open the Backstage by selecting File on the Outlook ribbon. Then select Open & Export. The Open window provides you with several commands. The Open Calendar command enables you to open a calendar file in Outlook, such as an exported iCalendar or Gmail calendar. To use the command, select Open Calendar. The Open Calendar dialog box opens. Navigate to the path that contains the calendar file and then click OK. The calendar is added to your My Calendars list under Other Calendars.

The Open Outlook Data File command enables you to open any Outlook .pst file. The folders and other data provided by an Outlook data file are added to your Outlook configuration when you open the data file.

The Import/Export command opens the Import And Export Wizard, which we look at in a moment. The Open command set is rounded out by the Other User's Folder command, which enables you to open an Outlook folder such as a Contacts folder when another user has shared it. This feature is limited to when you are working with Exchange email.

CHAPTER 22

If you want to import contacts or emails, use the Import/Export command, which opens the Import And Export Wizard. Follow these steps:

1.   Select Import/Export. The Import And Export Wizard opens (see Figure 22-9).

2.   Select the type of data you want to import (such as a vCard file or iCalendar file) or select Import From Another Program Or File for a data type not shown (for example, a comma-separated file exported from another program such as Excel). Then click Next.

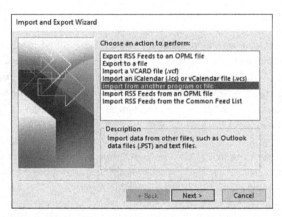

Figure 22-9   The Import And Export Wizard

3.   On the next wizard screen, select the file type to import; then select Next.

4.   On the next wizard screen, use the Browse button to select the file to import. You can also select options related to the import, such as Replace Duplicates With Items Imported, Allow Duplicates To Be Created, and Do Not Import Duplicate Items. Click Next.

5.   On the next screen, select the destination folder, such as Calendar or Contacts. Then click Next.

6.   The next screen lists the file to be imported and the folder that Outlook imports it into. At this point, you can choose to map custom fields. This enables you to match the field names used in the import file with those used in Outlook, such as those used in the Contacts folder. Select Map Custom Fields.

7.   (Optional) Drag the field names from the source file on the left of the Map Custom Fields box to the Outlook field names on the right (see Figure 22-10). When you have finished mapping the fields, click OK.

8.   Click Finish.

NOTE

The steps involved in exporting data from Outlook are similar to the steps for importing data. You specify the file type, the Outlook folder involved, and the location of the file to be created during the export.

Outlook places the imported data in the Outlook folder that you selected during the import procedure. For example, if you imported contacts, select Contacts in the Navigation pane to display the imported contacts.

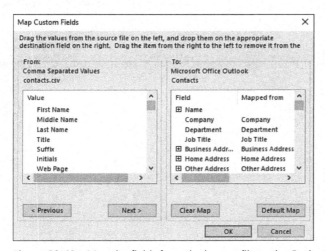

Figure 22-10   Map the fields from the import file to the Outlook fields.

Exporting data

You can also use the Import And Export Wizard to export Outlook data into a variety of file formats. Open the Import And Export Wizard from the Backstage Open window (select Import/ Export). On the first wizard screen, select Export To A File and then click Next.

On the next wizard screen, you can select the file format for the export. File types include tab- and comma-separated values. You can also export to Access and Excel file formats or export the data as an Outlook data file. When you have selected the export file type, all you have to do is select the Outlook folder containing the data you want to export. Specify an export file name and a location, and you can then export the data.

Navigating the Outlook workspace

Outlook is all about accessing and managing different types of items, so the Outlook application window makes it easy for you to access and manage your emails, calendar, contacts, and tasks. Figure 22-11 shows the default Outlook application window, with Mail currently selected in the navigation bar.

The various parts of the Outlook application window are as follows:

- **Folder pane:** The Folder pane enables you to navigate individual folders related to the currently selected Outlook item such as Mail (email), Calendar, or People (contacts). The Folder pane also provides a customizable area (at the top); you can drag your favorite folders to this area so that you have access to them no matter what Outlook items you currently have selected. If necessary, you can also minimize (hide) the Folder pane; select the Minimize Folder Pane arrow at the top of the pane.

Figure 22-11   Outlook gives you easy access to your email and other items.

- **Navigation bar:** The Navigation bar is a horizontal element near the bottom of the Outlook application window, and it serves as the main navigational tool for Outlook. A link to each of the Outlook items—Mail, Calendar, People, and Tasks—is easily accessible.

- **Reading pane:** The Reading pane enables you to view (and read) the currently selected email or task.

- **Details pane:** The Details pane provides a list of available items in a folder, such as your emails or tasks.

- **To Do bar:** The To Do bar provides a calendar and a list of appointments for the currently selected date (which, by default, is the current date). The To Do bar also provides a list of tasks for the day and enables you to add new tasks quickly. The To Do bar is off by default.

- **People pane:** The People pane gives you additional information about the currently selected email sender. For example, you can use the People pane to view other Outlook items, such as mail and meetings that are associated with the sender of the current selected email.

- **Status bar:** The status bar provides the View shortcuts and Zoom slider. You can add other information, such as quota information, to the status bar, and you can also remove features as needed via the Customize Status Bar menu (right-click on the status bar).

TIP

You can grab the top of the Navigation pane's button area and drag it upward to view more Outlook item buttons, such as the notes and the Folder list.

You can manipulate the layout of the various Outlook panes, such as the Folder pane and the To Do bar, on the ribbon's View tab. The Folder pane, Reading pane, and To Do bar have drop-down menus that enable you to view the panes in different views. You can also use the commands provided to turn off a particular pane and hide it from view.

Accessing Outlook items using the Navigation bar

The Navigation bar provides quick access to the different Outlook items. When you select a particular item, such as Mail, the Folder pane provides a list of folders associated with that item. In the case of Mail, you can access the Inbox, Drafts, and Junk Email, along with other associated mail folders.

The Navigation bar shows links to the Mail, Calendar, People, and Tasks items. At the bottom right of the Navigation bar, there is also an ellipsis (signifying More), which provides access to Other Outlook items and navigation options. For example, to open your notes, select the ellipsis (or More) and then select the Notes icon.

This menu also provides access to the Folders command. When you are in Mail view and select Folders (via the Navigation Bar ellipsis), all the Outlook folders become available in the Folder pane. The folders listed include Calendar, Contacts, Journal, and RSS Feeds. Select any folder to access that particular item. Having the folders listed in the Folder pane makes it easy for you to quickly switch from your Inbox to your contacts, then to your calendar, and finally back to your Inbox. To do this quick switching, you must select the folders in the Folder pane. If you select one of the navigation links, such as Calendar or People, the Folder pane goes back to the default list of folders (for example, your Inbox and Sent Items when Mail is selected).

You can access Outlook information by hovering the mouse over an Outlook item in the Navigation bar. For instance, if you place the mouse on Calendar, you are provided with a thumbnail calendar of the current month and a shortlist of upcoming appointments. Hover over People,

CHAPTER 22

and you get access to a Search People box and a list of any contacts you have added to your Favorites list. Place the mouse pointer on Tasks, and you can see a list of current tasks. As we work with Outlook in the Outlook section of this book, you learn that Outlook provides a number of enhancements that enable you to do your work quickly and efficiently, whether you are working with a keyboard and a mouse or on a device with a touch screen.

Customizing navigation options

You can use the Navigation Options dialog box to change the order in which Outlook items are displayed in the Navigation bar, as well as how many items are shown. By default, four items are visible—Mail, Calendar, People, and Tasks—but you can increase (or decrease) this setting as needed. Select More (the ellipsis) in the Navigation bar and then select Navigation Options. This opens the Navigation Options dialog box.

You can use the Move Up and Move Down buttons in the Navigation Options dialog box to change the order of the commands shown in the Navigation bar. You can also change the number of visible items using the spin box at the top of the dialog box (the default is four). If you select the Compact Navigation setting in the Navigation Options dialog box, the Navigation bar is "compacted" so that it fits neatly at the bottom of the Folder pane. Icons replace each of the text links that represent the various Outlook items, such as Mail, Calendar, and People.

> **TIP**
>
> **You can also open the Navigation Options dialog box via the ribbon's View tab. Select the Folder Pane command in the Layout group, and then select Options.**

You can return to the default settings for the Navigation bar at any time. Open the Navigation Options dialog box and select Reset. When you want to return to the default settings for the Navigation bar, you can select Reset.

Working with views in Outlook

As you work with the different items in Outlook, the Outlook panes provide you with a default view for each item type. For example, Outlook uses the Compact view as the default for mail. Other views for mail can be accessed using the Change View gallery on the ribbon's View tab. You can also view your mail using the Single and Preview views. In Compact view, each email's subject line and the first line of the message show in the email list. (By default, only the first line of the message shows, but you can increase the message preview to up to three lines.)

How your emails are listed in the Inbox will depend on whether you are using the Focused Inbox or not; the Focused Inbox is only available for Outlook.com and Microsoft Exchange email

CHAPTER 22

accounts. To enable the Focused Inbox, use the Show Focused Inbox command in the ribbon's View tab. When you use the Focused Inbox, you are working in a two-tier hierarchy:

- Emails that are listed as focused are considered important emails that you should attend to first.

- Emails that are listed under Other (the second option of the Focused Inbox) are considered lower-priority messages than the Focused emails.

Focused emails are considered focused based on the senders (and contacts) that you interact with the most. Messages from other sources, particularly emails that come as electronic newsletters or advertisements, will be placed in the Other list. Outlook determines the status of an email (Focused or Other), and as time goes by, how you interact with your emails will help Outlook do a better job of sorting and determining if an email is focused. You can help Outlook better determine a particular email's type by moving email that has not been categorized correctly. To move a Focused email to Other, right-click on the email and select Move To Other or Always Move To Other (so that the sender's emails always go to the Other list). To go from Other to Focused, right-click on the email and select Move To Focused or Always Move To Focused, as you require.

If you decide to turn off the Focused Inbox, select the View tab and then select Show Focused Inbox. Your messages are now listed individually by date, but you can change this by clicking the drop-down arrow (next to By Date) and selecting any of the view options, such as From, Categories, and Importance (we talk more about working with email in the next chapter). And if you yearn for the Conversation view introduced way back in Outlook 2010 (which arranged emails by conversation), you can select the Show As Conversations check box in the Messages group on the ribbon's View tab.

Each of the Outlook items has different views available. For example, the default view for your contacts is People. This view lists your contacts in the Details pane (including pictures, if available) and provides detailed information on the selected contact in the Reading pane. Other views are available for your contacts, including Business Cards and Card.

As already mentioned, the Change View command on the ribbon's View tab provides you with the different views available for the currently selected Outlook item. Figure 22-12 shows the People view for the Contacts folder and also shows the other view options for contacts in the Change View gallery (Business Card, Card, Phone, and List).

CHAPTER 22

Figure 22-12   Change the view for the Contacts folder.

You can also create custom views for the information in your Outlook folders. Select Change View on the View tab and select Manage Views to open the Manage All Views dialog box. The dialog box shows the preconfigured views for the current folder (such as Mail or Contacts). You can use commands in this dialog box to copy, modify, and rename views. You can also use the Reset button to change a view back to its default settings, which is useful when you have modified a view and want to put it back to the way it was by default.

To create a new view, select the New button to open the Create New View dialog box. In this dialog box, you supply the name for the new view, the type of view, and the folders on which Outlook can use the view. You have several options for the type of view you select for the new view:

- **Table:** Presents items in a grid of *n* rows and columns. Use this view type to view mail messages, tasks, and details about any item.

- **Timeline:** Displays items as icons arranged in chronological order from left to right on a time scale. Use this to examine journal entries and other items in this type of view.

- **Card:** Presents items such as cards in a card file. Use this to view contacts.

- **Business Card:** Presents items in a business card format that provides details for the contact, such as name, email, address, and so on.

- **People:** Presents items by photo plus name. Details for each entry are included in the Reading page. This view is used to view contacts.

- **Day/Week/Month:** Displays items in a calendar view in blocks of time. Use this type for meetings and scheduled tasks.

- **Icon:** Provides graphical icons to represent tasks, notes, calendars, and so on.

Obviously, most of the view types relate to a particular Outlook folder. For example, Business Card relates to contacts, whereas the Day/Week/Month type is suited for calendars. You can specify additional options related to the view, such as whether the view is used on the current folder and visible to everyone or visible only to you. Another option allows Outlook to use the view on all mail and post folders.

TIP

If you change the current view using the Advanced View Settings dialog box, you can save the "changed" view as a new view. Change the settings as needed and then select Change View on the ribbon. Select Save Current View As A New View. The Copy View dialog box opens; provide a name for the new view. You can then specify whether the view should be available to all mail and post folders or the current folder. When you have finished with the process, click OK to close the Copy View dialog box.

After you select the type of view (such as Table or Timeline) and folder options for the new view, click OK. The Advanced View Settings dialog box opens. You can use it to specify how information is grouped (by such things as creation date or categories), sorted, or filtered. You also can specify the fields that should be included in a new view (such as a table). Each field would represent a column, and each field column would provide specific information. The field column possibilities include Importance, Reminder, Icon, Flag Status, and Attachment (and there are many others).

After configuring the new view and clicking OK, you return to the Manage All Views dialog box. If you need to change a view you have created, select the view and select Modify. You can then modify the view as needed. When you close the Manage All Views dialog box, Outlook adds your new view to the Change View menu. You can select it when needed, as you do with the default views provided.

Categorizing Outlook items

You can assign categories to Outlook items to aid you in locating and organizing information in Outlook. When items have been assigned categories, Outlook can then organize the items in a particular view by a particular category. You can also use Search to locate items assigned to a category, and you can create Search folders that find items based on category.

By default, each Outlook category is color-coded. The categories have names such as Blue Category, Green Category, and so on. To open the Color Categories dialog box shown in Figure 22-13, select Categorize on the ribbon's Home tab and then select All Categories.

TIP

If you decide that you don't want a view you created, you can delete it in the Manage All Views dialog box.

You can rename the various color categories to assemble your own list of categories that you can then assign to your Outlook items. If you exhaust the default categories, you can create new categories in the Color Categories dialog box. You can open this dialog box no matter what type of item you are working with. For example, when you are working with an appointment, the Categorize command is on the Appointment tab of the ribbon. When you are working with an open email, you can access the Categorize command on the Message tab. The first time you assign one of the color categories to an Outlook item, the Rename Category dialog box opens. You can quickly rename the category by typing a new name in the Name box.

When you have renamed categories, you can assign them to your Outlook items as needed. Then when you select the ribbon's View tab in one of the Outlook folders, you can use the Categories command to arrange the items in the current folder by category. You can filter items in a particular view by using the Search box. Click in the Search box and then select the Categorized command provided in the Refine group (a set of contextual tools provided when you are using the Search box). When you select a category, the list of items is filtered by that category.

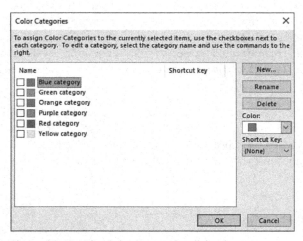

Figure 22-13   The Color Categories dialog box

Searching for Outlook items

Outlook provides you with some different possibilities for finding items in your various Outlook folders. The simplest way to search for items in the current folder is to click in the Search box, enter a search parameter (such as a name), and then select the Search arrow to run the search. The search tools will appear on the ribbon. Figure 22-14 shows the Search tab on the ribbon.

The Search tools provide a number of options. You can specify the scope for the search, such as the current folder, all subfolders, or all Outlook items. You can also use commands in the Refine group to search for items that have attachments, a particular subject, or a flag or importance level assigned to them.

After you specify the various options for the search, type your search terms into the Search box; Outlook provides the search results. You can modify the search on the fly and enable or disable search parameters on the ribbon as needed. When you finish the search, click the Close Search command to return to the current folder view.

Figure 22-14   The Search Tools

Using Advanced Find

If you want to create a more complex search, you can use the Advanced Find dialog box to conduct your search. Click the Search box; the Search Tools appear on the ribbon. Select the ellipsis (…) on the far right of the Search tab, select Search Tools (under Options), and then select Advanced Find. This opens the Advanced Find dialog box.

The Advanced Find dialog box enables you to specify the type of item you want to find and the location you want to search. You can also specify parameters such as who a message is from or its recipients. Advanced Find enables you to specify keywords for different fields, such as the subject field. Additional search parameters on the More Choices tab enable you to specify categories to be used in the search and other parameters, such as items that are unread or have a particular importance. The Advanced tab enables you to specify parameters by field, such as address fields and the date/time field.

When you have specified the parameters for the search, select Find Now. Outlook lists the items found by the search.

Using search folders

Search folders are containers that you can use to locate mail items in your email accounts. The search folders don't really contain mail items, but they provide you with a listing of email items that meet your search criteria, meaning the Search Folders criteria. For example, you could search for all unread emails or all emails from a particular person. Then, when you access the search folder in the Folders pane, you have access to the emails that meet your search criteria.

To create a new search folder for an account, right-click Search Folders in the Folders pane (it's probably directly under Tasks, if you haven't added any folders); then select New Search Folder. The New Search Folder dialog box opens, as shown in Figure 22-15.

Figure 22-15   The New Search Folder dialog box

You can select a search folder provided by the New Search Folder dialog box. Different categories, such as Reading Mail, Mail From People and Lists, and Organizing Mail, provide specific types of searches that you can assign to the folder. For example, select Unread Mail in the Reading Mail category to create search folder for unread mail. If you select a search folder such as Mail From Specific People, you must use the Customize Search Folder option to specify the person or persons you are talking about. (You can select the contact or contacts from your Contacts folder by using the Choose button.)

> **TIP**
>
> **You can create custom search folders by selecting Create A Custom Search Folder in the New Search Folder dialog box (it's at the bottom of the criteria under Custom; click Choose after selecting it). This opens the Custom Search Folder dialog box, which you can use to specify custom criteria for the search folder.**

After you have selected the type of search folder and supplied the additional information needed, click OK. The new search folder appears in your email folder list. Select the search folder to view the mail items that meet the folder's search criteria.

Printing Outlook items

You can print Outlook items in the Outlook Backstage. Select File on the ribbon. (You can access the Backstage from any item ribbon, such as the Message ribbon or Event ribbon.) Accessing the Backstage from any item type lets you quickly print the item you are working with (be it a message, contact, task, or event). Outlook also provides options for printing the entire contents of a folder, such as the People (contacts) folder. Because the Print window combines print settings, such as the selection of the print style and print preview, you can fine-tune your print job before printing.

Open a specific Outlook item, or open an Outlook folder, such as your mail or tasks. To access the Backstage, select File on the ribbon. Select Print to open the Print window. Figure 22-16 shows the Print window.

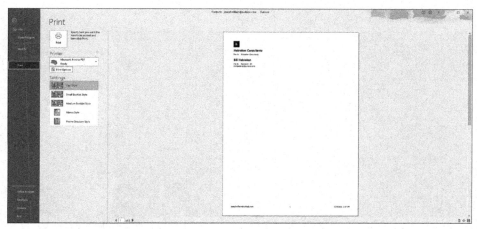

Figure 22-16   The Print window

You can select the printer for the print job by using the Printer drop-down menu. The Settings area of the window provides a list of the different styles available for the current item type that you want to print. The styles vary, depending on the type of item you are printing; for example, an email uses the Memo Style by default, and all the emails in a folder print using the Table Style. For contacts, individual contacts print by using the Memo Style, but an entire contacts list prints using the Card Style, Small Booklet Style, or Phone Directory Style. Because you are provided with a preview of your printout after you select a style, you can try different styles until you find the one most appropriate for the printout you want to create.

Select the Print Options button on the Print window if you want to control the number of copies, how the copies are collated, or other print parameters, such as the page range. This opens the Print dialog box.

You access print settings via the Print dialog box, where you can choose print options such as the fonts used in the printout and the paper type. You can even specify a header or footer to print on each page of the printout. Click the Page Setup button to set the format, paper, and header/footer settings in the Page Setup dialog box.

When you change options in the Print dialog box, it makes sense to click the Preview button to return to the Print window. This provides a print preview using the settings you configured in the Print dialog box. To preview your printout, you can use the various preview buttons, such as Actual Size, One Page, and Multiple Pages. When you are ready to send the print job to the printer, click the Print button on the window.

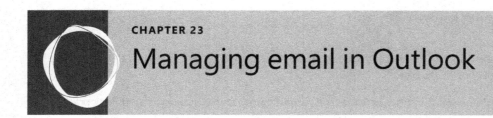

Working in the Outlook window   701

Creating an email message   704

Using the Outlook Address Book   706

Setting message options   708

Attaching files and items to a message   715

Using themes and email stationery   718

Adding a signature   719

Sending mail   720

Recalling a message   720

Working with received email   721

Managing email   724

Managing email accounts   724

Setting Outlook mail options   736

CHAPTER 23

Considering that most of us send and receive large volumes of email, Outlook takes the "mess" out of messages (as opposed to putting the "fun" in dysfunctional) and enables you to communicate with others in an organized and effective manner. As mentioned in Chapter 22, "Outlook configuration and essential features," Outlook's mail client supports a number of email account types, including internet mail (email provided by your ISP), Microsoft Exchange Server mail, Microsoft Outlook.com, and Gmail. In this chapter, we look at Outlook's email management tools and features, starting with basic concepts related to creating, sending, and receiving emails. We also look at Outlook's capabilities for managing and organizing emails and setting email account configurations and other email settings.

Working in the Outlook window

After you have configured the initial email account on Outlook's first start (as discussed in Chapter 22), you are ready to begin creating, sending, and receiving emails. Remember that you are not limited to a single email account in Outlook: You can configure multiple email accounts (and different types of email accounts), as discussed later in this chapter in the section "Adding an email account."

Your Outlook Mail folder provides access to the more specific email folders that hold different types of messages, such as received and sent messages (as well as deleted messages). Select Mail in the Navigation bar to view your default email folders. When you select the Inbox folder, the Details pane lists the emails in the Inbox. The Reading pane shows the contents of the currently selected email.

An optional To-Do Bar can also be added to the right side of the Outlook Reading pane. Select the View tab and then select the To-Do Bar command in the Layout group. If you are using the

Simplified ribbon, these options are accessed via a drop-down list. You can add three potential panes to the To-Do bar:

- **Calendar:** This pane provides the current month and a list of any schedule appointments found within a seven-day window.

- **People:** This pane allows you to accumulate a list of favorites. Right-click any person's name in Outlook (or the other 365 applications) to add them to the Favorites pane.

- **Tasks:** This pane provides a list of your current tasks. It also provides a New Task box, which you can use to add additional tasks to your Task list.

The To-Do Bar can contain one or all the bar content panes (Calendar, People, and Tasks). Select an item from the To-Do Bar drop-down menu to add that time to the To-Do Bar. You also have the option of turning the To-Do Bar off by selecting the Off command on the To-Do Bar menu.

As already mentioned, each Outlook email account has its own set of associated mail folders, such as the Inbox, Drafts, and Sent Items folders. You can collapse an email account in the Navigation pane to hide the folders associated with the account; click the Collapse button for the account. A second click expands the account, showing the associated folders. The default folders for your primary or default email account are as follows:

- **Inbox:** Outlook places received mail in the Inbox by default. When you select the Inbox, the Details pane lists emails by date order.

- **Drafts:** The Drafts folder can potentially contain any email that you compose and then close without sending. When you close an unsent email message, Outlook prompts you to save the email as a draft.

- **Sent Items:** Emails that you send from the email account are stored in this folder. Sent emails display in date order.

- **Deleted Items:** Outlook places deleted emails in this folder. You have the option of letting Outlook empty the Deleted Items folder when you exit the application.

- **Archive:** You can manually archive old messages to the Archive folder (which is part of the default Outlook configuration and cannot be deleted) using the Archive command in the Home tab's Delete group. Archiving messages reduces the size of your Outlook mailbox.

- **Conversation History:** This default folder (which cannot be deleted) is used to keep track of your Skype conversations. The Conversation History will include all the instant messages you have sent to or received from people in your Outlook Contacts list.

- **Junk Email:** This folder sequesters emails flagged as junk email by Outlook.

- **Outbox:** When you send a message, Outlook places it in the Outbox folder until sending the email by connecting to the outgoing email server.

- **RSS Feeds:** This folder is not mail related, but it gives you a way to access Really Simple Syndication (RSS) newsfeeds in Outlook. You can read content from an RSS feed in the Outlook window in much the same way that you read an email. We discuss RSS feeds at the end of this chapter.

- **Sync Issues:** There is no doubt that you (and Outlook) will experience issues from time to time related to syncing your email folders (particularly when you use multiple devices to access the same email account). Logs and other information related to synchronization error checking are kept in this folder, and it is used primarily by Outlook to track sync issues. It is a system folder and cannot be deleted. You can open it and look inside, but you should probably just leave it alone.

- **Search folders:** A search folder isn't an actual folder. Instead, it consists of search conditions that you can set so that emails meeting your conditions display in the search folder.

By default, Outlook uses a compact view format that arranges your emails in the Inbox chronologically. All emails are listed, and you can view only the unread messages by selecting Unread at the top of the email list. To access other filters and email arrangements, select the By Date arrow on the right-top of the email list. A gallery opens that provides a list of filters (such as Unread Mail and Flagged Mail), arrangements (such as Date, From, To, and Subject), and sorting options (Newest On Top or Oldest On Top). There is also an additional option available: Focused Inbox.

The Focused Inbox view categorizes and lists your email based on importance. There are only two categories: Focused and Other. Your important messages (based on interactions with your contacts) will appear when Focused is selected at the top of the email list. Messages considered unimportant are accessed by selecting Other at the top of the email list. If you don't like the Focused Inbox approach to viewing your email messages, you can turn this feature off by deselecting the Show Focused Inbox command on the View tab of Outlook's ribbon.

Two other possibilities provide alternative ways to view your Inbox's message list. You can use the Show As Conversations check box in the View tab's Message group, or you can list your emails by Date Received. Using the Conversations view makes it easy for you to view associated messages that relate to a particular mail message subject. However, if you prefer to list your messages by date, make sure you turn off the Focused Inbox and also toggle off the Conversations view (if necessary) by deselecting the Show As Conversations command. Whatever the case, experiment with the different ways to view your received emails and then select the option that works best for you.

Creating an email message

You can send an email message to anyone for whom you have an email address, whether that address is in your list of contacts or scribbled on a scrap of paper. You can even email groups of people listed in your various distribution lists.

You can attach Outlook items and other files to your emails. Because Word is the default email editor for Outlook, you can use all of Word's capabilities to create emails that include formatted text, charts, and SmartArt. You can use the Review tab's tools to check the message's spelling and grammar or open the Research pane to find information important to your message.

When you are in the Mail folder, you can quickly open a new email message; select the New Email command on the ribbon's Home tab. If you happen to be in one of the other Outlook folders, select the New Items command and then select Email Message. Whichever route you take (there are more possibilities than the two mentioned, which we discuss in a moment), a new message window opens, as shown in Figure 23-1.

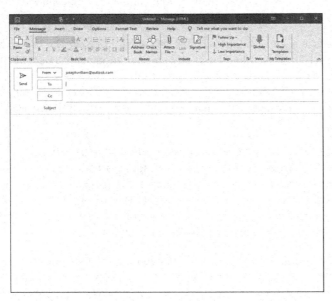

Figure 23-1   A new message window

If you have not changed the message type for Outlook, the new message appears in HTML format; Outlook sends the message from your default email account. You can change both of these settings via commands provided by the message ribbon. The list that follows provides a brief description of the command sets found on each of the message ribbon's tabs:

- **File:** Provides access to the Backstage. You can set permissions for the mail message and properties such as the importance, sensitivity, and delivery options.

- **Message:** Provides access to the Clipboard commands, basic text formatting, and the Outlook Address Book (Names). Other commands available include Attach File, Attach Item, Signature, and message tags such as Follow Up and High Importance.

- **Insert:** Provides commands for different types of attachments (including files and Outlook items such as Business Cards and Calendars). Other items, such as tables, pictures, shapes, and hyperlinks, can also be inserted from this tab.

- **Draw:** If you have a touchscreen device, this tab allows you to insert a drawing canvas in an email message and provides drawing tools that you can use on the canvas.

- **Options:** Enables you to assign a theme to the message. Other options available include additional fields for the message (BCC), voting buttons, delivery and received receipts, and options related to saving and delivering the message.

- **Format Text:** Enables you to change the format of the message (from HTML to plain text, for example). The various text-formatting options provided, such as font, paragraph, and style settings, are also available on this tab.

- **Review:** Provides proofing aids such as the Spelling & Grammar tool and the Thesaurus, and it includes language options such as Translate.

- **Help:** This tab provides access to the Outlook Help system and includes features for troubleshooting a problem and providing feedback to Microsoft.

TIP

You can create a new message as plain text, Rich Text, or HTML. Select New Items, point at Email Message Using, and then select Plain Text, Rich Text, or HTML for the message format.

No matter what enhancements or options you select for your message, you need to supply the body of the message, a subject for the message, and the recipient's email address (or addresses of the recipients). Obviously, you can type an email address in the To box to specify the recipient. You can also enter multiple email addresses by separating the addresses with a semicolon. A better way to address mail messages, however, is to use the Outlook Address Book.

CHAPTER 23

Using the Outlook Address Book

Outlook has the capability to access different stores or lists of information that can provide you with people's email addresses and other contact information, such as phone numbers and addresses. The Address Book is a catchall repository for address lists and can be used to access your Outlook Contacts list, contacts associated with a particular email account (such as your Microsoft Outlook.com account), and other directory lists, such as lists from mobile devices and lists provided by other email and communication servers. For example, in a corporate network, a Microsoft Exchange Server provides a global address list shared by all users on the Exchange network.

The different stores or collections of email addresses you have access to depend on the type of email account you use (Exchange Server email versus internet email). If you are using Outlook for home or small business email via an internet email account from your internet service provider, you won't have access to the Global Address List that an Exchange Server environment provides to a corporate user (although small business and home users can subscribe to Microsoft 365 and get Exchange email accounts).

The Address Book provides access to different collections of contact information (meaning email addresses), including the names that you place in the Outlook People (Contacts) folder. When you are composing a new message in the message window, you can open the Address Book by selecting To in the message window or selecting Names on the ribbon's Message tab. Figure 23-2 shows the Address Book dialog box.

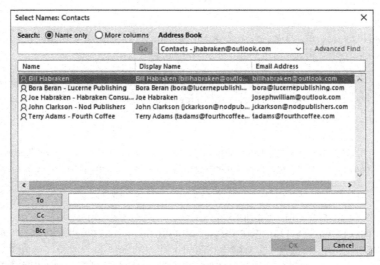

Figure 23-2   The Address Book dialog box

The Address Book drop-down menu in the Address Book dialog box enables you to select the list you want to access to address the email, such as your contacts, or an Exchange global address list. You can also search a selected address list using the Search box. By default, the Search feature is set to search the selected address list by name only. Enter a name and then click Go. Outlook highlights the first record in the current address list that matches the search term (such as a contact's first or last name). By default, the Search tool is set to Name Only; however, you can search other fields in the selected list's records by selecting More Columns and then running your search.

You can perform a more advanced search if you have access to address lists other than your default Outlook Contacts list (an advanced search has reduced functionality when used on the Outlook contacts list). An example of an address list that would allow you to take advantage of a full-featured, advanced search is an Exchange Global Address List. To open the Advanced Find dialog box, select the Advanced Find link.

The Find dialog box enables you to devise a more complex search than the Search box permits. Remember, this advanced form of search only works with shared address books such as an Exchange Global Address List. You can specify information in different fields and then click OK to search the address list. After you have located the email address you want to use to send the message, select the address and then click the To button in the lower part of the Address Book dialog box. Repeat as necessary to add email addresses. You can also add contacts to the Cc box or the Bcc box, as needed. After specifying the destination addresses for the message, click OK to close the Address Book dialog box.

NOTE

After you address the mail message, the People pane appears at the bottom of the message window, listing the recipients. If the recipient is one of your contacts, you can use the information provided in the People pane to view different interactions you have had with the contact, such as mail, meetings, and so on.

If you are using Microsoft Exchange Server as your email server, Outlook immediately checks the validity of the email addresses that you have entered in the To, Cc, and Bcc boxes. If you have entered an invalid address because of a typo or have entered an email address that is no longer on the Exchange Server, Outlook lets you know. It places a message below the ribbon in the message window stating that the email message cannot be delivered to the email address you have supplied because it is no longer valid.

Even if you do not use Exchange Server as your email server, you can check the email addresses that you have added to the address boxes in the message, such as To and Cc, to see whether you entered them correctly. Select Check Names on the ribbon's Message tab. This process checks internet email addresses for proper email format (*name@something*.com) and checks the email address against those you have listed in your Contacts folder. The Check Names dialog box opens if an incorrect or incomplete email address is entered in a To, Cc, or Bcc box. It attempts to provide a suggestion for the correct email address. The Check Names dialog box

CHAPTER 23

also gives you access to the Address Book so that you can check the email address manually and provide the correct one.

When you have the message addressed correctly, you can move on to the subject of the email and the actual body of the message. If you want to put the message aside and are not ready to complete and send the message, you can save it as a draft.

Click the Close button in the Message window. A message box opens and asks whether you want to save changes to the email; click Yes. Outlook places the message in the Drafts folder. Open the Drafts folder and double-click the message to open it in its window to access the message later. You can then complete the message and send it.

Setting message options

Outlook provides options that enable you to configure the email format, importance, sensitivity, and security settings for a message. You can also specify voting and tracking options for the message and specify delivery options, such as the email address to use when recipients send replies to the message. Other options relate to the format for the email and policies for the message with regard to archiving and retention.

In accessing these various message options, you'll find that they are not on a single ribbon tab but are somewhat dispersed among the tabs. A Properties dialog box for the message provides the greatest aggregate of the different settings, and we will look at the Properties dialog box in a moment.

Specifying email format

When you create a new email message using the New Email Message command, Outlook creates a new message in your default message type. (If you haven't changed the Outlook settings, the default is HTML.) You might have some mail recipients who prefer to receive email messages in a particular format, such as Plain Text, because of the email client that they are using. You can select the email format when you use the New Items command to create a new email. After clicking the New Items command (on the Outlook Home tab), select the Email Message Using submenu and select one of the email formats listed: Plain Text, Rich Text, or HTML.

You can also change the email type of an existing new message. Select the Format Text tab on the message's ribbon. The email format commands are located in the Format group. Outlook highlights the current format for the message in the group. To change the format of the message, select one of the other formats provided. If you select Plain Text as the message type, most of the Font and Paragraph commands on the Format Text tab are not available, nor are the Basic Text group commands on the Message tab.

Setting message flags, importance, and sensitivity

Outlook provides you with a number of ways to "label" messages related to follow-up (follow-up by you or the recipient), message importance, and message sensitivity. These message tools, including follow-up flags and message importance, are accessed via the ribbon's Message tab when you are working in the message window (with a new message or a message you are forwarding).

The commands for Follow Up and importance level (High Importance and Low Importance) are accessed via the Tags group on the Message tab. You can access additional tag options related to the current message by opening the message's Properties dialog box by selecting the dialog box launcher on the Tags group.

Let's take a look at using follow-up flags. We can then discuss the other tag-related features such as Importance and Sensitivity.

Message flags

You can add follow-up flags to a message as a reminder to you or the message recipient. You can also assign an importance level to the message so that the recipient knows whether the message is of high or low importance.

The message flag assigned to a message appears at the top of the message window. Messages that you have flagged and then sent are listed in your Sent Items folder and are marked by a flag. If the recipient also uses Outlook, any messages sent with flags are "flagged" in the recipient's Inbox folder.

To assign a follow-up flag to the current message (a message you are creating), select Follow Up on the ribbon's Message tab and then select one of the flags from the flag list, such as Today, Tomorrow, This Week, and so on. Outlook places the flag information at the top of the message window just above the From box.

If you want to set a custom flag for you or the message recipient (or recipients), select the Follow Up command and then select Custom. The Custom dialog box opens. You can use the dialog box to set a flag for yourself (in the Flag For Me section) and/or a flag for the recipients. Figure 23-3 shows the Custom dialog box with both the Flag For Me and Flag For Recipients check boxes selected.

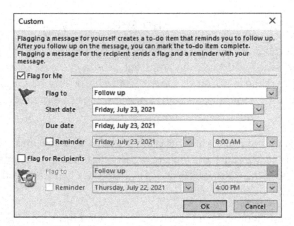

Figure 23-3 The Custom dialog box enables you to select flags for the message.

Use the Flag To drop-down menu to select the flag type, such as Call, Do Not Forward, Follow Up, For Your Information, and so forth. You can also specify a start date and a due date for the flag. If you want to set a reminder for the flag, select the Reminder check box and specify a date and time for the reminder.

To set a flag for the recipient or recipients, select the Flag for Recipients check box. Then use the Flag To drop-down menu to specify the flag type. You can also set reminders for recipient flags: Select the Reminder check box and specify the date and time for the reminder.

Importance level

There are three importance levels for Outlook messages: Low, Normal, and High. By default, Outlook assigns the Normal Importance level to all messages. You can change the importance level to High Importance or Low Importance, as needed. The High Importance and Low Importance commands are in the Message tab's Tags group.

Assigning an importance level to a message is a one-click process. Select either High Importance or Low Importance in the Tags group. If you assigned High Importance, you can toggle off the setting by clicking it a second time. This resets the importance level to Normal. (You can also toggle off the Low Importance setting in the same manner.)

Sensitivity level

You can set the Sensitivity level for a message that you are sending or forwarding. You can access the sensitivity settings and a number of other settings related to a message via the Properties dialog box. In the message window, select the dialog box launcher on the lower-left of the Tags group to open the Message Properties dialog box (for the current message).

TIP

If you are using Outlook in an Exchange Server environment, you can specify permissions for a message that enable you to set an expiration date for the message and control whether a recipient can forward a message. The Permission settings (if available) are accessed using the Permission command on the message window's ribbon (in the Options group).

By default, the Sensitivity level for a message is set to Normal. To change the sensitivity setting, select the Sensitivity drop-down menu (in the Properties dialog box) and then pick one of the options provided: Personal, Private, or Confidential. You can close the Message Properties dialog box by selecting the Close button. Marking the message with a Sensitivity level, such as Confidential, is only to suggest how the recipient should handle the contents of the message. The Sensitivity setting does not preclude the recipient from forwarding the message, for instance.

Configuring voting buttons, receipts, and delivery options

There are a couple of ways you can configure the tracking and delivery options for the current outgoing message. Select the Options tab on the message's ribbon; the Option tab supplies the Tracking group, which allows you to configure voting and receipt settings. The Tracking group contains the Use Voting Buttons options and options for requesting a delivery or read receipt.

You will also find the More Options group on the Options tab. This group allows you to configure delivery options, such as delaying delivery or saving the sent email to a particular Outlook folder.

The commands provided by the Tracking group and the More Options group can also be accessed in the message's Properties dialog box, including both Voting and Tracking options. Open the message's Properties dialog box by selecting the dialog box launcher on the Tags group (found on the Message tab of the email's ribbon).

The Voting and Tracking options are found in the second set of check boxes in the Properties dialog box and enable you to insert voting buttons on an email that allow the recipients to respond with a click on one of the options provided by your voting buttons. Voting buttons can include items such as Approve and Reject or Yes and No options. The Tracking options also include commands that enable you to receive notification that the recipient of the message has received the message or opened and read it.

Let's look at voting buttons and then discuss receipt requests and options related to message delivery.

Using voting buttons

Voting buttons enable you to make it easy for recipients to respond to your email content, such as a question that requires a yes or no answer or a suggestion for either approval or rejection. To add voting buttons to a message, select the Use Voting Buttons command in the Tracking group.

Select any of the following: Approve, Reject; Yes, No; and Yes, No, or Maybe. If you want to create a custom set of voting buttons, select Custom. This opens the Message Options/Properties dialog box for the message. You can type possible responses for the voting buttons in the Use Voting Buttons text box. Separate the selections using a semicolon.

When the recipient votes using the vote buttons on the received message, a message box opens and asks whether Outlook should send the vote response immediately or whether to allow the recipient to edit the message before sending. If the recipient closes the email without sending his or her vote, you won't get that vote even if the recipient used the voting buttons.

Requesting receipts

You can request receipts for your mail messages using the receipt commands in the Voting and Tracking options area of the message's Properties dialog box. As an alternative with the same result (as already mentioned in the previous section), you can go to the Tracking group provided by the email ribbon's Options tab. Whether you set up the tracking options in the Properties dialog box or in the Options tab's Tracking group, the options in the form of checkboxes are as follows:

- **Request a Delivery Receipt**: Selecting this tracking option requests that you receive a notification (in Outlook) when the message you send is received.

- **Request a Read Receipt:** Selecting this tracking option requests that you receive an email notification that the intended recipient has opened the message.

Even if you select either of these options, the recipient can choose not to send the receipt (the delivery receipt or read receipt). The dialog box that opens when the recipient opens the message provides them the opportunity to say no to the request for a receipt. Some email server systems can also be configured so that they do not send receipts. So, although delivery and read receipts seem like a good idea in terms of tracking important emails that you have sent, you will find that both recipients and email servers do not always share your enthusiasm for related to email receipts.

Setting delivery options

You can also set certain delivery options in a message's Properties dialog box or via the More Options group on the Message's Options tab. These options include the following:

- Where a sent message is saved (the folder used when it is saved upon sending—by default, this is the Sent Items folder)

- When the message is actually sent (Delay Delivery)

- The email address to which replies are directed

These options can be useful when you want certain emails placed directly into a folder related to a particular project rather than thrown in with all the other sent emails in the Sent Items folder.

These options are also handy when sending an email and you want all the replies to that email to go to a third party. An example is having all the replies to an invitation for a special event go to the person who is in charge of tracking who will attend the event; it's not uncommon for a department head or other supervisor to send an email invitation and then have a subordinate track the responses. These various delivery options are in the More Options group on the ribbon's Options tab.

To specify a folder as the location for a saved sent item, select the Save Sent Item To command (in the More Options group on the Options tab). By default, the message is saved to the Sent Items folder; to designate another folder, select Other Folder. The Select Folder dialog box opens, as shown in Figure 23-4.

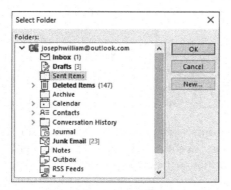

Figure 23-4   The Select Folder dialog box

Select a folder in the list. If you want to create a new folder, click the New button. The Create New Folder dialog box opens. Type the new folder's name and select where you want to place the new folder in the folder list; then click OK. After you have specified the folder (or created a new folder), select OK to close the Select Folder dialog box.

If you want to specify a delivery date for the message, select the Delay Delivery command. The Properties dialog box for the message opens. By default, Outlook selects the Do Not Deliver Before check box in the Delivery Options area of the Properties dialog box. Specify a date and time for the delivery, and then click Close to close the dialog box.

The Message Properties dialog box

Most of the message settings that we discussed in the previous sections—everything from flags to delivery options such as delay delivery—can also be accessed via the Properties dialog box for a new message, forwarded message, or message reply. If you are going to set a number of message options, you may want to select your settings in the message's Properties dialog box, rather than relying on the Options tab's Tracking and More Options groups.

You can launch the Properties dialog box from the dialog box launcher provided by the Tags group (on the Message tab), the Tracking group, or the More Options group (both Tracking and More Options are on the Options tab).

In the Settings area of the Message Options/Properties dialog box, you can set the Importance and Sensitivity of the message (which we already discussed). You can also configure other message properties that we have discussed, including the Voting, Tracking, and Delivery options.

> ➤ Security settings can also be set in the Properties dialog box; see Chapter 26, "Securing and maintaining Outlook."

Also, the Message Options dialog box enables you to link a contact or contacts to a message and assign categories to a message. Linking a contact to a message enables you to view the message on that contact's Activities page when you are viewing that particular contact's record in the Contacts folder.

When you associate contacts and categories to messages, you are just applying organizational tags to the emails. You can then view all the email sent to a particular contact in the Contacts folder or sort sent email by a particular category. The recipient of email that you have tagged in this manner does not know that you have assigned the contact or the category to the message.

To assign a contact to a message, click the Contacts button in the Properties dialog box. The Select Contacts dialog box opens. This dialog box shows all the people in your Outlook Contacts folder. Double-click a contact to add that person to the Contacts box on the message's Options dialog box. Repeat as necessary.

You can also add categories to a message from the Message Options/Properties dialog box. Click the Categories drop-down menu to assign a category to a message. You can select All Categories on the Categories drop-down menu to open the Color Categories dialog box. You can assign a category (or categories) to the message by selecting a category or categories in the Color Categories dialog box. You can also create new categories or rename existing categories, if needed. Click OK to close the Color Categories dialog box and return to the Options dialog box for the message. When you have finished setting options related to the message, select Close to exit the Options dialog box.

TIP

If you only occasionally set properties related to your email messages and you are not consistently using the same settings, you can use the various commands on the ribbon or the Options dialog box. If you find that you always use the same options for your mail (other than the defaults), change the Mail Options in the Outlook Options window. You can open this window from the Backstage by selecting Options. Later in this chapter, the Mail options are discussed in the "Setting Outlook mail options" section.

> ➤ More about categorizing Outlook items is available in Chapter 22.

Attaching files and items to a message

You can attach files and Outlook items to your email messages. You can send Word documents, Excel workbooks, a family photo, or any other file you want, including a collection of files in various archive formats, such as ZIP (which you can create using the Windows File Explorer). You can also send Outlook items, such as business cards of your contacts.

Commands for attaching files and Outlook items are available on the Message tab and the Insert tab of the message window's ribbon. On the Message tab, the Include group provides the Attach File, Link, and Signature commands. The Insert tab of a message also provides an Include group, which provides five commands: Attach File, Outlook Item, Business Card, Calendar, and Signature. If you are replying to a message or forwarding a message, the Message tab provides an Include group that provides the Attach File, Link, and Signature commands.

When you attach a file to a message, it appears as an icon in an attachment box that resides in the message window right below the Subject box. If you want to view an attachment in the parent application (such as an Excel workbook in Excel), double-click the attachment in the message; the attached file opens in the appropriate application.

You can attach multiple files to an email, as needed. Select the Attach File command on the ribbon's Message tab in the message window to attach a file to a message. A list of recent items will appear; you are also given the option to browse web locations (typically your OneDrive) or browse your local PC. When you select Browse This PC, the Insert File dialog box opens, as shown in Figure 23-5. By default, your Documents library folder opens.

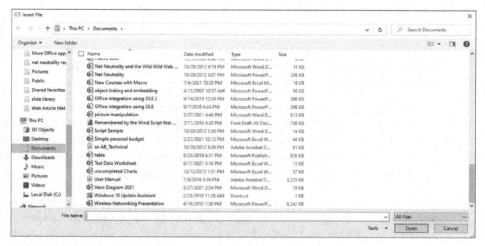

Figure 23-5   The Insert File dialog box

Select the file (or files) that you want to attach to the message, and then click Insert. The Attached box lists the attached file or files. If you attach a file and then decide that you don't want it to be attached to the message, select the attachment in the Attached box and delete it by pressing the Delete key.

If you are working in Windows Explorer and you want to send a file listed, right-click the file, select Send To, and then select Mail Recipient from the shortcut menu. This opens a new message in Outlook with the file attached.

CAUTION

The number and overall size of attachments can be problematic, particularly when you have an Internet email account that limits the size of attachments. The size allowed can vary from provider to provider, so read the provider's FAQ or call your provider to determine attachment limits before you try to send all your family reunion photos attached to a single email message. Technologies such as OneDrive and Microsoft Teams can be used to move big files from person to person.

In addition to attaching files from other programs, you can attach an Outlook item to a message. An Outlook item can be any item saved in one of your personal folders, including an appointment, a contact, a note, and so on. Outlook makes it easy for you to attach business cards of your Outlook contacts and calendars. The recipient can view calendar items even if he or she does not use Outlook.

To attach an item, select the Attach Item command on the Message tab. This command provides a menu of three possibilities: Business Card, Calendar, and Outlook Item.

Attaching a business card

To attach a business card of one of your contacts, select the Insert tab on your message and then select Business Card in the Include group. The submenu provided lists any contact cards that you recently attached to messages. To view a list of all your contacts, select Other Business Cards to open the Insert Business Card dialog box.

Use the Look In drop-down menu to select the Contacts list that you want to view in the dialog box. The list can include contacts on social media sites such as Facebook and LinkedIn (if you have connected Outlook to them). To preview a contact as a business card, select the contact. When you are ready to attach the business card, select OK. Outlook attaches the card to the message, and the card is inserted into the body of the message.

If you don't want to include the business card in the body of the message, select the business card and then press Delete. The card itself remains as an attachment in the Attached box. You can also delete it from the Attached box if you decide not to send the business card: Select the card in the Attached box and then press Delete.

Attaching a calendar

You can attach a calendar as an item to your mail message. The recipient need not use Outlook to view the calendar information. The attached calendar can consist of the current date (Today) or a range of dates. You also have control over the level of detail provided in the calendar.

To send a calendar with the message, select Calendar on the Insert tab. The Send A Calendar Via Email dialog box opens. Use the Calendar drop-down menu to select the calendar that supplies the information for the attachment (if you have multiple calendars in your Calendar folder). Select the Date Range drop-down menu to select the range of dates for the calendar. You can select a set range, such as Tomorrow or Next 7 Days, or you can click the Specify Dates button and provide the start and end dates for the range.

> ### TIP
>
> **You can select the Show Time Within My Working Hours Only check box, and then set your working hours in the Send A Calendar Via Email dialog box. This precludes any appointments or items outside your regular working day from being included with the calendar attached to the email message.**

The Detail settings for the calendar relate to the amount of detail you want to provide the recipient. By default, the detail level is set to Availability only, which shows time as Free, Busy, Tentative, and so on. Select the Limited Details setting if you want to include the availability and the subjects of your calendar items (within the date range). For full disclosure, you can select the Full Details setting.

If you select either the Limited Details or the Full Details setting, Outlook gives you additional options in the Advanced area of the dialog box. You can choose to include the details of items marked Private, and in the case of the Full Details setting, you can also include items attached to calendar items within the date range you have selected.

You can also specify the format of the attached calendar. Select the Show button to view the advanced settings. Select Email Layout to choose the layout for the calendar; you can select from Daily Schedule (the default) or List Of Events. When you have completed your selection related to the attached calendar, click OK to close the dialog box. Outlook inserts the calendar in the Attached box and attaches the details of the calendar into the body of the message. Users of Outlook can open the attached Calendar (.ics) file in Outlook. If you are going to send the calendar to someone who does not use Outlook, you might want to delete the calendar file in the Attached box and leave the calendar embedded in the body of the message. The calendar provides links from a calendar to a list of specific appointments it includes.

Using themes and email stationery

If you use the HTML or Rich Text message format for your email messages, you can take advantage of themes to make your messages look more interesting and appealing. A theme provides formatting attributes for the colors, fonts, and effects used in the message. Because you are using Word as your message editor, you are, in effect, applying a Word theme to the body text of the message. Themes are useful because they enable you to have a consistent look across a family of associated items, such as mail messages, Word documents, and Excel worksheets.

➤ **For information on using themes in Word, see Chapter 7, "Enhancing Word documents."**

Email stationery has been available in the last few versions of Outlook. Stationery gives you an overall look for the message's text and includes backgrounds for the body of the message. You can use stationery when you compose HTML emails. Let's look at assigning a theme to a message and then discuss creating a message using stationery.

To select a theme for the message, follow these steps:

1. Type the body of your message, or make sure that the insertion point is in the body of the message.

2. Select the Options tab of the ribbon.

3. Select the Themes command. You can preview any of the themes in the gallery by placing the mouse on a particular theme.

4. When you have decided on a theme, click the theme to assign it to the message.

You can fine-tune the themes by using the Colors, Fonts, and Effects commands to adjust the settings of the current theme. If you want to add a background color to the body of the message, use the Page Color command to select from the various theme colors. You can preview the colors by placing the mouse on a color in the palette.

If you want to use Outlook stationery for a new message, you must select the stationery as you initiate the new message. On the Home tab of any of the Outlook folders (Inbox, Calendar, Contacts, or Tasks), select the New Items command, point at Email Message Using, and then select More Stationery. The Theme Or Stationery dialog box opens, as shown in Figure 23-6.

This dialog box provides a list of available themes and installed stationery. The stationery is marked with the parenthetical tag (Stationery). Select the stationery (such as Currency), and a preview of the stationery displays in the dialog box. When you have found the stationery that you want to use, select OK to apply it to the new message and return to the message window.

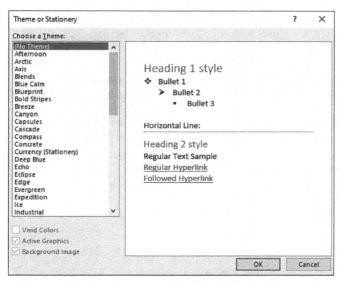

Figure 23-6   Select stationery for the new message.

Adding a signature

You can further personalize your emails by adding a signature to the message. A signature can be as simple as just your name. A signature can also include your phone number, extension, and other information. Some people even add a favorite quote to their signatures.

If you use HTML as your message format, you can insert a signature file that contains graphics, such as your picture. If you want, you can insert your electronic business card as the signature information (you should always include yourself in your Contacts list). Plain-text signatures (for use with plain-text messages) consist of text characters only.

You can create more than one signature for your mail messages. This enables you to have a different signature for your business emails and your personal emails. You can also create signatures for your plain-text messages and HTML messages.

> ## NOTE
>
> **Signatures for your emails are not the same as digital signatures. Digital signatures ensure that a mail message comes from a trusted source. Chapter 26 discusses digital signatures.**

To create a signature, select the Signature command on the message ribbon's Message tab and then select Signatures. The Signatures And Stationery dialog box opens. The Email Signature tab of the dialog box contains a list of your signatures in the Select Signature To Edit box. If you haven't created any signatures, there obviously won't be any signatures in the list.

To create a new signature, click the New button. The New Signature dialog box opens. Type a name for the new signature and then click OK. The signature appears in the signature list. Now you can edit the signature using the various tools shown in the Edit Signature pane.

Type the text for the signature and use the various drop-down formatting lists to format the text. You can also insert a business card or pictures and links in the signature. When you are finished creating the signature, you can repeat the process to create other signatures, as needed. When you click OK, the Signatures And Stationery dialog box closes. You can now use the Signature command to select from the list of the signatures that you have created and add them to the email.

Sending mail

When you have completed your email message, you can send it. Click Send, and Outlook places the message in your Outbox folder. If you have a persistent connection to your outgoing mail server, Outlook sends the message immediately and places a copy of the message in your Sent Items folder (or the folder that you specified using the Save Sent Item To command on the Options tab).

> ### TIP
> **You can also send an email by pressing Ctrl+Enter. The first time you press this key combination, Outlook asks you to verify it as a shortcut for sending email. Click Yes.**

If you are working offline, Outlook places the message in your Outbox folder. The message remains in the Outbox until you connect to your network (or the internet, if you are using internet email) and use the Send And Receive command. If you configured the message with delivery options that specified a delivery date, the message stays in the Outbox until the delivery date arrives.

Recalling a message

If you work on a network that uses Microsoft Exchange Server as your email messaging server, you can recall sent messages. You must recall the message before the recipient opens, deletes, or moves it to another folder. This feature is useful if you inadvertently sent an incomplete message or forgot to include an important attachment with the message.

The recall feature actually gives you two possibilities:

- You can recall the message and delete unread copies of the message.

- You can recall the message and replace it with a new message, such as a message that includes the attachment you wanted to send.

To recall a message, follow these steps:

1. With the Mail folder selected, select the Sent Items folder.

2. Double-click the message that you want to recall to open it.

3. On the ribbon's Message tab, select More Move Actions (in the Move group) and then choose Recall This Message. The Recall This Message dialog box opens.

4. Two options are available related to recalling the message: Delete Unread Copies Of This Message (the default) and Delete Unread Copies And Replace With A New Message. Select the option you want to use. Make sure that the Tell Me If Recall Succeeds Or Fails For Each Recipient check box is enabled.

5. If you use the default option to recall the message, select OK. The Recall Message dialog box closes. If you select the Replace With A New Message option, a new message opens. Create the message that replaces the recalled message, and then click Send.

You will eventually receive a notification in your Inbox folder (as new mail) notifying you of whether the recall was successful.

NOTE

Remember that this feature is for Exchange Server mail accounts; you cannot recall messages sent via internet or Outlook.com email accounts.

NOTE

By default, Outlook provides information on whether the recall succeeds for each message recipient.

Although you can't recall internet email messages, you can use this feature to notify the recipients of a particular email message that you want them to ignore. Use the message recall feature as detailed in the steps in this section. When you "recall" the message, Outlook sends a new message to the original recipients stating that you would like to recall the previous message. This doesn't remove the original message from the recipients' Inboxes, but it at least gives them a follow-up message that the original message is essentially invalid.

Working with received email

New email is downloaded when you open Outlook, and it connects to your mail server (you must be connected to the internet or your corporate network for this to happen). When Outlook opens, it selects your email Inbox (by default) and lists your emails in the Details pane, including any new email messages that have been downloaded from your mail server. The most recent message (the newest) in the Inbox appears at the top of the list and is also previewed in the Reading pane. This is because Outlook groups your email in your Inbox by date, by default.

Reading mail is really just a matter of selecting the message that you want to read; the message appears in the Reading pane. You can also open a message in a separate window: Double-click the message in the Details pane.

After you read a particular message, you typically answer it, forward it, or delete it. Outlook tracks each of these actions. For example, when you reply to a message, the original message in the Inbox folder is marked with a Replied symbol. Outlook saves the reply message in the Sent Items folder.

Deleting an email message is straightforward. Select the message (or messages) and then press the Delete key. When you delete a message, Outlook moves it to the Deleted Items folder. When you empty the Deleted Items folder, that message (and anything else in the Deleted Items folder) is gone.

Organizing messages in the Inbox

Earlier in this chapter, we discussed how Outlook provides different views for working with your email. For example, the default Focused Inbox differentiates emails as either Focused or Other. There is also the option of showing emails as Conversations, which we will discuss more in the next section.

If you prefer the old-school approach to your Inbox where you are viewing emails by date received (and turning off both the Focused Inbox and Conversations options), you can still modify the default view for the Inbox using the options at the top of the Details pane. By default, All is selected, and all your messages are shown in the Details pane. You can quickly filter the list to show only messages that you have not read; select Unread.

If you want to change how the emails are listed in the Details pane, you can select the drop-down arrow next to By Date and select other options for organizing the messages in the Inbox, such as From, Categories, Subject, and even Importance. (Now, you can see the value of using message tags and assigning messages categories.) If you want to change the order of the messages, you can use the command just to the right of the command list (the list that enables you to view by Date, From, and so on). Click the order arrow (it's called Newest when you sort the email by Date) to change the order of the messages. For example, if you select Newest when your email is sorted by Date, it changes to Oldest, and now the oldest email is at the top of the email list in the Details pane.

You can also change the current view of the Inbox using the Arrangement commands found on the Outlook ribbon's View tab. For example, you can select To or From to change how the messages are sorted. The Reverse Sort button changes the order of the messages (which is based on the Arrangement command you have selected, such as Date, To, and From Categories).

Other commands that you can take advantage of on the View tab are in the Layout group. These commands—Folder Pane, Reading Pane, and To-Do bar—enable you to determine whether these panes are shown in the Outlook application window. For example, by default, the Folder Pane and the Reading Pane are shown. If you also want to view your To-Do list (Tasks) when working with your Inbox messages, you can select the To-Do Bar command and then select Tasks. If you want to hide the To-Do Bar (or the Folder or Reading Panes), select the command, and then select Off.

Showing messages as conversations

Another potential and useful way to view your emails in the Inbox is to arrange the messages by conversation. But what does it mean to arrange messages in conversations? A conversation involves emails that are associated to a particular mail message subject. For example, if you received an email in your Inbox and then replied to it, both the original email and the reply would be shown in your Inbox as a conversation group. The conversations are listed by date and in convenient date groupings, such as Today, Last Week, Two Weeks Ago, and Older, enabling you to quickly locate messages that relate to a particular time period. You can collapse and expand a time period group, such as Last Week, to make it easier to concentrate on other date groupings of email conversations listed in the Inbox folder.

To arrange your messages in conversations, select the ribbon's View tab and then select the Show As Conversations check box (in the Messages group). A message box opens and asks you whether you want to apply the conversation view to all mailboxes or just this folder. Click the response that works best for you. (I usually just select This Folder so that the Inbox is in conversation view; I don't like my Sent Items or Deleted Items as conversations because it's too confusing.) Figure 23-7 shows the Inbox arranged in conversations, with a conversation titled "Heading to Cayman!" expanded to show the emails in the conversation. The conversations view arranges the emails very much like a threaded web conversation.

Figure 23-7   Messages in the Inbox can be arranged in conversations.

CHAPTER 23

You can expand a threaded conversation as needed to view all the messages in a particular conversation. Because the conversations are listed by date, you can also change the order of the messages from newest to oldest by selecting the toggle at the top-right of the Details pane.

If you are using Conversations view, the reply appears in the Inbox folder as part of the conversation when you respond to a message. The same is true for forwarded email, which is marked with a Forwarded symbol in the Inbox folder. (Remember, all these sent emails end up in your Sent Items folder.)

Filtering email

The Arrangement commands change how Outlook arranges the messages in a folder such as the Inbox, but you might also want to view a subset of the messages in the Inbox folder, based on certain criteria, such as only messages flagged as High importance or only emails that have attachments. You can filter email using the Filter Email command on the Outlook ribbon's Home tab. The command uses the Outlook Search feature to filter the messages in the Inbox folder.

Select Filter Email and then select one of the available filters, such as Unread, Has Attachments, or Flagged. The list filters based on your selection, and the Search Tools tab appears on the ribbon. This tab enables you to set the scope for the filter, such as the current folder or all sub-folders, and refine the search. Search refinements enable you to add criteria to the search. For example, if you filtered your Inbox folder by Has Attachments, you could select the Categorized command to add a category to your search filter. You could add another refinement, such as importance, by selecting the Important command.

Several filter-refinement commands (which add criteria to the search filter) are available in the Refine group of the Search Tools tab, including Categorized, Sent To, and Flagged. You can access additional refinement criteria by selecting the More command, which provides the Common Properties list. This list enables you to refine the search by all sorts of criteria, including Bcc, Cc, Due Date, From, and Received.

When you have finished your work with the Search Tools and want to remove the filter you have placed on the current folder, select the Close Search command. Outlook returns you to the folder, such as the Inbox, and removes the filter, showing the folder's entire contents.

Managing email

Managing email is really just a matter of determining what to do with your received email messages, although you can manage the Sent Items folder and messages that you save in other folders for later consideration. Whether you read your messages in the Reading pane or prefer to open them in a separate window, all the commands you need to manage individual messages are easily accessible via the ribbon.

If you are working in the Inbox folder, the Outlook ribbon provides most of the message-management commands on the Home tab. If you are working with a received message that you have opened in its own window, the message-management commands are on the ribbon's Message tab (which is the only tab available, other than the File tab that takes you to the Backstage). More commands related to dealing with a message are on the Message tab of the message window's ribbon. So, you might want to open a message if you want to quickly perform an action related to that message. Figure 23-8 shows the message window's ribbon with the Message tab selected.

Figure 23-8   The ribbon's Message tab

Outlook dedicates most of the command groups on the Message tab to managing your received messages. For example, the Delete group provides options for dealing with messages that you no longer want, and the Respond group provides different commands for replying to or forwarding a message.

Using Quick Steps

Quick Steps are commands that combine multiple actions in one click. For example, the Move To Quick Step (one of the default Quick Steps) enables you to mark an email as read and move it into a particular folder. The Reply & Delete Quick Step opens a reply message for a selected message and, after you have completed and sent your reply, deletes the original message. To view all the default Quick Steps in the Quick Steps gallery (on the Message tab), select the More button.

Some of the default Quick Steps, such as the Move To and Done commands, require a brief setup the first time you select them. For example, if you are working in a message window and then select the Move To Quick Step, the First Time Setup dialog box opens, as shown in Figure 23-9.

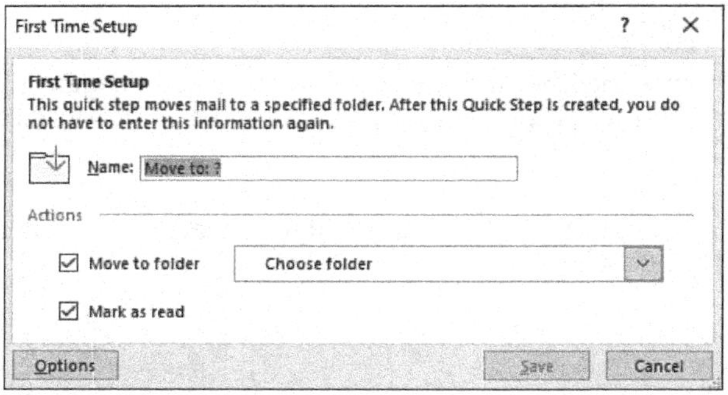

Figure 23-9   The First Time Setup dialog box for the Move To Quick Step

By default, this Quick Step moves items to the specified folder and marks them as read. Use the Choose Folder drop-down to specify the folder that the Quick Step should use. The name of the Quick Step changes to the name of the folder that you select. However, you can change the name as needed in the Name box. When you have finished setting up the Quick Step, click Save.

You aren't limited to the default Quick Steps provided in the Quick Steps group. You can create additional Quick Steps by selecting the dialog box launcher in the Quick Steps group. This opens the Manage Quick Steps dialog box, shown in Figure 23-10. You can use the dialog box to edit, duplicate, and delete existing Quick Steps. You can also change the order in which the Quick Steps appear in the Quick Steps group. Use the Move Up and Move Down buttons in the Manage Quick Steps dialog box, as needed.

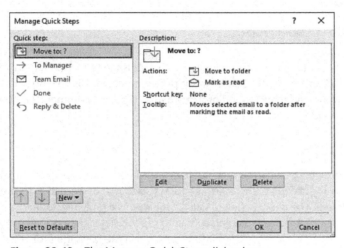

Figure 23-10   The Manage Quick Steps dialog box

You can also create custom Quick Steps. To create a new Quick Step, follow these steps:

1. In the Manage Quick Steps dialog box, click the New button and then select the type of Quick Step you want to create, such as Move To Folder, Categorize And Move, Flag And Move, and so on. When you select the Quick Step type, the First Time Setup dialog box appears.

2. Click the Options button in the First Time Setup dialog box (refer to Figure 23-9) to expand the dialog box. This enables you to see the current actions for the Quick Step and to add actions, if needed.

3. Specify options related to the actions. For example, if the action is Move To Folder, select the folder the mail should move to.

4. (Optional) If you want to add an action to the Quick Step, click the Add Action button; then select the action you want to take place (such as Categorize Message or Flag Message) from the Choose An Action drop-down menu for the new action.

5. (Optional) Select a shortcut key for the Quick Step from the Shortcut Key drop-down menu.

6. (Optional) Type text in the ToolTip text box (which appears when you hover the mouse over the Quick Step).

7. Type a name for the Quick Step in the Name box.

8. Click the Save button and then click Finish.

TIP

The Quick Steps group is also available on the Home tab of the Outlook ribbon. Quick Steps aren't reserved for working with mail messages; you can create Quick Steps that also enable you to manage other Outlook items, such as Tasks or Contacts.

Outlook adds the Quick Step to the Quick Step group. You can also edit, duplicate, and delete Quick Steps in the Manage Quick Steps dialog box, as needed.

Answering a message

Answering or replying to a message can take the form of a simple reply to the sender of the message or can encompass a reply that goes to everyone who received the original message and the sender of that message. The Respond group on the ribbon's Message tab provides several commands related to responding to a message.

To simply reply to the sender of the message, select the Reply command. A new message window opens, containing the original message text. Type your response to the message and then select Send.

If you want to reply to the sender and all the recipients of the original message, select Reply All. This opens a new message window addressed to the sender and all recipients, including those listed in the Cc or Bcc address boxes.

The next time you open a message to which you've replied, a reminder at the top of the message window tells you the date and time you sent your reply. Don't forget that the Replied To arrow next to a message in the Inbox window also shows that you have responded to the message.

CHAPTER 23

Forwarding a message

You can forward mail you have received as needed to coworkers or other concerned parties. When you forward a message, you can add text to the email and include new attachments if you choose. Forwarded mail includes any attachments that were part of the originally received message.

NOTE

Attachments are not included when you simply reply to a message.

Open the message that you want to forward or select the message in the Inbox folder. Select the Forward command in the Respond group. A new message window opens. Provide the addresses of the individuals that you want to receive the forwarded message. Select Send to send the forwarded message. Outlook places a copy of the forwarded message in your Sent Items folder and tags the original message as forwarded.

TIP

You can right-click a message and then select Reply or Reply All from the shortcut menu that appears.

Saving an attachment

When you receive messages with attachments, you might want to save those attachments to folders on your computer for later examination or reference, or even for editing. You can pick out messages with attachments in your Inbox because a paper clip icon beside the message subject represents a message attachment.

CAUTION

Attachments can pose a security hazard. Do not open attachments from unknown email senders. Even email from known parties merits at least some scrutiny. Save attachments to your computer, and then scan them with antivirus software before opening.

Select (in the Inbox) or open the message that contains the attachment you want to save. The attachment appears as a thumbnail above the message area. Select the attachment thumbnail, such as a picture, to preview it. Outlook previews the attached item either in the Reading pane (if you have not opened the message) or in the message window. When you are previewing the image, an Attachments tab appears on either the Message or Outlook ribbons. The Attachments tab provides tools related to printing, removing, saving, or copying the attachment.

The Actions group on the Attachments tab allows you to open, quick print, or remove the attachment. The Save To Computer group provides a Save As command. For emails containing multiple attachments, a Save All Attachments command is provided. If you want to immediately save a copy of the attachment (or attachments) to your OneDrive, select either the Upload or Upload All attachments in the Save To Cloud group.

If you want to select and then copy an attachment or attachments, select the Select All command in the Selection group and then select Copy (also in the Selection group). You can then paste the attachment or attachments into any of the other 365 applications as needed. To return to the message from the attachment preview, select the Show Message command on the Attachments tab. You can also use the Back To Message link at the top of the Preview pane to return to the message.

➤ **For more about attachments and Outlook security settings, see Chapter 26.**

Translating messages

An Outlook feature with great potential is the new Translate feature, which can be used to translate received messages that have been sent or forwarded to you in another language. Although you might read any number of languages, this feature is designed to help you with emails sent in languages you are not conversant in.

So, let's say you received an email in French and want to translate it into English. First, select the message in your Inbox. Then select the Translate command on the Outlook ribbon's Home tab and click Translate Message on the Translate menu. The message will be translated to English (or the language you have selected as your preferred language for your Microsoft 365 installation).

You can also translate selected words or phrases in the email as needed. Right-click a word and select Translate to view an English (or other language if your default 365 language is other than English) translation of the word. You can also select a phrase or an entire text block, such as a paragraph, and translate the selection using a right-click.

TIP

You can manage the language(s) you use for authoring and proofing in Outlook. In the Outlook Backstage, select the Options link to open the Outlook Options dialog box. Then select Language. The Office authoring languages and proofing settings can be used to add or remove languages from your 365 installation and designate your preferred language.

Deleting messages

You have options when you delete messages. (This is true for messages in your Inbox folder and the other mail folders). As already mentioned, the commands related to deleting mail messages are in the Delete group (this group is available on the Home tab of the Outlook ribbon and the Message group of a message window's ribbon). The most straightforward way to deal with a selected message or group of selected messages that you no longer want is to select the Delete command. The message or messages are moved to your Deleted Items folder. Outlook provides three other possibilities in the Delete group:

- **Ignore:** This command moves the currently selected message and any future messages in the conversation (based on the subject) to the Deleted Items folder.

- **Clean Up:** This command provides a list of three related commands: Clean Up Conversation, Clean Up Folder, and Clean Up Folder & Subfolders. If you select Clean Up Conversation, Outlook moves redundant messages in the conversation to the Deleted Items folder. Remember that the Conversation view can include messages that are present in other Mail folders, not just the Inbox folder. The Clean Up Folder and Clean Up Folder & Subfolders commands remove redundant messages in the current folder, as well as its subfolders, respectively.

- **Junk:** This command provides an options list that enables you to block the sender or to never block the sender or the sender's domain (such as @whatever.com). This command also enables you to access the Junk Email Options dialog box for your email account.

➤ **For more about dealing with junk email, and using message rules, see Chapter 26.**

The various commands provided in the Delete group make removing items from the Inbox folder or another mail folder a more constructive process in terms of keeping the Inbox free of unwanted, redundant, and spam email. Email messages can also be managed using rules, which are discussed later in the book.

When your emails are in the Deleted Items folder, they are destined for oblivion (although you can move a message in the folder to another folder if you decide you want to keep it). To permanently delete a message in the Deleted Items folder, select the message (you can select multiple messages) and then click the Delete command. A message appears asking whether you want to delete the selected item or items permanently. Click Yes to delete the message or messages permanently.

If you are confident about the status of messages that you delete (you don't want to undelete them), you can empty all the messages in the Deleted Items folder instead of deleting it message by message. Right-click the Deleted Items folder and select Empty Folder. Click Yes to verify the permanent deletion of the items in the Deleted Items folder.

You can also configure Outlook so that your Deleted Items folder empties when you exit Outlook. Select File to open the Backstage, and then select Options. In the Outlook Options window, select Advanced and navigate to the Outlook Start and Exit settings. Select the Empty Deleted Items Folders When Exiting Outlook check box. Outlook empties your Deleted Items folder (or folders, if you have multiple email accounts) when you exit.

Printing mail

You can print your email messages in multiple ways. To send a message to the printer without previewing it, right-click the message and select Quick Print from the shortcut menu. This sends the message directly to your default printer.

If you want to specify the printer, the print options, or the print style for the printout, select File and then Print. The Print window opens and provides a preview of the message. You can change the settings related to the print job, such as the printer and the print style, as required.

Moving email

You can also organize your mail messages by moving them from your Inbox folder to other folders. You can use the Move command on the Home tab of the ribbon to move and copy messages from one folder to another. This provides you with alternative places to store items and can make finding them in the future easier than having all your messages languish in the Inbox folder in one huge mess.

> ### TIP
>
> **You can create your own message filters directly in the Search box. Just type your key-words for the filter, and the messages that meet your criteria are listed in the Details pane.**

To move a message, select the message in the Details pane. Then select the Move command on the ribbon's Home tab. If you want to move the selected messages to another folder, select Other Folder (you also have the option of copying the email to another folder). The Move Items dialog box opens.

> ### TIP
>
> **If you have a lot of messages in the Inbox, you might want to filter the messages using particular criteria and then move those messages en masse to another folder, such as a folder where you keep all your excess emails.**

Specify the folder that you want to move the items to. If you need to create a new folder, select the New button. The Create New Folder dialog box opens. Type a name for the new folder, and then select the location in the folder list where you want to place the new folder. Click OK to close the Create New Folder dialog box; you return to the Move Items dialog box. Click OK to move the items and to close the Move Items dialog box.

If you don't like working with the Move Items dialog box, you can create folders directly in the Navigation pane's folder list and drag items from the current folder, such as the Inbox, to another folder. Right-click a particular email account and select New Folder from the shortcut menu. Provide a name for the folder, and it's ready to go. You can then select items in the current mail folder in the Details pane and drag them to the new folder.

Managing email accounts

As we discussed in Chapter 22, Outlook makes it easy for you to configure your default email account the first time you run Outlook. You can also add or delete email accounts as needed (you aren't stuck with a single email address or the email address you first configured in Outlook). You can also change the configuration settings for any existing email accounts. Outlook makes it pretty simple to add several types of email accounts to your account settings:

- **Microsoft 365:** If your organization or business uses Microsoft to host email or other network services through a Microsoft 365 subscription, your company's IT folks will determine your email account name and other settings. These accounts are similar to Exchange Server accounts in terms of how the account holder logs in and interacts with the account. If you have your email name and the password, that is typically enough information to set up the email account in Outlook.

- **Outlook.com or Exchange ActiveSync–compatible service:** This possibility enables you to configure an Outlook.com account for use in Outlook. Exchange ActiveSync was originally developed so that Microsoft Exchange email users could access their email on smart devices such as smartphones. The bottom line with this service is that it gives you access to your Outlook.com account, including your contacts and calendars. It also gives you the option of connecting Outlook to other web-based email services such as Gmail.

- **Microsoft Exchange Server (or compatible service):** This type of account makes Outlook an Exchange Server client; mailboxes and other resources, such as shared public folders, are managed on the Exchange Server on your network. Your network system administrator likely will configure this or provide you with the settings for an Exchange account. The current version of Outlook is also compatible with legacy Exchange Server installations, including Exchange 2013 and earlier.

- **POP account:** POP3 (Post Office Protocol 3) is a protocol that most ISPs use, which allows a POP3 email server to function as a mail drop. This means that your incoming email arrives at the POP3 server and sits there until you connect with your email client (Outlook) and download the mail to your computer. The home email accounts provided by your Internet service provider are almost always POP3 accounts.

- **IMAP account:** IMAP (Internet Message Access Protocol) is a protocol that allows Outlook to download email from an IMAP mail server. IMAP differs from POP3, in that your email is not removed from the mail server when you connect to the server with Outlook. Instead, Outlook provides you with a list of saved and new messages, which you can then open and read. IMAP is particularly useful when more than one device, such as your computer and a smartphone or other mobile device, can access a single email account. Other examples of IMAP-type accounts are Yahoo and Google mail.

NOTE

Both POP3 and IMAP accounts have to be configured with the outgoing mail server information, which is the SMTP server. SMTP is the Simple Mail Transport Protocol and is used to get your mail from your computer to your provider's SMTP mail server and then on to the internet for delivery.

To access your Outlook account settings, select File and then Info. In the Backstage Account Information window, select Account Settings. If you are using Outlook for internet email only (POP3), only Account Settings and the Social Network Accounts are available on the Account Settings menu. If you use Outlook as an Exchange Server client, you also have access to Delegate Access, Download Address Book (the Global Exchange Address Book for your Exchange Server network), and Manage Mobile Notifications. Select Account Settings on the menu. The Account Settings dialog box opens. The Email tab of the Account Settings dialog box lists your currently installed email accounts, as shown in Figure 23-11.

TIP

An excellent way to keep your mail messages organized is to use rules that automatically determine what happens to an email message or messages that meet particular conditions. These rules move or delete messages, depending on the rule actions. See Chapter 26 for more about rules.

Figure 23-11   The Account Settings dialog box with the Email tab selected

Editing email account settings

To view the current settings for an email account, double-click the account (in the Account Settings dialog box). The Change Account dialog box opens (which you can also open by selecting the account and then clicking the Change icon on the toolbar). You can view the user information, server information, and log-in information for the account. You can edit account settings, if necessary, and then use the Test Account Settings button to see whether the new account settings work correctly.

Change your account settings only if your email provider sent you a notice to change settings or if the account is not working correctly. When you open the Account Settings dialog box for an email account, the information that can be edited will depend on the type of email account you are working with. Username and other account options, such as the mail server, can be changed for an Exchange ActiveSync service email, such as an Outlook.com account or POP3 and IMAP accounts. Again, make sure that you have the correct information from your email provider before making any changes to your email account settings.

If an account is not working correctly, you can also use the Repair command to open the Auto Account Setup tool in the Repair Account dialog box. Auto Account Setup is the same tool you use when you add a new account to Outlook. It walks you through all the steps of setting up the account, which might be useful when correcting problems with the account, particularly if you have entered information incorrectly that is required for Outlook to set up the mail account.

If an email account that you no longer have or use is listed in the Account Settings dialog box (for instance, you have changed ISPs), you can delete that account from the list. Select the account and then click the Remove button. Outlook asks you to verify the removal. If you truly want to remove the account, select Yes.

TIP

Both POP3 and IMAP accounts have to be configured with the outgoing mail server information, which is the SMTP server. SMTP, the Simple Mail Transport Protocol, is used to get your mail from your computer to your provider's SMTP mail server and then on to the Internet for delivery.

You have complete control over which of your email accounts is considered the default account for Outlook. Typically, you send new mail messages from the default account (so keep this in mind when selecting your default account). Select an account in the account list, and then click the Set As Default button. Outlook designates the default account with the default icon (a circle with a check mark). This change does not take place until you close the Account Settings dialog box and then restart Outlook.

Adding an email account automatically

You can add email accounts to the Outlook configuration as needed. All you have to do is select Add Account in the Outlook Backstage Info window. Outlook will do a search for email accounts on your system and list any valid email addresses in the Outlook Add Account window. If the email address you want to add is not listed in the Email Address box, type in the email address and then click the Connect button.

You will be asked to provide the password for the account and then an Account Setup Complete message appears. If you look in the Folder pane, you will see that the email address has been added and that an Inbox, Drafts, Sent Items, and Deleted Items folders have been set up for the new account as well.

> TIP
>
> **If you are having a problem adding an Exchange Server email account to Outlook (particularly if you configured an Internet email account as your first Outlook email account), you might have to close Outlook and open the Account Settings dialog box using the Mail command in the Windows Control Panel. Open the Control Panel, select User Accounts, and then select the Mail icon. In the Mail Setup–Outlook dialog box, click the Email Accounts button. This opens the Account Settings dialog box, and you can select New to add the Exchange mail account.**

Adding a mail account manually

If auto-setup doesn't work for you, or if you just want to set up an email account yourself, you can manually configure your account. This can be very useful when internet email from an ISP just doesn't seem to want to go the automatic route. Your ISP should supply you with the POP3, IMAP (Internet Message Access Protocol), and SMTP (Simple Mail Transfer Protocol) server names. With these types of email accounts, your ISP also typically provides you with a master log-in name and password; you can then specify the username and password for emails that you create using the master logon as needed.

To add an account manually, select Add Account on the Outlook Backstage Info page. The Outlook Mail Setup window will open. Enter your email address and then select the drop-down arrow next to Advanced options. In the center of the dialog box, select the Let Me Set Up My Account Manually check box and then select Connect. The Choose Account Type window will open.

Select the icon for your account type: Microsoft 365, Outlook.com, Google, Exchange, POP, or IMAP. Add the required information for the email type you are installing. For example, with a POP account, you will need to enter the name of the incoming mail POP server in the Incoming Mail Server box. Enter the SMTP server in the Outgoing Server box. If your ISP provided you with specific port numbers for the incoming mail and outgoing mail servers, enter that information in the appropriate Port box.

Once you have entered the POP account or other email account type settings, you can enter the password for your email account and then select Connect. It might take a few moments, but if the settings were entered correctly for the email account, the Account Setup Is Complete window will open. Click OK to return to Outlook. When adding an email account manually is successful, Outlook adds mail folders (Inbox, Drafts, Sent Items, Deleted Items, Junk Email, Outbox, and Search Folders) for the account to the Folder pane. If you are adding an Outlook.com account, the Calendar for the account is added to your My Calendars list; the Contacts (People) list from the account is added to your People lists; and any tasks that you created using the Outlook.com account are available in the My Tasks list when you select Tasks on the Navigation bar.

CAUTION

Outlook email accounts and Outlook profiles are closely connected entities. I recommend that you look over Chapter 22 and read the "Configuring Outlook at first start" and "Understanding Outlook profiles" sections before you add email accounts to Outlook's configuration.

Setting Outlook mail options

We have already discussed options that can be set for individual Outlook mail messages, such as tracking options and delivery options. You also have the option of configuring different email settings using a more "global approach" by accessing the Outlook Options window. You access these various settings and options via the Backstage. Select File and then Options; the Outlook Options window opens. Select Mail to access the mail-related options, as shown in Figure 23-12.

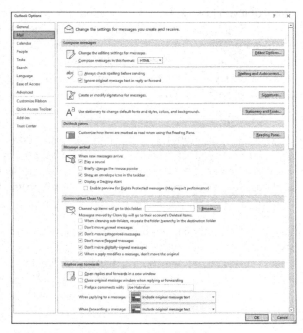

Figure 23-12   Outlook Options dialog box

The Mail Options window provides a number of categories of options:

- **Compose Messages:** These settings include the default message format (HTML, Rich Text, or plain text) and whether Outlook spell-checks messages before sending them. Other options involve the creation and modification of signatures and address whether Outlook uses personal stationery when creating new messages.

- **Outlook Panes:** This group provides access to the Reading Pane dialog box. You can select options such as when items are marked as read and whether to enable single-key reading using the spacebar.

- **Message Arrival:** These options relate to what happens when a new message arrives in the Inbox folder. Options include playing a sound, changing the mouse pointer, and displaying an envelope icon in the taskbar. You can also enable an automatic preview for messages that have been assigned rights protection.

- **Conversation Cleanup:** These options relate to how Outlook cleans up the Inbox folder when you select the Clean Up command. You can specify the folder that cleaned-up items are move to. Also, you can specify that Outlook not move messages that meet certain criteria, such as unread, categorized, or flagged messages.

- **Replies And Forwards:** These options include an option for automatically closing the original message window when you reply to or forward the message. You can also specify whether the original message text is included in your replies or forwarded messages.

- **Save Messages:** These options relate to saving drafts and whether Outlook saves forwarded messages in the Sent Items folder. You can set when a draft of a message should be saved, based on the minutes it has been opened and not yet sent. You can also determine whether forwarded messages should be saved if copies of sent messages are being placed in the Sent Items folder.

- **Send Messages:** These options enable you to specify the default importance and sensitivity levels and to specify an expiration date for messages. Other settings include automatic name-checking (of email addresses) and whether Outlook should delete meeting requests and notifications from your mailbox as you respond.

- **MailTips:** These options allow you to specify when MailTips display. You make settings in the MailTips options dialog box and can assign them to specific email accounts. MailTips options include those for special message circumstances, such as when the recipient address is not valid, when the message is too large to send, and when the recipient is external to your MailTips. MailTips are only available as options if you are using Outlook for an Exchange Server email account.

CHAPTER 23

- **Tracking:** These options enable you to require delivery and read receipts for all your messages, and always to send a read receipt when you receive a message with Read Receipt Required specified.

- **Message Format:** These options primarily relate to HTML emails. You can send HTML messages using cascading style sheets and reduce message size by removing formatting that is not essential to display the message properly.

- **Other:** These options include shading message headers when you are reading messages and specifying whether Outlook shows the Paste Options button when you paste content into a message.

Two additional options are related to the Inbox and Deleted Items folders. When you select Advanced in the Outlook Options window, look at the Outlook start and exit options. By default, Outlook starts with the Inbox folder selected. You can change this to one of the other Outlook folders, if you want, such as the Calendar or Contacts folder. However, because email seems important to everyone, why not leave it set to the Inbox folder? A check box related to the Deleted Items folder is also available in this set of options. If you want to empty your Deleted Items folder, select Empty Deleted Items Folders When Exiting Outlook. Then click OK to close the Outlook Options window.

Using the calendar for appointments and tasks

Navigating the calendar   739

Scheduling an appointment   743

Searching the calendar   748

Sharing calendars   750

Setting calendar options   757

Working with tasks   758

Staying organized can often seem like a futile endeavor. However, Outlook provides a relatively painless way for you to keep track of both your busy personal and work life. Outlook's calendar provides an effective yet easy-to-use environment for managing your schedule. In fact, Outlook can help you juggle multiple calendars so that you can easily track both your work and personal appointments and events. You can keep track of one-time appointments and events and also schedule recurring appointments and tasks.

The fact that Outlook can manage multiple calendars means that you can use it to manage your professional and personal calendars or manage calendars related to different projects. For example, you can have a calendar associated with each email account that you manage using Outlook. You can also create calendars that enable you to manage different types of events. For example, you can have a calendar for work-related events and a calendar for personal appointments and events. In this chapter, we look at navigating the calendar and working with multiple calendars, including shared calendars. We also look at working with appointments and tasks, as well as setting calendar and task options.

Navigating the calendar

To access the Outlook calendar folder, select Calendar in the navigation bar. By default, the calendar is in Month view. The Folder pane shows the current and next month and also provides a list of all your calendars in the My Calendars list. The Details pane shows the current month, and the current day is highlighted. Figure 24-1 shows the default view for the calendar.

Figure 24-1   The Outlook Calendar in the Month view

Any appointments or other events that you have entered are now visible on the calendar. (Some events might have been assigned to you by coworkers, supervisors, or administrative assistants, particularly if you share your calendar with these individuals). Each event on the calendar provides you with the start time, the name of the event, and its location. If you place the mouse on a particular appointment or other event, a ScreenTip appears and provides the details for the appointment, including the start and end times, the location, the name of the meeting organizer (if it is someone other than you), and whether a reminder has been set for the event.

As already mentioned, thumbnail versions of the current month and the next month appear on the Folder pane. This area is referred to as the Date Navigator. The current date is highlighted on the Date Navigator. Any dates that have scheduled appointments or events are shown in bold.

If you select a date on the Date Navigator, the calendar switches to Day view, which shows the currently selected day in detail. It lists the appointments and events that you have scheduled for the day. You can scroll through the hours of the day to view scheduled appointments as needed.

When you view a particular date in the Day view that does not contain an appointment(s), two navigation tools appear on the page for that day: Previous Appointment (on the left) and Next Appointment (on the right). You can click Previous Appointment to move backward through the calendar to the closest (to the current day) appointment. If you click Next Appointment, you move forward in the calendar to the next scheduled appointment or event. You will find that the options to move to the next scheduled appointment (or back to the next previous appointment) are available in all the calendar views except for the Schedule view. You can also navigate Day view using the Back and Forward buttons on the left corner of the calendar.

You have also probably noticed that the weather is provided for the next three days starting with the current day. The current and the following day are shown as Today and Tomorrow respectively. The weather information will appear at the top of the calendar when you work in any calendar views. By selecting the drop-down arrow next to the current city, you can change the location for the streamed weather (depending on your Outlook window size, you can see up to three days of weather). Select Add Location and provide the city and state information. You can select any of the locations in the list as you require. If you want to remove a location from the list, place the mouse on the location and click the X.

TIP

To view more months in the Date Navigator, drag the border between the navigator and the calendar list downward in the Navigation pane to expand the navigator area. Do the opposite if you want to see fewer months.

Changing the calendar view

You can quickly change your view of the calendar information by using the commands in the Arrange group. These commands are available on both the ribbon's Home tab and the View tab when you are working with the calendar. The calendar views are as follows:

NOTE

If you have multiple email accounts, such as an Exchange account and an Outlook.com account, multiple calendars appear in the My Calendars list and in Month view (by default).

- **Day:** This view shows the current day. You can use the Calendar Navigator to quickly change the current day shown in the Reading pane. You can use the Back and Forward buttons to move back or forward in the calendar, day by day.

- **Work Week:** This view shows the current workweek of Monday through Friday. Select any date on the Calendar Navigator to view a different workweek.

- **Week:** This view shows the current week. Use the Calendar Navigator to specify a different week for this view.

- **Month:** This view shows the current month. When you change the month in the Calendar Navigator, that particular month is shown in the Reading pane.

CHAPTER 24

- **Schedule View:** This view is designed for comparing multiple calendars. If you have multiple email accounts configured in Outlook, these accounts also have associated calendars. For example, you might have a work email account configured in Outlook and a personal account such as an Outlook.com account. Schedule view lists the time across the top of the calendar in a horizontal layout. The calendars shown in this view are arranged vertically along the left side of the view. Use the horizontal scrollbar along the bottom of the Reading pane to scroll through the time scale.

When navigating within a particular calendar view, you can use the Back and Forward buttons at the top left of the Reading pane to change to one of the other views, such as Work Week or Month. Select the appropriate command in the Arrange group.

The calendar folder's ribbon also provides a Go To group on the Home tab that can be useful for going to a particular day or range of days. To return to the current day (no matter which view you are currently using), select the Today command. If you want to view the next seven days, which uses a format similar to the Work Week and Week views, select the Next 7 Days command in the Go To group.

TIP

You can add other users' shared calendars (this is pretty typical in an Exchange Server environment) to your Outlook Calendar folder. Select the Add A Calendar button in the lower part of the Schedule view. Sharing calendars is discussed in more detail later in this chapter in the section "Sharing calendars."

If you select the Dialog Box Launcher at the bottom-right of the Go To group, the Go To Date dialog box opens. This dialog box enables you to specify both a date and a view. You can use the Date drop-down menu to open a Calendar Navigator and then specify the date that you want to go to. You can then use the Show In drop-down menu to specify the view that you want to use, such as Week Calendar, Month Calendar, and so on.

Change the time scale and time zone

When you are working in a particular view, you might want to change the time scale that is currently being used in that view. By default, the time scale is set to 30 minutes. You can change the time scale using the Time Scale command in the Arrangement group on the View tab (the Time Scale command is not available on the Home tab).

If you decrease the time scale, you have more space for viewing the details related to your various scheduled appointments and events. If you increase the time scale, you have less space to view the details related to your appointments but are able to condense the timeline for that particular view and see a greater range of time.

You can change the time scale in the following views: Day, Work Week, Week, and Schedule view. To change the time scale, select the Time Scale command and then select a different time scale interval, such as 60 minutes, 15 minutes, and so on.

You can also use the Time Scale command to change the current time zone. This is particularly useful when you are on the road and are operating in a different time zone. Changing the time zone ensures that any set appointment or task alarms are operating correctly. The default time zone set for Outlook is based on the time zone you selected for your Windows installation. The time zone information is located in the Outlook options for the calendar, which are typically accessed via the Options command in the Backstage.

NOTE

You can add a second time zone to the Outlook calendar. Select the Show A Second Time Zone check box in the Time Zones pane of the Outlook Options window. You can then select the time zone using the Time Zone drop-down menu. This can be useful if you work with people who are located in a different time zone.

You can quickly access the calendar options via the Time Scale command. To change the current time zone, select the Time Scale command and then select Change Time Zone. The Outlook Options window opens with the Calendar Options selected.

Click the Time Zone drop-down menu and select a new time zone for Outlook. Then click OK. This closes the Outlook Options window and returns you to the calendar.

Scheduling an appointment

You can quickly create appointments in any calendar view. You also have different options for creating appointments; two possibilities are using the New Appointment command on the ribbon's Home tab and double-clicking a specific day and time in the Reading pane. Either option opens the Appointment dialog box, shown in Figure 24-2.

Enter a subject for the appointment in the Subject box. You can also enter a location. Make sure the appropriate date and start time are entered in the Start Time box. You can use the Start Time drop-down menu to access a Calendar Navigator and specify the appointment date. You can also set the time. If you double-click a particular time in the calendar in the Reading pane, the date should be correctly specified when the Appointment dialog box opens.

You might also want to adjust the end time for the meeting. By default, Outlook schedules each appointment for one time slot, which by default, is 30 minutes. Use the End Time box's time drop-down menu to specify the end time for the appointment.

Each appointment has a body text area that enables you to add notes related to the appointment. You can also insert business cards, Outlook items, pictures, or other items related to the appointment using the various commands on the Insert tab. You can also attach files to an appointment if needed.

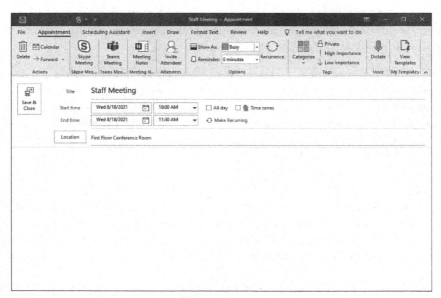

Figure 24-2   The Appointment dialog box

Select the Time Zones command in the Options group if you want to specify a time zone for the start time or end time, which can be extremely useful if you are traveling between time zones. (If you have reduced the size of the appointment window, you might not see the whole ribbon; click Options and then Time Zones.) This places Time Zone drop-down menus to the right of the Start Time and End Time boxes. You can select a time zone from the appropriate time zone drop-down menu, as you require.

When you create an appointment, you have control over how the appointment is shown on the calendar. Appointments are shown on the calendar as Busy, by default. To change this setting, select the Show As drop-down menu in the Options group to select an option other than Busy for the appointment; other status possibilities include Working Elsewhere, Tentative, and Out of Office.

> **TIP**
>
> **Use the Browse button to locate a different sound file if you want to use a sound other than the default. If you do not want a sound to play when the reminder opens, deselect the Play This Sound check box in the Reminder Sound dialog box.**

You can also set a reminder for the appointment. By default, Outlook automatically specifies a 15-minute reminder. You can select the Reminder command to choose from a list of different time increments (5 Minutes, 10 Minutes, 1 Hour, 1 Day, and so on). By default, a reminder sound is played when the Reminder box opens for the appointment. You can select the Sound command at the bottom of the Reminder list to open the Reminder Sound dialog box.

You can also tag an appointment with categories, specify importance levels, or mark the appointment as private using the commands available in the Tags group (on the Appointment tab). When you mark an appointment as private, the details of the appointment are not shown to other users with whom you have shared your calendar.

After you have specified the various parameters and options for your new appointment, select the Save & Close command on the Appointment tab. The appointment is added to the calendar.

Scheduling a recurring appointment

If you have a weekly, monthly, or otherwise consistently recurring appointment, you can quickly schedule it on your Outlook calendar. The appointment must recur at a set time interval, such as Weekly or Monthly. To create a recurring appointment from the calendar folder, select the New Items command on the Home tab, point at More Items, and then select Recurring Appointment. The Appointment Recurrence dialog box opens, as shown in Figure 24-3.

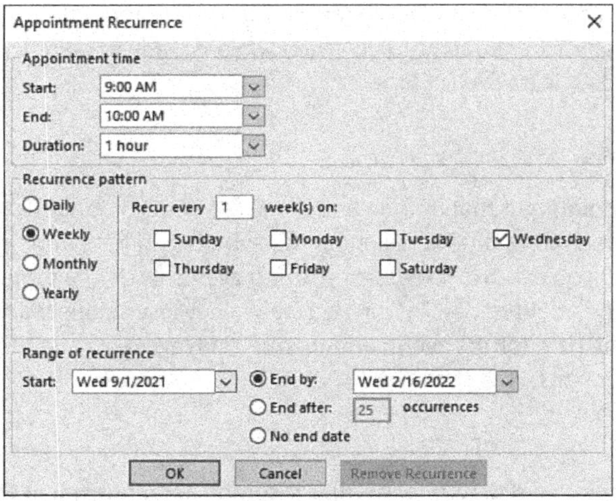

Figure 24-3   The Appointment Recurrence dialog box

In the Appointment Time area, enter the start and end times for the appointment. Outlook calculates the duration of the appointment for you. In the Recurrence Pattern area, indicate the frequency of the appointment: Daily, Weekly, Monthly, or Yearly. After you select the recurrence pattern, you are provided with options such as day of the week (for a weekly recurring appointment) and day of the month (for a monthly recurring appointment). Specify how often the appointment recurs and the time period (such as day of the week).

CHAPTER 24

In the Range Of Recurrence area, enter appropriate time limits using the following guidelines:

- **Start:** Select the date on which the recurring appointments begin.

- **End by:** Select this option and enter an ending date to limit the number of recurring appointments.

- **End after:** Select this option and enter the number of appointments if there is a specific limit to the recurring appointments.

- **No End Date:** Select this option if the recurring appointments are not on a limited schedule.

After you have set all the recurrence options for the appointment, click OK to close the Appointment Recurrence dialog box. This takes you to the Appointment dialog box for the recurring appointment. The start and stop options for the appointment have been replaced by recurrence information, which specifies when the appointment recurs, when it starts (an Effective Date), and the time for the recurring appointment.

Enter a subject for the appointment; you can also add a location and other information in the appointment body. Also, you can specify the reminder settings for the appointment and tag the appointment as you would any other appointment. When you are ready to place the recurring appointment on the calendar, select Save & Close.

Scheduling an event

An event is really just an appointment that lasts an entire day (24 hours or longer). You can use events to block out larger timeframes on your calendar than you would for a normal appointment. As with appointments, you can also schedule recurring events, such as a monthly seminar or some other event that lasts an entire day. To quickly create a new event, select a time slot in the calendar (to specify the date for the event) and then select New Items and then All Day Event. The Event dialog box opens.

TIP

You can make any appointment (new or existing) a recurring appointment. In the appointment window (new or existing), select the Recurrence command on the Appointment tab to open the Appointment Recurrence dialog box.

The Event dialog box is almost the same as the Appointment dialog box, but the Start Time and End Time boxes are deactivated because the event lasts all day. You can edit the date for the Start Time and End Time boxes (the same day) if required. Specify a subject for the event and an optional location. As with appointments, you can set reminder options for the event and assign tags to the event, such as categories and importance levels.

You can also make the event a recurring event. Once you designate the appointment an event, select the Recurrence command on the ribbon's Event tab, which opens the Appointment Recurrence dialog box (even though this is still technically an event). Set the recurrence parameters and click OK to close the dialog box and return to the event. When you are ready to add the event to the calendar, select Save & Close.

When viewing your calendar, you have probably noticed that appointments appear in their specific time slots. Events are listed just below the day designation in the calendar when you are using the Day, Work Week, or Week view. When you use Month view, you can tell events from appointments because events are shown in bold on the calendar day.

Editing and managing appointments

You can edit appointments (or events) in the calendar, as you require. Double-click an appointment in the calendar, and the appointment's dialog box opens. You can change the subject, location, date, and time for the appointment. You can also add information to the appointment body or change other settings related to the appointment using the various commands on the ribbon. After making changes to an appointment, recurring appointment, or event, select the Save & Close command.

You can also manage appointments directly on the calendar. To change the appointment subject, select the appointment on the calendar and then click inside the subject text. You can edit the text as needed.

You can also move an appointment to a different time or day on the calendar. To change either of these parameters, drag the appointment to a new location (in terms of date and time). If you want to change the time for the appointment by dragging, make sure that you are in the Day, Work Week, or Week view. You can also drag an appointment to a different date in Month view, but you cannot change the time of the appointment. However, you can quickly edit the time by double-clicking the appointment and then editing the time in the Appointment dialog box. You can view the time range for an appointment in any of the calendar views; hover the mouse over the appointment.

When you do select an appointment in the calendar, the Calendar Tools appear with the Appointment tab. Options such as the Reminder settings and Tags can be quickly selected for the appointment.

You can also delete unneeded appointments from the calendar. Select the appointment and then press the Delete key. You can also delete a selected appointment or event from the calendar using the Delete command in the Actions group on the ribbon. In either case, the appointment is removed from the calendar.

Searching the calendar

Outlook provides a robust and flexible Search tool that you can use to search your calendar or any shared calendars. The Search Calendar box is on the top right of your calendar (no matter what view you are using).

You may have to collapse the ribbon if you currently have it expanded and close the Task list. Both items can obscure the Search Calendars box.

TIP

About dead center in the upper part of the Outlook window is another search box that is directly above the Address Book icon. This is the Search People box. It searches through your contacts and address lists. This search box does not allow you to search your calendar.

Once you click in the Search Calendar box, the Search tab will appear as an option on the ribbon. Select Search, and the Search tabs become available on the ribbon, as shown in Figure 24-4.

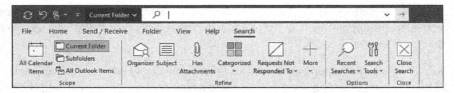

Figure 24-4   The ribbon's Search Tools

One way to search the calendar is to type keywords into the Search box. The appointments and events that match the search terms are displayed in the Reading pane sorted by date. Appointments are listed in a tabular format that provides field names such as Subject, Location, Start, and End as the field column headings. You can reorder the list of appointments found by clicking any of the field headings. To clear the search, click the X to the right of the Search box.

As already mentioned, a number of commands are provided by the Search Tools, which are activated on the ribbon as soon as you click in the Search box. You can use commands in the Refine group to conduct a new search or refine a search that was based on keywords. For example, you can view appointments that have file attachments by selecting the Has Attachments command. If you have categorized appointments or events, you can use the Categorized command to select a specific category; then only messages that have been assigned that category will appear in the search results.

You can also refine your search using parameters related to whether you have responded to or accepted an appointment. The Requests Not Responded To command (in the Refine group) allows you to limit the search to accepted appointments, tentative appointments, or appointment requests that you have not responded to.

You can access additional properties for your search criteria by selecting the Advanced Find command. Select Search Tools in the Options group (on the Search tab) and then select Advanced Find. The Advanced Find dialog box will open, as shown in Figure 24-5.

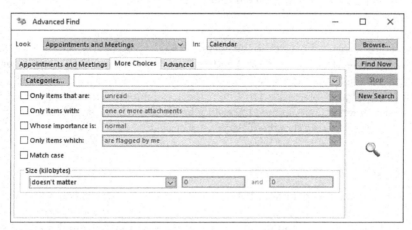

Figure 24-5   The Advanced Find

The More Choices tab of the Advanced dialog box provides the most possibilities for designing an advanced search. Parameters are set using a series of check boxes that are associated with a drop-down menu containing a list of possibilities. There are five check box/drop-down menu combinations in the Advanced Find dialog box:

- **Only Items That Are:** This check box has an accompanying drop-down menu that provides two choices: Unread or Read.

- **Only Items With:** This check box option offers two choices: One Or More Attachments or No Attachments.

- **Whose Importance Is:** This check box box provides three possible levels of importance: Normal, High, and Low.

- **Only Items Which:** This check box has a drop-down menu that provides four different parameters: Are Marked Completed, Are Flagged by Someone Ese, Have No Flag, and Are Flagged By Me.

- **Match Case:** This check box allows you to search for items in the calendar that match the case of your search term.

NOTE

Calendar appointments and meetings can be flagged just like email messages. For example, you can flag a meeting using the importance flags such as High Importance or Low Importance. You can add the flag when you first create the appointment or meeting or can add the flag by opening up the appointment or meeting. Flags are discussed in more detail in Chapter 23 in the section "Setting message flags, importance, and sensitivity."

Once you have set up your search in the Advanced Find dialog box, select the Find Now button. This will run the search (Advanced Find) and list the matching appointments and meetings in a results pane at the bottom of the Advanced Find dialog box. You can access any of the items in the results pane by double-clicking that item; the appointment or meeting window will open for that item. When you are finished reviewing the items in the Advanced Find dialog box, you click the X in the upper-right of the dialog box to close it.

Sharing calendars

Outlook gives you different options for sharing your calendar information with coworkers, colleagues, friends, and family. One of the easiest ways to share calendar information, such as an appointment, is to select the appointment on the calendar and then use the Forward command on the Actions tab to quickly send the appointment to a coworker or colleague.

Outlook was originally designed as the email client for the Exchange (email) Server environment and enables you to share your calendar and also allows others to share their calendars with you. Exchange environments have typically been restricted to bigger companies and institutions, though Microsoft 365 subscriptions for small business combine the power of Exchange with Outlook at the smallest businesses. Other possibilities for sharing your Outlook calendar include the capability to email calendar information and to publish your calendar online.

Even if you subscribe to Microsoft 365 as a home user, you can still take advantage of many of the features described in the "Creating a calendar share invitation" section that follows. If you have configured Outlook with a free Outlook.com email account, you will find that you can both share your calendar and share the calendars of colleagues, collaborators, and even family members.

Creating a calendar share invitation

If you are using Outlook as an Exchange Server client, your calendar is stored on the Exchange server, making it easy to share your calendar with coworkers on the Exchange network.

To share your calendar, select the Share Calendar command on the Home tab. The Calendar Properties dialog box opens, as shown in Figure 24-6. Select the Permissions tab (if it is not already selected) and then select Add. The Global Address List opens in the Add Users dialog box. (If you are using an Outlook.com email account, select your Contacts list in the Address Book drop-down menu.) Add a recipient or recipients from the list; select a recipient or recipients, and then select the Add button. You can also access recipients from your Contacts and other address lists that are provided by your Exchange Server network. Once you have added the names to the shared calendar list, select OK. This will close the Add Users dialog box and return you to the Permissions tab of the Calendar Properties dialog box. You can set the permission level to Can View (the default) or Can Edit.

Figure 24-6   Sharing a calendar via the Calendar Properties dialog box

Once you set the permission level, select OK. An invitation to share the calendar will be sent automatically to everyone you added to the shared calendar list. The invitation email will provide an Accept link and will also describe the share level (View or Edit).

Inside OUT

Not all email client calendars are created equal.

Sharing your calendar with other users (and vice versa) can be very useful in work environments in which you closely collaborate with colleagues who are not housed in the same location that you are. If you use Outlook as your email client in an Exchange Server environment, you will have no problem using the Share Calendar command in the ribbon's Share group to share your calendar with other users on your network.

If you are using an Outlook.com email account in Outlook, you also can share your calendar using the Share Calendar command as you would if you were using an Exchange client installation of Outlook. This is a relatively new wrinkle in Outlook. Past versions of Outlook.com email accounts (including Hotmail accounts) were treated like POP or IMAP accounts, which do not allow the direct sharing of the Outlook calendar. Outlook.com accounts now work like Microsoft Exchange accounts and fundamentally function as email accounts that are provided to you by your company via Microsoft Exchange Server.

Unfortunately, POP and IMAP email accounts (such as Gmail or a POP account from your ISP) do not provide you with a calendar that you can share, and the Share Calendar and Calendar Permissions commands are unavailable.

You can control the amount of detail shown when the recipient views your calendar. Select the Details drop-down menu; the default setting is Availability Only, but you can also select Limited Details or Full Details. Obviously, Full Details shares all the information on the calendar, including appointment body notes. After you have addressed the sharing invitation and set the other options, select Send. The invitation is sent to the recipient or recipients.

Opening a shared calendar

If coworkers or colleagues share a calendar with you, you receive a sharing invitation email. To add the calendar to your Calendar list, select the link provided in the Sharing Invitation email. You may have to verify the calendar addition to your Outlook configuration, and then the calendar is added to the Shared Calendars group in the Navigation pane.

The level of detail you can view in the calendar depends on the detail setting that was selected by the user who is sharing the calendar. You can view the shared calendar as you would your own calendar using the various Arrange and View commands provided on the ribbon.

Viewing multiple calendars

Multiple calendars can be opened in the Reading pane. Select the check box for each calendar that you want to view (in the Folder pane). Each calendar you have opened resides in its own pane in the Reading pane. When you are working with multiple and shared calendars, Outlook provides two useful tools that enable you to compare your appointments and events with another user's calendar (or users' calendars). These two tools are the Overlay feature and calendar groups (although the Schedule view that we discussed earlier in the chapter is also useful when viewing and comparing multiple calendars).

The Overlay feature enables you to superimpose calendars. This can be useful if you want to take a quick look at multiple calendars to check for overlapping or conflicting appointments. To overlay multiple calendars, select the calendar in the Folder pane. On the ribbon's View tab, select the Overlay command. The calendar is then superimposed over the other selected calendar, as shown in Figure 24-7.

Both calendars are color-coded, and you can switch between the calendars using the tabs provided on the upper right of the Reading pane. You can click the tab for a calendar to bring it to the forefront. Select the Close Calendar button (X) on that calendar if you want to close it.

If you often view several shared calendars in Outlook throughout the course of your workday, you might want to create calendar groups. A calendar group is a listing of multiple calendars. You can quickly open the calendars in a group by selecting that group (instead of the individual calendars).

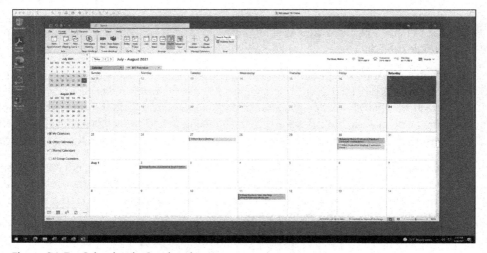

Figure 24-7 Calendars in Overlay view

> **NOTE**
>
> **You can set permissions for calendars shared on an Exchange network. Use the Calendar Properties dialog box to set permissions for your shared calendar. Click the Calendar Permissions dialog box on the Calendar Home tab to open the current calendar's properties.**

The easiest way to create a new calendar group is to first open the calendars you want to include in the group in the Reading pane and then select each calendar in the Folder pane. On the Home tab, select Calendar Groups and select Save As New Calendar Group. The Create New Calendar Group dialog box opens. Provide a name for the new group and then click OK. In the future, you can quickly open all the calendars in the group by selecting the group in the Folder pane (the group appears as another calendar category in the Folder pane along with My Calendars and Shared Calendars).

Emailing calendar items

If you want to share items on your calendar with coworkers, colleagues, or family members who are not using Outlook or an Outlook.com email—meaning situations where you can't share the entire calendar—you can forward appointments, meetings, or events to any valid email address. Depending on the calendar program that the recipient is using, they might be able to add an item, such as an appointment, directly to their calendar.

For example, if you forward an appointment to a Gmail recipient, the received email provides the date and other information related to the appointment in a when, where, and who (the sender of the appointment) format. An Add To Calendar link below the appointment or event information allows the recipient to use the link to add the appointment to their Google calendar. (All that is required after opening the appointment link is to save the appointment to the Google calendar.)

If you are sharing an appointment, event, or meeting with someone using an iCloud email account, it is provided as an attachment in a received email. The Recipient can double-click the attachment, which will open an attachment mail window. To add the item to their Apple calendar, the email recipient can right-click the attachment and select Open Attachment. The Apple calendar will open, and the appointment or meeting will be added to the recipient's calendar.

Obviously, collaborating with others who use Outlook as their email client (or who use Outlook.com online) is an easy option for sharing information. This is particularly true with your Outlook calendars and calendar items because the actual sharing requires just a few steps, including setting permission levels.

> ### NOTE
>
> **Outlook "packages" calendars and calendar items in the ICS file format. This format is compatible with Outlook, Apple Calendar, and Google Calendar. This makes it easy for you to share calendar items from Outlook because they are compatible with most popular web-based calendars.**

Emailing a calendar

If you are using an IMAP or POP3 account as your primary email account, you won't have access to all the calendar-sharing capabilities provided by an Exchange Server or Microsoft 365 email account. However, you can email content from your calendar to others. The Email Calendar command is in the Share group on the ribbon's Home tab (when you are in the Calendar folder).

With your calendar open in the Reading Pane, select the Email Calendar command. The Send A Calendar Via Email dialog box opens.

In the Date Range drop-down menu, select the calendar range that you want to include in the email message. You choose details such as Today, Tomorrow, and Whole Calendar. You can also specify a range of dates.

Use the Detail drop-down menu to specify the level of detail you want to provide in the calendar information: Availability Only, Limited Details, or Full Details. You can also choose to show only time within your working hours by selecting Show Time Within My Working Hours Only. Click the Show button to set advanced parameters related to the Calendar, such as the layout in the email: Daily Schedule, or List Of Events.

After you have specified the settings for the email calendar, click OK. The calendar information is embedded in the email message and attached as an .ics calendar file. Click Send to send the calendar information to the recipient(s).

Publishing a calendar online

Another way to share a calendar is to publish it online. Again, this is a way of sharing calendar data if you are using a POP or IMAP email account that does not provide the calendar item–sharing capabilities that you get with an Exchange server, Microsoft 365, or Outlook.com email account. In fact, The Publish Online feature is not available in the Home tab's Share group when you have Outlook configured with a primary email account that is an Exchange server, Microsoft 365, or Outlook.com email type.

The Publish Online option for sharing your calendar comes with some challenges. The main challenge is finding a WebDAV (Web Distributed Authoring and Versioning) server to which you can publish your calendar. If you already have access to a WebDAV server, you have met the first challenge and can then concentrate on the challenges related to actually getting the calendar online.

Publishing your calendar online is a two-part process. You publish the calendar to a specific WebDAV server, and then you invite users to subscribe to the calendar. On the ribbon's Home tab (with the calendar that you want to publish open), select Publish Online, and then select Publish To WebDAV Server. A Publish Calendar To Custom Server dialog box will open (see Figure 24-8). This dialog box is very similar to the Send A Calendar Via Email dialog box and allows you to set the timespan and level of detail to be shown in the published calendar.

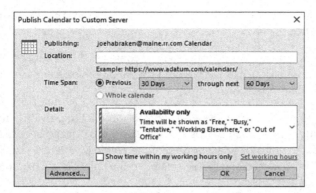

Figure 24-8   Set the parameters for publishing your calendar online.

More importantly, this dialog box allows you to specify the location for the published location. After specifying the various details for the published calendar, enter the URL for your custom server in the Location box in the Publish Calendar To Custom Server dialog box. Set the level of detail you want to provide to coworkers or colleagues who will have access to your published calendar. Click the OK button, and Outlook will contact the web server you specified for the calendar upload.

> **NOTE**
>
> Web Distributed Authoring and Versioning (WebDAV) is an extension of the HTML tag language used to build websites. WebDAV's purpose is to provide a collaborative environment for users who want to share files (such as a published Outlook calendar). Some free WebDAV servers are available on the web (do a search). If you have your own server (and the inclination and time), you can also set up your own WebDAV server using different web server software platforms, such as the Apache web server and Microsoft's Internet Information Server (IIS).

A Send A Sharing Invitation dialog box will open once the calendar has been published to the WebDAV server URL you specified. This allows you to share the published calendar's URL with other people.

To send a sharing invitation, select Yes. A new email will open that includes a link to the published calendar. Enter the contact names in the To box for all contacts you want to share the published calendar with. Once your contacts have received the email, they can select the link and access the published calendar.

Users who select the link will have the option of publishing the calendar to their default calendar management client. Remember that the published calendar is really only a snapshot of a specified range in your calendar. If you want to provide coworkers or colleagues with a more interactive scheduling environment, your best bet is to share the calendar in Outlook.

Setting calendar options

The calendar options can be accessed via the Outlook Options window. Select File to access the Backstage, and then select Options. The Outlook Options window opens. Select Calendar in the options list to access the Calendar options. Figure 24-9 shows the Outlook Options window with Calendar selected.

The calendar options enable you to set your work time, reminder defaults, and other options, such as the current time zone. The calendar options categories are as follows:

- **Work Time:** These options enable you to set the start time and end time for your work hours, as well as specify the days in your workweek. You can also set the first day of the week and the first week of the year.

- **Calendar Options:** These options include the default reminder time and settings related to meetings, such as allowing attendees to propose new times for meetings. You can also add holidays to the calendar, set permissions for the viewing of Free/Busy times, and enable an alternative calendar (useful if you keep separate work and personal calendars).

- **Display Options:** These options enable you to control the default calendar color and also specify the Date Navigator prompt. Other settings include switching from vertical layout to Schedule view based on the number of opened calendars.

Figure 24-9   The Calendar options

- **Time Zones:** These options enable you to set and label (give it a descriptive name) the current time zone. Options are also available for showing a second and even a third time zone.

- **Scheduling Assistant:** These options enable you to show calendar details in a ScreenTip when using the Scheduling Assistant and also specify whether calendar details are shown in the scheduling grid.

- **Automatic Accept Or Decline:** This feature enables you to configure the calendar so that meetings are automatically accepted or declined (declined based on time conflicts), and canceled meetings are automatically removed from the calendar.

➤ Meetings are discussed in Chapter 25, "Working with contacts and planning meetings."

- **Weather:** The Weather bar, which shows at the top of the calendar by default, can be "turned off" by deselecting the Show Weather On The Calendar option. You can also choose to show the temperature in either Celsius or Fahrenheit (the default in the United States).

When you have finished setting the various Calendar options, click OK to close the Outlook Options window and return to Outlook.

Working with tasks

There always seems to be a task at hand, and Outlook makes it easy for you to add tasks to the Task list and manage them. You can include a reminder when you create a task, and you can assign tasks to coworkers and colleagues (the downside is that you can be assigned tasks as well).

We have already worked with email messages in Chapter 23 and appointments and events in this chapter. So, we've used the navigation pane to access Outlook tools such as your email and your calendar. The navigation pane also provides an icon for the Task List, and when you select it, the entire reading pane is devoted to a list of your tasks. This view is fine if you are only working on tasks, but if you want to be able to view a task list while working with your email, you need to modify the view. An easy way to include tasks in Outlook's default view is to add the To-Do Bar to the Outlook window.

Select the ribbon's View tab. The To-Do Bar command is in the Layout group. Select the command, and then select the options you want to appear in the To-Do Bar: Calendar, People, and/ or Tasks. Because we are talking about working with tasks in the To-Do Bar, I recommend that you add both the Calendar and Tasks to your To-Do Bar. That way, you can access the calendar (even though it's not a full-screen calendar) as you manage your tasks.

Another benefit of using the To-Do Bar is that you can use it to quickly create a task. Click in the Type A New Task box near the top of the To-Do Bar and then enter a subject for the task. When you press Enter, the task is added to the Task list in the To-Do Bar. Creating a task in this way doesn't open the New Task dialog box, which provides you with access to all the fields for a task (such as Start Date, Due Date, and Status). So, while this is a quick way to get a task in the list; it requires that you return to the task later to add its details. Another option (and perhaps a better choice) is to create a new task via the To-Do Bar by double-clicking just below the last entry in the Task list to open the New Task dialog box, as shown in Figure 24-10.

Figure 24-10   The Task dialog box

Follow these steps to create the new task in the Task dialog box:

1.   Enter the subject of the task into the Subject box.

2.   Enter a date on which the task should be complete or click the Due Date list arrow to open the Date Navigator and then choose a due date.

3.   Enter a start date or use the Date Navigator to select a start date.

4.   From the Status drop-down menu, choose the current status of the project: Not Started, In Progress, Completed, Waiting On Someone Else, or Deferred.

5.   Enter any comments, descriptions, or other information related to the task in the body of the task.

You can use the Task tab of the ribbon to set other attributes related to the task (in much the same way that you assign options to an appointment). You can use the Categorize command to assign a category or categories to the task. You can also tag the task with a flag using the Follow Up command. If the task is private, high importance, or low importance, use the appropriate command in the Tabs group to set options for the task. When you are ready to place the task on the Task list, click Save & Close. The task is listed in the Task list on the To-Do Bar.

Using the Tasks folder

You can also create, view, and manage tasks from the Tasks folder. Select Tasks in the Navigation bar. Your tasks (grouped by date ranges such as Today, Next Week, and so on) are listed in the Details pane in a To-Do list. Select a task to view its details in the Reading pane. When you use the Tasks folder to manage your tasks, you can work with the To-Do list (as shown in Figure 24-12). Alternatively, you can select Tasks in the Folder pane, and your tasks are then listed in a columnar format, with the different fields (such as Subject, Due Date, and Categories) as the column headings.

TIP

If you want to add the calendar (or Date Navigator, as it also is referred to) to the Tasks folder, select the View menu, click the To-Do Bar, and select Calendar.

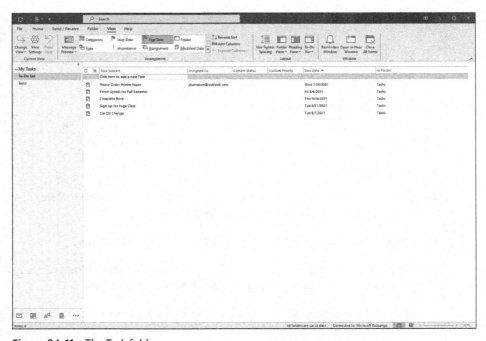

Figure 24-11   The Task folder

Creating a new task from the Tasks folder

You can also create tasks when you are working in the Tasks folder. One option is to select the New Task command on the ribbon's Home tab. This opens the untitled (meaning new) Task dialog box. All you have to do is enter the necessary information for the task and then click the Save & Close command. You can also open the New Task dialog box by double-clicking in the empty part of the To-Do list or below your listed tasks when you have Tasks (instead of the To-Do list) selected in the Folder pane.

Another possibility for quickly adding a task without entering all the details for that task (we talk about editing a task a little later in the chapter) is to click the Type A New Task box at the top of the To-Do list and then enter a subject for the task. Press Enter, and the task is added to the Today group tasks.

Creating a recurring task

You can create recurring tasks. For example, you might have to provide a weekly report each Friday, so it makes sense to schedule a recurring task that reminds you to get that weekly job done. Recurring tasks can easily be created to recur daily, weekly, monthly, or yearly.

You can create a recurring task from an existing task or by creating a new recurring task. Just open an existing task or create a new task. If you aren't in the Tasks folder (you can create a task or recurring task from any Outlook folder), select the New Items command on the Home tab and then select Task. A New Task dialog box opens. Type a subject for the task; then select the Recurrence command on the task's ribbon. The Task Recurrence dialog box opens.

In the Task Recurrence dialog box, set the recurrence pattern by selecting Daily, Weekly, and so on, and then specify the Recur Every increment (such as 1 Week or 2 Weeks). Also specify the day that the recurring task recurs using the day check boxes (Sunday through Saturday). You can specify when a new task should be regenerated as the previous recurring task was completed.

In the Range Of Recurrence area of the Task Recurrence dialog box, specify the start date for the task. You can then specify the end date for the task using the following options:

- **End By:** Specify an end date for the recurring task.

- **End After:** Specify the number of occurrences that should take place before the recurring task is ended.

- **No End Date:** No end date is specified for the recurring task.

When you have finished setting the options for the recurring task, click OK to return to the Task dialog box. The recurrence information for the task (and the next due date) appears above the subject of the task. You can assign policies (on an Exchange Server network), categories, and other tags, such as follow-up flags, to the recurring task, as needed. When you have finished setting the options for the task, select Save & Close.

Assigning and accepting tasks

There is probably no greater joy in the workplace than being able to pass off a task to a coworker or colleague. You can assign tasks to other people, such as coworkers or subordinates, but be advised that your coworkers (and even your subordinates) can also assign you an Outlook task. Everyone using Outlook has the power to create a task and then assign it to another user. Assigned tasks (meaning tasks you assign to others) appear in your Task list and on the To-Do Bar (if you have it open in other folder views, such as Mail). An assigned task also appears on the To-Do list of the person to whom you assigned the task.

To assign a task to a coworker or colleague, follow these steps:

1. Select the New Task command (from the New Command group when working in the Tasks folder) or double-click the To-Do list or the To-Do Bar. (Also, you can use the New Items command if you are in a folder other than the Tasks folder.) A New Task dialog box opens.

2. Enter the subject and other details for the task.

3. Set options for the task using the appropriate commands on the ribbon.

4. Select Assign Task in the Manage Task group. A To: box (just like the To: box that appears on a new email) appears above the Subject box so that you can address the task.

5. Select To or Address Book on the ribbon to open the Address Book. You can use the Global Address List on an Exchange Server network to add the recipient or recipients of the assigned task, or you can switch to your Contacts list and select the names as needed. Click OK to close the Address Book.

6. When you are ready to assign the task, select Save & Close.

The task can now be managed by the assignee of the task (although you can view it). By default, you receive a status report (via email) when the task is complete. Also, by default, an updated copy of this task is kept on your Task list so that you can view any changes that have been made to the task, such as whether the task has been started and the percentage of the task that has been completed.

Paybacks can be nasty, and in the case of tasks, there is no doubt that those who give shall also receive. When a coworker or manager assigns you a task, the assigned task is sent as a mail message. Double-click the message to open the task. The Respond group on the ribbon provides the necessary commands for you to respond to the assigned task, including Accept and Decline. Select the Accept command to accept the task. If you select Accept, the Accepting Task message box opens. This dialog box enables you to immediately send a response that you are accepting the task. It also gives you the option of editing the Accept response before it is sent. Click OK in the Accepting Task message box, and the task will be added to your Task list.

> **NOTE**
>
> **You can reply to a task "invitation" before accepting it. Use the Reply command in the Respond group. This enables you to get more information on a task before you decide to "own" it.**

If you want to decline the task, select Decline. The Declining Task dialog box opens. When you decline a task, a message is sent to the originator of the task, and the task is moved to your Deleted Items folder. You also have the option of editing your response (that you are declining the task) before sending it.

Viewing and managing tasks

Outlook provides you with different options for viewing your tasks. As mentioned earlier, when you work in the Tasks folder, you can view the tasks in a To-Do list or in a columnar format (by selecting Tasks in the Folder pane). Outlook provides you with commands that enable you to further manipulate the view of your Tasks folder. The Arrangement group on the View tab provides commands that enable you to arrange the Task list by Categories, Start Date, Due Date, and Importance. The Reverse Sort command can be used to quickly reverse the sort order of the To-Do list.

The ribbon (when you are in the Tasks folder) provides other commands for managing your tasks. These commands include Delete, Mark Complete, and various commands in the Follow Up, Actions, and Tags groups.

Viewing the Task list

When you select Tasks in the Folder pane, your tasks are listed in a tabular format; this view includes field columns for Subject, Due Date, and Categories. The tasks are listed by due date in ascending order. You can use a column heading to quickly sort the list by subject or category and change whether the tasks are listed in ascending or descending order by that field. In this default Simple List view of the Task list, you are provided with basic information for each task, and each task has a check box that makes selecting that task easy.

You can change the Simple List or the To-Do List view of the Task list (depending on which one you are using) to a different view using the Change View group commands on the ribbon. Figure 24-12 shows the various views available in the Change View gallery.

CHAPTER 24

Figure 24-12   The Change View gallery

Each view provides a different tabular view of the tasks, including different fields. The different views available on the Change View gallery are as follows:

- **Detailed:** Displays the subject, Status, Date Modified, Date Completed, In Folder, and Categories.

- **Simple List:** Shows the Subject, Due Date, and Categories.

- **To-Do List:** Changes to To-Do List view (which can also be accessed via the Navigation pane).

- **Prioritized:** Groups the tasks by priority.

- **Active:** Shows the active tasks, including the Status, Due Date, Percent Complete, and Categories.

- **Completed:** Filters the list to show completed tasks only.

- **Today:** Lists the tasks with "today" as the Due Date.

- **Next 7 Days:** Lists the tasks with a due date that falls within the next seven days, and includes the Status, Percent Complete, and Categories.

- **Overdue:** Filters the Task list and lists overdue tasks only.

- **Assigned:** Filters the Task list to show tasks that others have assigned to you.

- **Server Tasks:** Lists tasks stored on your mail server. In the Microsoft Exchange server environment, all tasks that you have created and been assigned from other users on the Exchange server network are stored on the server. POP and IMAP accounts can also take advantage of this view, though this view only shows tasks that are stored locally on your PC, not the mail server itself.

You can add columns to any of the tabular views provided in the Change View gallery, as you require. Select the ribbon's View tab and then select Add Columns (in the Arrangement Command group). The Show Columns dialog box opens, as shown in Figure 24-13.

Select a column in the Available Columns list, and then click the Add button to add the column to the current view. By default, frequently used fields are shown in the list, but you can use the drop-down menu to select other field categories, such as Info/Status Fields, Date/Time Fields, and All Task Fields.

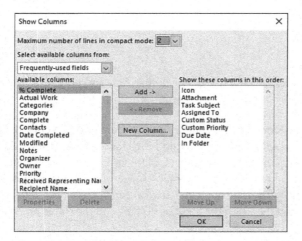

Figure 24-13   The Show Columns dialog box

When you click OK, the Show Columns dialog box closes, and you return to the Task list. The column or columns you added using the Show Columns dialog box appear in your current view of the tasks.

TIP

When you view other items, such as emails or contacts, in a tabular view, you can use the Add Columns command to add columns as required.

If you want to return a particular view to its default, you can reset any view that you have modified using the Show Columns dialog box. On the View tab, select the Reset View command. A message box opens. Select Yes to reset the current view.

Editing tasks

You can edit any task in the Task list or the To-Do list. Double-click the task, and the task's dialog box opens. You can edit any of the fields related to the task, and you can also tag the task with categories, follow-up flags, and a level of importance.

When you want to add information to a task—particularly the number of hours required to complete the task or other information such as mileage or the company you did the work for—select the Details command on the Task tab. Fields are provided for total work, actual work, mileage, and billing information. Enter the information as needed, and be sure to select Save & Close when you finish editing the task's details.

In the case of tasks that you have assigned to others, you can rescind the task. Open the task first; then on the Task tab of the ribbon, select Cancel Assignment. The name of the assignee or assignees is removed from the task. The task still exists; however, it is now your task and is no longer assigned to a coworker or subordinate. To save changes that you have made to a task in the task's dialog box, select Save & Close.

> **NOTE**
>
> **By default, assigned tasks generate a status report when they are completed. The report is forwarded to the assignor of the task.**

You can generate a status report for your tasks and then send the report to a coworker or colleague. This is particularly useful when you are working with a task that has been assigned to you, and you want to provide an update to the assigner of the task. In the task's dialog box, select the Send Status Report command (on the Task tab). A new email message appears, including the status of the task in the body of the message. Address the message to the appropriate recipient or recipients, and then click the Send button to send the status report.

Managing tasks

Outlook also provides tools for managing your tasks. When you select the check box for a particular task, that task is marked as complete. You can also mark a selected task or tasks using the Mark Complete command on the Home tab. If you want to remove a task or tasks from the list, select the Remove From List command.

You can also mark tasks for follow-up using the various flags provided in the Follow Up group. For example, if you wanted to follow up on a particular task in your Task list tomorrow, you could mark it with the Tomorrow follow-up flag.

In some situations, you might want to move tasks from the Tasks folder to an Outlook folder that you have created. For example, you might want to keep tasks that you consider personal (perhaps you have even categorized them as personal) in a "personal" folder. You can create your own folders within any of the default Outlook folders. For example, you can create a new subfolder in your Tasks folder. You can create the folder using the New Folder command on the Folder tab, or you can create the folder during the process of actually moving the tasks (or any other Outlook items) to their new home.

TIP

You share your tasks with other users (just as you can share your calendar). If you work in a network environment that provides Exchange or SharePoint, you can share tasks using the Share Tasks command on the ribbon's Folder tab. You can also open tasks that others have shared with you using the Open Shared Tasks command.

To move specific tasks, select those tasks in the Task list; then select the Move command on the ribbon's Home tab. Select Other Folder to open the Move Items dialog box, which lists the default Outlook folders, such as Calendar or Inbox, and any folders you have created. You can use the New button to create a new folder, if necessary. To move tasks from your Tasks folder to another folder, select the folder in the Move Items dialog box and then click OK. The dialog box closes, and the tasks are moved to the folder you selected.

Setting Tasks options

The Tasks options settings can be accessed in the Outlook Options window. Select File to open the Outlook Backstage, and then click Options to open the Outlook Options window.

When you select Tasks in the Outlook Options window, a limited number of options specifically relate to tasks. In fact, there are only two groups of options—Task Options and Work Hours—as shown in Figure 24-14.

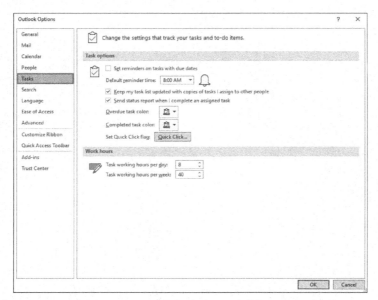

Figure 24-14   The option settings for Outlook tasks and work hours

CHAPTER 24

The Task Options group includes settings related to task reminders, reports, and task flags. You can choose to set reminders for all tasks with due dates and set a default reminder time. In relation to tasks that you assign to other people or that are assigned to you, you can choose to keep updated copies of tasks that you assign in your Task list and have a status report sent automatically when you complete an assigned task. Both settings are enabled by default.

You also have control over the color of overdue and completed tasks. Select the overdue task color or the completed task color to change the default color for either of these task types. You can also set a Quick Click flag for flagging tasks with a particular flag type. This feature enables you to add a flag to a task in the Task list with a single click. To specify the flag type for the Quick Click Feature, select Quick Click and then use the Set Quick Click dialog box to choose the Flag Type, such as Today, Tomorrow, or Complete.

TIP

You can copy tasks from your Task list to another folder using the Copy To Folder option on the Move command's menu.

The other options group for Tasks is the Work Hours group. There are two possible settings: Task Working Hours Per Day and Task Working Hours Per Week. The default settings for these two options are 8 Hours Per Day and 40 Hours Per Week, respectively. You can use the spin boxes for either of these settings to change the defaults if required.

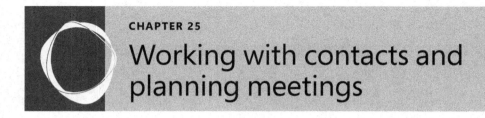

Working with contacts and planning meetings

Navigating the Contacts List   769

Creating a new contact   772

Editing contact information   776

Searching the Contacts folder   780

Organizing contacts with groups   781

Forwarding and sharing contacts   782

Communicating with contacts   785

Contact actions   787

Printing contact information   788

Setting contact options   788

Scheduling meetings   789

Responding to meeting requests   793

Although Outlook is seen primarily as an email application, it is also a powerful contact-management tool that enables you to easily communicate with your coworkers, clients, and friends. Outlook also enables you to access contact information in a variety of lists, including your Contacts list, Exchange global address lists, and social media websites such as LinkedIn and Facebook. Outlook doesn't just provide access to contact information; it also provides you with tools for better communicating with these contacts. For example, you can quickly send a group email to your customers or schedule a meeting with your coworkers.

In this chapter, we take a look at the possibilities for creating and managing contact data in Outlook and explore how the Contacts folder's data becomes a key part of using Outlook to communicate with others. Outlook also provides a number of tools related to scheduling meetings with your contacts, and we examine both how meetings are scheduled and managed.

Navigating the Contacts list

The Outlook Contacts folder is accessed via the Navigation bar. Select People to open the Contacts folder in the Outlook window, as shown in Figure 25-1. Contacts are selected in the Folder pane. The selected contacts information is shown in the Reading pane.

Figure 25-1   The Outlook Contacts folder

The default view for the Contacts folder is the People view. The Contacts list is provided in the Details pane. Information for the currently selected contact is provided in the Reading pane. You can quickly change the view using the commands in the Current View group on the ribbon's Home tab. These views are as follows:

- **People:** The default view for the Outlook People folder (Contacts) provides a photo (if available) and the name of the contact. When the contact is selected in the Details pane (Contacts list), additional information (in a tabbed format) is provided for the contact in the Reading/Preview pane, such as the email address, mobile phone number, and instant messaging address. If you are using Outlook in an Exchange Server or SharePoint Server environment, you can also see whether the contact is currently available.

- **Business Card:** This default view provides the name, phone number, title, company, and address of the contact. A photo of the contact can be included, too.

- **Card:** This view provides more detail than the Business Card view and includes more field information, including assigned categories and notes. This view does not show photos of contacts (when you have inserted a digital photo of the contact in the Contact Information).

- **Phone:** This view provides a tabular view of your contacts and includes field columns for the business phone, business fax, home phone, and mobile phone. It is extremely useful for making phone calls to your contacts.

- **List:** This view provides a tabular format for the contacts and includes a number of field columns, such as Full Name, Job Title, Company, Department, and Business Phone.

You can further manipulate the view (whatever view you have selected in the Current View gallery) using the commands provided on the ribbon's View tab (see Figure 25-2). The amount of fine-tuning you can do to the Contacts list depends on the view you have selected. For example, if you have List selected as the current view, you can use the commands in the Arrangement group to sort contacts based on a common element. For example, select Company if you want to group your Contacts list by company.

Figure 25-2   Set the view using the Change View group commands.

The Arrangement group commands include grouping commands, such as Categories, Company, and Location. Also, commands are available for reversing the current sort direction and adding columns to the current view. The Arrangement commands, such as Company and Location, are not available when you are using the People, Business Card, or Card views. When you group your Contacts list by Categories or Company, make sure that Show In Groups is selected in the Arrangement gallery. This lists categories or company names and then lists contacts in the appropriate group.

The Reverse Sort command works no matter what view you are currently using. When you are in a tabular view, such as the List or Phone view, you can also use a field column heading (such as Full Name or Department) to sort the list by that particular field.

If you want to change the view when you have the ribbon's View tab selected, use the Change View command in the Current View group. If you modify a particular view and want to reset it, select the Reset View command. A message box opens and asks you to verify the reset of the view; select Yes.

Creating a new contact

You can create a new contact in Outlook either from scratch or based on another item, such as an email. To create a new contact from scratch, you can use the New Contact command on the Home tab of the Contacts folder's ribbon, or you can create a new contact from any of the Outlook folders using the New Items command (and then selecting Contact).

As already mentioned, you can also add a contact to the Contacts folder based on information found in another Outlook item. For example, you can right-click an email address in the From, Cc, or Bcc field of a received message and then select Add to Outlook Contacts; this opens a new Contact dialog box, and the name and email information is automatically entered for the contact. All you have to do is supply the other information you want to enter.

Depending on the type of email accounts you use in Outlook, entering a contact's information might not be the only possibility for adding contacts and contact field information. In an Exchange server environment where a global address list exists, your coworkers and colleagues probably already appear in that list. Contacts can also be shared by other colleagues when you use Outlook as an Exchange Server client. We discuss the sharing of contacts with others later in this chapter.

Let's take a look at creating a new contact from scratch. In the Contacts folder, select New Contact on the Home tab. A Contact dialog box opens, as shown in Figure 25-3.

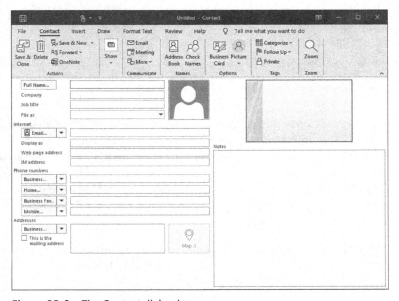

Figure 25-3 The Contact dialog box

A wide variety of information can be added for the contact. You don't have to use all the fields provided in the dialog box, but it does make sense to enter the information that is useful to you in terms of communicating with the contact. To make the Contacts folder more than just a glorified email address list, I recommend entering the following field information:

- Name

- Company

- Job title

- Email address

- Web page address

- IM address

- Phone numbers (business, home, business fax, mobile)

- Address (street, city, state, ZIP Code, and country)

When you are working in the various fields in the Contact dialog box, you can use the Tab key to quickly navigate from field to field (or Shift+Tab to move backward from field to field). Some fields, such as Full Name and Addresses, provide you with dialog boxes that make it easy for you to enter (and check) all the information possible for that particular field. For example, when you select the Full Name field box/button, the Check Full Name dialog box opens.

This dialog box enables you to enter a contact's title, such as Miss, Ms., Dr., or Mr., and the first, middle, and last name, including a suffix such as Jr. After you have entered the information in the Check Full Name dialog boxes, click OK to return to the Contact dialog box.

As you enter the information for the contact, a business card is built for the contact on the right side of the dialog box. Depending on the purpose of your Contacts list, you might want to include images of your contacts, which then appear in the Contacts folder when you use People view or Business Card view. This can be particularly useful when you have clients or customers in your Contacts folder you don't see often and need a reminder of their appearance (you can't remember everyone's face).

CAUTION

If you have saved and closed a contact's record and you are using People view, you might be going crazy trying to get the Contact dialog box open for that contact (or any contact in the list). When you are in People view, the details for the currently selected contact are shown in the Reading pane. To work on the current contact exclusively, double-click on the Contact's name in the contact list. This will open the Contact dialog box, where you can make additions or changes as needed.

CHAPTER 25

To add a digital photo of the contact to the Contact dialog box, select the Add Contact Picture box, which appears as a person's silhouette. The Add Contact Picture dialog box opens. Navigate to the folder that contains the picture, and then select the picture. Click OK to add the picture to the contact's information. You are returned to the Contact dialog box.

Inside OUT

Resizing a window can affect the appearance of that window's ribbon commands.

When multiple windows are open on the Desktop (say an application window and a dialog box or two), moving or resizing one or more of the windows is a common practice for the multitasker looking for more work room on the desktop. If you make a window or dialog box that has a ribbon smaller when resizing it, you will find that it changes how the commands on that window's ribbon are displayed because it compresses the ribbon.

At "normal" size, the Contact dialog box shows all the commands in each of its ribbon's command groups: Actions, Show, Communicate, Names, Options, Tags, and Zoom. However, resize the Contact box to make it smaller, and group commands will disappear from the ribbon. For example, the Show group provides commands such as General, Details, Certificates, and All Fields. When you make the Contact dialog box smaller, the Show group disappears, and the ribbon provides a Show command (like a drop-down menu) that is used to access the various commands normally found in the Show group. If you continue to make the Contact dialog box smaller, more command groups will disappear and become represented by a drop-down menu. All the commands are still there; they are just hidden because you have compressed the space available to the ribbon. You might also experience this hidden command phenomenon when resizing a new Message window or new Task window in Outlook.

Entering contact details

The level of detail you enter for a particular Outlook contact is up to you; however, I think that, in most cases, having more information about a contact makes the listing more useful to you. You can enter all sorts of information related to a contact, such as department, office, title, and manager's name—even a nickname. Personal information about the contact, such as spouse/partner or birthday, can also be included (all these fields are included by default in the Contact dialog box). To enter additional information related to a contact (when you are in the contact's dialog box), make sure the Contact tab is selected on the ribbon, and then select Details in the Show group. Figure 25-4 shows the details fields.

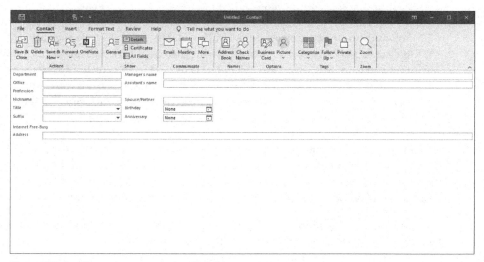

Figure 25-4   The new contact's details fields

Adding fields for a contact

You also have the option to add fields to the contact's information. This can be useful if you want to include information that isn't included as a default field, such as the contact's children's names or the contact's assistant's phone number. To add fields, follow these steps:

> **TIP**
>
> **You don't necessarily have to worry about the file size of the picture that you use for a client; it is sized appropriately to appear in the Contact dialog box. If you want to change the picture after you have inserted it, use the Picture command in the Options group.**

1. Select the All Fields command in the Show group. A blank field pane opens in the Contact dialog box.

2. Use the Select From drop-down menu to select a field category, such as Frequently Used fields, Miscellaneous fields, or Personal fields. When you select one of the field groups, specific fields are listed in the Field pane. For example, the Personal field group supplies fields such as Birthday, Children, Hobbies, and Language.

3. Select a field (on the All Fields screen) and then enter the information for the field in the Value column. You can return to the Select From drop-down menu to view other fields and enter information in those fields.

4. When you have finished working with the additional fields, you can return to the general contact information for the contact by selecting General in the Show group.

CHAPTER 25

TIP

You can also create user-defined fields. This enables you to include any data you want in the contact information. To create a user-defined field, click the New button at the bottom of the Contact dialog box (when All Fields is selected). Provide a name, type, and format for the new field in the New Column dialog box. Any fields you create are added to a contact's data using the user-defined fields in this item category (via Select from the drop-down menu when All Fields is selected in the Show group).

Adding field data only strengthens your informational IQ for the contacts you place in your Contacts folder. Viewing the information placed in these additional fields requires you to use the All Fields command. You can then select the category of fields you used (via the Select From drop-down menu) when you entered additional field information for the contacts.

After you enter all the information for a new contact, select Save & Close, which places the contact in the Contacts list and returns you to the Contacts folder.

Editing contact information

You can open a contact's record to access field data and add information or edit specific fields. Double-click any of the records listed in your Contact list and edit as needed in the Contact window.

Another option for editing and entering contact information is to view your contacts in the List view. Select the List command in the Current View group of the ribbon's Home tab. You can then edit any of your contacts' information inline; click in any of the field columns, such as Full Name or Email, and enter the field information as you require.

If you find the inline editing too restrictive and you want to update or edit a contact's information in the Contact dialog box, switch to one of the other views, such as Business Card or List (any view other than People works), and then double-click the contact. The Contact dialog box for that contact opens. Enter new data or edit the existing data for the contact. Remember that you can access additional fields using the commands available in the Show group (such as All Fields).

If you want to enter information about a more narrative contact (meaning that it needs more space), you can use the Notes box, which is located on the right of the Contact dialog box. You can enter any type of information in the Notes box, such as notes on a conversation that you had with the contact or the fact that the contact is not very good at golf (no golf invitation for that contact). Editing contact information typically relates to making sure that the contact's information is accurate, but it also pertains to having any and all information that you can accumulate for that contact.

If you prefer to work with your contacts in a view that enables you to edit and enter contact data in a more table-like environment (columns and rows), you can switch to List view (select List in the Current View gallery). Using the field column names as a reference, click in one of the field positions in a contact's record (each row of information in the list is the record for a specific contact), and then enter the information for that field. Working in List view also enables you to quickly update information in multiple records without having to open the Contact dialog box for each individual contact.

Editing a business card

When you enter the information for a contact, a default business card is created for that contact. You can edit the layout and fine-tune the field information in the business card. Creating a more custom layout for contact business cards can be useful if you have a contact listing for each of your employees and colleagues. When you provide their information to a potential customer or client, you furnish an electronic business card that is extremely informational and also visually appealing. It also makes sense to create your own contact entry and then build your own electronic business card for inclusion with your own emails.

Make sure that you are in the Business Card, Card, Phone, or List view for the Contacts folder (these settings are in the Current View group); the People view doesn't allow access to the full dialog box for a contact, so switch out of that view if you are currently in it.

To edit the business card for a contact, double-click the contact in the Contacts list to open the contact's dialog box. Then select the Business Card command in the Options group (on the ribbon). The Edit Business Card dialog box opens, as shown in Figure 25-5.

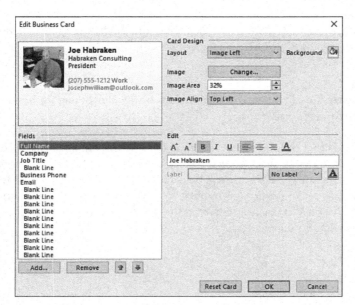

Figure 25-5 The Edit Business Card dialog box

The Edit Business Card dialog box gives you control over the fields shown on the business card, the position of the image, and the fonts used on the business card. Let's start with the fields.

The fields currently used on the business card are listed in the Fields box. You can select a field and then use the Remove button to remove the field from the card. You can also add fields to the business card. Select the Add button. A menu appears and provides categories of fields that you can add to the card. For example, the Organization group provides the Company, Department, and Job Title fields. The Address group lists the Business Address, Home Address, and Other Address fields.

Use the Add Field menu to add fields to the business card as needed. This menu also provides you with a Blank Line option and a Custom Field category. After removing or adding fields, you can use the Move Field Up and the Move Field Down buttons to rearrange the fields on the business card.

If you have not added an image to the business card or you want to change the image on the business card, select the Change button to open the Add Card Picture dialog box. Locate the image, select it, and click Open.

You also have control over the layout of the business card in terms of where the image is positioned and whether you use a background color. You can use the Layout drop-down menu to position the image as follows: Image Left (the default), Image Right, Image Top, Image Bottom, Text Only, or Background Image. If you want to add a background color to the card, select the Background button and choose a color from the Color dialog box.

Depending on the layout setting that you select for the image in the Layout drop-down menu, you can select the actual alignment of the image using the Image Align drop-down menu. For example, if you choose the Image Bottom Layout setting, you can then align the image on the bottom of the card using the Bottom Right alignment setting.

TIP

You can also open the Edit Business Card dialog box by double-clicking the business card preview in the contact's dialog box.

You can use the various font and alignment settings in the Edit area of the dialog box to change the attributes for the text on the business card. For example, you might want the company name to be in italic, or you might want to use a bold, red font for your name. Having text color and appearance options can be particularly useful if you have used a background color or used the image as a background (not unlike a watermark). Make sure you use a text color and size that is readable on the background.

TIP

If you don't like the changes you have made to a business card, you can use the Reset Card button in the Edit Business Card dialog box to reset the card to the Outlook defaults.

When you have finished editing the business card, click OK to return to the contact's dialog box. The new layout for the business card appears in the business card preview to the right of the various contact fields in the contact's dialog box.

Tagging contacts with flags and categories

Although you are not actually editing the contact's information, tags such as categories and follow-up flags can enhance (informationally) a contact's record. When you are working in the Outlook Contacts folder, the various tag commands are provided in the Tags group on the Home tab of the Outlook ribbon. To add a category to a contact, select the Categorize drop-down menu and choose a color-coded category from the list that appears.

TIP

You can set the Quick Click command, which allows you to quickly add a specific type of flag when clicking the Flags column in the Contacts folder. Select Follow Up and then specify the flag type in the Set Quick Click dialog box.

You can also flag contacts for follow-up. For example, you might have had an appointment with a contact recently and want to follow up with that contact sometime this week (whatever week you are in). You then can flag the contact with the This Week flag. To select a flag for a contact, select the Follow Up command.

Although a follow-up flag serves as a visual reminder that you need to follow up with the contact, you might also want to create a reminder to accompany the flag. That way, Outlook reminds you to follow up with the contact. Select Follow Up and then Add Reminder. The Custom dialog box opens.

In the Custom dialog box, specify the flag type in the Flag drop-down menu. You can also specify a Start Date and a Due Date for the follow-up. Use the Reminder Date and Time settings to specify when you want to receive the reminder related to the flag. Select OK to return to the contact's dialog box.

NOTE

Using follow-up flags is just one way to tag a contact for follow-up. You can also create a task or a specific appointment in the Calendar, which reminds you to follow up with that contact.

Mapping a contact's address

Despite the fact that we rely on email, texting, instant messaging, and social media to commu-nicate with customers and colleagues, sometimes you still need to meet face to face. Outlook can help you on your journey by mapping the contact's address.

In the contact's dialog box (to the right of the contact's address), select Map It. Your default web browser opens a map of the address using Bing.com. You can select the Directions link on the left side of the website and then enter your location to get directions to the contact's address. You can then use the Send command to send the directions to an email address or to a mobile device. You can also print the directions from the web browser window. When you close the web browser window, you return to Outlook.

Searching the Contacts folder

If you have a large number of contacts in the Contacts folder, you might need a tool to help you locate a particular contact quickly. If you are in the People, Business Card, or Card view, you can jump alphabetically around your Contacts list using the index on the left side of the Preview pane. This, however, doesn't help you find a specific contact or a group of contacts that satisfy the same search criteria such as those who work at the same company or reside in the same state.

In terms of conducting searches in the Contacts folder, there are options. You can do a quick search (such as a person's last name or company name) using the Search People box in the Find group on the Home tab. Enter a search string; matching contacts (to your search string) will appear in a results pane.

If you find the Search People limited in terms of its search capabilities, you can access additional search-related commands on the ribbon's Search tab. Place the insertion point in the Search box at the top of the Outlook window. The Search Tools become available on the Outlook ribbon's Search tab. These tools allow you to search by categories and other parameters and include the ability to search in specific Contact folders.

The various Search commands provided on the Search tab enable you to control the scope of the search (you can search in the current folder and include subfolders), refine the search, and set options related to the search. The Refine group is particularly useful and enables you to refine a search. For example, you can do a search by business name by typing the business name in the Search Contacts box. Use the Has Address command in the Refine group to show only contacts who work at the company (entered in the Search Contacts box) or who work at a particular branch (based on the business address). Figure 25-6 shows the Search Tool, including the Refine group commands.

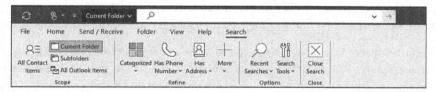

Figure 25-6   The Search Tools' Refine group

The Refine commands provided for searches in the Contacts folder are as follows:

- **Categorized:** This command allows you to search for contacts by category.

- **Has Phone Number:** Enables you to filter the Contacts list by the phone fields: business phone, home phone, or mobile phone. For example, if you select Has Business Phone, only the contacts listed with a business phone are shown in the Reading pane.

- **Has Address:** Filters the Contacts list based on whether specific address fields contain information. The possibilities are Has Email Address, Has IM Address, Has Business Address, and Has Home Address.

- **More:** If you are using Outlook on a corporate network (Microsoft Exchange) or using a corporate Microsoft 365 subscription, this option can provide Enterprise forms (including templates) related to various Outlook items such as contacts and email. If you don't use Outlook in a corporate environment, the More choice will certainly not give you more.

You can also access recent searches and other search tools via the Search Tools command groups. Select the Recent Searches command and select a search from the list provided to access recent searches you have used.

If you want to access advanced search tools, select the Search Tools command. A particularly useful search tool in relation to a large Contacts list is the Indexing Status command. Select this command to have Outlook index your contact entries. This makes your searches faster and more efficient. When you have finished working with the Search feature, you can quickly return to the contacts by selecting the Close Search command.

Organizing contacts with groups

We have already discussed ways to visually organize your Contacts folder using different views and the Search box. You can also quickly sort contacts in Phone or List view using the field headings to sort the list by name, company, or category, for example.

Another way to organize your contacts is to use contact groups. By default, the Contacts list is one big list with no real subdivisions. You can use contact groups to group contacts by company or location, for example. You can also create a personal group and a business group, to provide some functional division between the types of contacts you store in your Contacts folder.

You can create contact groups, no matter what type of email account you are using in Outlook. Even users with a POP or IMAP email account can create contact groups, just like users who have a corporate or institutional Exchange email account. To create a new contact group, select New Contact Group on the ribbon's Home tab. The Contact Group dialog box opens.

Type a name for the new group in the Name box. You can then add contacts to the group. Select the Add Members command, and then select From Outlook Contacts. (You can also add contacts from the Address Book.) The Select Members: Contacts dialog box opens, with your Contacts list selected.

Select a contact or contacts in the list, and then click the Members button. When you have finished adding members to the new group, click OK to close the Select Members: Contacts dialog box. You return to the Contact Group dialog box, and the new members are listed. If you want to remove any members, select the member (or members) and then click the Remove Member command.

To close the new Contact Group dialog box, select Save & Close. The new contact group appears in your Contacts folder (meaning in the Reading pane) with your contacts. To view the contacts in a contact group, open the contact group. You can open a specific contact in the group by double-clicking the contact.

NOTE

You can assign categories and flags to contacts in contact groups, and you can assign categories and flags to contact groups. Contact groups can also be forwarded to other users.

Including a contact in a contact group does not remove the contact from your Contacts list. It basically creates a shortcut to the contact. So, if you remove a contact from a contact group, you are not removing the contact from the Contacts folder. The great thing about contact groups is that you can basically treat them like a contact. If you find that you are sending email messages or assigning tasks to the same group of recipients, create a contact group and then address the email to that group. Contact groups can also be used to send multiple meeting invitations. (Scheduling meetings is discussed later in this chapter in the section "Scheduling meetings.")

Forwarding and sharing contacts

You can share your Outlook contacts with coworkers and colleagues when you use Outlook in an Exchange Server email environment. Even if you don't use Outlook in a business environment (meaning you use a personal Outlook.com email or Internet email from your ISP), you can forward contacts to other users. In Exchange Server environments, not only can you share your Contacts folder with other network users, they can also share their Contacts folder with you.

The Share group on the Contacts folder ribbon's Home tab provides commands for sharing and viewing shared contacts and includes the following commands: Forward Contact, Share Contacts, and Open Shared Contacts. These commands are available in any of the Contact list views provided in the Current View group on the ribbon. These commands can also be accessed via the ribbon when you are working in the dialog box for a particular contact. The Share group is located on the Contact tab of a contact dialog box's ribbon in the Contact dialog box.

Forwarding contacts

When you forward a contact or contacts to other people, the contact information comes in the form of an email attachment. The contact information can be attached to a message in two different formats:

- **Business Card:** This format is also known as a vCard and uses the vCard file extension .vcf. The vCard is considered the standard for electronic business cards and can be interpreted by most email and contact-management software packages.

- **Outlook Contact:** You can also attach a contact or contacts to a message as an Outlook Contact item. Contacts attached as an Outlook Contact item can be opened by both recipients who use Outlook and recipients who use an email client that supports the Outlook Contact file format.

You can also forward contact groups via a mail message. However, contact groups can be sent only as Outlook Contact items. You cannot send an Outlook contact group as a vCard attachment.

To forward a contact or contacts from the Contacts folder, select the contact or contacts in the Contacts list. Select the Forward Contact command in the Share group, and then select one of the commands on the menu provided: As A Business Card or As An Outlook Contact. A new message opens.

When you forward a contact via email, the business card is also embedded in the body of the message. When you forward the contact information as an Outlook Contact item, the contact information is not embedded in the body of the message.

Specify the recipient or recipients for the message as you would any other email message. You can include explanatory text (or other text) in the body of the message. You can also choose to attach other files to the message, as needed. When you are ready to forward the contact information, select Send.

As already mentioned, you can forward a single contact or multiple contacts using the Forward Contact command. In fact, you can use the Search Contacts tool to specify a subset of your contacts (based on a category you have assigned those contacts). Once you have your search results, select the contacts you want to forward and then select the Forward Contact command to open your message for the contacts.

NOTE

If Outlook has been configured for text messaging (in an Exchange Server environment or if you subscribe to Microsoft 365 or a third-party text message service), you can also forward contact information in a text message. When you select the Forward Contact command, a Forward As Text Message choice is included on the menu (again, if Outlook is configured for text messaging).

If you are the recipient of contact information as a business card (vCard) or as an Outlook item, double-click the attachment in the received message. This opens the forwarded contact's dialog box. Select Save & Close, and the contact is added to your Contacts list.

Sharing contacts

You can also share your Contacts folder directly with other users in an Exchange Server environment (this includes folks with a Microsoft 365 subscription). Remember that the Share Contacts command shares all your contacts in the Contacts folder. Let me rephrase that: When I say *all* your contacts, I mean all your contacts in the "main" Contacts list. So, you might want to consider a couple of possibilities for protecting contact information that you don't really want to share. One possibility is to tag specific contacts as private. Users with whom you share your Contacts list cannot view the details for any contacts you have tagged as private. Therefore, select those contacts in the Contacts list and then select the Private command on the Home tab.

Another possibility is to create a new folder in your Contacts folder and move contacts you don't want to share to this new folder. In the Navigation pane, right-click the Contacts icon and then select New Folder. Use the Create New Folder dialog box to specify a name for the new folder and then click OK. Drag contacts that you do not want to share from your Contacts list to this new folder.

Now you can share the Contacts list. Select Share Contacts on the Home tab. A sharing invitation message opens, as shown in Figure 25-7.

Specify the recipients for the sharing invitation by addressing the message as you would any other email message. You can also add text to the body of the message, if needed. A check box in the message specifies that you allow the recipient (or recipients) of the invitation to view your Contacts folder. You can also select the Request Permission To View Recipient's Contacts Folder check box if you want to be able to view the recipient's Contacts folder. Click Send. A message box opens and asks you to verify that the Contacts folder is shared as Reviewer/Read Only (which is a good thing, in most cases). Click Yes, and the invitation is on its way.

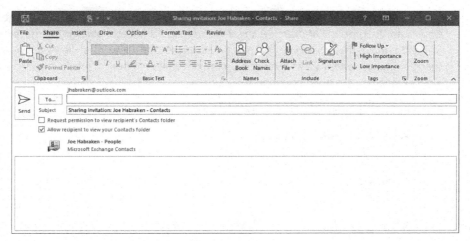

Figure 25-7   Share your contacts with others.

When the recipient receives the sharing invitation and opens it, all they have to do is select the Open This Contacts Folder command at the top of the email (in the Reading pane). This places your Contacts list on the recipient's Folder pane in a Shared Contact group folder.

If you also requested that the recipient share contacts with you, the recipient needs to select the Allow command on the Share message's ribbon. An Outlook message box opens and asks whether the user wants to share the Contacts folder with you (a read-only version). When that person clicks Yes, a sharing message is sent to you. All you have to do is use the Open This Contacts Folder command when you open the message, and you can view the shared contacts. Now everybody is happy. Shared contacts appear as a group in your Contacts list in the Outlook Navigation pane (when you have People selected in the Navigation pane).

> **TIP**
>
> If you have opened a sharing invitation email, make sure the message's Share tab is selected on the ribbon; then click the Open This Contacts Folder command to switch to Contacts and view the shared Contacts folder.

Communicating with contacts

Creating and maintaining a contact list in Outlook really has one purpose: We accumulate people's contact information so that we can communicate with them. The Contacts folder's ribbon (the Home tab) provides the Communicate group commands. These commands provide different options for communicating with your contacts, including emails, meeting requests, and task assignments.

When you are in People view, you are not provided all the commands available in the ribbon's Communicate group. (For example, the Call command is not available on the More gallery.) Switch to one of the other views, such as the Business Card view or List view (any view other than People), to access all the available Communicate commands. We talk in a moment about what I mean by "available" commands.

The full set of Communicate commands follows:

- **Email:** This command opens a new Email window addressed to the currently selected contact in your Contact list.

- **Meeting:** This command opens a new meeting request for the selected contact or contacts.

- **Assign Task:** This command opens a new Task message for the selected contact or contacts.

- **Reply With IM:** You can get in touch with the selected contact via instant messaging using Skype For Business, which works seamlessly with the Microsoft Office application suite.

- **Call:** You can have Outlook (with a little help from Windows) dial a phone number for a client if you have a modem or other telephony connection to your computer. This command can be used to dial any of the phone numbers listed for the selected contact.

The Communicate group commands available in your installation of Outlook depend on your Outlook configuration and your computer hardware. For example, if you don't have a dial-up modem or some other type of telephony connection to your computer, you won't be able to dial a contact's phone number and talk to them by phone.

At the outset of this discussion related to the Communicate group, I stated that not all the Communicate commands are available on the ribbon when you are in People view (for example, the Call command is not available). However, when you are in People view and have selected a contact, you can access a number of communication-related commands directly in the Reading pane (which shows the contact's information). Commands just below the selected contact's name include the Start Audio Call, Start Chat, and Send Email. An ellipsis (...) provides more commands such as Edit Contact, Add To Favorites, and Schedule A Meeting. Again, the communication options you have available when working in Outlook will depend on your computer hardware and service connection options (provided by your company or one of the Microsoft 365 subscriptions).

Contact actions

The Contacts folder ribbon also provides you with the Actions group. The commands in this group enable you to interact or "take action" relative to a contact or contacts. Two Actions group commands that you may want to take advantage of are Move and Mail Merge.

The Move command is self-explanatory; you can use it to move contacts from the primary Contacts list to other folders within the main Contacts folder. When you select Move, then Other folder, a list of your Contacts folders is shown. You also have the option of copying selected contacts to a folder.

The Mail Merge command enables you to merge all your contacts or selected contacts into a Word document. Figure 25-8 shows the Mail Merge Contacts dialog box, which opens when the Mail Merge command is selected.

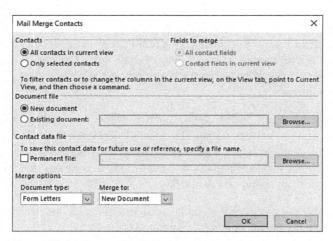

Figure 25-8   Create a mail merge using your contacts.

The Mail Merge Contacts dialog box provides options for merging the contact date to a new or existing document. You can also specify that the contact data be saved as a Word data source. You can then use the data source for future merges by selecting the file when using Microsoft Word.

When you select OK, the Outlook data is provided to Word, and a new or existing document (depending on the option you selected in the Mail Merge Contacts dialog box) opens in the Word application window. You can use the Mailings tab to enter the merge fields into the new letter as needed and then complete the merge.

➤ For a discussion of the Word mail merge feature, see Chapter 9, "Managing mailings and forms."

Printing contact information

You can print your contact information in a variety of formats. These formats include an alphabetical card style, a memo style, and a phone directory style.

To print the current Contacts list (this can be the main Contacts list or any lists that you have created in separate folders), select File to access the Outlook Backstage. Then select Print. The Print window opens with a preview of the default print style. A number of print styles are available in the Settings box. You can choose from different print formats for your Contacts list, such as Card Style, Small Booklet Style, and Phone Directory Style. You can also specify the printer for the print job and set print options as needed. When you are ready to print the Contacts list, click the Print button.

Setting contact options

The setting options for the Contacts folder are found in the Outlook Options window, which is accessed in the Outlook Backstage. Select File on the ribbon; then in the Backstage, select Options. To view the options for people (contacts), select People in the Options list. You will find that the options for how you work with your contacts are fairly sparse and pretty straightforward. The options are as follows:

- **Names And Filing:** These options include the full name order for contacts, as well as the default order for filing contacts (by name). The default Full Name order is First (Middle) Last. The Default File As order is Last, First. Use the drop-down menus to change the default settings. The Names And Filing options also include a check box that has Outlook check for duplicates when saving new contacts.

- **Contacts Index:** You can specify that an additional index be shown for the contacts in a language other than the default language configured for Outlook.

- **Online Status And Photographs:** These options allow you to monitor the online status of your Outlook contacts and show user photographs when available. Select Display Online Next To Name to monitor whether a particular contact is online. (This status will appear when you have the People pane activated when viewing the Outlook Email folder.) The Show User Photographs When Available option will display the users' photograph in received email messages and other Outlook items, such as meetings. Both the Display The Online Status Of Your Contacts and the Show User Photographs When Available options are enabled by default in the Outlook options.

When you have finished working with the People options, select OK. The Outlook Options window closes, and you are returned to the Outlook application window.

Scheduling meetings

This chapter has already discussed communicating with your Outlook contacts and taking various actions related to a contact or contacts. We've looked at sending messages to contacts and using other communication methods, such as task assignments and instant messaging. You can also schedule meetings quickly and efficiently using the information in your Contacts folder. Because scheduling meetings also relates to the Outlook Calendar, you can sort out who is available for a particular meeting using the Scheduling Assistant. In environments that enable you to share calendars on the network, such as an Exchange Server or SharePoint environment, you can accurately tell when a contact is available and when a contact is busy.

➤ For more about the Outlook Calendar, see Chapter 24, "Using the calendar for appointments and tasks."

When you create a new meeting, you provide the time and date of the meeting, identify the subject and location of the meeting, and invite contacts to attend the meeting. You can create a new meeting from any of the Outlook folders using the New Items command. When you create a new meeting from the Contacts folder, you can select the contacts you want to invite to the meeting in the Contacts list before you select the Meeting command.

So, when you are in the Contacts folder (or any other folder that contains contacts), select the contacts you want to attend the meeting. (Press and hold the Ctrl key as you select multiple attendees, or better yet, create a group and use it to add attendees to the meeting.) Next, select the Meeting command in the Communicate group, which opens the Meeting dialog box, as shown in Figure 25-9.

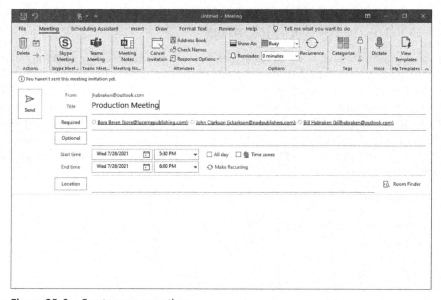

Figure 25-9   Create a new meeting.

The contacts you preselected in your Contacts list appear in the To box. You can add contacts using the Address Book command in the Attendees group. This means that you can invite attendees to the meeting who are not in your Contacts list but are in other lists in the Address Book, such as the global address list that is provided to you when you use Outlook as an Exchange Server client. You might also have lists in your Address Book that you imported from other software applications that can be accessed to build the list of attendees for the meeting. When you use the Address Book dialog box to specify attendees for the meeting, you can specify both required and optional attendees for the meeting.

Enter a subject for the meeting in the Subject box. You can also specify a location for the meeting in the Location box, such as a particular conference room, building location, or site external to your company or institution (say, a local coffee or doughnut shop). You should also specify the start and end times for the meeting (including the date and the time). If you are scheduling an all-day event, select the All Day Event check box.

As with any Outlook item, you can use the Options and Tags group commands to specify options related to the meeting. For example, you can specify when the reminder for the meeting should be provided, details on whether the meeting is recurring (use the Recurrence command), and any possible multiple time zones for the meeting (particularly if it is a video-conference or an online meeting). You can also tag the meeting with categories and importance level flags.

Because the meeting information is sent to the potential attendees as an email message (these are invitations, after all), you can provide additional information regarding the meeting in the message body box. You can tell attendees more about what the meeting entails and whether they should bring anything to the meeting.

Selecting the meeting location

If you are using Outlook as an Exchange Server client, you can click the Location button in the Meeting dialog box. The Select Rooms dialog box opens, showing the global address list for your Exchange Server network (or SharePoint environment). This list might also include a listing of meeting rooms for your corporation or institution. To select a room for the meeting, select the room in the list and then select the Rooms button at the bottom of the dialog. The room will be selected for the meeting. Click OK to return to the Meeting dialog box. The meeting room is listed in the Location box and the To box because the room itself becomes a participant (albeit a location) for the meeting.

CAUTION

Many people use Outlook as an Internet email client but do not get to take advantage of all of Outlook's bells and whistles that are provided for those who use Outlook on an Exchange Server network. Don't be disheartened when you can't take advantage of absolutely every Outlook feature. If you take advantage of an Outlook.com email account, you can access much of what Outlook has to offer. Even if you are using Outlook as an email client for a POP or IMAP email account, you can still schedule meetings, specify the meeting locations, and invite attendees.

An alternative to the Location command is the Room Finder pane, which you can open using the Room Finder command on the far right of the Location button in the Meeting dialog box. The Room Finder command opens a calendar of the current month and also opens a list of available rooms (again, if you are working in a networked environment that provides this information). You can use the date selector (the calendar), the available room list, and the suggested times list (all these tools are in the Room Finder pane) to determine the best room availability based on the date and time.

Using the Scheduling Assistant

Although finding a conference room or other venue for a meeting might be an issue, one of the biggest headaches related to scheduling a meeting is finding a date and time that works for all the participants. The Scheduling Assistant can help you ferret out potential conflicts and schedule your meeting when most, if not all, participants are available.

To open the Scheduling Assistant, select the Scheduling Assistant tab on the Meeting dialog box's ribbon. This tab only houses a single command—Scheduling Assistant—so, when you select it, the Scheduling Assistant opens, as shown in Figure 25-10.

The Scheduling Assistant lists the participants in the All Attendees list. The date (the meeting date) is broken down in a tabular format, with the column headings defined by hours. Each attendee's free/busy time for the date is shown on the timeline.

A blue vertical line shows the start time and end time for the meeting. You can drag the start and end timelines on the time grid to specify a meeting time without conflicts. You can also cross-reference information provided in the Room Finder task pane to make sure there is no room conflict at the newly specified meeting time.

The Scheduling Assistant also enables you to add attendees and rooms so that you can build a meeting directly from the Scheduling Assistant before you add an attendee or other information to the meeting. This means you can open a new Meeting dialog box and enter the attendees, meeting time, and room from the Scheduling Assistant.

When you have finished fine-tuning the meeting time and other settings in the Scheduling Assistant, select the Appointment command in the Show group to return to the Meeting dialog box. Before you send the meeting invitations, you might want to alter the response options available on the Response Options command in the Attendees group. By default, a response is requested to the invitation, and attendees are provided the option of proposing a new time for the meeting. If you do not want to allow new time proposals, deselect the Allow New Time Proposals option.

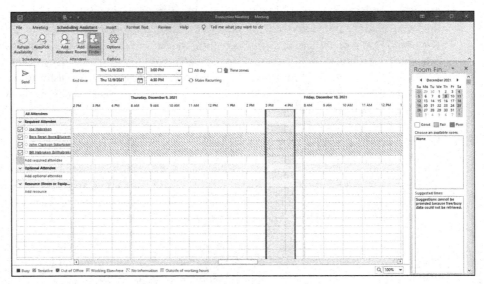

Figure 25-10   The Scheduling Assistant

If you send the invitation to possible attendees for whom you manually entered the email address or when you are not sure whether an email address is valid, select the Check Names command (in the Attendees group). If there is a problem with an address or name, Outlook provides a message box detailing the problem.

When you are ready to send the meeting, click Send. The meeting invitations are sent to the attendees. The meeting is also added to your Outlook Calendar as an appointment.

Viewing and editing meeting information

You can open a meeting on your Calendar and view or edit the meeting details as needed. Double-click the meeting in the Calendar (which appears as an appointment), and the Meeting dialog box opens.

If you want to quickly track responses for the meeting invitations that were sent, select the Tracking command in the Show group (the Tracking command is available only for sent meetings) and then select View Tracking Status.

A list of the attendees and the status of their responses displays. If an attendee has not responded, the response is labeled as None. Attendees can also respond to the invitation using Accept, Tentative, or Decline.

You can also edit the meeting parameters. You can change the time and date of the meeting, and you can edit the list of attendees for the meeting. If necessary, you can use the Scheduling

Assistant to reschedule the meeting and specify a new location for the meeting. You can even use the Cancel Meeting command to cancel the meeting.

If you make substantive changes to the meeting, you can send these changes to the attendees. When you have finished making your changes, select the Send Update button. Updated invitations are sent to the attendees. If you have changed the date or time for the meeting, the meeting also is moved on your Calendar.

When you do receive a meeting response message from an attendee, the message details whether the specific attendee has accepted, tentatively accepted, or declined the invitation. The email also provides tracking information related to the number of accepted, tentative, and declined responses you have received related to the meeting.

Responding to meeting requests

When you are a potential attendee for a meeting, you receive a meeting invitation from the meeting organizer. The invitation comes in the form of an email. The invitation provides the meeting details and enables you to accept or decline the meeting invitation. If you accept the meeting invitation, the meeting is automatically added to your Outlook Calendar.

Double-click a meeting invitation in your Inbox to open it. Figure 25-11 shows a meeting invitation message.

The Respond group on the ribbon provides five alternatives for responding to the meeting: Accept, Tentative (accept tentatively), Decline, Propose New Time, and Respond. The Propose New Time command enables you to either accept tentatively and propose a new time or decline and propose a new time. The Respond command enables you to reply to the sender of the invitation or forward the invitation without accepting or declining the invitation. The respond commands provided in the Respond group are also provided inside the Meeting window to the left of the sender's name and email address.

TIP

If you select a meeting invitation in your Inbox, you can also respond to the invitation using the response commands at the top of the Reading pane.

When you select the Accept, Tentative, or Decline command, you are provided with three options related to your response to the originator of the meeting:

- **Edit The Response Before Sending:** This command enables you to include additional comments with your response message. Selecting this command opens a new message, and you can add text to the body of the message, attach files, or do anything that you can normally do to an email message, such as address or copy the message to other recipients.

CHAPTER 25

- **Send The Response Now:** This command sends a response immediately without additional comments or information.

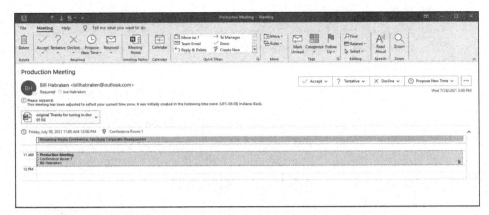

Figure 25-11   A meeting invitation message

- **Do Not Send A Response:** This command adds the meeting to your Calendar, in the case of an acceptance or tentative acceptance response from you, but does not provide a response to the meeting planner. If you decline the meeting and use this option, the originator can track your response in the meeting's tracking information.

You can propose a new time and accept tentatively or decline the message. When you select the Propose New Time command, you have two options:

- Tentative And Propose New Time

- Decline And Propose New Time

When you select either of these possibilities, the Propose New Time dialog box opens (see Figure 25-12).

This dialog box is basically a compact version of the Scheduling Assistant. You can use the Start and End lines (drag them to a new position on the timeline) to propose a new start and end time for the meeting. You can also use the AutoPick Next button to find the next available time slot for all the participants. AutoPick Next enables you to search forward in the timeline. The Back button to the left of the AutoPick Next button enables you to search backward in the timeline.

After you have specified your proposed time for the meeting, click the Propose Time button. A new message opens with both the current and proposed times for the meeting detailed. You can add information to the body of the message as needed. When you are ready to send the message, click Send.

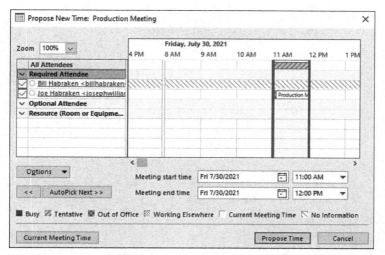

Figure 25-12   You can propose a new time for the meeting.

CHAPTER 26

Securing and maintaining Outlook

Security overview   797

Configuring Outlook security settings   801

Encrypting email and using digital signatures   804

The perils of HTML email   806

Dealing with message attachments   807

Coping with junk email   810

Creating email rules   813

Managing rules   818

Archiving Outlook items   819

Configuring an autoreply message   824

Outlook's capabilities for communication are based on the fact that Outlook is connected to a data network. Whereas some Outlook users take advantage of Outlook's features in controlled and secure corporate network environments, many of us use Outlook as an email, calendar, and contacts tool to communicate directly over the internet. And although we have virus protection and other security software on our computers (and perhaps on our home or small business internet router), we are still potentially open to outside attack by viruses and other malware. Even the most secure network environments fail to completely protect Outlook users from malicious email file attachments and junk email.

In this chapter, we take a look at some of the ways to secure Outlook. This chapter also discusses some of the maintenance tools you can use to keep your Outlook environment more organized, such as email rules and the Outlook archiving feature. We even look at how to configure Outlook to autoreply to messages that you receive when you are out of the office.

Security overview

The fact that Outlook receives data from other people (in some cases, people unknown to you) makes Outlook a potential source of attacks on your computer. These attacks can include the appropriation of information that you store in Outlook, such as your Contacts list. Nothing is more embarrassing (and potentially damaging) than having an infected file attachment "take over" Outlook and send copies of itself to everyone in your address book.

Attacks on your computer are not limited to email attachments and code embedded in HTML messages (which we discuss later in this chapter). Hackers have been known to exploit imperfections in software packages such as Microsoft Outlook and the other Office applications. Operating systems (such as Windows) and applications use TCP/IP ports for communication between your computer and the internet. Remember that most of us now use persistent internet connections, such as broadband and DSL, which means our computers are constantly connected to a public network. This gives hackers the ability to potentially invade our computers.

NOTE

The TCP/IP (Transport Control Protocol/Internet Protocol) protocol stack is the set of rules that your computer uses to communicate on IP networks such as the internet.

Protecting your computer potentially involves a number of different measures. Attacks via TCP/IP port exploits can be repelled by using a firewall and/or the firewall capabilities of your Wi-Fi router. A firewall is software or a device that sits between your computer (or computer network) and the Internet. A firewall examines both incoming and outgoing data and can filter out data that does not adhere to the firewall's rules. Windows provides a firewall—Microsoft Defender Firewall—that is just one of Microsoft Defender's strategies for protecting your computer.

Although this chapter primarily looks at what Outlook has to offer in terms of security features, it's not a bad idea to have a good feel for some of the types of threats you might face. Let's discuss viruses and other malware a little more closely and also look at some basic things beyond using the Outlook security settings that you can do to protect your computer.

Malware and antivirus software

It seems that malware—software designed to do your computer harm, such as a virus—has been around as long as personal computing. All of us who use Windows as our computer operating system know that we must install some sort of antivirus and antimalware software that helps defend our computer and the information stored on it from attack.

Inside OUT

Microsoft provides you with security features in Outlook and Windows.

Outlook provides you with some tools that can help you avoid email hacks and malware. Outlook automatically blocks a lot of file extensions that prevent you from receiving malware attachments. For example, program files such as .exe, .com, and .app files are blocked, as are Active Server Pages (.asp) and Basic Source Code (.bas). Outlook also makes it easy for you to categorize unwanted email as junk and to block specific email senders.

As already mentioned, Windows also has your back in regard to your computer security. The Windows Defender Security Center provides you with virus protection, account protection, a built-in firewall, and app and browser control settings. It makes sense to take advantage of these different security tools rather than ignore them. You can access the Windows Defender Security Center in Windows by selecting the Start button and then Settings. The Windows Settings window will open; select Update & Security and then Windows Security.

Malware (or "bad software") comes in a variety of flavors. There are self-replicating viruses, which can easily spread from computer to computer via infected email attachments. Viruses typically require that you activate them, so don't open attachments in emails from senders you don't know. However, even a friend can inadvertently send you an infected file.

Worms also can infect your computer and do not require you to activate them. They can quickly spread to computers on the same network (yes, even a home or small business network). Trojan horses are malware programs that are disguised as something else. For example, you might receive a file that claims it is a slideshow of firework displays from around the world. If the file is a Trojan horse, there will be fireworks, but just in terms of the havoc that will be wreaked on your PC.

The best way to protect against viruses and other malware is to use an antivirus program. Windows has Defender built into the operating system; it provides you with antivirus protection without adding third-party software. However, if you are particularly fond of a particular third-party vendor's antivirus software or feel otherwise compelled to purchase additional protection, there are a number of other antivirus software for Windows; you can check the web for reviews and other information related to these antivirus software packages.

Strong password protection

Your email account is password protected. After you configure an email account for use in Outlook, you don't have to re-enter that password to access the account—but that password is still protecting the email account. Windows 10 gives you the option to password-protect your computer by requiring that you enter a log-in name and password. This log-in name and password can be a Windows Live account name, such as your Outlook.com username and password. Your computer's protection really relies on the strength of the password that you use, as does your Outlook email account.

Not all attacks on your email account and your computer are related to nefarious and complex viruses attempting to infiltrate Outlook and your operating system. Many hackers rely on extremely weak and easily guessed passwords to hijack your email account or gain access to your computer. If you use a weak, easily guessed password (or no password), nearly anyone can log on to your computer and access your data. If someone knows your email account name (which is easy to find online) and a little bit about you (also found online), a hacker can probably guess your "easy" password.

The only way to avoid the easy password hack is to protect your computer and your email account or accounts with strong passwords. A strong password (as defined by Microsoft) is a password with at least eight characters. The strong password also uses a combination of numeric and alphanumeric characters and does not include easy-to-guess or personal information. For example, if I use the password "joseph" as my Windows account password, I'm making it easy for someone else to guess my password. Create a more complex, strong password, but make sure that you remember the password. Of course, scribbling passwords on scraps of paper that are easily accessible by anyone walking in the door doesn't set up a very secure environment either, even if you have created the strongest of passwords.

You probably have noticed that a log-in password is not required when you start Outlook (unless you use Outlook in a work environment where the network administrator has configured the software to require a log in at startup). If your computer is running, and you are away from the computer, anyone can start Outlook and poke around in your Mail, Contacts, or Calendar folders.

You have two options for requiring a log in when you start Outlook. If you are using Outlook in an Exchange Server environment (which includes those of you with Office 365 subscriptions), you can configure Outlook so that it always requires user identification upon startup. If you use Outlook for internet email (such as a POP3 account), you can password-protect your Outlook data file. Both Outlook log-in-protection schemes are set up in the Outlook Account Settings dialog box, which is accessed in the Outlook Backstage.

To configure Outlook to require user identification (when you are using an Exchange email account), follow these steps:

1. Select File to open the Backstage.

2. With Info selected in the Backstage, select Account Settings and then select Account Settings (again) on the menu. The Account Settings dialog box opens.

3. Select the Data Files tab in the Account Settings dialog box.

4. Select your Exchange email account data file in the list provided by the Data Files tab.

5. Click Settings. The Microsoft Exchange dialog box opens.

6. Click the Security tab.

7. On the Security tab (in the User Identification area of the dialog box), select the Always Prompt For Logon Credentials check box. Click OK to close the Microsoft Exchange dialog box.

CAUTION

If you work in an institutional or business environment, your IT department might configure Outlook so that the Security tab is not available to you.

You can close the Account Settings dialog box to return to the Outlook application window. When you start Outlook in the future, you are required to log in by entering your username and password.

If you are using Outlook for Internet email, you can password-protect Outlook by actually password-protecting your Outlook data file (.pst file). You are then required to provide the data file password when you start Outlook. Don't password-protect the Outlook data file unless you really feel it necessary (for example, when you share a computer with others).

The Outlook data file is accessed via the Account Settings dialog box. Open the Account Settings from the Backstage using the Account Settings button (just as you did in the steps provided several paragraphs ago).

On the Data Files tab of the Account Settings dialog box, select the data file for your Internet email account; then select Settings. In the Settings dialog box, select Change Password to open the Change Password dialog box. Enter a new password, and then verify the new password (also make sure you remember this password; if you do write it down, keep it in a safe and secure place). To save the password in your Windows password list, select the Save This Password In Your Password List check box. Then click OK to close the Change Password dialog box. You can also close the Account Settings dialog box.

The data file is now password-protected. The next time you start Outlook, you are asked to provide the Outlook data file password. Enter the password, and then click OK to open Outlook.

CAUTION

If you don't share your computer with other people or don't work in an environment where others can access your computer, there is no real advantage to requiring a log in when starting Outlook (in an Exchange Server setting) or password-protecting your Outlook data file (when using internet email). And if you forget the password, it is a real disadvantage. Also, in corporate Exchange Server environments, the network administrator probably does not want you to change any of your Outlook settings.

Configuring Outlook security settings

Microsoft Office has bundled the security settings for each of the member applications in the Trust Center. Each application, such as Outlook, has its own Trust Center where you can view and configure the various security settings.

➤ **For an overview of the Trust Center, see "Using the Trust Center," in Chapter 2.**

To access the Outlook Trust Center, follow these steps:

1. Select File to open the Outlook Backstage.

2. In the Backstage, select Options. The Outlook Options window opens.

3.   Select Trust Center; an Options window opens that provides a link related to information about the Microsoft Trust Center. Also, Microsoft recommends that you do not change the settings in the Trust Center if you want to keep your computer secure.

4.   To access the Trust Center settings, select the Trust Center Settings button. The Trust Center opens.

The Trust Center provides different categories of privacy and security settings. Figure 26-1 shows the Automatic Download settings. Categories such as Trusted Publishers and Macro Settings are found in the Trust Center of other 365 applications, such as Word and Excel. Trusted publishers are discussed in Chapter 2, "Navigating and customizing the 365 interface," and the Macro Settings options are discussed in Appendix B, "365 macros."

➤ **For an overview of the macro-related Trust Center settings, see Appendix B.**

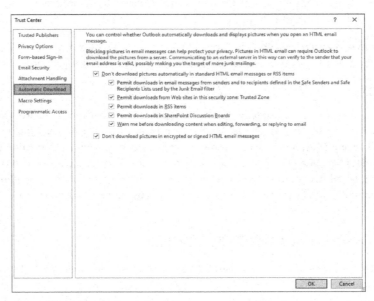

Figure 26-1   The Outlook Trust Center

The Trust Center categories that are directly related to the Outlook application environment are as follows:

- **Privacy Options:** The privacy options are related to connecting Office applications to the internet (for software updates), the Microsoft Customer Experience Improvement program, and installing new services for the Research task pane. You can determine which privacy options you disable. The options for updating content should remain updated. The Privacy Options window also provides settings for research and reference. You have the option to select language pairs for translation (Translation options), and you can select the reference books and research sites used by the Reference task pane using the Research options.

- **Email Security:** The security options provide encrypted mail settings and the capability to manage digital IDs for sending encrypted and secure mail. You can also choose to read all your standard mail in plain text. We talk about encrypted email options in the next section.

- **Attachment Handling:** These options relate to including personal information when sending Office documents as attachments and previewing attachments for received emails. These options are discussed in more detail in this chapter's "Dealing with message attachments" section.

- **Automatic Download:** These options relate to the download and display of pictures in email messages. Junk email senders can use pictures in HTML messages to increase the number of junk emails you receive. See "The perils of HTML email, " for more about these settings," later in this chapter.

- **Programmatic Access:** These settings allow you to enable warnings that alert you when another program accesses the Outlook address book. For example, you might use a smartphone or smart device that syncs with your contacts, calendars, or email. This is considered to be access by another program, but it is okay. Other access might be the work of a virus or other malware. You can also set a warning for your antivirus program; Outlook can tell you whether it is inactive or outdated. If your antivirus software is currently up to date and deemed valid by the Trust Center, the Programmatic Access settings might be unavailable.

CAUTION

If you are going to send an encrypted email to another person using Outlook, then that person also needs to have a digital ID. You and the other party must then exchange emails that are digitally signed. When you add that person to your contacts (or update the contact information), the digital certificate is added to the contact information. The person on the other end must also add you to the Contacts folder in the same manner.

Many of these Trust Center options can be left with the default options enabled. Change the security settings only if you have a compelling reason to do so. In some networking environments (such as an Exchange Server environment), the network administrator determines the settings for your Outlook mail client.

Encrypting email and using digital signatures

You can choose to raise the bar for email security by encrypting your email. Encrypted email is mail that has been transformed using a mathematical algorithm. The only way to read encrypted mail is to decrypt the mail. Outlook uses digital certificates to verify the sender of encrypted email. If you don't want to encrypt your emails, you can use a digital certificate (also known as a digital ID) to verify the authenticity of the email that you send.

To send encrypted email, you must obtain a digital certificate. If you work at a company that wants you to encrypt your email, it should provide you with a digital certificate. If you run a small business or work at home and feel the need to encrypt messages, you need to obtain a digital certificate from a certificate authority. A number of certificate authorities are available online, including the following:

- IdenTrust (*https://www.identrust.com/certificates/*)

- Entrustdatacard (*https://www.entrustdatacard.com/products/digital-signing-certificates/code-signing-certificates*)

- Digicert (*https://www.digicert.com/*)

The settings related to encrypted email and digital certificates are in the Outlook Trust Center's Email Security options. Figure 26-2 shows the Email Security options.

Before you use the Encrypted Email settings, you need to either import an existing digital ID or get a digital ID online. If you need a digital ID, click the Get A Digital ID button. This starts your web browser and opens a Microsoft-sponsored web page that provides a list of certificate authorities. Select a certificate authority, and you are walked through the process of obtaining (meaning "paying for") a digital certificate.

If you have a digital ID that your company has provided, it might have already been configured on your computer. If a digital certificate has been exported from another computer, you can import the ID into the Trust Center. Click the Import/Export button and then use the Import/Export Digital ID dialog box to specify the certificate's file name, password, and digital ID name. Then click OK.

If you have purchased your own digital ID, you need to install it on your computer. The certificate installation process is typically provided to you in an email from the certificate authority. Many certificate authorities provide a link that takes you to an installation web page.

Encrypted email uses a private key and a public key. The email is encrypted by the public key associated with your digital ID. The private key, which is then used on the receiving end to decrypt the message, is stored in the recipient's Contacts folder in your contact entry. Anyone intercepting or otherwise pirating the message cannot decrypt the message content or attachments.

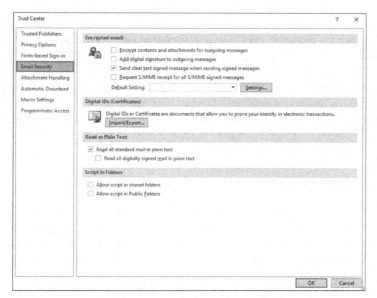

Figure 26-2   Email Security options

Options for encrypting email

You have options for encrypting your email. If you want to encrypt all outgoing email and attachments, you can specify that fact in the Encrypted Email section of the Email Security options (open the Trust Center via the Trust Center link in the Outlook Options window). Select the Encrypt Contents And Attachments For Outgoing Messages check box.

> ### TIP
>
> You can check to see if a digital certificate is installed and available to Outlook. In the Email Security Options window, click the Settings button. The Change Security Settings dialog box should list your digital ID in the Signing Certificate and Encryption Certificate boxes.

You can also choose to encrypt individual emails. This makes more sense than sending all your email encrypted, particularly if you need to share encrypted messages with only one or two recipients. Remember that you and the recipient must share digital ID information before you can send encrypted emails.

When you have a new message open that you want to encrypt, select the ribbon's Options tab. In the Permissions group, select the Encrypt command. Prepare your mail message, including attaching files or items as needed. You can then send the message.

CHAPTER 26

NOTE

If you don't have a digital ID, the Options tab does not list the Encrypt and Sign commands.

If you send an encrypted message to an individual who does not have a digital signature (or if you haven't added the individual to your Contacts folder), Outlook opens an Encryption Problems dialog box and lists recipients of the email. You can click the Send Unencrypted button to send the email as a regular message. Otherwise, click Cancel, and make sure that the recipient is in your Contacts folder. Then attempt to send the message again.

Digitally signing emails

You can also use your digital ID to digitally sign email. This does not encrypt the message content or attachments, but it does verify you as the sender. You can choose to send a digital signature with all your outgoing messages by selecting the Add Digital Signature To Outgoing Messages check box in the Encrypted Email section of the Email Security options.

Because you are using a digital signature as a security measure, it makes sense to receive confirmation that your digital signature is validated by the recipients and that messages are received unaltered. This notification can also tell you when a message was opened and by whom. In the Encrypted Email section of the Email Security options, select the Request S/MIME Receipt For All S/MIME Signed Messages check box.

You can also choose to digitally sign specific messages (instead of signing all messages). With a new message open, navigate to the ribbon's Options tab; then select the Sign command in the Permission group. When you send the email, a message box opens and asks you to grant permission to use the key (associated with the digital ID) to sign the message. Click Grant Permission, and then click OK to send the message. When the recipient receives the email, it provides a Signed By statement and includes a digital certificate image in the header of the message. The recipient can click the digital certificate to view details related to the digital ID.

The perils of HTML email

HTML email can included links, graphics, and other elements that make your emails look more appealing and interesting (at least when compared to a plain-text email). However, HTML email can actually pose a threat to your computer. HTML email can include active content such as Active X controls and scripts, and these can potentially be malware. HTML email can also include graphic images. These images can include a web beacon.

NOTE

Believe it or not, Outlook can serve as your RSS (Really Simple Syndication) feed reader. Right-click the RSS Feed folder in your Mail folder, and then select Add a New RSS Feed. You can copy and paste the URL for any website that provides an RSS feed into the New RSS dialog box. You can then use Outlook to read the feeds from the RSS source.

A web beacon is basically HTML code that is typically used on websites to count the number of people who access the website; however, web beacons can also be used to send information to a website. Web beacons in HTML emails can verify that your email address is valid (you activate the web beacon when you open or view the email). The verification of your email address is sent to the "owner" of the web beacon and results in you receiving much more junk email.

To turn off HTML email as the format for received messages, select the Read All Standard Mail In Plain Text check box in the Read As Plain Text section of the Email Security options. Even if you choose to receive plain-text messages, you can quickly switch a message from plain text to HTML when viewing the message. The message infobar displays this message: "We converted this message into plain text format." Click the infobar icon and select Display As HTML to view the message in HTML.

If you still decide to receive messages as HTML email (I mean, who really wants to receive text-only email messages?), Outlook blocks automatic picture downloads for external sources, by default. And because many web beacons are associated with images, you are protected, to a certain extent. The settings related to picture download and other download-related options, such as RSS item downloads, are in the Automatic Download options of the Outlook Trust Center. Because you can specify safe senders and safe recipients in the Junk Email filter (which we discuss later in this chapter in the section, "Coping with junk email"), you can leave the Don't Download Pictures Automatically In HTML Email Message Or RSS Items setting enabled. You can then place friends and family members (or other trusted individuals) in the Safe Senders and Safe Recipients lists (as discussed in "Coping with junk email").

Dealing with message attachments

Outlook blocks many file types as mail attachments. When a blocked file type is included in a message that you receive, Outlook provides a message that a potentially unsafe file type was blocked. Message attachments can certainly contain malware, so blocking file types that are programs or executable files makes sense. Table 26-1 lists some of the blocked file types.

Table 26-1 A subset of blocked file types

File Extension	Description
.app	Executable application file
.asp	Active Server page
.bat	Batch processing file
.chm	HTML Help file
.com	Command file
.crt	Certificate file
.hlp	Windows Help file

CHAPTER 26

.js	JavaScript source code
.jse	JScript encoded script file
.msh	Microsoft Shell
.prf	Windows System file
.prg	Program file
.scf	Windows Explorer command
.scr	Windows Screen Saver
.vbp	Visual Basic project file
.vbs	Microsoft Visual Basic for Applications script (or Visual Basic script)

These file types and a number of others are blocked because they are considered potential vehicles for malware. If you glance at the subset of blocked files listed in Table 26-1, you can see why these file types are on the blocked list. Malware masquerading as any of these file types can do a lot of bad things to your computer.

CAUTION

In an Exchange Server environment, your administrator can tweak the blocked file list. If you are using Outlook for internet email, you can change settings in the system Registry to unblock specific file types. This is not a good idea unless you are very familiar with editing the Windows Registry. The Microsoft Support website (*https://support.microsoft.com*) provides the steps for editing the Registry. Search for "Outlook blocked unsafe attachments."

In terms of sending emails that have attached files that are blocked by Outlook (when you are receiving these emails), Outlook has no problem sending them.

You can attach any type of file to an Outlook email, including file types on the block list. (Look back at Table 26-1.) When you click the Send button and attempt to send an email that has a potentially unsafe file attachment (such as a .com or .vbs file), Outlook opens a message box stating that the email attachment(s) is potentially unsafe and that any recipient using Microsoft Outlook might not be able to open the attachment(s).

You are provided with three options by this Microsoft Outlook alert box. You can select Yes and send the message with the attachment. Or you can select No, and you will be returned to the message window where you can remove the unsafe attachment or attachments. If you are unsure as to whether you should choose Yes or No, you can also select Help in the alert box. This will open the Outlook Help window. Links to articles on how best to share files safely and a section on the file types blocked in Outlook can be accessed via Help.

If you want to send blocked file types without receiving this alert box each time you send an email containing a file attachment that is on the block list, place the file in a zipped folder (archive), and then send the zipped file as the attachment. Outlook does not block files with the zip extension, so the recipient will not have the attachment blocked when they receive your email. The recipient can then unzip the file and access the original file.

In Windows, you can right-click any file in the File Explorer and access a shortcut menu. Point at Send To, and then select Compressed (Zipped) Folder. This compresses the file(s) (or a folder) into a ZIP archive. Before we end our discussion of attachments and Outlook, we need to address two settings in the Attachment Handling options of Outlook's Trust Center. Figure 26-3 shows the Attachment Handling options.

When you select the Add Properties To Attachments To Enable Reply With Changes check box, you allow Outlook to send personal information placed in a document that you have edited using the Track Changes feature. Information such as your name or email address can easily end up in the properties of an Office file that you have worked with.

If you don't want Outlook to share this personal information in the file's properties, be sure to clear the Add Properties To Attachments To Enable Reply With Changes check box (it is cleared by default). This keeps your personal information out of the attached document; however, this also makes it impossible for you to track changes that others might make to a document that you send them. You must decide whether it's more important to track changes or protect your personal information.

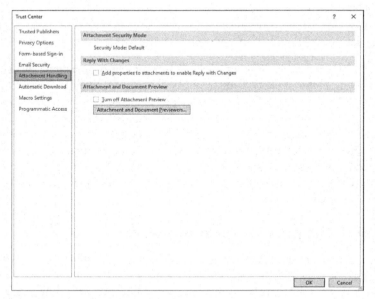

Figure 26-3   Attachment Handling options

One other setting that can help protect you from security issues with attachments is the Turn Off Attachment Preview check box. If you want to negate a preview of attached files, make sure that the check box has been cleared.

Coping with junk email

Junk email is certainly a scourge. It fills up your Inbox with a lot of spam that you just don't want, and taking the time to delete this stuff is a pain. Junk email can be more than just a nuisance—it can also potentially serve as part of a phishing scam. In a phishing scam, you receive what appears to be a legitimate email message from a business that you frequent on the web (Amazon, eBay, or any other website where you buy stuff or perform financial transactions). These businesses typically keep your personal information, including credit card numbers, on file. The phishing email asks you to update personal information or provides a link that takes you to a fake website where you are asked to supply your password or other personal information. When the phisher has the info, all sorts of bad things can happen.

Outlook's junk email filtering relies on message content, including keywords and phrases, to determine whether a message is junk. Sometimes it places a legitimate message in the Junk Email folder.

The Junk Email filter can also block senders in your blocked sender list. Although Outlook tries its best to ferret out junk email, you can help it by providing information such as safe senders, safe recipients, and blocked senders, to make the Junk Email filter more efficient.

The Junk Email filter can provide different levels of protection from junk email. By default, the filter is set to No Automatic Filtering. If you have blocked email senders, mail from them is moved to the Junk Email folder. By default, you are not taking advantage of Outlook's ability to move suspected junk email automatically. The other settings include Low and High. Low moves messages received in the Inbox to the Junk Email folder only if they are obvious junk email messages (at least, obvious to Outlook in terms of content and overall structure). The High setting does a better job of catching junk email, but it might also move "regular" email to the Junk Email folder. You can change the level of protection using the Junk Email Options dialog box, which we will discuss shortly.

Working with the junk email commands

The commands for dealing with individual messages and their junk email status (whether they are or aren't) are in the Delete group of the ribbon's Home tab (when the Mail folder is selected in the Folder pane). Figure 26-4 shows the Junk command and its menu of associated commands.

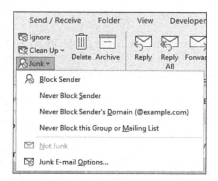

Figure 26-4   The Junk commands

You can use the commands on the Junk command's menu to specify the "junk" status of a message, no matter what mail folder you are working in (meaning the Inbox or the Junk Email folder). First, let's look at options related to legitimate messages that are marked as junk and placed in the Junk Email folder.

As you receive email, the Junk Email filter moves any email that it considers junk to the Junk Email folder. You can view mail that has been placed in the Junk Email folder by selecting Junk Email in the Navigation pane (when the Mail folder is selected).

If you find a message listed in the Junk Email folder that is not junk, you can mark it as Not Junk and have it moved to the Inbox. Select the message in the Junk Email folder, and then select Junk and then Not Junk. The Mark As Not Junk dialog box opens, letting you know that the message was moved back into the Inbox folder. An option box is also included in the dialog box that enables you to always trust email from the sender of the message. This option adds the sender of the message to your Safe Senders list; you have to decide whether you want to leave this check box selected (by default) or choose to deselect it. To close the Mark As Not Junk dialog box, select OK.

You can also add email senders to the Safe Senders list by selecting any message in any folder (including the Junk Email folder) and then selecting the Never Block Sender on the Junk command's menu. A message box opens, letting you know that the sender has been added to your Safe Senders list. Using this Junk option does not move the email from the Junk Email folder.

Using the Never Block Sender's Domain command, you can also place a sender's entire domain on the Safe Senders list. This command also does not move the email from your Junk Email folder to the Inbox (same as the Never Block Sender command); you need to drag the email (or emails) to the Inbox or use the Not Junk command, as discussed earlier.

When you are working in the Inbox, you can specify one or more messages as junk. Select the message or messages and then select Block Sender. The sender of the message (or messages) is added to the blocked sender list. The message is also moved to the Junk Email folder.

CHAPTER 26

Setting junk email options

You can set the level of protection that the Junk Email filter provides and work with your safe senders, safe recipients, and blocked senders lists. Select the Junk command, and then select Junk Email Options. The Junk Email Options dialog box opens, as shown in Figure 26-5.

Figure 26-5   The Junk Email Options dialog box

The dialog box provides five tabs:

- **Options:** The Junk Email options are a series of option buttons and check boxes (see Figure 26-5). The Low, High, and Safe Lists Only option buttons determine the level of protection. Obviously, in terms of effective Junk email filtering, No Automatic Filter is the lowest setting, and Safe Lists Only is the highest level. The higher the protection level settings, the greater the number of received messages that will end up in your Junk Email folder. The Options tab also enables you to specify whether junk email should be deleted rather than moved to the Junk Email folder. By default, links are disabled in phishing messages, and you are also warned when a suspicious domain name appears in an email address. By default, your sent emails are postmarked to help the receiver distinguish them as regular emails.

- **Safe Senders:** This tab provides a list of safe senders that you might have created using the Never Block commands on the Junk menu. You can also add, edit, or remove senders from the Safe Senders list on this tab. You can import a list of safe senders from a delimited text file or export your list to a text file. Two other options provided by this tab are two check boxes: Also Trust Email From My Contacts and Automatically Add People I Email To The Safe Senders List. Both check boxes are designed to keep your frequent contacts' and email recipients' messages out of the Junk Email folder.

- **Safe Recipients:** This list might seem a little odd because you are receiving the message that must be either marked as junk or not. If you receive emails that include other recipients (such as a particular contact group the sender has created), you can specify that any or all these recipients be added to the safe recipients list. This gives Outlook another parameter in determining a received message's junk status. You can add, edit, or remove safe recipients as needed. You can also import a list from a file. This tab works in much the same way as the Safe Senders tab.

NOTE

When a message is postmarked, it is tagged with unique information related to that message, such as the list of recipients and the time the message was sent. The postmark is valid only for that message. Postmarking a message means that the message takes a little longer to be processed and to leave your Outlook Outbox. Outlook does not view postmarked emails as junk. Spammers would find it a burden to postmark all their messages; sending tons of spam requires a lot of computing power, and postmarking all spam would take increased computing power. This means that postmarking spam would cost spammers money.

- **Blocked Senders:** This is your rogues' gallery of blocked senders. You can add, edit, and remove blocked senders on this tab. You can also import a list of blocked senders or export your list. Remember, any messages from an address or domain name on the blocked senders list are treated as junk email.

- **International:** This tab enables you to block top-level domains, meaning that you can block emails from senders who are from specific countries or regions. Countries have their own top-level domain designation, such as .aq (Antarctica), .br (Brazil), and .nz (New Zealand)—all places I want to go. To block all emails ending in a specific top-level domain, click the Blocked Top-Level Domain List button. Select from the list provided, and then click OK. You can also block emails that are encoded in a particular character set; this means that you can block email sent in specific languages. Click the Blocked Encodings List button, and then specify by language the mail you want to block.

The strength of the Junk Email filter is directly related to the time you take to fine-tune the various options provided in the Junk Email Options dialog box. If you are fairly diligent about specifying safe senders and blocked senders, and if you increase the level of junk email protection on the Options tab, you should see a decrease in junk email. However, remember that spam email is an industry, and those in this industry are constantly looking for ways to get around junk email filters and other types of spam protection. I doubt whether any of us will ever be completely free from spam.

Creating email rules

You can automate the management of your Mail folder using Outlook rules. A rule can delete, flag, or move messages. For example, a rule can be used to automatically move messages in the Inbox from a particular sender to a particular mail-related folder. This can help you keep organized, particularly if you need to place mail from a particular sender in a folder other than the Inbox. Although rules can't necessarily be considered a security feature, they do give you control over the disposition of the email messages that you receive.

An Outlook rule is basically a set of conditions. When the conditions of the rule are met by an email message, the rule acts on the message. A rule can take all sorts of things into account, such as sender, message subject, and message body content. A rule can be simple or complex; it all depends on what you want the rule to do.

Creating a quick rule for a specific sender

Outlook makes it easy for you to create rules based on the properties of a selected email. For example, you can quickly create a simple rule that moves email from a particular sender from your Inbox to another specified location. Follow these steps:

1. Select a message from a sender in your Inbox.

2. Select the Rules command in the Move group.

3. Select Always Move Messages from *Name of Sender*. The Rules And Alerts dialog box appears, as shown in Figure 26-6.

4. Select a folder in the Rules And Alerts dialog box, or use the New button to create a new folder using the Create New Folder dialog box (and then select the new folder).

5. Click OK.

The new rule is created. The selected message moves to the folder that you specified when you created the rule. Messages in the Inbox that also meet the conditions of the rule (the single condition of a specified sender) move to the folder you chose in the Rules And Alerts dialog box.

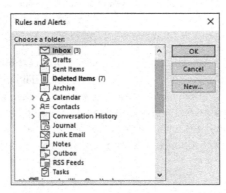

Figure 26-6   The Rules And Alerts dialog box

Creating complex rules

You can also create rules that are more complex. Rules can use multiple criteria and perform multiple actions. Outlook provides a Rules Wizard that makes it fairly straightforward to create rules with multiple criteria and multiple actions.

If you have an email message that meets the criteria (or maybe just a criterion or two, such as the subject or the sender) that you want to include in a rule, you can speed up the creation of the rule by selecting that message. To open the Create Rule dialog box, select the Rules command and then select Create Rule. Figure 26-7 shows the Create Rule dialog box.

The Create Rule dialog box provides a number of check boxes and other options that enable you to create a rule based on the currently selected message. The criteria for the rule can consist of the sender, the subject text, and the message recipient (or recipients, if the message was sent to more than one recipient). To set the criteria or conditions for the rule, select the appropriate check boxes and provide additional information, as required (such as subject text).

Because rules need to perform actions based on your rule's conditions, you are provided with several check boxes in the Do The Following area of the dialog box. You can have the rule provide a new alert window when a message is received that meets the conditions of the rule. You can also choose to have a sound be played when the rule's conditions are met. You can use the Browse button to use any .wav sound file on your computer for this purpose.

You also specify that the rule move the item to a particular folder. The Select Folder button specifies a folder as needed.

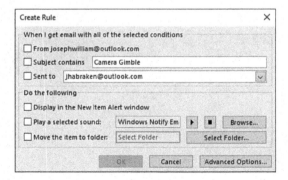

Figure 26-7   The Create Rule dialog box

The Create Rule dialog box limits you to three different conditions (sender, subject, and receiver) and can open an alert window, play a sound, and/or move the message to a specified folder. This doesn't seem much better than the rule we quickly created in the previous section based on the sender of the email. There has to be a tool that enables you to beef up a rule with more conditions and multiple actions. There is—read on.

The Rules Wizard

Complexity and functionality can be added to a rule using the Rules Wizard. With the Create Rule dialog box open, select the Advanced Options button in the lower-right corner. The Rules Wizard opens, as shown in Figure 26-8.

The first wizard screen asks you to select all the conditions to be used by the new rule. These conditions can be related to sender, subject, message importance, specific words in the body, flags, categories, and messages with an attachment. Many of the conditions you select in the conditions list require you to provide additional information in the Edit The Rule description box of the Rules Wizard to flesh out that particular condition. Select conditions using the check boxes provided in the Step 1: Select Condition(s) box.

> ### NOTE
>
> **Rules can be created for your RSS feeds. See the RSS feed conditions provided by the Rules Wizard on the condition screen.**

In the Step 2: Edit The Rule Description box, select any underlined items associated with the conditions you selected in the Step 1 box. Provide the information required by each condition; for example, the Specific Words In The Body condition requires that you click the Specific Words link and supply a list of words for the rule to use. At this point in the process, you are provided only the conditions for the rule, not what the rule will do. After providing and fine-tuning your conditions, click Next.

Figure 26-8   Setting conditions using the Rules Wizard

On the next wizard screen, you specify the actions you want the rule to perform. The Rules Wizard: The What Do You Want To Do With The Message? screen is shown in Figure 26-9.

Select an action or actions in the Step 1: Select Action(s)box. If you select an action that contains a link, you need to provide the details for the action in the Step 2: Edit The Rule Description box. For example, if you select the Forward It To People Or Public Group action in Step 1, you need to specify the people or public group in Step 2 (specify the people using the Address Book).

NOTE

Although the Rules Wizard provides a separate screen for the rule's conditions, actions, and exceptions, configuring each of these items for a rule is similar. You specify a condition, action, or exception in Step 1. Then you provide the details for the condition, action, or exception in the Step 2 box.

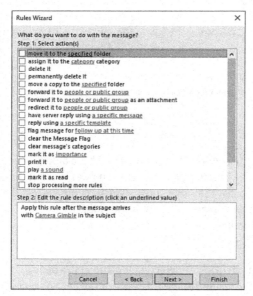

Figure 26-9   Specifying the actions for the rule using the Rules Wizard

After you specify the action or actions for the rule and provide the details for the action, click Next. The next wizard screen enables you to configure any exceptions you want to have for the rule. These exceptions could relate to mail from specific people, messages that are flagged for a particular action, or messages with specific words in the subject or body. Use the check boxes in the Step 1 box to select individual exceptions to the rule. For example, if you create a rule that moves messages to a particular folder (the action) based on the subject line or keywords in the body (the condition), you can set an exception for the rule, such as ignoring the rule if the message is from a particular person.

You are certainly not required to specify an exception (or exceptions) for a rule. However, if there are exceptions, use the exceptions check boxes in the Step 1 box to specify them. Then provide the underlined value information for any exception you have selected for the rule in the Step 2 box. For example, if you have created a rule where you want messages received from a particular person to be marked High importance, you would need to specify the importance level in the Step 2 box.

When you are ready to continue the rule-creation process, click Next. The Finish Rule Setup screen appears.

Specify a name for the new rule (or you can go with the default, which is based on the first action you selected when you started this process). The Turn On This Rule check box is selected by default, so the rule is enabled. You can choose to run the rule on messages already in the Inbox by selecting the appropriate check box. This screen also enables you to review your rule, including the conditions, actions, and exceptions. When you are sure that everything is configured correctly, click the Finish button. The rule is created and added to your Rules And Alerts list. If you chose to have the rule act on messages already in the Inbox, the rule does its stuff based on your rule settings.

You can run rules that you have created at any time by accessing the Clean Up commands on the ribbon's Folder tab. Select the Run Rules Now command to run all your rules.

Managing rules

You can manage your rules using the Rules And Alerts dialog box. This dialog box enables you to edit existing rule settings, delete rules, create new rules, and run rules in the Rule list. It also enables you to determine the specific order that rules run in, which is important if the rule sequence is of consequence to your overall plan related to using rules. To open the Rules And Alerts dialog box, select the Rules command and then select Manage Rules & Alerts. Figure 26-10 shows the Rules And Alerts dialog box.

The rules are listed on the Email Rules tab. You can select a message in the dialog box and then use the Rule description area to edit the values for the rule's conditions, actions, or exceptions. Other commands provided in the Rules And Alerts dialog box are as follows:

- **New Rule:** This command opens the Rules Wizard so that you can create a new rule. When you open the Rules Wizard from the Rules And Alerts dialog box, you have the option of starting the new rule by choosing a rule template from one of three different categories: Stay Organized, Stay Up-To-Date, or Start From A Blank Rule. After you select a rule template, the process for creating the rule is the same as discussed earlier in this chapter.

- **Change Rule:** This menu enables you to edit a rule's settings, rename a rule, change the alert for the rule, and move or copy the rule to a folder.

- **Copy:** You can copy the rule to another Outlook message folder.

- **Delete:** You can delete the selected rule.

- **Move Up/Move Down:** Use these buttons to change the order of the rules. Remember that the rules perform their actions in the order they are listed in the Rules list.

- **Run Rules Now:** This command opens the Run Rules Now dialog box. You can select a rule or rules in the dialog box and specify a folder in which the rules run. You can apply the rule (or rules) to all messages, unread messages, or read messages. After making your choices in the Run Rules Now dialog box, select Run Now to run the rules.

- **Options:** This command opens the Options dialog box. You can use the commands in this dialog box to export or import Outlook rules.

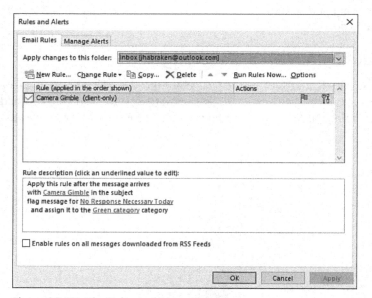

Figure 26-10   The Rules And Alerts dialog box

CHAPTER 26

If you make changes to your rules, you can immediately apply the changes by selecting Apply. When you are finished working in the Rules And Alerts dialog box, and you want to close the dialog box, click OK.

Archiving Outlook items

Another Outlook management tool is the AutoArchive feature. Older mail messages can be periodically and automatically archived in an archival Outlook data file. This archive.pst file is kept in the same location on your computer's hard disk as the Outlook data source file that holds your Outlook profile information. You can archive mail messages and calendar items, such as appointments and tasks.

The point of archiving is to save email messages for later reference but also to remove some of the older items that are floating around your mail folders.

Archived messages are still accessible, however. You can access them as needed from the Archive folders that are made available in the Folder pane when you enable the AutoArchive feature. You have a couple of options for archiving information in an Outlook mail-related folder. You can use the AutoArchive feature, or you can manually archive specific folders.

The great thing about using the AutoArchive feature is that you can specify global archiving settings that affect all your Outlook mail folders. If you don't like a one-size-fits-all approach to folder archiving, you can breathe a sigh of relief: You can also set the AutoArchive settings for individual folders if required.

Configuring AutoArchive settings

The AutoArchive feature is configured in the AutoArchive dialog box. You can open this dialog box from the Outlook Advanced options window (select Options in the Backstage and then Advanced) using the AutoArchive Settings button. Figure 26-11 shows the AutoArchive dialog box.

Figure 26-11   The AutoArchive dialog box

By default, the AutoArchive feature is disabled. To enable the feature, select the Run AutoArchive Every 14 Days check box. This means that, every fourteenth day, the AutoArchive feature automatically archives the contents of the Inbox and other email folders. You can use the day spin box to specify a different interval for running the AutoArchive feature. You have probably noticed that a lot of settings are crammed into the AutoArchive dialog box:

- **Prompt Before AutoArchive Runs:** If this item is enabled, Outlook displays a dialog box each time it is about to perform the AutoArchive; you can click OK to continue or Cancel to stop the operation.

- **Delete Expired Items (Email Folders Only):** Check this box to have Outlook delete messages from the Inbox after archiving them.

- **Show Archive Folder In Folder List:** This option makes the archive folder available from the Mail Folder list, making it easier to access archived files.

- **Clean Out Items Older Than:** Use this spin box to specify the increment, and then use the drop-down menu to specify Months, Weeks, or Days. The default age for older items is six months.

- **Move Old Items To:** This setting provides the path and file name for the archive file. The default name is archive.pst, and the location is My Documents\Outlook Files. You can use the Browse button to specify another location (or file name) if needed.

- **Permanently Delete Old Items:** Select this option if you want to delete old items rather than archive them.

When you have specified the settings for the AutoArchive feature, you can apply these to the Outlook folders (those that can be archived, such as the Inbox, Tasks, and Calendar folders). Click the Apply These Settings To All Folders Now button and click OK to close the dialog box.

Setting AutoArchive options for a folder

If you do not want to apply the AutoArchive options that you set in the AutoArchive dialog box to all Outlook folders (such as the Mail, Tasks, and Calendar folders), you can set AutoArchive options for each folder individually.

Select a folder in the Folder pane (you can list all your folders in the Folder pane by selecting More and then Folders in the Navigation pane), and then select the AutoArchive Settings command on the ribbon's Folder tab. Figure 26-12 shows the AutoArchive tab of the Inbox Properties dialog box.

CHAPTER 26

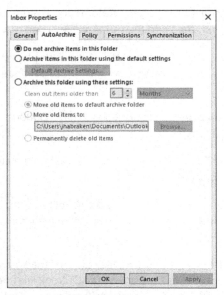

Figure 26-12   The AutoArchive tab of the Inbox Properties dialog box

To set custom archiving options for the folder, select the Archive This Folder Using These Settings button. You can then set the increment and time frame (months, weeks, or years) for the age of items to be archived. By default, the Move Old Items To Default Archive Folder option is selected. You can choose to use the Move Old Items To option button to specify another archive file and/or path, or you can choose the Permanently Delete Old Items option button to delete the old items rather than archive them. Click OK to close the dialog box.

Archiving manually

If you don't want to use the AutoArchive feature or you feel the need to archive a folder outside the archiving cycle that you have established in the settings for the AutoArchive feature, you can choose to archive folder items manually. This feature enables you to archive one folder at a time (and any subfolders it might hold). The manual archive can be run using the current AutoArchive settings for a folder (such as the age of items that should be archived), or you can select new age parameters while doing the manual archive.

To open the Archive dialog box, select File on the ribbon and then select Info in the Backstage. On the Info window, select the Tools button (next to the Mailbox Settings heading) and then select Clean Up Old Items. The Archive dialog box appears, as shown in Figure 26-13.

Figure 26-13   The Archive dialog box

Choose one of the following options in the Archive dialog box:

- **Archive All Folders According To Their AutoArchive Settings:** Use this option to manually archive all the Outlook folders using their individual AutoArchive settings. Using this option is no different from running an AutoArchive, except that you are prompting Outlook to archive the folders immediately.

- **Archive This Folder And All Subfolders:** Select this option to archive the selected folder. Using this option requires that you provide an age date for items to be archived. You can also specify the path for the archive to be created.

If you opted to archive the folder selected in the Folder list, provide an item age (Archive Items Older Than) using the drop-down menu. You are specifying the age by an actual date. You can also choose to include items that have been flagged as Do Not AutoArchive (in their own Properties dialog boxes). You can also specify an archive file other than the default using the Browse button. When you have finished specifying your settings for the manual archive, select OK.

> **NOTE**
>
> Another tool that you might find useful is the Mailbox Cleanup tool, which is available in the Backstage Cleanup tools. Use it to find old and large items and manage the size of your mailbox.

Whether you use auto-archiving or manual archiving is up to you. After you archive items in Outlook, an Archive group appears in the Navigation pane and provides a list of folders that have been archived. You can access archived items by selecting the appropriate archived folder and then selecting the item.

Configuring an autoreply message

The following Outlook users can take advantage of the Automatic Replies command in the Outlook Backstage (on the Info window) to configure an automatic out-of-office reply:

- Outlook users who work in an Exchange Server environment at a corporation or institution

- Outlook users who subscribe to Microsoft 365 Small Business or Enterprise

The same goes for those of you using Outlook with an Outlook.com email account. The automatic reply is sent in response to any received messages. The autoreply message can be useful if you are going to be away for a period of time when you cannot check your Outlook email using another device.

TIP

You can apply rules to an automatic reply that you have configured in the Automatic Replies dialog box. Click the Rules button (at the bottom of the dialog box), and the Automatic Reply Rules dialog box opens. Use the Add Rule button to create new rules that apply to incoming messages while you are out of the office. For example, you might want to create a new folder and have a new rule move all emails you received during the automatic reply time span to that folder. When you come back from your vacation, you can go right to that folder and deal with any pressing messages.

You will not see the Automatic Replies option on the Info page of a POP or IMAP email account. This option is only available to Exchange Server clients (which includes Outlook.com email accounts).

When you select the Automatic Replies (Out Of Office) command, the Automatic Replies dialog box opens, as shown in Figure 26-14. To configure your automatic reply, select the Send Automatic Replies option button. You can then specify a start and end time for the time span during which the automatic reply should be active.

The Automatic Replies dialog box also lets you configure a separate out-of-office reply for people inside your organization and outside your organization. Select the Inside My Organization tab to enter an internal message. To create an autoreply message for outside your organization, select the Outside My Organization tab.

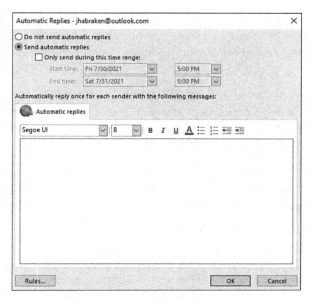

Figure 26-14   The Automatic Replies dialog box

By default, the Outside My Organization reply is configured to autoreply to all message senders outside your organization. You can specify that the autoreply go to only your contacts by selecting the My Contacts Only option button.

When you finish configuring your automatic reply, you can click OK to close the Automatic Replies dialog box.

If you use Outlook for internet email (such as a POP3 account), you don't have the option to use the Automatic Replies dialog box to configure an autoreply message (the Automatic Replies command isn't even on the Info window in the Backstage). You can, however, use an Outlook rule and template to create an automatic reply system for when you are out of the office. This helps keep your Inbox from being crammed to the max upon your return because message senders receive a reply message that you are out of the office. This might make them hold back additional messages until your return (or so we can hope). For this scheme to work on your POP or IMAP internet service provider email account, you will need to leave the Outlook application running on your computer while you are away.

The first task you should do to create your automatic reply is to open a new mail message. Because you want the reply to reach everyone who sends you a message, it makes sense to create the email as a plain-text message. On the ribbon, select New Items and then point at Email Message Using; then select Plain Text.

Type a subject for the new message, such as "Out of Office," "On Vacation," or any subject that works best for you to let recipients know that you are currently unavailable. Also enter body text for the message to provide any other information that you feel is required for the automatic reply being created.

After you have entered the subject and the message body text, save the message as an Outlook template. Select File to open the Backstage; then select Save As. In the Save As dialog box, change the Save As Type entry to Outlook Template. Supply a file name and path for the message, and then select Save. You can then close the message without saving it.

Now you can create the rule, which uses the template as the automatic reply message. In the ribbon's Move group, select Rules and then Create Rule. In the Create Rule dialog box, select Advanced Options. The Rules Wizard opens. In the condition box, select the Sent Only To Me check box; then select Next.

On the Action screen, select the reply using the specific template check box. In the Step 2 box of the Action screen, select the specific template value to open the Select A Reply Template dialog box. In the Look In box, select User Templates In File System. Select the template that you created in the template list (use the Browse button if you saved your template to a folder other than the default path for user templates).

After you have selected the template, click Open. The Select A Reply Template dialog box closes, and you return to the Rules Wizard. The path and template name now appear in the Step 2 box with the Reply Using action. Click Next. You can add any exceptions to the autoreply rule on this wizard screen. Then click Next.

You are almost finished; provide a name for the rule. By default, the Turn On This Rule check box is selected. All you have to do is click Finish. Now when you receive a message in your Inbox, your autoreply rule sends a response to the sender using your mail template.

Publisher

CHAPTER 27
Essential Publisher features 829

CHAPTER 28
Advanced Publisher features 861

Essential Publisher features

Introducing Publisher   829

Planning your publication   830

Working with publication templates   831

Creating a new publication   833

Creating a business information set   841

Working with text   843

Inserting illustrations   852

Using building blocks   857

Printing publications   858

Most desktop publishing applications are developed for well-schooled designers who create complex publications using fairly complicated software tools. These complex software applications were not designed for the average person and required a steep learning curve to take full advantage of the software's capabilities. Microsoft introduced Publisher in 1991 as an easy-to-use publication design application that enabled even the novice user to create a wide variety of publication types.

Microsoft Publisher has evolved over the years from a somewhat basic application for creating simple publications into a powerful desktop publishing tool. This chapter looks at the features you need to know to begin creating your own publications in Microsoft Publisher.

Introducing Publisher

In the past, Microsoft Publisher was a bit of an outlier in terms of its look and feel when you compared it to the other Microsoft 365 applications, such as Word, Excel, and PowerPoint. Publisher now provides you with a similar application geography and the same ribbon-centric interface provided by the rest of the 365 applications.

Publisher provides you with tools that are geared toward document layout and the use and placement of images. For example, you can quickly select a photo or other image file to serve as a page background in your publication. The selected picture can either fill the background or be tiled, depending on your needs. Publisher also makes it easy for you to insert online pictures from your OneDrive. In fact, you can drop multiple pictures from an online source onto the scratch area (the gray area surrounding the current publication), making it easy to access multiple images quickly.

Publisher also has you covered if you want to take advantage of a commercial printer for your Publisher product, such as a brochure or flyer. In fact, you can also prepare your publications for printing at a photo center. Publications can also be exported as PDFs, which can be downloaded by your clients via the web.

TIP

Publisher makes it easy to swap two photos on a publication page: Just drag a picture onto another picture on the page. When the outline of the picture frame turns pink, drop the picture (you are dragging), and the two photos exchange positions—they are swapped—on the page.

Whether you use Publisher for simple in-house publications or more complex output, you will find that Publisher provides all the tools you will need. Let's take a look at some thoughts on planning a publication and then dive into Publisher publication templates.

Planning your publication

Although Publisher makes it easy to create a variety of publication types, you should still plan your new publication before you actually assemble it in Publisher. If you know you want to create a business card, newsletter, or flyer, you have already established that you have a need for a particular publication type. However, it also makes sense for you to consider the core purpose of the publication and determine how to best approach its overall look, feel, and theme. For example, a newsletter for your book club might have a colorful, friendly look that emphasizes light, playful content. On the other hand, a publication for business clients would likely have a more "professional" layout, color scheme, and tone.

Another important aspect of planning a new publication is assembling the different objects and text that make up the publication. Because Publisher is a design and layout tool, it makes sense to have a folder on your computer that contains all the pictures, images, and perhaps even pre-typed text blocks to use as you create the layout for the publication. Of course, you can create these items (particularly the text) as you assemble the publication, but doing so takes some of your concentration away from creating a professional and eye-catching publication.

Here are some other points to keep in mind as you get ready to create a new publication in Publisher:

- **Consider print publications versus electronic paper publications.** As already mentioned, the printer you use can affect the overall quality of a printed Publisher publication. Publisher provides alternatives to a printed publication. You can save your publication as either a PDF or an XPS document. These file types preserve your fonts, formatting, and images as you laid them out. Publisher also gives you the option to create an HTML version of your publication, which you can publish directly to a web page. Consider using these electronic publication possibilities if you don't need to distribute hard copies of your publications to your target audience.

- **Know your printer.** Printers differ in the amount of whitespace they require on the outside edge of a printed page. Inkjet and laser printers have different requirements as well. If you plan to do bleeds off the page for brochures or flyers, you need to know whether your printer is capable of this task before you set up the publication with that particular design feature. If you need professional-looking results for your finished publication and your printer isn't up to the task, consider using the Export possibilities in the Backstage Export page. You can save the publication pages as a JPEG or TIFF file and then print the pages at a center that provides photo printing. The Export page also gives you the option to save your publication for a commercial printer that has the proper equipment.

- **Balance objects on the page.** Effectively using the white space on a page is important in creating an eye-catching layout. Consider balancing the layout of a page on the diagonal (the upper-left part of the page should balance with the lower-right part of the page) and align items with respect to the outside borders of the page instead of in the center of the page. A publication with everything centered on the page looks unprofessional and doesn't use the page space effectively. The best way to get a feel for balanced publications is to examine flyers, brochures, or ads you feel are designed well and then adapt these overall layout concepts to your own Publisher publications.

- **Size items according to their importance.** The relative size of an item on the page reflects the importance of that item. Make sure that the objects on the page that are important to the overall theme or message of the publication are sized to have maximum impact.

These are just a few of the points to keep in mind when designing a new publication. Ultimately, you must remember the importance of emphasizing the purpose of a particular publication while also exercising your artistic sensibilities. Even the most eye-catching publication ultimately will fail if it doesn't get its message across.

Working with publication templates

When you begin a new publication in Publisher, you typically start by selecting one of the many publication templates available. Publisher has a library of built-in templates and also provides access to a huge number of templates on Office.com. When you start Publisher, you are greeted by the Home page (see Figure 27-1). This page gives you access to recently opened publications (select a publication to open it). It also provides access to a subset of available publication templates. Select a template, and a box will open with more information about that particular template, such as the provider (in many cases, Microsoft), size of the publication created, and even the paper sizes the template uses (such as business cards or other specialty publication sizes). To use a particular template, select it to open its information box and then click the Create button.

Editions of Publisher prior to Publisher 2013 provided a larger collection of built-in templates; if you haven't updated your Publisher edition for a while, you will find that Publisher now provides a rather sparse collection of built-in templates. But don't worry—there are a huge number of templates available online.

To view more templates, select the More Templates link on the right of the Home page. This command takes you to the New page, which provides a Search For Online Templates box (on the left side of the window). You use the Search Online Templates box in the upper part of the template window to view templates available online.

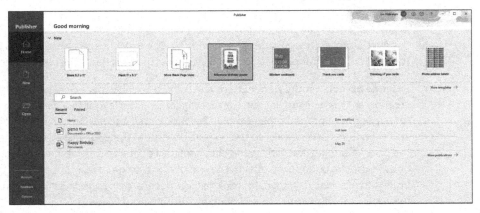

Figure 27-1   The Publisher Home page

Whether you are working on the Publisher Start page or the New page in the Backstage, finding the right template for your purpose is going to come down to your search terms. For example, if you wanted to create business cards, you would type **business cards** in the Search box and then click the Search icon. Figure 27-2 shows the New landing page in Publisher with the results from a search for "business cards."

Note in Figure 27-2 that business card templates that resulted from the keyword search are displayed as thumbnails on the New page. You will get the same results if you were working on the New page accessed via the Publisher Backstage. It also provides a search box for templates and will list "found" templates as thumbnails.

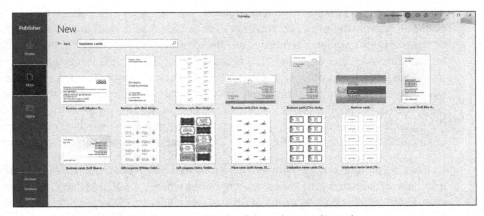

Figure 27-2   Find your Publisher template by doing a keyword search.

Before we walk through the process of creating a new publication using a template, an explanation of the difference between a page and a sheet is in order. A page is exactly what you think a page is: It is represented in the Publisher workspace as a white space (in the dimensions that you selected when you selected the template) where you place the objects to appear in the publication. You can navigate from page to page in the publication by using the Page pane.

A publication can have multiple pages. You can modify page dimensions by using the Page Setup commands on the Page Design tab and the Page Setup dialog box.

A sheet is the actual piece of paper that you use when you print the publication. You can specify the sheet size, whether to print one or two sides on the paper, and other settings for the sheet in the Backstage Print window. If you use a template based on a paper size, the paper and the sheet are the same. In some cases, the sheet size can be bigger than the actual publication. For example, when you create a business card, the page is the size of one business card, with the understanding that you print multiple pages on a single sheet.

Creating a new publication

Selecting a route for creating your new publication depends on your experience with Publisher and the particular design requirements of your publication. The various publication templates give you a lot of help as you initially design your publication: They create placeholder objects in your new publication that you can replace with your own pictures or design elements.

Creating a new publication using a blank template requires more initial layout and design work, but depending on your desktop publishing abilities, you might find that creating your own publications from scratch gives you greater creative freedom, and you get the end product that you desire.

Using a template

We have already discussed the overall geography of both the New "landing" page (when you first open Publisher) and the New page you can access in Publisher's Backstage when you are already working in the application. In terms of template selection, you will need to search for your template, and the results of your search appear as thumbnails on the Start Page or New page (refer to Figure 27-2). When you find the online template that you want to use, select it. A template window opens and provides the name (and provider) of the template. A Create button is also provided in the template window, but you are not offered the customization options that are provided for the built-in templates. Any modifications you make to the template must be made in the Publisher workspace after you have downloaded the template. Select the Create button. The template downloads, and your new publication opens in the Publisher workspace, as shown in Figure 27-3.

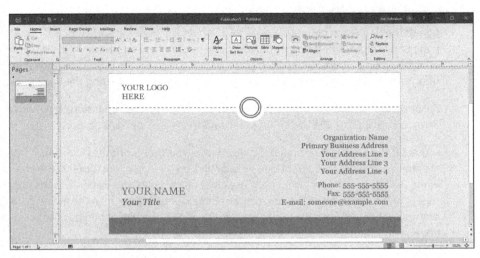

Figure 27-3 Your selected template opens in the Publisher window.

Using blank sizes

You can also create a publication from scratch based on sheet size and orientation. You will find that blank templates are available on the New landing page or the New page (which you access by selecting File on the ribbon and then New in the Backstage). The two most easily accessed blank templates are available in the Featured (template) list and consist of the Blank 8.5"×11" and Blank 11"×8.5" templates. These provide a blank portrait and blank landscape page, respectively. If you want to access more, select More Blank Page Sizes. Figure 27-4 shows the blank sizes available on the More Blank Page Sizes page.

At the bottom of the More Blank Page sizes page, you will find template folders provided in two broad categories: Publication Types and Manufacturers. The Manufacturers folders make it easy for you to select a blank publication template that is compatible with the box of forms you have purchased. For example, if you purchased Avery labels, use a template from one of the Avery folders provided; if you already have blank business cards made by Staples, select your template from the Staples folder.

When you locate the blank template you want to use, select it. You can then customize the color or font scheme or change the business information to be used for the publication in the Customize pane. This pane is shown in Figure 27-4 on the right side of the More Blank Page Sizes page. Note that drop-down boxes allow you to select template colors and font sets from drop-down menus. There is also a drop-down box labeled Business Information. The Business Information set is used to dictate what Publisher places into your publication templates by default. For example, for business cards, you would want your name, title, address, phone number, and so on to go automatically into the form. You need to create at least one information set for Publisher to use. The great thing is that you can actually create more than one information set, which makes it easy to make publications for other people or to create your professional publications and personal publications on the same PC.

Creating a business information set is covered in this chapter in the section "Creating a business information set." If you don't already have a business information set, you may want to skip ahead and create that before creating your publication.

When you are ready to create a new publication from the selected blank template, click Create. The new publication (based on the template) opens in the Publisher workspace.

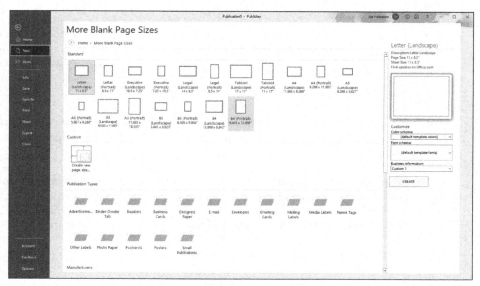

Figure 27-4   Blank templates are available for your publications.

Creating a new template

If you want to base new publications on a publication you have already created, you can save that publication as a template. Your custom template is then available in the template list provided in the Backstage. Before you can take advantage of your own templates, you need to let Publisher know where you want to save any personal templates you create.

CAUTION

If you don't specify a default folder for your personal templates in the Publisher Save options, Publisher will not provide a Personal heading on either the New page that opens when you start Publisher or the New page in the Backstage.

Go to the Backstage (File) and then click Options. This opens the Publisher Options window. Select Save in the options list on the left of the window. Type the complete path for your personal template folder in the Default Personal Templates location box. You can use any folder on your computer. For example, I created a folder called templates in the Documents folder. I then let Publisher know that the path is `C:\Users\`*my user name*`\Documents\templates`, where `C:` is my hard drive letter. You can also use the default folder for Publisher templates Publisher if you want, which is `Users\`*your user name*`\AppData\Roaming\Microsoft\Templates`. Where you keep your Publisher templates is up to you; just make sure you type the correct path in the Default Personal Templates location box. After you have specified the folder location, select OK.

Now you can base a new template on any publication you have created (or create a new one). And although this is a little like putting the cart before the horse (because I haven't discussed all the ins and outs of the various Publisher commands and tools), here is how you do it:

1. Create a new publication or open an existing publication.

2. In the Publisher workspace, modify the current publication as needed. You can insert objects, including pictures and page parts. You can also modify the page setup and color scheme settings on the Page Design tab.

3. When you have modified the publication to meet your needs (meaning that you are ready to save it as a template), select File to access the Backstage.

4. In the Backstage, select Save As and then select Computer in the Places list.

5. Select Browse on the Save As page. The Save As dialog box opens.

6. Select the Save As Type drop-down menu and select Publisher Template. The Save As dialog box automatically navigates to your default Publisher template folder (as you specified in the Publisher Options).

7. Provide a file name for the template, and then click Save to save the template. The new template is saved to your default template folder.

Now when you go to either the New page upon starting Publisher or the New page in the Backstage (both these pages are where the templates are accessed), a new heading, Personal, appears between the Office and Built-In headings. Select Personal, and any template you have saved to your template folder is listed. To start a new document from one of these templates, select the template.

Navigating the Publisher workspace

When you select a template (preformatted, blank, or your own), a new publication opens in the Publisher workspace. The ribbon borders the top of the workspace, and the status bar is at the bottom. The View shortcuts (Single Page and Two-Page Spread) and the Zoom slider are on the right side of the status bar, which makes it easy to change the current view of the publication and to zoom in or out of the publication page. Figure 27-5 shows the Publisher workspace.

The Pages pane on the left side of the workspace helps you navigate the various pages in the publication. A thumbnail is provided for each page in the publication. The gray area surrounding the current publication page is the scratch area. You can drag items from a publication page and place them on the scratch area. Objects in the scratch area are available even when you switch between pages in the publication or open a different publication. Think of the scratch area as a place to leave logos, headings, or other items you use as you work on a particular publication. Parking the object on the scratch area is also the easiest way to move an object from one page to another.

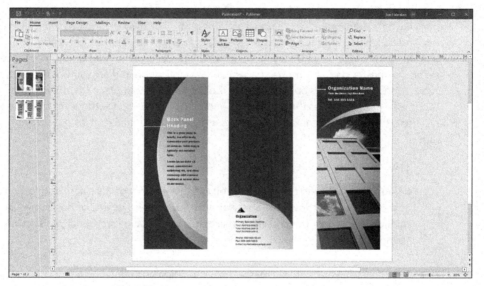

Figure 27-5   The Publisher workspace

Using the rulers and guides

Bordering the top and left sides of the scratch area are the horizontal and vertical rulers, respectively. You can use the rulers to place objects on a publication page. When you move the mouse on the page, the vertical and horizontal positions of the mouse pointer are shown as tick marks on the vertical and horizontal rulers. When you drag an object on the publication page, the position (horizontal and vertical) of the mouse pointer also displays on the Publisher taskbar. Thus, you can precisely place objects on a page.

You can also drag horizontal and vertical guides from the rulers onto the publication page. Place the mouse on the horizontal or vertical ruler edge and drag the ruler guide onto the publication when you see the guide mouse pointer. These light-green ruler guides are nonprinting, and you can use them to align objects on the page more precisely. In fact, when the Align To Guides check box is checked on the ribbon's Page Design tab, objects dragged onto the publication snap to a grid line, making it easy to align the object (such as an image). Just move an object near a guide, and the guide is highlighted as the object snaps onto it.

If you want to remove a ruler guide, drag it off the publication page. Grabbing a guide is easiest if you select it in one of the page margins. That way, you aren't inadvertently selecting objects that are within the confines of the page itself.

At this point, I should mention that Publisher provides you with another category of guide (other than the ruler guide): the layout guide. Layout guides are also used to position objects precisely on a publication page. There are different kinds of layout guides: margin, column, row, and baseline. These types of guides appear as light-blue lines on the publication page (by default); however, you can't drag them off the page as you do a ruler guide. The layout guides are on the master page (or master pages) of the publication and appear on all the pages in the publication. (Ruler guides appear only on the page where you place them.) The master page, as its name implies, provides the page setup and other publication settings for new pages inserted into the publication. The next chapter talks more about using layout guides and editing master pages.

TIP

If you don't like using ruler guides, you can move either of the rulers right onto the publication page. Hold down the Shift key and drag a ruler (vertical or horizontal) onto the publication. Repeat the process to place the ruler back in its original position adjacent to the scratch area.

➤ **You can use layout grids on master pages to help you align objects in a publication. For more about master pages and layout grids, see the "Working with master pages" section of Chapter 28, "Advanced publisher features."**

If you want to add ruler guides to a particular publication page, you can quickly drag a new ruler guide from either the horizontal or the vertical ruler. Several preset ruler guide configurations are provided in the Guides gallery, making creating ruler guides less of a drag. To open the Guides gallery, select the ribbon's Page Design tab and then select the Guides command in the Layout group. The Guides gallery opens, as shown in Figure 27-6.

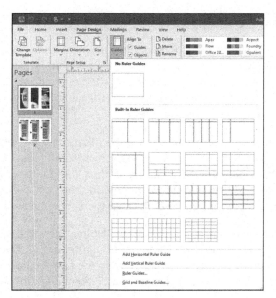

Figure 27-6   The Guides gallery

You can choose from any of the built-in ruler guides provided in the Guides gallery. If you want to add a single horizontal or vertical ruler guide, use the Add Horizontal Ruler Guide or Add Vertical Ruler Guide command, respectively.

If you find that the built-in ruler guides don't give you the guide layout you want, you can create your own custom ruler guides. Select Ruler Guides in the Guides gallery to open the Ruler Guides dialog box.

The Ruler Guides dialog box provides both a Horizontal tab and a Vertical tab. To set the guide position on the Horizontal tab, specify a position in the Ruler Guide Position box (for example, enter **4** for 4 inches) and then click the Set button. Each time you specify a position and click the Set button, Publisher adds a guide to the guide list.

You can select the Vertical tab of the Ruler Guides dialog box and set vertical guides as needed by providing a position and then clicking the Set button. You can clear individual guide positions on either tab by selecting a position and then clicking the Clear button. (Clicking Clear All clears all the guides.) When you click OK, the Ruler Guides dialog box closes and the guides you specified appear on the publication.

You can quickly clear all the guides (those selected from the gallery or those that you created) on the publication page by using the Guides command. Select Guides and then select No Ruler Guides in the gallery.

CHAPTER 27

Options for viewing the publication

As already mentioned, the Pages pane provides a thumbnail of each page in your publication. You can use the Pages pane to quickly move from page to page in your publication. You can also collapse or expand the Pages pane by using the button at the top of the pane. If you want to increase the size of the page thumbnails on the Page pane, you can drag its border (on the left side of the vertical ruler) toward the scratch area as needed.

Because the Publisher workspace contains both your actual publication and other tools, such as the ribbon, the rulers, the Pages pane, and (potentially) guides, it makes sense that you might want to manipulate the view in the Publisher workspace. The ribbon's View tab provides command groups for changing the view and the items shown in the workspace, and for manipulating the current zoom level for the publication. Figure 27-7 shows the ribbon's View tab.

The Views group on the View tab enables you to switch between Normal view (the view of your publication pages) and Master Page view (the next chapter covers master pages). The Layout group enables you to view a single page or two facing pages using the Two-Page Spread Command. The Show group has check boxes that enable you to view different items in the workspace. These commands are as follows:

- **Boundaries:** This command enables you to view the boundaries for the objects on the page, such as images, text boxes, and shapes.

- **Guides:** To view guides on your publication, this command must be enabled. (It is enabled by default.)

- **Fields:** Select this command to show fields in the publication. The mail merge process uses fields as placeholders for names and addresses in your recipient list.

- **Rulers:** Enabled by default, this command shows or hides the rulers.

- **Page Navigation:** When you select this command, the Page pane displays on the left side of the Publisher workspace. Clear the Page Navigation check box to hide the Page pane.

- **Scratch Area:** Enabled by default, this command shows the scratch area and any objects you might have dragged to the scratch area.

- **Graphics Manager:** This command opens the Graphics Manager task pane. The Graphics Manager provides a list of pictures on the publication. You can select from the picture list to select a picture in the publication.

- **Baselines:** This command shows the baseline guides set for the publication. You can use baseline guides to align text to the guides, which controls the spacing between text lines in a story (we discuss text and stories later in this chapter).

Figure 27-7   The ribbon's View tab

The other command groups on the View tab include the Zoom commands and the Window group. The Zoom commands include 100%, Whole Page (the default), and a drop-down menu of percentage zoom settings. If you want to change the zoom on a particular item or items, select the item (or items) and then click the Select Objects command.

You use the Window commands to arrange open publication windows. You can tile (Arrange All) or cascade (Cascade) the open publication windows, which is particularly useful if you want to drag an object from one publication to another or do a copy-and-paste between publications.

Creating a business information set

Before you get too far into the publication-creation process, you will want to create one or more business information sets. A business information set is a collection of information about you (and your company). Publisher uses the information in the business information set to automatically fill in the information needed by Publisher templates, such as for business cards, brochures, and envelopes.

The best part of a business information set is that you enter the information once and then can use it again and again as you create your various publications. Publisher even enables you to create multiple business information sets, which is extremely useful if more than one person uses Publisher on the computer or if you create publications for both personal and business on the same computer.

Creating a new business information set

You can create a new business information set or edit an existing business information set in the Publisher Backstage (if you have already created one). You have the option to select or create a new business information set every time you select one of the built-in templates to create a new publication (in the Start or New Backstage pages). Let's assume you haven't created the default information set: In the Backstage, select the Info command and then click the Edit Business Information button. The Create New Business Information dialog box opens, as shown in Figure 27-8.

Provide the information required in each field of the Create New Business Information Set dialog box (Individual Name, Tagline or Motto, Address, and so on). You can also specify a logo for your company: Simply select the Change button, use the Insert Picture dialog box to specify

CHAPTER 27

the new logo for your company, select a new image file, and then select Insert. Publisher places the new logo in the Logo box. When you have finished editing the information set, specify the name for the set in the Business Information Set Name box (the default is Custom 1); then click Save to save the information. If you are currently working on a publication that uses the default business information set, you are asked to update the publication (with the information you just placed in the information set); select Update Publication.

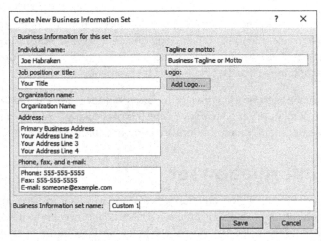

Figure 27-8   The Create New Business Information Set dialog box

Now you have your initial (and default) business information set. If you need to edit the information, go to the Info page of the Publisher Backstage. To access your default business information, select Edit Business Information. The Business Information dialog box opens. Use the drop-down menu to select an existing business information set (for editing), and then select Edit. The Edit Business Information Set dialog box opens; it is basically the same as the Create New Information Set dialog box. After you have edited the business information set, you can click the Save button to save your changes and close the Edit Business Information Set dialog box. You then return to the Business Information dialog box. If you want to update the information used in the current publication, click the Update Publication button; otherwise, click Close.

Creating additional business information sets

If you use Publisher to create publications for both personal and business use, or if multiple people use the same computer (and Publisher), you might want to create multiple business information sets. As already mentioned, you can open the Business Information dialog box from the Backstage by clicking the Edit Business Information button in the Info window.

You can also open the Business Information dialog box as you work on a publication. Select the Business Information command on the ribbon's Insert tab (in the Text group), and then select

Edit Business Information. A Business Information dialog box opens (if you have already created your business information set) that shows your default business information set and allows you to edit or delete it. If you have not created (and saved) an information set, these actions on the ribbon will open the same Business Information dialog box that we accessed from the Publisher Backstage (refer to Figure 27-8).

Let's assume that you have created your default business information set in the Backstage and would like to edit it or create an alternative business information set as you work in the Publisher application window. (Select Edit Business Information on the ribbon's Insert tab.) This opens the Business Information dialog box in the Publisher application window.

To create a new business set, click New. The Create New Business Information Set dialog box opens (refer to Figure 27-8). Supply the information for the set using the various field boxes. You can also specify a logo for the new information set. Type a new name for the set in the Business Information Set Name box, and then click the Save button to save the new information set.

When you open the Business Information dialog box in the future, you can specify the business information set you want to use. Use the drop-down box to select a specific information set. You can change the information set for the current publication by selecting the information set from the list and then clicking Update Publication.

You can also edit the current business information set, create a new set, or select a different information set for the current publication from the Publisher workspace. Select the ribbon's Insert tab and, in the Text group, select the Business Information command.

You can use the Business Information Fields list to insert any of the field information in the information set directly into the publication. If you want to edit the business information set or create a new set, select the Edit Business Information command on the Fields list. The Business Information dialog box opens. Use the Edit or New command in the dialog box, as needed. You can delete an information set by selecting the set in the drop-down menu and then clicking the Delete button.

Working with text

When you work with text in Publisher, a text box called an object frame encloses the actual text. Publisher gives you complete control over the look and formatting of the text in the object frame, including the font style, font size, font attributes (such as bold and italic), and color of your font. You can edit any or all these font parameters for a particular text box.

Working with text in Publisher is more than just typing inside boxes. You have control over the format of the text within the box, including the text direction and special text effects; also, you have control over the formatting of the text box itself, including outside borders and fill color. You can create text boxes as "space-holders" as you design your publication and then add the text to the box at your convenience. You can even insert text files into your publication that you have typed in other applications.

Editing text in a text box

If you use a template containing text boxes with placeholder text, you need to edit the text in each text box. Select the text in a specific text box and then type the text that replaces the placeholder text. The new text uses the same font attributes as the placeholder text. If you want to change the font or paragraph attributes for text, select the text that you want to format (in the text box) and then use the Font and Paragraph commands on the Home tab, as needed. You can also create bulleted and numbered lists inside a text box by using the Bullets and Numbering commands in the Paragraph group.

When you use templates to create your publications, you might also find two or more linked text boxes. If you click the text in one of the text boxes on the publication page, the text in more than one text box is selected. This means that the text actually flows from one text box to the other. (It can flow through several text boxes.) The text in a text box or linked text boxes is also referred to as a *story*. We will look at creating linked text boxes shortly.

Creating your own text boxes

You can insert a new text box on any publication page, as needed. The Draw Text Box command is on the ribbon's Insert tab. Follow these steps:

1. Select the Draw Text Box command.

2. Place the mouse pointer on the page and drag diagonally to create the text box (in the required dimensions).

3. Release the mouse button. The insertion point appears in the text box.

4. Use the Font commands on the Format tab for the text box tools to set the font size and attributes for the font, such as font color. Alternatively, switch to the Home tab to use the font, paragraph, and styles commands that it provides.

5. After specifying your font attributes, type the text that you want to place in the box.

When you have finished entering the text into the text box, click outside the text box to deselect it. You might find that it makes sense to zoom in on the text box when you are entering the text. This is particularly true if you are looking at a large publication page in Whole Page view.

Formatting text boxes

As already mentioned in the discussion of text boxes, you have control over the text inside the box and the text box itself. When you click inside a text box to select text, two sets of contextual tools appear on the ribbon: drawing tools and text box tools. You use the drawing tools (available when you select Format under the Drawing Tools tab) to format the text box itself, including the shape, style, fill, outline, and special effects.

TIP

You can format selected text in a text box using WordArt Styles. Publisher provides different style formats in the WordArt Styles gallery.

The text box tools (available when you select Format under the Text Box Tools tab) enable you to change text, font, and alignment settings. This set of tools also provides the commands for linking text boxes and adding effects to your text. Typography settings are available that enable you to use the Drop Cap feature and special typographic features such as ligatures.

Using the drawing tools

To format the text box itself, select the text box and then click Format under the Drawing Tools tab to access the various tools for formatting an object (remember that text boxes, pictures, and clip art are all Publisher objects). You will find that the drawing tools are uncomplicated yet sophisticated. The Drawing Tools command groups are as follows:

- **Insert Shapes:** This group provides a Shapes gallery divided into categories that include Lines, Basic Shapes, and Callouts. You can insert the shapes in the gallery onto the current page by selecting a shape and then "drawing" it (clicking and dragging) on the page. Inserting a new shape does not affect the currently selected text box or other shapes. You can use the Edit Shape command to edit the currently selected text box (or other object). On a text box, you can edit wrap points, which enable you to change the shape of an object (such as a rectangle) and determine how the text wraps within the edited object (which is why they are called *wrap points*). The Insert Shapes group also provides the Change Shape gallery, which enables you to change the current shape of the object (a rectangle, for a text box). If you want to edit the text in a text box or add text to a new shape that you have inserted into the page, use the Edit Text command when the object is selected.

- **Shape Styles:** This group provides a gallery of Shape styles that you can assign to the currently selected text box (or the currently selected shape). Click the More button (underneath the Shape Styles scroll arrows) to see the entire gallery, which provides shape styles with color gradients and other shading possibilities. The Shape Fill command provides access to a Scheme Colors palette that enables you to change the current color scheme. You can also add gradient textures and patterns using this command. The Shape Outline command enables you to specify a new scheme color (which affects the lines, including the outside lines) of the object. You can also use this command to specify tints, line weight, dashes, and patterns for the currently selected shape.

TIP

The Shape Fill command provides the Sample Fill Color tool (which looks like an eye-dropper). You can use it to clone a color from any object in your publication and then use that color as the fill for the currently selected object. Select Sample Fill Color and then click an object on the page.

- **Arrange:** This command group enables you to change how the text wraps around other objects on the page (if you have a large text box containing other objects). Wrapping options include Square (the text wraps around the object in a square), Top and Bottom, and Through. The Wrap Text command also provides access to the Edit Wrap Points command and the More Layout Options command, which opens the Format Text Box dialog box. The dialog box gives you control over all aspects of a text box related to colors, lines, size, and layout. The other commands in the Arrange group relate to arranging a text box on the page in layers with other objects. You can change the layer position of an object using the Bring Forward and Send Backward commands.

  The Align command enables you to change the alignment of an object in relation to the page margins (such as Align Left or Align Top). You can also choose to distribute multiple selected objects using the Distribute Horizontally and Distribute Vertically commands. The Group and Ungroup commands enable you to either group or ungroup several selected objects. Grouping objects helps maintain their position in relation to each other. A Rotate command is also provided in this group and can be used to either rotate or flip a selected object, such as a text box or picture.

- **Size:** This command group provides measurement spin boxes that adjust the height and width of the text box. You can also access the Format Text Box dialog box by selecting the dialog box launcher at the bottom of this command group.

All the commands we discussed that relate to a text box apply to another Publisher object: the shape. Aligning and layering multiple objects on a page can be complicated, so we revisit the Arrange command group in the next chapter when we look at working with multiple objects on a page.

➤ **Aligning and layering multiple objects can be tricky. See the "Manipulating publication objects" section of Chapter 28, "Advanced Publisher Features."**

Using the text box tools

As already discussed, you can use any of the font and paragraph attributes to format the text in a text box using the commands on the Home tab. If you want to use special formatting attributes, use the text box tools. These tools go beyond the settings for basic font attributes and enable you to do more complex manipulations, such as specifying the text's direction and how it fits in the box (including special alignment commands). You can also add effects and special typography settings to the text, including WordArt Styles. Figure 27-9 shows the Text Box Tools tab.

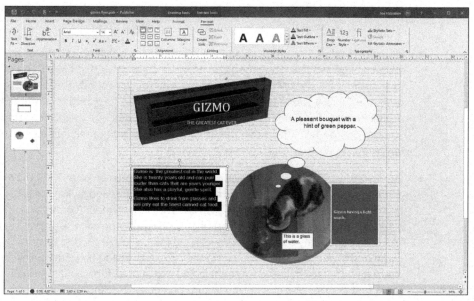

Figure 27-9   Format the text in the text box using the text box tools.

The command groups provided on the Text Box Tools tab are as follows:

- **Text:** These commands fit text in the box, change the text directions, and set the hyphenation for the text. The Text Fit command enables you to use Best Fit to change the size of the text so that it fits in the box. You can also choose to grow the text box or shrink text upon overflow. The Text Direction command enables you to rotate the text from horizontal to vertical. The Hyphenation command opens the Hyphenation dialog box, where you can change the hyphenation zone or manually hyphenate text.

- **Font:** This command group provides font attribute settings (such as size, bold, italic, and font color) and enables you to adjust the character spacing (normal, tight, loose, and so on). The Clear Formatting command enables you to clear all formatting on the selected text.

- **Alignment:** These commands enable you to align the text in reference to the borders of the text box. For example, the Align Top Left command moves the text to the top-left corner of the text box. Nine alignment options exist. The Columns command enables you to create columns in the text box. You can select from one to three columns on the Columns menu or select More Columns to open the Columns dialog box. The Margins command allows you to set the margins for the text (the margins in the box) using presets such as Narrow, Moderate, and Wide. You can select the Custom Margins command to open the Format Text Box dialog box and set custom margins for the text box.

- **Linking:** The Create Link command links two or more selected text boxes. We look at linking text boxes in the next section.

- **WordArt Styles:** This group provides a WordArt Styles gallery with styles that you can assign to selected text. The group also provides commands that enable you to fine-tune the currently selected WordArt style formatting. You can modify the fill color for the text using the Text Fill command. To manipulate the outline color or the weight of the font border, use the Text Outline command. If you want to change the text effect for the text, you can use the Text Effects command, which enables you to manipulate the shadow, reflection, glow, and bevel of the text characters.

- **Typography:** These commands allow you to add a drop cap to text, set the number style, and add special typography formatting, such as ligatures and stylistic sets. Ligatures are text characters tied together using a common design element (common to the text characters). The Drop Cap command provides a gallery of drop caps, as shown in Figure 27-10. You can preview any of the drop cap styles in the gallery or use the Custom Drop Cap command to set your own drop cap in the Drop Cap dialog box. The stylistic sets provide alternative character shapes for the selected text. Not all font families provide this option; some font families also enable you to turn on flourishes using the Swash command.

If you want additional control over settings related to the text box and the text inside the text box, you can go "old school" and open the Format Text dialog box. On the Text Box Tools tab, select the dialog box launcher at the bottom of the Text group. Figure 27-11 shows the Format Text Box dialog box.

The Format Text Box dialog box has five tabs that provide control over things such as text box lines and fill, size, layout, alignment, and margins. The Color and Lines tab enables you to set the fill color and level of transparency and the line color, style, and weight. You can use presets or set your own borders. You can even use the Border Art button to select from a list of available borders with titles such as Apples, Baby Pacifier, and Candy Corn.

Figure 27-10   Select a drop cap style.

Figure 27-11   Set text box options in the Format Text Box dialog box.

The Size tab provides settings for the size and rotation of the text box. It also provides scale settings for the height and width and enables you to lock the aspect ratio. The Layout tab provides settings for the position of the text box on the page and the wrapping style if an image is included in the text box. The Text Box tab is where you set the margins for the text box and specify the vertical alignment of the text in the box. The Alt Text tab is reserved for alternative text descriptions of the objects on your publication page, which are useful to people with impairments (such as vision) who want to view your publication.

> **NOTE**
>
> Because you can add text to any shape you insert into a publication, both the drawing tools and text box tools discussed in this chapter are applicable to any shapes you place.

Linking text boxes

You can link the text boxes if you want text to flow from one text box to another. Publisher then considers the text that fills the text boxes to be a single story. You might find many linked text boxes in the flyer and brochure templates, among other Publisher preformatted templates. Linking the text boxes makes it easier for you to keep the text formatting consistent in a longer or more complex publication.

To create your own linked text boxes, follow these steps:

1. Use the Draw Text Box command to create a new text box and enter text into that text box as needed.

2. Create a second text box using the Draw Text Box command.

3. Select the first text box.

4. Select the Text Box Tools tab on the ribbon.

5. Select the Create Link command in the Linking group. An ellipsis symbol appears on the selected text box.

6. The mouse pointer becomes a pitcher (like a pitcher of water). Navigate to the text box that you want to link to the currently selected text box, and then click the mouse. The text boxes are now linked.

You can tell when two (or more) text boxes are linked because when you select a linked text box, the Next symbol (a right-pointing arrow) or the Previous symbol (a left-pointing arrow) appear on the edge of the text box frame. You can use these buttons on the text box frame to move to a linked text box from its partner.

NOTE

If you don't like typing text in the text boxes, create your text in Word and then copy and paste the text into your Publisher text boxes. You can link as many text boxes as necessary in a publication.

After you fill the first text box with text (either by typing the text or by inserting a text file, which will be discussed in a moment), the text flows into the next text box. Figure 27-12 shows three linked text boxes. Note the Previous and Next symbols on the middle text box (showing that it is linked to both the top and the bottom text boxes).

One point to keep in mind is that as you size either of the boxes, the amount of text in the boxes shifts from one box to the other, particularly if you make the primary box in the linked set larger or smaller.

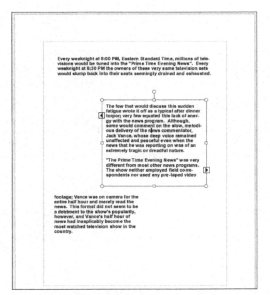

Figure 27-12   Linked text boxes

When you enter more text into a text box than it can hold (or copy and paste more than it can hold), an ellipsis (...) button appears on the text box frame. This means that the text box contains more text than it can accommodate. This also means that the Do Not Autofit command is selected on the Text Fit command menu. You can fix this problem by creating another text box and then clicking the ellipsis button. The mouse pointer shows the Create Link icon (the pitcher); click the pitcher icon on a text box to link the boxes. The overflow text (the text that you can't see) flows into the second text box.

NOTE

If you misjudge the size of your text box (or linked text boxes) to accommodate all the text in an inserted text file, Publisher creates an additional linked text box to make sure that all the imported text is taken care of. Resize your original text boxes and then delete the added text box.

Inserting a text file

You can insert text files directly onto a publication page. This is extremely useful when someone is creating the publication copy (the text) as you design the publication in Publisher. You can easily insert files created in Word. The Word document can even have images and other objects embedded in the text (such as pictures or even Excel worksheets). If you are using some other word processor, you should save the text document as plain text (.txt) or in Rich Text Format (.rtf).

CHAPTER 27

You can insert a Word document or text file directly onto a publication page, and the Insert feature creates its own text boxes to accommodate the text as needed; however, you have greater control over the process if you create your own text box and then insert the file text directly into it. If you know that the text file requires more than one text box, create the text boxes and then link them. You can then have the story flow from the initial text box into the other text box (or boxes). To insert a text file into your publication, follow these steps:

1. Draw a text box (or linked text boxes) on the publication page.

2. Click inside the text box (or in the first of the linked text boxes).

3. Select the Insert tab on the ribbon.

4. In the Text group, select the Insert File command. The Insert Text dialog box opens.

5. Locate the file using the Insert Text dialog box, and then select the file you want to insert.

6. Select OK.

Publisher inserts the text into the text box (or linked text boxes). You can modify the formatting for the text as needed by using the font- and paragraph-formatting attributes on the Home tab or the additional text-formatting tools on the Text Box Tools tab.

Inserting illustrations

Publisher provides a lot of options in terms of the types of illustrations you can add to your publication pages. You can add a picture file in many image file formats, and you can add an image from the web. You can also add a variety of shapes to your publication pages using the Shapes gallery. Publisher makes it easy for you to add your own pictures to publications via the Online Pictures command. You can use Bing to do an image search on the web, or you can insert a picture from your OneDrive.

Images on a publication page add interest to the publication and greatly enhance the probability that your publication will get its intended purpose across to the reader. Although adding graphic elements to a publication is fun, make sure you place and size key graphics, particularly important pictures or logos, for maximum visual impact.

Options for inserting pictures

Publisher supports a wide variety of picture file formats that you can insert into a publication. Some of the commonly used file formats that do not require you to add a graphics filter are as follows:

- Windows Bitmap (.bmp)

- Graphics Interchange Format (.gif)

- Joint Photographic Expert Group (.jpg)

- Portable Network Graphics (.png)

- TIFF, Tagged Image File Format (.tif)

- Windows Metafile (.wmf)

> ➤ **More details related to working with pictures and other graphics in the Office applications are provided in Chapter 4, "Using and creating graphics."**

When inserting a picture into your publication, you can insert the picture directly onto the publication page, or you can insert a picture placeholder. Inserting a large image onto a page requires that you size and/or crop the image to get it into a manageable size. Of course, the size of the image on the page depends on the size of the image file. I think using the picture place-holder is preferable. The picture placeholder provides an already cropped and sized version of the picture that conforms to the picture placeholder. You have the option to move the crop markers (if you want to make the placeholder bigger), and you can also move the picture within the picture placeholder to make sure that you determine the center of the photo in relation to the placeholder. By default, the placeholder places the center of the inserted picture in the cen-ter of the placeholder box. Whether you insert your pictures directly on the page or into picture placeholders is up to you. Let's look at both options, starting with inserting a picture.

Inserting a picture

Inserting a picture is really just a matter of selecting a picture file and having Publisher plop it onto the current publication page. To insert a picture, follow these steps:

1. Navigate to the page where you want to insert the picture.

2. Select the Insert tab of the ribbon.

3. Select the Pictures command. The Insert Picture dialog box opens.

4. Navigate to the folder that holds the picture you want to insert; then select the picture file.

5. Click Insert.

Publisher places the picture on the publication page. The picture tools become available on the ribbon. You can size the picture and position it on the page as needed.

Inserting a picture placeholder

We have already discussed that the alternative to inserting a picture directly onto the page is to insert a picture placeholder. You can insert a picture into the placeholder frame. This enables you to pre-size the picture based on the picture placeholder size.

On the Insert tab, select the Picture Placeholder command, and then size and position the picture placeholder as needed. When you click the picture icon in the middle of the picture placeholder, the Insert Picture dialog box opens. Locate your picture file, select it, and then click Insert. Figure 27-13 shows an inserted picture on the left and the same picture placed directly into a picture placeholder.

Figure 27-13   Inserted picture versus picture in a placeholder

Notice that Publisher sized the picture in the placeholder appropriately for the publication page. The picture on the left is quite large and needs some work in terms of sizing and placement. You don't have to use picture placeholders, but they allow you to design the layout of a page before adding photos or other images. Placeholders also help by pre-sizing and pre-cropping the picture for you.

After you place a picture on a page, you might find that you want to replace it with another picture. If both pictures are already on the page, you can drag one image onto the top of the other to have the two pictures swap positions. This maneuver is a little tricky, so make sure you are dragging the picture by the picture icon that appears in the center of the picture when you select it. Also, don't let go of the picture you are dragging until the pictures actually swap places. In addition, you can select two pictures and then swap them using the Swap command on the Picture Tools tab (which appears when you have selected a picture or pictures). The Swap command also enables you to swap the formatting between two pictures. Swapping formatting means that any adjustments you made to a file using the Adjust group commands are swapped between the photos.

NOTE

When you replace a picture with another picture, the new picture uses any changes you made to the frame around the picture, such as a picture style or sizing. If you made any adjustments to the original picture, such as corrections or recoloring, these settings are not adopted by the replacement picture.

If you want to replace a picture on the page with a picture that is on your computer, OneDrive, or somewhere on the web—you can search with Bing using the Online Pictures command on the Insert tab—you simply select the picture and then select the Change Picture command in the Adjust group of the Picture Tools tab. Select Change Picture on the menu to open the Insert Pictures dialog box. Select one of the options for pictures (such as From a File, Office.com Clip Art, or your OneDrive). Then insert the "replacement" picture. The inserted picture replaces the current picture and conforms to the frame that was inhabited by the "replaced" picture. The picture that was replaced is put in the scratch area for subsequent use.

Formatting a picture

After you have inserted a picture onto the publication page, you are provided with the picture tools, which enable you to enhance and fine-tune the picture (and the frame around it). Select any picture, and then click Format under the Picture Tools tab to make the various picture tools available on the ribbon. Figure 27-14 shows the picture tools.

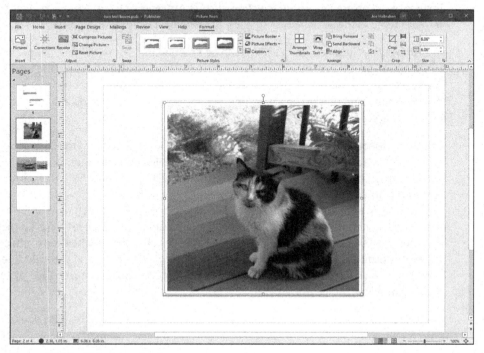

Figure 27-14   The picture tools

CHAPTER 27

You can use the various commands to adjust the picture and its border as needed. The Picture command on the far left of the Picture Tools tab enables you to insert another picture onto the page. The Adjust group of commands, which includes Corrections (brightness and contrast) and Recolor, can enhance the image itself. This group also includes the Compress Pictures (which reduces the picture file sizes to keep the publication file size down), Change Picture, and Reset Picture (resets all your changes) commands. The Picture Styles group provides commands that enable you to change the shape and style of the picture frame (the Picture Styles Gallery) and control the picture border's line color and weight. Additionally, you can add special effects to the photo and its frame using the Picture Effects command. This group also makes it easy to add a caption to a picture using the Add Caption command. The Picture Tools tab includes command groups that were available on the Text Tools tab (which we discussed earlier). The Arrange group provides commands that enable you to layer objects on the page and rotate objects. The Crop and Size groups allow you to crop and size the picture, respectively. For a primer on working with pictures and other graphics, see Chapter 4.

➤ For an overview of working with graphics in Microsoft 365, see Chapter 4.

Inserting clip art

Another way to add pictures to your publication pages is to use clip art (or pictures, illustrations, and the like) that can be sourced from the web using Publisher's Online Pictures command in the Illustrations group on the Insert tab. Publisher uses Microsoft's Bing search engine to locate images based on your category selection, such as Airplane, or by using your keyword search terms entered in the Search box at the top of the Online Pictures dialog box.

Inserting clip art into your publications can be entertaining, but remember, images you add to your publications are meant to enhance your publications. Don't overdo the cutesy clip art. Always gauge the tolerance of your audience for clip art, and use it as much as you want in your personal publications. Use clip art sparingly in any publications that you are creating for use in a professional context.

Select the ribbon's Insert tab to insert clip art or other web images into the current publication page. Then select the Online Pictures command in the Illustrations group. The Insert Pictures window opens. You can select any of the categories (such as Animals, Fish, Flowers, or Man) to find clip art and other Web images using Bing. If you want to find clip art specifically, you will need to do a search using the Bing Image Search box. Type a search term and also enter the words *clip art* in the search box. For example, if I wanted to search for a clip art picture of a pumpkin, I would enter `pumpkin clip art`. Your search results will be shown as a group of thumbnail pictures. Select the clip art image that you want to insert and then click the Insert button. When you select the inserted clip art image on the publication page, the picture tools become available on the ribbon.

One last word about web-based images such as clipart: By default, when Bing does an image search via the Online Pictures dialog box, it sources Creative Commons images. Creative

Commons is a nonprofit organization that provides licenses to rights holder to protect their intellectual property (such as clip art), as well as to make it available for use by others. Typically, Creative Common licenses allow you to use images for personal or nonprofit purposes. In most cases, you can't use a shared Creative Commons licensed image for your own profit. To get a better understanding of how Creative Commons licenses work, visit *https://creativecommons. org*.

Inserting shapes

You can insert any of the shapes available in the Shapes gallery. These shapes include lines, arrows, and flowchart parts, among other possibilities.

To insert a shape, select the Shapes command (on the Insert tab). Locate the shape in the gallery that you want to use and then select the shape (such as Rectangle, Arrow, or Rounded Rectangular Callout). A drawing tool replaces the mouse pointer. Drag on the page to create the shape. You can size and position the shape on the page as needed.

When you select the shape, the drawing tools become available on the ribbon. These are the same tools that become available when you select a text box on a page. We discussed formatting text boxes earlier in this chapter, and the same commands and tools apply to formatting shapes. If you want to place text in a shape (and, in effect, turn it into a text box), select the shape on the page and then select the Edit Text command in the Insert Shapes group. This places the insertion point in the shape.

Using building blocks

Another option for adding graphical elements to a Publisher publication is the building block. The Building Blocks group on the Insert menu provides premade graphics that you can use to enhance your pages. These items range from headings and pull quotes to calendars and advertisements. The commands in the Building Blocks group are as follows:

- **Page Parts:** The page parts comprise a gallery of items that include ready-made headings, sidebars, and stories. The stories are preformatted text boxes containing placeholder text and an image; you can replace these placeholders with your own text and objects. The page parts are well designed and provide items that you can add to your publications to make them look more professional.

- **Calendars:** This command provides a gallery of calendars that you can insert into your publication. Calendars are available for the current month (This Month) and the next month (Next Month). If you want more control over the month and year for the calendar, select the More Calendars option on the bottom of the Calendars gallery. The Building Block Library window opens. It offers a large number of calendar designs and enables you to set the month and year for the calendar you insert into the publication page.

- **Borders & Accents:** This command provides a gallery of box frames and accents that you can use to enhance your publication. Selecting More Borders takes you to the Building Block Library window, which provides additional borders and accents, as well as frames and lines.

- **Advertisements:** The advertisements range from simple graphic elements, such as attention-getters, to more complex advertisements that are predesigned text boxes containing pictures, text, and other graphic elements. You can modify the text in even the simplest of the attention-getters if required. You open the Building Block Library window by selecting More Advertisements in the Advertisements gallery. The library provides other items as well, including coupons.

Inserting a building block is just a matter of selecting one of the building block commands, such as Page Parts or Advertisements, and then selecting a particular item provided in that command's gallery.

Printing publications

When you are working in Publisher, you are, in effect, always seeing each page as it will print. This means that objects, pictures, and text boxes appear on the Publisher pages as they look on printed pages.

The best strategy for previewing your publication is to go from the general to the specific. Zoom in and make sure that individual objects are correctly set up, and that text boxes do not contain typos.

TIP

Don't forget to take advantage of the Spelling feature on the ribbon's Review tab; you can correct any typos or misspellings before you print your publication.

When you zoom out on the publication, you can check the placement of objects, the overall design of the publication, and the use of color.

When you are ready to print your publication, select File to open the Backstage. In the Backstage, select Print. The Print page opens, as shown in Figure 27-15.

As with any other Office application, you can use the printer settings to specify the printer for the print job and specify properties for your printer. The actual settings for the publication specified in the Settings area depend on the type of publication you are printing. For example, if you are printing a flyer, the setting of one page per sheet makes sense. However, if you want to print multiple business cards to a blank sheet of perforated business cards, select multiple copies per sheet and then specify the number of items that should be printed on each sheet.

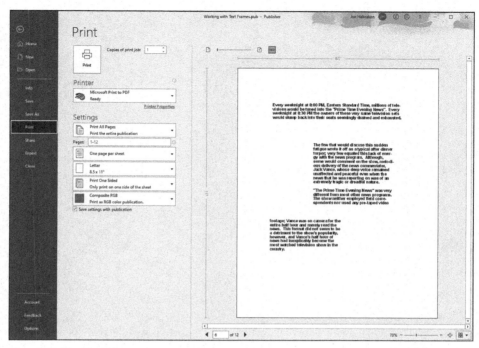

Figure 27-15   The Print page

For double-sided printing, you have the option of flipping the page on the long edge or on the short edge. Select the option that makes it easiest for the recipient of your publication to read the front side and then the flip side without rotating the page.

In most cases, it is assumed that you will print your publication to a color printer. However, switch the publication color from composite RGB (red, green, blue) to composite grayscale if you plan to print to a black-and-white printer. This results in a more readable product than just sending the RGB print job to a black-and-white printer.

When you are ready to print your publication, click the Print button. This closes the Print window and sends your publication to the specified printer.

CHAPTER 28

Advanced Publisher features

Adding pages to a publication   861

Configuring page settings   863

Changing the current template   866

Working with master pages   868

Using tables in publications   872

Manipulating publication objects   874

Merging data into a publication   877

Fine-tuning your publications   882

CHAPTER 28

Microsoft Publisher provides templates for all the common publication types, such as brochures, flyers, newsletters, and business cards. And you probably figure that using a template is the way to go if you want a professional-looking product. However, always relying on Publisher templates means that your publications are going to look similar to the publications created by other Publisher users. So, how do you make your publications stand out and look unique? Publisher offers advanced tools and features that can greatly enhance even the simplest of publications.

In this chapter, we look at some of the more advanced features of Microsoft Publisher. We start with an exploration of features related to the pages in a publication, including master pages. Master pages make it easy to include design elements and ensure consistent layout options across the pages of a publication. We also look at using tables in a publication and manipulating multiple objects on a page. We close the chapter with a look at merging information into a publication and fine-tuning your publications.

Adding pages to a publication

At some point, you may need to add blank pages to your publication. Whether you created your publication from scratch (using a blank template) or used one of Publisher's preformatted templates (such as a newsletter or menu), the process for adding pages to a publication is straightforward and risk-free. The Page command is on the ribbon's Insert tab in the Pages group. The Pages group contains only two commands: Page and Catalog Pages. We discuss the Catalog Pages command later in this chapter.

When you select the Page command, you have three possibilities: Insert Blank Page, Insert Duplicate Page, and Insert Page. The Insert Blank Page command inserts a blank page after the currently selected page. The page is the same size and has the same orientation and margins as the page selected in the Pages pane (before you inserted the new page). Other than the fact that the page is blank, it is the same as the original page in terms of the page setup.

The page has the same page settings because Publisher bases these on the master page for the publication, which dictates the page setup for all the pages in the publication (unless you have more than one master). We talk more about master pages later in this chapter. For now, you just need to know that the master page contains the page-layout information for the pages in the publication and can contain other elements that you want to appear on every page, such as a logo or information in headers and footers. Each publication has a single master page by default (although you can create additional master pages for a more complex publication).

If you are using a template that provides objects that you don't think you can duplicate, you can choose the Insert Duplicate Page option on the Page command to create a duplicate of the currently selected page. You can then remove the objects that you don't need or rearrange the objects to create your new page.

TIP

To delete a page from a publication, right-click the page in the Pages pane and select Delete from the shortcut menu.

When you want to add multiple pages before or after the current page, and you want to have control over the objects (duplicates and otherwise) that appear on the new pages, use the Insert Page command on the Page gallery. This opens the Insert Page dialog box, shown in Figure 28-1.

Figure 28-1   The Insert Page dialog box

Specify the number of new pages needed, and then select the appropriate option button to designate whether you want the new pages to be added before or after the currently selected page. For objects, you have three options for the new page or pages: You can insert blank pages (with no objects), create one text box on each new page, or duplicate all the objects on a specified page in the publication. After setting the options in the Insert Page dialog box, click OK. Publisher adds the pages (based on the options you chose) to the publication.

You will find that when you are working on a publication that has facing pages, such as a publication based on one of the newsletter templates, the options available in the Insert Page dialog box are different from those shown in Figure 28-1 (which shows the choices available for a document that does not contain facing pages). With the facing pages selected in the Pages pane, the Insert Page dialog box provides the Before Left Page, After Right Page, and Between Pages options, which enable you to specify where a new set of facing pages is inserted into the publication in reference to the currently existing two-page spread. If you have a publication that employs more than one master (the master provides the page settings for a page or pages in the publication), you will also find that a Master page drop-down menu is provided in the dialog box, which you can use to specify the master to use for the new page.

Configuring page settings

The commands for formatting your publication pages are on the ribbon's Page Design tab. The command groups Template, Page Setup, Layout, Pages, Schemes, and Page Background populate this tab. The Page Setup group provides commands that enable you to quickly and easily change page attributes such as margins, page orientation, and size. For example, the Orientation command has two possibilities: Portrait and Landscape. However, if you have a publication in landscape and you want to change the orientation of a single page (the currently selected page) to portrait, all the pages change orientation when you select Portrait on the Orientation gallery.

CHAPTER 28

> ### NOTE
>
> **You can have more than one master page for a publication, which means that you can mix pages that use different page setup attributes in the same publication. We discuss master pages later in this chapter.**

You may agree that using the term "Page Setup" as the name for this command group is a little misleading because you are changing the settings for the master page on which your document pages are based. When you make changes to the master page using the Page Setup commands, Publisher applies the changes you make to all the pages in your publication that are based on that particular master page.

Other commands in the Page Setup group are the Margins and the Size commands. Each of these commands provide a number of presets. For example, the Margins command provides a gallery of margin possibilities. You can select from the margin presets: Wide, Moderate, Narrow, and None. There is no preview provided for the margin changes, so you need to select one of the presets to see how it affects the objects currently on the page. If you don't like the margin change, you can use the Undo command to return to the previous margin settings. If you want to set custom margins, select the Custom Margins command in the Margins gallery. The Layout Guides dialog box opens (see Figure 28-2).

Use the margin spin boxes to set the margin guides for the pages in the publication. Remember, you are setting the margins for the master page for the publication. When you have finished configuring the margin guides, click OK. The new margin guides appear on the pages of the publication.

The Size command (in the Page Setup group) also provides a list of preset page sizes, such as A5 (Landscape), Letter (Landscape), and Tabloid (Landscape). The available preset page sizes depend on the template you used for your publication.

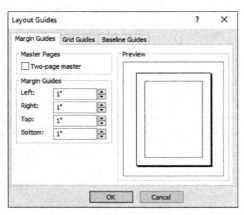

Figure 28-2   Set custom margins in the Layout Guides dialog box.

Remember that any selection in the Size gallery changes the size of all the pages in the publication (because you are formatting the master page). If you select More Preset Page Sizes, the Preset Page Sizes window opens. This window offers different publication sizes in folders (such as Standard, Booklets, and Postcards). The contents of these page size folders are the blank page sizes and the manufacturer's blank page sizes that you have access to when you are using the New page (either in the Backstage or Publisher's initial landing page) to create a new publication using a blank template (of a particular page size). To view the page sizes in a particular page size group, select that group by clicking the folder. Figure 28-3 shows the page sizes available when you select the Standard group.

When you find the page size you want to use, select it and then click OK. You return to the Publisher workspace, and the page size you selected is applied to the pages in the publication.

The Size gallery also provides a Page Setup command, which opens the Page Setup dialog box. This dialog box, shown in Figure 28-4, gives you settings for all the various page options.

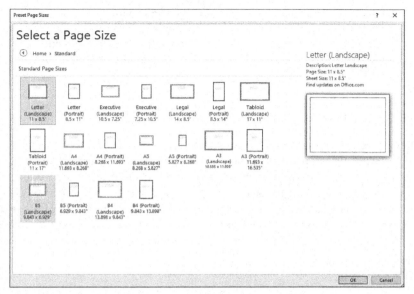

Figure 28-3   Select a page size from the Preset Page Sizes window.

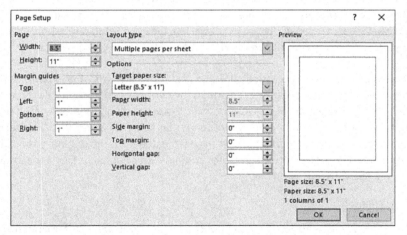

Figure 28-4   Set the page configuration options in the Page Setup dialog box.

The Page Setup dialog box gives you access to the page size and margin guides settings. It also provides you with settings for the number of pages per sheet and the settings for the target paper. Remember that sheets are what the printer produces; each sheet in the publication can have multiple pages (think of mailing labels or business cards). To set the number of pages per sheet, use the Layout Type drop-down menu.

CHAPTER 28

To set the options for the printer paper that is used, select a target paper size in the drop-down menu, or select Custom and then use the Page Option spin boxes to set the width, height, margins, and so on for the target paper. As you change the Page Setup dialog box settings, the results display in the preview pane. When you finish setting the Page Setup options, click OK to apply the settings and close the Page Setup dialog box.

Changing the current template

Whether you use a blank page size or a preformatted template, you still are using a template to build your publication. You also have the option to change the current publication's template. This can be a little tricky, particularly if you have already placed objects such as text boxes and pictures on the pages of the publication. However, there is no risk because if you choose to apply a new template to the current publication, Publisher can create a new publication based on the change in template; so the current publication is unaffected. In fact, you can then decide whether you want to save the new publication and continue to edit it or discard it and return to your original publication.

TIP

The Size gallery also provides access to the Create New Page Size dialog box. This dialog box is exactly the same as the Page Setup dialog box, except it provides a Name box so that you can name your new page size. Use the Create New Page size dialog box when you want to create a new custom page size. Use the Page Setup dialog box when you want to modify the current page size.

Making a template change successfully (instead of starting over with a new template) will depend on the number of changes you made to the current document and the type of template you used when you began the publication-creation process. If you used one of the preformatted templates, such as a brochure or business card template, you are probably better off starting a new publication and copying the objects you created from the original publication to the new publication. The preformatted templates contain a lot of default objects that might not translate well to a different template.

CAUTION

Apply the template to your current publication only if you are sure it will not negatively affect the publication layout. It really makes more sense to create a copy; you can discard it later if you don't like it.

To change the current template, select the Change Template command on the Page Design tab. This opens the Change Template window (which is similar to the New page in the Backstage). The window defaults to a listing of various flyer templates, but you can select Home at the top of the window to access any of the built-in templates or search for templates on Office.com. If you use one of the built-in templates, you can use the Customize settings to change the color scheme, font scheme, or business information set for the publication.

Select your new template and then click OK. The Change Template dialog box appears, as shown in Figure 28-5.

By default, the Change Template dialog box specifies that a new publication is to be created using the new template. This is probably the best way to proceed. When you are ready to create the copy of the current publication based on the new template, click OK. It might take a moment, but the new publication displays in the Publisher workspace.

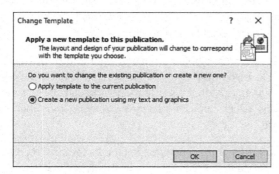

Figure 28-5   The Change Template dialog box

How successful the template change was in relation to the layout and look of the new publication is a matter of how well the new template was able to "digest" the objects that you placed in the original publication. If Publisher was unable to place objects on the pages (mainly due to available space or page formatting), the Extra Content task pane appears.

The Extra Content task pane lists all the objects that did not fit into the changed publication. You can choose to view subsets of different object types not placed using the Show check boxes: Text and Tables, Images, or Shapes and WordArt.

TIP

You can save items in the Extra Content task pane to the Building Block library. Select the object arrow and then select Save As Building Block.

To place an object in the new publication from the Extra Content task pane, select the arrow to the right of the object and then click Insert. You can repeat this process as needed to place all the unused objects on the publication page or pages. If you find that most of the objects you inserted on the original publication pages are showing up in the Extra Content task pane, you might want to abort this entire mission and try again with a different substitute template. If you don't want the new publication based on the new template, close the publication. A message box opens to let you know that you have not used all the items in the Extra Content task pane.

Click OK to close the message box. Another message box appears, alerting you that you have not saved changes to the publication (meaning the new publication); select Don't Save, and the publication closes.

Working with master pages

The term *master page* was already introduced in our discussion of page setup attributes such as margins and page orientation. When you create a new publication, whether based on a blank template or a preformatted template, Publisher creates a master page that supplies basic page-formatting attributes to the pages in the publication. If you create a simple publication consisting of pages with the same formatting, this single master page approach (meaning that every page uses the master page settings) can probably work for you.

Master pages can also include information and objects that you want to be repeated on every page of the publication. For example, if you want to include a logo in the top-right corner of every page, it makes sense to place that logo on the master page. You can also place header and footer items on the master page, which can include page numbering and other information, such as a draft number or date.

You are not responsible for making sure that the master page (and its settings) is applied to the page or pages in your publication. By default, Publisher assigns the default master page to the pages. However, suppose you have pages in the publication that you do not want affected by changes to the master page. In that case, you can select those pages and then choose None on the Master Pages gallery (select Master Pages on the Page Design tab). This breaks the tie between the page and the master page. You can always associate the page with the master page (if required) by selecting the master page in the Master Pages gallery.

NOTE

Although many of the commands on the ribbon's Page Design tab affect all the publication pages because they change the master page settings, the Background command in the Page Background group changes only the background on the selected page.

Even though you have the option of whether to apply master page settings to the pages in the publication (because you can specify None as the master page setting for a page), you might still need to create multiple master pages. Multiple master pages can be useful when you are working with a more complex publication that requires different page setup values (such as page orientation) for some of the pages. Each master page you create can have its own settings and objects, which repeat on the pages assigned that master page. You can even create a two-page master for publications that contain facing pages (such as a booklet).

Placing objects on the master page

If you want to place a repeating object on your publication pages, such as a logo, you can place the object on the master page. Any page in the publication that has been assigned the master page (which is all the pages, by default) "inherits" the object(s). Any object (and I do mean *any* object) that you place on a master page is placed on all the pages that are associated with the master.

To edit a master page (in most situations, it is the only master page for the publication), select the Master Pages command on the Page Design tab and then select Edit Master Pages. This switches you to Master Page view. Publisher lists the master page (or pages) for the publication in the Pages pane, and the Master Page tab appears on the ribbon. The current master page displays in the Publisher workspace. Figure 28-6 shows Master Page view.

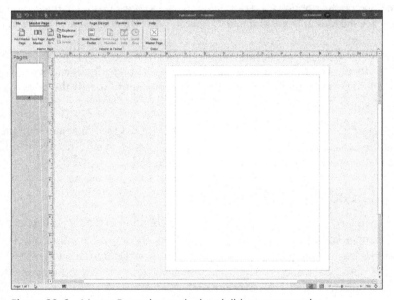

Figure 28-6   Master Page view and related ribbon commands

Master pages are designated by letters of the alphabet. For example, the default master for a publication is master page A. You can change the name or ID of a master page using the Rename command, but Publisher provides only a one-character ID (so you can't create a descriptive ID for a master page).

In many respects, a master page is no different from a "regular" publication page. You can use the various tools on the ribbon's Insert tab to add objects to the master page. These objects, such as a text box or a logo, are displayed on each page in the publication (controlled by the master you are working on).

Select the Insert tab and add objects to the master page as needed. If you want to have repeating page parts, borders, accents, or advertisements in the publication, use the Building Blocks group commands (on the ribbon's Insert tab) to insert items. You can also insert pictures, clip art, and shapes as needed (as you would on any page in a publication).

The Apply To command on the Master Page tab enables you to apply the master page (and the changes you have made to the master) to all the pages in the publication, the current page, or a specific range of pages. Use the Apply To All Pages option to assign the change to all pages in the publication. Apply To Current Page affects only the page that was selected when you switched to the Master Page view.

TIP

You can also quickly apply a master page (or None) to the pages using the Master Pages command on the ribbon's Page Design tab. Select a page or pages in the Pages pane, and then click the Master Pages command. You can select a master page or None, as needed.

To specify a range of pages, select Apply Master Page; the Apply Master page dialog box opens. It has options for all pages, a range of pages, or the current page. To set a range of pages, select the Pages option button and then use the From and To boxes to specify the page range. When you are done working in the dialog box, click OK.

When you have finished working with the master page (or pages, if there are multiple masters), select the Close Master Page command on the Master Page tab. This returns you to your publication.

Inserting headers and footers

You can use headers and footers to add repeating information to the pages in your publications. For example, you can insert page numbers, dates, and any other information that you want to repeat. The header or footer for a publication (a publication with only one master) resides in the master page and propagates to the pages assigned that master page (typically, all the pages in a publication with one master page).

You can add headers and footers to a master page in the Master Page view; the related commands are in the Header & Footer group. To show the header on the selected master page, select the Show Header/Footer command. Publisher selects the header area on the master page; it appears as a selected text box. You can type text into the header or use the Insert tab to insert objects such as pictures or other items. To move to the footer area of the master page, select the Show Header/Footer command a second time. Each time you select this command, you toggle between the header and footer (or vice versa).

Three other commands in the Header & Footer group are extremely useful. The Insert Page Number command inserts the page number symbol (#) in a header or footer. This places the appropriate page number on the pages in the publication. You can add text before or after the page number symbol. For example, you can type the word *Page* before the inserted page number symbol.

The Insert Date command enters the current date, and the Insert Time command enters the current time. You can use these commands to add information in either the header or the footer. When you have finished working in the header or footer of a master page, click in the body of the master page to deselect the header or footer box.

TIP

You can also access the header and footer for a publication using the Header and Footer commands in the Insert tab's Header & Footer group. This group includes a handy Page Number command that provides a gallery of page number positions, including Top Left, Bottom Left, and Center. This gallery also gives you access to the Page Number Format (select Format Page Numbers), which enables you to select the number format and specify the start number for the page numbering in the publication.

Creating master pages

You can add master pages to your publication in the Master Page view. You can also rename and/or delete master pages, if needed. One option for adding a new master page is the Add Master Page command on the Master page tab. When you select the Add Master Page command, the New Master Page dialog box opens, as shown in Figure 28-7.

NOTE

If you want to create a new master page that is a duplicate of an existing master page, you can use the Duplicate command in the Master Page group. This creates a new master page with a new ID that is a duplicate of the currently selected master. You can then edit the duplicate master as needed and assign it to pages in the publication.

By default, Publisher sets the page ID to B (which you might as well leave as is) because the original master page is considered the A master. If you want, you can add a description for the new master page. When you click OK, Publisher adds the new master page to the Pages pane. The new master page is also selected so that it is the active page in the Publisher workspace. You can modify the master page as already discussed and then use the Apply To command to apply the new master page to specific pages in the publication.

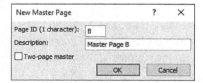

Figure 28-7 The New Master Page dialog box

Having more than one master page enables you to create a publication that contains pages with different layouts and default objects, including different headers and/or footers. For example, you can have a master page that does not include a header or footer and a master page that does include a header or footer. Assigning the master page without a header or footer to the first page in the publication enables you to follow the general rule that page numbers and headers/footers are not typically included on the first page of a publication. All the subsequent pages in the publication can be assigned a master page that includes header and footer information, such as page numbering. Remember that you can assign master pages to selected publication pages when you are working on the pages in the workspace. Use the Master Pages command on the Page Design tab to assign a master page to the current publication page by selecting from the master page gallery.

Using tables in publications

You can use tables on your publication pages to arrange objects on the page. When you place a table on a page, you are inserting a Publisher object, just like a text box or picture. You can thus size and move the table on the page as needed. You can place text in the table cells, and you can place other objects, such as pictures, in the cells. Although you might think of a table as columns and rows that enable you to enter text information into a cell, you can also consider a table as a potential layout tool for positioning objects on the page. This can be an especially useful strategy when working with pages that have a lot of objects.

You insert a table into a page using the Table command on the ribbon's Insert tab. You have two options for creating the table. First, you can select the Table command and then use the table grid to specify the number of columns and rows for the table using the mouse. When you release the mouse button, Publisher inserts the table into the publication.

Second, if you want to specify the number of rows and columns for the table without having to drag the mouse onto the table grid, you can select the Insert Table command below the table grid. Selecting Insert Table opens the Create Table dialog box. It provides a spin box for both the number of rows and the number of columns. Specify the number of columns and rows as needed and then click OK.

When you insert the new table, the table is the selected object on the page. The Table Tools appear on the ribbon. The Table Tools consist of two different tabs: Design and Layout.

Table design commands

The Table Tools, Design commands consist of commands related to the table's overall look, such as the table's format, the fill color, and border parameters for the table. You can use the Table Formats gallery to select a format for the table from the supplied gallery. Place the mouse on a format in the gallery to preview the format on your table. If you do not want to use a table format, you can use the Fill command to select a fill color for the table. The commands in the

Borders group enable you to select a line weight and color and specify the border's location in the table.

When you are working with text in the table, you can use the WordArt styles to add interest to all the text in the table or specific cells. The Text Fill, Text Outline, and Text Effects commands in the WordArt Styles group modify the WordArt style you assign to the table text.

The Typography group enables you to add drop caps, select different number styles, and change the stylistic set for the current style being used. The Table Design commands share a great deal of similarities with the Text Box Tools Format group of commands. Both command groups include the WordArt Styles and Typography group.

Because you are working with a table that consists of separate cells, you can format the entire table by selecting the table frame. If you want to format specific cells or ranges of cells in the table, select those cells and then use the commands provided in the various Design groups as needed.

Table layout commands

Publisher also provides commands related to the layout of the table, which include commands for inserting rows and columns and aligning text (or other objects) within the table cells. To access the Layout commands for a table, select the table and then click the Layout tab under Table Tools (see Figure 28-8).

Figure 28-8   The Table Tools, Layout commands

The Table Tools, Layout command groups are as follows:

- **Table:** This group provides the Select command. You can use the options on the Select command menu to select a cell, column, row, or entire table. The View Gridlines command shows the gridlines in a table that does not have formatted borders. The Delete command provides options for deleting columns, rows, or the entire table.

- **Rows & Columns:** This group provides insertion commands for rows and columns. You can insert above or below a row and to the left or right of a column. Select multiple rows or columns to add a like number using these commands.

- **Merge:** The Merge Cells command merges selected cells. If you want to split merged cells, use the Split Cells commands. The Diagonals command enables you to divide a cell or cells on the diagonal either downward (Divide Down) or upward (Divide Up).

- **Alignment:** This group controls how the text is aligned in the current cell or selected cells. The specific commands are Align Top Left, Align Top Center, Align Top Right, Align Center Left, Align Center, Align Center Right, Align Bottom Left, Align Bottom Center, and Align Bottom Right. This group also provides the Text Direction and Cell Margins commands. The Text Direction command toggles the orientation of the text from horizontal to vertical (and vice versa). The Cell Margins command allows you to set the table's default cell margins.

- **Arrange:** These commands enable you to control the text-wrapping properties in the table or selected cells. Other commands in this group relate to changing the layer position of an object in a table cell and grouping or ungrouping objects. A Rotate command enables you to rotate or flip an object.

- **Size:** You can change the height or width of the table using the appropriate spin box. The Grow To Fit Text check box is enabled by default and allows the table cells to group to accommodate text that you type. The dialog box launcher for this group opens the Format Table dialog box, which gives you control over the table's color, lines, size, and layout.

Remember that a table is more than just a container for text. It is a structured layout tool that you can use to arrange a variety of object types on a page.

Manipulating publication objects

Publisher enables you to manipulate the objects on a page. You can group objects, layer objects on a page, and even swap images between two picture frames and maintain the size settings for each of the picture placeholders involved in the swap.

Grouping objects

Grouping objects lets you fine-tune the positioning of any number of objects on the page. For example, after you have placed objects on a page, you might want to adjust the overall positioning of all of them in relation to the top or bottom of the page or some other special element on the page (such as a large heading). Moving each object individually can be time-consuming and frustrating, especially if you have the objects currently positioned exactly where you want them to be in relation to each other.

To group objects, use the mouse to click and drag a selection box around the objects. If you don't want to select all the objects on a page, select the first object and then select subsequent objects by holding down the Ctrl key as you click them. After you select all the objects you want to include in the group, select the Group command on the Home tab. Figure 28-9 shows three shapes that have been grouped on a page.

A group has its own frame, and you can use the frame to move the entire group on the page. Place the mouse on the group frame and then drag it to a new position. You can also use the group frame to size the entire group of objects at the same time; click and drag the sizing handles as needed.

CHAPTER 28

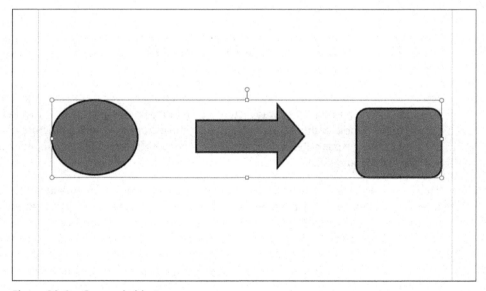

Figure 28-9   Grouped objects

You can delete a group and all the objects in the group at once or copy the objects and then paste them on another page in your publication. When you finish manipulating the grouped objects, click anywhere outside the group to deselect it.

Layering objects

You can also layer objects in a stack. For example, you might use a combination of shapes, text boxes, and pictures to build a custom logo or other layered item. You can also overlap adjacent objects by layering to provide the page with more visual interest.

Layering objects is just a matter of dragging the objects onto each other and then sorting out the layers using the commands in the Arrange group. You can use the Bring Forward command to bring an object forward in the stack (one object) or to bring it to the front of the stack (on top). The Send Backward command enables you to send a selected object backward (one layer) or to send it to the bottom of the object pile using the Send To Back option.

> TIP
>
> **Use the Ungroup command to separate the objects in a selected group.**

When you have the objects layered correctly, select the entire stack (drag the mouse around the object stack). You can then group the layered objects using the Group command. This enables you to move the stack without messing up the layers.

Swapping images

When working with multiple pictures, a very useful feature is the Swap command on the Picture Tools, Format tab. It enables you to swap the pictures in two selected picture frames or swap the formatting of two selected picture frames.

You can actually swap two pictures without ever accessing the Swap command on the ribbon. Select a picture on a page; the Swap Picture icon (a right-pointing arrow over two triangles) will appear in the middle of the selected image. Drag the picture over another picture or picture placeholder on the page. Release the mouse, and the two images will be swapped, including their formatting and effects.

You can also swap two pictures or their formatting using the Swap command on the Picture Tools Format tab. Select an image and then hold down the Ctrl key to select a second image on the page with the mouse. The Swap command becomes active on the Picture Tools Format tab as soon as you select the second picture. Select the Swap command. A drop-down menu offers two options: Swap or Swap Formatting Only. To swap the images, select Swap. If you only want to swap the formatting of the two selected images (and not their position on the page), select Swap Formatting Only.

Whether you drag a picture using the swap picture icon to swap it with another image or select two images and use the Swap command to swap the images, you will find that the pictures adapt to the size of their new frames, rather than the frames being resized to accommodate the swapped pictures. For example, if you swap a larger picture with a small picture (in terms of the picture frame size), the large picture takes the place of the smaller picture and, in effect, becomes the smaller picture. The real value of being able to swap the pictures without disturbing the placement and formatting of the picture frame is that you don't disrupt the overall balance of your publication page.

When you want to swap the formatting of the picture frames between the two selected pictures, select Swap Formatting Only on the Swap command menu. This swaps the formatting of the frames but does not change the content or placement of either frame.

Merging data into a publication

You can perform a variety of data merges into Publisher publications. You can do a mail merge to envelopes, mailing labels, addressable brochures, and other publications. You can also perform email merges to an email publication. A catalog merge enables you to merge text or picture entries into a publication. For example, you might want to generate a product list using a data file that contains the name and perhaps even pictures of your products. Publisher merges each product and any accompanying information related to the product to a new publication page.

When you conduct a merge, whether a mail merge or a catalog merge, you need two items: the publication that you want to merge the information into (such as a postcard that you send to multiple clients) and the information that you merge, such as names and addresses. This information is saved in a data file. Publisher inserts the information in the data file (known as the data source) into the postcard, envelope, or mailing label using placeholder codes called merge fields. Each merge field in the merge publication relates to a piece of information in the data source, such as first name, last name, or street address.

NOTE

The data file used for a merge in Publisher can be created in Microsoft Excel, in Microsoft Word, or directly in Publisher as you perform the merge.

The publication that you use as the destination for the merged information can be any publication that you create in Publisher. For example, you might want to use an envelope template if you want to do a merge of client name and address information to envelopes that you can then print. The merge publication is only the model for the merge, and Publisher creates multiple copies of the merge publication (such as an envelope or a catalog page)—one for each record (or each person, in the case of clients) in the data file.

Performing a mail merge

To perform a mail merge, create the new publication that will be the destination for the merged information. For example, you can create a new postcard using one of the postcard templates and then merge name and address data to any number of cards . Most of the envelope, postcard, and other mail-related templates (such as mailing labels) have reserved areas on them for the recipient's address. You want to place the merge fields (which are codes that correspond to field information in your data source) in the publication area. Delete the text box text reserved for the address information on the publication. The commands that you use to perform the merge are on the Mailings tab.

TIP

If you are entering individual fields using the Insert Merge Field command, you can put spaces or blank lines between fields, as needed. Line up the fields as you would the address information on an envelope or other publication to be mailed.

For the merge, you first must supply an address list, or a data source, for the merge. You can create it or use an existing list. Publisher saves the data source in the Microsoft Access database format with the extension .mdb.

To begin the merge and create a new address list, follow these steps:

1. Select the Mail Merge command (in the Start group on the Mailings tab) and then select Mail Merge. The Select Recipients command in the Start group becomes active.

2. Click the Select Recipients command. You can specify the recipients for the merged publication in either a new list or an existing list.

3. Let's assume that you need to create a new list. Select Type New List. The New Address List dialog box opens, as shown in Figure 28-10.

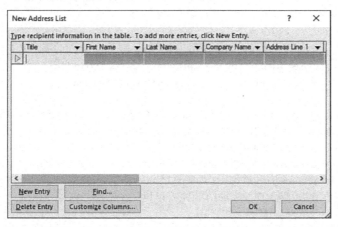

Figure 28-10 The New Address List dialog box

4. Each column in the address list is a different field. Each row is a different record. Type the field entries for the first recipient (first name, last name, and so on).

5. To enter additional records, select the New Entry button as needed.

6. When you have finished entering the recipients in the address list, click OK. The Save Address List dialog box opens.

7. Specify a name and location for the list, and then click Save. The Mail Merge Recipients dialog box opens. You can preclude recipients in your address list from the merge by clearing specific recipient check boxes.

8. Click OK to close the dialog box.

TIP

When working in the New Address List dialog box, use the Tab key to move forward a field, and use Shift+Tab to move back.

After you have specified the recipient list for the merge, the commands in the Write & Insert Fields group, such as Insert Merge Field, Address Block, and Greeting Line, become active. This is because you have provided the merge fields for the merge by creating the recipient list. You can enter individual field names from the Insert Merge Field command; it provides a list of all the field names in the recipient list.

NOTE

The Mail Merge Wizard walks you through the steps of the merge, but using it is more trouble than just using the commands supplied on the Mailings tab and your own common sense.

If you are creating envelopes or mailing labels, the easiest way to get the name and address on the envelope or label publication is to use the Address Block command. Position the insertion point on the publication where you want the recipients' names and addresses to reside—for example, in a text box on an envelope; then select the Address Block command. The Insert Address Block dialog box opens, as shown in Figure 28-11.

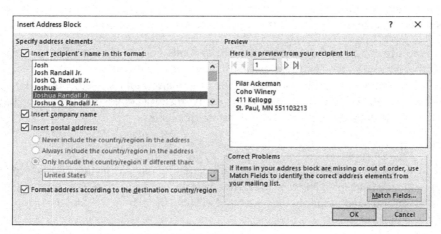

Figure 28-11   The Insert Address Block dialog box

Select a recipient name format and then deselect items that you do not want to include in the address block, such as Insert Company Name. You can also specify that the country/region should not be included in the address. A preview appears on the right side of the dialog box. When you are ready to return to your publication, click OK. The address block field appears on the publication page as <<AddressBlock>>.

When the merge fields are on the publication, you are ready to perform the merge. You can select the Preview Results command and then preview each of the merged publications (such as individual envelopes) if you are unsure of how the merge results will look. When you are ready to complete the merge, select the Finish & Merge command.

The Finish & Merge command provides three options: Merge to Printer, Merge to New Publication, and Add to Existing Publication (in an email merge, it supplies Send Email Messages). I recommend merging to a new publication, which enables you to closely examine the merge results before you print the merged publication pages. When you complete the merge and create a new publication, a multipage publication opens in Publisher. A copy of the publication is created for each of the recipients. For example, if you used a two-page postcard publication as your starting material, a two-page postcard would be created for each recipient.

Performing a catalog merge

The Catalog Merge feature is another Publisher tool that allows you to merge a date into a publication. This merge tool creates product lists in catalogs. The data placed into the catalog comes from a data source of products. You can use an existing list or create the list when you create the catalog pages.

To begin a catalog merge into the current publication, select the Insert tab and then select Catalog Pages. A catalog merge area (in the form of a text box) appears on a new, blank page in the publication. The new page appears as a stack of pages in the Pages pane because Publisher considers it a catalog. The Catalog tools become available on the ribbon. These commands walk you through the process if you start on the left (with the Start group) and then take advantage of the subsequent commands as they become active on the ribbon.

You can size or move the catalog merge area as needed on the blank publication page. Remember that it contains the fields that specify what information to merge into the catalog pages using the information in the data source. You cannot insert tables or other objects in the catalog merge area. You can specify the number of entries that will appear on each catalog page, but not until you get a little further along in the merge process.

TIP

To specify pictures for the product list, you need to type the picture file name into the Picture field, including the file extension for the picture (such as .jpg, .png, and so on). You also need to specify the folder that will hold the picture files, but that happens later in the process.

The next step in the process is to specify a product list for the merge. This serves as the data source. Select the Add List command (on the Catalog Tools Format tab). You can type a new list or use an existing list. Again, let's assume that you need a new list. Select Type New List. The New Product List dialog box opens, as shown in Figure 28-12.

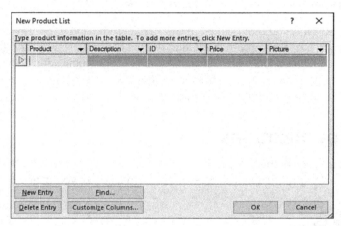

Figure 28-12   The New Product List dialog box

Enter the field information into each of the fields for your first product. Repeat as needed to build your product list. If you want to add fields to the product information, select the Customize Columns button. The Customize Product List dialog box opens. You can add fields, rename fields, or delete fields as needed. When you click OK, you return to the New Product List dialog box.

When you have completed your data entry, click OK. The Save Address List dialog box opens. Specify a name and location for the list and then click Save. Publisher saves the file, and the Catalog Merge Product List opens. You can deselect records that you do not want to include in the merge by deselecting the check box for each item. Click OK to close the dialog box.

After you have specified the data source for the catalog merge (or created it), many of the catalog tools become active on the ribbon. You can use the various layout commands, such as the Layout gallery, to specify how you want the catalog entries to appear on the page, including the number of entries per page. You can also use the Rows And Columns command to manually set the number of columns and rows in the catalog merge area if you do not like any of the presets in the Layout gallery.

When you have a layout selected, you can insert the merge field codes into the catalog merge area. When you select the layout, Publisher inserts placeholder text into the catalog merge area; you can replace this text with merge fields. Select the appropriate placeholder text and then use the Text Field command to enter the field name. Repeat this process as necessary to add all the field codes to the catalog merge area.

If you included a picture field in the product list, a picture placeholder appears in the catalog merge area. Click the picture placeholder; the Insert Picture Field dialog box opens. Select the Picture field and then click the Specify Folders button. You can specify the folder that holds your pictures by using the Add button. This opens the Browse dialog box; use it to specify the folder that contains the pictures (such as the My Pictures folder) and then click OK.

You are almost finished. Now you can use the Preview Results command to preview the results of the merge. When you are satisfied with the results, use the Merge To New or Add To Existing command to merge the catalog to a new publication or an existing publication document, as needed. I recommend merging to a new publication. When you are sure that the catalog data has merged correctly into the new publication, you can print the results.

Fine-tuning your publications

Before you print a hard copy of the final product, be sure to correct all the publication errors and check the overall design. Publisher offers several tools that enable you to fine-tune your publication.

The Spelling feature

The Spelling feature checks your documents for misspellings and typos. It is available in the Proofing group of the ribbon's Review tab. The Proofing group also provides access to the Research task pane and the Thesaurus, which you can use as resources for finalizing text in your publication.

You can set spelling options for Publisher in the Publisher Options window. Select File to open the Backstage, and then select Options. Click Proofing to select (or deselect) settings related to spelling, such as Flag Repeated Words and Ignore Words That Contain Numbers.

Hyphenation

Another element of fine-tuning a publication is determining where words hyphenate in your text boxes. You can have Publisher automatically hyphenate the text in your text frames, which means it determines where to break words with a hyphen and continue the remaining portion of the word on the next line. Because Publisher enables automatic hyphenation by default, it places hyphens only as needed. The great part about the feature is that if you edit the text, Publisher automatically removes unnecessary hyphens and places new hyphens as needed.

You can also specify the hyphenation zone for new text boxes in the Publisher Options window. Go to Publisher Backstage (File) and then click Options. In the Publisher Options window, select Advanced; the hyphenation-related settings display in the Editing Options area. By default, Publisher automatically hyphenates text. You can set the hyphenation zone as needed.

If you want, you can manually hyphenate text in a text box by selecting the Hyphenation command in the Text group of the Text Box Tools, Format tab. When you select Hyphenation, the Hyphenation text box appears. You can clear the Automatically Hyphenate This Story check box and then change the hyphenation zone. To manually hyphenate the story, click Manual.

Design Checker

The Design Checker is another great tool for helping you fine-tune your publications. The Design Checker looks at your publication's design elements and objects and helps you find empty frames, improperly proportioned pictures, font problems (such as too many fonts), and other design problems. The Design Checker also offers you help when it identifies a potential design problem.

To run the Design Checker on the current publication, select File to access the Backstage; then select Info. In the Info window, select the Run Design Checker button. The Design Checker reviews your publication. When it is finished, you return to the Publisher workspace. The Design Checker task pane appears on the right side of the workspace, as shown in Figure 28-13.

Figure 28-13   The Design Checker task pane

By default, the Design Checker runs a general design check. Any problems it unearths display in the Select An Item To Fix list. The Design Checker flags problems on publication pages as well as master pages associated with the publication. You can quickly go to a flagged item in the publication by selecting the item in the list. As soon as you fix the problem, such as placing text in an empty text box or deleting the empty text box, Publisher removes the item from the Design Checker list.

If you want to run additional tests, which include design checks for commercial printing (Run Final Publishing Checks) and web publishing (Run Website Checks), select the appropriate check boxes in the Design Checker task pane. When you select one of the additional test possibilities, the Design Checker immediately begins inspecting the publication. Although it does not check the entire publication and only works on the current page, the Design Checker can run an email check, which verifies whether email addresses on the current page are valid. Select the Run Email Checks (Current Page Only) box in the Design Checker pane to activate this feature and check any email addresses on the current page.

If you want to fine-tune the type of problems that the Design Checker flags, you can open the Design Checker Options dialog box. To do so, click the Design Checker Options link in the task pane. The Design Checker Options dialog box has two tabs: General and Checks. The General tab enables you to specify the display options for the list of problems and the page range to examine when you run the Design Checker (you can select all pages or the current page).

The Checks tab lists the items that the Design Checker uses when it checks the publication. It looks for problems such as Picture Is Missing, Object Is Overlapping Text, and Text Is Too Big To Fit In The Frame. You can clear any of the check boxes, if necessary. The Design Checker then no longer flags items that meet that particular condition as items to fix. When you are done with the Design Checker Options dialog box, click OK. You can close the Design Checker task pane by clicking its Close button.

PART VII

Appendixes

APPENDIX A
Microsoft 365 application integration 887

APPENDIX B
Microsoft 365 macros 903

Microsoft 365 application integration

Sharing application data   887

Understanding object linking and embedding   888

Linking objects   891

Updating and breaking links   895

Embedding objects   898

Editing embedded objects   901

Sharing data with Outlook using actions   901

The Office application suite provides specific software applications for specific jobs: Word for documents, Excel for spreadsheets, PowerPoint for presentations, and Outlook for email management. However, Office isn't just a collection of unrelated software tools; it is a suite of well-integrated applications.

In this appendix, we look at how you can integrate information from an Office application into another application. For example, you might want to insert an Excel workbook into a Word document. We also look at the two different ways of sharing data between applications: linking and embedding.

Sharing application data

Many of us share information on corporate networks via network shares and file servers. Users on a corporate network or users taking advantage of the Enterprise 365 subscription can also typically access SharePoint sites that provide a place for users to share files. Office fully integrates the use of SharePoint sites into the suite applications.

Users not attached to a corporate network can take advantage of the file-sharing capabilities provided by Microsoft's OneDrive, including the use of the 365 Web Apps. And we all fall back on the use of emails with file attachments as a way for sharing files with others.

➤ Microsoft's OneDrive and the Online apps are discussed in Chapter 5, "Using the 365 Online apps."

Sharing files is certainly not rocket science, considering all the connectivity possibilities that corporate networks and the Internet provide, including SharePoint sites and OneDrive. However, all these shared files are not worth a lot if we cannot massage all that information into some kind of meaningful output.

As the Microsoft 365 applications have evolved over time, Microsoft has grown and fine-tuned its ability to share files in the cloud and allow for real-time collaboration. Microsoft Office suite's ability to share information from one application to another is one that we often take advantage of but don't really think about all that much. Being able to pull together information that resides in different applications into a report or a presentation without converting any of the data is really priceless. For example, you can perform a mail merge in Microsoft Word, which uses recipient information contained in your Contact folder in Outlook, to generate form letters or a group email.

➤ **Mail merges are discussed in Chapter 9, "Managing mailings and forms."**

Consider other examples of the cooperative capabilities of Word and Outlook. Word functions as the Outlook email editor (providing you with all of Word's features when composing emails), and Smart Tags in Word documents can be used to automatically input information into Outlook. Word and Outlook are truly integrated into their capability to work together.

These collaborative capabilities in Word and Outlook are certainly not the exception. As already mentioned, the capability to seamlessly share information between applications is a huge benefit—you can share information in Excel with Word (or vice versa) and application data with PowerPoint or Publisher. All the 365 applications provide a platform for comingling data from the various suite members. The basis for much of this data sharing is called object linking and embedding.

Understanding object linking and embedding

Microsoft's object linking and embedding, or OLE, has been around since the early 1990s. With OLE, you can create "compound" documents that consist of data from more than one application. Breaking down the name (object linking and embedding) into its component parts is the easiest way to define what OLE actually is. An object can be anything from worksheet data or a chart in Excel to a slide in PowerPoint to an image in a Word document to pretty much any selectable entity in any of the Office applications. OLE works with application objects.

Now let's tackle linking. When you link an object to a document or other application file, you are creating a connection between the source file and your current document, the container file. The object does not reside in the container; it is represented there by a linking code. When you update the object, the update occurs in the original source application, and the results of the update are reflected in the container. For example, you can link a Microsoft Excel worksheet to a Word document. When you activate the workbook with a double-click (or by right-clicking the worksheet and selecting Open Source), its source application (Microsoft Excel) is started, and the linked workbook is opened in it. Figure A-1 shows a linked workbook from Excel that has been linked to a Word document.

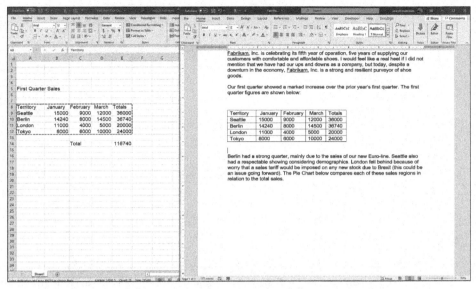

Figure A-1   A linked worksheet in a Word document with the Excel source data

Embedding gets the data into a document or presentation, but the information is no longer linked to the original source information in the other application, such as an Excel worksheet or chart. An embedded object becomes part of the destination file and increases that file's size. It is basically a transplanted copy of the original data. Because the embedded file resides in the destination file, updating the original file in the original application does not update the embedded copy; there is no link between the two.

Embedded objects can be edited even though they are no longer communicating with their sources. However, because they now reside in a destination application such as Word or PowerPoint, the information is edited or manipulated within that particular destination application, in a rather unusual way. When you activate an embedded object (double-click it), the server application opens inside the current application. For example, if you activate an Excel object such as an embedded worksheet in Word, the Word ribbon is replaced by the Excel ribbon while the worksheet object is activated. So, in essence, you are running the server application (Excel) from inside the application (Word) that holds the embedded object.

Another example of an embedded object is an Excel workbook (such as sales figures for your company) embedded in an Outlook appointment. You double-click the embedded Excel object to activate it. Figure A-2 shows an embedded Excel worksheet that has been "activated" in an Outlook event (appointment).

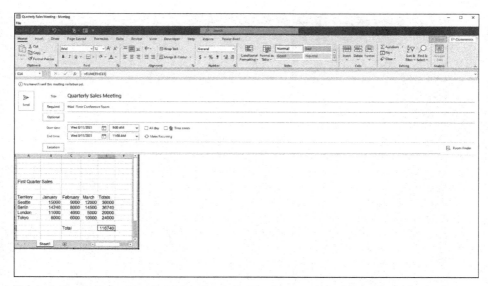

Figure A-2   An embedded Excel workbook that has been activated in an Outlook appointment

Note in Figure A-2 that the ribbon typically found in the Appointment window has been replaced with the Excel ribbon. When you click outside the embedded worksheet, the various Appointment commands return to the ribbon.

Choosing between linking and embedding

You might be wondering when it's best to link and when you should embed. This depends on the type of information you want to place in a particular file and how you plan to collaborate with other users as you work on the file. This is particularly important if someone else "owns" the object (such as an Excel worksheet) that you want to link to a report you are writing in Word.

You should link objects that are dynamic (the information in them updates continually), such as worksheets built into Excel or reports written in Word, to your container file. This enables you to update the object in the application you created it in and have the current results linked to several containers. For example, the same Excel worksheet (which is being updated weekly) could be linked to a Word report (container one) and a slide in a PowerPoint presentation (container two).

Objects such as Excel worksheets that contain information from past quarters or a completed PowerPoint presentation attached to an upcoming meeting appointment in Outlook—that is, any items that are static and not updated over time—can be embedded into your application files, making them part of the file rather than linked content.

Linking objects

There are different approaches available for linking objects from one application to another. One option uses Copy and Paste Special, a tried-and-true method of quickly linking data (it has been around nearly as long as the Office applications).

Another possibility takes advantage of the Paste Options gallery, which is available when you select the Paste command in the Clipboard group. Interestingly, a link created by using one of the Paste Options does create a link to external content but does not create the same kind of link that Paste Special does (we look at the differences in a moment).

The third possibility for creating a link to external data is to use the Object command on the ribbon's Insert tab. This allows you to insert a new object from a list of object types (such as an Excel worksheet or PowerPoint slide). Or, you can specify a file name for an existing object (you can actually browse to locate the file) that you want to link to the current document. For example, you might want to link an existing Excel worksheet to a Word document or PowerPoint slide. Let's take a look at the mechanics of each of these linking possibilities.

Linking with Paste Special

When an object copied in an application is pasted into a document or other file type with the regular Paste command, the data is dropped in with no information about its origin. In contrast, when an object is pasted into a document using Paste Special options such as Paste Link, several pieces of information about the object are stored in the container file. These include the source file's name and location, the server application, and the location of the object within the source file. This extra information makes it possible for the linked object to update whenever the source file updates.

Open the application that serves as the destination (container file) for the linked information. Then to link with Paste Special, follow these steps:

1. Open the application that contains the information you want to link (such as an Excel workbook).

2. Select the information that will serve as the object.

3. Select the Copy command on the Ribbon's Home tab.

4. Return to the application (click the Application's icon on the taskbar) that will receive the linked information.

5. Select the Paste command (in the Clipboard group) and then select Paste Special. This opens the Paste Special dialog box, shown in Figure A-3.

6. In the dialog box, select the object that you want to place into the current application.

7. Select the Paste Link option button.

8. Click OK.

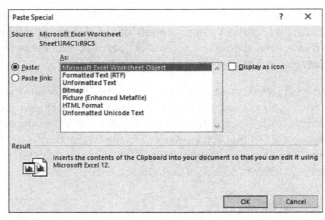

Figure A-3 The Paste Special dialog box

The object is pasted into the application file (such as a Word document). The object that you have linked looks no different from any information that you have pasted into a document or other file. However, the information is linked into the file; you can view the link at any time by pressing Alt+F9, which enables you to view field codes in a document or other file. Figure A-4 shows the linking field code that was inserted into a Word document using the steps discussed in this section.

You can toggle off the field view by pressing Alt+F9. Linked content differs from information that you've pasted in that you can select it (when you click it) only as a complete object. For example, clicking linked Excel worksheet data selects all the data; you don't have the option of changing individual cells in the container application.

TIP

If you want to display the linked object as an icon instead of as the data itself, select the Display As Icon check box in the Paste Special dialog box. This is useful if you are pasting sound and image files into an application and don't want the image files to display in the document as you work on the document itself.

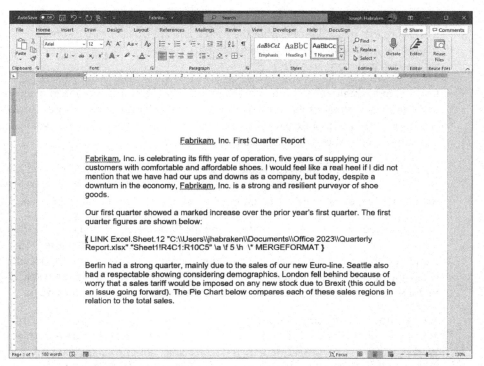

Figure A-4 The linking field code for a linked object in a Word document

Linking with the Paste Options gallery

You can also paste a link using two of the commands in the Paste Options gallery. After you select and copy the object to be inserted as a link (in the source file), return to the application and the file that serves as the linking container.

In the container application, select Paste (on the Home tab). The Paste Options gallery opens, as shown in Figure A-5. The two option commands of interest in the gallery are the third and fourth icons from the left.

Figure A-5 Create the link using the Paste Options linking commands.

The third Paste Options command is Link & Keep Source Formatting. If you hover over this command with the mouse, you see what the pasted link will look like in the container file. Select this option if you want to have the link created and keep the formatting for the object that was assigned to it in the source file.

If you want to create the link but take advantage of styles and formatting in the destination file (the container file), select the fourth command: Link & Use Destination Styles. For example, if you are pasting a link for Excel worksheet data into Word, the pasted information is formatted using the default table style for the current document.

Either of these Paste Options commands inserts the link into the document. You can view the link code by pressing Alt+F9. However, both these links are different from the link that you get when you use the Paste Special dialog box discussed in the previous section.

When you double-click the link created using the Paste Special dialog box, the source application opens, and you can update the data as needed. When you use the Paste Options commands, double-clicking the linked information does not open the source application. However, when you update the information in the source file, the linked information is still updated. This might seem odd, but this is the way these two different linking techniques work.

You can, however, still open the source file for a link even if you have used the Paste Options command. Right-click the linked object and then point at the object name (such as Linked Worksheet Object) on the shortcut menu. Select Links, and the Links dialog box opens. Select the link in the Links list and then click the Open Source button to open the source file for that particular link.

Linking using the Object command

You have a third option for creating links: You can create a link using the Object command on the Ribbon's Insert tab. This option enables you to link an entire file to the container (destination) file. Because Word is often used as a container file, let's look at how to link into a Word document. Follow these steps:

1. Place the insertion point where you will place the linked object.

2. Select the Insert tab.

3. Select the Object command (in the Text group) and then select Object. The Object dialog box opens.

4. Select the Create from File tab in the Object dialog box, as shown in Figure A-6.

5. Use the Browse button to locate the file you want to link into the current document. In the Browse dialog box, select the file and then click Insert.

6. Select the Link to File check box in the Create from File dialog box.

7. Click the OK button.

The information links into the current document. When you double-click the linked object, the source application opens, showing the linked file data.

Figure A-6   Create the link using the Create From File tab.

Updating and breaking links

When you link an object to a file, you have complete control over that link; you can configure how the link data should update, and you can break the link while retaining the currently shown information from the data source in your container file. Links (by default) update when you open the container file; any changes made in the source file should be present in the linked content when you open it. For example, if an Excel worksheet links into a Word document, any changes made to the Excel data since the last time you opened the Word document update when you open the Word document.

You have control, however, over whether the link updates when you open the document. A Microsoft Word information box opens (see Figure A-7) and asks whether you want to update the links in the document. Click Yes or No, depending on whether you want the links to update. If you don't update the link, don't worry; you can update the links manually (which we discuss in a moment) or update the link the next time you open the container file.

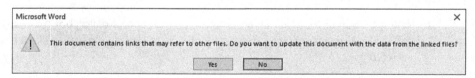

Figure A-7   You determine whether the link should be updated.

In some cases, you might want to configure a link so that it is updated only when you want (and need) to see the updated content. This is particularly useful when you have linked source files that might be updated by a number of collaborators. You can wait until you are sure that the source data is in its final form before you manually update a link.

You can specify the update settings for links in a file in the file's Info window. Let's look at a Word document containing links as an example. Select File to open the Backstage; then click Info.

The Info window provides access to settings related to permissions and sharing settings for the current document. To access the Links dialog box, select the Edit Links to Files command in the Related Documents area of the window (the bottom right). Figure A-8 shows the Links dialog box.

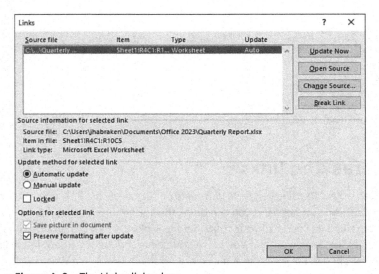

Figure A-8   The Links dialog box

The Links dialog box gives you complete control over the links in your document or another file. Four buttons in the dialog box provide commands related to your links, as follows:

- **Update Now:** You can update a selected link by clicking the Update Now button.

- **Open Source:** If you want to view the source file for a particular link, select the link, and then click Open Source.

- **Change Source:** This command opens the Change Source dialog box. You can browse for a file in the dialog box and then open the file to replace the source file in the currently selected link.

- **Break Link:** You can break the current link to the source file. This enables you to retain the current content in the source file in your container document, but it no longer updates when the source file is edited.

NOTE

You can prevent a link from updating (automatically or manually) in a document by locking the link. This can be useful when you are not sure about the linked content and whether it originates with a trusted source. Select the link and click the Locked check box in the Links dialog box.

For our discussion in this section relating to automatic versus manual updates, two option buttons provided in the Links dialog box are important: Automatic Update and Manual Update. By default, the Automatic Update option button is selected for each link. If you want to change a link to manual updating, select the link and then click Manual Update. When you finish working in the Links dialog box, click OK.

In the future, you can update links manually from the Links dialog box (select a link and then click Update Now). You can open the Links dialog box from the Backstage as previously discussed. Alternatively, you can right-click an object in the container file, point at the object name on the shortcut menu (such as a linked Worksheet object), and then click Links on the shortcut menu.

You can also update a link within the container file, such as a Word document, without opening the Links dialog box: Right-click the linked object in the document and then click Update Link on the shortcut menu.

When breaking links, you might want to keep the data currently provided by the link in your container file (such as a Word document or PowerPoint slide) and not allow the object to be updated when the source file is edited (such as an Excel worksheet). This enables you to take a snapshot of the current data and include it in your document.

To break a link, open the Links dialog box and select the link you want to break. Click Break Link. A message box opens, asking whether you are sure you want to break the selected link (or links). Click Yes to break the link and then click OK to close the Links dialog box.

Editing linked objects

After you create a linked object, you might want to edit and update the information in the object. Once you update a linked object you will definitely realize the full benefit of an OLE link because your updated linked object will appear (updated) in every document to which it is linked.

You can edit a linked object in two ways. The first is to start at the source file, using the server application to make changes to the object. The second is to start at the container file and let the link information lead you to the correct source file and server application. With the second method, you do not have to remember the source file's name or even which server application created it.

TIP

You can select multiple links in the Links dialog box if you want to change multiple link settings, such as configuring the links for manual update. Select the first link, and then hold the Ctrl key as you select other links as needed.

To edit a linked object starting from the source file, start the server application and then open the source file that contains the object you want to edit. Edit and make changes to the object as needed. When you open the container file containing the linked object, the link updates (or you can update it manually), and the most current version of the data's object is provided in the container file.

NOTE

Linked objects provide a great way to get multiple sources of information from different users into a particular destination application.

Editing from the container file is quick and easy because you do not have to find and open the server application manually. To edit a linked object from the container file, double-click the linked object that you want to update. The server application starts and displays the source file. If double-clicking the object does not start the server application, right-click the object and point at the object name on the shortcut menu. Then select Links to open the Links dialog box. Select the link you want to edit and then click the Open Source button. The server application starts.

Edit the information in the server application and then save the changes you have made. You can then close the server application. When you return to the container application, the data should have been updated in the linked object.

Embedding objects

If you want to embed data into a destination file, you can do so with the Paste Special dialog box or use the Object command on the Insert tab. Remember that embedding places the information into the destination file but does not link to the source, so editing embedded objects is different from editing linked objects. After you embed information, it becomes a part of the destination file (such as an Excel worksheet that you have embedded in a Word document).

Embedding with Paste Special

Embedding information from one application into another application using Paste Special is similar to linking an object. However, no actual link is created. Only a copy of the information in the source file is placed into your destination file. Follow these steps to embed information using Paste Special:

1. Open the application that contains the information you want to embed.

2. Select the data, text, or other item that will serve as the object.

3. Select the Copy command in the Clipboard group, or press Ctrl+C.

4. Open (or navigate to) the application that provides the file that will serve as the destination for the embedded object. If necessary, open the specific file.

5. In the destination file, select the Paste command and then select Paste Special. The Paste Special dialog box opens.

6. Select the object type in the As box (such as Microsoft Excel Worksheet Object).

7. Select OK.

The Paste Special dialog box closes, and the object is embedded into the current document. Note that when you click the object, particularly if the object is Excel worksheet data, you cannot place the insertion point in any of the sheet cells. You can select only the entire object.

Embedding using the Object command

If you want to embed an entire file as an object or create a new object, you can use the Object command. For example, let's say that you want to insert an Excel worksheet into a PowerPoint slide. You can use the Object command to do this.

You might wonder why you would want to create a new object in a destination file. If you look back at the description of embedding, it creates an object in a destination file that is then edited using the server application. Suppose you want to put a very complex table in a PowerPoint slide or Word document. You want to have the capabilities of Excel (in terms of Excel functions) available when you edit the object. It makes sense to embed an Excel object. The real power of embedded objects is that they are edited using all the capabilities of the server application without leaving the destination application.

To embed an existing file as an object into a destination file, open the destination file. Sticking with our Excel object on a PowerPoint slide example, make sure you have the presentation that contains the destination slide for the Excel object. Make sure you are on the specific slide, and then select the Object command on the Ribbon's Insert tab. The Insert Object dialog box opens.

Select the Create From File option button (in PowerPoint) and then use the Browse button to locate the file you want to embed.

After you locate the file in the Browse dialog box, select the file and then click OK. The file name appears in the File box on the Insert Object dialog box, as shown in Figure A-9.

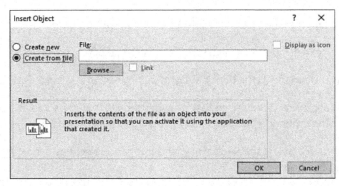

Figure A-9   The Insert Object dialog box in PowerPoint

To embed the object and close the Insert Object dialog box, click OK. The object appears in the container file (a document, slide, or another file type). You can relocate the object as needed. For example, on a PowerPoint slide, the object can be repositioned like any other object—such as an image or chart that can be dragged and sized.

NOTE

In Word, the Object command opens the Object dialog box, as opposed to the Insert Object dialog box found in PowerPoint.

Embedding new objects

You can also embed new objects in a destination application file, such as a document or presentation. Use the Object command to open the Object (Word) or Insert Object (PowerPoint) dialog box. In PowerPoint, select the Create New option and select an object type in the Object Type list. Then click OK to insert the object. In Word, use the Object Type list on the Create New tab of the Object dialog box to select an object type, and then click OK.

In either case (PowerPoint or Word), a new object is placed in the file. The server application's ribbon (an application such as Excel) replaces the destination application's ribbon. Edit the new object as needed. To return to the destination application's ribbon, click outside the object.

Editing embedded objects

Editing embedded objects is extremely straightforward. Remember that, although the object doesn't have any association with specific content in a source file, it is a copy of that source file and is still tied to the server application that was used to create it.

To edit an embedded object, double-click the object. This action evokes the server application and provides you with the ribbon and commands in that application. For example, when you double-click an Excel object in a PowerPoint slide, Excel basically takes over the PowerPoint application window. You are still in PowerPoint, but you now have all the capabilities of Excel to edit the object.

When you finish editing the object using the server application tools, you can return to the destination application. Click anywhere outside the object. The ribbon for the destination application returns, and you can continue to work in the application as needed.

Sharing data with Outlook using actions

You can share data between Word and Outlook using actions. Several actions are available in Word, including the Date, Person Name, and Telephone Number actions. An action such as the Date action or Person Name action requires that you right-click a text item (such as a date or person's name) to complete the action; the action is actually scheduling an event in Outlook (related to the date) or adding a person's name to your Outlook people folder. Unfortunately, there isn't a visual cue (such as underlining or highlighting) to let you know that a particular type of information can be manipulated by an action. You can tell only by right-clicking an item (again, such as a date or a person's name) and checking whether Additional Actions is one of the choices on the shortcut menu.

Placing the mouse on Additional Actions shows you the available actions. For example, right-clicking a date and then pointing at Additional Actions provides actions such as Schedule A Meeting and Show My Calendar. Both possibilities open Outlook, and either opens a new event to schedule a meeting or open your calendar to that particular date.

To take advantage of the actions provided in Word, you need to enable them. This is accomplished via the AutoCorrect dialog box, which you access via the Word Options window. To enable actions in Word, follow these steps:

1. In Word, select File to open the Backstage.

2. Select Options to open the Word Options window, and then select Add-Ins. The Word Add-Ins options are listed.

3. To enable the available actions, select the Manage drop-down menu at the bottom of the Add-Ins window and then select Actions from the menu.

4. Click the Go button (to the right of the Manage drop-down menu). The AutoCorrect dialog box opens.

5. Select the Enable Additional Actions In The Right-Click Menu check box, as shown in Figure A-10.

6. You can enable any of the available actions listed, such as Date, Person Name, Place, and Telephone Number, by selecting the appropriate check boxes.

7. After making your selections, click OK to return to the Word application window.

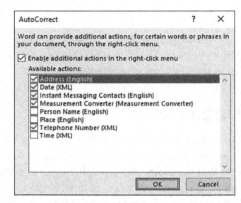

Figure A-10   Enable actions in the AutoCorrect dialog box.

To use an action to place information in Outlook, place the mouse on an item, such as a name or date, and then right-click. On the shortcut menu, point at Additional Actions. The Additional Actions submenu gives you choices related to placing the information into Outlook or allowing Outlook to use the information to perform a particular action. For example, in the case of right-clicking a name (the Person Name action), you are provided with choices such as Send Mail, Schedule a Meeting, Open Contact, and Add to Contacts. All the choices request that Outlook perform an action based on the text in the Word document.

TIP

You can also access the AutoCorrect options via the Proofing page of the Word Options. Open the Word Options from the Backstage (Options) and then select Proofing. Select the AutoCorrect Options button. In the AutoCorrect dialog box, select the Actions tab.

Enabling the Word AutoCorrect actions is worthwhile. It is just another possibility for quickly taking information in a Word document and using it to interact with another Office application—in this case, Outlook.

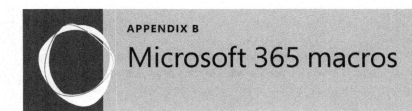

Microsoft 365 macros

Macros and Office   903

Understanding macros   908

Creating a macro   910

Running macros   914

Editing recorded macros   914

Digitally signing macros   917

The 365 applications provide easy access to commands and features via the ribbon, which is the standard command-and-control tool for the productivity software suite. File management and print commands (as well as access to an application's options settings) have been nested in the Backstage. Although it might seem that getting things done in your Office applications does not require anything other than the standard commands and features, you might find an occasion when you want to have more control over a process. You might want to automate a particular series of commands by recording a macro.

In this appendix, we take a basic look at the process of recording your keystrokes and mouse clicks as part of a macro script. This macro primer includes information on adding the Developer tab to the ribbon and enabling macros in the Office Trust Center.

Macros and Office

The ability to record software commands via keystrokes (and, eventually, mouse clicks) and save them in the form of a short script or mini-program has been available in the Office applications for years. This series of recorded commands that is saved as a short script or routine is called a *macro*. The great thing about macros is that they can help you automate repetitive tasks.

Another great thing about macros is that you don't have to be a programmer to create some useful ones. You don't have to write the code for the macro; you simply record it. (Although a special form of the Visual Basic programming language is designed for use with the Office applications.)

All the Office applications provide you with the capability to create your own macros. Even simple macros can reduce the drudgery associated with certain tasks. For example, you might create a macro in an Excel worksheet that helps you insert a new row into a spreadsheet and then copy the necessary formatting and formulas into the new row from the previous one in the sheet. This macro is extremely simple to create and enables you to make a routine Excel task more efficient. Or let's say that you create a macro in Word that saves and prints a form based on a template that you created. This type of macro greatly simplifies the task of completing an online survey for your network users.

In terms of creating macros, you can write the code for a macro or record a macro (depending on the application you are working with). Word and Excel allow you to record macros; PowerPoint, Publisher, and Outlook require that you write the macros. So, you might want to start exploring macros in Word and Excel because recording them, doesn't require a great deal of knowledge of the coding language (Visual Basic for Applications).

The types and complexity of the macros you ultimately create are up to you. Macros provide you with a great deal of flexibility in automating routine tasks in the Office applications; definitely consider them as a resource in reducing the number of steps for often-required tasks.

Adding the Developer tab to the ribbon

The various macro-related commands are on the ribbon's Developer tab; however, by default, the Developer tab is not included as one of the ribbon's tabs. (This is true for all the Office applications.)

If you want to record a macro in Word or Excel, you need to add the Developer tab to that application's ribbon. For example, in Excel, follow these steps to add the Developer tab to the ribbon:

1. On the ribbon, select File to open the Backstage.

2. Select Options to open the Options window for the application.

3. In the application's Options window, select Customize ribbon.

4. Make sure that Main Tabs is selected in the Customize the ribbon drop-down menu (on the right of the Options window).

5. In the Main Tabs list, select the Developer check box.

6. Click OK to close the application's Options window.

Inside OUT

Start your macro journey by recording your own macros.

Although recording macros might seem like an advanced feature that may be beyond your capabilities, it is actually fairly simple to create your own macros in Excel and Word by recording them. Recorded macros provide you with a fairly straightforward tool for automating repetitive tasks that you do in Excel or Word. Unfortunately, PowerPoint, Publisher, and Outlook do not provide you with the ability to record macros.

So, even though PowerPoint, Publisher, and Outlook do not allow you to record macros, all the Office applications provide you with the ability to create your own macros by writing your own macro code. Visual Basic for Applications (VBA), a hard-wired programming tool and interface into the various Office applications, allows you to write your own macro scripts. Unfortunately, VBA does have a learning curve. One way to get familiar with the overall look of VBA scripts is to record your own macros and then open them in the Visual Basic editor. This allows you to inspect the VBA code that was automatically written when you recorded your macro. If you do want to learn more about VBA, you will find that there are a number of books available, though many of them are specific to Excel. (Excel is the Office application that lends itself best to the use of macros, though Word probably runs a close second.)

APPENDIX B

You are returned to the application window. The Developer tab is now included on the ribbon.

Enabling macros in the Trust Center

Macros can be a security risk; remember that macros are, in effect, programs. This means that a macro can contain all sorts of code, including code that can do bad things to your installed applications and, potentially, your computer. What's more, antivirus software isn't always capable of catching malware (malicious software) that comes in the form of a macro.

Because macros pose a potential security risk to your computer, they are disabled in your 365 applications by default: The default setting in the Trust Center is Disable All Macros With Notification. This means that a security box notifies you if you open a file that contains macros. You are given the opportunity to keep the macros disabled or allow them to be enabled in the file. This gives you complete control over whether the macros remain disabled when you open a particular document, presentation, or workbook.

CAUTION

Macro viruses have long been the bane of email users around the world; macro viruses can spread like wildfire and are somewhat easy to create. (Look up the Melissa virus on the web; this macro virus infected thousands of computers via email.) You should certainly be careful opening emails in Outlook with unknown attachments because they can contain macros. Also, be careful opening files that contain macros that you have downloaded from the web. Remember, macro viruses were the first cross-platform viruses to appear and spread between computers running both Windows and Mac OS.

Depending on the environment you work in, the macro settings in the Trust Center might have been changed from the default settings to protect the computers on the network. For example, if you work on a corporate network, your network administrator might have changed the setting in the Trust Center to Disable All Macros Except Digitally Signed Macros. This requires you to digitally sign your macros before using them.

If you work in a home office environment and plan to use only macros that you create, you might want to change the macro setting for a particular 365 application to the Enable All Macros (Not Recommended; Potentially Dangerous Code Can Run) option. This gives you the most flexibility in running your own macros, but it can potentially open your computer to attack via a macro virus if you run macros in other files, particularly those that you download from the web.

How you approach your application security is up to you. If you are going to be working with your own macros in an application, you might want to edit the macros using the Trust Center. To access the Trust Center for an application (such as Word or Excel), follow these steps:

1. On the application's ribbon, select File to open the Backstage.

2. Select Options to open the Options window for the application.

3. In the application's Options window, select Trust Center.

4. In the Trust Center pane, select Trust Center Settings, which opens the application's Trust Center.

5. To change the macro settings for the application, select Macro Settings. Figure B-1 shows the Word Trust Center and the default macro settings.

6. Select the macro setting you want to use for the application and then click OK.

The Trust Center closes, and you return to the application's Options window. Click OK to return to the application window.

➤ For more about the Trust Center, see Chapter 2, "Navigating and customizing the 365 interface."

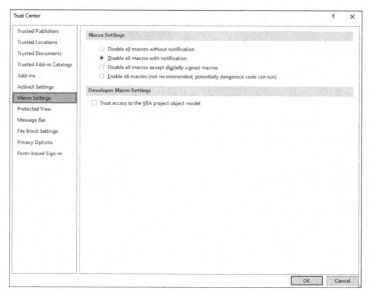

Figure B-1   The Word macro settings in the Trust Center

APPENDIX B

Creating macro-enabled Office files

An alternative to adjusting the macro settings in the Trust Center is to save your Word document or Excel workbook in a file format that enables the macros that you have created and stored in the file. With the exception of Microsoft Outlook, all of the Office applications provide you with this capability. This approach to enabling macros in a file does not present the same level of risk as allowing an application to enable all macros via the Trust Center macro settings.

So, let's say that you want to save a PowerPoint presentation as a PowerPoint macro-enabled presentation. You can create a new presentation and save it in the macro-enabled file format, or you can use the Save As command to save a macro-enabled copy of any presentation that you have previously created.

The Save As dialog box opens whether you are saving a presentation for the first time (with Save) or using Save As to create a macro-enabled version of the presentation. In the Save As Type drop-down menu, select PowerPoint Macro-Enabled Presentation, as shown in Figure B-2.

Then all you have to do is supply a file name (if you are saving the presentation for the first time) and a location for the saved file. Then click Save. Now you can create macros as needed in this presentation, and they will be enabled.

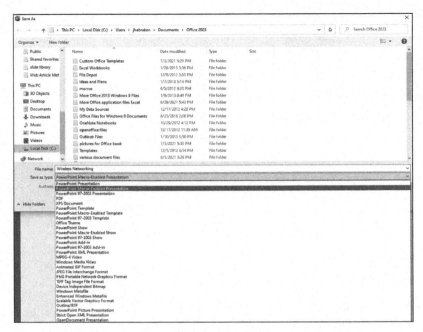

Figure B-2   Saving a macro-enabled presentation

Understanding macros

Macros created in the Office applications are saved in a scripting language called Microsoft Visual Basic for Applications, or VBA. Creating macros in VBA only scratches the surface of what you can accomplish using the VBA scripting language. Developers use VBA to create add-ons and other special tools for the various Office applications. VBA can be used to enhance the user interface for an Office application by creating new ribbon tabs and commands for those tabs.

VBA is an object-oriented programming language. This means that it is designed to manipulate different classes of objects, which is exactly what is necessary for a programming language to work in the Microsoft 365 environment where many different object types are found in the different 365 applications. In fact, VBA is designed so that developers can create new object classes, if necessary, as they design and code tools and application add-ons.

When you record VBA code for a macro, the code is contained in what is referred to as a *module*. Each application has its own module for the macros you create for that application.

Each macro consists of a subroutine that dictates what the macro does when you run it. Figure B-3 shows the subroutine code for a simple Excel macro.

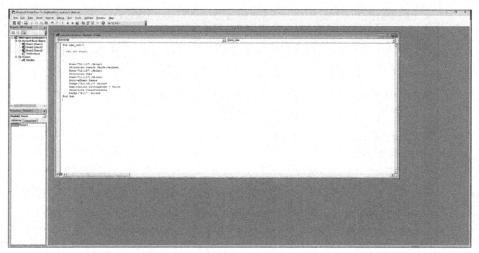

Figure B-3   Macros consist of VBA code subroutines.

Because we are primarily exploring the recording of macros (rather than writing code), you don't have to worry too much about the actual code created during the process. However, you can edit the code in the Microsoft VBA editor (which we touch on later in this appendix). You only need to enable the macro recorder and then perform the steps that make up the macro's routine.

NOTE

A complete discussion of VBA as a programming tool and language is far beyond the scope of this appendix and this book. If you want to delve further into VBA programming, I recommend acquiring a book specifically on VBA; you can check out VBA-related titles at the Microsoft Press Store (*www.microsoftpressstore.com*).

Another subject area that you should understand before you begin creating your macros relates to where your macros are saved after you create them. Each Office application offers slightly different options. The following list provides the options for each member of the Office suite discussed in this book (precluding OneNote, as already mentioned):

- **Word:** Macros recorded in Word can be saved to the Normal template (Normal.dotm), which makes the macros available to all documents based on that template. You can also save macros to a specific template or to the current document.

- **Excel:** Macros recorded in Excel can be stored in the current workbook, a new workbook, or a macro catch-all workbook called the Personal Macro workbook. Macros stored in the Personal Macro workbook are available globally, meaning in all your Excel worksheets.

- **PowerPoint:** Macros in PowerPoint can be saved in the current presentation or all currently open presentations (when you use the macro recorder). Using the macro-enabled file types, you can also use the Save As Type list to save presentations, templates, and even shows (meaning that the macros can be run while you show the presentation).

- **Outlook:** Outlook saves macros with the application's dataset so that you can access any macros you create in Outlook any time you need them.

- **Publisher:** Macros in Publisher are stored in the Publisher publication that is open when you record the macro. You can also use the Save As command to save a Publisher file as a Word document containing the recorded macros using the Word Macro-Enabled Document file type.

One other important point relates to macros: They require a great deal of trial and error because they do not always work as intended. For example, sometimes the VBA code you create when you record a macro doesn't define an object correctly (such as a range you selected in an Excel worksheet), or the macro (when played) has a problem relocating a particular object.

Simple, well-thought-out macros typically work as you intended. More complex macros might require more research into VBA if you want to create and troubleshoot them.

Creating a macro

The macro-related commands are in the Developers tab's Code group. Word and Excel don't provide the same macro-related commands; however, some commands are common to both. For example, you use the Record Macro command to record a new macro in Word or Excel. Other macro-related commands common to Word and Excel are as follows:

- **Visual Basic:** This command opens the Visual Basic editor. The editor has its own toolbar that you can use to create VBA modules and subroutines from scratch.

- **Macros:** This command opens the Macros dialog box. It enables you to view the list of macros. Commands are available for editing, deleting, and running macros in the list. The Macros dialog box also provides access to the Organizer, which you can use to copy macros from one file to another.

- **Record Macro:** This command starts the macro-recording process.

- **Stop Recording:** In Word and Excel, you use the Stop Recording command when you have finished recording the macro.

- **Macro Security:** This command opens the Trust Center's macro settings.

Before recording steps in the macro, you must supply a name for the macro, and you have the option of specifying a shortcut key for the macro. Keyboard shortcuts for macros can include the use of the Ctrl, Alt, and Shift keys; function keys; and the alphanumeric keys on the keyboard. As already discussed in the previous section, you might also have the capability to choose where the macro is stored, depending on the specific Office application you are using. (You definitely have options in Word and Excel.)

In terms of naming conventions for macros, you must follow some rules. First, the macro name can be up to 80 characters and must begin with a letter or an underscore. The remaining characters in the macro name can be letters, numbers, or the underscore symbol. You cannot use spaces in your macro names or special characters (such as *, /, and :). Finally, your macro name cannot be a duplicate of an Excel built-in name or an object that already exists in the workbook. If you violate any of these rules, a warning box opens to let you know that the name you entered is not valid. This is no big deal because you can close the box and re-enter a name for the macro that follows all the rules.

One other aspect of creating your macro to take into account before you turn on the macro recorder relates to planning. It makes sense to plan a macro in terms of the series of commands and actions that you will record. You should consider practicing—or even writing down—the steps in the macro before you record it.

If you create a macro that doesn't function correctly, it is certainly no big deal. You can easily delete a macro that doesn't operate properly. You also have the option of editing a macro, which we discuss later in this appendix—but you might find that deleting a bad macro and attempting to record it again is as easy (particularly for short macros) as trying to debug and edit your problem-child macro.

Recording a macro

The macro-recording process is pretty much the same for Excel and Word (which are two of the most often used Office applications). Let's walk through how you record a macro in Excel and then create a macro in Word and assign it to the Quick Access Toolbar as a button. Follow these steps:

NOTE

When the macro recorder is running, you lose some functionality normally attributed to the mouse; for example, you cannot select text in a Word document. Use keyboard shortcuts as much as possible when you are recording your macros.

1. In the Developer's tab's Code group, select Record Macro. This opens the Record Macro dialog box, shown in Figure B-4.

2. Enter a name for the macro in the Macro Name box.

3. Set the shortcut key for the macro.

4. Use the Store Macro In drop-down menu to select where you want to store the macro.

5. Provide an optional description for the macro in the Description box and then click OK.

6. Perform the actions that will be recorded in the macro. You can access the various ribbon tabs as needed to access commands, and you can use the keyboard or mouse to move within the worksheet.

7. When you have finished recording the macro, click Stop Recording.

NOTE

The Record Macro dialog box in Word provides the Button command, which enables you to assign the macro you are recording to a button, which in turn can be placed on a toolbar such as the Quick Access Toolbar. You are also provided the option of assigning a keyboard shortcut to the macro (using the Keyboard button).

Figure B-4   Excel's Record Macro dialog box

The macro is stored as you specified in step 4. You can view the list of macros available, including the new macro that you have recorded, by selecting Macros in the Code group.

Assigning a macro button to the Quick Access Toolbar

Word makes it easy to create a new macro and assign it to the Quick Access Toolbar. This is extremely useful if you create a macro that opens a weekly report form or an invoice that you use frequently. You can use the macro to open a new document based on a template that you have created (such as an invoice template).

TIP

If you are creating a macro in Excel to move a certain number of cells from a cell of origin (but for use with a variable starting cell), select the Use Relative References command in the Code group before recording the macro.

➤ For more on creating forms using form controls, see Chapter 9, "Managing mailings and forms."

To create a macro in Word and assign it to a button on the Quick Access Toolbar, follow these steps:

1. In the Developer's tab's Code group, select Record Macro. This opens the Record Macro dialog box.

2. Enter a name for the macro and provide an optional description.

3. Select Button. This opens the Word Options window with the Quick Access Toolbar settings selected.

4. In the Command pane, choose the icon that represents your new macro.

5. Click Add to add the macro button to the Quick Access Toolbar pane, and then click OK.

6. Perform the actions that are included in the macro, and then click Stop Recording.

CAUTION

When the macro recorder is running in Word, you may lose some of the functionality of the mouse (such as selecting text or double-clicking in the header area). The best practices to getting around this issue are to use keyboard shortcuts, ribbon commands, and even the arrow keys (if necessary) to record the proper sequence of actions for the macro.

The new macro is stored in the Normal template. The button for the new macro is included on the Quick Access Toolbar. You can run the macro using the button.

TIP

If you want to create a template in Word that contains its own macros, such as for an online form, save the template as a Word Macro-Enabled Template file type.

You can also add macros to the Quick Access Toolbar in the other Office applications, such as Excel, Outlook, and PowerPoint. Open the Backstage (select File, Options) in the application and select Quick Access Toolbar. In the Choose Commands From drop-down menu, select Macros.

You can add any of the macros listed to the Quick Access Toolbar. Select a macro and then click the Add button.

APPENDIX B

Running macros

Macros can be run in a variety of ways. You can run a macro using the shortcut key that you have assigned to that macro. You can also run a macro from an assigned button on the application's Quick Access Toolbar.

TIP

You can specify a Quick Access Toolbar button for your macro other than the default in the Quick Access Toolbar settings (in Options). Select the macro in the Quick Access Toolbar list and then click Modify. Select a new button and then click OK.

Before you run a macro, you need to make sure you provide the appropriate conditions in your application required by the macro. For example, if the macro performs a particular task in an Excel worksheet, you need to be in the correct cell so that the macro navigates the sheet correctly as it performs its tasks.

You can also run macros from the Macros dialog box. To view available macros, select the Macros command (on the Developer tab). The Macro dialog box opens, as shown in Figure B-5.

Figure B-5   The Macro dialog box

To run a macro from the Macros dialog box, select the macro. Then all you have to do is select the Run button to have the macro run.

Editing recorded macros

As already mentioned in the previous section, macros can be accessed via the Macros dialog box. The Macros dialog box also enables you to open a macro in the VBA editor.

TIP

You can open the Macros dialog box at any time by pressing Alt+F8.

Although it isn't exactly editing, you can delete unwanted macros from the list. To delete a macro from the Macros dialog box, select a macro and then click Delete. A message box opens and asks whether you want to remove the selected macro; click Yes to confirm the deletion.

Exploring the VBA Editor

To view the VBA code in a macro and edit it, you need to open the VBA Editor. Select a macro in the Macros dialog box and then click Edit. The VBA Editor opens, as shown in Figure B-6.

The VBA Editor window in Figure B-6 shows the NewMacros module, which contains the sub-routines for a Word macro: page_number_spell_check (note that the macro name does not use special characters or spaces). The editor is basically a standalone application and provides its own menu system and command toolbar structure.

Figure B-6   The VBA Editor

The VBA Editor window is divided into three panes:

- **Project Explorer:** This pane provides a list and is used to access the projects available in the current application session. You can use it to navigate (and select) available objects in the projects. These objects include modules such as the NewMacros module and other objects, including the current document (or worksheet) and references to other objects, such as templates.

- **Properties:** This pane provides a list of the properties for the object currently selected in the Project Explorer.

- **Code Window:** This is the largest pane of the editor's window and contains the actual VBA code for the selected module.

TIP

The geography of the VBA code in the macro is straightforward; each subroutine (for a macro) begins with the Sub **line followed by the name of the macro. Directly under the** Sub **line, the name of the macro is repeated (followed by the word** Macro**). The next line consists of the description that you provided for the macro.**

Below the macro's name and description (which typically appear in a green font), the actual lines of code that make up the macro (and relate to the actions that you performed) are listed. The macro subroutine ends with the code line, End Sub.

In terms of editing the code lines, one of the simplest possibilities is changing references to specific files or objects specified in the macro. For example, if the macro opens a new file from a template named cyclone.dotm, and you have modified the template and renamed it to newcyclone.dotm, you can change the reference within the specific code line that refers to the template. Or let's say that you have a macro that inserts a particular building block into an Excel worksheet. You can edit the name of the building block in the macro to refer to any building block in your building block galleries, as long as you only edit the name and do not delete or disturb any of the other text in the code line.

Any addition of code lines to a macro requires that you enter the VBA code in the correct syntax and in the appropriate context. For example, the Selection code is used to specify a command from the keyboard. If you want to specify that the selected text be cut by the macro, you add a code line:

```
Selection.Cut
```

Obviously, you have to specify the text to be selected in a code line that comes before Selection.Cut. To specify the text selection, use the code line Selection.Extend followed by Selection.MoveDown Unit:=wdLine, Count:=3. This means that you turn on the Extend feature (which is F8; you can't drag with the mouse to select text when the Macro Recorder is on) and then use the down-arrow key to move down three text lines to select that text. You see that you can read and understand the VBA code lines. As you add more code vocabulary to your repertoire, you will have more confidence in editing macros and potentially writing your own VBA code.

Stepping through a macro

A good way to troubleshoot a macro that is not working correctly is to step through it. This process enables you to go through the code lines one at a time. The best way to perform a step debugging is to open the VBA Editor window and then rearrange the open windows so that you can see the editor and the application window (such as Word) either side by side or top and bottom. This enables you to see what happens in the application window as you execute each line of code.

Open the Macros dialog box and then select the macro you want to step through. Click Edit to open the VBA Editor. When you have the editor and the application arranged on your screen so that you can see them both, follow these steps to step through the macro:

1. Place the insertion point in the macro subroutine where you will begin stepping through.

2. Press F8 to execute that line of code. The code is highlighted yellow.

3. To step to the next line of code, press F8.

4. Continue to press F8 to execute each line of code until you come to the End Sub line.

5. To end the debugging process, click the Reset button (the button with the blue square in the middle) on the editor's toolbar.

As you step through each line of code, take note of what is happening in the application window as each code line executes. This enables you to find the specific line of code that is misbehaving in a macro that does not work correctly.

Digitally signing macros

We have already discussed the fact the macros can be a security risk and that the security settings for the Office applications are geared toward not allowing macros to run by default. So, another alternative for verifying that your macros are not malware is to digitally sign the macro project (which can contain a number of macros). This enables you to use and share the macros without enabling macros in the Security Center and lessens the possibility of executing a "bad" macro.

After you digitally sign your macro projects, you can change the macro settings in the Trust Center to use the Disable All Macros Except Digitally Signed Macros option. Collaborators and other users who might use your templates or other files that contain macros can also use this setting, which enables you to share the macros but doesn't open any of your colleagues to a macro attack.

Digitally signing a macro project requires that you obtain a digital certificate. Digital certificates can be provided by a certificate authority. For example, you can obtain digital certificates from online certificate authorities such as Symantec (www.broadcom.com) and Entrust Datacard (*https://www.entrust.com/digital-security/certificate-solutions/products/digital-signing/code-signing-certificates*). Some companies and institutions also have their own in-house certificate authority, so talk to your IT folks if you are creating macros that you will share with others.

CAUTION

If you are going to distribute your macro-enabled documents or workbooks to other users, you really need to have a digital certificate from a certificate authority. Using the Office selfcert application to self-certify macros is fine if you are only creating macros for yourself. When you share self-certified macros (in your Office files, such as Word or Excel) with other users, they will receive a security warning when they open those files.

You can purchase a digital certificate from a certificate authority for your VBA code, or you can ask your digital certificate overlord (a network administrator or CIO, perhaps) at your company for a digital certificate for your VBA projects. If neither of these options is open to you, you can still create your own digital certificate using an Office utility program named Digital Certificate for VBA Projects. The process of creating a digital certificate is very straightforward; follow these steps:

1. On the Windows 10 Desktop, open the File Explorer using the icon on the taskbar.

2. Click in the Search box on the right side of the File Explorer window.

3. Type **selfcert** in the Search box and then click the This PC command on the left side of the ribbon.

4. When the search has finished, double-click the SELFCERT file to open the Create Digital Certificate window, as shown in Figure B-7.

5. Type a name for the new digital certificate and then click OK.

6. A dialog box opens and states that your certificate was successfully created. Click OK to close the message box.

Figure B-7   Create a digital certificate to sign your macros.

Once you have a digital certificate (self-generated or provided by a certificate authority), you can use it to digitally sign your macro projects. This process takes place in the VBA editor. Follow these steps:

1. On the Developer's tab, click the Macros command to open the Macro dialog box.

2. Select a macro in the Macro Name list and then click Edit to open the VBA editor.

3. In the Project Explorer, select the name of the VBA project (it is in the project tree under the Modules folder) that you want to digitally sign.

4. Select the editor's Tools menu and then select Digital Signature. This opens the Digital Signature dialog box.

5. Select the Choose button in the Digital Signature dialog box. A Windows Security box opens showing a certificate from a certificate authority (provided by your employer or one that you were provided directly by a certificate authority) or the certificate that you created using the SELFCERT application (see Figure B-8).

6. Click OK, and you are returned to the Digital Signature dialog box. The name of your certificate is now listed as the certificate name in the dialog box.

7. Click OK.

Figure B-8   The Windows Security box lists your digital signature certificate.

You can now close the VBA Editor. The Project module (and all the macros that it contains) is now digitally signed.

You have now digitally signed the macro project so that it is easy for others to use your macros in templates or other documents, worksheets, and so on. If you plan to share it on the network or email it to another user. You have a problem, however.

Because you generated the digital signature certificate, it is not considered a certificate from a trusted source. When a user on another computer attempts to open the document or use the template, the Office application being used checks the certificate to see if it is from a certificate authority on the trusted list. Because you aren't really a certificate authority, any user opening your document or template containing the macros sees a security message in the application (just below the ribbon) detailing that the macros have been disabled.

A quick workaround can remedy this problem. Users can add your certificate to their trusted root certificate authority's store. The macros can then be enabled. Therefore, this set of tasks should be performed on the computer of the other users.

Select the Options button in the security warning that has appeared in the application. This opens the Microsoft Office Security Options dialog box. At this point, there is no way to activate the macros. In the dialog box, click the Show Signature Details link. This opens the Digital Signature Details dialog box, which shows the details related to your digital certificate. To view the certificate, select the View Certificate button.

The Certificate dialog box doesn't really provide any more information than the Digital Signature Details dialog box, but it does grant access to the Certificate Import Wizard, which is where you need to be to add the certificate to the trusted store.

Select the Install Certificate button in the Certificate dialog box. The Certificate Import Wizard opens. By default, the certificate store is set to Current User. This means that the certificate is installed for the current user only. If you want to authorize the certificate for all users, select Local Machine in the Store Location box. Click Next to move to the next wizard window.

In the next wizard window, click the Place All Certificates In The Following Store option button and click the Browse button. This opens the Select Certificate Store dialog box.

In the certificate store list, select the Trusted Root Certification Authorities folder. Then click OK. Now you can click Next. The final wizard screen appears, showing the settings that you have selected, including the certificate store. Click Finish.

A security warning dialog box opens and indicates that you are about to install a certificate and that Windows cannot validate that the certificate is authentic. Select Yes to install the certificate. A Certificate Import Wizard message box opens and lets you know that the import was successful. Click OK. Then click OK two more times to return to the Microsoft Office Security Options dialog box, which is where you started this entire process.

When you return to the macro, the related options available have been expanded because the digital certificate was added to the store. The possibilities are as follows:

- **Help Protect Me From Unknown Content (Recommended):** Initially, this option was the only possibility in the dialog box. It is still the default but can be changed to allow the macro to run in the application.

- **Enable Content For This Session:** This option enables the macros for this session. When you open the file in the future, the macros will be disabled, and the application will provide a warning. However, you can use this same option (each time) to enable the macros.

- **Trust All Documents From This Publisher:** This option enables the user to open files with the macros enabled, and no macro-related warning appears when the user opens the file in an application.

After you have changed the security settings related to the macros in the document or file, you can click OK. If you have selected the second or third possibility, the security warning closes in the application. Now the macros can be run in the application as needed.

Index

Symbols

3D models, PowerPoint, 586

A

Access, 12
  importing to Excel, 484–485
Accessibility Checker task pane,
  67
Accessibility group (Shape
  Format tab), 92
Account command, Backstage,
  30
Add A Service dialog box, 102
add-ins, 41–42
addresses
  envelopes (Word), 232
  mapping, 780
Adobe Acrobat
  PDF files, PowerPoint presen-
    tations, 663
Adobe Reader, 51
Advanced Options settings,
  40–41
.aiff (Audio Interchange File
  Format), 626
alignment
  Word
    charts, 180
    paragraphs, 147
    pictures, 180
    tables, 219
  Excel, 362
    text, 346
  PowerPoint, 546–547, 558

Publisher
  fonts, 847
  tables, 874
Animation Painter (PowerPoint),
  622
antivirus software, 799
applications, 108
  add-ins, 41
  Advanced Options settings,
    40–41
  collaboration, 888
  data sharing, 887, 888
  file sharing, 887
  Online apps, 97
  options, customizing, 38, 40
  Options window, 38
  updates, 128
  Web apps, 8
application window, 22
  dialog box launcher, 23
  Outlook, 690–691
  Quick Access Toolbar, 23
  ribbon, 23
  ruler, 24
  shortcut menus, 23
  status bar, 24
  task panes, 23
  title bar, 22
Arrange group (Shape Format
  tab), 92
artistic effects, pictures, 84
attachments (Outlook)
  security, 803
  saving, 728–729
Attach Template dialog box, 136

AutoArchive (Outlook), 819
  folder options, 821–822
  settings, 820–821
AutoComplete, Excel, 320, 321
AutoCorrect, Word, 199
AutoFilter, 470–473
AutoRecover, 56, 62
AutoSum (Excel), 394, 395
AutoText (Word), 196

B

background removal, pictures,
  83
Background Removal tool, 86, 88
Backgrounds (PowerPoint),
  themes, 574–575
Backstage, 3, 28
  Account command, 30
  Account page, 17
  Add A Service, 103
  Close command, 30
  Connected Services list, 17
  entering, 17
  Excel
    Backstage Info page, 309
    Check For Issues, 315
    Home page, 113
    Info page, 113
    New page, 113
    new workbook, 303
    Open page, 113
    Print page, 340–342
  Export command, 30
  Export page, 53

Feedback command, 31
File tab, 28
Help and, 17
Home command, 29
Home page, 28
Info command, 30
New command, 29
New page, 58
Open command, 29
Options command, 31
Outlook log in, 800
PowerPoint, 532
Print command, 30
Publisher, business information set, 841–843
Save As command, 30
Save As dialog box, 53
Save command, 30
saving files to cloud, 105
Share command, 30
Transform command, 30
Word
  New page, 132
  Print window, 157–159
  Proofing Options, 193
Word Online, 107–108
backward compatibility, 49
bar charts, 184
Excel data bars, 365
bibliographies (Word), 274
citations, 274–275
inserting, 277–278
Source Manager, 276–277
style, 275
Bing
Online Pictures browser, 183–184
Search box and, 6
Bing Maps, 42
Blank Document template (Word), 130
.bmp (bitmap) files, 81, 852
bold text
PowerPoint, 556
Word, 126

bookmarks, Word, 269, 288–289
borders
Excel, 362
Word, 166–168
Borders and Shading dialog box, Word, 167
Borders gallery, Excel, 358–359
browsers, Online apps, 99
building blocks (Word), 197
built-in styles, Word TOCs, 259–260
bulleted lists, 75
icons as bullets, 596
PowerPoint, 549, 551, 556
Word, 162, 164
business cards (Outlook), 716
business information set (Publisher), 841–843
buttons
Import/Export, 34
New Group, 34
New Tab, 34
Rename, 34
Reset, 34
Ribbon Display Options, 26

C

CAcert, 66
Calendar (Outlook), 687, 691, 702
appointments, 743–747
attachment to Outlook message, 717
Date Navigator, 740
Day view, 740–741
Email Calendar option, 754
emailing calendars, 754–755
emailing items, 754
event scheduling, 746–747
meetings, 789–791
Month view, 741
multiple, opening, 752–753
My Calendars list, 739
navigating, 739–743
Options window, 757
Overlay, 753

publishing calendars online, 755–756

Publish Online feature, 755

responding to meeting requests, 793–794

Schedule view, 742

scheduling assistant, 758

ScreenTips, 740

searches, 748–750

sharing, 750

  invitations, 750, 752

  opening shared calendars, 752

sharing invitation, 756

time scale, 742

time zones, 743–744, 758

weather, 741

Week view, 741

work time, 757

Work Week view, 741

Calendars gallery (Publisher), 857

Calls (Teams), 9

Captions (Word), 266–268

Cartesian coordinates in charts, 431

catalog merges (Publisher), 880–882

certificate authorities, 66, 918

Changes group (Review tab), 19

character formatting (Word), 141–142

Chart Design tab (Word), 185

charts, 70

  bar, 184

  column, 184

  doughnut, 184

  line, 184

  pie, 184

  PowerPoint, 586

    slides, 602–606

  radar, 184

  Word, 179–180

    Excel datasheets, 185

    inserting, 180–186

charts (Excel)

  3D area charts, 429

  Add Chart Element, 444–445

Analysis Toolpak, 433

area charts, 429

axes, 424, 442, 449

background, 425

bars, 450, 452

bubble charts, 432

Cartesian coordinates, 431

categories, 424

Change Chart Type dialog box, 456

Change Colors gallery, 444

chart area, 424

Chart Elements button, 439

Chart Filters button, 439

chart objects, 440

Chart Styles button, 439

Chart Styles gallery, 441

Chart Tools, 425, 441

color, 448

column/bar charts, 427–428

combination, 425, 454

  custom, 455–457

copying, 440

creating, 435–436

customizing, 439–440

data, changing, 441–443

data labels, 424, 447

data points, 447–449

Data series, 424

deleting, 440

doughnut charts, 432

drop lines, 450, 452

elements

  Chart Elements pane, 446

  selecting, 445

error bars, 452–453

Format Data Series task pane, 448–449

Format Legend task pane, 448

Format tab, 441

Format Trendline task pane, 451

gridlines, 424, 449

high-low lines, 452

histogram charts, 433
inserting from ribbon, 436
layout, 443–444
legend, 424, 447–449
line charts, 425–428
   x-axis, 428
   y-axis, 428
Move Chart command, 440
moving, 440
Pareto charts, 433
pie charts, 428–429, 455
plot area, 424
Quick Analysis gallery, 438
Quick Layout button, 443
radar charts, 433
Recommended Charts, 437
scatter charts, 430
secondary charts, 456
Select Data Source, 443
sparklines, 366, 457
   creating, 457–458
   modifying, 459
stock charts, 431–432
styles, 443–444
sunburst charts, 434
surface charts, 432
titles, 447
trendlines, 450–452
type
   Change Chart Type, 442
   changing, 441–443
up/down bars, 452–453
waterfall charts, 434
X Y (scatter) charts, 430
charts (Excel Online), 116
Chat (Teams), 9
Check For Issues button, 67
citations (Word), 274
   creating, 274–275
   Source Manager, 276–277
   style, 275

Click-to-Run, 13
clip art, 69
   Publisher, 856–857
clipart, 74
Clipboard
   Excel, 329
   Excel Online, 116
Clipboard group (Home tab), 20
Close command, Backstage, 30
cloud
   files, Online apps, 101, 103
   sharing saved files, 104–106
cloud storage, 59
collaboration, 6, 8
   applications, 888
   calendar sharing, 750, 752
   Excel, 310
      comments, 354–355
      data validation, 504
      prepping workbooks, 315–317
   Microsoft Teams, 9
   modern comments, 6
   OneDrive, 8
   PowerPoint, 665–666
   Word, 128
      private copies of shared documents, 11
      tracking changes, 280–285
color
   borders and shading, 168
   Excel, 357
      background color, 360
      color scales, 366
   hex color codes, 11, 297
   Outlook
      categories, 695–696
      themes, 718
   pictures, correcting, 84
   PowerPoint
      slides, 547
      text, 564
      themes, 572

SmartArt, 79
themes, 170
column charts, 184
columns, Word documents, 226–228
Columns dialog box (Word), 227
comments
Excel
deleting, 355–356
inserting, 354–355
moving between, 355
viewing, 355–356
Word, 289
contextual view, 128
modern comments, 128
Word Online, 111
Comments group (Review tab), 19
Compare group (Review tab), 19
compatibility
backward, 49
conversion utilities, 49
file formats, 49
Compatibility Checker, 67
compatibility functions (Excel), 417
Connected Services (Backstage), 17
Contacts (Word), mail merges, 236
Contacts (Outlook), 691, 769
Actions group, 787
address mapping, 780
Arrangement group, 771
business cards, 777–778, 783
Business Card view, 770
Card view, 770
categories, 779
Communicate commands, 786
Communicate group, 785
Contact dialog box, 772
Contacts folder, 780–781
creating, 772–776
Edit Business Card dialog box, 778
editing, 776–777
entering details, 774

fields
additional, 775–776
business cards, 778
filing options, 788
follow-up flags, 779
forwarding, 783–784
groups, 781–782
importing, 688
index, 788
List view, 771
mail merge, Word and, 787
Meeting command, 789
meetings
editing, 792–793
location, 790–791
scheduling, 789–790
Scheduling Assistant, 791–792
viewing, 792–793
moving, 787
online status, 788
options, 788
People view, 770
Phone view, 771
photograph, 788
photos, 774
printing, 788
Search People box, 780
sharing, 784–785
sorting, 771
tagging, 779
Tags group, 779
Contextual tabs, 21
copying
files, new file type, 54
links, sharing from cloud, 106
Copy options, 40
copyright laws, pictures, 70
Creative Commons licensing, 71, 74, 183
Crop command, 86
cropping pictures, 86
cross references, Word, 269–270

cube functions (Excel), 416

Customize Quick Access Toolbar button, 35–36

Customize Quick Access Toolbar menu, 28

Customize Ribbon window, 33

custom styles (Word), TOC and, 261–262

custom tabs, 34

Cut options, 40

D

databases, 461
  Excel, connecting to, 488
  flat file, 462
  ODBC (Open Database Connectivity), 491
  relational, 462

data (Excel)
  external sources, 488–489
  what-if analysis, 510–511
    Goal Seek, 510

data files (Outlook), 680–681
  folder, 682
  repairing, 685–686

data merges (Publisher), 877
  catalog merges, 880–882
  mail merges, 877–880

data series
  Excel, stock charts, 431
  pie charts, 429

data sharing
  between applications, 887–888
  Outlook, 901–902

data tables (Excel), 511

data validation (Excel), 503
  criteria specification, 504–506
  error checking, 509
  invalid data, circling, 508–509
  templates and, 509
  tips, 509
  validation rules, 503–504
    creating, 504
    error alerts, 506–508
    input message, 506–508

date and time, Excel functions, 414

Date Navigator (Outlook), 740

dates
  Excel, 320
  Word, fields, 252

Default Local File Location box, 56

Defender, 799

Design Checker (Publisher), 883–884

Designer pane (PowerPoint Online), 117

Design tab
  PowerPoint Online, 118
  SmartArt, 79
  Word, 170

Developer tab, 34
  adding to ribbon, 904–905
  commands, 910–911
  macros, 910–912

Developer tab (Word), 136

diagrams, SmartArt, 71–76

Dictate command, 109

Dictation (Word), 127

Digicert, 66

digital certificates, 918

digital IDs, 804

digital pictures, 70, 81
  file compression, 81
  file formats
    .bmp, 81
    .gif, 81
    .jpg, 81
    .png, 81
    .tif, 81
    .wmf, 81

digital signatures
  email, 804, 806
  Excel, 311
  files, 66
  macros, 917–920

Display options, 41

document formatting (Word), 140
  character formatting, 141
  editing, 203–204

managing, 204–207

manual, 142

paragraph formatting, 141

Quick Styles gallery, 201–202

styles, 200

Document Info command (Word), 175, 177–178

Document Inspector (Excel), 315–316

documents (Word), 155

columns, 226–228

insertion point, 138

keyboard, 139

large, 257

margins, 155

master, 257

Master Document, 290–294

mouse, 138

navigating, 137–140

saving as templates, 135

section breaks, 228–230

section formatting, 230

sections, 257

split window, 192

templates, attaching, 136

TOC (table of contents), 258–266

Word Online, 107

Documents library, 60

Document Views group (Word), 187–189

doughnut charts, 184

Draw tab (PowerPoint Online), 118

DRM (Digital Rights Management), 66

drop caps, text boxes (Publisher), 848

drop-down arrow, 25

E

editing files, restricting, 65–66

Editing options, 40

Editor command, 4, 19, 109

Editor pane, 4

Editor (Word), 192–194

Editor (Word Online), 111

effects, themes, 170

Outlook, 718

Effects (PowerPoint), 562

animation, 615–616

motion path, 616–622

options, 623

themes, 574

email

IMAP protocol, 672

Internet email, 672–673

Outlook, 718

Outlook.com, 672

POP3 account, 672

POP (Post Office Protocol), 672

SMTP (Simple Mail Transport Protocol), 672

email accounts

Exchange, 676–677

Google, 676

IMAP (Internet Message Access Protocol, 677

Microsoft 365, 676

Outlook, 670–671

adding, 671, 674, 676–677

Advanced Setup window, 676

manual setup, 675

settings, 680

Outlook.com, 676

Outlook profile, 677–680

POP, 676

email (Outlook)

focused, 693

messages, deleting, 729–730

importing, 688

items to calendar, 754

security, 803

signatures, 719–720

embedding objects, 898

editing, 901

new objects, 900

Object command, 899–900

Paste Special, 899

encrypted email, 804–806

endnotes (Word), 269, 278–279
engineering functions (Excel), 416
envelopes (Word), 232, 234, 251–252
error alerts, Excel data validation, 506–508
error checking, data validation, 509
error messages (Excel), 417–418
Excel, 12
  3D models, 297
  Access and, importing data, 484–485
  access restriction, 311
  alignment, merging cells, 370–371
  Analysis Toolpak, charts, 433
  Analyze Data tool, 301
  auditing tools, 419–420
  AutoComplete, 320–321
  AutoFill, 323
  AutoSum, 394–395
  Backstage
    Backstage Info page, 309
    Check For Issues button, 315
    Home page, 113
    Info page, 113
    New page, 113
    new workbook, 303
    Open page, 113
    Print page, 340–342
  Borders gallery, 358–359
  calculations, 383
  cell ranges
    borders, 358
    permissions, 314
    protecting, 313–315
  cell references, 402–404
  cells
    annotating, 356
    borders, 358–359
    clearing contents, 332
    color, 360
    copying formatting, 362
    deleting, 332
    editing content, 333

    inserting, 369–370
    locking, 311, 313
    merging, 370–371
    moving, 331–332
    permissions, 314
    protecting, 313–315, 362
    style creation, 361–362
    styles, 360–361
  Cell Styles gallery, 360–361
  charts, 70
    Add Chart Element, 444–445
    Analysis Toolpak, 433
    axes, 424, 442, 449
    background, 425
    bars, 450, 452
    Cartesian coordinates, 431
    categories, 424
    Change Chart Type command, 442
    Change Chart Type dialog box, 456
    Change Colors gallery, 444
    chart area, 424
    Chart Elements button, 439
    Chart Elements pane, 446
    Chart Filters button, 439
    chart objects, 440
    Chart Styles button, 439
    Chart Styles gallery, 441
    Chart Tools, 441
    color, 448
    column/bar charts, 427–428
    combination, 425, 454–457
    copying, 440
    creating, 435–436
    customizing, 439–440
    data, changing, 441–443
    data labels, 424, 447
    data points, 447–449
    data series, 424
    datasheets, 185
    deleting, 440
    drop lines, 450, 452

elements, selecting, 445
error bars, 452–453
Format Data Series task pane, 448–449
Format Legend task pane, 448
Format tab, 441
Format Trendline task pane, 451
gridlines, 424, 449
high-low lines, 452
in PowerPoint slides, 602
inserting from ribbon, 436
layout, 443–444
legend, 424, 447–449
line charts, 425, 428
Move Chart command, 440
moving, 440
pie charts, 455
plot area, 424
Quick Analysis gallery, 438
Quick Layout button, 443
Recommended Charts, 437
secondary charts, 456
Select Data Source, 443
sparklines, 366, 457–459
styles, 443–444
titles, 447
trendlines, 450, 452
type, changing, 441, 443
up/down bars, 452–453
Chart Tools, 425
Circular Reference Warning, 418
Clear command, 332
Clipboard, 329
collaboration, 310
    data validation and, 504
    prepping workbooks, 315–317
color
    background color, 360
    color scales, 366
    hex color codes, 297
Colors gallery, 357

columns
    AutoFit Column Width, 373
    Column Width dialog box, 374
    deleting, 375
    freezing, 375–377
    hiding, 375
    inserting, 374
    width, 373–374
comma style, 350
Comment group, 355–356
comments, 354–356
Comments button, 302
Comments pane, 355–356
Commission Percentage, 400
conditional formatting, 363
    color scales, 366
    copying rules, 367–368
    creating rules, 367–368
    data bars, 365
    highlight cells rules, 364–365
    icon sets, 367
    top/bottom rules, 365
Conditional Formatting command, 363
Copy command, 327, 404
Cut command, 327, 404
data, external sources, 488–489
data bars, 365
databases, SQL Server, 488
data series, pie charts, 429
datasheets, charts, 185
Data tab, 462
Data Table dialog box, 512
data validation, 503
    circling invalid data, 508–509
    collaboration and, 504
    criteria specification, 504–506
    error checking, 509
    templates and, 509
    tips, 509
    validation rules, 503–508
Data Validation dialog box, 506, 508

dates, 320
decimals, increase/decrease, 350
Delete command, 375
digital signatures, 311
Document Inspector, 315–316
enhancements, 299
Error Checking, 418
Euro Currency Tools, 398
external data, 493–494
files
   saving, 307
   types, 50
   .xlsx format, 309
Fill handle, 321–325
Find And Replace, 371–373
Flash Fill, 326–327
Fonts gallery, 357
Forecast Sheet, 523–524
Format Cells, 311
Format Cells dialog box, 346–347, 350–351, 362
Format Painter, 362
formulas, 383
   arithmetic operators, 389
   comparison operators, 390
   copying, 404
   creating, 389–390
   editing, 389–391
   editing cell references, 392
   entering, 391
   error messages, 417–418
   moving, 404
   operands, 390
   operator precedence, 390–391
   proofing, 417–421
   range names in, 399–400
Formulas tab, 397
   Calculation, 398
   Defined Names, 397
   Formula Auditing, 397
   Function Library, 397
Freeze Panes command, 376

Function Arguments, 398
Function Arguments dialog box, 393
Function Library, 397–399
functions, 319, 384, 387, 392
   arguments, 392–393
   AutoSum, 394–395
   categories, 396
   compatibility, 417
   copying, 404
   cube, 416
   date and time, 414
   engineering, 416
   entering, 393
   error messages, 417–418
   financial functions, 405–407
   Function Arguments, 401
   information, 416
   Insert Function command, 396–397
   logical functions, 407–409
   Lookup & reference, 410–413
   math & trig, 416
   moving, 404
   proofing, 417–418
   range names in, 399–401
   resources, 387
   searching for, 396
   statistical functions, 395, 409–410
   SUM, 392, 394
   text, 414–416
Goal Seek, 510, 518–519
Greater Than dialog box, 364
Group command, 480–482
Home screen, 299
Illustrations group, 71
Import Data dialog box, 487
Insert Chart dialog box, 436
Insert dialog box, 370
Insert Function command, 396–397
Insert Sheet Columns, 374
Insert tab, 381
labels, 318–319

Linked Data Types, 298
Lookup function, 10
macros, 909
Manage Workbook area, 317
Merge & Center command, 370–371
Microsoft account, 299
Microsoft Power BI and, 10
Name box, 302
New Formatting Rule dialog box, 367
notes, 356
Number Format gallery, 350
number formats, 351–354
Number group, 350
numeric formats, 350
outlines, 480–482
page breaks, 335
Page Layout, 335
Page Setup group, 337–338
passwords, 310
Paste command, 327, 404
Paste gallery, 328–329
Paste Special, 329–331
percent style, 350
pivot tables, 494–502
PowerPoint and, 319
Protect Sheet dialog box, 313
Protect Workbook command, 310
range names, 378–379
  formulas, 399–400
  functions, 399–401
  naming from selection, 379–380
Range Password text box, 314
ranges
  Edit Name dialog box, 380
  edit ranges, 313–315
  moving, 331–332
  Name Manager, 380
  text formatting, 346
  transposing, 331

references
  absolute references, 388
  absolute referencing, 386–387
  editing in formulas, 392
  mixed references, 388
  relative referencing, 385
ribbon
  Analysis tab, 301
  Data tab, 301
  Formulas tab, 301
  Help tab, 301
  Home tab, 300
  Insert tab, 300
  Page Layout tab, 301
  Review tab, 301
  View tab, 301
rows
  AutoFit Row Height, 373
  deleting, 375
  freezing, 375–377
  height, 373–374
  hiding, 375
  inserting, 374
  Row Height dialog box, 374
Save This File dialog, 307
Scenario Manager, 511, 514
  cell specification, 515
  creating scenarios, 513–515
  naming, 514
  PivotTable reports, 517
  scenario summaries, 517
  Scenario Values dialog box, 515–516
  viewing scenarios, 516–518
Search box, 302
series, 322
  AutoFill, 323, 325
  custom, 325–326
  custom fill lists, 324–325
  date, 325
  Fill handle, 322–325
  filling, 321–322

Flash Fill, 322
growth, 325
linear, 325
Series dialog box, 325–326
Share button, 302
sheets, 299
  associated sheets, 509
  custom, tables and, 478–479
  deleting, 307
  external data, 298
  freezing rows and columns, 375–377
  graphics, 381–382
  hiding, 377
  images, 381–382
  inserting, 306
  inserting into workbooks, 306–307
  Insert Sheet Columns, 374
  navigating, 302–303
  Online Pictures, 381
  ordering, 306–307
  page breaks, 339–340
  Page Layout, 337–339
  passwords, 313
  permissions, 310
  printing, 337–343
  print titles, 340
  protecting, 311
  real-time data, 298
  renaming, 307
  shapes, 381
  Sheet1 tab, 302
  sheet references in cells, 402–404
  SmartArt, 381
  splitting, 377
  viewing, 334–336
Sheet View, 478
Sheet View group, 334
Show Formulas command, 384
Solver, 519–522
sorting, 468
Split command, 377

status bar, 302
Style dialog box, 361
styles, 362
Styles group, 360–361
subtotals, 483
tables, 461
  AutoFilter, 470–473
  AutoFilter Search box, 471
  columns, 462
  Create Table dialog box, 464
  creating, styles, 464–465
  criteria range, filters and, 476
  custom sheet views, 478–479
  data forms, 479–480
  data tables, 511
  defining ranges, 463–464
  External Table Data group, 466
  fields, 462
  Filter command, 479
  filtering, 470–471
  filters, advanced, 475–478
  Format as Table command, 463
  queries, 490–494
  slicers, 474–475
  Sort commands, 467
  Sort dialog box, 468–469
  sorting, 467–468
  Table Design Tools, 465–466
  Table Styles gallery, 464
  web tables, importing, 486
templates
  Blank Workbook, 299
  data arrangement, 306
  listing, 299
  new workbook, 304
  Office.com, 304–306
text
  alignment, 346
  entry, 318
  fonts, 345–346
  formatting, 345–348

orientation, 345, 348
  wrapping, 370–371
text files, importing, 486–487
themes, 357
Themes gallery, 357
time, 320
values, 318–319
View tab, 334
vlookup function, 10
Watch Window, 420
web tables, importing, 486
what-if analysis, 510–511
  Goal Seek, 510
Wolfram and, 10
workbooks
  inserting sheets, 306–307
  new, 303
  new, blank, 304
  permissions, 310
  protecting, 309, 311
  recovering unsaved, 317
  template, 304
Workbook Views, 334
Workbook Views group, 335
Zoom command, 336
Excel for the Web, 11
Excel Online, 112–116
Exchange ActiveSync, 671–672, 732
Exchange Server
  email accounts, 676
    Exchange before 2013, 677
  Outlook, 673
    account management, 732
    configuring, 682–684
    email address validity, 707
    Exchange ActiveSync, 671–672
    recalling messages, 720
Export command (Backstage), 30
exporting data, Outlook, 687, 689
Export page (Backstage), 53

F

Feedback command (Backstage), 31
field codes (Word)
  mail merge, 245
  TOC creation, 264–266
  viewing, 271
Field dialog box, 177–178
fields
  Contact (Outlook), 775–776
  mail merges (Word), 240
  Word
    date, 252
    Field Names list, 252
    form controls, 254
    inserting, 253
    page numbers, 252
file compression
  image files, 81
  lossless, 81
  lossy, 81
  resolution, 82
File Explorer, 60
  libraries, 60
  New Folder button, 61
  Search box, 63
file formats, 49
  blocked, 798
    security and, 807–809
  .bmp (bitmap), 70, 852
  compatibility, 49
  conversion utilities, 49
  converting, 53–54
  Excel, 50
  .gif (Graphics Interchange Format), 70, 852
  HTML files in email messages, 705, 708
  .jpg (Joint Photographic Experts Group), 70, 852
  PDF files, 51
  pictures, 82, 180
    .bmp (bitmap), 70, 81
    .gif (Graphics Interchange Format), 70, 81

.jpg (Joint Photographic Experts Group), 70, 81
.png (Portable Network Graphics), 70, 81, 852
.tif (Tagged Image File Format), 70, 81
.wmf, 81
Plain Text files, email messages, 705, 708
PowerPoint, 50
Publisher, 50
Rich Text files, email messages, 705, 708
.tif (Tagged Image File Format), 70, 852
web pages, 53
.wmf (Windows Metafile), 852
Word, 50
XML (eXtensible Markup Language), 49

file management, 59–60

files
access, 66
creating
Start screen, 56
templates, 58
themes, 58
digital signatures, 66
DRM (Digital Rights Management), 66
Editing, restricting, 65–66
macro-enabled, 907
message attachments (Outlook), 715
opening, 131
passwords, 65
Protect Document settings, 65
Add A Digital Signature, 66
Always Open Read-Only, 65
Encrypt with Password, 65
Mark as Final, 66
Restrict Access, 66
Restrict Editing, 65–66
read-only, 65
Recovered Unsaved File, 63
saving
as different file type, 52–53
AutoRecover and, 62
Default Local File Location box, 56
location, 55–56

options, 55–56
to cloud, 101
to OneDrive, 103
to OneDrive for Business, 103
searches, 63
templates, 56–57
text
importing to Excel, 486–487
inserting in Publisher, 851–852
themes, 57
versions, 62
AutoRecover and, 62
Manage Document (Word), 62
video, PowerPoint, 639

file sharing, 6
between applications, 887
Check For Issues button, 67
files saved to cloud, 104–106
PDF files, 51
Word
older versions, 107
private copies of shared documents, 11
XPS (XML Paper Specification) format, 51

Files (Teams), 9

File tab
Backstage, 28
Excel Online, 113
PowerPoint Online, 118
Word Online, 107

fills
Excel, 362
PowerPoint, 574
Publisher, 846

filters
Outlook messages, 724
tables (Excel), 470–478

financial functions (Excel), 405–406

Find And Replace (Excel), 371–373

Find And Replace dialog box, 139

firewalls, 798

flat file databases, 462

folders, 59–61

fonts

Excel, 345–346, 357, 362

OpenType, 142, 146

PowerPoint, 557, 573

proportional, 142

Publisher, 847

themes, 170, 718

Word, 132, 142–143, 146

Word Online, 109

footers

Excel, 342–343

PowerPoint, 576–577

Publisher, 870–871

Word, 172–179

footnotes (Word), 269, 278–279

Forecast Sheet (Excel), 523–524

Format tab

SmartArt, 79–80

Word, 185

formatting

character formatting, 141

paragraph formatting, 141

templates, 132

forms (Word), 254

Formula dialog box, 226

G

galleries, 20

Excel, 357–359

Header, 174

PowerPoint, New Slide, 536

Number Format, 350

Paragraph Spacing, 171

Picture Styles, 83

Quick Analysis, 438

Shapes, 71

Style Set, 170

Table of Contents, 260

Themes, 169, 571

Excel, 357

.gif (Graphics Interchange Format), 81, 852

PowerPoint, 11

Gmail calendar (Outlook), 687

Goal Seek (Excel), 518–519

Google email accounts, 676

grammar checking

PowerPoint, 643

Word, 194

Word Online, 111

graphics, 69

benefits, 69

copyright laws, 70

Excel Online, 115

Excel sheets, 381–382

HTML email, 806

icons, 71

online pictures, 70

PowerPoint, 585–586

3D models, 586

charts, 586

icons, 586

Online Pictures, 590

photo album, 591–593

pictures, 586–589

screenshots, 586

shapes, 586

SmartArt, 586, 596, 599–600

stock images, 586, 589–590

Word Art text boxes, 587

Publisher, 852–856

ribbon, Insert tab, 71

Screen Clipping tool, 93

screenshots, 93–94

shapes, 71

SmartArt, 69, 71

diagrams, 69

gallery, 75–76

lists, 75

stock images, 70

WordArt, 71

graphics card requirements, 15

Graphics Manager (Publisher), 840
gridlines (PowerPoint), 546
grouping shapes, 90

H

handouts (PowerPoint), 576
hard drive requirements, 14
hardware requirements, 14
Header & Footers Tools Design tab (Word), 175
Header gallery, 174
headers
    Excel, 342–343
    PowerPoint, 576–577
    Publisher, 870–871
    Word, 172–179
headings (Word), 269
Help system, 16–17
hex color codes, 297
Home command (Backstage), 29
Home tab
    Clipboard group, 20
    PowerPoint Online, 118
    Style group, 25
Home window, Start screen, 129
horizontal scrollbar, 24
HTML documents (Publisher), 830
HTML email, 806–807
HTML files in email messages, 705, 708
hyperlinks
    PowerPoint, 608–609
    table of contents (TOC), 262

I

iCalendar (Outlook), 687
icons, 71
    bulleted lists, 596
    PowerPoint, 586, 595
Illustrations group
    Excel, 71
    Word, 71

images, 69
    clip art, 74
    compressing, 85
    Creative Commons license, 74
    cropping, 86
    Excel sheets, 381–382
    files, compression, 81
    HTML email, 806
    Online Pictures command, 74
    Publisher, 852–856
    resolution, 82
    stock images, 10, 70, 129
    text layout around, 88
    Word, 182–187, 266–267
Images and Illustrations (PowerPoint), 72
IMAP (Internet Message Access Protocol), 677, 732
IMAP protocol, email, 672
Immersive Reader view (Word Online), 106
Import/Export (Outlook), 687
Import/Export button, 34
importing data to Outlook, 687–689
indexes (Word), 271–273
Info command (Backstage), 30
information functions (Excel), 416
Insert Chart dialog box (Word), 184
insertion point, Word documents, 138
Insert Picture dialog box, 72, 82
Insert Shapes group (Shape Format tab), 92
Insights task pane, 23
Inspect Document option, 67
installation, Microsoft 365, 15
interface
    application window, 22–24
    Contextual tabs, 21
    customizing, 31
    galleries, 20
    Home tab, 20
    ribbon, 19
Internet email, 672–673
ISP (Internet Service Provider), 672

italic text
  PowerPoint, 556
  Word, 126

J–K

Journal (Outlook), 691
.jpg (Joint Photographic Expert Group), 81, 852

keyboard, text selection, 140

L

labels
  Excel, 318–319
  Word, 234–235, 251–252
landscape orientation, 156, 863
Language group (Review tab), 19
Language options, 38
Layout tab (Word)
  Breaks, 228
  Columns dialog box, 226–227
  Page Setup group, 155–157
libraries, 60
  creating, 61
  File Explorer, 60
  Function Library (Excel), 397–399
  Pictures, 72
  Stock Images, 72–73, 183
licensing, 12–13
line charts, 184
line spacing
  Word, 146–149
  Word Online, 110
linking objects between applications, 891
  Object command, 894–895
  Paste Options gallery, 893–894
  Paste Special, 891–892
links
  breaking, 895–897
  copying, sharing from cloud, 106
  text boxes (Publisher), 848–851

updating, 895–897
web tables to Excel, 486
Links dialog box, 896–897
lists, SmartArt, 75
Live Preview, 25
logarithmic scale, chart axes, 449
lossless compression, 81
lossy compression, 81

M

M4A files, 626
macros, 903–905
  button, Quick Access Toolbar, 912–913
  commands, 910–911
  creating, 910–911
  Developer tab, 910–911
  digitally signing, 917–920
  editing, 915–916
  enabling, Trust Center, 905–906
  Excel, saving, 909
  macro-enabled files, 907
  naming conventions, 911
  Normal template, 913
  Outlook, 910
  PowerPoint, 910
  Publisher, 910
  recording, 911–912
  running, 914
  saving, 909–910
  VBA Editor, 915–917
  VBA (Visual Basic for Applications), 905
  viruses, 906
  Word, 909
mail merges (Publisher), 877–880
mail merges (Word), 236–238
  address block, 245
  commands, 238–239
  Compete The Merge, 250
  document type, 237
  envelopes, 251–252
  fields, 240

greeting line, 246
labels, 251–252
Mail Merge Wizard, 237–238
merge fields, 245–247
Outlook Contact list, 241
Outlook Contacts, 787
previewing, 249
recipient list, 238–245
records, 240
Rules, 248–249
Mail Options window (Outlook), 737–738
mail-related documents (Word), 231
address block, 245
Complete The Merge, 250
envelopes, 232, 234
merged, 251–252
greeting line, 246
labels, 234–235
merged, 251–252
mail merges, 236–239
mass mailings, 236–238
Contacts list, 236
merge fields, 245–247
merge preview, 249
merge rules, 248–249
Outlook Contact list, 241
recipient list, 240–245
malware software, 798–799
HTML email, 806
margins
Excel, 337
Word, 132, 155
master documents (Word), 257, 290, 294
inserting existing documents, 293–294
Outline view, 290–291
subdocuments, 292–293
master pages (Publisher), 838, 868–872
**meeting requests (Outlook), responding to,
793–794**
Meetings (Teams), 9
memory requirements, 14

menus, shortcut menus, 23
Merge Shapes command, 90–91
Microsoft 365
account, 732
email accounts, 676
installation, 15, 670
Office Home & Student, 13
purchasing, 13
subscription, 5
Microsoft 365 Business premium, 14
Microsoft 365 Business standard, 14
Microsoft account
Excel, 299
OneDrive and, 97
Microsoft Azure Information Protection, 14
Microsoft Defender Application Guard, 129
Microsoft ID, 15
Microsoft Intune, 14
Microsoft Office subscriptions, 13
Microsoft Power BI, Excel and, 10
Microsoft Query, 490–494
Microsoft SQL Server, 461
Microsoft Teams, 9, 12
**MIDI (Musical Instrument Digital Interface) files,
626**
Mini Toolbar (Word), 145
modern comments, 6
monofont type, 142
mouse
text selection, 140
Word documents, 138
MP3 files (Moving Picture Experts Group), 626
MP4 files, 626
Music library, 60

N

naming system, folders, 59
navigating documents (Word), 137–139
Navigation bar (Outlook), 690–692
Navigation pane (Word), 189–190
New command (Backstage), 29

new features, 8
New Group button, 34
New page (Backstage), 58
  Excel, 113
  Word, 132
New Slide dialog box, 119
New Tab button, 34
Normal template
  macros, 913
  Word, 132
note pages (PowerPoint), 576
notes (Excel), 356
numbered items, 75
  PowerPoint, 551–552, 556
  Word, 162, 164, 269

O

Object command, linking objects, 894–895
objects, PowerPoint slides, 542, 606–607
ODBC (Open Database Connectivity), 491
Office, perpetual version, 5
Office 365 Family, 13
Office 365 Personal, 14
Office.com (Excel), 304–306
Office for the Web, 7
Office Home & Student, 13
Office Presentation Service, 658
OLAP (Online Analytical Processing), 494
OLE (object linking and embedding), 888–890
  editing linked objects, 897–898
  embedding objects, 898–901
  linking objects, 891–895
  linking versus embedding, 890
  links, breaking, 895–897
  Links dialog box, 896–897
OneDrive, 8, 59
  as default location, 102
  Excel, 299
  Microsoft account and, 97
  Microsoft ID and, 15

Online Pictures dialog box, 74
  paid versus free version, 98
  Personal Vault, 99
  Personal version, 98
  pictures, 73, 181
  PowerPoint presentations, 665
  saving files to, 103
  SharePoint and, 104
  Word, new files, 107
OneDrive for Business, 8, 103
Online apps, 7, 97
  browsers, 99
  Excel, 112–116
  file saving to cloud, 101, 103
  location, 99–100
  PowerPoint, 117
  PowerPoint Online, 98
  viewers, 100
  Wi-Fi and, 100
  Word, 100, 106–112
Online Pictures, 70, 74
  Creative Commons license, 71
  Excel sheets, 381
  PowerPoint, 590
Online Pictures browser (Word), 183–184
Open command (Backstage), 29
OpenType fonts, 142, 146
Open window, Start screen, 129
Open window (Word), 131
operator precedence, Excel formulas, 390–391
Options command (Backstage), 31
Options window, 38, 55
Organizer window (Word), 206
.ost (Offline Store) files, 682
outlines
  Excel, 480–482
  PowerPoint slides, 542
  Word, 290–294
Outline view (Word), 190, 192

Outlook, 12

account management

  account setup, 674

  adding accounts automatically, 735

  adding accounts manually, 735–736

  Exchange ActiveSync, 732

  Exchange Server, 732

  IMAP account, 732

  Microsoft 365 account, 732

  Outlook.com, 732

  POP3 account, 732

  settings, editing, 734

Address Book, 706

Address Book dialog box, 706

address validity, 707

Advanced Setup window, 676

application window, 690–691

Archive, 702

archiving

  AutoArchive, 819–822

  manual, 822–823

Arrangement commands, 724

Attached box, 715

Attach Item command, 716

attachments, 715–716

  blocked file formats, 807–809

  business cards, 716

  calendars, 717

  files, 715

  Outlook items, 716

  saving, 728–729

  security, 807–810

Attachments tab, 728–729

Automatic Replies command, 824–826

Backstage, log in, 800

blocked files, 798

blocked senders, 813

Calendar, 691

  appointment reminders, 744

  appointment scheduling, 743–747

  Contacts, meetings, 789–790

Date Navigator, 740

Day view, 740–741

editing meetings, 792–793

Email Calendar option, 754

emailing calendars, 754–755

emailing items, 754

event scheduling, 746–747

meeting location, 790–791

meetings, responding to requests, 793–794

Month view, 741

multiple, viewing, 752–753

My Calendars list, 739

navigating, 739–743

opening shared calendars, 752

Options window, 757

Overlay, 753

Publish Online feature, 755

publishing calendars online, 755–756

Schedule view, 742

Scheduling Assistant, 758, 791–792

ScreenTips, 740

searching, 748–750

sharing calendars, 750

sharing invitations, 750, 752, 756

time scale, 742

time zones, 743–744, 758

viewing meetings, 792–793

weather, 741

Week view, 741

work time, 757

Work Week view, 741

Calendar pane, 702

calendars

  Gmail, 687

  iCalendar, 687

  opening files, 687

categories, 695–696

Check Names dialog box, 708

command sets, 705

Compose Messages options, 737

configuring, 673
  Exchange Server, 682–684
Contacts, 691, 769
  Actions group, 787
  Arrangement group, 771
  associating with messages, 714
  business card attachments, 716
  business cards, editing, 777–778
  Business Card view, 770
  Card view, 770
  categories, 779
  Communicate commands, 786
  Communicate group, 785
  Contact dialog box, 772
  creating, 772–776
  Edit Business Card dialog box, 778
  editing, 776–777
  entering details, 774
  fields, additional, 775–776
  fields, business cards, 778
  filing options, 788
  follow-up flags, 779
  forwarding, 783–784
  groups, 781–782
  index, 788
  List view, 771
  mail merges, 236, 241
  mail merge, Word and, 787
  mapping address, 780
  Meeting command, 789
  meeting location, 790–791
  meeting scheduling, 789–790
  meetings, editing, 792–793
  meetings, Scheduling Assistant, 791–792
  meetings, viewing, 792–793
  moving, 787
  online status, 788
  options, 788
  People view, 770
  Phone view, 771
  photograph, 788

  photos, 774
  printing, 788
  Search People box, 780
  sharing, 784–785
  sorting, 771
  tagging, 779
  Tags group, 779
  vCards, 783
Contacts folder, searching, 780–781
Conversation Cleanup options, 737
Conversation History, 702
Data File dialog box, 683
data files, 680–681
  folder, 682
  .ost (Offline Store) files, 682
  .pst (personal storage file) files, 682
  repairing, 685–686
data sharing, 901–902
Deleted Items, 702
Details pane, 722
dictation toolbar, 11
Drafts, 702
email
  calendar items, 754
  focused, 693
email accounts, 670–677
  settings, 680
email rules, 814–819
Exchange ActiveSync, 671–672
Exchange Server, 673
exporting data, 687–689
Find dialog box, 707
Focused Inbox, 703, 722
Follow Up, 709
forwarding messages, 728
Import/Export command, 687
importing data, 687–689
Inbox, 702–703, 722
Inbox Repair Tool dialog box, 686
international filter, 813
Junk, 730

Junk command, 810–811

Junk Email, 702, 810–813

macros, 910

Mail folder, 701

Mail Merge Contacts options, 787

Mail Options window, 737–738

MailTips options, 737

Message Arrival options, 737

Message Format options, 738

messages

   attachments, 704

   categories, associating, 714

   contacts, associating, 714

   conversation cleanup, 730

   creating, 704–705

   deleting, 729–730

   delivery options, 712–713

   downloading, 721

   file formats, 708

   filtering, 724

   flags, 709–710

   ignoring, 730

   importance, 709–710

   moving, 731

   printing, 731

   recalling, 720–721

   saving sent, 712

   sending, 720

   sensitivity level, 710–711

   stationary, 718

   themes, 718

   time sent, 712

   translating, 729

   types, 705

Navigation bar, 690–692

Navigation Options dialog box, 692

New Email command, 704

Open Calendar command, 687

Outbox, 703

Outlook Panes group, 737

People, Address Book, 706

People pane, 702

personal folders, 684–685

POP3 accounts, 671–672

printing, 698–699

profiles, 677–678

   creating, 678–679

   data files, 680, 682

   loading, 681

   managing, 679–680

   multiple, 678

   Use This Profile, 681

Properties dialog box, 713–714

Quick Click command, 779

Quick Steps, 725, 727

   creating, 726

   Done, 725

   gallery, 725

   Manage Quick Steps, 726

   Move To, 725

   Reply & Delete, 725

reading messages, 721

   as conversations, 723–724

   filtering, 724

   Inbox organization, 722

   threaded conversations, 724

Reading pane, 722

receipts, delivery, 712

receipts, read, 712

reminder follow-ups, 779

Replies and Forwards options, 737

replying to messages, 727

RSS Feeds, 703

Save Messages options, 737

Scheduling Assistant, 789

searches, 696–697, 707

   Advanced Find, 697

   search folders, 697–698

Search folders, 703

security, 797

   attachments, 803

   digital IDs, 804

digital signatures, 804, 806
downloads, 803
email, 803
encrypted email, 804–806
HTML email, 806–807
junk mail, 810–813
log requirement, 800
message attachments, 807–810
password, 799–801
safe senders, 807
settings, 801, 803
Send And Receive command, 720
Send Messages option, 737
Sent Items, 702
Show As Conversations, 723
signatures, 719–720
spelling and grammar, 704
stock images, 670
Sync Issues, 703
Tasks, 759–760
  accepting, 762
  assigning, 762–763
  creating, 761–763
  marking complete, 766
  moving, 767
  options, 767–768
  recurring tasks, 761
  Task list, 763, 765
  tasks, 766
  Tasks folder, 760
  To-Do Bar, 758
  views, 763
Tasks pane, 702
templates, automatic replies, 826
text messaging, 784
Themes command, 718
To-Do Bar, 701–702
Tracking group, 711
Tracking options, 738
Translator, 669
Trust Center, 801–803

updates, 669
views, 692–695, 703
View tab, 694
voice commands, 11
voting buttons, 711–712
Outlook.com
  account management, 732
  email accounts, 672, 676

P

Page Break command, 110
page breaks
  Excel sheets, 339–340
  Word, 157
page numbers (Word), 178–179
  fields, 252
  TOC and, 258–259
paragraph formatting, 141
  PowerPoint, 558
    alignment, 558
    SmartArt, 558
    text direction, 558
  Word, 146–147
    alignment, 147
    double spacing, 149
    exact spacing, 149
    indents, 151–152
    line spacing, 148–149
    multiple spacing, 149
    single spacing, 149–150
    tabs, 152–154
paragraph spacing, themes, 170
Paragraph Spacing gallery, 171
passwords, 799–801
  Excel, 310, 313
  files, 65
Paste options, 40
Paste Options, linking objects, 893–894
Paste Special
  embedding objects, 899–900
  linking objects, 891–892

pattern fills (PowerPoint), 575
PDF documents, 51
  Publisher, 830
  PowerPoint presentations, 663
People pane (Outlook), 702
perpetual version of Office, 5
Personal Vault, 99
phishing email, 810
photographs in Outlook Contacts, 788
picture fills (PowerPoint), 574
picture placeholders (SmartArt), 77
pictures
  artistic effects, 84
  Background Removal tool, 86, 88
  clip art, 74
  color correction, 84
  copyright law, 70
  corrections, 83
  Creative Commons license, 74
  cropping, 86
  digital, 70
  Excel sheets, 381
  file compression, 85
  file formats, 180
    .bmp (bitmap), 70
    .gif (Graphics Interchange Format), 70
    .jpg (Joint Photographic Experts Group), 70
    .png (Portable Network Graphics), 70
    .tif (Tagged Image File Format), 70
  icons, 71
  inserting, 82
  Insert Picture dialog box, 72
  modifying, 83
  OneDrive, 73, 181
  online, 70
  Online Pictures command, 74
  photo file types, 82
  Picture Tools Format tab, 74
  PowerPoint, 586–593
  PowerPoint Online, 120
  removing background, 83

  screenshots, 71
  Search Pictures box, 72
  shapes, 71
  sizing, SmartArt, 78
  stock images, 10, 70, 180
  Word, 179–180
    Image Search browser, 183
    inserting, 180–182
    online pictures, 184
    Online Pictures browser, 183–184
    stock images, 182–184
    text and, 186–187
Pictures command, 72, 82
  Word, 180–182
Pictures library, 60, 72
Picture Styles gallery, 83
Picture Tools, 181
Picture Tools Format tab, 74, 83
pie charts, 184
Pinned headings, 129
PivotTable reports (Scenario Manager), 517
placeholder text, templates, 133
Plain Text files, email messages, 705, 708
.png (Portable Network Graphics), 81, 852
POP3 accounts, 671–672, 732
POP (Post Office Protocol), 672, 676
portrait orientation, 156
PowerPath, animation, 622
PowerPoint, 12, 529
  3D models, 586
  access tools, 645
  action buttons, 656
  Advanced Animation group, 622
  animation, 611–614
    additional, 624–625
    assigning, 615
    Effect Options, 619, 623
    effects, 615–622
    motion path, 616–622
    sound effects, 625–627

timings, 627–628
triggering, 622
Animation Exit group, 614
Animation gallery, 614–616
Animation Painter, 622, 625
Animation pane, 628–629
Animations tab, 614
Backstage, 101, 532
bulleted lists, 549, 551, 556
Bullets and Numbering dialog box, 550, 552
Bullets gallery, 550
Chart command, 602–604
charts, 70, 586, 602–606
collaboration, 665–666
Custom Slide Show command, 649
Effect Option command, 623
Effects, 562
Effect tab, 621
Excel sheets, 319
Eyedropper tool, 560
file types, 50
Font dialog box, 558
Font group, 557
footers, 576–577
Format Shape task pane, 561, 564–566
GIFs, animated, 11
grammar checking, 643
graphics, 585–586
    3D models, 586
    charts, 586
    icons, 586
    Online Pictures, 590
    pictures, 586–589
    screenshots, 586
    shapes, 586
    SmartArt, 586, 596, 599
    stock images, 585–586, 589–590
    WordArt text boxes, 587
gridlines, 546
guides, 546
handouts, 576, 659–663

Header And Footer dialog box, 576
headers, 576–577
hyperlinks, 608–609
icons, 586, 595
Images and Illustrations, 72
Insert Picture dialog box, 587
Layout commands, 567–568
Layout gallery, 543
layout masters, 581–582
Layout tab, 567
line types, 561
macros, 910
Mail Setup dialog box, 680
New Slide command, 540
New Slide gallery, 536
note pages, 576
notes, 659
    Notes Master, 661
    printing, 661, 663
numbered lists, 551–552, 556
Numbering command, 552
objects, 606
    grouping, 607
    layering, 607
Office Presentation Service, 658
Options window, 538
Outline view, 541
Paragraph dialog box, 558
Paragraph group, 557
photo albums, 591–593
pictures, 587–589
Pictures command, 587
Picture Tools, 588
PowerPoint Export tools, 663
presentations
    appearance, 539
    audience considerations, 642
    copies, 531
    creating, 530–536
    creating from existing, 535
    exporting, 663–664

from existing, 531
interactive, 656–658
PDF file, 663
place, 642
planning, 641–642
printing, 661, 663
purpose, 642
run through, 644–645
saving as template, 538
self-running, 652–656
sharing, 665–666
slideshows, 545
themes, 535
viewing during editing, 552–554
windows, 548
Presentation Views, 543
  Normal, 543–544
  Notes Page, 543–544
  Outline, 544
  Reading View, 544
  Slide Sorter, 544, 549
Presenter Coach, 645–646
Presenter view, 646–648
Proofing option, 643
quick styles, 559
Recent list, 535
Record Slide Show command, 654
Reuse Slides task pane, 536
rulers, 546
screenshots, 586
Section command, 582
Set Up Show dialog box, 652
shape attributes, 559
Shape Effects, 559–561
Shape Fill, 559–561
Shape Format tools, 559
Shape Outline, 559–561
shapes, 586, 593–594
  Effects, 562
  File or Line options, 561

fill, 559–561
  formatting, 561, 563
shape styles, 559
Shape Styles group, 561, 563
Skype for Business, 658
Slide Master command, 578
Slide Master tab, 579–580
slides
  black and white, 547
  Blank option, 540
  color, 547
  custom slide show, 649, 651–652
  deleting, 549
  from Word outline, 542
  grayscale, 547
  hidden slides, 648–649
  inserting, 540, 542
  layout modification, 543
  layout type, 540
  master slide creation, 579–581
  master slides, 577–579
  objects, inserting, 542
  rearranging, 549
  reusing, 536
  sound, 634–635
  tables, inserting, 566
  text entry, 541–542
  Title and Content option, 540
  Title Slide option, 540
  video, 636, 639–640
slide sections, 582, 584
slideshows, 545
  recording, 654–656
Slide Sorter, 582
SmartArt, 586, 596–601
smart guides, 546
Snap Objects To Grid option, 546
sound, trimming audio, 636
Start screen, 529
stock images, 589–590
Symbol dialog box, 550

Table Design commands, 568, 570
Table Design tab, 567
tables
  3D effects, 570
  formatting, 567–570
  on slides, 566
templates, 531–534
text
  alignment, 558
  effects, 564–566
  fill, 563
  font attributes, 557
  outline, 564
  paragraph attributes, 558
  SmartArt, 558
  text direction, 558
  WordArt, 563
Text Box command, 556
text boxes, 559
  fill, 559–561
  Fill or Line, 561
  inserting, 556–557
  photo albums, 592
  Word Art, 587
Text Effects command, 564
Text Fill command, 563
Text Options, 564
Text Outline command, 564
themes, 570–571
  applying, 571
  backgrounds, 574–575
  colors, 572
  considerations, 570
  custom, 575
  effects, 574
  fills, 574
  fonts, 573
  photo album, 593
  Variants gallery, 571
timings, 654
transitions, 611–614, 630–633

Trim Audio command, 636
Video Tools, 640
Zoom, 651–652
zooming, 545
PowerPoint Designer, 609–610
PowerPoint for the Web, 11
PowerPoint Online, 98, 117
  Designer pane, 117
  Editing View, 119
  New Slide command, 119
  Notes, 119
  pictures, 120
  presentations, new, 119
  ribbon, 98
    Animations tab, 118
    Design tab, 118
    Draw tab, 118
    File tab, 118
    Help tab, 119
    Home tab, 118
    Insert tab, 118
    Review tab, 118
    Slide Show tab, 118
    Transitions tab, 118
    View tab, 118
  Slides, new, 119
  Slide Show, 119
  Slide Sorter, 119
  SmartArt, 120
  status bar, 119
Prezi, 540
Print command (Backstage), 30
printers, Publisher and, 831
printing
  Outlook, 698–699
    Contacts information, 788
    email messages, 731
  PowerPoint
    handouts, 661, 663
    notes, 661, 663
    presentations, 661, 663

Publisher, 831, 858–859
white space and, 831
Word, 157–159
   envelopes, 234
Excel worksheets, 337–343
Print options, 41
processor requirements, 14
profiles (Outlook), 677–678
creating, 678–679
data files, 680, 682
loading, 681
managing, 679–680
multiple, 678
Use This Profile, 681
Proofing group (Review tab), 19
Proofing option (PowerPoint), 643
Proofing options, 38
proportional fonts, 142
Protect Document, 65
Add A Digital Signature, 66
Always Open Read-Only, 65
Encrypt with Password, 65
Mark As Final, 66
Restrict Access, 66
Restrict Editing, 65–66
Protect group (Review tab), 19
Protect tab, Proofing group, 19
.pst (personal storage file) files , 682
Publisher, 12, 829–830
advertisements, 858
balanced documents, 831
baseline guides, 840
blank pages, 834
borders, 858
boundaries, 840
Building Blocks group, 857–858
Business Information, 834
business information set, 841–843
Calendars, 857
clip art, 856–857
Customize pane, 834

data merges, 877–882
Design Checker, 883–884
Drawing Tools
   Arrange command, 846
   Insert Shapes group, 845
   Shape Styles group, 845
   text boxes and, 845–846
Draw Text Box command, 844
fields, 840
file formats
   .bmp (bitmap), 852
   .gif (Graphics Interchange Format), 852
   .jpg (Joint Photographic Expert Group), 852
   .png (Portable Network Graphics), 852
   .tif (Tagged Image File Format), 852
   .wmf (Windows Metafile), 852
Graphics Manager, 840
guides, 840
Guides gallery, 839
Home page, 831
HTML documents, 830
hyphenation, 882
illustrations, 852–856
Layout guide, 838
macros, 910
Mailings tab, 878
master pages, 868
   creating, 871–872
   footers, 870–871
   headers, 870–871
   Layout guide, 838
   object placement, 869–870
Master Page view, 840
More Blank Pages option, 834
Normal view, 840
object alignment, 846
object arrangement, 846
objects
   groups, 875
   layers, 876
   swapping, 876–877

Page Design tab, 863–864, 866
Page Navigation, 840
page settings, 863–864, 866
Pages group, 861
page size, 864
Pages pane, 837, 840
PDF documents, 830
picture placeholder, 853–854
pictures, 852–856
  clip art, 856–857
  formatting, 856
  swapping, 876–877
printing, 831
printing publications, 858–859
print versus electronic publications, 830
.pub files, 50
publications
  adding pages, 861–863
  duplicate pages, 862
  margins, 863
  orientation, 863
  Page Setup group, 863
  planning, 830–831
  saving as template, 835
  viewing, 840–841
ribbon, 836
Ruler Guides option, 839
rulers, 837–838, 840
scratch area, 840
shapes, 857
  fills, 846
  styles, 845
  wrap points, 845
Shapes gallery, 845
Spelling feature, 882
status bar, 836
tables, 872
  alignment, 874
  arranging, 874
  columns, 874
  Design commands, 872–873

Layout commands, 873–874
  merging cells, 874
  rows, 874
  sizing, 874
Table Tools, 872–874
templates, 831–833
  blank, 834
  changing, 866–867
  creating, 835–836
  Manufacturers folder, 834
  More Templates link, 832
  Publication Types folder, 834
  saving publication as, 835
  searching for, 832
text boxes
  alignment, 847
  creating, 844
  drawing tools and, 845–846
  drop caps, 848
  editing text, 844
  fonts, 847
  formatting, 844–846
  linking, 848–851
  sizing, 846
  text size, 847
  typography, 848
  WordArt Styles, 848
Text Box Tools tab, 846–849
text files, inserting, 851–852
View shortcuts, 836
View tab, 840
windows, 841
Word documents, inserting, 851
XPS documents, 830
Zoom, 841

Q

queries, Excel tables, 490–494
Quick Access Toolbar, 23
  Customize Quick Access Toolbar, 28, 35–36
  customizing, 35–37

keyboard shortcuts, 28

macro button, 912–913

Save button, 53

Quick Analysis gallery, Excel charts, 438

Quick Parts (Word)

AutoText entries, 196

building blocks, 197

Building Blocks Organizer, 177

footers, 177

headers, 177

Quick Steps (Outlook), 725–726, 727

Quick Styles (Word), 200–205

Quick Tables, 211

R

radar charts, 184

RAM requirements, 14

Reading view (Word Online), 106

Read Mode (Word), 132

read-only files, 65

Recent headings, Shared With Me list, 129

Recent list, 56

Pinned headings, 129

recording macros, 911–912

records, mail merges (Word), 240

Recovered Unsaved File, 63

Redo button, 23

relational databases, 462

Rename button, 34

repairing data files, Outlook, 685

Reset button, 34

resolution, file compression and, 82

Resume Assistant (Review tab), 19

Review tab

Changes group, 19

Comments group, 19

Compare group, 19

Language group, 19

PowerPoint Online, 118

Proofing group, 19

Resume Assistant, 19

Speech group, 19

Tracking group, 19

Word, 193

Word Online, 111

ribbon, 19, 23

Customize Ribbon window, 33

customizing, 32–33

Developer tab, 904–905

Excel Online, 112–116

Insert tab, 71

keyboard shortcuts, 27

minimizing, 26

PowerPoint Online, 98, 118–119

Word, 125, 136

Word Online, 107–112

Ribbon Display Options button, 26

ribbon tabs, 25

Rich Text files, email messages, 705, 708

RSS Feeds (Outlook), 691

ruler, 24, 32

PowerPoint, 546

Publisher, 837–838

Word, 151, 153

running macros, 914

S

Save As command (Backstage), 30

Save As dialog box, 52

Change File type option, 54

file type conversion, 53

folders, 60

Save As Type drop-down, 52

Save button, 23

Save command (Backstage), 30

Save This File dialog box, 104

saving files

as different file type, 52–53

AutoRecover and, 62

Default Local File Location box, 56

location, 55–56

options, 55–56

Quick Access Toolbar, 53
web page formats, 53
scanpst.exe file, 685
Scenario Manager (Excel), 511, 514–518
Scheduling Assistant (Outlook), 791–792
Screen Clipping tool, 93–94
screenshots, 71, 93–94, 586
scrollbars, 24
Search box, 5
searches
Bing and, 6
Calendar (Outlook), 748–750
closing, 17
Excel, 302
File Explorer, 63
files, 63
functions (Excel), 396
Get Help On area, 17
Help and, 16
Open dialog box, 64
Outlook, 696–698, 703, 707, 780–781
Tell Me What You Want To Do, 4
templates
Publisher, 832
PowerPoint, 532–533
Word, 195
Search Pictures box, 72
security
blocked files, 798
Defender, 799
digital IDs, 804
Excel, 310, 362
Excel workbooks, 309
firewalls, 798
Outlook, 797, 800–813
passwords, 799–801
phishing, 810
software, 798–799
Trust Center, 45
Trusted Locations list, 46–47
Trusted Publishers list, 45

viruses, 798–799
web beacons, 807
Send Link dialog box, 105
Shape Format command, 91, 93
Shape Format tab
Accessibility group, 92
Arrange group, 92
Insert Shapes group, 92
Shape Styles group, 92
Size group, 92
Text group, 92
WordArt Styles group, 92
shapes, 69
Excel sheets, 381
grouping, 90
inserting, 71, 88
multiple, 89–91
PowerPoint, 586, 593–594
formatting, 561, 563
Publisher, 857
fills, 846
Shapes command, 88
Shapes gallery, 71, 88
multiple shapes, 89–91
PowerPoint, 593
Shape Styles group (Shape Format tab), 92
Share command (Backstage), 30
SharePoint, OneDrive for Business, 8
sharing data (Outlook), 901–902
sharing files, 8
saved to cloud, 104–106
Word, older versions, 107
workbooks in cloud, 105
shortcut menus, 23
Show/Hide command (Word), 141
signatures, email (Outlook), 719–720
Size group (Shape Format tab), 92
Skype for Business, 658
slicers (Excel), 474–475, 502
SmartArt, 71
Cycle category, 75
Design tab, 79, 601

diagrams, 75–77
Excel sheets, 381
Format tab, 79–80, 601
gallery, 76
Hierarchy category, 76
inserting, 76–78
Layouts gallery, 79
List category, 75
lists, 75
Matrix category, 76
modifying, 79, 81
Office.com category, 76
Picture category, 76
picture placeholders, 77
PowerPoint, 558, 586, 596–601
PowerPoint Online, 120
Process category, 75
Pyramid category, 76
Relationship category, 76
sizing, 78
Text pane, 77
WordArt Styles gallery, 80, 602
SmartArt command, 76–78
SmartArt graphics, 69
SMTP (Simple Mail Transport Protocol), 672
Solver (Excel), 519–522
sound (PowerPoint), 634–635
animations (PowerPoint), 625
editing options, 635
Trim Audio command, 636
Source Manager, 276–277
sparklines (Excel), 366
Speech group (Review tab), 19
spelling
Editor (Word), 192
email messages, 704
Publisher, 882
Word, 194
Word Online, 111
SQL Server databases, connecting to, 488
Start menu (Word), 128

stationary, email (Outlook), 718
statistical functions (Excel), 409–410
status bar, 24
customizing, 37
Excel, 302
PowerPoint Online, 119
stock images, 70, 129
Outlook, 670
PowerPoint, 585–586, 589–590
Word, 182–184
Stock Images library, 10, 72–73, 180, 183
Style group, 25
styles
Excel, 360–362
PowerPoint backgrounds, 574
shapes (Publisher), 845
templates, 134
Word, 142, 200
built-in, TOC and, 259–260
creating, 171
custom, TOC and, 261–262
editing, 203–204
managing, 204–207
Quick Styles, 200
Quick Styles gallery, 201–202
tables, 220–222, 223
TOC and, 258–262
Style Set gallery, 170
Styles window, 203
subscriptions, 12–13
Microsoft 365, 5
Microsoft 365 Business premium, 14
Microsoft 365 Business standard, 14
Office 365 Family, 13
Office 365 personal, 14

T

tab groups, 35
Table Design tools (Word), 216
alignment, 219
cell format, 219–220

columns, 217–218
merge cells, 219
rows, 217–218
styles, 220–223
text direction, 220
Table Of Contents gallery, 260
table of contents (TOC)
adding entries, 263
field codes, 264–266
generating, 265
hyperlinks, 262
inserting, 261
page numbers, 258–259
previewing, 262
styles, 258–262
Table of Contents dialog box, 261
updating, 263
Word, 258
table of figures (Word), 267–268
Table Tools (Word Online), 110
tables (Excel), 461
AutoFilter, 470–473
AutoFilter Search box, 471
Create Table dialog box, 464
creating, styles and, 464–465
data forms, 479–480
data tables, 511
External Table Data group, 466
Filter command, 479
filtering, 470–471
advanced, 475–478
criteria range, 476
slicers, 474–475
Format As Table command, 463
pivot tables, 494–495
creating, 497, 499–500
Design tab, 501
PivotTable Analyze tab, 500–501
Recommended Pivot Tables, 496–497
slicers and, 502
queries, 490–494

ranges, 463–464
sheets, custom views, 478–479
Sort commands, 467
Sort dialog box, 468–469
sorting, 467–468
sort order, 467
Table Design Tools, 465–466
Table Styles gallery, 464
web tables, importing, 486
tables (PowerPoint)
3D effects, 570
formatting, 567–570
in slides, 566
tables (Publisher), 872
alignment, 874
arranging, 874
columns, 874
merging cells, 874
rows, 874
sizing, 874
Table Tools, 872–874
tables (Word)
alignment, 219
AutoFit, 212
captions, 266–267
cell format, 219–220
column width, 212
converting text to, 211, 214
design, 126
drawing, 210, 213
Excel spreadsheet, 211
formulas, 225–226
inserting, 210–213
layout, 126
merge cells, 219
navigating, 214
positioning, 215–216
Quick Tables, 211
selecting, 215–216
sorting data, 224
styles, 220–223

Table Design tools, 216–220
Table Drawing tool, 213
table grid, 210
text deletion, 214
text direction, 220
text entry, 214
tables (Word Online), 110
tabs
Contextual tabs, 21
custom, 34
ribbon tabs, 25
Word, 153–154
Tabs list, 34
task panes, 23
Tasks (Outlook), 702, 759–760
accepting, 762
assigning, 762–763
creating, 761–763
editing, 766
marking complete, 766
moving, 767
options, 767–768
recurring tasks, 761
Task list, 763, 765
Tasks folder, 760–763
To-Do Bar, 758
views, 763
TCP/IP (Transport Control Protocol/Internet Protocol) port, 797
Teams channel (Teams), 9
Tell Me What You Want To Do search box, 4
Template And Add-in dialog box, 136
templates, 56–58
Excel
Blank Workbook, 299
data arrangement, 306
data validation and, 509
listing, 299
new workbook, 304
Office.com, 304–306
formatting, 132

New window, 130
Normal, macros, 913
Outlook, automatic replies, 826
placeholder text, 133
PowerPoint, 531–534
Blank Presentation, 532
creating, 537–539
previewing, 534
saving presentations as, 538
searches, 532–533
Publisher, 831–833
blank, 834
changing, 866–867
creating, 835–836
Manufacturers folder, 834
More Templates link, 832
Publication Types folder, 834
searching for, 832
sample text, 133
styles, 134
Word, 130, 132
attaching to documents, 136
creating, 134–136
folders, 135
Normal, 132
themes, 169
Word Online, 107
text
Excel, 318
alignment, 346
fonts, 345–346
formatting, 345–348
functions, 414–415
importing files, 486–487
orientation, 345, 348
wrapping, 370–371
PowerPoint
alignment, 558
converting to SmartArt, 600
effects, 564–566
fill, 563
font attributes, 557

outline, 564
paragraph attributes, 558
quick styles, 559
shape attributes, 559
SmartArt, 558
text box fill, 559–561
text box formatting, 559
text direction, 558
WordArt, 563
Publisher
  drop caps, 848
  editing in text boxes, 844
  fonts, 847
  formatting text boxes, 844–846
  liking text boxes, 851
  linking, 848
  linking text boxes, 849–850
  size, 847
  text box creation, 844
  Text Box Tools tab, 846–849
  typography, 848
  WordArt Styles, 848
selecting
  keyboard, 140
  mouse, 140
slides (PowerPoint), 541–542
templates, 133
text boxes (PowerPoint)
  inserting, 556–557
Word
  converting to a table, 214
  tables, 214, 220
WordArt, 94–95
text boxes
PowerPoint
  hyperlinks, 608
  photo album, 592
  Word Art, 587
Publisher
  alignment, 847
  creating, 844

drawing tools and, 845–846
drop caps, 848
editing text, 844
fonts, 847
formatting, 844
linking, 848–851
sizing, 846
Text Box Tools tab, 846–849
text size, 847
typography, 848
WordArt Styles, 848
Text Effects gallery, 95
Text group (Shape Format tab), 92
Text pane (SmartArt), 77
texture fills (PowerPoint), 574
themes, 57–58
color, 170
default, 170
Document Formatting group, 170
effects, 170
email (Outlook), 718
Excel, 357
fonts, 170
paragraph spacing, 170
PowerPoint, 535, 570–575
  photo album, 593
Save As dialog box, 169
style sets, 170
templates, 169
Word, 142, 168–172
  deleting, 172
  email, 718
  Save Current Theme dialog box, 172
Themes gallery, 169
Excel, 357
PowerPoint, 571
.tif (Tagged Image File Format), 81, 852
time
Calendar (Outlook), 758
Excel, 320
title bar, 22

titles (Excel), 338
To-Do Bar (Outlook), 701–702
Track Changes (Word Online), 111
Tracking group (Review tab), 19
Transform command (Backstage), 30
Transitions tab (PowerPoint Online), 118
Translate (Word Online), 111
Translator (Outlook), 669
Trojan horses, 799
TrueType fonts, 142
Trust Center, 43
   accessing, 906
   macros, 905–906
   opening, 43
Trust Center (Outlook), 801–803
Trusted Locations list, 46–47
Trusted Publishers, 45
typography, text boxes (Publisher), 848

U

Undo button, 23
updates, 4, 128

V

VBA (Visual Basic for Applications), 905, 908
   macros
      editing, 915–916
      saving, 909–910
      stepping through, 916–917
   modules, 908
vCards (Outlook), 783
vertical scrollbar, 24
video (PowerPoint), 636
   online video, 636
   slides
      files, inserting, 639
      modifying clips, 640
Videos library, 60

views (Outlook), 692, 703
   advanced settings, 695
   Change View command, 693
   creating, 694
   custom, 694
   Focused Inbox, 692–693
   sorting, 703
   types, 694
   View tab, 694
View tab (Word), 187–189
View tab (PowerPoint Online), 118
View tab (Word Online), 112
viruses
   macros, 906
   software, 798–799
vlookup function (Excel), 10
voice commands (Outlook), 11
voting buttons (Outlook), 712

W

Watch Window (Excel), 420
.wav (Waveform Audio) files, 625
Web apps, 8
   Excel for the Web, 11
   PowerPoint for the Web, 11
web beacons, 807
WebDAV (Web Distributed Authoring and Versioning), 756
what-if analysis (Excel), 510–511
white space, 155
   printing and, 831
Wi-Fi, Online apps and, 100
Window group (Word), 187
windows
   Options, 55
   Options window, 38
   resizing, 774
Windows Defender Security Center, 798
Windows Reader, PDF files, 51
.wma (Windows Media Audio) files, 626
.wmf (Windows Metafile), 81, 852

Wolfram, Excel and, 10

Word, 12

AutoCorrect, 199

Backstage (Print window), 157–159

bibliographies, 274–278

blank documents, 130

bookmarks, 269, 288–289

borders, 166–168

building blocks, 197

bulleted lists, 162, 164

captions, 266–267

character formatting, 142

Chart Design tab, 185

charts, 179–186

citations, 274–277

collaboration, 128

  private copies of shared documents, 11

comments, 289

  contextual view, 128

  modern comments, 128

Compare, 285–287

cross references, 269–270

date fields, 252

Developer tab, 136

Dictation, 127

document formatting, 140

  character formatting, 141

  manual, 142

  paragraph formatting, 141

  styles, 142

  themes, 142

Document Info command, 175

  Field dialog box, 177–178

Document Information, 252

documents

  columns, 226–228

  inserting in Publisher, 851

  insertion point, 138

  keyboard, 139

  large, 257

  layout, 155

  Master Document, 290–294

  mouse, 138

  navigating, 137–140

  orientation, 156

  saving as templates, 135

  section breaks, 228–230

  section formatting, 230

  sections, 257

document window, splitting, 192

Editor, 19, 192

  Grammar checker, 194

  navigation buttons, 194

  running, 193

  spelling, 192

  Spelling pane, 194

  Thesaurus task pane, 195

endnotes, 269, 278

  inserting, 279

  moving between, 279

  number format, 279

  numbering, 278

  styles, 278

Envelopes And Labels dialog box, 232

field codes

  TOC building, 264–266

  viewing, 271

Field dialog box, 252

Field Names list, 252

fields, 252–253

figures, table of figures, 267–268

files

  new from OneDrive, 107

  opening, 131

  sharing, older versions, 107

file types, 50

Font dialog box, 145–146

fonts, 132

footers

  creating, 172–174

  inserting, 174–175

page numbering, 178–179
tools, 175–178
footnotes, 269, 278
inserting, 279
moving between, 279
number format, 279
numbering, 278
styles, 278
Format tab, 185
formatting styles, 200
forms, 254
Header & Footers Tools Design tab, 175
headers
creating, 172–174
inserting, 174–175
page numbering, 178–179
styles, 174
tools, 175–178
headings, 269
Home tab, 126
Clipboard group, 126
Font group, 126, 143
Paragraph group, 126
Illustrations group, 71
images
captions, 266–267
Image Search browser, 183
stock images, 129, 182–184
text and, 186–187
indents, 146
indexes, 271–273
Insert tab, 126
Draw Table, 213
Page Break, 157
Table group, 210–211
interface, 125
Label Options dialog box, 235
macros, 909
mailings
address block, 245
Complete The Merge, 250

document type, 237
envelopes, 232, 234, 251–252
Envelopes and Labels dialog box, 234
greeting line, 246
labels, 234–235
mail merges, 236–239
Mail Merge Wizard, 237–238
mass mailings, 236–238
merge fields, 245–247
merge preview, 249
merge rules, 248–249
Outlook Contact list, 241
recipient list, 240–245
recipients, 238
Manage document, file versions, 62
margins, 132, 155
Mini Toolbar, 145
multilevel lists, 165–166
Navigation pane, 189–190
numbered items, 269
numbered lists, 162, 164
Online Pictures browser, 183–184
Organizer window, 206
outlines, PowerPoint slides, 542
Outline view, 190, 192, 290–291, 293–294
Page Layout view, 132
page number fields, 252
Page Setup dialog box, 155–156
Paragraph dialog box, 146
alignment, 147
Decrease Indent, 151–152
Line and Page Breaks, 150–151
Line And Paragraph Spacing, 148–149
Tabs, 152–154
paragraph formatting, 146–147
alignment, 147
double spacing, 149
exact spacing, 149
indents, 151–152
line spacing, 148–149
multiple spacing, 149

single spacing, 149–150
tabs, 152–154
pictures, 179–182
Picture Tools, 181
printing, 157–159
Proofing Options, 193
Quick Parts, 196
Read Mode, 132
Recent list, 129
ribbon, 125–126, 136
Ruler
    indents, 151
    tabs, 153
scrollbars, 138
Search Documents box, 131
Search feature, 195
shading, 166–168
Start menu, 128
Start screen
    Home window, 129
    New window, 129
    Open window, 129, 131
styles
    creating, 171
    editing, 203–204
    Manage Styles dialog box, 205
    managing, 204–207
    Quick Styles gallery, 201–202
    TOC and, 258–262
Styles window, 203
table of contents (TOC), 258
    adding entries, 263
    field codes, 264–266
    generating, 265
    hyperlinks, 262
    inserting, 261
    page numbers, 258–259
    previewing, 262
    styles, 258–262
    Table Of Contents dialog box, 261
    updating, 263

table of figures, 267–268
tables
    alignment, 219
    AutoFit, 212
    captions, 266–267
    cell format, 219–220
    columns, 217–218
    column width, 212
    converting text to, 211, 214
    design, 126
    drawing, 210, 213
    Excel spreadsheet, 211
    formatting, 216–218
    formulas, 225–226
    inserting, 210–213
    layout, 126
    merge cells, 219
    navigating, 214
    positioning, 215–216
    Quick Tables, 211
    rows, 217–218
    selecting, 215–216
    sorting data, 224
    styles, 220–223
    Table Design tools, 216–220
    Table Drawing tool, 213
    table grid, 210
    text deletion, 214
    text direction, 220
    text entry, 214
tabs, 146
Tabs dialog box, 153–154
templates, 130, 132
    attaching to documents, 136
    Blank Document, 130
    creating, 134–136
    folders, 135
    forms, 254
    Normal, 132
    themes, 169

text formatting, 143
  bold, 126
  case, 144
  effects, 143
  font color, 126
  font size, 126, 143
  fonts, 142
  images and, 186–187
  italic, 126
  typography, 143
text selection
  keyboard, 140
  mouse, 140
themes, 168–172
  deleting, 172
  email, 718
Track Changes, 280, 282–283
  accepting, 285
  comments, 280
  rejecting, 285
  reviewing changes, 284–285
  Reviewing Pane, 282
  Simple Markup view, 280
  viewing changes, 283–284
View tab, 187–189
Word Options window, 901
WordArt, 69, 71, 80, 94–95
  PowerPoint, 563
  Smart Art, 602
  Text Effects gallery, 95

styles
  PowerPoint, 563
    text boxes (Publisher), 848
WordArt Styles gallery, 80
WordArt Styles group (Shape Format tab), 92
Word Count (Word Online), 111
Word for the Web, 7
Word Online, 100, 106, 110
  Backstage, 107–108
  Comments, 111
  Editor, 111
  Grammar, 111
  Immersive Reader view, 106
  Reading view, 106
  Ribbon, 107–112
  Save As page, 107
  Spelling, 111
  tables, 110
  Table Tools, 110
  Track Changes, 111
  Translate, 111
  Word Count, 111

X–Y–Z

XML (eXtensible Markup Language), 49
XPS (XML Paper Specification) format, 51
  Publisher, 830

Zoom group (Word), 187
zoom, PowerPoint, 545, 651–652

Plug into learning at

MicrosoftPressStore.com

The Microsoft Press Store by Pearson offers:

- Free U.S. shipping

- Buy an eBook, get three formats – Includes PDF, EPUB, and MOBI to use with your computer, tablet, and mobile devices

- Print & eBook Best Value Packs

- eBook Deal of the Week – Save up to 50% on featured title

- Newsletter – Be the first to hear about new releases, announcements, special offers, and more

- Register your book – Find companion files, errata, and product updates, plus receive a special coupon* to save on your next purchase

 Pearson